MEASURING THE COSTS OF PROTECTION IN EUROPE

European Commercial Policy in the 2000s

MEASURING THE COSTS OF PROTECTION IN EUROPE

European Commercial Policy
in the 2000s

Patrick A. Messerlin

Institute for International Economics
Washington, DC
September 2001

Patrick A. Messerlin, visiting fellow, is professor of economics at the Institut d'Etudes Politiques de Paris and director of the Groupe d'Economie Mondiale de Sciences Politiques, a Paris-based research organization. He has been a consultant to various international organizations and firms and served as a senior economist at the research department of the World Bank from 1986 to 1990. He is also a member of the Advisory Committee on Competition Issues (French Ministry of Economics) and of the Shadow G7-G8 Group. He has written several books on global trade policy, in addition to numerous articles for professional journals, including *Economic Journal, European Economic Review, Weltwirtschaftliches Archiv, World Economy, Economic Studies* (OECD), *European Economy* (European Commission), and *Revue Economique.*

INSTITUTE FOR INTERNATIONAL ECONOMICS
1750 Massachusetts Avenue, NW
Washington, DC 20036-1903
(202) 328-9000   FAX: (202) 328-5432
http://www.iie.com

C. Fred Bergsten, *Director*
Brigitte Coulton, *Director of*
    Publications and Web Development
Brett Kitchen, *Director of Marketing*

Typesetting by BMWW
Printing by Kirby Lithographic
    Company, Inc.

Printed in the United States of America
03 02 01   5 4 3 2 1

Library of Congress Cataloging-in-Publication Data

Messerlin, Patrick A.
    Measuring the costs of protection in Europe / Patrick A. Messerlin.
    p. cm.
    Includes bibliographical references and index.
    ISBN 0-88132-273-3
    1. Protectionism—Europe—Case studies. 2. Nontariff trade barriers—Europe—Case studies. 3. Tariff—Europe—Case studies. 4. European Economic Community countries—Commercial policy—Case studies. 5. European Union countries—Commercial policy—Case studies.
    I. Title.

HF2036 .M47 2000
382'.7'094—dc21   00-039702

Tables

Figures

Boxes

Preface

This is the fifth study in the Institute's series on the costs of trade protection in major countries and regions around the world. The goal of these studies is to provide objective, internationally comparable analyses of the impact of trade barriers on some of the most important participants in the global economy. Directed by Reginald Jones Senior Fellow Gary Clyde Hufbauer, the series began in 1994 with *Measuring the Costs of Protection in the United States* by Hufbauer and Research Fellow Kimberly Ann Elliott. This was followed by *Measuring the Costs of Protection in Japan* by Yoko Sazanami, Shujiro Urata, and Hiroki Kawai in 1995, *Measuring the Costs of Visible Protection in Korea* by Namdoo Kim in 1996 and *Measuring the Costs of Protection in China* (1998) by Zhang Shuguang, Zhang Yansheng, and Wan Zhongxin, copublished with the Beijing-based Unirule Institute of Economics. We believe these studies can be particularly useful as partial foundations for any new trade liberalizing negotiations in the World Trade Organization or at the regional level.

In this study, Patrick Messerlin uses partial equilibrium methods to assess the costs to consumers of all the major instruments of protection in the European Community and to evaluate the political economy of European protection. He studies the relationship between domestic (intra-EC) policies—notably the Common Agricultural Policy and the Single Market in Services—and EC trade policy, and asserts that the high political content of EC trade policy, and the absence of any other means for EC international actions, has induced the EC to carve out zones of political influence with the intensive use of discriminatory trade agreements.

The domestic policies of the EC and its trade policy will continue to evolve. This study looks at their future evolution, given the impending accessions of the Central European economies and the ongoing debate over European political union. It also offers valuable insights into the EC agenda for the WTO ministerial in Qatar in November 2001.

The study concludes that the EC will be more comfortable in the world scene if it chooses the "community" option of political integration for a multifaceted, multicultural Europe of the 21st century instead of the 19th century federation option. A key advantage of going the "community" route is that such a *political* European Community will free *economic* integration of Europe to develop on *economic* grounds. On external issues, a fully-fledged Community would be inclined to finally devote to strategic issues the full attention they deserve. This evolution could then shift the focus of the EC-US dialogue away from trade issues toward more global problems, such as the European technological gap in military equipment or security issues in the Asia Pacific.

The Institute for International Economics is a private nonprofit institution for the study and discussion of international economic policy. Its purpose is to analyze important issues in that area and to develop and communicate practical new approaches for dealing with them. The Institute is completely nonpartisan.

The Institute is funded largely by philanthropic foundations. Major institutional grants are now being received from the William M. Keck, Jr. Foundation and the Starr Foundation. A number of other foundations and private corporations contribute to the highly diversified financial resources of the Institute. About 31 percent of the Institute's resources in our latest fiscal year were provided by contributors outside the United States, including about 18 percent from Japan.

The Board of Directors bears overall responsibilities for the Institute and gives general guidance and approval to its research program, including the identification of topics that are likely to become important over the medium run (one to three years), and which should be addressed by the Institute. The Director, working closely with the staff and outside Advisory Committee, is responsible for the development of particular projects and makes the final decision to publish an individual study.

The Institute hopes that its studies and other activities will contribute to building a stronger foundation for international economic policy around the world. We invite readers of these publications to let us know how they think we can best accomplish this objective.

C. Fred Bergsten
Director
June 2001

Acknowledgments

I would like to acknowledge the contributions of the many who shared their time and expertise during the course of this study. C. Fred Bergsten and Gary Hufbauer were constant sources of encouragement and patience. I benefited enormously from the many comments on preliminary drafts and suggestions of Bernard Hoekman, Petros Mavroidis, André Sapir, and Alan Winters.

I would also like to thank all those who spent their time providing data and/or explaining aspects of the EC commercial policy: Pierre Buigues, Dimitris Diakosavvas, Kimberly Elliott, Carl Hamilton, Joe François, Sam Laird, Louis-Pascal Mahé, Per Molander, Guiseppe Nicoletti, François Ortalo-Magné, Thierry Pouch, Carl-Christian Schmidt, Dean Spinanger, Leonard Waverman, and Dimitri Ypsilanti.

I am also grateful to Virginia Braunstein for collecting some of the data, and to Alfred Imhoff and Madona Devasahayam for their patience and expert editing of the manuscript.

This book is the best opportunity for me to express my deep gratitude to Mike Finger who introduced me to the fun of trade policy. Of course, I alone am responsible for any errors that remain.

Political Stresses, Legal Constraints, and Old-Fashioned Economic Views

The European Community (EC) is an entity in formation, not a fully fledged state, unlike the United States and the other countries examined in this series of studies on the costs of protection.[1] This feature gives EC trade policy a very distinctive flavor: it has a high proportion of political content, because the EC has no other way (foreign policy or army) to express its political views; it can be sticky and chaotic, because it is based on cast-iron, sometimes inconsistent, often poorly drafted (with regard to external relations) Treaties; and it relies on an institutional process that tends to be intrinsically biased toward old-fashioned ways of economic government.

This chapter is devoted to examining these features because they have had (and still have) a profound impact on the scope, magnitude, and structure of EC trade barriers, and hence on the costs of protection in the EC (examined in part I of this book); and because they shape the possibilities for the evolution of EC trade and commercial policies (examined in part II).

First, a high proportion of political content means that a protectionist trade policy is seen by many Europeans as a price "readily" paid for political objectives, be it territorial expansion of the Community through "preferential" trade agreements or accessions or internal unification ("deep integration," in EC parlance).

---

1. "European Community" is the correct legal expression when dealing with the economic policies examined in this book (trade, transport, agriculture, competition, etc.). The term "European Union" has no legal existence; it is a "chapeau" covering the European Community and intergovernmental cooperation (which has no international legal substance) in the fields of the Common Foreign and Security Policy, and Justice and Home Affairs.

Second, the Treaty-based constraint makes EC trade policy particularly prone to selective sectoral protection, a source of large distortions in European economies. It also makes almost impossible, bold EC initiatives for multilateral liberalization, even though the EC has often had (and still has) recourse to the General Agreement on Tariffs and Trade (GATT) and to its successor, the World Trade Organization (WTO), even for solving *intra*-EC problems.

Third, the institutional process of revising the EC cornerstone—the 1957 Treaty of Rome—has not produced only desirable outcomes. Revisions have offered renewed opportunities for the EC member-states, in which a demand for economic government based on old-fashioned concepts is still alive, to "react" to the expansion of market-oriented policies induced by the natural development of the Community—and these "reactionary" provisions tend to increase the costs of protection in the EC.

The High "Political Content" of EC Trade Policy

The principle guiding the formation of modern Europe so far has been to use an economic process for a fundamentally political goal. The economic integration of the Community thus is the privileged instrument for getting "an ever closer union of the peoples of Europe" (Treaty of Rome, preamble, first paragraph). The Treaty of Rome itself is the best illustration of this principle: it was an economic response to the political collapse of the European Defense Community (involving the same founding countries) a few years earlier.

The Treaty of Rome defines the political goal of the Community in vague terms. An "ever closer union of the peoples of Europe" can cover a wide range of possible alternatives—from peaceful coexistence between European states to their political unification—all of which are compatible with the "sense of mission" (Winters 1993a, 224), far beyond the attainment of mere economic benefits, that characterizes European integration. In fact, referring to the peoples of "Europe" in 1957 was amazingly ambiguous; including the peoples then living under the Soviet regime of central planning and high protection could, at that time, be seen as an expression of defiant political repossession, or as a murky compromise between markets and the rule of the state.

Such a high proportion of political content has an impact on the level of EC trade barriers. There is an implicit—unconscious in many European minds—trade-off between the acceptable economic costs associated with a highly political trade policy and the political goals to be reached, with their perceived political benefits. Europeans eager to create some kind of federal Europe have been, and probably still are (as shown by the ongoing debate on the European political "constitution," see chapter 7), ready to adopt a much less open trade policy than Europeans interested "merely" in peaceful coexistence between European states.

The search for such a balance has been a permanent part of the Community's history. It started with the debate on the EC Common Agricultural Policy (CAP) in the mid-1960s (see chapter 4). In the late 1980s, it was highlighted by the slow pace at which the external dimension of the Single Market Program was taken into consideration (Eeckhout 1994). It is at the core of the "Euroskeptic" approach in Britain. For instance, Hindley and Howe (1996) argued that the economic costs of the EC for the British economy in the mid-1990s were higher than the economic and political gains they perceive from British membership—hence concluding that Britain should withdraw from the Community. Since then, other Euroskeptics have argued that Britain should join the North American Free Trade Agreement (NAFTA, the free trade area between Canada, Mexico, and the United States) as an alternative to the EC (Hulsman 2001).

The debate has crossed the Channel with the emergence of the *souverainistes* in France, who argue that Brussels is "too" powerful, but also that the Community is not protectionist enough, and is being diluted into a "mushy" free trade area. But it would be wrong to limit the search for a balance between economic costs and political gains to the Euroskeptic or *souverainiste* groups. It is a constant preoccupation of the EC governments—as is illustrated by persistent references made in Germany to the Atlantic dimension of the Community (e.g., G. Schröder, *International Herald Tribune*, 19 July 1998), or by the world dimension of trade routinely emphasized in Britain (e.g., the title of the British White Paper, *Free Trade and Foreign Policy: A Global Vision*, 1996).

There is an essential—though often ignored—corollary to this balance between economic costs and political benefits. To say that the EC is, at bottom, about politics, not economics, and to use this argument for justifying costly decisions from the economic perspective, is a one-sided approach. The argument also implies that any decreasing perception of the political gains from European integration requires a decrease in the economic costs of European unification, to keep the balance even. In trade policy, that means a push for a more open Community.

This case can be illustrated by many intra-EC key issues, such as the reform of the EC Common Agricultural Policy. If during the Cold War the explicit European goal of "self-sufficiency" in agriculture was perceived by a large majority of Europeans as an acceptable cost to be paid for a united Community confronted with the military threat of the Soviet Union, the current perception (wrong or not) that such threats have disappeared is contributing to the undermining of the existing CAP, and to its reform. In sum, because politics are in permanent flux, tomorrow's politics will not necessarily sustain economic costs adapted to yesterday's politics.

Its high political content has made EC trade policy an obvious substitute for foreign policy, to an extent unsurpassed in other industrial countries. (In this respect, EC trade policy is a not too distant cousin of the trade policies of newly independent countries.) Of course, the United States may also use its trade policy for political purposes (after all, the constitutional external powers of the US federal government are broader than its purely domestic powers). But having an operational diplomacy and army, the United States has a much wider range of possible instruments than the EC.

In contrast, the high political content of the EC trade policy, *and* the absence of any other means for EC international actions, have induced the EC to carve out zones of political influence through the intensive use of discriminatory trade agreements (see chapter 6). All these agreements have had almost no economic impact on the EC. Rather, their role has been to strengthen the hegemony of certain EC member-states or to establish the EC hegemony. During the past 40 years, EC trade policy has been the privileged support for EC territorial expansion—from the 6 founding members in 1951 to 9 (1973), 10 (1981), 12 (1986), and 15 (1995) member-states (leaving aside the direct enlargement to eastern Germany in 1990, which had been prepared for since the Community's birth, and confirmed by special trade arrangements between the former German Democratic Republic and the EC since the 1960s).

Today's elaborate EC hierarchy of trade treaties reflects the subtle graduation of countries from the status of trading partner to the situation of full member-state: reciprocal or nonreciprocal agreements; free trade agreements of several vintages and types, or customs unions; and ultimately accession agreements. Each of these agreements is associated with a well-codified set of trade barriers between the Community and its trading partners: quantitative restrictions or not, preferential tariffs in all sectors or not, antidumping actions or not, "approximation" of laws and regulations in accordance with EC rules ("*acquis communautaire*") or not, and so on. Indeed, these trade agreements manifest an increasingly clear political dimension, often reflected in the title of the Treaties. For instance, the January 2000 draft of the agreement signed with Mexico is entitled "Economic Partnership, Political Coordination, and Cooperation Agreement."

A Treaty-Based Trade Policy

The EC relies on Treaties between sovereign member-states. Treaty after Treaty, the coverage of activities subject to the European integration process has continuously expanded: the 1951 Treaty of Paris on coal and steel; the 1957 Treaty of Rome on all products and services, generating the 1964 Common Agricultural Policy and the 1992 Single Market Program (SMP) in services; the Treaty on the Single European Act (1986); the Maastricht Treaty (1992), covering monetary and economic union; the Amsterdam Treaty (1997), entered into force in May 1999, and tinkering with social rights; and, following the Intergovernmental Conference (IGC) of Nice in December 2000, the Nice Treaty (2001) focusing on the voting rights of member-states and other institutional arrangements related to the accession of the Central European countries (CECs) to the Community.[2] Box 1.1 summarizes the key provisions of EC trade policy since the Treaty of Rome, and its major subsequent revisions, which constitute, in EC parlance, the "Treaty establishing the European Community" (TEC).[3]

The TEC constitutes the Community's "fundamental law" (Zuleeg 1997). But it also imposes specific constraints on EC trade policy, because it does more than lay down pure constitutional rights and obligations of member-states. Its successive versions (Rome, Maastricht, Amsterdam, Nice) lock in key specific "deals," which have been necessary for reaching a consensus, and cannot be substantially modified afterward without due renegotiations. This "stickiness" is not specific to trade policy. For instance, it is also illustrated by the "convergence criteria" of the Treaty of Maastricht, which state that member-states can participate in the monetary union only if they meet certain criteria (such as a budget deficit not higher than 3 percent of GDP) at a given period of time. Almost everyone agrees that these convergence criteria have no economic meaning and that they can be harmful to economic growth and efficiency in Europe. However, renegotiating them is seen as so costly (in time, signals sent to the markets, etc.) that they remain in place and will have to be met, despite their costs.

Examples of stickiness abound in trade policy. In 1957, a protocol on the banana import regime was attached to the Treaty of Rome: it excluded this product from the European common market, and kept it under exclusive member-state competence. It required 36 years, two GATT panels, and pressure from the Uruguay Round negotiations to substitute (in 1993) a unique EC import regulation for the existing member-state import schemes. But this regulation was so unacceptable to EC trading partners that, five years later, a new panel of the WTO condemned it. Although the April 2001 agreements between the EC, the United States, and Ecuador are a first step toward settling the case, they do not really modify the costs of protection imposed on EC consumers. In fact, the case will definitely be settled only by 2006, that is almost in time for the 50th anniversary of the Treaty of Rome, when the final EC tariff on banana imports will be implemented (see appendix A, case 19).

---

2. These matters could have been handled by the Accession Treaties. Another intergovernmental conference is scheduled for 2004 with a focus on questions of the European Constitution (see chapter 7).

3. The TEC is "Pillar One" of the Treaty on the European Union. Pillar Two and Pillar Three of the Treaty deal, respectively, with the Common Foreign and Security Policy, and with Justice and Home Affairs.

Box 1.1 The Common Commercial Policy

The Treaty of Paris left little scope for a European common trade policy. In accordance with Articles 71 to 73, the key trade instruments (tariffs, specific quotas, and trade agreements) remained under the jurisdiction of member-states. The "High Authority" until 1967 and the Commission since then could take only a narrow range of trade measures, considered as marginal and exotic in the 1950s, but with a great future—antidumping, antisubsidy, and safeguard actions (Article 74).

In sharp contrast to the Treaty of Paris, the Treaty of Rome made trade policy an "exclusive competence" of the Community—a logical consequence of the fact that the EC was set up as a customs union, with member-states abandoning their national tariffs vis-à-vis the rest of the world and adopting a common tariff schedule. It imposed de jure a large power devolution from member-states to the Community. Decisions shall be made on a "qualified majority vote" basis (or even on a simple majority basis for a limited set of decisions); they are enforceable without prior ratification by national parliaments; and they shall be based on "uniform principles" to be followed by all member-states. But the Treaty of Rome left unclear the exact scope of the Community's exclusive competence for the Common Commercial Policy (CCP). The cornerstone provision, Article 133 (ex 113),[1] defined CCP coverage only with an illustrative list—mostly tariffs, antidumping or antisubsidy measures, and trade agreements.

This indicative definition of the scope of the Community's exclusive competence has generated many conflicts between the Commission and member-states (Meunier and Nicolaidis 1999), and it has necessitated a series of rulings by the European Court of Justice. In 1993, the introduction of services and intellectual property rights in the Uruguay Round reignited the conflict between the Commission and member-states over competence. In its 1994 ruling, the court adopted the following distinction: Cross-border trade, whether in goods or services, is subject to the "exclusive competence" of the Community; by contrast, member-states retain competence (jointly with the Community) for trade issues involving commercial presence and factor movements (non-cross-border services, investment, labor, and property rights).

The Nice version of the TEC (2001) has tilted the balance somewhat toward exclusive Community competence, by expanding the majority rule to a range of services and trade-related intellectual property issues. However, this change is much more modest than it appears at first glance—for legal and political reasons. Legally, following the so-called "parallelism approach," the unanimity rule in services will continue to prevail for all the provisions of an international agreement that require unanimity in the adoption of intra-EC decisions (e.g., on taxation or on social issues).

Politically, the history of EC trade policy has amply shown that consensus is still the de facto rule. In many cases, member-states "trade" their signatures on agreements under the majority rule for their signatures on agreements under the unanimity rule. Moreover, the range of services left under the unanimity rule (audiovisuals, education, health, and social services, to which one should add transport, which remains governed by specific treaty provisions) is large enough to leave many decisions de facto under the unanimity rule. The Nice version of the TEC has not brought investment issues under the majority rule (except for services, to be consistent with WTO Rules), nor the other traditional conflictual topics between the Commission and member-states, particularly the EC export policy, which is not yet clearly defined (Eeckhout 1994). Still pending are issues such as export subsidies or exports of dual-use (military and

---

[1] The approach by successive versions of the TEC has necessitated renumbering all the articles of the Treaty of Rome. In this book, the new numbers (after Amsterdam) precede the old numbers (in parentheses).

(box continues next page)

Box 1.1 *(continued)*

commercial) goods despite the limited progress brought by the enforcement (in September 2000) of the Community General Export Authorization for dual-use goods exported to "friendly" countries.

In addition to Article 133 (ex 113), the Maastricht version of the TEC (1992) has maintained only Articles 131 (ex 110), 132 (ex 112), 133 (ex 113), and 134 (ex 115) from the initial provisions of the Treaty of Rome (for more detail, see Devuyst 1992). Articles 132 (ex 112) and 134 (ex 115) have been kept, partly because they deal with issues related to the "transitory" period in case of accession; they are thus necessary for new member-states. They have been maintained for additional reasons. Article 132 (ex 112) deals with progressive harmonization of export policies, which have proven difficult to unify. Article 134 (ex 115) allows the Commission to authorize a member-state to take measures restricting intra-EC trade when it faces problems because of trade deflection (when imports from non-EC countries limited by a member-state could enter this state after a first entry in another member-state) or "economic difficulties." Article 134 (ex 115) was particularly necessary when the founding member-states enforced national quotas or equivalent protectionist measures. Such quotas have been almost completely eliminated. But the Community can take protective measures limited to one member-state (the so-called "regional" trade measures), at the request of the member-state(s) in question and conditional to the Commission's authorization.

Another example is the Common Agricultural Policy (see appendix A, cases 15 to 18). In 1964, its adoption was a condition imposed by the French government for starting the second phase of dismantling intra-EC trade barriers in manufacturing. In 1973, the CAP was already so enmeshed in the web of intra-EC deals that it was impossible to use the opportunity of the British accession to begin to dismantle it—despite the many early warnings about the CAP's perverse impact on European farmers in the long run (see chapter 4), and despite the fact that British farm policy was better conceived than the CAP, from an economic *and* social point of view. In the 1980s, similar difficulties emerged in getting rid of the special rules in steel and coal (see appendix A, case 11). In the 1990s, similar problems were raised by state-owned firms in services and the elusive notion of "service of general interest" (see chapter 5, and appendix A, cases 20 to 22).

The stickiness of EC trade policy increases the costs of EC trade protection in two ways. It keeps high barriers on products and services for which long delays are necessary before including them in a move to trade liberalization (often very slow, as is best illustrated by services; see chapter 5). And it makes EC protection less "uniform," because, meanwhile, other goods and services have been subject to liberalization policy, or to technical progress equivalent to such liberalization. The sectoral selectivity of EC trade policy is mirrored by a relatively wide range of EC nominal rates of protection for goods (from 0 percent to more than 1,000 percent; see chapter 2), which are likely to generate even larger differences in effective rates of protection, and hence, large distortions and costs of protection in EC economies.

Last, the progressive expansion of the activities covered by the Treaties has had two opposite consequences. On the one hand, it has extended the coverage of EC trade policy from goods to services—creating wider trade-offs in trade negotiations. This evolution tends to make EC trade liberalization easier because trade negotiators with a wide scope of possible trade-offs are generally better equipped to reach successful outcomes than negotiators with a narrow scope. In the highly legalistic EC context, this benefit has an important *internal* corollary. Moreover, wider coverage of EC Treaties means an enlarged choice among alternative TEC provisions on which to base a trade-related initiative, and the choice of the appropriate legal basis for an initiative is often critical for its success (as is illustrated by labor issues; see chapter 5) and for the exact magnitude of its economic costs and benefits.

On the other hand, the deepening of European integration has made EC trade policy related to, and hence dependent on, deals involving other policies, with possibly negative consequences. For instance, the extent to which too restrictive monetary and budgetary policies have been associated with the creation of the euro in an environment of rigid factor (labor and capital) markets may have contributed to slow growth and unemployment, and generated a macroeconomic climate hostile to trade liberalization. Such costs could be particularly important in the years to come, when the bulk of intra-EC and extra-EC liberalization of services will occur.

The "Statist" Bias in the TEC

The successive versions of the TEC have a *statist* bias, which has increased in *relative* terms since the late 1980s or early 1990s. "Statist" means that the Treaties stick to an old-fashioned economic role for governments, based on *direct* public interventions on prices and quantities in the markets of goods and labor, in contrast to a more indirect and lighter approach based on free markets relying on governments acting as competitive rulemakers and strict law-enforcers.[4] "Relative" means that the level of statism in the EC is not assessed in absolute value but on the basis of a comparison with the level of statism in the rest of the world. In this respect, Koedijk and Kremers (1996) have provided evidence that, during the past 20 years, the *relative* level of EC statism—in comparison with non-EC countries that are members of the Organization for Economic Cooperation and Development (OECD)—has increased, although its *absolute* level may have decreased. Their conclusion echoes well the evolution of the successive TEC versions.

---

4. Statism does not necessarily imply a hierarchical structure; in fact, the EC is unique in its lack of hierarchies, its huge variety of actors involved in any decision, and the absence of agents or institutions specialized in "deal-striking" (Bomberg and Peterson 1996).

The statist nature of the Treaty of Paris may seem of secondary importance today, because the Treaty should be eliminated by 2002. But the Treaty involves such powerful vested interests that it remains to be seen whether some kind of "special treatment" beyond 2002 will not be granted to EC steelmakers, all the more because the Treaty's statism, in tune with the planning approach fashionable in the early 1950s, was also related to a still existing force: a strong tradition of collusion between steel firms backed by their governments.[5] The Treaty provisions were, in many cases, influenced by the "Entente Internationale de l'Acier" (International Steel Cartel), which was set up in 1926 by steelmakers from Belgium, France, Germany, Saarland, and Luxembourg. The "Entente" was the best illustration of the general approach, promoted during the 1920s by the very active Pan-European Movement, which was advocating the idea of political union in Europe, according to which cartels were the best compromise between trade liberalization and "market stability" (Bonnefous 1952). The "Entente" has exerted a deep influence on the interwar European trade policies, in particular on the Franco-German Treaty of Commerce (Rieben 1954).[6] The Paris Treaty pricing rules, broadly similar to the Entente price provisions and to the US Pittsburgh basing-point system abandoned in 1924 following an antitrust order, have been (and still are) potential substitutes for trade barriers between the member-states (see appendix A, case 11).

The Treaty of Paris is a good illustration of the trade-off mentioned in the introduction, that is, economic costs readily paid for political goals. It *had to* be a masterpiece of baroque trompe l'oeil. Six years after World War II, intra-EC free trade revealing German comparative advantages in steel would have hardly been acceptable to the other member-states. Substituting private for public barriers thus has made a lot of political sense. But the price paid for launching the formation of modern Europe in these two highly symbolic sectors has been the inhibition of competition in these sectors for the next five decades, an almost complete collapse of world trade in steel (to be fair, the United States contributed heavily to this evolution by imposing the first voluntary export restraints and antidumping measures), and a long-lasting "attraction" for industrial policy in other EC manufacturing sectors.

The Treaty of Rome represents a marked departure from the Treaty of Paris. It was much ahead of its time, with bold moves toward regulatory

---

5. The text (December 2000) of the Treaty of Nice includes a provision imposing the maintenance of specific data on steel and coal after the end of the Treaty of Paris. Although (provisionally) limited in time, this extension could easily be one aspect of the "special treatment" invoked in the text.

6. In addition to the heavily procartel, interwar legacy, the Treaty of Paris was negotiated under the pressure of a request by Germany in 1950 to increase its steel production from 11 million to 14 million tons. France was opposed to this request, but the United States was ready to accept it in the Cold War environment. The French government and industrialists saw the Treaty of Paris as a way to handle the situation (Preda 2001).

reform in several respects. For instance, the neutral stance of Article 295 (ex 222) on public ownership has helped open the door to service liberalization; and the antisubsidy provisions included in competition policy in Article 87 (ex 92) have been extremely useful in constraining European governments so inclined to subsidize and to tax. The Treaty of Rome reflects the strengthening of the market-economy option, boosted by the "German miracle" emerging in the mid-1950s. It portends a new vision of the "ideal" government, shifting from a direct actor in markets to a "referee" setting the rules according to which the market will freely function.

But the Treaty of Rome has an important downside. In many instances, it is flexible or vague enough to allow recurrent attempts to introduce old-fashioned ways of economic government, including by the Commission, as is illustrated by its efforts to build European industrial policies in high-technology sectors or in trans-European networks during the mid-1990s. How this flexibility can open the door to setbacks is best illustrated by Article 3 (ex 3), which provides a list (reproduced in table 1.1) of the Community's trade activities. It is remarkable that only 3 of the 11 items on the list are unambiguously market-oriented: the elimination of intra-EC barriers (a), the intra-EC "four freedoms" (c), and the need for a competition policy (f).[7] That the ambiguity be embodied in the Treaty is crucial because it allows the use of judicial activism to reintroduce statism, without a necessary recourse to legislative action (see chapter 5 on services).

The clear statism of the Treaty of Paris and the ambiguities of the Treaty of Rome largely reflect the economic consensus of their times. During the 1980s this consensus profoundly shifted in favor of market forces and in favor of states as vigilant and efficient law-enforcers but prudent and restrained law-producers. However, *despite* this evolution, the two versions of the TEC written in the 1990s were still (sometimes increasingly) statist, mirroring a "reactionary" attitude among member-states against the market-oriented reforms of the late 1980s and early 1990s.

Such a reactionary attitude can be illustrated by the following examples. As shown by table 1.1, the Maastricht TEC version (1992) includes a revised list of Article 3 (ex 3) with almost twice as many items as the 1957 list. All new items are of direct interest for international trade issues: out of the nine new items, not one is unambiguously market-oriented. Moreover, the Maastricht TEC version reaffirms the need for *direct* state intervention in labor markets (for instance, by keeping references to minimum wages), and it includes a series of new provisions devoted to culture, industry, technology, and so on, stating the strong and *direct* role of the member-states and the Community in these matters, in accordance with

---

7. Item f deserves two remarks. Its "nonstatist" dimension is not absolute (although consistent with economic analysis). It is the *only* nondiscriminatory item with respect to the rest of the world, but it was necessary for the Treaty of Rome to comply with GATT national treatment (and with economically sound analysis).

Table 1.1 An entity in formation: The European Community's goals, as listed in Article 3 of the Treaty establishing the European Community (TEC)

The Rome version of TEC, 1957	The Maastricht version of TEC, 1992	The Amsterdam version of TEC, 1997
a. Elimination between member-states of customs duties, quantitative restrictions on imports and exports of goods, and all measures having equivalent effects	a. Unchanged	a. Prohibition between member-states of customs duties, quantitative restrictions on imports and exports of goods, and all measures having equivalent effects
b. Establishment of a common tariff and a Common Commercial Policy	b. A Common Commercial Policy	b. Unchanged
c. An internal market characterized by the abolition between member-states of obstacles to the free movement of goods, persons, services, and capital	c. Unchanged	c. Unchanged
d. A common policy in agriculture	d. Measures concerning the entry and movement of persons subject to Article 100c	d. Measures concerning entry and movement of persons subject to Title IV
e. A common policy in transport	e. A common policy in agriculture and fisheries	e. Unchanged
f. A system ensuring that competition in the internal market is not distorted	f. Unchanged	f. Unchanged
g. Enforcement of procedures for coordinating economic policies and avoiding disequilibria of balance of payments	g. Unchanged	g. Unchanged
	No direct equivalent	No direct equivalent
h. Approximation of the member-states' laws to the extent required for the functioning of the common market	h. Unchanged	h. Unchanged
		i. Promotion of coordination between employment policies of the member-states with a view to enhancing their effectiveness by developing a coordinated strategy for employment

(table continues next page)

Table 1.1 An entity in formation: The European Community's goals, as listed in Article 3 of the Treaty establishing the European Community (TEC) *(continued)*

The Rome version of TEC, 1957	The Maastricht version of TEC, 1992	The Amsterdam version of TEC, 1997
i. Creation of a European Social Fund to improve job opportunities and standard of living	i. A policy in the social sphere comprising a European Social Fund	j. Unchanged
j. Creation of a European Investment Bank to facilitate the Community's economic growth by creating new resources	No direct equivalent	No direct equivalent
	j. Strengthening of economic and social cohesion	k. Unchanged
	k. A policy on environment	l. Unchanged
	l. Strengthening of the competitiveness of European industry	m. Unchanged
	m. Promotion of research and technological development	n. Unchanged
	n. Encouragement of the establishment and development of trans-European networks	o. Unchanged
	o. Contribution to the attainment of a high level of health protection	p. Unchanged
	p. Contribution to education and quality training and to the flowering of cultures of member-states	q. Unchanged
	q. Policy in development cooperation	r. Unchanged
k. Association of the overseas countries and territories to increase trade and promote jointly economic and social development	r. Unchanged	s. Unchanged
	s. Contribution to strengthening consumer protection	t. Unchanged
	t. Measures in energy, civil protection, and tourism	u. Unchanged

Sources: The successive versions of the TEC.

items (l), (o), (s) and (p) of Article 3 (ex 3). For instance, Article 151 (ex 128) on culture provides a legal basis for direct actions by the member-states and the Community in these matters, with the Community supplementing "if necessary" member-states' actions. Article 157 (ex 130) on industry does not use the term "industrial policy," but one of its aims is to "encourage an environment favorable to cooperation between undertakings." Five years later, as shown in table 1.1, the Amsterdam (1997) version of Article 3 (ex 3) insists anew on a "social Europe" based on direct public intervention in labor markets (item i), and Article 16 (ex 7d) devotes much attention to the notion of "services of general economic interest."

Why do these more recent versions of the TEC not reflect the move toward regulatory reform observed outside the Community (and to some extent in some EC member-states), nor echo more clearly the fall of the Berlin Wall and the collapse of centrally planned economies? It seems that, to a large extent, the revised versions of the Treaty of Rome are "reacting" to the 1992 Single Market Program (SMP) of liberalization and regulatory reforms. They have been written by and for the member-states to stop (and to get back under control) the spread of the SMP's market-oriented concepts, which had been first shaped by the European Court of Justice during the late 1970s and the early 1980s, then relentlessly promoted by a few influential industrialists (see chapters 4 and 5), and finally translated into legal means by the Commission during the late 1980s and early 1990s.[8]

The statist bias of the more recent versions of the TEC raises two specific problems for EC trade policy. First, because trade policy has been much more dependent on the Treaty and on member-states' decisions than on the Court of Justice's rulings, it has benefited less from the strong (but relatively short-lived) "market-oriented push" of the Court than other EC policies (box 1.2 and table 1.2 underline the heavy dependence of EC trade policy on member-states). For instance, the Court has felt compelled to cancel only one antidumping measure (in 1992) on the substantive ground of competition issues, despite the fact that many other antidumping cases could have been canceled for the same reason (see appendix B). Another illustration could be the Court's treatment of technical barriers to trade; its nondiscriminatory dimension (so crucial for imports from outside the Community) has never been made explicit in legal terms (see chapter 4).

The second problem of the statist bias is that it does not affect the sectors uniformly. It is heavy in sectors that the Treaties of Paris and Rome deal with in detail (steel, agriculture, transport), whereas it is lighter in sectors that these Treaties have not ticked as "special," such as manufacturing (steel excluded) or market services (except transport). In other words, the statist bias reinforces the selectivity (nonuniformity) of EC protection—and hence its costs.

---

8. In fact, since the early 1990s, the court itself has shifted to a less market-oriented approach, such the scope for "public service" and the protection of public monopolies from competition (see chapter 5).

Box 1.2 Making of the Common Commercial Policy

The typical decision process in EC trade policy could be described as an ongoing "fast-track" regime, with the Commission acting as the US president, and the Council of Ministers, which represents the view of the member-states, as the US Congress. By drafting negotiating directives or more informal proposals, the Commission tables terms of reference (for opening new negotiations, imposing new barriers, etc.) that the Council examines, alters, and adopts—or not. Once the requests have been approved, the Commission can negotiate or implement the measures. The Commission goes back to the Council for approval of the results of the negotiations, or for information about enforcement. The Parliament's opinion is required for free trade agreements under Article 133 (ex 113) and Article 300 (ex 228). Moreover, the Nice Treaty has granted the Parliament the power to ask the Court of Justice for an opinion on the compatibility of an international agreement with the TEC.

This brief parallel shows that the communitarization of EC trade policy is not synonymous with a unique decision maker (the Commission). Rather, it is a complex process de facto involving 16 partners—the Commission and the 15 member-states—in an environment characterized by no central government, no clear parliamentarian role, no hierarchies, and no strong institutions for conciliation. These complexities have been increased by the emergence of nongovernmental organizations increasingly keen to be involved in trade policy as a way to promote their specific agendas. Last updated in 1998, the Commission's directory of interest groups lists 800 associations (WTO, *Trade Policy Review: The European Union*, 2000).

The key decision maker is thus the Council, which has the legislative and decision-making powers. In accordance with Article 133 (ex 113) of the Treaty of Rome, the Council shall appoint special committees to assist the Commission. This so-called "133 (ex 113) Committee" is the only operational body of this kind mentioned in the Treaty of Rome, reflecting the key importance of trade policy. Though legally only consultative, the 133 Committee, which is supported by an ever-increasing set of expert groups, operates in practice in place of the Council on many trade issues. It acts as a clearinghouse for all aspects of the Community's trade policy, ratifying deals prepared by previous informal bargaining between a set of actors that varies for each trade problem. The 133 Committee increases its considerable power by the fact that it can meet during ongoing negotiations, and be briefed by the negotiating commission at intervals of a few hours. The committee is chaired by the rotating (on a six-month basis) EC Presidency, and it can provide indicative votes—but only the Council can formally vote.

The Council votes on trade issues under the majority rule (see box 1.1). Table 1.2 provides the weighting votes in the Council, and seats in the Parliament, for each present and expected member-state, with the thresholds defining a "qualified" majority or a "blocking" minority. As explained in the text, the Council still largely works on a consensus basis, because the majority rule does not protect trade policy from being held "hostage" by deals in other domains that remain subject to the consensus rule—hence making trade policy subject to "indirect" vetoes. For instance, the final approval by France of the Uruguay Round was made conditional on the adoption of new "comitology" rules, and on granting of additional EC subsidies to French farmers.

The Commission's main source of power with respect to the Council and to the 133 Committee is tactical. The Commission is always in possession of all the facts, and it is often alone in this situation. It decides when and how to present its cases to the 133 Committee. And it is the hub of the many specialized trade committees where the Council is often (but not always) represented.

Table 1.2 deserves two last comments for the future. First, the current EC, with 15 member-states, is probably the most free-trade-oriented possible. The 1990s did not allow classifying the future member-states as staunch supporters of free trade, with the exception of Estonia. In this perspective, it is interesting to observe that, all together, the future member-states could constitute a blocking minority. Second, although recognized as a candidate country by the Community since 1999, Turkey is not included in the list of table 1.2, which shows the ambiguity of the EC approach with respect to this country, an unsustainable situation in the long run (see chapter 6).

Table 1.2 The EC decision making process: Weighting votes in Council of Ministers and seats in European Parliament

	Current situation						Situation at the end of enlargement					
	Votes in Council of Ministers		Seats in Parliament		Population		Votes in Council of Ministers		Seats in Parliament		Population	
Country	Units	Percent	Units	Percent	Millions	Percent	Units	Percent	Units	Percent	Millions	Percent
Britain	10	11.5	87	13.9	59.9	15.9	29	8.4	72	9.8	59.9	12.4
France	10	11.5	87	13.9	59.6	15.8	29	8.4	72	9.8	59.6	12.3
Germany	10	11.5	99	15.8	82.1	21.8	29	8.4	99	13.5	82.1	17.0
Italy	10	11.5	87	13.9	57.9	15.3	29	8.4	72	9.8	57.9	12.0
Spain	8	9.2	64	10.2	39.5	10.5	27	7.8	50	6.8	39.5	8.2
Poland	—	—	—	—	—	—	*27*	*7.8*	*50*	*6.8*	*38.7*	*8.0*
Romania	—	—	—	—	—	—	*14*	*4.1*	*33*	*4.5*	*22.5*	*4.7*
Netherlands	5	5.7	31	5.0	16.0	4.2	13	3.8	25	3.4	16.0	3.3
Belgium	5	5.7	25	4.0	10.2	2.7	12	3.5	22	3.0	10.2	2.1
Greece	5	5.7	25	4.0	10.5	2.8	12	3.5	22	3.0	10.5	2.2
Portugal	5	5.7	25	4.0	9.9	2.6	12	3.5	22	3.0	9.9	2.1
Czech Republic	—	—	—	—	—	—	*12*	*3.5*	*20*	*2.7*	*10.3*	*2.1*
Hungary	—	—	—	—	—	—	*12*	*3.5*	*20*	*2.7*	*10.1*	*2.1*
Austria	4	4.6	21	3.4	8.1	2.1	10	2.9	17	2.3	8.1	1.7
Sweden	4	4.6	22	3.5	8.9	2.3	10	2.9	18	2.5	8.9	1.8
Bulgaria	—	—	—	—	—	—	*10*	*2.9*	*17*	*2.3*	*8.2*	*1.7*
Denmark	3	3.4	16	2.6	5.3	1.4	7	2.0	13	1.8	5.3	1.1
Finland	3	3.4	16	2.6	5.2	1.4	7	2.0	13	1.8	5.2	1.1
Ireland	3	3.4	15	2.4	3.8	1.0	7	2.0	12	1.6	3.8	0.8
Lithuania	—	—	—	—	—	—	*7*	*2.0*	*12*	*1.6*	*3.7*	*0.8*

(table continues next page)

Table 1.2 The EC decision making process: Weighting votes in Council of Ministers and seats in European Parliament *(continued)*

	Current situation						Situation at the end of enlargement					
	Votes in Council of Ministers		Seats in Parliament		Population		Votes in Council of Ministers		Seats in Parliament		Population	
Country	Units	Percent	Units	Percent	Millions	Percent	Units	Percent	Units	Percent	Millions	Percent
Slovakia	—	—	—	—	—	—	*7*	*2.0*	*13*	*1.8*	*5.4*	*1.1*
Luxembourg	2	2.3	6	1.0	0.4	0.1	*4*	*1.2*	*6*	*0.8*	*0.4*	*0.1*
Cyprus	—	—	—	—	—	—	*4*	*1.2*	*6*	*0.8*	*0.8*	*0.2*
Estonia	—	—	—	—	—	—	*4*	*1.2*	*6*	*0.8*	*1.4*	*0.3*
Latvia	—	—	—	—	—	—	*4*	*1.2*	*8*	*1.1*	*2.4*	*0.5*
Slovenia	—	—	—	—	—	—	*4*	*1.2*	*7*	*1.0*	*2.0*	*0.4*
Malta	—	—	—	—	—	—	*3*	*0.9*	*5*	*0.7*	*0.4*	*0.1*
EC-15	87	100.0	626	100.0	377.6	100.0	237	68.7	535	73.1	377.6	78.1
EC-27	—	—	—	—	—	—	345	100.0	732	100.0	483.5	100.0
Majority conditions[a]	62	71.3	—	—	—	—	258	74.8	—	—	299.8	62.0
Blocking minority	26	29.9	—	—	—	—	88	25.5	—	—	—	—

EC = European Community.

a. As of today, 62 votes (cast by at least 10 member-states, when not on a proposal from the Commission required by the TEC). After 2004, a decision must pass a "triple majority" test: a majority of the total number of member-states, the support of 71 to 74 percent of weighted votes in the Council, and, upon request by a member-state, the support of member-states representing 62 percent of the EC population.

Note: Countries in italics are candidate countries to the European Community.

Sources: Nice Intergovernmental Conference, December 2000; Eurostat; International Monetary Fund.

"Why Did the Dog Fail to Bark?"

The above description of the systemic pressures on EC trade policy leads to the following question: why has the EC not become more protectionist in the recent years, after almost a decade of sluggish growth and high unemployment in Continental Europe? In other words, "Why did the dog fail to bark?" (M. Wolf 1996)

A first answer has been the personal influence of Leon Brittan as EC commissioner for external trade policy, as illustrated by his proposal for a "Millennium Round." Legally speaking, launching new trade negotiations at the WTO on agriculture and services is a commitment signed by the Community and its EC member-states at the end of the Uruguay Round in 1994.[9] However, shifting from this narrow legal aspect to the political level of a commitment to a fully fledged round is Brittan's achievement—and it is not a minor one. As is often underlined, Brittan's proliberalization stance has faced many, sometimes strong, negative reactions from member-states (see chapter 6). But it has also mirrored European public opinion, which seems amazingly more open-minded in trade matters than most European politicians: indeed, despite a decade of slow growth, free traders roughly match protectionists in the four large EC member-states (a better score than in the United States and in the world as a whole) (*The Economist*, 2 January 1999, 53–54).

There are two other answers. As shown in chapters 2 and 3, and in many appendix A cases, the communitarization of trade policy has been achieved at the cost of substituting new instruments of protection (e.g., antidumping actions) for traditional barriers (e.g., tariffs or nontariff barriers). Reassured by this perspective, protectionist groups in Europe have abstained from massive action, except when under immediate pressure. In other words, the dog did not bark, but it has bitten in careful "surgical strikes." Another reason is that, as shown in chapters 2 and 3, the level of liberalization achieved by the Uruguay Round has been small in the highly protected agricultural and manufacturing sectors (in fact, many EC farm products were *more* protected during the second half of the 1990s than before) and almost nil in services (dominated by standstill provisions, including the 1997 protocols on telecommunications and financial services; Dobson and Jacquet 1998).

The various pressures on EC trade policy described above will be important for the next round of multilateral trade negotiations in two re-

---

9. The EC and its 15 member-states joined the WTO (and the "plurilateral" Agreements on Government Procurement and on Civil Aircraft) as founding members on 1 January 1995. The Uruguay commitments of the 12 EC member-states and the Uruguay Round commitments of the three new member-states have been consolidated, as well as the Uruguay Round commitments of WTO members with respect to the EC (after renegotiations under GATT Article XXIV: 6).

spects. First, the Treaty-based structure handicaps the EC's ability to launch bold multilateral trade liberalizations. Such initiatives require a consensus among member-states that still have huge differences in appraising what is the "best" trade policy. Consensus means compromises—not a good recipe for bold initiatives. It induces member-states to trade their support for "compensations" in other deals, as is best illustrated by the 1996 negotiations on the first Information Technology Agreement in which the EC was hardly able to play an unequivocal role because its negotiators were stuck by constant requests from member-states for (not necessarily clearly defined) compensation.

Of course, this situation is not specific to the EC. It is frequent in the context of vote-based decisions, as is illustrated by the US Congress. The difference is that a member of Congress represents one vote out of several hundred, with no veto right, whereas (until 2004) a member-state represents between 2 and 10 votes out of 87, and has an indirect veto right through the de facto consensus rule (see box 1.2).

Second, this EC handicap is counterbalanced, to a certain extent, by the EC's strong capacity to launch *internal* liberalizations. Because intra-EC deals may leave certain member-states unsatisfied, the GATT-WTO framework can provide additional concessions for these unsatisfied states, without hurting the interests of the other member-states.

The first illustration of such a GATT "intercession" in EC internal problems was the Kennedy Round (1962–67), which helped to solve certain difficult questions raised by the substitution of the Common External Tariff for EC member-state tariffs. The Treaty of Rome defined the Common Tariff as the unweighted average of the four (Belgium, Luxembourg, and the Netherlands being members of the Benelux customs union) existing tariffs for every tariff item. But this automatic rule raised serious conflicts between member-states for a substantial number (roughly a fifth) of tariff items, for which member-states were implementing very different tariff rates. Tariff cuts adopted during the Kennedy Round were essential for overcoming these difficulties, because they reduced the differences between the tariffs of the most and least protected member-states. The problem was not minor, as is illustrated by the evolution of the German average tariff on dutiable imports; from the late 1950s to 1968, it increased from 6.5 to 10.4 percent, coming back to its pre-EC level only after the Kennedy Round (Weiss 1992, 135).

There are other illustrations of the GATT-WTO intercession in internal EC problems. First is the Uruguay Round negotiations on agriculture and the 1992 Reform of the Common Agricultural Policy (see chapter 4). Another more recent example is the WTO negotiations on telecommunications, which reduced certain transitory exceptions that the most advanced member-states grudgingly granted to less advanced ones when the SMP (i.e., *intra-EC* liberalization) was adopted.

I

MEASURING THE LEVEL AND COSTS OF EC PROTECTION DURING THE 1990s

Chapter 2 aims to provide the available information on the level of EC protection using a systematic approach that encompasses all the sectors producing goods. It aggregates all the forms of protection imposed at EC borders: ad valorem tariffs, ad valorem equivalents of specific tariffs, non-tariff barriers, and antidumping duties and measures. Chapter 3 estimates the costs of protection for 22 sectors—most of them defined at a more dis-aggregated level than that used in chapter 2—to get a better measure of the peaks of protection. It uses two partial-equilibrium models to cross-check the results obtained.

2

The Level and Evolution of EC Overall Protection in the 1990s

This chapter presents a quantitative assessment of the level of overall protection granted to the European output of farm and industrial goods. (A brief conclusion touches upon services that have been, and still are, protected by instruments having little in common with trade barriers imposed on goods.) "Overall" protection refers to all the key trade barriers—tariffs, nontariff barriers (NTBs), and antidumping measures—granted to the EC output of goods. The chapter also gives a sense of the recent evolution of EC protection, because it covers the years 1990, 1995, and 1999 (the last year giving an accurate measure of the post-Uruguay Round tariff protection, because most EC tariff commitments had by then been implemented).[1]

The chapter provides two major results, which echo the main features of EC trade policy underlined in the previous chapter. First, the level of overall protection for the whole EC economy (see table 2.1) was roughly 13 to 14 percent from 1990 to 1997 (for simplicity's sake, the year 1997, very similar to 1995, is not provided) and still almost 12 percent in 1999, that is, a much higher level (two to three times) than generally stated. This level of EC protection will remain unchanged at least until 2005—most EC commitments on trade barriers in goods taken during the Uruguay Round were implemented in 1999, except the dismantling of the quota regime in textiles and clothing, which will take place in 2005. Second, EC protection is very selective. Rates of overall protection exhibit wide differences by sector, and these differences tended to remain stable during the period examined.

---

1. This can be shown by comparing the committed tariffs for 2001 (available in the annex of the WTO's *Trade Policy Review: The European Community*, 1998) and the tariffs enforced in 1999 (from the annex of the WTO's *Trade Policy Review: The European Union*, 2000).

Table 2.1 An overview of EC protection, by industry, 1990, 1995, and 1999

					1990		
					Antidumping measures		Rate of overall
		Number of tariff	Average MFN tariffs[a]	Non-tariff barriers[b]	Number of tariff	Rates[c]	protec-tion[d]
ISIC4	Sectors	lines	(percent)	(percent)	lines	(percent)	(percent)
100a	Cereals (rice excluded)	16		63.0			63.0
100b	Meat (bovine and ovine)	44	20.0	74.0			94.0
100c	Dairy products	67		1,04.0			104.0
100d	Sugar	7		1,17.0			117.0
100e	Other agriculture	443	10.1	10.5			20.6
200	Mining	110	0.5	65.0	3	24.0	2.9
311–12	Food products	483	15.5	15.0	5	15.8	30.6
313	Beverages	52	17.5	5.0			22.5
314	Tobacco	7	66.6				66.6
321	Textiles	1,081	9.9	11.0	23	22.0	21.4
322	Apparel	219	12.3	19.0			31.3
323	Leather and leather products	102	4.7	5.0			9.7
324	Footwear	68	10.9	5.0	3	6.7	16.2
331	Wood products	124	5.3		6	16.1	6.1
332	Furniture and fixtures	27	6.0				6.0
341	Paper and paper products	196	7.6		3	4.6	7.7
342	Printing and publishing	43	6.1		3	0.0	6.1
351	Industrial chemicals	881	7.1		68	16.5	8.4
352	Other chemicals	361	6.2		1	46.9	6.3
353	Petroleum refineries	40	4.6				4.6
354	Petroleum and coal products	13	2.6				2.6
355	Rubber products	80	5.9				5.9
356	Plastic products, nec	139	8.9				8.9
361	Pottery, china, etc.	24	8.4		1	17.5	9.1
362	Glass and products	131	8.3		8	17.5	9.4
369	Nonmetallic products	121	4.5		7	27.7	6.1
371	Iron and steel	469	4.8	15.0	64	15.7	21.9
372	Nonferrous metals	262	4.6		6	8.1	4.8
381	Metal products	524	5.8	n.a.	6	14.0	6.0
382	Machinery	924	4.1	n.a.	28	21.8	4.8
3825	Office and computing equipment			n.a.			
382x	Other machinery			n.a.			
383	Electrical machinery	501	5.8		30	20.3	7.0
3832	Radio, TV, and communication			n.a.			
383x	Other electrical machinery			n.a.			
384	Transport equipment	342	6.1		2	15.0	6.2
3841	Shipbuilding			n.a.			
3842	Railroad equipment			n.a.			
3843	Motor vehicles			n.a.			
3844	Motorcycles and bicycles			n.a.			
3845	Aircraft			n.a.			
3849	Other transport equipment						
385	Professional goods	352	8.3	n.a.	9	16.0	8.7
390	Other industries	263	5.5	2.0	3	18.1	7.7

Block A: All sectors

Total number of tariff lines		8,516			279		
Average level of trade barriers							
Simple average			7.4			17.5	13.8
Labor weighted average			8.1				17.1
Value-added weighted average			8.2				15.3

Block B: Industrial goods (ISIC 314 to ISIC 390)

Total number of tariff lines		7,294			271		
Average level of trade barriers							
Simple average			6.8				10.8
Labor weighted average			6.8				9.7
Value-added weighted average			7.2				9.5

Block C: Agriculture

100	Whole agriculture[d]	577					38.3

n.a. = Ad valorem tariff equivalents of these NTBs are not available.
ISIC = International Standard Industrial Classification.
MFN = most favored nation
nec = not elsewhere classified
OECD = Organization of Economic Cooperation and Development.

	1995							1999						
		MFN tariffs		Non-tariff	Antidumping measures		Rate of overall		MFN tariffs		Non-tariff	Antidumping measures		Rate of overall
Number of tariff lines[d]	Average rates[a] (percent)	Maximum rates (percent)	barriers[b] (percent)	Number of tariff lines	Rates[c] (percent)	protec-tion[d] (percent)	Number of tariff lines	Average rates[a] (percent)	Maximum rates (percent)	barriers[b] (percent)	Number of tariff lines	Rates[c] (percent)	protec-tion[d] (percent)
21			48.0			48.0	21	14.0	15.2	5.0			19.0
41	20.0	20.0	29.0			49.0	26	11.2	12.1	64.8			76.0
91			108.0			108.0	61	9.7	10.3	100.3			110.0
7			106.0			106.0	7			125.0			125.0
417	9.6	25.0	2.2	1	5.6	11.8	538	8.9	179.7	11.2	4	5.3	20.0
132	0.8	1.4	71.3	14	9.4	3.5	137	0.2	8.0	71.3	10	7.1	2.3
618	15.4	42.0	15.0			30.4	1,586	19.5	236.4	5.0			24.5
52	17.5		5.0			22.5	180	8.6	64.0				8.6
7	66.6	117.0				66.6	9	47.3	81.9				47.3
1,087	9.8	25.0	9.0	200	23.3	26.2	1,059	8.5	13.0	8.0	141	18.9	22.1
216	12.4	14.0	19.0			31.4	225	11.6	13.0	19.0			30.6
105	4.8	12.0				4.8	102	3.2	9.7	·	9	27.9	5.7
53	8.4	20.0		2	0.0	8.4	58	7.4	17.0		5	17.5	8.9
131	4.8	10.0				4.8	181	2.6	10.0		3	6.8	2.7
35	5.7	7.0				5.7	38	1.8	5.6				1.8
198	7.6	12.5		2	0.0	7.6	200	3.8	7.5				3.8
42	6.2	12.0		3	12.3	7.1	41	3.0	8.0		1	18.6	3.5
959	7.4	20.0		49	25.0	8.7	1,153	5.3	41.7		32	24.5	6.0
392	6.4	17.6		10	17.4	6.8	423	3.4	22.0		3	19.0	3.5
46	4.3	7.1				4.3	62	2.1	6.5				2.1
18	1.4	9.0				1.4	17	0.4	6.0		1	30.0	2.2
88	7.8	20.0				7.8	105	5.5	17.0				5.5
34	7.7	8.6				7.7	35	5.9	6.5		3	0.0	5.9
24	8.4	13.5				8.4	25	5.9	12.0				5.9
146	7.0	12.5				7.0	137	4.8	11.0		2	0.0	4.8
124	4.5	10.0		6	2.6	4.6	132	2.4	7.0		1	0.0	2.4
542	5.3	10.0	7.0	63	21.3	14.8	521	2.7	7.0	4.0	51	24.0	9.0
258	4.5	10.0		4	25.3	4.9	255	2.9	10.0		6	15.3	3.3
339	5.5	17.0		9	32.8	6.4	354	3.0	8.5		17	31.0	4.5
930			n.a.				1,017			n.a			
58	4.6	12.0	n.a.	10	20.7	8.2	76	0.8	3.0	n.a.	1	13.5	1.0
872	4.2	12.0	n.a.	9	7.7	4.3	941	1.8	9.7	n.a.	3	0.0	1.8
534							679						
225	7.3	15.0	n.a.	40	24.6	11.7	321	3.6	14.0	n.a.	45	37.7	8.9
309	4.9	8.5	n.a.	10	23.1	5.6	358	2.6	6.9	n.a.	3	19.5	2.7
323							354						
57	3.0	10.0	n.a.			3.0	63	1.6	6.2	n.a.			1.6
35	4.7	7.5	n.a.			4.7	40	1.8	3.7	n.a.			1.8
149	8.5	22.0	6.1			14.6	164	6.3	22.0	4.0			10.3
31	8.7	17.0		1	28.4	9.6	34	6.1	15.0		6	24.5	10.4
45	2.9	15.0	n.a.			2.9	47	1.7	7.7	n.a.			1.7
6	4.6	4.9				4.6	6	1.5	2.7				1.5
362	5.6	16.1	n.a.	4	0.0	5.6	381	2.2	6.7	n.a.	1	0.0	2.2
303	5.8	20.0		3	27.1	6.1	308	3.1	17.0		2	31.5	3.3
8,675					440		10,427					350	
	7.4				21.8	13.7		7.0				22.4	11.7
	7.9					14.4		6.4					12.8
	8.5					15.1		6.6					12.3
7,296					425		7,871					336	
	6.7					11.0		4.3					7.7
	6.7					10.0		4.3					7.1
	7.5					10.1		4.7					6.8
577						32.0	653						31.7

a. Many specific tariffs in agriculture (ISIC 100a to 100e) are not taken into account.
b. For agriculture, defined as global rate of protection minus MFN tariff and antidumping barriers.
c. Ad valorem estimates of antidumping measures terminating cases.
d. For agriculture (sectors 100a–100d), based on three-year averages of OECD "CSE-based tariffs" (see text).

Sources: GATT Secretariat, WTO, *WTO Trade Policy Reviews*; EC, *Official Journal*, appendix A; author's computations.

These results are based on three very conservative assumptions: (1) They rely on tariff averages, which, even by sector, cover tens or even hundreds of different tariff lines, so that peak protection rates are largely eroded by the averaging process. (2) They include the major *border* nontariff barriers (quantitative restrictions and antidumping measures), but they are based on the most conservative estimates. (3) They ignore almost all the *non-border* barriers to trade (which would be very difficult to quantify), in particular technical regulations (norms and standards; see chapter 4), public procurement, and production and export subsidies (see chapter 5).

These results deserve three general comments. First, the Uruguay tariff commitments are less dramatic than has often been said (and still is) because EC tariff reductions have been concentrated on already low tariffs (a key point when assessing the costs of protection; see chapter 3). Second, the high level of EC overall protection flows from the systematic incorporation of NTBs and antidumping measures, which are not included in the official figures usually reported. It reveals that a substantial proportion of *industrial* goods is still highly protected, a point often hidden by the focus on protection of farm products. For instance, in 1999, the rate of overall protection was higher than 10 percent in industrial sectors amounting to almost 24 percent of the EC industrial value added; it was higher than 20 percent for almost one-sixth of the EC industrial value added; and it was higher than 30 percent in the clothing sector, the value added of which was equivalent to the combined value added of the sugar and meat sectors.

Third, the almost complete stability of the EC rate of overall protection from 1990 to 1997 is interesting, because it shows that both the fear of Fortress Europe and the hope of a more open EC after the 1992 Single Market Program are equally wrong. Rather, the stability reflects that the communitarization of member-state trade policies—which was ongoing between the mid-1980s and mid-1990s—has allowed the Community to substitute its own trade barriers (mostly antidumping measures) for the old ones run by the member-states. The completion of the Single Market (and the hope that it will improve the competitive position of EC producers and induce the EC to open its borders), the dismantling of the barriers between the EC and the European Free Trade Area (EFTA) countries in 1993, and the accession of three new member-states in 1995 have had no noticeable (indirect) influence on EC barriers.[2]

---

2. A direct impact was impossible, because the EC has imposed on new member-states a strict adoption of the *"acquis communautaire"* in trade policy (meaning the EC trade barriers). This point is important when assessing the global welfare effects of the 1995 EC enlargement: EC producers may have been "deprotected" vis-à-vis their EFTA counterparts (chapter 3 examines this point, and concludes that the EC gains have been modest, even under the most favorable assumptions), but EFTA producers may have been "reprotected" when their countries adopted the EC trade regime (chapter 4 provides some evidence of this aspect for manufactured products).

This broad picture of EC overall protection suggests two points that are at the core of chapter 3. First, large pockets of such high protection in agriculture, industry, and services imply very high costs of protection. Second, such an entrenched position of highly protected sectors means that the coming WTO negotiations will be very difficult: they aim to open sectors that have been very successful at remaining highly protected through all the previous GATT rounds. In this respect, this chapter reveals the raison d'être of the next round, which is not well perceived by public opinion, nor by many decision makers, who wonder why a new round is needed if the previous one was so successful. In fact, this chapter shows that there is still serious work to be done to eliminate high trade barriers, including in manufacturing.

EC Tariff Protection Between 1990 and 2000

Table 2.1 presents the EC most-favored-nation (MFN) *bound* tariffs for all the sectors producing goods (agriculture, mining, and manufacturing) for the three years 1990, 1995, and 1999 (the question of applied tariffs under preferential agreements is examined at the end of the section). This information is drawn from the various WTO *Trade Policy Review* reports on the EC which is the best source available because it has been approved by the EC Commission and EC member-states and subject to inquiries by the WTO Secretariat and EC trading partners.

Common Agricultural Policy has been divided into five groups of products: the four large, highly protected products (from cereals to sugar) at the heart of the Common Agricultural Policy, and the rest of the farm products ("other agriculture"). For the four sectors, the columns labeled "MFN tariffs" report only the ad valorem average and maxima tariffs which are far from covering all the tariff lines (specific tariffs are a very frequent instrument in these sectors). For "other agriculture," ad valorem tariffs and ad valorem equivalents of specific tariffs made available to the WTO and provided in the annexes of *Trade Policy Review* are reported.[3] The same is done for industrial goods.

Table 2.1 provides five major results. First, the simple average of all EC existing tariffs on goods was 7.4 percent in 1990 and in 1995, and still 7 percent in 1999 (see "block A" toward the bottom of the table). These figures are significantly higher than the averages generally reported. This difference can be explained by the fact that the generally reported estimates cover only a narrowly defined set of industries excluding a substantial proportion of the EC output of goods, that has been, and still is,

---

3. In fact, most of the high maximum MFN tariffs in table 2.1 are ad valorem equivalents of specific tariffs.

protected by opaque instruments (in particular, farm and food products representing 20 percent of EC total value added in goods). This limited coverage introduces a systematic underestimating bias both in the estimated level of protection and in its evolution.

These biases can be shown by comparing blocks A and B at the bottom of table 2.1. The simple tariff average of the narrowly defined set of industries (block B is based on International Standard Industrial Classification [ISIC] sectors 314 to 390 which are covered by the usual estimates of EC protection) starts at only 6.8 percent for 1990 and 1995. It declines to 4.3 percent in 1999, and it is expected to decline to 4 percent in 2001, when all existing EC commitments on tariffs will be implemented.[4] In sum, the widely disseminated impression of the low level of EC protection depends on incomplete (not all sectors are covered) and imperfect (not all instruments of protection are included; see below) coverage of EC protection.

Second, the simple average of all EC existing tariffs declines by a small amount (from 7.4 to 7 percent). This result is due to the fact that EC tariff reductions have been concentrated on already low tariffs, as can be shown with table 2.1: the sectoral tariffs higher than 7.4 percent in 1995 declined, on average, by 23 percent in 1999, whereas the sectoral tariffs lower than this threshold declined by 53 percent.

Third, as is well known, economy-wide tariff averages are crude indicators with limited economic meaning. Foreign exporters look at the tariff imposed on the specific product(s) they want to sell in Europe, not at an EC-wide average. Because looking at the 8,000 to 10,000 individual tariffs the EC imposed in the late 1980s and 1990s would make little sense, a more suitable measure of EC protection is to look at average and maximum tariffs by *sector*.[5] Sectors in table 2.1 are defined at the 3-digit level of ISIC codes, except for three industries (machinery, electrical machinery, and transport equipment), which, when possible, are presented at a more meaningful 4-digit level.

As table 2.1 shows, the EC average tariffs by ISIC sector vary widely—mirroring the existence of very different maxima tariffs (for almost all ISIC sectors, the minimum tariff is 0 percent). Since the Uruguay Round, such maxima tariffs can still reach astronomical rates: higher than 100 percent (live bovines, milk, cheese, bananas, wheat, rice, fruit, and starch), up

---

4. The only noticeable tariff declines implemented in 2000 were the elimination of tariffs agreed to under the Information Technology Agreement of 1997, and of those on certain pharmaceutical products and alcoholic beverages. All these expected declines rely on the assumption that the EC does not significantly reshuffle its tariff classification (see text below).

5. Table 2.1 does not provide minima tariffs by sector because, for almost all sectors, tariffs are zero (for details, see the table in the annex of the appropriate WTO *Trade Policy Review*). Standard deviations by sector are not reported either (see the same source).

to 826.2 percent or 1,009.9 percent in 1997 for certain meat products or prepared animal feeds. (The WTO Secretariat, which relies on computations of ad valorem equivalents of specific tariffs done by the EC Commission, does not provide similar details for 1999.) Maxima tariffs in the industrial sectors can also be very high—and even *increased* after 1995 (e.g., chemicals) as a result of specific tariffs.

Fourth, the number of tariff lines is not stable, in particular, between 1995 and 1999. There is an almost continuous "reshuffling" of the tariff schedule during the whole period. This phenomenon, well known by practitioners, is neglected by most studies of protection, despite its importance. Of course, reshuffling tariffs does not necessarily have a protectionist intent; it can be related to new products or technologies, and it aims to make the product list of the tariff schedule closer to the set of products effectively available on the markets.

But tariff reshuffling makes possible tariff increases on new (and not so new) products for protectionist motives—particularly important motives in a technologically developed economy facing difficulties in following the fast course of modern technical progress, such as the EC. For instance, before 1983, compact-disk players were considered by the EC tariff schedule as "record players," with a 9 percent tariff. In 1984, they were granted a specific tariff line in the EC schedule, with a tariff increase to 16.5 percent (to be reduced to 13.5 percent in 1988 and to 9.5 percent in 1989). As a result, it is not surprising that unilateral decisions on tariff reshuffling can lead to serious frictions with trading partners, and ultimately possibly to WTO panels and Appellate Body rulings (e.g., the 1995 EC decision to reclassify local area network equipment) and to consultations and renegotiations under GATT Article XXVIII. As shown in table 2.1, tariff reshuffling was particularly intense for farm, food, and chemical products between 1995 and 1999.

Fifth, being based on simple tariff averages, our estimates are higher than figures usually reported, which are import-weighted averages. Import-weighted estimates have two shortcomings that lead to a systematic underestimate of the level of protection: they weigh high tariffs by restricted (hence smaller than they would be in the absence of protection) import flows and low tariffs by unrestricted (even possibly magnified by substitution effects) import flows. In a study of protection from the perspective of new WTO negotiations, such as this one, a better approach is thus to weight tariffs in a way that mirrors the essential fact that protection is granted to *domestic producers*; hence, it should ideally reflect the relative weight of vested interests.

Table 2.1 uses two different weights: value added and employment of EC sectors in 1990 and 1995 (data are from OECD 1997a, and from annual EC *Reports on Agriculture*). It shows that both EC-wide labor-weighted or value-added-weighted *tariff* averages are larger than simple tariff averages if one includes farm products (see block A), but not necessarily if one excludes them (see block B). This result may be partly due to a statistical problem—the aggregation of the whole universe of manufacturing products in only 35 ISIC sectors. But it is also not so surprising. Protecting with NTBs and antidumping measures is much more attractive for vested interests than trying to modify a whole schedule of bound tariffs.

All the above observations are based on MFN tariffs. One could argue that such an approach overstates the level of EC protection, because the many preferential agreements between the EC and its trading partners (see chapter 6) imply EC *applied* tariffs that are lower than MFN tariffs. This argument deserves a too often forgotten caveat: the MFN treatment of WTO members by the EC was *expanded* during the late 1990s, from Australia, Canada, Japan, New Zealand, and the United States, to Hong Kong, South Korea, and Singapore after their graduation from the Generalized System of Preferences in May 1998. As a result, the import share of EC trade under MFN tariffs *increased* from 35 percent (1990) to 39 percent (1999).

Notwithstanding this argument, it may still seem that a possibly better indicator of the EC *average* tariff rate would be the ratio of tariff duties paid (almost €14 billion in 1996) to total imports (roughly €596 billion for the same year), that is, 2.3 percent. However, such a figure ignores the fact that the EC economy does not produce many goods (oil, tropical food, etc.) that are imported under zero *MFN* tariffs. According to Sapir (1998), 30 percent of EC imports were under zero MFN tariffs in 1996. A better indicator of the average protection of EC production would thus be the ratio of tariff duties paid to *all* dutiable imports, that is, 3.4 percent. This figure for 1996 should be compared with the 6.7 percent (1995) and 5.1 percent (1997, not shown in table 2.1) simple average tariffs of block B in table 2.1 (*not* to the block A average tariffs, because the EC preferential agreements give very limited [if any] preferences for farm goods from temperate countries and food products; see chapter 6).

At this stage, a last question needs to be examined. How do foreign exporters that benefit from EC preferential tariffs really behave? Do they pass through their tariff preferences to EC consumers, or do they keep forgone tariff revenues for themselves (except a small portion "abandoned" to EC consumers in order to be slightly cheaper than producers subject to full MFN tariff rates), either as pure rents (if they are as competitive as producers under MFN conditions) or as cost differentials (if they are less competitive than producers under MFN conditions)? Profit maximization suggests the rent/cost differential option as the most likely situation. In this case, the best indicator of the average tariff rate would be the ratio of tariff duties paid to *MFN* dutiable imports. On the basis of Sapir's computations—which suggest that 25 to 30 percent of EC imports are under preferential tariffs—this last indicator would range from 5.9 to 5.2 percent, that is, a figure close to block B results for 1995 and 1997.

EC "Overall" Protection Between 1990 and 2000

As is well known, EC trade protection is far from relying exclusively on tariffs. NTBs, such as variable levies in agriculture, voluntary export restraints (VERs) in industrial sectors (e.g., those imposed by the Multi-Fiber Agreement [MFA] in textiles and clothing or by the EC car agreement with Japan), quotas on imports from centrally planned economies, antidumping measures, and technical barriers to trade have played or are playing a significant role. Table 2.1 includes only "core" NTBs: import quotas, VERs, minima prices, and specific tariffs for which there are available ad valorem equivalents.

The other NTBs have been ignored, because they are too difficult to assess or too marginal—for instance, entry price system (fresh fruit and vegetables), excise duties imposed by EC member-states (beer, wine, and cigarettes), and state-trading enterprises (gas, electricity, and minerals in France; tobacco in Italy; one may also wonder whether EC domestic policies, such as the CAP, have not created de facto state-trading enterprises; see chapter 4). There are two exceptions: crude tariff equivalents of technical barriers to trade have been introduced for the food and car sectors because of their importance.[6] To combine all the NTBs taken into account in order to estimate the EC-wide and sectoral rates of overall protection requires two steps: (1) arriving at a better understanding of interactions between tariffs and other trade barriers through the communitarization process of EC trade policy, and (2) defining the method for combining tariffs and "tariff equivalents" of the NTBs and antidumping measures taken into account in table 2.1.

"Communitarizing" Trade Policy in Industrial Goods, 1977–97

In the early 1980s, protection of farm products was already almost entirely communitarized under the Common Agricultural Policy (see chapter 4 and appendix A, cases 15 to 19). By contrast, things have been more recent and complex in manufacturing. Until the early 1980s, NTBs on industrial

---

6. The reason is that both sectors are covered by the EC "Old Approach" in terms of technical harmonization (*Single Market Review* 1997c, 66), which is particularly rigid and prone to be captured by protectionist interests (see chapter 4). According to the scant available information for food products (*Single Market Review* 1998, vol. 1, 224), technical barriers could represent up to 20 to 25 percent of unit prices in the food sector; table 2.1 is based on a very conservative estimate of 5 percent. Similarly, an estimate of 4 percent has been used for the car sector, which is covered by 200 directives on technical regulations, out of a total of slightly more than 500 directives (see appendix A, case 12). This figure is very conservative: estimated cost equivalents of technical regulations imposed on certain auto parts range from 15 to 30 percent (in the case of Japanese exports to the EC) (OECD 2000g).

goods were introduced (although more and more rarely) and enforced by individual member-states.[7] The 1987–97 decade has witnessed the end of these practices and the communitarization of NTBs on imported industrial goods. What follows shows that this long process has exacted a price in protection costs because Community protection has been substituted for member-state protection, mostly through antidumping measures.

The 1974–85 steel depression offered the first major opportunity to communitarize trade policy on steel products—which, according to Articles 71 to 73 of the Treaty of Paris, was still a member-state competence (see box 1.1). In 1977–79, the Commission let fly a broadside of almost a hundred Community antidumping complaints, getting strong leverage on most foreign exporters to impose EC-wide VERs and price arrangements. Steel trade policy reached its full communitarization with the 1994 ruling of the European Court of Justice (see box 1.1) stating that, when included in an agreement of "general nature" with third countries, steel under the Treaty of Paris is subjected to the Community's exclusive competence, as defined by the Treaty of Rome.

For the other industrial products, the first steps toward communitarized trade NTBs occurred in 1982–83, when member-states agreed to freeze their existing national NTBs in two lists embodied in Regulation 288/82 (NTBs against exports from market economies) and Regulation 3420/83 (NTBs against nonmarket country exports). After the adoption of these regulations, the few tentative moves by member-states to impose new national NTBs were either stopped or undercut by Community measures, as is best illustrated by videocassette recorders (see appendix A, case 8).

In 1988, about 1,000 quotas (most of them imposed on imports from centrally planned economies) were still enforced by member-states—excluding the textile and clothing quotas under the MFA, which were negotiated by the Community, but on a member-state basis (Langhammer 1990). However, only a small proportion of these quotas triggered frequent requests under Article 134 (ex 115) mostly by France, Ireland, Italy, and Spain: during the 1980s only 100–150 derogations from intra-EC free circulation were granted every year.

The early 1990s witnessed the almost complete communitarization of the trade policy in four major steps. First, between 1989 and 1992, under the pressure from the bold, nondiscriminatory, unilateral trade liberalization undertaken by Central European countries, the EC eliminated almost

---

7. This feature raised the issue of whether or not it was possible to isolate completely a member-state market from the EC markets by using Article 115. In particular, Hamilton (1986) has argued that, in most of the cases, Article 115 has been unable to generate a perfect segmentation of the member-state markets, and hence that the lowest member-state NTBs were de facto the only relevant restrictions.

all member-state NTBs against exports from Central European countries when signing with them the Europe Agreements (see chapter 6). Second, the 1991 Japan-EC consensus on cars imposed an EC-wide VER, coupled with specific VERs for five member-states (see Appendix A, case 12). Third, in 1994, under the Uruguay Agreement on Safeguards, the EC committed itself to eliminate all its remaining "grey area" measures (except the Japan-EC car consensus, which was to be eliminated 31 December 1999, and indeed was eliminated at this time). Fourth, since 1995, the EC has imposed EC-wide restrictions following the Uruguay Agreement on Textiles and Clothing (see appendix A, cases 13 and 14). Since 1997, the EC has done the same on steel from certain Eastern European countries that are still not WTO members (Russia, Ukraine, and Kazakhstan). As a result, in mid-2001, the only major exceptions to complete communitarization of border instruments of protection are antidumping measures enforced only with respect to certain "regional" EC markets ("regional" generally meaning a certain member-state territory).

Combining NTBs and Antidumping Measures with Tariffs

Combining NTBs and antidumping measures with tariffs in table 2.1 imposes getting the ad valorem tariff equivalents of the NTBs, an exercise that requires looking separately at agriculture and industry. In agriculture, the only available estimates of *non*-tariff protection for 1990 and 1995 consist of the various "subsidy equivalents" calculated by the OECD Secretariat (see box 2.1). In 1999, tariffs had been substituted for the existing NTBs (variable levies, quotas, etc.) as a result of the implementation of the Uruguay Round. But *transparent* EC protection is still lacking, because many EC tariffs (almost one-half of farm tariff lines; WTO, *Trade Policy Review: The European Union*, 2000) are totally or partly expressed in specific terms (euros per physical unit of output), not in ad valorem terms. (Hence the level of protection effectively granted by such specific tariffs varies with world prices.) In other words, NTBs in EC agriculture include many specific tariffs (at least, those for which there has been no ad valorem equivalents made available to the WTO Secretariat by the EC Commission).

As a result, the subsidy equivalents calculated by the OECD still constitute the key source of information on which computations have to be calibrated. Table 2.1 combined these various sources of information as follows. For the four key farm products (cereals, meat, dairy products, and sugar), the sectoral CSE-based tariffs (more precisely, the average for the three years ending the year under scrutiny) are used as the estimates of the rates of overall protection. Then, the ad valorem tariff equivalents of the NTBs in these four sectors are calculated as the differences between

Box 2.1 Measuring the level of protection and support in agriculture

The OECD Secretariat provides two basic estimates of protection and support in agriculture: "consumer subsidy equivalents" or CSEs (which measure the transfers from domestic consumers to producers, resulting from agricultural policies); and "producer subsidy equivalents" or PSEs (which include all the transfers that farmers receive from farm policies). Because this study is interested in the costs of protection for consumers, it focuses on CSEs. The CSEs and PSEs used in this study are based on the "old" OECD method of measuring support, which is better suited for estimating the level and costs of protection than the "new" method (for a description of both methods, see OECD 1999a). However, the CSE and PSE data used in this study have been updated so that they benefit from all the corrections introduced through February 2000.

CSEs are available under two different forms: as a percentage of the consumption values at domestic prices, and as a percentage of world prices. In what follows, this latter form is called the CSE-based ad valorem tariff equivalent—for short, the CSE-based tariffs. The OECD Secretariat does not provide CSE-based tariffs directly; rather, it provides NACs ("Nominal Assistance Coefficients") defined as $[1 + (T/p^*)]$, where p^* is the world price and T the CSE in ECUs per unit (i.e., the tariff equivalent in ECUs per unit). In other words, CSE-based tariffs are defined by (T/p^*). NACs (and hence CSE-based tariffs) have often been disregarded because world farm prices could depend substantially on the farm policies of all the large OECD countries (introducing a circular causality when estimating costs of protection). However, chapter 3 provides evidence that the EC (alone) is not a much larger world producer of farm goods than of industrial products.

Table 2.1 is based on the CSE-based tariffs. The fact that Hufbauer and Elliott's study of US protection (1994) relies on simple CSEs (and not on CSE-based tariffs) is without any serious consequence for comparing the two studies, because CSEs and CSE-based tariffs are close in the US case (except for dairy and sugar). By contrast, using CSEs (instead of CSE-based tariffs) in the EC case would have led to severe underestimates of the costs of protection in the EC.

---

the MFN tariffs and the sectoral CSE-based tariffs. For the rest of agriculture ("other agriculture"), a more global procedure has been followed.[8]

In manufacturing, because ad valorem equivalents of NTBs (essentially import quotas and voluntary export restraints) are notoriously difficult to estimate, this study has not tried to generate such estimates systematically. Rather, it draws on existing information (the various sources are

---

8. This more global procedure adopted has three steps. First, the average rate of overall protection of the whole agriculture has been estimated (see block C of table 2.1) as the weighted sum of the overall CSE-based tariff estimated by the OECD (for detail, see table 4.2) and the average MFN tariff for the rest of agriculture. The weights used are drawn from the production: 60 percent for the overall CSE-based tariff (the OECD Secretariat estimates that the CSE-based tariffs cover roughly 60 percent of EC farm production) and 40 percent for the rest of agriculture. Second, the average rate of overall protection for "other agriculture" has been defined as the weighted difference between overall protection for the whole of agriculture and overall protection for the four sectors (in this case, the weights are the number

mentioned in the detailed case studies provided in appendix A).[9] Concerning antidumping measures, they can first consist of ad valorem duties; in this case, it is simple to combine them with tariffs. They can also consist of specific tariffs, minimum prices, or quantitative restrictions. In these cases, ad valorem equivalents of such measures have been estimated on the basis of the dumping margins (always expressed in ad valorem terms in EC antidumping procedures; see appendix B) multiplied by a (conservative) coefficient of 0.5 (this coefficient replicates the proportion observed, on average, in the cases that provide appropriate information). Antidumping cases initiated between 1980 and 1989 have been combined with the 1990 tariffs; those initiated between 1986 and 1994, with the 1995 tariffs; and those initiated between 1992 and 1999, with the 1999 tariffs.[10]

The last step is to aggregate all these equivalents of NTBs and antidumping measures with tariffs in order to get the rates of "overall" protection by industrial sector and for the whole EC economy. The method used differs for NTBs and antidumping measures. Concerning NTBs, the available ad valorem estimates have been added to the average tariffs of the sectors in question. Concerning antidumping, the aggregation procedure is as follows: For each sector, the share of tariff lines under antidumping measures (table 2.1 provides the number of tariff lines under antidumping measures) has been computed to get the share-weighted average ad valorem antidumping duty, which then has been added to the existing sectoral average tariff.[11] One could argue that this method as-

---

of tariff lines). Third, the NTBs for "other agriculture" are the differences between the rate of overall (CSE-based) protection and the average MFN tariff. It is interesting that this procedure provides a rate of overall protection for "other agriculture" for 1999 (20 percent) very close to the rate of protection (aggregating ad valorem tariffs and ad valorem equivalents of specific tariffs) estimated by the WTO Secretariat (17.3 percent) for the same year.

9. In the case of coal (not included in the appendix A cases), ad valorem equivalents of NTBs are derived from estimates (Anderson 1995; Fundación de Economía Analítica 1998) of the German subsidies (weighted by the production share of German coal in the EC). It is assumed that there are no subsidies in the rest of the EC coal sector, a very conservative assumption for Belgium, France, Spain, and (since the recent arbitrage between coal and gas) Britain.

10. Combining 7 to 9 years of antidumping cases may seem inconsistent with the sunset clause in EC antidumping regulations, which requires the automatic expiration of antidumping measures after 5 years of enforcement. But, as shown in appendix B, there is strong evidence that the time span of antidumping measures has lasted more than 5 years (on average, 7–8 years, at least) because of delays, legal disputes, and "reviews" of all kinds, so that the effective impact of the sunset clause is limited.

11. Conservative methods have been used to count the number of lines. Double counting has been eliminated (tariff lines concerning two or more cases have been counted once). This approach explains almost entirely the decline in the number of tariff lines between 1995 and 1999 shown in table 2.1. Ignoring double counting would give 475 lines in 1995 and 449 lines in 1999 (comparing the latter figure with the 336 lines given in table 2.1 gives an indication of the intensity of harassment in certain sectors—mostly textiles and steel). Tariff lines

sumes that antidumping measures are applied on an MFN (nondiscrimi-natory) basis, whereas they are imposed only on certain countries. How-ever, available evidence shows that de facto, they apply to all sources of competitive producers, and have a powerful "chilling" effect on the rest of the producers (Messerlin 1989).

Overall Protection: Level and Evolution

The estimated rates of overall protection suggest five observations. First, the estimated *level* of EC *overall* protection is still high; the EC-wide aver-age rate of overall protection until 1997 was roughly 13 to 14 percent, almost double the EC-wide average tariff. Moreover, following the Uru-guay Round, this level declines only by a small amount, because it was still close to 12 percent in 1999. This modest decline is due to the fact that liberalization has been concentrated on already low rates of overall pro-tection, as can be shown with table 2.1; sectoral rates of overall protection higher than 13 percent in 1995 declined by 18 percent in 1999, whereas sectoral rates lower than this threshold declined by 40 percent—note that these declines are *smaller* than those observed for the tariffs alone (23 and 52 percent, respectively; see above).

These results are far from being exclusively due to the heavily NTB-based protection of farm (ISIC 100) and food (ISIC 311 to 313) products. Of course, the rate of overall protection in agriculture was still high in 1999—more than 30 percent for the whole agricultural sector (see block C of table 2.1). If it declined between 1990 and 1995 (due to the increases of key world farm prices in 1995), it remained stable between 1995 and 1999, although the shift from border protection (reflected in the CSEs) to nonborder pro-tection (mirrored in the PSEs) after the Uruguay Round is *not* captured in table 2.1 (which relies entirely on CSE-based tariffs). But NTBs and an-tidumping measures also increase the rate of overall protection of *indus-trial* goods *stricto sensu* by a third or two-thirds—from 6.7 to 11 percent in 1995, and from 4.3 to 7.7 percent in 1999 (see block B of the table).

Second, NTBs and antidumping measures tend to be *concentrated* in the same sectors: The decline in NTBs (imposed by EC member-states) ob-

---

involved in cases terminated by a "no dumping" conclusion have been ignored but not those included in cases terminated by a "no injury" or in withdrawn cases, in order to take into account the "chilling" effect of antidumping complaints. Last, tariff lines specified with only six digits have been counted as only one tariff line: for instance, tariff line *xxxx.xx*00 (where *x* represents numbers) has been counted as one tariff line, even if it includes two tariff lines *xxxx.xx*10 and *xxxx.xx*20. One case (cotton fabric) has been treated in an ad hoc way. The 1994 version of this case has had much wider coverage than cases in subsequent years. De-spite the fact that no measures have terminated the 1994 case, the tariff lines included in this case but not in the subsequent cases have been counted as if subjected to an antidumping "measure" of 3 percent, in order to take into account the "harassment" associated with the 1996 and 1997 versions of the same case.

served between 1990 and 1999 has often been compensated for by the expanding product coverage of Community antidumping measures (particularly in the cases of consumer electronics and textiles, but also in fisheries and mining) and by increasingly high antidumping measures (see appendix B)—again putting back to back the Fortress Europe and Open Europe arguments (Pelkmans and Carzaniga 1996, 99).[12] This evolution is worrisome, all the more because the average ad valorem tariff equivalent of antidumping measures increased from 17.5 percent (on a per tariff line basis) in 1990 to 22.4 percent—that is, almost three times the average MFN bound tariff—in 1999.

Of course, one could argue that the average antidumping ad valorem equivalent is only 0.8 percent when spread across *all* manufacturing sectors (in other words, antidumping contributes only 7 percent to the overall rate of protection). But this argument misses the point that this instrument has been used (so far) in 350–450 tariff lines only (of a total of almost 11,000). When one considers only the manufacturing sectors that have been effectively subject to antidumping procedures, antidumping contributes 13 percent to the rate of *overall* protection of these sectors.

The few sectors where NTBs have not been (so far) replaced by antidumping measures are cars and other transport equipment (ships, trains, aircraft, etc.), which could still rely on even more powerful alternative instruments of protection, such as norms, repressed competition at the distribution level, subsidies, tied contracts, and public procurement. A last source of re-protection is the permanent, substantial tariff "reshuffling" after 1995; creating more tariff lines allows getting tailor-made protection of existing domestic production (note that farm [ISIC 100] and food [ISIC 311–12] products, textiles [ISIC 321], and industrial chemicals [ISIC 351]—all very actively protected industries—are among the sectors with the highest number of tariff lines by unit of value added).[13]

Third, the most heavily protected sectors (farm and food products, textiles, and apparel) exhibit almost *constant* rates of protection between 1990 and 1997 (not shown in table 2.1), and the decline was very limited (if there was any) between 1997 and 1999. It should be added that a *declining* simple average rate of protection by sector can be consistent with a *constant* level of protection granted to domestic production if the imple-

---

12. Our conservative method for reporting the number of tariff lines in antidumping cases has led to the elimination of more than a hundred lines in textiles for the years 1995 and 1997. If one takes into account this point, the trade coverage of antidumping cases in terms of nonfarm tariff lines is increasing from 3.5 percent (1990) to 4.6 percent (1997).

13. Indeed, there was a noticeable hike of the EC protection rate between 1995 and 1997 (13.9 to 14.3 percent). This hike is the arithmetical consequence of averaging over tariff lines (when calculating simple averages); there is no hike if one combines the level of protection in 1997 and the number of tariff lines in 1995. But it is important to emphasize that this hike has a real economic meaning, to the extent that it mirrors the protectionist impact of a much more detailed tariff schedule.

mented protectionist instruments are increasingly "better" targeting the domestic output to be protected—a hypothesis quite compatible with the "optimal" use (from the complainants' point of view) of antidumping measures.

Fourth, the *dispersion* between rates of overall protection by sector is larger than the dispersion between sectoral tariff averages, because NTBs and antidumping measures vary between sectors more widely than tariffs (antidumping measures reach levels rarely achieved by industrial tariffs, even maxima tariffs, such as 80 or 100 percent).

Fifth, labor-weighted rates of overall protection are higher than the corresponding simple averages—suggesting that EC *overall* protection is concentrated in labor-intensive sectors, a result consistent with the perception of the EC as a relatively capital-abundant economy, and confirming the suggestion that protecting with NTBs and antidumping measures is much more attractive to vested interests than trying to modify tariffs. However, the differences between simple and labor-weighted averages appear to be smaller in 1999 than before. This evolution may reflect the fact that what counts in recent antidumping cases is sheer political clout and legal expertise, which reduce the need to demonstrate job losses and make the antidumping instrument equally available to capital-intensive as well as labor-intensive industries.

Concluding Remarks

The above results complement, refine, and generalize those reached by two recent studies (Hoeller, Girouard, and Colechia 1998; Daly and Kuwahara 1998) by looking at a much more detailed production structure and by introducing the tariff equivalents of major trade barriers (NTBs and antidumping measures). When comparing the EC to the three other Quad countries (Canada, Japan, and the United States), the two other studies conclude that EC tariff protection is higher than in the United States and Japan (including after the full implementation of the Uruguay Round commitments).

The above exercise has two main limits. First, it relies exclusively on *nominal* tariffs (and tariff equivalents). *Effective* rates of protection (which take into account the impact of trade barriers imposed on inputs imported by domestic producers) are not provided in this study, because there is no input-output table available for the EC at the disaggregation level reached by table 2.1. Indeed, effective rates of protection based on the information provided in this chapter are unlikely to be very different from nominal tariffs, because the peaks of EC protection are largely eroded by the level (ISIC 3-digit) used for defining sectors (the "averaging" effect). That being said, it is clear that the EC production structure must face some very large effective rates of protection, because tariffs higher than 50 or 100 percent are not so rare.

Second, the chapter provides no estimates of the level of protection for all the services. On the basis of appendix A, cases 20 to 22, chapter 3 provides estimates of the level of EC protection for three services (films, passenger air transport, and telecommunications) that range from 40 to 100 percent—suggesting huge costs of protection in EC services. These estimates of the level of protection are high when compared with other available estimates, which suggests that protection in services is no more than double the average merchandise protection (Hoekman 2000). This may be due to the fact that the absence of effective liberalization in services makes it very hard to find a good "free trade" benchmark in services, because links between prices and production costs are much looser in services than in manufacturing. For instance, retailers may not seem very well protected because the price of their services does not differ much between countries; but that tells little about potential differences in their production costs, which should constitute the basis for measuring the level of protection (and which are much better captured in the manufacturing sector).

3

The Costs of Protection in the European Community

A study of EC trade policy in the coming decade should focus on the remaining peaks of protection because they are generating the highest domestic costs, and hottest international *and* domestic tensions. There is an additional reason for such a focus: most of the highly protected EC activities examined in detail in this chapter are similar to those listed by the study on the costs of protection in the US economy done by Hufbauer and Elliott (1994), suggesting that almost the *same* sectors in the OECD countries have been able to resist past trade liberalization. Many of these highly protected products are intermediate goods (used as inputs by EC producers) in which developing countries have comparative advantages. This concentrated survival of protection may reflect the limited participation of developing countries in past rounds of WTO negotiations, and the capacity of EC firms to "pass through" peaks of protection downstream to consumers.

During the WTO negotiations of the coming decade, reciprocity is unlikely to work with such round-immune, worldwide troublemaking sectors, which always argue that they are being hurt by a liberalization that they have been successful at aborting. *Unilateral* actions are necessary to cope with them. The first step in such actions is to recognize the problem at stake by revealing the domestic costs of protection of these highly protected sectors. This is the topic of this chapter.

The focus on EC high protection during the 1990s pinpointed 22 products and services (5 in agriculture, 14 in manufacturing, and 3 in services) characterized by a high rate of overall protection. The absence of available information on the relations between these products and services, and between them and the rest of the economy, has made necessary the use of partial-equilibrium models to estimate the costs of protection, although such models can neither catch income effects nor the feedback effects from a better allocation of resources generated by freer trade (including dynamic interactions between economic growth and trade).

But a general-equilibrium approach requires quantitative information on the existing links between sectors—hence it is forced to rely on "prefabricated" sectors (generally derived from national accounts). This is a severe constraint when one focuses on trade negotiations because prefabricated sectors aggregate products under low and high levels of protection. The resulting *average* rates of protection by sector do not reflect peak rates, and thus they generate systematic and possibly large underestimates of protection costs (because those costs increase more than the level of protection; e.g., they are a function of the *square* of the rates of protection in the case of linear supply and demand functions).

The chapter provides two major results about the *magnitude* of the costs of protection for EC consumers. (The reasons for using the costs of protection for consumers as the preferred measure, in sharp contrast to the traditional approach, are explained in the section estimating the costs of protection in the perfect competition case). First, the estimated costs of protection in agriculture and manufacturing for EC consumers amount to 6 percent of the value added generated by these two sectors, when perfectly competitive markets are assumed in the protected sectors.

However, almost all the industrial products (12 of the 14) and a significant portion of the farm goods examined in detail in this chapter are produced under imperfect competition. Taking into account this aspect increases by one-third on average the protection costs of the highly protected goods involved, despite conservative assumptions about the extent to which trade liberalization would allow shifting to more competitive domestic markets. As a result, the protection costs of the *whole* EC agriculture and manufacturing sectors (including all the products not pertaining to the 19 highly protected goods examined) would amount to 7 percent of the corresponding value added.

Second, estimating the costs of protection in the three services examined in detail suggests even higher figures—almost one-sixth of the corresponding value added. Introducing imperfect competition doubles these estimates. However, because the three services represent only a small proportion of all tradable services, these estimates have not been extrapolated to the whole EC service sector. But they suggest that the costs of EC protection (goods *and* services) could easily represent 7 percent of the *entire* EC GDP—the equivalent of the Spanish GDP.

These results deserve a caveat and a remark. The caveat is that the above estimates assume that the Single Market is working effectively— that there are no substantial nonborder barriers left in *intra-EC* trade. This assumption is still not fulfilled for a noticeable number of goods because norms, standards, and other kinds of technical regulations still constitute substantial barriers to trade (see chapter 4). And it is a heroic assumption for services, simply because intra-EC liberalization in services is only two to three years old, and quite incomplete (see chapter 5). This caveat suggests the following remark. The *level* of EC protection may be similar to what exists in the other Quad countries (see chapter 2), but this does not imply that the *costs* of protection are similar. Relatively high and frequent remaining intra-EC barriers are likely to allow more imperfect competition in the EC Single Market than in the "single" markets of the other Quad countries. Hence they are likely to make protection more costly in the EC than in the other Quad countries.

Asking for protection (and granting it) has one essential motive: to generate domestic income *transfers*. Analyzing protection would thus be incomplete without assessing the main winners and losers in the EC. In this respect, the chapter provides two major results. First, contrary to a belief widespread in Europe, protection is a costly instrument for "saving" jobs. Only a few jobs—roughly 3 percent of the total number of jobs existing in the 22 sectors involved—are estimated to have been possibly saved by the high protection granted to these sectors. The combination of high costs of protection for EC consumers and few jobs saved leads to an astronomical average annual cost per job saved: roughly €220,000, or 10 times the European average wage of the sectors in question. If saving jobs is the issue at stake, it must—and can—be addressed by more efficient policies than trade protection.

Second, the instruments of import protection used by the EC have the crucial—and very undesirable—feature of granting large rents to vested interests. In fact, estimated rents are *larger* than tariff revenues collected by the EC authorities. For the 22 products and services examined in detail, rents represent 30 percent (if one minimizes the likelihood of the existence of such rents) to 40 percent (if one makes more plausible guesses about existing rents) of the total costs of protection for EC consumers—relative to 24 and 13 percent, respectively, for tariff revenues.

Of course, the existence of such rents is not specific to the EC, as is illustrated by the following remark made in the US context: "Special interests seeking protection have 'captured' trade policy and moved it away from the domain of public good" (Krueger 1992). But again their magnitude might be specific to the EC, to the extent it reflects more frequent situations of imperfect competition—hence EC protection is more "captured" by vested interests with strong incentives and means to keep the external protection unchanged *and* to slow down the emergence of more competitive EC markets (for a description of such vested interests in the EC, see Pedler and van Schendelen 1994).

These conclusions fly in the face of the traditional views about protection and liberalization in Continental Europe, where protection is often perceived, and justified, as an expression of some kind of "public interest" (e.g., strategic goods, cultural differences, social stability, etc.) and where free trade is widely seen as favoring narrow-minded "private" interests. The above results suggest that the reality of European protection is quite the opposite. Massive private rents are derived from protection by a happy few, and resulting large costs are imposed on many European consumers, who may be beginning to realize this point, as is illustrated by the tone less favorable to farmers during the March 1999 debate on reforms in EC agriculture (see chapter 4). However, vested interests may be quick to adjust to this recent evolution by adopting a "smiling" face to promote protection—for instance, by flaunting themselves as protectors of the environment or food safety, despite the abundant evidence showing quite the contrary.

This chapter is organized as follows: the first section below presents a brief review of the 22 highly protected sectors examined in detail. The second section estimates the costs of protection for these sectors, and for the rest of the EC output of goods aggregated in one sector, in a perfect-competition framework that allows comparisons with the Hufbauer-Elliott study (1994) on the costs of US protection. The third section reestimates these costs for an imperfect-competition environment more appropriate to the EC economy. Last, the fourth section looks at three adjacent issues: the stability of protection in the 22 sectors during the 1990s, the possibility of terms-of-trade effects reducing the costs of protection for the EC, and the relative impact of "preferential" (compared with multilateral) liberalization.

Twenty-two Highly Protected EC Sectors: A Presentation

Table 3.1 lists the 22 EC products and services highly protected in 1990, and appendix A gives a detailed description of protection for each. The list does not cover all the EC highly protected sectors. Ideally, at least half a dozen manufacturing sectors (fishing, beverages, coal, nonferrous metals, footwear and leather products, glass, machine tools, pharmaceuticals, shipbuilding, and aerospace) could have been added, as well as many service sectors.[1] However, lack of data about the exact level of protection and the economic performances of these sectors has prevented doing so. Because the 22 sectors involve both intermediate and final goods or services (in fact, most are intermediate), EC consumers should be understood as both households (consumers of final goods and services) *and* firms (consumers of intermediate goods and services)—a key point, because trade in intermediate goods accounts for a substantial percentage of EC and world trade.

---

1. WTO, *Trade Policy Review: The European Union*, 2000, provides information on some of these highly protected sectors (electrical equipment, pharmaceuticals, shipbuilding, and aerospace).

Table 3.1   Characteristics of 22 highly protected sectors, 1990

Sector	Additional protection initiated by European Community (period)	Domestic shipments (millions of euros)	Imports (c.i.f. and duties paid) (millions of euros)	Average annual percentage change of imports, 1988–90	Number of workers (thousands)	Estimated value added[a] (millions of euros)	Estimated average wages[b] (euros)
Cement	1985	9,171.8	291.2	35.2	58.0	3,810.5	23,466
Fertilizers	1980	1,413.4	1,937.9	8.0	28.0	488.4	34,361
Low-density polyethylene	1982	6,957.6	1,407.0	25.9	34.0	2,404.1	34,361
Polyvinyl chloride	1981	4,069.6	597.7	35.6	18.0	1,406.2	34,361
Hardboard	1986	7,904.2	2,635.7	5.5	71.0	2,845.2	15,038
Newsprint[c]		1,782.7	2,436.9	3.2	14.0	778.1	25,026
Chemical fibers	1960s	9,117.2	1,942.0	8.1	71.8	3,150.3	34,361
Videocassette recorders	1982	1,794.4	710.8	−28.8	16.0	797.8	27,464
Integrated circuits	1987	1,989.8	4,606.0	4.1	41.6	715.4	25,481
Photocopiers	1985	1,274.9	962.1	7.4	24.0	667.9	23,909
Steel	1970s	58,588.7	4,994.2	11.7	379.4	18,584.3	26,086
Passenger cars	1970s	92,702.5	10,567.4	9.5	1,229.0	27,359.6	28,404
Textiles	1960s	112,580.5	21,353.0	8.5	1,636.5	43,539.4	15,508
Clothing	1960s	64,569.8	18,096.4	15.1	1,234.6	25,112.0	12,213
Cereals	1960s	22,572.0	1,382.4	−0.2	1,134.0	15,013.8	13,725
Meat	1960s	24,864.0	2,767.0	7.5	946.1	16,538.3	16,063
Dairy products	1960s	27,597.9	1,462.4	1.7	36.9	18,356.8	18,760
Sugar	1960s	5,073.0	1,789.0	2.3	275.1	3,374.3	13,680
Bananas[d]	1993	376.4	1,188.0	17.1	25.0	250.4	7,000
Films (France)	1986	206.9	563.5	15.9	21.7	137.9	25,000
Air transport[c]		27,536.6	18,869.9	6.8	296.8	18,357.7	30,000
Telecoms[c]		62,751.0	4,700.6	17.6	703.3	41,834.0	25,562

(table continues next page)

Table 3.1   Characteristics of 22 highly protected sectors, 1990 *(continued)*

Sector	Additional protection initiated by European Community (period)	Domestic shipments (millions of euros)	Imports (c.i.f. and duties paid) (millions of euros)	Average annual percentage change of imports, 1988–90	Number of workers (thousands)	Estimated value added[a] (millions of euros)	Estimated average wages[b] (euros)
Totals for the 22 sectors, by economic activity							
Agriculture		80,483.3	8,588.8	5.1	2,417.1	53,533.6	14,642
Manufacturing		373,917.1	72,538.3	9.6	4,855.9	131,659.2	19,632
Market services		90,494.5	24,134.0	9.1	1,021.8	60,329.7	26,839
Total		544,894.9	105,261.1	9.2	8,294.8	245,522.4	19,066
Sectors, in percentage of the corresponding activities							
Agriculture		40.1	17.7		29.3	40.1	97.6
Manufacturing		11.0	15.7		14.9	10.9	85.4
Market services[e]		2.4	13.4		2.3	2.4	117.2
Total		7.4	15.2		9.6	6.4	86.3

c.i.f. = cost, insurance, freight
ISIC = International Standard Industrial Classification.

a. Estimates for manufacturing sectors are based on the ratio (value-added/production) for the corresponding ISIC sectors. For farm products, they are based on the ratio (value-added/production) for the whole agricultural sector. For services, they are based on the ratio (value-added/production) for the whole service sector.
b. Estimates based on ISIC average wages (manufacturing), and on sectoral data for the other sectors.
c. Member-state protection still dominant by 1990.
d. Both production and distribution.
e. Excluding nonmarket services.

Sources: Case studies in appendix A; European Commission (1995).

Table 3.1 shows that protectionist measures at the Community level were granted to these sectors a long time ago (mostly during the 1960s and early 1970s). Table 3.2 shows that barriers are very high (with protection peaks in ISIC sectors that table 2.1 did not present as highly protected): 15 of the 22 sectors have an overall protection rate higher than 30 percent, and 19 sectors have an overall protection rate higher than 15 percent. The fourth section below provides detailed information showing the stability of protection in these 22 sectors during the 1990s. It shows that the estimated costs of protection in terms of value added are stable since the relative sizes of the sectors examined have not substantially changed during the past decade (highly protected services taking the little room left by less highly protected agriculture and manufacturing sectors), and since there is no reason to believe that other parameters, e.g., elasticities or degree of labor mobility, have profoundly changed.

As table 3.1 shows, domestic shipments of the 22 sectors represent almost 7.5 percent of total EC production. This coverage varies widely by economic activity. The farm sectors on the list cover almost 40 percent of EC farm output, whereas the manufacturing sectors represent 11 percent of EC industrial production (mostly because of steel, passenger cars, and textiles and clothing), and the three service sectors account for only 3 percent of the EC production of "market services."[2] However, looking at the *relative* magnitude of these sectors is also important for getting a sense of the costs of protection to be expected. The combined production of the 14 listed industrial sectors is almost five times larger than the combined output of the listed farm sectors, and the combined production of the three service sectors is larger than the farm output. In other words, manufacturing and service sectors with such large pockets of high protection should be expected to be a substantial source of high costs of protection.

In manufacturing, the coverage of protection in terms of workers is higher than in terms of production, mirroring the concentration of EC protection in labor-intensive industrial sectors. This is not the case in the farm and service sectors; but in the early 1990s, none of these sectors was exposed to domestic regulatory reform, not even to mention liberalization and foreign competition.[3] Although less precise, the evidence about average wages provided by table 3.1 is consistent with the above remarks. Wages in the highly protected manufacturing sectors are, on average,

---

2. Market services range from distribution to transport, financial services, professional services of all kinds, market-based health, and education services. They represented more than 52 percent of the EC GDP in 1990 (more than 57 percent in 1995–96) (OECD 1998b). Their importance explains the small coverage (in percentage) of the three sectors examined. Nonmarket services represented less than 13 percent in 1990 (as in 1995–96).

3. The figure for farmers deserves a remark. In 1990, of a total of 8.2 million farmers in Europe, there were only 4.5 million "professional" farmers (i.e., farmers selling to markets on a regular basis). The other farmers produced for their own consumption (retired people or gardeners), but were nevertheless entitled to some benefits of the Common Agricultural Policy.

Table 3.2   Estimated welfare effects of liberalizing the 22 protected sectors: The perfect-competition case

Sector	Overall ad valorem tariff equivalent (percent)	Induced increase in (c.i.f.) imports (millions of euros)	Consumer surplus gain		Breakdown of the consumer surplus gain (A2)				Net national welfare gain[b] (F = D + E) (millions of euros)
			A1[a] (millions of euros)	A2[b] (millions of euros)	Producer surplus[b] (B) (millions of euros)	Tariff revenue[a,b] (C) (millions of euros)	Quota rent[a,b] (D) (millions of euros)	Efficiency gain (E) (millions of euros)	
Cement	22.8	84.3	99.3	78.0	14.4	9.0	45.0	9.6	54.7
Fertilizers	32.7	479.7	829.2	641.6	86.0	477.3	0.0	78.5	78.5
Low-density polyethylene	12.5	557.0	265.6	300.0	108.9	156.3	0.0	34.8	34.8
Polyvinyl chloride	12.5	252.0	120.0	132.0	49.8	66.4	0.0	15.7	15.7
Hardboard	25.0	798.4	830.1	739.1	112.8	239.6	286.8	99.6	386.4
Newsprint	7.0	159.9	82.2	191.5	26.6	159.4	0.0	5.6	5.6
Chemical fibers	22.9	686.0	433.1	580.1	138.9	362.4	0.0	78.7	78.7
Videocassette recorders	30.2	442.3	289.4	313.1	81.7	164.7	0.0	66.7	66.7
Integrated circuits	47.6	2,373.3	3,462.6	2,187.4	138.6	547.7	936.4	564.2	1,500.6
Photocopiers	33.7	394.2	287.1	313.5	4.8	242.4	0.0	66.4	66.4
Steel	21.9	3,043.8	2,423.1	1,626.1	396.5	228.7	667.7	333.1	1,000.8
Passenger cars	17.1	3,223.9	2,402.5	2,100.8	277.9	978.5	568.5	275.8	844.3
Textiles	21.4	6,275.0	5,954.0	7,095.6	2,677.7	1,742.4	2,007.2	668.3	2,675.5
Clothing	31.3	6,891.4	7,655.4	7,102.8	1,711.9	1,695.6	2,618.5	1,078.5	3,697.1
Cereals	63.0	2,996.8	2,792.0	3,211.9	1,770.2	497.7	0.0	944.1	944.1
Meat	95.0	2,766.6	4,998.8	4,108.4	1,599.5	1,194.9	0.0	1,314.0	1,314.0
Dairy products	104.0	1,842.1	3,643.6	2,717.2	1,061.7	697.7	0.0	957.8	957.8
Sugar	117.0	3,942.1	4,040.6	4,268.3	979.5	982.7	0.0	2,306.1	2,306.1
Bananas	81.9	448.4	1,076.5	824.6	106.0	136.6	398.3	183.7	582.0

Films (France)	76.8	280.0	547.9	406.4	54.1	35.0	209.7	107.5	317.3
Air transport	71.0	2,289.5	9,414.3	8,761.3	113.2	1,654.9	6,179.9	813.3	6,993.2
Telecom	45.2	5,740.6	5,887.8	3,929.7	1,169.0	0.0	1,463.3	1,297.4	2,760.7
Totals for the 22 sectors, by economic activity[c]									
Agriculture	90.4	11,996.0	16,551.4	15,130.4	5,516.8	3,509.5	398.3	5,705.7	6,104.1
Manufacturing	22.2	25,661.2	25,133.7	23,401.7	5,826.5	7,070.4	7,130.2	3,375.6	10,505.8
Market services	53.1	8,310.1	15,850.0	13,097.4	1,336.4	1,689.9	7,852.9	2,218.2	10,071.1
All 22 sectors	37.4	45,967.3	57,535.1	51,629.5	12,679.7	12,269.9	15,381.5	11,299.5	26,680.9
The sector producing the rest of the goods[d]									
Tariffs and nontariff barriers	6.1	54,679.6	35,352.5	41,162.3	15,212.2	13,848.6	10,482.3	1,661.8	12,144.2
Only tariffs	3.4	30,755.4	13,263.0	22,984.9	8,603.7	13,840.8	0.0	540.3	540.3

c.i.f. = cost, insurance, freight

a. Based on Francois-Hall (1997) model.
b. Based on Hufbauer-Elliott (1994) model.
c. Tariffs are shipment-weighted tariffs of the corresponding 22 sectors.
d. This sector excludes all services.

Sources: Case studies in appendix A; European Commission (1995); author's computations.

lower than the average industrial wage—mirroring the expected wage differentials between export (capital-intensive) sectors and import-competing (labor-intensive) sectors in a relatively capital-abundant economy like the EC. The same relation holds, less clearly, in agriculture, but not in market services (again probably reflecting the highly regulated environment of these activities).

All 22 sectors but one have experienced (and are still experiencing) severe problems with intensity of competition in EC markets. Farm products are covered by the "common market organizations" (see chapter 4) and by a host of related institutions that severely limit competition (from farm trade unions to cooperatives in banking, in input purchasing, and in product marketing) and by a trade regime that generates anticompetitive situations (particularly in distribution; see Abbott 1998 and appendix A, cases 15, 18, and 19) to such an extent that many observers consider EC major farm goods as subject to a quasi state-trading regime. In manufacturing, all the listed sectors have been subject to long-lasting "crisis cartels" (chemical fibers, steel), to fines for repeated collusive or anticompetitive behavior (cement, basic chemicals, passenger cars), or to both, leaving only clothing as a sector not too much plagued by anticompetitive behavior.

Last, the three listed market services illustrate the three main imperfectly competitive situations existing in EC services: public firms in a highly regulated environment (air transport); public monopolies or dominant firms (telecommunications); and a small oligopoly with a fringe of tiny competitive firms in a hyper-subsidized and -regulated environment (filmmakers). These observations strongly suggest the merit of estimating the costs of protection for European consumers not only in a perfect-competition situation (see the next section) but also in an imperfect-competition environment (see the following section). The difference between these two estimates could be interpreted as reflecting at least partly the additional costs of the absence of a fully functioning Single Market, given prevailing EC external barriers on imports from the rest of the world.

Costs of Protection:
The Perfect-Competition Case

Table 3.2 presents the costs of EC protection estimated with two alternative models. Using the Hufbauer-Elliott model (1994), adopted in the study on the costs of protection in the United States, allows a direct comparison with their results for the US economy. The model, described in more detail in appendix C, assumes that domestic and imported goods are not perfect substitutes, that the supply of imported goods is perfectly elastic, and that the supply of domestic goods is less than perfectly elastic. (Appendix A provides detailed information about the elasticities used for each product and service). The cross-elasticities of demand have been calculated by using the modified Cournot aggregation condition (Tarr 1990) based on three basic price elasticities (for total domestic demand, domestic supply, and foreign supply) and on the elasticity of substitution between domestic and imported goods.

The fact that such a model cannot take into account input costs (by construction) has two implications. First, it misses an important reason for asking for protection: in order not to be squeezed by high protection on their inputs, producers request high protection on their outputs (for lowering effective protection). Second, the production-generated rents revealed by the model may be captured not by the producers directly involved, but by input owners—as is best illustrated by the case of farm products (most of the rents are going to landowners and other providers of essential inputs, e.g., capital, distribution services, or holders of licenses to produce; see chapter 4). The use of the Francois-Hall model (1997) has two motives (also described in appendix C): first, it allows for testing the robustness of the results obtained by the Hufbauer-Elliott model; second, it allows for analyzing two important adjacent issues, namely, the possible impact of terms-of-trade effects on the costs of protection in the EC, and the gains from "preferential" liberalization compared with those from multilateral liberalization (see the last section, below).

This section (and the rest of the chapter) highlights one measure of the costs of protection: those costs paid by EC consumers. This focus deserves an explanation because, as is well known, costs for consumers are the widest possible definition of protection costs; they include tariff revenues and rents to firms that are usually analyzed as pure transfers between nationals of the country in question, and consequently usually are not considered costs for the economy. By contrast, the traditional approach limits protection costs to the "efficiency gains" (the Harberger triangles) generated by the elimination of the misallocation of resources imposed by protection. However, this usual approach does not fit the EC case very well, for two reasons.

The first reason is related to nontariff-barrier rents. Are these rents transfers between domestic consumers and producers, are they collected by foreign (or even "domestic") firms shifting them to the rest of the world, or do they consist of real trade costs? Three observations can be made: (1) Certain nontariff barriers (NTBs) for the 22 products and services are equivalent to voluntary export restraints generating rents captured by foreign firms (see appendix A). (2) Other NTBs are closely related to technical regulations aimed at raising rivals' costs (see chapter 4). (3) The upholding of many NTBs during the long communitarization process has required a lot of effort and money-wasting resources and created "directly unproductive profit-seeking" activities. For all these reasons, adding rents to efficiency gains in order to get the "net national welfare gain" (following the Hufbauer-Elliott [1994] terminology) in a substantial number of the 22 products and services provides a better indicator of gains from trade liberalization than narrowly defined efficiency gains.

The second reason relates to tariff revenues. It flows from the fact that the EC is not (yet) a "country." Are tariff revenues then a transfer from "Europeans" to the Community budget, or are they a transfer from consumers of one member-state to the budget of another member-state—and hence a cost of protection from the first state's point of view? One could argue that this question is irrelevant because the pooling of tariff revenues by the EC implies that, ultimately, consumers in one member-state benefit from tariff revenues raised from consumers in another member-state. However, such an outcome is far from being assured. EC decisions in trade-related matters are also the outcome of hard bargaining between member-states; hence, they increase real trade costs and/or generate directly unproductive profit-seeking activities. Moreover, a substantial proportion (40 percent) of EC tariff revenues is spent on EC international actions or on costs for levying tariffs (as a matter of fact, low EC tariffs do not cover the costs of levying them). For all these reasons, including tariff revenues in the costs of protection does not appear, in the EC case, an unreasonable approach.

In sum, the costs of protection for European consumers look, on the whole, like a more accurate indicator than the usual narrowly defined efficiency gains. In any case, table 3.2 provides separate estimates for all basic components of the costs of protection, so that the reader can find his or her preferred measure. Globally, it shows that the estimated "efficiency gains" from liberalizing trade in the 22 sectors represent one-fourth, and the estimated "net national welfare gain" one-half, of the estimated "costs of protection for EC consumers."

Overview of Costs

In 1990, the estimated costs of protection for European consumers in the 22 sectors and in the rest of the EC goods-producing sector amounted to €92–93 billion—depending upon the model used, and taking into account the NTBs imposed in the EC sector producing the rest of the goods.[4]

---

4. The "sector producing the rest of the goods" consists of the farm and industrial goods not listed in the 22 sectors, but excludes services (as in the Hufbauer-Elliott [1994] study). It deserves a remark because chapter 3 is based on *applied* tariffs (not on MFN-bound tariffs, as in chapter 2). According to Sapir (1998), 21.3 percent of EC imports (subject to MFN nonzero tariffs) are coming from sources benefiting from an EC "preferential" zero tariff, and 8.3 percent from GSP sources. The GSP complexity makes it difficult to estimate the average applied tariff (see chapter 6); what follows assumes that half of GSP trade benefits are from an EC zero tariff, and the rest from no preference at all. As a result, 25 percent of the imports of goods (21 percent for zero-tariff trade and 4 percent for GSP trade) competing with the sector producing the rest of the goods have been assumed to be subject to an EC zero tariff, leading to an *applied* tariff of 3.4 percent (corresponding to the MFN-bound tariff of 4.6 percent).

This sum represents roughly 6 percent of the corresponding value added, and 55 to 60 percent of these costs are due to the protection of the 22 sectors alone—underlining the necessity of focusing on protection peaks during the next round.

These estimates are larger than the costs of protection in the United States estimated by Hufbauer and Elliott (1994) at $70 billion (€55 billion, at the 1990 exchange rate) for the same year (1990). However, this difference is substantially reduced by two adjustments. First, the Hufbauer-Elliott study does not take into account NTBs and antidumping measures existing in the sector producing the rest of the goods; it estimates the costs of protection in this sector on the basis of the average tariff (3.5 percent) alone. The same approach in the EC would reduce the estimated costs of protection for European consumers to €71–74 billion by using a 3.4 percent average tariff (instead of a 6.1 percent rate of overall protection). Second, estimating the costs of protection in agriculture on a CSE basis (and not on the basis of CSE-based tariffs), as was done in the Hufbauer-Elliott study, would further reduce the EC costs of protection to €60–65 billion (as is mentioned in chapter 2, CSEs and CSE-based tariffs are very different in the EC case). These two adjustments lead to relatively similar costs of protection for the two countries—if one assumes a perfectly competitive environment within the EC (a key caveat, as seen below).

Costs by Sector

Table 3.2 provides three results. First, it confirms the importance of the costs of protection for European consumers of farm products (a well-known result). The costs of protecting the five farm sectors examined in detail represent roughly a fourth of the costs of EC protection in goods only, or almost a third of the value added for the five sectors. Assuming that the level of protection for other farm products is similar to the level (6.1 percent) for the sector producing the rest of the goods (a conservative assumption), the costs of EC protection for all farm products represent roughly 12 percent of EC total farm value added.

Second, the costs of protection in the 14 listed manufacturing sectors represent almost one-fifth of the value added of these sectors—and they are higher (in euros) than the costs for farm products. The costs of protection for the whole manufacturing sector (the 14 listed sectors plus the industrial activities included in the rest of the goods-producing sector) amount to roughly 5 percent of the corresponding value added. These results strongly suggest that industrial products should be an important component of the negotiations of the coming round—not for the sake of reciprocity (as is often said), but as a source of large additional welfare gains for the EC. If one adds together agriculture and manufacturing, the protection costs for

European consumers amount to roughly 6 percent of the total EC value added in all the goods-producing sectors of the Community.

The last result for sectors provided by table 3.2 concerns services. Lack of data on the most efficient world service producers imposes a different interpretation of the models used. The costs of protection are estimated on the basis of the lowest *prices* available in the world, with no assurance that these prices reflect the lowest possible *costs* of production (in contrast to sectors producing goods).[5] Moreover, the small number of services included in the 22-sector list requires additional caution about the interpretation of the results obtained. Bearing these caveats in mind, the costs of protection for European consumers in the three service sectors considered represent 16 percent of their value added (with a huge peak in the French film case, where costs for French viewers are larger than the value added, and where the efficiency gains alone represent 80 percent of the value added).

Major Beneficiaries of Transfers from Protection

The preceding section focused on the losers from protection: European consumers (again, households *and* firms). What follows looks at the beneficiaries of protection-based transfers. Table 3.2 is based on three very conservative assumptions for splitting protection costs between tariff revenues and rent-based barriers in each sector: (1) The CSE-based tariffs are interpreted as "real" tariffs (see chapters 2 and 4). (2) Antidumping measures are assumed to generate no rents, despite the fact that antidumping cases are often terminated (at least partly) by "undertakings" that consist of voluntary export restraints in terms of maxima quantities or minima prices, hence in rent-generating instruments, as documented in appendix B. (3) Certain tax revenues (e.g., seat taxes in movie theaters) are conceived of as equivalent to tariffs, although they are not registered as such.

Under these assumptions—which maximize tariff revenues and minimize rents—table 3.2 shows that roughly only 24 percent of the costs of protection in the 22 highly protected sectors is collected in the form of tariff revenues, whereas estimated NTB rents amount to 30 percent of these costs. Less conservative assumptions about the breakdown between tariffs and rents in fertilizers, chemical fibers, consumer electronics (videocassette recorders and photocopiers), agriculture, and services would boost quota rents to 40 percent of the costs of protection for EC

---

5. An important lesson of recent regulatory reform in services is that costs have often been cut by much more than initially expected, as is illustrated by the long and wide British experience (Amstrong, Cowan, and Vickers 1994) or by EC telecommunications (see appendix A, case 21).

consumers (and reduce tariff revenues to 14 percent) in the 22 sectors examined in detail.[6]

Again, this last result is essential in the European context, where protection is often justified on the basis of the "public interest," whereas free trade is often considered as favoring "private" interests. In fact, vested private interests are able to benefit from a large proportion of the protection costs imposed on EC firms and households. Hence, they are strongly induced to keep untouched the level and instruments of protection.

Small Domestic Price Increases, High Costs of Protection

European debates on protection often rely on the assertion that a small change of 1 or 2 percent in domestic prices generates insignificant protection costs. This argument is routinely illustrated by the many EC antidumping proceedings, which, when the "interest of the Community" not to impose antidumping measures is discussed, state that high antidumping measures create no severe damage to the EC economy because they generate only small price changes (see the antidumping proceedings published in the EC *Official Journal* reporting the discussion about the interest of the Community clause). In sharp contrast to this frequent assertion and in accordance with economic analysis, connecting the costs of protection (table 3.2) to the corresponding price changes (table 3.3) shows that indeed, small price changes can generate high costs of protection.

Protection and Jobs

A frequent argument for protection (and a particularly powerful one in the sluggish European continental economies of the 1990s) is that protec-

---

6. Tariff revenues officially reported for 1990 amount to only €13 billion (Court of Accounts, EC, *Official Journal*, 1996, C340, 25). Under the initial assumptions about the breakdown between tariff revenues and rents (24 and 30 percent, respectively), the estimated tariff revenue losses would amount to €25 billion. Under the revised assumptions (14 and 40 percent, respectively), they would still amount to €18–19 billion. Further adjustments could be made on the basis of preferential tariffs in textiles and clothing under the GSP or Lomé conventions, and in all manufactured goods under the European Economic Area (EEA) Agreement (see chapter 6). Such preferential tariffs would reduce tariff revenues by €2–4 billion more, without reducing protection costs (exporters enjoying such preferential tariffs are induced to keep them for their own profits, and to limit the passthrough to EC consumers as much as possible). All these adjustments suggest tariff revenues estimated at €14–16 billion, a figure close enough to the official figure to be seen as mirroring the real situation. Hagdahl (1996) has underlined the fact that many tariffs will not be profitable for the Community by the year 2005. All this suggests that the main raison d'être of tariffs is not to provide revenues but to hide peak protection rates (protecting well-targeted sectors) behind a forest of low tariffs. However, low tariffs may still generate a costly protection if there is multiple crossing of borders due to the fact that the successive stages of the production process are located in different countries (in order to get the full benefits of comparative advantages).

Table 3.3 Estimated price and employment effects of liberalization: The perfect-competition case

Sector	Changes in domestic prices		Decrease in jobs[b]		Consumer gain per saved job[b]		Efficiency gain per saved job[b]	
	Francois-Hall model[a] (percent)	Hufbauer-Elliott model[b] (percent)	Number	As percent of jobs	Thousands of euros	As a proportion of average wage	Thousands of euros	As a proportion of average wage
Cement	−0.15	−0.16	91	0.2	857.1	36.5	105.5	4.5
Fertilizers	−2.37	−6.49	3,514	12.6	182.6	5.3	22.3	0.7
Low-density polyethylene	−1.60	−1.59	1,072	3.2	279.9	8.1	32.5	0.9
Polyvinyl chloride	−1.27	−1.24	443	2.5	52.9	1.5	35.4	1.0
Hardboard	−2.24	−1.43	511	0.7	611.1	40.6	194.9	13.0
Newsprint	−1.18	−1.50	210	1.5	800.2	32.0	26.7	1.1
Chemical fibers	−1.62	−1.53	1,102	1.5	526.4	15.3	71.4	2.1
Videocassette recorders	−4.87	−4.89	746	4.7	419.7	15.3	89.4	3.3
Integrated circuits	−3.35	−7.52	6,027	14.5	366.4	14.4	93.6	3.7
Photocopiers	−4.92	−0.38	90	0.4	3,483.3	145.7	737.8	30.9
Steel	−0.72	−0.68	5,152	1.4	315.6	12.1	64.7	2.5
Passenger cars	−0.31	−0.30	3,694	0.3	568.7	20.0	74.7	2.6
Textiles	−2.42	−2.41	39,383	2.4	180.2	11.6	17.0	1.1
Clothing	−2.88	−2.69	33,160	2.7	214.2	17.5	32.5	2.7

Cereals	−10.42	−8.01	46,341	4.1	69.3	5.0	20.4	1.5
Meat	−7.58	−6.54	40,695	4.3	116.5	7.3	32.3	2.0
Milk (manufactured)	−4.78	−3.89	837	2.3	3,246.4	173.0	1,144.3	61.0
Sugar	−34.90	−20.41	29,129	10.6	146.5	10.7	79.2	5.8
Bananas	−29.27	−30.71	4,190	16.8	196.8	28.1	43.8	6.3
Films (France)	−30.40	−30.91	6,721	30.9	60.5	2.4	16.0	0.6
Air transport	−2.31	−0.41	609	0.2	14,386.4	479.5	1,335.5	44.5
Telecommunications	−2.23	−1.90	19,933	2.8	197.1	7.7	65.1	2.5
Totals for the 22 sectors, by economic activity[c]								
Agriculture	−17.39	−13.91	121,192	5.0	124.8	8.5	47.1	3.2
Manufacturing	−2.14	−2.34	95,195	2.0	245.8	12.5	35.5	1.8
Market services	−11.65	−11.07	27,263	2.7	480.4	17.5	81.4	3.0
Total	−6.90	−6.16	243,650	2.9	211.9	11.1	46.4	2.4
Sector producing rest of the goods								
Tariffs and nontariff barriers	−0.47	−0.49	179,636	0.5	229.1	10.3	9.3	0.4
Only tariffs	−0.26	−0.28	101,732	0.3	225.9	10.1	5.3	0.2

a. Based on the Francois-Hall (1997) model.
b. Based on the Hufbauer-Elliott (1994) model.
c. Unweighted averages
Sources: Case studies in appendix A; European Commission (1995); author's computations.

tion "saves" jobs, despite economic analysis showing the poor capacity of protection to save jobs. It is thus important to estimate the number of jobs that would have been eliminated in the highly protected sectors, if protection had been removed. (Of course, a partial-equilibrium analysis focusing on import-competing sectors ignores the number of jobs that would have been *created* in the exporting sectors by a more open European economy; and it treats changes in jobs as proportional to changes in shipments, because factor incomes are assumed fixed.) Under these assumptions, table 3.3 shows that EC protection has saved very few jobs, even in the highly protected sectors—roughly 250,000 jobs, or 3 percent of the total number of jobs existing in these 22 sectors. The number of jobs saved as a percentage of the total number of jobs varies widely by sector (in certain sectors, it is almost negligible).

Dividing the estimated protection costs by the estimated number of jobs saved provides the average cost of protection by job saved. Table 3.3 shows that, in many sectors, this average cost amounts to several hundreds of thousands of euros—roughly 10 times the corresponding sectoral wage, with huge peaks in some sectors. Relating the number of jobs saved to efficiency gains (the narrowest definition of protection costs) reduces the costs per job saved by one-fourth, but it does *not* change the conclusions for policy: saving jobs by protecting the 22 sectors would cost 2.5 times the average wage. These results strongly suggest that, if saving jobs is the issue at stake, it has to (indeed, it can) be addressed by more efficient policies than trade protection.

Costs of Protection:
The Imperfect-Competition Case

Jacquemin and Sapir (1991) have provided clear evidence that extra-EC—*not* intra-EC—liberalization has been the key factor in introducing more competitive disciplines into the EC economy. Only extra-EC imports have exerted a significant disciplinary effect on price-cost margins. (Intra-EC imports have exerted some noticeable disciplinary effects in only a few sectors with high intra-EC NTBs, but none of these sectors pertains to our 22-sector list.) This result echoes studies showing the continuing existence of "border effects" *within* the Community (Krugman 1991; Sapir 1996). The ad valorem tariff equivalent of such effects has been recently estimated as large: roughly 37 percent (Head and Mayer 1999). Different consumer preferences *and* restrictive business practices (including alliances among EC firms aimed at keeping stable market shares in the various EC member-states in the context of weak EC anticartel enforcement; see chapter 5) are major candidates for explaining these intra-EC obstacles.

The section thus aims to estimate the costs of protection in the EC in an imperfect-competition environment. It is based on a partial-equilibrium model elaborated by Atje and Hufbauer (1996). The model estimates the effects of a decrease in protection *cumulated* with a shift from imperfectly competitive market structures to more competitive ones by considering four alternative basic market structures: perfect competition (in this case, the model boils down to the above Hufbauer-Elliott model [1994]), monopolistic competition between eight firms, monopolistic competition between four firms, and monopoly.

Assessing Market Structures

A preliminary task is to assess the market structure prevailing under protection (the "initial" market structure), and to define the market structure that would prevail after trade liberalization in the EC market in question (the "final" market structure). Six sectors (textiles, clothing, cereals, meat, dairy, and sugar) of the 22 sectors examined in detail have been excluded from this exercise because the number of existing producers seems large enough to ignore the possible interactions between protection and competition in these markets. This is a conservative hypothesis, which leaves aside the possible consequences of imperfect competition existing at the distribution level. For instance, the emergence of few worldwide trademarks in textiles or clothing or the existence of few large world grain, sugar, or banana traders could have some impact on markets at the production stage (see appendix A, cases 15, 18, and 19).

For 11 of the 16 remaining sectors, the available information suggests beginning by defining the "final" market structure (the structure associated with *no* protection). This is because these 11 sectors have all been (and still are) subject to antidumping measures, which constitute the core of existing protection. EC antidumping proceedings provide some information about the market structure prevailing *before* the imposition of these antidumping measures; it seems reasonable to assume that once protection is removed, markets will go back to this structure. In particular, antidumping proceedings give the number of allegedly dumping firms and the number of EC firms, as well as the global market share of these two groups of firms.

This information allows us to calculate a "partial" Herfindahl Index (PHI), which permits us to classify the "final" market structure according to the following procedure. Because an eight-firm market structure has a minimal "complete" (i.e., based on complete information) Herfindahl Index (CFI) of 0.125 (when the eight firms have exactly the same market share), any of the 11 sectors with an estimated PHI smaller than 0.125 has been classified as "returning" to a "competitive" market structure, once protection is removed.[7] For a four-firm market structure with a minimal CFI of 0.250, any of the 11 sectors with an estimated PHI higher than 0.125 and smaller than 0.250 has been classified as returning to an eight-firm market structure.

The next step is to define the "initial" market structure for these 11 sectors. There is almost no information available giving a sense of the degree of additional imperfect competition brought on by protection. This lack of information suggests adopting the following conservative hypothesis. Existing protection in the 11 sectors in question has induced the market to function under the *next less* competitive structure. For instance, existing protection forces a competitive market to function as an eight-firm market, an eight-firm market as a four-firm one, and so on.

For the five remaining sectors that have not been subject to antidumping measures (newsprint, cars, films, air transport, and telecommunications), two procedures have been followed. For newsprint, cars, and films, the information about CFIs under protection is available, and it has been assumed that eliminating protection in these four sectors would allow the market in question to function under the *next more* competitive structure. Last, for air transport and telecommunications, the initial and final situations have been arbitrarily defined as four- and eight-firm markets (respectively) to present minima estimates of the impact of more competition in a liberalized environment.

Costs under Imperfect Competition

Table 3.4 focuses on the costs of protection for EC consumers in the 16 sectors that have been considered as operating under imperfect competition. These costs are larger (sometimes in considerable proportion) than those estimated under perfect competition, and estimated excess profits accruing to protected sectors are massive—underlining again the huge vested interests willing to keep peaks of EC protection unchanged.

The "amplification" factor generated by imperfect competition (the costs under imperfect competition as a percentage of the costs under perfect competition) ranges from a few percent to almost 900 percent. Focusing on the 12 industrial goods operating under imperfect competition, the average amplification factor is about 135 percent. As a result, for the whole EC manufacturing sector, the costs of protection would amount to roughly 7 percent of EC total industrial value added. The amplification factor seems much more important for services; it corresponds to a

---

7. PHIs are defined as the sum of the square of the *average* market share held by the allegedly dumping firms and of the square of the *average* market share held by EC firms (nondumping foreign firms are ignored). By construction, they tend to underestimate the level of concentration; in the three sectors where PHIs can be compared with CFIs, PHIs are half or two-thirds of the corresponding CFIs.

Table 3.4 Estimated welfare effects of liberalizing the 14 highly protected sectors under imperfect competition

Sector	Assumed change of market structure[a]	Consumer surplus gain (millions of euros)		Efficiency gain (millions of euros)		Producer surplus loss (millions of euros)		Excess profits[b] (millions of euros)
		Imperfect competition case[b]	Perfect competition case[c]	Imperfect competition case[b]	Perfect competition case[c]	Imperfect competition case[b]	Perfect competition case[c]	
Cement	8 → PC	673.8	78.0	50.0	9.6	565.2	14.4	1,118.6
Fertilizers	4 → 8	716.2	641.6	108.1	78.5	43.4	86.0	103.7
Low-density polyethylene	8 → PC	617.8	300.0	63.9	34.8	236.7	108.9	534.8
Polyvinyl chloride	8 → PC	341.0	132.0	33.5	15.7	144.2	49.8	340.4
Hardboard	8 → PC	974.4	739.1	126.0	99.6	558.0	112.8	780.2
Newsprint	8 → PC	276.1	191.5	13.6	5.6	98.0	26.6	177.4
Chemical fibers	8 → PC	1,020.1	580.1	120.8	78.7	505.7	138.9	922.5
Videocassette recorders	4 → 8	363.0	313.3	88.2	66.7	76.0	81.7	116.2
Integrated circuits	8 → PC	2,239.9	2,187.4	575.3	564.3	50.2	138.6	99.5
Photocopiers	4 → 8	363.0	313.5	76.8	66.4	64.2	4.8	104.2
Steel	8 → PC	4,403.4	1,626.1	543.9	333.1	2,054.1	396.5	4,658.6
Passenger cars	4 → 8	5,417.9	2,100.8	945.8	275.8	4,545.0	277.9	7,234.4
Textiles	No change	7,095.6	7,095.6	668.3	668.3	2,677.7	2,677.7	—
Clothing	No change	7,102.8	7,102.8	1,078.5	1,078.5	1,711.9	1,711.9	—
Cereals	No change	3,211.9	3,211.9	944.1	944.1	1,770.2	1,770.2	—
Meat	No change	4,108.4	4,108.4	1,314.0	1,314.0	1,599.5	1,599.5	—
Milk (manufactured)	No change	2,717.2	2,717.2	957.8	957.8	1,061.7	1,061.7	—
Sugar	No change	4,268.3	4,268.3	2,306.1	2,306.1	979.5	979.5	—
Bananas[d]	No change	1,327.1	824.6	391.5	183.7	131.3	106.0	

(table continues next page)

Table 3.4 Estimated welfare effects of liberalizing the 14 highly protected sectors under imperfect competition (continued)

Sector	Assumed change of market structure[a]	Consumer surplus gain (millions of euros)		Efficiency gain (millions of euros)		Producer surplus loss (millions of euros)		Excess profits[b] (millions of euros)
		Imperfect competition case[b]	Perfect competition case[c]	Imperfect competition case[b]	Perfect competition case[c]	Imperfect competition case[b]	Perfect competition case[c]	
Films (France)	4 → 8	408.2	406.4	112.4	107.5	2.6	54.1	3.2
Air transport	4 → 8	20,105.9	8,761.3	3,251.3	813.3	3,370.2	113.2	11,772.9
Telecommunications	4 → 8	10,410.9	3,929.7	2,839.6	1,297.4	2,499.8	1,169.0	7,755.0
Totals for the 22 sectors, by economic activity								
Agriculture		15,632.9	15,130.4	5,913.5	5,705.7	5,542.2	5,516.8	n.a.
Manufacturing		31,605.2	23,401.7	4,492.7	3,375.6	13,330.3	5,826.5	16,190.5
Market services		30,925.0	13,097.4	6,203.3	2,218.2	5,872.5	1,336.4	19,531.1
All sectors		78,163.0	51,629.5	16,609.4	11,299.5	24,745.0	12,679.7	35,721.6
The sector producing the rest of the goods								
Tariffs and nontariff barriers	No change	41,162.3	41,162.3	1,661.8	1,661.8	15,212.2	15,212.2	
Only tariffs	No change	22,984.9	22,984.9	540.3	540.3	8,603.7	8,603.7	

PC = perfect competition; 8 = 8 firm market; 4 = 4 firm market.
n.a. = not available

a. 8 → PC: cases from 8-firm market to perfect competition; 4 → 8: cases from 4-firm market to 8-firm market.
b. Atje-Hufbauer model (1996).
c. Hufbauer-Elliott model (1994).
d. For the assumed change of market structure, see appendix A, case 19.

Sources: Case studies in appendix A; European Commission (1995); author's computations.

doubling of the costs of protection, despite the very conservative assumptions adopted about changes in market structures.

These results reveal what could be the main source of divergence between the costs of protection in the United States and the EC. These two large economies may differ less in their level of protection (hence, when estimated under perfect competition, the costs of protection in the two economies may be relatively similar, as shown above) than in their level of *effective* internal competition. For decades, the US economy has been a well-integrated "single market" without too much public interference—partly because many US states are smaller economically relative to the whole US economy than EC member-states are to the whole EC economy, and as a consequence, US states tend to have a more competition-oriented behavior than the EC member-states. In sharp contrast, the EC economy has only started the process of establishing its single market, and it is doing so under the heavy influence of "large" ("dominant" in competition-policy parlance) member-states.[8] In other words, the estimated amplification factor could be interpreted as reflecting the additional costs of the absence of a fully functioning Single Market, given prevailing external barriers on imports from the rest of the world.

Variations on Three Important Related Issues

Three important issues could significantly change the magnitude of the results achieved so far. Has the level of protection in the 22 highlighted sectors decreased substantially since the early 1990s? Are there reasons to believe that the EC is a large market (at least for some of these 22 products) relative to the rest of the world—so that the EC could benefit from terms-of-trade effects that would reduce net gains from liberalization? And are there reasons to believe that the EC's propensity for "preferential" liberalization (the EC's "addiction to discrimination," examined in chapter 6) has provided noticeable gains, in comparison with those to be expected from multilateral liberalization?

Protected Sectors: Stable during the Past Decade

What follows shows that none of the 22 heavily protected sectors experienced a substantial and definite decline of protection between the early and late 1990s. Table 3.5 is devoted to farm goods growing in a temperate

---

8. This is best illustrated by the steel sector. Although both the EC and US steel sectors have been quite protected during the past two decades, the US steel industry has made a quicker adjustment to new and more efficient technologies than its EC counterpart (see appendix A, case 11).

Table 3.5 Trade and nontrade barriers for selected farm products (percent)

	Period	Wheat[a]	Coarse grains	Beef	Pork	Poultry	Dairy[b]	Sugar
Tariff equivalents, bound and applied tariffs								
1. Tariff equivalents (reference period)	1986–88	103.0	133.0	83.0	40.0	51.0	177.0	234.0
2. Uruguay MFN bound tariffs	1995	155.6	134.4	125.0	51.7	44.5	288.5	297.0
3. Applied (out-of-quota) tariffs	1995	34.8	99.2	80.9	40.3	16.3	147.5	n.a.
4. Applied (in-quota) tariffs	1995	n.a.	45.7	20.0	13.3	8.1	33.2	n.a.
5. Applied (out-of-quota) tariffs	2000	55.5	78.1	36.8	19.2	12.7	103.8	248.1
6. Negative tariff escalation: level	1995	Serious	Serious	Severe	Nil	Moderate	Small	Moderate
Negative tariff escalation: change	2001/1995	None	None	Decrease	None	None	None	Increase
Production and export subsidies								
7. Share in EC farm budget	1985	11.6 ←→		13.8	0.8	0.2	30.0	9.1
	1990	14.6 ←→		10.7	0.9	0.7	18.8	5.3
	1995	43.5 ←→		11.7	0.4	0.6	11.7	5.3
	1998	42.4 ←→		14.5	0.9	0.2	7.3	4.1
8. Export subsidy equivalents	1996–97	12.5	27.0	53.0	252.5	16.0	125.0	157.5
9. Share (subsidized/total) exports	1996–97	99.0	109.5	116.5	37.0	72.5	102.0	69.5
10. Subsidized exports/commitments (volume)	1996–97	73.5	80.0	102.0	48.5	102.0	48.0	99.0
11. Subsidized exports/commitments (outlays)	1996–97	12.0	23.0	68.0	28.0	102.0	34.0	99.0
12. Self-sufficiency rate	1960	85	85	92	n.a.	n.a.	101	104
	1979	112	90	98	100	105	123	125
	1991	141	116	113	106	106	116	122
	1995	113	106	109	105	109	106	140
	1998	126	113	112	107	111	106	138

n.a. = not available
MFN = most favored nation

a. Common wheat.
b. Butter (except for line 7: all dairy products).

Sources: Rows 1 and 2: Ingco (1996). Row 4: Tangermann (1998, table 232) and WTO, *Trade Policy Review: The European Community,* 1997. Rows 3 and 5: author's computations. Row 6: OECD, 1997b. Row 7: Court of Auditing, EC, *Official Journal.* Rows 8 to 11: OECD, 2000e. Row 12: *EC Report on Agriculture,* various years.

climate.[9] The first part of the table provides four kinds of key information about the EC Uruguay Round commitments on tariffs: (1) the estimated tariff equivalents (row 1) of the border protection enforced during the period 1986–88, as the reference period for the "tariffication" exercise; (2) the MFN-bound tariffs (row 2) listed in the EC Uruguay Round commitments on agriculture; (3) the "out-of-quota" and "in-quota" (rows 3 and 4) ad valorem equivalents of the tariffs applied in 1995; and (4) the ad valorem equivalents of the tariffs applied in 2000 (row 5, like row 3, is based on the average of OECD price estimates—for Australia, Canada, New Zealand, and the United States—for the farm product and year in question).

Four major lessons emerge from table 3.5. (1) The substantial differences between the tariff equivalents of the reference period and the Uruguay Round bound tariffs (rows 1 and 2) reflect the magnitude of the "dirty" tariffication process (see chapter 4). (2) The similarities between the tariff equivalents of the reference period and the applied tariffs in 1995 (rows 1 and 3) mirror the absence of any real liberalization in 1995. (3) The similarities between the tariffs applied in 1995 and 2000 (rows 3 and 5) reflect the absence of any real liberalization until 2000, in particular if one takes into account food safety measures amounting to import bans (beef) or other severe barriers (pork and poultry).[10] (4) In-quota tariffs (amplified by complex or opaque quota-management regimes) have been high enough to keep rates of fulfillment of the existing (very small) quotas at a low rate; the average fill rate on all quota lines imposed by the EC decreased from 75 percent (1995) to 66 percent (1997) (OECD 2000d).

The second part of table 3.5 deals with domestic and export farm subsidies. Row 7 shows limited changes in the domestic subsidy concentration by product, except in favor of dairy products in the mid-1980s and of cereals in the Uruguay Round aftermath (in this case, reflecting the increasing gap between CSE- and PSE-based tariffs during the late 1990s following the 1992 CAP Reform; see chapter 4). Row 8 provides estimates of the ad valorem rates of export subsidies.[11] Row 9 gives the share of sub-

9. Appendix A, case 19, shows that the conclusions drawn from table 3.5 can be extended to bananas, the only tropical farm product examined in this study; in fact, protection of EC bananas increased in 1993 relative to 1990.

10. The increase in the applied tariff for wheat between 1995 and 2000 mirrors the combination of decreasing world prices and specific tariffs (see chapter 4). Recent estimates (Gibson, et al. 2001) on tariffs (for products more widely defined than those included in table 3.5) tend to confirm the magnitude of the estimated tariffs for 2000 that are presented in table 3.5. The same conclusion can be drawn from the estimated ratios of EC/world prices made public by the European Commission during the launch of the "Everything but Arms" initiative (see chapter 6) (European Commission, 2000c).

11. Export-subsidy rates should be roughly equal to the corresponding ad valorem tariff equivalents; both mirror the same wedge between world and EC prices. This is the case except for wheat, coarse grains, and pork. The discrepancy for the first two goods may be due to the fact that export-subsidy rates have been calculated for 1996 and 1997, which were characterized by high world prices (to such an extent that the EC has imposed export taxes). The third case (pork) was largely determined by the 1997 crisis in the Netherlands.

sidized exports in total EC exports, rows 10 and 11 provide the ratio of subsidized exports with respect to EC commitments in the Uruguay Agreement (respectively, in volume and value), and row 12 recapitulates the effect of import and export protection on EC "self-sufficiency" rates. Two major lessons emerge: (1) EC exports still depend heavily on export subsidies, and the EC clearly has difficulties fulfilling its commitments, notably in beef, poultry, and sugar. (2) Self-sufficiency rates have not substantially declined since their 1970s peak, revealing how little has been achieved in trade liberalization by the EC in recent years (see chapter 4).

Table 3.6 on the industrial goods pertaining to the 22-sector list provides the 1990 and 1999 bound tariffs, which are also the tariffs applied by the EC (with minor exceptions). It also reports the voluntary export restraints (VERs) existing during the late 1980s and 1990s, and it gives the number of antidumping cases in force for the same periods, including "ambiguous" ones.[12] For the period 1995–99, ad valorem tariff equivalents of antidumping measures have been estimated with the method adopted in chapter 2, whereas ad valorem tariff equivalents of the VERs are explained in the corresponding cases in appendix A.

The key lesson from table 3.6 is that the reduction of the overall level of protection during the 1990s was modest (if there was any) for all these industrial products. In many cases, one observes a mere substitution of focused instruments of protection (e.g., antidumping measures) for more rigidly or broadly defined instruments (e.g., tariffs or VERs). This change is far from meaning that existing EC products are less protected; it could mean that the protection has been better "designed," with a higher level of protection granted to a smaller but better defined coverage of EC production.

The apparent exceptions to the stability of protection during the 1990s would require extensive research to be confirmed. For instance, the long history of private collusive behavior in cement, polyvinyl chloride, newsprint, and steel (see appendix A, cases 1, 4, 6, and 11) due to insufficient anticartel enforcement makes it far from certain that the apparent decline of the overall level of protection corresponds to an effective opening of EC markets, and not to a shift from public to private barriers—and hence from tariff revenues to private rents.

The car industry raises different issues. Protection by technical regulations may have been substituted for trade barriers—the number of EC directives dealing with norms and standards for cars increased by 50 percent during the 1990s relative to the 1970s, and doubled relative to the 1980s. And the protection granted by the massive subsidies of the 1980s and early or mid-1990s (particularly in France) may have had long-term

---

12. These cases consist of antidumping complaints withdrawn by the complainants before the end of the official investigation. It is hard to interpret such withdrawals; they could cover private restrictive actions (cement), interactions between antidumping measures and collusive behavior (low-density polyethylene [LdPE] and polyvinyl chloride [PVC] in the first period), or shifts from basic to derived products (LdPE in the second period), etc.

Table 3.6 The evolution of EC global protection of the 14 highly protected industrial sectors

	1990				1999			
	GATT MFN-bound tariffs (percent)	Types of NTBs		Rate of overall protection (percent)	GATT MFN-bound tariffs (percent)	Types of NTBs		Rate of overall protection (percent)
Sector		Voluntary export restraints	Antidumping cases (number)			Voluntary export restraints	Antidumping cases (number)	
Cement	3.2		5	22.8	1.7		6[a]	n.a.
Fertilizers	5.2		19	32.7	4.3		23	26.0
Low-density polyethylene	12.5		4	12.5	5.9		3[b]	14.7
Polyvinyl chloride	12.5		4	12.5	7.8			7.8
Hardboard	10.0		16	25.0	7.6		7	20.2
Newsprint	7.0		2	7.0	2.5			2.5
Artificial/synthetic fibers	8.9		23	22.9	6.4		18	22.7
Videocassette recorders	12.5		4	30.2	12.0		2	27.7
Integrated circuits	13.5		2	47.6	0.0		1	30.0
Photocopiers	7.2		2	33.7	3.1		7	35.3
Steel	4.8	VERs	43	21.9	2.7	VERs	67	9.0
Cars	10.2	VERs[c]		17.1	9.8	VERs[c,d]		13.8
Textiles	9.9	VERs[e]		21.4	8.5	VERs[e]	35	22.1
Clothing	12.3	VERs[e]		31.3	11.6	VERs[e]		30.6

EC = European Community.
GATT = General Agreement on Tariffs and Trade.
MFN = most favored nation
NTBs = nontariff barriers
n.a. = not available

a. Antidumping measures unknown.
b. Derived products targeted by antidumping measures.
c. VERs eliminated by 31 December 1999, plus an ad valorem tariff equivalent for technical regulations.
d. Threats of antisubsidy cases for certain vehicles.
e. See text for the ad valorem equivalents of VERs.

Sources: Appendix A, various cases; EC, *Official Journal*; author's computations.

effects, which are possibly still being felt (first, by closing the EC markets to Japanese cars during the period of disbursement; second, by allowing artificially surviving EC carmakers to become shareholders of Japanese carmakers—as is best illustrated by the Renault-Nissan deal—because the Japanese government decided not to subsidize its domestic automakers in difficulty, contrary to what has been done in Europe).

In services, observed protection has not substantially declined during the past decade. There has been no multilateral liberalization (existing WTO agreements in services are standstill agreements); and intra-EC liberalizations, only a couple of years old, are incomplete and reversible (for details, see chapter 5). In fact, information on the three services examined in detail (see appendix A, cases 20 to 22) raises doubts even about the standstill commitments: (1) The subsidization rate of French films has increased, and there are similar changes in most EC member-states. (2) Intra-EC liberalization in airlines seems to have been counterbalanced on most routes by route-sharing agreements between the very few firms present on those routes. (3) If the telecommunications sector may have operated under lower barriers and with more competition in the late 1990s than the early 1990s, recent benchmarking studies suggest that price differences with respect to the most efficient countries (a proxy for the rate of protection) did not substantially change (see appendix A, case 22).

Is the EC a "Large" Country?

A "large" country is big enough to have "market power" in the world market of the good in question. When such a country imposes border protection, it improves its terms-of-trade (increases its export prices, or reduces its import prices). As a result, if the EC were a large country, EC trade liberalization would generate terms-of-trade losses for the EC, and the net gains estimated in the previous sections would be reduced.

Identifying the situations in which the EC would be a "large" country is beyond the scope of this study. As a result, the costs of protection with terms-of-trade effects have been systematically estimated for the 22 products. Table 3.7 presents available information on EC market shares of world production for these 22 products; market shares larger than 25 and 40 percent of world consumption could be interpreted as two crude thresholds for possible EC market power.[13] None of the 22 sectors passes the 40 percent threshold. Only a handful pass the 25 percent threshold: hardboard, cars, textiles, clothing, and dairy—all goods (except maybe hardboard) subject to intensive product differentiation, a feature that tends to reduce the plausibility of large terms-of-trade effects.

---

13. In EC competition-policy enforcement, the 40 percent threshold is almost systematically associated with a dominant position (not to the abuse of such a position), whereas it has been less often the case for the 25 percent threshold.

Table 3.7　Estimated welfare effects of liberalizing in cases of terms-of-trade effects and regional liberalization

Sector	Tariff equivalent (percent of world price, 1990)	Terms-of-trade effects[b]					Regional liberalizations[b]			
		Consumer surplus gain[a] (millions of euros)	EC share of world output (percent)	Consumer surplus gain[c] (percent)	Increase in world prices (percent)	Terms-of-trade losses (millions of euros)	Central European countries		1995 EC member-states	
							Share of EC imports[d] (percent)	Antidumping measures[e] (percent)	Shares of EC 1990 imports (percent)	Consumer surplus gain[c] (percent)
Cement	22.8	99.3	12.0	66.6	7.0	15	92.6	83.3	8.0	2.8
Fertilizers	32.7	829.2	12.0	70.2	8.9	127	32.8	28.6	8.9	5.4
Low-density polyethylene	12.5	265.6	20.0	26.1	6.2	77	37.6	0.0	30.1	2.1
Polyvinyl chloride	12.5	120.0	20.0	25.3	6.5	22	34.7	0.0	9.4	0.6
Hardboard	25.0	830.1	25.0	60.5	7.0	150	16.8	71.4	30.6	14.4
Newsprint	7.0	82.2	25.0	34.9	1.8	40	2.4	0.0	65.1	36.1
Chemical fibers	22.9	433.1	15.0	36.5	7.9	150	20.5	0.0	20.8	3.2
Videocassette recorders	30.2	289.4	16.0	34.5	12.4	68	6.7	0.0	10.1	1.4
Integrated circuits	47.6	3,462.6	5.0	57.3	14.7	458	0.0	0.0	5.5	2.5
Photocopiers	33.7	287.1	10.0	42.0	9.9	71	0.2	0.0	0.5	0.0
Steel	21.9	2,423.1	21.0	48.5	10.0	411	42.7	42.8	36.6	13.2
Passenger cars	17.1	2,402.5	35.0	49.1	6.4	617	18.7	0.0	11.7	0.9
Textiles	21.4	5,954.0	25.0	58.5	6.9	1,148	23.3	20.0	9.4	1.8
Clothing	31.3	7,655.4	25.0	61.2	8.7	1,064	29.4	20.0	3.2	0.0
Cereals	63.0	2,792.0	16.0	41.8	30.9	270	5.5		0.7	0.0
Meat	95.0	4,998.8	22.0	52.0	28.9	364	2.9		10.1	2.2
Milk (manufactured)	104.0	3,643.6	27.5	49.9	37.6	252	13.0		13.4	0.4
Sugar	117.0	4,040.6	14.5	60.8	27.8	234	0.6		1.8	0.0
Bananas	81.9	1,076.5	4.0	72.6	14.7	96	0.0		0.0	0.0

(table continues next page)

Table 3.7 Estimated welfare effects of liberalizing in cases of terms-of-trade effects and regional liberalization *(continued)*

Product category	Terms-of-trade effects[b]						Regional liberalizations[b]			
							Central European countries		1995 EC member-states	
	Tariff equivalent (percent of world price, 1990)	Consumer surplus gain[a] (millions of euros)	EC share of world output (percent)	Consumer surplus gain[c] (percent)	Increase in world prices (percent)	Terms-of-trade losses (millions of euros)	Share of EC imports[d] (percent)	Antidumping measures[e] (percent)	Shares of EC 1990 imports (percent)	Consumer surplus gain[c] (percent)
Films (France)	76.8	547.9	5.0	71.8	15.5	49	5.0		2.0	0.7
Air transport	71.0	9,414.3	18.1	92.1	4.5	500	7.0		11.0	3.6
Telecommunications	45.2	5,887.8	24.0	48.1	19.3	625	7.0		9.7	3.8
Totals for the 22 sectors, by economic activity										
Agriculture	90.8[f]	16,551.5[g]	16.8[h]	53.3	28.0[h]	1,216[g]	4.4[h]		5.2[h]	0.7
Manufacturing	22.2[f]	25,133.7[g]	19.0[h]	56.4	8.2[h]	4,420[g]	25.6[h]		17.9[h]	3.0
Market services	55.2[f]	15,850.0[g]	15.7[h]	75.1	13.1[h]	1,174[g]	n.a.[h]		8.6[h]	3.5
All 22 sectors	37.5[f]	57,535.1[g]	18.1[h]	60.6	13.3[h]	6,809[g]	18.2[h]		13.6[h]	2.5
Sector producing rest of the goods[h]										
Tariffs and nontariff barriers	7.2	38,085.2	n.a.	48.6	2.8	11,155	7.0		11.0	3.4
Only tariffs	4.6	16,641.1	n.a.	27.7	1.8	7,196	7.0		11.0	0.3

EC = European Commission.

a. Table 3.2 estimates, based on the Francois-Hall (1997) model.
b. Estimates based on the Francois-Hall model.
c. In percentage of table 3.2 estimates based on terms-of-trade effects.
d. Unweighted average share in 1994–96 EC imports.
e. Percentages of antidumping cases enforced against the Central and Eastern European countries (for 1990–98).
f. Import-weighted average tariffs.
g. Sums.
h. Unweighted averages.

Sources: Case studies in appendix A; European Commission (1995); OECD, 1999a, table 3.2; author's computations.

To introduce terms-of-trade effects, table 3.7 arbitrarily sets the foreign supply elasticity at the low level of 3.[14] It presents the costs of protection for European consumers under terms-of-trade effects as a percentage of the costs of protection that would have existed in the absence of such terms-of-trade effects (for simplicity's sake, only results based on the Francois-Hall model are reported). If terms-of-trade effects occur in all sectors (an unrealistic assumption), gains from trade liberalization would be, on average, 60 percent of those existing in the absence of terms-of-trade effects. Limiting the possibility of terms-of-trade effects to the five sectors for which EC shares of world markets are higher than 25 percent would generate gains from trade liberalization roughly equal to 82 percent of those without terms-of-trade effects. This result suggests that the estimated European consumers' costs provided in the section on the costs of protection under perfect competition are unlikely to be substantially modified by the possible existence of terms-of-trade effects.

"Preferential" Liberalizations: A Large Impact?

The 1990s witnessed few noticeable changes in the level of EC protection, both in economywide terms (see chapter 2) and in terms of the 22 listed products and services (see the above section). However, these results take into account only the EC liberalization in a *multilateral* context. They ignore the impact of two "preferential" liberalization processes involving the EC during the 1990s: (1) with EFTA countries, under the auspices of the European Economic Area (1993) and leading to the accession of Austria, Finland, and Sweden to the EC in 1995; and (2) with Central European countries (CECs) under the auspices of the "Europe Agreements" (signed in the early and mid-1990s), which should lead to the progressive accession of all the CECs to the EC at still undecided dates.[15] However, table 3.7 shows that, as of 1999, CEC trade with the EC may have been free from tariffs, but that it was still hampered by severe trade barriers, precisely in products for which CECs are noticeable suppliers of EC imports—suggesting that the EC-CEC preferential liberalization is still very incomplete (see chapter 6), and can be left aside for the time being.

---

14. This very low elasticity of 3 has been adopted to be consistent with the Hufbauer and Elliott study (1994). Recent studies tend to use an elasticity of 5, which would lead to smaller terms of trade effects, and hence to smaller reductions in gains from liberalization because of these effects.

15. Iceland, Liechtenstein, Norway, and Switzerland are left aside, because they are very small economies or do not produce a significant amount of the 22 listed products, or because there are still important barriers (e.g., in services). The CECs included in this exercise are Bulgaria, Croatia, Czech Republic, Estonia, Hungary, Latvia, Lithuania, Poland, Romania, Slovakia, Slovenia, and Turkey. This unusually wide definition of Central Europe includes Croatia and Turkey (under the Customs Union Treaty) because trade between these countries and the EC is large enough not to be ignored.

As a result, what follows focuses on the accession of the three new EC member-states, and estimates the *maximum* positive impact of preferential liberalization limited to these three countries. It purposely leaves aside the robust economic arguments underlining the costs associated with preferential liberalization (see chapter 6), and it ignores legitimate doubts about the high risks of capturing partial liberalizations (there are powerful incentives for EC importers and EC preferential partners to keep prices under the umbrella of EC tariffs imposed on nonpreferential imports, in order to capture as private rents what used to be tariff revenues).

Instead, table 3.7 relies on the two following hypotheses, which *maximize* the impact of preferential liberalization: (1) The three new member-states are assumed to be always among the most efficient world producers. (2) The elimination of trade barriers between the EC and the new member-states allows for the introduction of world prices in European trade. In other words, table 3.7 sees preferential liberalization from the most favorable perspective possible (risks of trade diversion are largely eliminated); that is, as equivalent to a multilateral liberalization, except for the fact that EC preferential partners have much smaller supply capacities than the entire world.

Table 3.7 provides the gains from preferential liberalization based on the Francois-Hall (1997) model. For farm and industrial goods, a crude (and indirect) indicator of supply availability from the three new member-states (NMSs) is their trade share in EC imports. Such shares are not available for services, so proxies have been used: the ratio of NMSs to EC production for films, the ratio of NMSs to EC GDP for air transport, and the ratio of NMSs to EC revenues for telecommunications. Last, supply elasticities of the NMSs have been set at the level of EC elasticities. Under these working hypotheses, which are the most favorable possible to preferential liberalization, table 3.7 shows that preferential liberalization would bring only a very modest proportion of the gains to be expected from a multilateral liberalization; for the 22 products, the gains from the accession of the three NMSs would amount to only 3 percent of the gains from multilateral liberalization.

This result is not very surprising. It reflects the small size of the NMSs relative to the EC's huge economy (their aggregated GDP is roughly 11 percent of the EC GDP). This observation suggests that the same result should be expected for the preferential liberalization between the EC and CECs, because the aggregate GDP of all CECs is roughly 7 percent of the EC GDP—a conclusion consistent with available estimates of the EC net benefit from enlargement (Baldwin, François, and Portes 1997).

EC TRADE AND COMMERCIAL POLICY IN THE 2000s: CONSTRAINTS AND DYNAMIC FORCES

Chapters 4 and 5 aim to give a sense of what the EC's attitude could be in the multilateral trade negotiations of the coming decade. They examine what has been done—or not—by the EC to fulfill its Uruguay Round commitments, and try to spot the dynamic forces that could change the course of EC protection. Chapter 4 deals with trade policy and focuses on agriculture and manufacturing. Chapter 5 deals with commercial policy, which covers topics of increasing importance for the coming round, such as services, trade and labor issues, public procurement, and competition.

Chapter 6 describes the EC's addiction to discriminatory policy based on preferential trade agreements, and tries to assess the possibility of a slow shift away from this stance and toward a more multilateral approach. It also looks at the use of the various dispute settlement mechanisms available to the EC, particularly the WTO dispute settlement procedure.

4

The Dynamics of EC Trade Policy

If EC trade policy is now largely communitarized, its impact will never be. Common EC trade barriers have different effects on member-state economies with different production patterns. Each EC member-state has a different mix of sectors, the relative prices in which are modified by EC trade policy, all other things being constant. These differences are magnified in the medium (politically key) term by the fact that member-states are diversely exposed to world trade: extra-EC trade represents more than 40 percent of total trade only for Germany and Britain—meaning that trade shocks will not occur simultaneously with the same strength in all member-states. Member-state goals and strategies in trade policy thus will continue to differ—perhaps more than ever, because similar effects on member-state economies can no longer be achieved by a differentiated use of trade instruments.

As for the foreseeable future, the Community will have no supreme arbitrator (as the United States has with its president) and no institution able to generate deals on a routine, nonconsensual basis (as the US Congress does with majority voting). Therefore, the differentiated effects of EC trade barriers on member-state economies will continue to make EC trade policy dependent on ad hoc deals struck by coalitions among members. This situation will erode de facto the difference—based on the Treaty of Rome—between the Community's exclusive competence in trade policy and the joint competence of the Community and its member-states in commercial policy (see box 1.1 and chapter 5).

Modern trade policy deals with more than border barriers (tariffs or quantitative restrictions). Its coverage extends to nonborder barriers, such as technical regulations (TRs, that is, mandatory norms and voluntary standards), which, intentionally or not, can have a severe direct or indirect impact on trade flows. Since its origin, the Community has acknowledged this wide scope of trade policy, and the Treaty of Rome includes provisions for coping with it—although such preoccupations materialized only in the 1970s when the Common Market focusing on internal tariffs on goods was achieved.

In the early 1980s, a small group of major industrialists—the European Roundtable of Industrialists (ERT), led by the Volvo chief executive, Pehr Gyllenhammar—began to promote the concept of the Single (or Internal) Market. The ERT first set a vast agenda to eliminate intra-EC nonborder barriers, such as technical standards, customs and border facilities (trade facilitation), and inadequate physical infrastructure, ultimately reaching topics pertaining to commercial policy (see chapter 5) (Cowles 1995; Richardson 2000).[1] Later, the ERT plan—benefiting from the legal precedents established by the EC Court of Justice during the previous decade—was relaunched by another influential ERT member (the Philips chief executive, Wisse Dekker) in January 1985. This renewed plan gave birth, within a few weeks, to the Single Market Program (SMP, also often called the 1992 Program). The SMP, which was developed by the Commission and the Council between 1985 and 1993, has had (and still has) an important impact on nonborder barriers imposed on intra-EC trade in goods, and large effects on EC trade policy vis-à-vis the rest of the world, as is underlined below.

The dynamics of EC trade policy for the next decade will be dominated by three questions. First, to what extent has the EC fulfilled its Uruguay Round commitments on trade in goods? Second, to what extent have EC member-states been preparing for the coming WTO round with appropriate domestic reforms? (Chapters 2 and 3 underline how much the coming round will require serious preparation, because it will deal with the EC's most entrenched protectionist sectors.) Third, have recent years witnessed evolution in the position of some member-states on trade policy issues, making possible coalitions among them that would be more favorable to liberalization during the next round? The chapter outlines contrasting answers to these questions.

---

1. The key role of Gyllenhammar (who was also a member of the Leutwiler Group set up in the GATT to cope with the—often forgotten—disastrous attempt to launch a new round of talks in 1982) should remind us that European integration is much less EC-centered than often stated. It has been argued (e.g., see Baldwin 1995) that increased integration in the EC has negatively affected non-EC countries, thereby prompting their application for EC membership. This view presents the EC as the *source* of change. The ERT role shows that some EFTA leaders have been *instrumental* in EC integration. It suggests that investment diversion from the EFTA to the EC may have been more a reaction to the *future* integration of the *whole* of Western Europe than to the actual level of integration already reached by the EC at that time (a point consistent with the poor state of the Single Market Program at that time and the fact that empirical studies suggest 1988–89 as the first years for investment diversion (Baldwin, Forslid, and Haagland 1995; Sapir 1997).

On the one hand, the chapter shows that the EC has done little homework in its highly protected sectors, leading even to doubts about its capacity to fulfill some of its Uruguay Round agricultural commitments after 2000–01, or to stop an endless drift in antidumping measures for some industrial sectors. In addition, the late 1990s witnessed the increasing use of underlying fears in Europe about the environment or food safety as a source of high or even prohibitive trade barriers—including *within* the EC—in food products (e.g., meat or dairy products) *and* in industrial goods (e.g., asbestos, soft polyvinyl chloride).

On the other hand, the chapter suggests changing attitudes among member-states on trade policy. Certain states that so far have traditionally been staunch supporters of protection could shift to a much freer trade attitude at any time in the future, whereas others that have traditionally supported a free trade approach may have been captured by EC protection enough to have lost their energy for promoting EC openness. Because these changing attitudes in various member-states are so complex, and to some extent may go in opposite directions, it is hard to predict their ultimate influence on the course of EC trade policy—in particular, whether they will push for deeper liberalization than during the past decade.

Box 4.1 and table 4.1 reveal the implicit preferences of the three major European institutions (the Commission, the Council, and the Parliament) on the seven topics of trade policy by examining the texts released by these institutions just before the Seattle WTO Ministerial. (In February 2001, the EC Council reduced the hope among EC trading partners of a more accommodating EC stance, raised by the Commission's statements in late 2000, by making clear that the Council text adopted before Seattle remains the basis for the EC approach for a new WTO round.) Box 4.1 suggests a rationale for organizing the chapter in five sections. The first and second sections below (on agriculture and industry, respectively) describe the homework done, or not done, by the EC after the Uruguay Round and in preparation of the coming round. The third section focuses on the potentially new source for severe trade barriers, namely, technical regulations (norms and standards), with a special attention to food safety and health concerns. The fourth section examines whether there are signs that attitudes on trade policy are evolving in certain member-states. A concluding section summarizes a few proposals that the EC ideally should table.

Agriculture: An Incredibly Slow Liberalization Process

The texts released for the Seattle WTO Ministerial by the three European institutions send a rather negative message on agriculture. They insist on the aspects of Article 20 of the Uruguay Agriculture Agreement that can

Box 4.1   The EC trade policy revealed at the 1999 Seattle WTO Ministerial

Table 4.1 presents the seven topics concerning trade policy covered by the texts released for the Seattle WTO Ministerial by the three European institutions (Council, Commission, and Parliament). In February 2001, the Council confirmed that its text remains the basis for the EC approach toward a new WTO round. Table 4.1 assumes that the length of the text devoted to a topic reveals the relative importance of this topic for the European institution in question. This length is measured by the number of words as a percentage of the total number of words for each text (excluding the introductory and concluding general remarks). Table 4.1 also gives the rank of each trade policy topic among the total of 14 topics covered in the three texts (the seven other topics pertain to commercial policy or refer to the trade and development relations between the EC and developing countries; see chapters 5 and 6).

These crude measures of the relative importance of the various topics dealt with by EC trade policy suggest three major lessons. First, the Commission and Council have relatively similar agendas, with the same preeminent issues. They differ on the less important topics, for reasons that may either reflect a joint strategy vis-à-vis the rest of the world or underlying conflicts between them. The Commission has put more emphasis on technical issues (technical barriers to trade and trade facilitation), on which it may want to expand its influence and which are particularly sensitive for developing countries. The Council, conversely, is more interested in trade defense instruments (on which it may want to show its grip), which are also a major concern of US trade policy. Second, the Parliament differs in its huge emphasis on trade and environment. Third, the topics related to technical barriers to trade and trade-related health and environment issues have globally received the largest amount of attention from the Parliament and Commission—but not from the Council.

For each of the seven topics covered, table 4.1 also aims to capture the economic "tone" of the Commission text by looking at the frequency with which 15 key terms (and their variations) have been used: five proliberalization terms (competition, liberalization, market access, mutual recognition, and reduction of barriers), five terms associated with more "neutral" views with respect to liberalization (barriers, disciplines, nondiscrimination, subsidies, and transparency), and five terms reflecting a reluctant approach to liberalization (progressive, harmonization, regulation, safeguard, and reciprocity). The general impression that can be drawn from this exercise is that all the topics are rather loaded with neutral or reluctant terms—except industrial tariffs.

For the sake of minimizing quotes, this chapter refers to the Commission text, limiting references to the two other sources only to cases of noticeable differences among the three texts.

---

be easily used for protectionist purposes, in particular by focusing on the effects of implementing the reduction commitments made under the agreement, and by taking into account the "nontrade" concerns and special treatment for developing countries. Moreover, they do not mention the basic fact that Article 20 is entitled "Continuation of the Reform Process," and starts by recognizing [..] the long-term objective of substantial progressive reductions in support and protection."

Three aspects of the texts merit noting. First, the EC texts offer no perspective about further EC tariff or export subsidy reductions or tariff-quota increases (despite the fact that, in 2000, 186 key EC cereal, meat, and

Table 4.1 Trade policy topics in EC preparatory texts for 1999 Seattle WTO Ministerial

Topic and ranking criteria	Commission		Council		Parliament	
	Share	Rank	Share	Rank	Share	Rank
Topic importance by source[a]:						
Text length devoted to topic						
Agriculture	9.2	4	14.4	2	12.3	3
Industrial tariffs	8.8	6	9.1	4	7.4	6
Trade and environment	8.9	5	8.3	5	12.3	2
Trade defense instruments	2.2	14	4.9	9	4.1	11
Trade facilitation	6.9	7	3.9	12	0.7	14
Technical barriers to trade	5.7	10	2.8	13	1.8	12
Trade and consumer health	3.0	12	1.8	14	6.8	8
Reminder:						
Commercial policy issues[b]	42.6		42.9		47.4	
Trade and development[c]	12.6	2	13.3	3	7.0	6

"Tone" by topic[d]:	Agriculture	Industrial tariffs	Technical barriers	Health and environment	Trade facilitation	Trade instruments
Term frequencies						
Proliberalization terms	33.3	60.0	0.0	42.9	0.0	20.0
Neutral terms	44.4	0.0	37.5	42.9	55.6	40.0
Reluctant terms	22.2	40.0	62.5	14.3	44.4	40.0
Number of observations	9	3	8	7	9	5

EC = European Community.
WTO = World Trade Organization.

a. Decreasing order in the Council text.
b. For details, see table 5.1.
c. For details, see chapter 6.
d. Proliberalization terms: competition, liberalization, market access, mutual recognition, (barrier) reduction. Neutral terms: barriers, disciplines, nondiscrimination, subsidy, transparency. Reluctant terms: harmonization, progressivity, reciprocity, regulation, safeguard.

Source: See box 4.1.

dairy products were expected to still be subject to EC duties higher than 80 percent; Bureau and Bureau 1999). Moreover, the texts take for granted the current definition of acceptable and unacceptable subsidies (in particular, the "blue" box) and all the existing special safeguard provisions included in the Uruguay Agriculture Agreement.

Second, the texts state that the coming negotiations should lead to the renewal of the "peace clause" (a provision that de facto excludes farm subsidies from the WTO dispute settlement regime) and should deal with the elimination of specific barriers, such as state-trading companies, export credit schemes, food aid, and loan deficiency payments—all barriers used more by EC trading partners than by the EC (at least for the time being), although the EC intervention agencies running the Common Agricultural Policy and the EC intervention price mechanism have many common features with state-trading firms and the US marketing loan regime, respectively.

Third, the texts insist on the recognition, in the future, of "non trade concerns" as legitimate restrictions in farm trade. Some of these nontrade concerns are relatively new, and may be quite acceptable for all WTO members, such as the consequences of the fact that past and existing farm policies have caused severe environmental deterioration—particularly in Europe. But other concerns, such as the "multifunctional" role of agriculture, are vague, to say the least, whereas a last group of concerns, such as food security, is quite traditional, and heavily loaded with a protectionist content (it is generally a synonym for self-sufficiency).[2] The texts provide no clues about the EC's choices from among all these interpretations.

This initial EC approach could be seen as tough negotiating tactics, consisting, at the beginning of the talks, of offering no concessions and demanding maximal concessions from its partners. It could also reflect specific circumstances of the late 1990s: the Asian and Russian crises making European farmers (particularly large cereal growers or pig exporters) more reluctant about trade liberalization than a few years ago; the coming EC enlargement to include Central European countries with good potential for farm products (see chapter 6); the wrong but widespread and well-entrenched perception among European leaders that EC agriculture has no comparative advantages under market conditions (see below).

The latest news from the ongoing negotiations on agriculture in Geneva (launched in the context of the Built-in Agenda of the Uruguay Round) suggests that indeed there may have been a tactical element in the initial EC toughness. In November 2000, the EC approved a negotiating proposal including reduction of tariffs, export subsidies, and domestic support.

---

2. From an economic perspective, multifunctionality should be conditional on the existence of robust evidence showing that farmers make more of a nonmarketed contribution to social welfare than other producers (Anderson, Erwidodo, and Ingco 1999), and it could largely rely on instruments other than subsidies that could be much better monitored than state aid (Mahé and Ortalo-Magné 2001).

Though the proposal shows EC's willingness to negotiate, its offers are still very limited: an overall average reduction of tariffs, with a minimum reduction per tariff line (contrary to the traditional EC approach toward manufacturing tariffs); only "further reductions" (not elimination) of export subsidies; and the maintenance of the existing domestic support (subsidy) regime. Moreover, the proposal keeps many of the EC points tabled in Seattle, particularly on "nontrade concerns" (the question being whether this expression represents a real improvement over the previous expression of multifunctionality) and on trade barriers imposed on farm imports by EC trading partners. It remains that the EC proposal has been perceived by EC trading partners as open enough that they decided in March 2001 to start the second phase of agriculture talks in the WTO.

However, the constant reference of the three EC Seattle texts to the decisions of the 1999 Berlin European Council on agriculture suggests another reason for the very defensive position of the texts. It reflects, *above all*, the very limited *domestic* reforms achieved by the EC since the Uruguay Round. (The same could be said for fisheries, another source of conflict between the EC and its trading partners, for reasons explained in box 4.2.) As a result, the rest of the section focuses on the Common Agricultural Policy and, in particular, on its evolution since 1992. After a brief presentation of the CAP initial framework, the section underlines the fundamental gap between the 1992 CAP Reform and the Uruguay Agriculture Agreement—a gap that has cast serious doubts on the EC's ability to fulfill some of its Uruguay Round farm commitments in the coming years. In March 1999, the European Council held in Berlin (hereafter, the Berlin Council) made far too modest decisions; it reduced (not eliminated) the risks of EC failure in implementing its Uruguay Round farm commitments, but left the Community in a defensive position in the WTO negotiations, as mirrored by the Seattle texts.

The Initial CAP: A Brief Review

The Treaty of Rome devotes Articles 32 (ex 38) to 38 (ex 46) to the design of the CAP, which was then seen as necessary for creating a common market in agriculture.[3] Article 33 (ex 39) lists the key CAP goals: (1) to increase

---

3. These 10 initial articles represent one-tenth of the 69 pages of the Treaty of Rome devoted to economic governance—a proportion roughly in line with the GDP share of EC agriculture in the late 1950s. After the late 1960s, the Community's resources (time, budget, and regulations) devoted to farm issues became increasingly out of line with the size of the farm sector: more than 50 percent of the EC budget during most of the past 30 years (and still 45 percent in the late 1990s), more than one-fourth of the EC directives adopted between 1958 and 1998 (including those devoted to standards for farm products). Three articles (ex 44, ex 45, and ex 47) of the initial version of the Treaty of Rome have disappeared in the Amsterdam TEC version, because they were dealing with the mechanisms for establishing the CAP and the implementation procedures during the period of transition.

Box 4.2   The Common Fisheries Policy: Another Loch Ness monster?

Article 32 (ex 38) of the Treaty of Rome defines fisheries as agricultural products—hence, no wonder that the Common Fisheries Policy (CFP) has many common legal points with the CAP: a common market organization for fish adopted in 1981, the same year as for sugar; minimum prices for domestically caught fish; and, above all, a vast set of subsidies of all kinds (from financing stocks to modernizing the fleet).

However, there are two key differences between the CAP and the CFP: if no adequate measure is taken, fish is an exhaustible resource. Until the mid-1970s, seas were "commons," without clear property rights (in sharp contrast to farmland). Fish were then doomed to disappear sooner or later, because every fisherman had an incentive to catch as much fish as he could, and to rely on other fishermen to avoid fish exhaustion. In 1977, following the UN Conference on the Law of the Sea, the EC coastal member-states expanded their sovereignty to "exclusive economic zones" (EEZs), defined as 200 nautical miles from their North Sea and Atlantic coasts (instead of a few miles, as before). These EEZs have empowered EC member-states to define and enforce annual "total allowable catches" (TACs, i.e., the maximum quantity of fish to be caught to ensure the sustainability of the fish resource) for roughly 120 different species. TACs have generated (and still do) severe conflicts about the scientific basis justifying them, as witnessed in December 2000, when the Commission proposed drastic cuts in catches of cod and hake for the years to come.

TACs determine the quantity of fish to be caught, and hence to be traded, for a given consumption pattern. Obstacles to getting TACs can thus inhibit trade in the fishery sector as strictly as could trade barriers on fish per se. This feature explains why tariffs and trade instruments on the product (fish) have a limited role in the fishery sector—in contrast to the CAP. In fact, since the 1962 Dillon Round, EC fish products have been subject to bound (completely since 1995) and moderate (9.6 percent in 2000 on average, with a substantial tariff escalation) tariffs, with substantial tariff preferences for developing countries (Shirotori 1997).

By contrast, constraints on TACs abound in almost all the countries implementing them (including the EC). Only nationals can get them, domestic firms having received TACs cannot hire the services of foreign vessels or harbors, foreign fishermen are not allowed to invest in the domestic fishery sector, and so on. Such restrictions prevail even within the EC. EC TACs may be initially defined on biological (sustainability) grounds, but their ultimate level and breakdown between member-states rely on arcane considerations with little biological rationale: traditional fishing rights and activities, the political balance between regions, restrictions on EC fishing capacities due to the creation of EEZs by non-EC countries, etc. Member-state TACs are then split between vessels according to various schemes, from professional unions (Britain) to administration (France). In sum, EC TACs boil down to fishing quotas granted on a vessel basis through an allocation system severely limiting extra- and intra-EC competition.

If EC TACs address the sustainability issue of the fish resource, they have thus a key limit from an economic point of view: They do not permit screening the most efficient EC fishermen—in determining the fish allowed to be caught—from the least efficient ones. They thus waste resources, from vessels to harbors and fishery logistics. This intrinsic flaw has been greatly amplified by the very generous subsidies granted by the CFP to EC fishermen who are unable to assess correctly market evolution because they are protected by minimum prices. In 1997, the average rate of subsidization in EC fisheries was 15 percent—ranging from 5 percent (Belgium) to 90 percent

(box continues next page)

Box 4.2 *(continued)*

(Finland), relative to 4 percent (Iceland) and 25 percent (Canada) in the rest of the OECD countries (OECD 2000e). Such subsidies are fundamentally inconsistent with the objective of sustainable fish resources because they create strong incentives for overfishing, particularly in member states with lax enforcement of TACs, which leads to periodic excess supply and financial crises in the EC fishery sector.

Because of these flaws, the EC TAC regime has fueled many trade conflicts. The EC has tried to ease TAC-generated constraints by getting access to EEZs held by non-EC countries for EC (often Portuguese or Spanish) vessels. This has often led to bitter situations, as is best illustrated by the conflicts with Morocco and Chile. Moreover, constrained by GATT-bound tariffs, the EC has increasingly used nontariff barriers to limit access to its fish markets in four ways: (1) Costly conditions on fishing techniques have been imposed, such as banning certain types of fishing nets (1998). (2) Complex rules define fish country of origin by the nationality of the vessel, crew, staff, and captain, and even members of company boards (in 1992, fish caught by a Mauritian firm were no longer considered EC fish because a Japanese citizen had become a member of the company's board, following the acquisition of the Mauritian firm by a Japanese company). (3) Recurrent antidumping and antisubsidy measures (consisting of minimum prices on foreign Atlantic salmon) have been routinely imposed for years. (4) Last but not least, there are a half-dozen WTO dispute settlement cases on fish products, with the EC involved in five.

Improving EC TACs requires two key measures. First, to promote the efficiency of the fishing sector, TACs should be transferable between vessels, as they are in Iceland (Gissurarson 2000) and, to a lesser extent, in the Netherlands. "Individual transferable quotas" (ITQs) could then be bought by more efficient fishermen from less efficient fishermen, leaving both operators (and the whole country) in a better situation. Second, trade liberalization should make ITQs transferable among the fishermen of the *whole world* (and not only from the country in question), that is, tradable between countries—with all their components of services and investment.

---

farm productivity, (2) to ensure a fair standard of living for the agricultural community, (3) to stabilize markets, (4) to assure the availability of supplies, and (5) to ensure that supplies reach consumers at reasonable prices. This list reveals the basic problem of the CAP: too biased in favor of producers. Even point 5, which is the only one mentioning consumers, refers to "reasonable"—not low—prices. Moreover, until the early 1990s, the CAP was essentially based on using *one* instrument (price support) to reach *all* these objectives, and that has been an important additional source of distortions and costs.

The CAP began to be implemented in July 1964, three months after the beginning of the Kennedy Round negotiations. During the following 30 years, all agricultural goods have been progressively subjected to 26 different common market organizations (CMOs), leaving less than 12 percent of EC total farm output de facto not regulated by CMOs (with potatoes as the only important product).[4] Until the CAP Reform was adopted

---

4. Grant (1997) reports European farmers' pressures to get fully operational CMOs (with floor prices and quantity regulations), even for minute products, e.g., bergamot or honey.

in 1992, all the CMOs relied essentially on a set of multiple guaranteed prices determined on an annual (or half-yearly) basis by the Council of Ministers (appendix A gives details for the five farm products examined in chapter 3). Because these guaranteed prices were unrelated to world prices, they required two-sided protection—first on import, then on export. Since its origin, the CAP has imposed variable levies on imports, that is, adjusted specific tariffs that vary on a daily basis raising world prices to the level of EC domestic prices (which are guaranteed on an annual or half-yearly basis)—making imports prohibitive. A decade later, export subsidies have become routinely necessary to dump into world markets the growing EC excess supply generated by the too-high, rigidly guaranteed EC farm prices.

In an effort to limit the effects of such guaranteed prices, two other instruments—supply control and market-support payments—became increasingly important in the late 1970s. Supply control (stock management) was expected to suffice to cope with excess supply. But inflated stocks—generated by the cumulation over years of continuous excess supply—have imposed such a budgetary burden on the Community that it has been necessary to have increasing recourse to additional tools to control supply, such as quantitative limits on production (e.g., mandatory production quotas on milk, introduced in 1984) or on essential inputs (e.g., voluntary set-aside programs for cereals or planting rights in wine). Last, market-support payments were granted under the form of demand subsidies (for low-income consumers) or supply subsidies for private storage (which tend to increase food supply) and for the cessation of production or for early retirement of farmers (which tend to decrease food supply).

Table 4.2 provides some sense of the long-term evolution of EC farm protection and support with the progressive accumulation of CAP instruments, and a comparison with three other OECD countries. This section is also based on the old OECD methodology for estimating CSEs and PSEs; see chapter 2.) Although there are no CSE or PSE estimates for the years before 1979, available studies suggest that the average nominal rate of protection in Western Europe increased from 30 percent (in the early 1950s) to 40 percent (late 1950s) and 60 percent (late 1960s) (Gulbrandsen and Lindbeck 1973). These figures give a sense of the ever-increasing trend of EC protection in agriculture from the immediate aftermath of World War II to the mid-1990s—leading to the striking situation (see table 4.2, bottom rows) that the total domestic support (as defined by the OECD) granted to EC agriculture represents more than 90 percent of the farm gross value added after 1993.[5]

---

5. For international comparisons, only ratios in terms of farm value added or GDP are meaningful. It is hard to compare the average domestic support per farmer or per hectare between countries because it is largely determined by differences in average farm size and labor intensity. The ratio of total domestic support to GDP allows us to take into account the fact that a portion of this support may be captured by the nonfarm sector.

Table 4.2 Consumer and producer subsidy equivalents and total farm support, 1979–99ª (percent)

Group or country	1979–86	1986–88	1989–90	1991–92	1993–95	1996–98	1999
Consumer subsidy equivalents (CSEs) (percent)							
European Community	30	44	36	42	32	29	37
Japan	42	57	49	51	51	50	52
United States	11	13	10	10	9	7	6
Australia	7	9	8	9	6	6	6
Producer subsidy equivalents (PSEs) (percent)							
European Community	37	49	43	50	46	47	55
Japan	63	73	68	70	75	71	68
United States	21	30	22	21	18	22	29
Australia	11	10	10	11	10	9	9
CSE-based tariffs (ad valorem tariff equivalents of the CSEs, percent)							
European Community	45	80	57	74	47	42	58
Japan	76	134	97	103	103	100	116
United States	13	15	11	12	10	8	6
Australia	7	10	9	10	7	6	6
EC total domestic support							
As percent of farm value-added	72.9	89.8	77.7	97.0	92.2	86.6	90.7
As percent of GDP	2.4	2.6	2.1	2.3	1.9	1.5	1.5
In euro per full-time farmer	6,204	10,975	11,983	16,383	15,450	16,413	17,211
In euro per hectare	894	1,394	1,382	1,769	1,578	1,504	1,571
In euro per EC inhabitant	233	311	304	364	318	303	316
EC consumer subsidy equivalent							
As percent of farm value-added	34.0	47.1	34.7	40.6	31.9	24.6	28.3

a. Based on the old method (see text).

Sources: OECD, *Economic Accounts for Agriculture*, Agricultural policies in OECD countries, various years; author's computations.

This initial version of the CAP has generated two major distortions in EC agriculture. First, because the CAP has relied on instruments providing support proportional to production or input volumes, it has essentially benefited large farms. In the early 1990s, the top 25 percent of EC farms, representing 72 percent of EC farm output, received 68 percent of EC price-support subsidies (OECD 1999b). Second, as shown by economic analysis, guaranteed price increases have had two opposite effects. On the one hand, they have increased farmers' income, but only on a transitory basis, because in the long run, farmers' incomes have followed the skill-adjusted average income prevailing in the rest of the EC economies. On the other hand, guaranteed price increases have progressively accumulated, in the form of rents attached to the fixed factors necessary for farm production—in particular, to land prices. In other words, if farmers as *producers* have enjoyed only transitory income increases from the CAP, farmers as *landowners* (and owners of other key fixed inputs, e.g., the rights to produce milk under the quota regime) have benefited from rents increasing in the long run.

The perverse impact of the CAP instruments explains the apparent paradox of recurrent and violent demonstrations by farmers who have been, and still are, receiving massive CAP transfers. The farmers who demonstrate are most often small farmers. They earn modest incomes from their farm activities and benefit from CAP rents only on limited assets (small landholdings or cattle). Although they receive limited benefits from the CAP, they are very dependent on it (they often have to do other business to survive). In addition, they feel threatened by the trend to larger farms, substitution of capital for labor, and accelerating rural depopulation—all developments that the CAP instruments are exacerbating because of their built-in biases in favor of large farms.

By contrast, large farms earn higher incomes because of their larger size and increased intensity in skilled labor, and they benefit from CAP rents on their large assets. In these circumstances, it is crucial for these large farmers to keep alive the popular myth in Europe of "one" agriculture based on small farms, to maintain a strong coalition with small farmers so that they do not become too politically isolated, and can keep pressure on elections in rural constituencies. As a result, large farmers strongly support the "one trade union" approach, and behind the scenes, they contribute substantially to the demonstrations of the small farmers.

1992 CAP Reform and the Uruguay Round: A Crucial Gap

The 1992 CAP Reform (also called the MacSharry Reform, from the then EC agriculture commissioner, Ray MacSharry) was adopted in May 1992, after the rejection, by the Netherlands and Britain, of a bolder plan including the possibility of subsidies degressive on a farm basis, and after

Box 4.3   The 1992 Common Agricultural Policy Reform

The 1992 Reform covered arable crops (cereals, oilseeds, and protein seeds), beef, and milk, that is, almost one-fourth of EC farm production in 1992 (one-fifth in the late 1990s). Table 4.3 summarizes the evolution of key guaranteed prices and compensatory subsidies under the reform, with all prices and subsidies expressed in euros (because prices and subsidies were published until 1995 in "green euros," they have been multiplied by a conversion factor of roughly 1.2 to get series consistent for the whole period). Table 4.3 deserves three comments, which for simplicity's sake are only presented for arable crops (with figures rounded). First, the "intervention" price (the other types of guaranteed prices have been abolished) was reduced in three annual steps (1993, 1994, and 1995). The intervention price for 1995 was set for an indefinite period (it was changed by the 1999 Berlin Council for the years 2000–06).

Second, compensatory land-based subsidies (€54 per ton in 1995) have also been increased in three annual steps. These subsidies are defined by ton, but they are paid on a per-hectare basis. This required complex calculations to determine historic regional yields. Each member-state had to specify "cereal growing regions"; for each of these regions, it had to determine an average annual yield based on past (pre-1991) performance; then the yield (in tons per hectare) was multiplied by the subsidy (in euros per ton) to determine the payment by eligible hectare. The whole system was specified by type of crop, productivity level, irrigation method, and so on. Not surprisingly, such a complicated system, in combination with weak monitoring, has allowed massive overcompensation for price cuts.

Third, mandatory set-aside obligations have been imposed on large (but not on small) farmers who have also been compensated with subsidies (€57 per ton in 1995), with a similar regime of reference yield to get the payment per hectare set aside.

Table 4.3 shows that the reform of the beef sector was based on the same format of decreased guaranteed prices combined with compensatory factor-based subsidies (called "premiums"), with some limits imposed on the number of possible claims (cattle head) eligible for subsidies.

The 1992 Reform also introduced environmental measures, but marginally and ambiguously. Depending on the precise circumstances of implementation, these measures have played the role of pure subsidies (in the absence of effective monitoring, as for pork in Brittany), or they have been implicit market-support payments to a "new farm" product—"nature," announcing the theme of "multifunctionality" in agriculture.

the withdrawal of an alternative scheme, supported by Germany, based on the generalization of the milk production quota regime to major farm products. The reform introduced two key changes (see box 4.3 and table 4.3): (1) reduction of guaranteed prices for arable crops, beef, and milk; and (2) full compensation of the income losses caused by lower guaranteed prices through "compensatory payments," consisting of "factor-based" subsidies defined on a per-hectare or cattle-head basis.

This package of measures reveals a crucial gap between the CAP Reform and the Uruguay Agriculture Agreement. The farm trade liberalization launched by the Uruguay Round aims to generate substantial decreases of production costs, and changes in the varieties of farm goods produced. By contrast, the 1992 Reform introduced no strong incentives to *reduce* EC costs. What follows provides evidence confirming the as-

Table 4.3 1992 CAP Reform and 1999 Berlin Council: Select guaranteed prices and compensatory subsidies

Commodity, price, and subsidy		1992	1993	1994	1995	1996	1997	1998	1999
				1992 CAP Reform					
Cereals, oilseeds, and protein seeds									
Intervention price[a]	Euros/ton	184.7	137.7	127.1	119.2	119.2	119.2	119.2	119.2
Market price[b]	Euros/ton	167.2	163.6	151.8	150.8	150.0	136.8	125.4	n.a.
Set-aside rate (mandatory)	Percent	n.a.	15.0	15.0	12.0	10.0	5.0	5.0	10.0
EC compensatory subsidies ("payments")									
Cereals	Euros/ton	n.a.	29.8	41.7	54.3	54.3	54.3	54.3	54.3
Oilseeds[c]	Euros/cereal-ton	n.a.	83.7	88.4	89.5	89.5	83.9	87.6	94.2
Protein seeds	Euros/ton	n.a.	77.5	77.5	78.5	78.5	78.5	78.5	78.5
Set-aside	Euros/ton	n.a.	53.6	67.9	68.8	68.8	68.8	68.8	68.8
Meat (bovine)									
Intervention price	Euros/ton	4,088	3,833	3,632	3,475	3,475	3,475	3,475	3,475
EC compensatory subsidies ("premiums")									
Bulls (first age)	Euros/head	48	72	89	109	109	135	135	135
Steers (first age)	Euros/head	48	72	89	109	109	109	109	109
Suckler cows	Euros/head	60	83	113	145	145	145	145	145
Slaughter (adults)	Euros/head	n.a.	n.a.	n.a.	n.a.	n.a.	n.a.	n.a.	n.a.
Additional member-state aid									
Suckler cows	Euros/head	42	30	30	30	30	30	30	30
Milk									
Increase in milk quotas[d]	Percent	0.0	0.0	0.0	0.0	0.0	0.0	0.0	0.0
Intervention prices[e]									
Butter	Euros/ton	3,490	3,342	3,240	3,282	3,282	3,282	3,282	3,282
Skimmed milk powder	Euros/ton	2,055	2,029	2,029	2,055	2,055	2,055	2,055	2,055
Sugar beet									
Minimum price (A sugar)[f]	Euros/ton	46.7	46.1	46.1	46.7	46.7	46.7	46.7	46.7
CAP budget[g]									
"Fund guarantee"[h]	Millions of euros	31,068	34,748	32,970	34,503	39,108	40,423	38,748	40,440
"Rural development"	Millions of euros	2,895	3,386	3,335	3,609	3,935	4,132	4,367	5,565
Average CAP budget									
Per full-time farmer[i]	Euros/farmer	4,757	5,269	5,265	5,224	6,070	6,502	6,391	6,617
Per hectare	Euros/hectare	505	537	524	507	567	589	n.a.	n.a.

CAP = Common Agricultural Policy.
EAGGF = European Agricultural Guidance and Guarantee Fund.
n.a. = not available
VAT = value-added tax

a. Based on 155 green euros/ton in 1992.
b. Producer prices (excluding VAT).
c. From 1992 to 1996, converted from a euro/hectare basis (conversion factor of 4.6).
d. A third increase of 0.5 percent is scheduled for 2007.
e. A third decrease of 5 percent is scheduled for 2007, with a compensatory subsidy of 17.24 euros/ton.

sessment already made in 1995 (Johnson 1995) that the 1992 Reform represented a significant change in the *structure* of farm support in Europe, but not a change in the *level* of support, a situation meaning troubles ahead for the EC. The absence of incentives for cost cutting flows from the principle of full compensation of price cuts included in the 1992 Reform— following a tradition dating from the very first years of the CAP (in the mid-1960s, German farmers were fully compensated for German price decreases following the CAP's introduction in Germany).

In fact, the implementation of the 1992 Reform witnessed a massive *over*-compensation of cereal price decreases caused by two factors. First,

Berlin Council: Decisions for 2000, proposals for 2000–06							Change (percent)		
2000	2001	2002	2003	2004	2005	2006	1995/ 1992ᵃ	2006/ 1996	2006/ 1992ᵃ
110.3	101.3	101.3	101.3	101.3	101.3	101.3	−35.5	−15.0	−45.2
n.a.	n.a.	n.a.	n.a.	n.a.	n.a.	n.a.	−9.8	n.a.	n.a.
10.0	10.0	10.0	10.0	10.0	10.0	10.0	−20.0	0.0	−33.3
58.7	63.0	63.0	63.0	63.0	63.0	63.0	82.4	15.9	111.4
81.7	72.4	63.0	63.0	63.0	63.0	63.0	6.9	−29.6	−24.7
72.5	72.5	72.5	72.5	72.5	72.5	72.5	1.3	−7.6	−6.4
58.7	63.0	63.0	63.0	63.0	63.0	63.0	28.3	−8.5	17.5
3,240	3,010	2,780	2,780	2,780	2,780	2,780	−15.0	−20.0	−32.0
160	185	210	210	210	210	210	128.0	93.2	340.5
122	136	150	150	150	150	150	128.0	38.0	214.6
163	182	200	200	200	200	200	143.1	38.0	235.6
27	53	80	80	80	80	80	n.a.	n.a.	n.a.
50	50	50	50	50	50	50	−27.6	65.6	19.9
0.0	0.0	0.0	0.0	0.0	0.5	0.5	0.0	n.a.	n.a.
3,282	3,282	3,282	3,282	3,282	3,118	2,954	−6.0	−10.0	−15.4
2,055	2,055	2,055	2,055	2,055	1,952	1,850	0.0	−10.0	−10.0
46.7	46.7	46.7	46.7	46.7	46.7	46.7	0.0	0.0	0.0
40,526	39,605	39,570	39,430	38,410	37,570	37,290	11.6	−5.0	20.0
2,618	4,495	4,330	4,340	4,350	4,360	4,370	16.6	20.1	50.9
6,183	6,599	6,907	7,027	7,005	7,009	7,106	9.8	17.1	36.0
n.a.	n.a.	n.a.	n.a.	n.a.	n.a.	n.a.	0.4	n.a.	n.a.

f. EC price (Italy, Ireland, Portugal, Finland, Spain, and Britain have slightly higher prices).
g. Member-state subsidies are not taken into account.
h. EAGGF effective expenses until 1998, forecasts afterwards.
i. Assuming a 2 percent annual rate of decrease of the number of full-time farmers (from 1998 to 2006).

Note: From 1992 to 1994, prices and payments are expressed in commercial euros, based on a conversion factor of 1.2 euro per green euro.

Sources: The Agricultural Situation in the EU, various years. European Commission: The CAP Reform: A Policy for the Future, 1999.

producer prices (paid at the farm gate, excluding the value-added tax) declined by much less than intervention prices (e.g., common wheat market prices declined by 10 percent, relative to 35 percent for intervention prices, as shown by table 4.3), so that the compensatory subsidies that were largely based on the decline of *intervention* prices were excessive. Second, the detailed provisions of the 1992 Reform allowed "generous" calculations of compensations, which seriously contributed to minimizing the impact of the 1992 Reform and preserving the initial CAP (see box 4.3 and, for details, Chambres d'Agriculture 1994b or Swinbank 1997). This overcompensation has been estimated at 11 percent of the granted compensatory subsidies (*excluding* set-aside subsidies) for 1993–94, 30 percent for 1994–95, 42 percent for 1995–96, and 21 percent in 1996—a total of €8.5 billion for the four years (European Commission 1997b). More important, the CAP Reform has penalized low-cost farm production in the long run, in several ways: efficient farmers and those with good land (whose yields are higher than average) have been penalized by the fact that compensatory subsidies are based on an average yield, stricter set-aside obligations for large farms have limited low cost production made possible by these farms, and so on.

Skyrocketing compensatory subsidies could not last forever. They reactivated another EC tradition dating from the waiver granted in 1984 to Britain for its contribution to the CAP budget. In the late 1990s, member-states became increasingly obsessed by their individual budgetary "rate of return" (*taux de retour*; i.e., how much money a member-state can get back from its contribution to the EC budget). This concern led to the 1999 Berlin Council decision to "stabilize" the EC farm budget for 2000–06. But such a stabilization can only impose a "soft" constraint: it corresponds in fact to an increase in the subsidy rate *by farmer*, because the number of EC farmers is continuously decreasing (see box 4.5 below). As a result, it is unlikely to induce remaining EC farmers to cut their production costs, and to change their product mix.

Full compensation and budgetary stabilization have allowed the EC to escape the difficult decision about which farmers should be entitled to receive subsidies. From the perspective of the Uruguay Agriculture Agreement, the raison d'être of subsidies is to be *transitory* compensation for those farmers who have been induced to make wrong decisions in the past because of the CAP, and of the farm policies of other countries. Ideally, such subsidies should thus be granted only to *incumbent* farmers; they should not be available to entrant farmers, who should make market-based decisions, and they should not be based on production factors, in order to be "de-coupled" as much as possible from farm production. Ideally, the level of subsidies should mirror the length of time during which the farmers in question have been induced to make wrong decisions—meaning that subsidies should have some determined endpoint.

Not only did the compensatory subsidies introduced by the CAP Reform have none of these desirable features, but they have amplified (and still do) the negative effects of the initial CAP regime. They also tend to be capitalized in land and other input values—increasing once more the value of land for arable crops, relative to land for pastures, forests, or other environmentally friendly uses (Mahé and Roe 1996). And they are also biased in favor of large farms—favoring the heirs of incumbent farmers to the detriment of entrant "farm entrepreneurs" coming from the rest of the economy, and hence generating long-term losses in entrepreneurial capacity in the EC farm sector (Mahé and Ortalo-Magné 2001). Ironically, this basic issue of who should be entitled to get compensation has resurfaced in the context of the EC's enlargement to Central European countries—to the great confusion of the EC, which has provided inconsistent solutions and arguments (see chapter 6).

Two mutually reinforcing reasons have contributed to further limiting the impact of the Uruguay Round on the CAP Reform. First, most European governments looked at the Uruguay deal in terms of what they could gain from US reforms—not of what they could gain from the EC's own reforms. This approach greatly underestimated the potential EC benefits from the round, as illustrated by the following estimates: in 1990, the cost of US farm policy for EC farmers was roughly $800 per farm, whereas the cost of the CAP for EC consumers was roughly $11,100 per farm—that is, an underestimating factor of almost 14 (the cost of the CAP for US farmers was roughly $3,400 per farm) (Tyers and Anderson 1992).

Second, defining the reference period for tariffying existing border barriers is a key element of the Uruguay Agriculture Agreement (for a general description of the agreement, see Josling 1998 or Swinbank 1999). As shown by table 4.2, the main reference period used (1986–88) corresponds to peak farm protection in the EC. Hence, the EC Uruguay Round commitments for tariff reductions rely on the highest possible initial base—making effective liberalization minimal, and full compensation the most expensive possible. Indeed, in 1992–94, EC member-states were still largely underestimating CAP overall costs, and thus the subsidies necessary to implement the full-compensation principle. Table 4.2 mirrors this point, showing the widening gap between EC PSEs and CSEs after 1993—this divergence reflecting the increasingly intensive use of compensatory subsidies by the EC.

Implementing EC Uruguay Round Commitments: Trouble Ahead

The very limits of the CAP Reform raise a question: could the EC face difficulty in meeting its Uruguay Round commitments (which are briefly described in appendix A for the five farm products covered in chapter 3) on export subsidies, market access, and aggregate measures of support (these topics are ranked by decreasing order of expected trouble in the future)?

Export Subsidies

Difficulties have been faster to emerge and are most severe in the domain of export subsidies—a worrisome situation from the world perspective, for two reasons. The EC accounts for roughly 90 percent of export subsidies notified to the WTO, and the bulk of EC export subsidies is devoted to the major farm products of interest for almost all WTO members (grains, beef, dairy products, and sugar). Between 1995 and 1998 (the years for which EC official notification of export subsidies is available), the EC exceeded its Uruguay Round commitments for beef (1996), olive oil (1996), other milk products (1996–97), rice (1996–97), poultry (1997), sugar (1997–98), coarse grains (1998), pork (1998), and eggs (1998) (OECD 2000d). This evolution was expected to continue and spread over more products for 1999 and 2000 (Tangermann 1999; OECD 2000d).[6]

As underlined in chapter 3 (table 3.5), export subsidy rates and tariff rates should be similar for the same product (they both reflect the same wedge between domestic and world prices), and indeed they generally are. This means that increasingly low EC tariffs will increasingly constrain the level of export subsidies that the EC can grant. In the absence of serious adjustment (due to the full-compensation principle), this evolution will lead to increasing EC domestic stocks *and* to declining world shares of EC farm exports. This dark perspective was behind the attempt to make further CAP reforms in 1999 (see below).

Market Access: Barriers to Imports

The 1992 CAP Reform has connected world and intervention prices, import duties, and compensatory subsidies in such a way that the EC could not have faced any noticeable difficulty in meeting its market-access Uruguay Round commitments in the late 1990s. But this political tour de force was achieved at a huge cost: the absence of noticeable economic incentives for change in the agricultural sector, an illustration of the French saying *"plus ça change, plus c'est la même chose"* (the more it changes, the more it is the same). Comparing the post-Uruguay Round, postreform year 1995 to the pre-Uruguay Round, preform years 1991–93 for common wheat offers the best illustration of this remark (for simplicity, figures have been rounded, and the complications related to wheat quality ignored).

First, the EC commitments on bound tariffs have been de facto irrelevant since 1995, as is best illustrated by what happened in 1995–96. On the basis of the 1995 world average wheat price of €93 per ton forecast by the Commission in 1994, the 1995 bound specific tariff (€140 per ton) would have generated a level of protection of 150 percent for 1995—a level judged unacceptable by the major EC trading partners during the Uruguay Round negotiations. As this situation has persisted in the following years,

---

6. Because the EC did not exhaust its allowed export subsidies in 1995 (because of very high world prices), it has invoked a "forward" mechanism (the possibility of compensating for excess export subsidies during a year with export subsidies unused in past years, as is possible in other agreements, such as in the Multi-Fiber Agreement). That could be an expediency, but could not be a solution for the recurrent problems faced since 1996. It should be added that an approach in terms of effective (rather than nominal) rates of export subsidies would be useful to get a more complete assessment of the EC situation (export subsidies have been granted to the EC food industry as compensation for high protection of basic farm products).

despite the scheduled progressive reduction of EC bound tariffs (see below), the EC has had to use the alternative definition (included in the Uruguay Agriculture Agreement) to determine its external tariff, namely to cap the tariff to be paid at 55 percent of the wheat *intervention* price. Since 1995, this formula has been de facto the operational definition of the EC tariff on wheat.

Second, the tariff-cap formula has maintained a substantial level of protection, even when world prices have been unusually high. For instance, in 1995, the duty-paid price was €185 per ton (1.55 times the 1995 intervention price of roughly €119 per ton), that is, a rate of protection of almost 100 percent when based on the Commission forecast of €93 per ton for the 1995 world price, and still a rate of protection of almost 30 percent when based on the unusually high world price of roughly €150 per ton prevailing in the 1995–97 world markets. (It is important to note that, by definition, any decrease in world prices generates an *increase* of the tariff-cap-based rate of protection).

Third, the full-compensation principle has ensured that no significant change could occur in basic domestic support to farmers. For instance, the sum of the EC 1995 intervention wheat price (€119 per ton) and the associated compensatory subsidy (€54 per ton) comes close to the prereform floor price of roughly €195 per ton.

Following all these measures, access to EC markets seems already tightly locked. However, the Uruguay Agriculture Agreement allows for "special agricultural safeguard" measures in case of unexpected difficulty with import prices or volumes. In the EC case, the potential application of these safeguards covers 539 tariff lines—almost one-third of the total number of lines for farm products in the EC tariff schedule. Effective price-based safeguards ("snap-back tariffs") have been imposed on 12 (1995), 14 (1996 and 1997), and 12 (1998) items (mostly sugar, poultry, and molasses); volume-based safeguards have been imposed on 47 (1996), 46 (1997), and 27 (1998) items (mostly fruit and vegetables) (OECD 2000d).

The Uruguay Round negotiators were so aware of the limits imposed on market access liberalization that they took care to introduce tariff quotas: 3 percent of domestic consumption could be imported at tariffs lower than bound tariffs, and this share should be progressively increased to 5 percent over 6 years. However, despite the fact that the EC "in-quota" tariffs were roughly one-third of the bound tariffs, the average "fill" rate steadily declined from 76 percent (1995) to 72 percent (1996) to 71 percent (1997) to 66 percent (1998) to 68 percent (1999) (OECD 2000d). This evolution mirrors the protectionist impact of the EC quota-management system, which relies on licenses on demand—a mechanism opaque enough to reduce the awareness of cheaper world prices among EC consumers.

All these relations between world prices, domestic prices, and the various instruments of protection were bound to evolve progressively under the pressure of two forces independent of the post-1995 EC farm policy:

(1) the evolution of world prices, and (2) the committed decreases of EC bound tariffs (by 36 percent, i.e., from €140 per ton in 1995 to €95 per ton in 2000 in the wheat case). In such a framework, the only instrument left at the disposal of the EC decision makers was the intervention price— leaving two alternatives for post-1995 situations.

One alternative would be for world prices to *increase* more than the scheduled decrease of EC bound tariffs. In this case, the tariff-cap formula remains the only effective constraint, bound tariffs are redundant, and farmers enjoy overcompensation—high world prices coupled with subsidies rigidly based on too high intervention prices. This alternative prevailed in 1995–96, with unusually high world prices—even leading the EC to impose export *taxes* (on wheat and barley) for a few months, in an effort to reduce EC prices relative to world prices.

The other alternative would be for world prices to *decrease* enough to make the progressively *reduced* bound tariffs the effective trade barrier (the tariff-cap formula becoming then redundant). For instance, a hypothetical world price of €90 per ton in 2000, combined with the committed 2000 bound tariff of €95 per ton, would have given a duty-paid import price of €185 per ton (corresponding to a tariff equivalent of 106 percent, i.e., *more* than the average tariff equivalent for the years 1994–98). Since 1997, this second alternative has prevailed, and the world prices for 2000 leave some—but now small—redundancy of EC bound tariffs, except for low-quality wheat and barley (Tangermann 1999). In other words, the 6 years since the end of the Uruguay Round have witnessed the elimination of the initially huge and "redundant" tariff protection incorporated into the EC Uruguay Round commitments on market access. This redundancy is now limited, and any new tariff reduction may trigger some *effective* liberalization.

These observations on wheat can be expanded to the other major farm products (Tangermann 1999). In all cases, EC commitments on market access have been so minimal that the EC will remain a difficult partner in the coming WTO negotiations—in particular for all products whose intervention prices have been left untouched by the 1992 Reform, or have not been subject to further reductions since 1995 (by the Berlin Council; see below), such as sugar.

Aggregate Measures of Support

Prospects in the domain of aggregate measures of support are better than those for export subsidies and tariffs. For 1995 and 1996, the EC aggregate measures of support (AMS) levels represented 64 and 67 percent, respectively, of EC commitments in this domain (€73.5 billion in 1995, to be progressively reduced to €61.2 billion by 2000) (OECD 2000d).

However, this positive note deserves a serious caveat: it relies on the assumption of the stability of the existing definition of domestic support, an assumption that will almost certainly be challenged by all EC trading partners in the coming negotiations in two respects. First, the current AMS coverage of dairy products refers only to milk used in butter and skimmed milk powder; as a result, it ignores €6 billion out of €19 billion in subsidies paid to the EC dairy sector. Second, the AMS is just a portion of the total domestic support for the farm sector. Total support also includes the blue and green boxes of subsidies (plus a de minimis component and a special and differentiated component, which are small and can be ignored in what follows). In particular, the EC favorable situation in AMS mirrors the current definition of the blue box, which includes the €16 billion compensatory subsidies paid to arable crops.

Changing these definitions will generate severe difficulties for the EC. The most serious challenge concerns the blue box—the EC being the only WTO member (with Norway) to intensively use this implicit escape clause to the Uruguay Agriculture Agreement. The blue box represents 23 percent of the EC's total domestic support granted from 1995 to 1998 (34 percent for Norway), in sharp contrast with 4 percent for the United States, and 0 percent for Japan or South Korea, the EC's traditional allies in agricultural matters (OECD 2000d). If the blue box subsidies had been included in the AMS definition in 1995–96, the EC would have already been dangerously close to its AMS commitments (by 10 to 5 percent).

The EC compensatory subsidies currently included in the blue box deserve two additional remarks. On the one hand, they could be seen as a powerful instrument for further reforms in the long run. Even French taxpayers are beginning to find expensive the total domestic support to agriculture, amounting to more than €17,000 per farmer in 1999 (with a peak of €18,000 in 1998), whereas the French minimum *wage* is €10,000 per year.[7] This emerging reluctance will be boosted when it will be more widely known that the average total income of agricultural households is higher than the average income of other households in the rich EC member-states—by 5 to 10 percent in Belgium, to more than 50 percent in France, to more than 100 percent in the Netherlands, the only important exceptions being Germany and Italy, where farm income is 10 to 20 per-

---

7. This figure is based on OECD "total domestic support," which serves as a basis for estimating the share of domestic support in farm value added in table 4.2 (the figure of roughly €6,500 per farmer in table 4.3 takes into account only the transfers financed by the CAP budget). Similar figures are available at the member-state level (e.g., in 1997, total transfers to French farmers amounted to €18 billion [a figure that includes the often ignored support for fruit and olive oil, but also reflects the fact that the price support for cereals was smaller than usual because of high world prices] represented 75 percent of the French value added in farming, or twice the level of net farm income [Bureau and Bureau 1999]). The impact of such information is best illustrated by the opposite fate of two Parliamentary reports. In 1993, the Devedjian Report (which was the first one to courageously underline the CAP costs) was pilloried by almost all French politicians. In 1998, the Marre Report stressed this point again, and the unfairness of the subsidy regime (in 1997, 938 French farms received subsidies larger than €115,000 each, whereas 200,000 farmers received less than €7,500 each; it was well received.

cent short of the nonfarm income (OECD 1999b). Indeed, this increased transparency had already changed the tone and content of the debate about the CAP in France and several other member-states before the 1999 Berlin Council—leading these countries to focus more on questions of the intrinsic soundness of the CAP regarding global resource allocation, income distribution among farmers, and environmental damage by farm activities, and to look for ways to reduce subsidies.

On the other hand, the fact that massive farm subsidies are considered acceptable as long as they respect budgetary stabilization is unhealthy. It endangers the Treaty of Rome: excluding farm goods from the state-aid rules of the treaty is anachronistic—and inconsistent at a time when all manufactured goods *and* services are increasingly subjected to such disciplines. Far from being an instrument of change, such massive subsidies have inhibited (and still do) the adjustment efforts that the EC farm sector should make before the new round of negotiations, to become more competitive by world standards. They will inevitably generate more inefficiencies (even in those EC farm segments considered efficient today) and ultimately fuel demand for more protection. In this subsidy domain, as for the rest of farm policy, the EC should aim to benefit from New Zealand's and Sweden's experiences of bold moves (described in box 4.4), with their positive effects on efficiency, product diversification, and consumer gains.

1999 Berlin Council: Another Missed Opportunity

In March 1999, the Berlin Council adopted several decisions (see box 4.5 and table 4.3), which have been presented as a "new" CAP reform for the years 2000–08. In fact, the Council was close to collapse on farm issues, and has been unable to go very far. In particular, reductions in intervention prices range from small to nil, leading to three consequences: (1) Intervention prices in sectors left untouched by the 1992 Reform and the Berlin Council, such as dairy products (until 2005) and sugar, will be increasingly unsustainable; (2) further EC tariff reductions will be difficult without further reductions of intervention prices; and (3) the EC will find it increasingly hard to fulfill its existing commitments on export subsidies. In sum, the Berlin Council has left the EC in a defensive position in the coming negotiations—in many ways, not in a much better position than before the 1992 Blair House negotiations (for a modestly more optimistic view, see Tangermann 1999).

In sum, the outcome of the Berlin Council is too modest to substantially change the major trends of EC production and consumption, and hence of domestic stocks and trade (for information, stock cereals in mid-1998 were back to their 1990 level). In particular, it would still be hard for the EC to fulfill its commitments (with adverse secondary effects on the EC mix of farm products), if and when the euro becomes stronger or world farm

Box 4.4   Swedish farm policy reform: A blueprint for future CAP reform?

New Zealand is the most frequently mentioned illustration of farm policy reform in an OECD country because it has the longest experience with "life in agriculture after subsidies" (Chambres d'Agriculture 1993; Federated Farmers of New Zealand 1999; Johnson 2000). The Swedish experience of the early 1990s is less well known, but it is very interesting in the EC context, because of the many similarities between Sweden and the rich EC member states (Britain, France, Germany) that block the farm reform process in the EC: Sweden has a farm share of less than 2 percent of GDP and employment, an acreage per head equal to the EC average, CSEs and PSEs 50 to 150 percent higher (during the 1980s, before its accession to the EC) than the corresponding figures for the EC (and with a similar evolution during the 1980s), and so on. In sum, Sweden shows that the so-called specificities of the EC farm sector do not resist scrutiny (for a careful analysis of this point and a detailed presentation of Swedish reform, see Molander 1994).

The Swedish farm policy reform, which was launched in 1989, was founded on four basic principles: (1) the dismantlement of domestic regulations (price guidance and milk quotas similar to those of the CAP), (2) the elimination of export subsidies, (3) the use of variable-import levies as the main instrument for protecting Swedish farmers (pending the tariffication process under negotiation in the Uruguay Round), and (4) budget-financed support to take care of the environmental, social, and regional aspects of farm production.

The proposed policy devoted special care to transitional measures: (1) The dismantlement was set at the beginning of the process (July 1991). (2) A transitional floor price on grain (set so that the average marginal farmer should be neutral between continued production and leaving the sector) was guaranteed for three years. (3) The price decrease was compensated for by stepwise-reduced, de-coupled income support providing 75, 50, and 25 percent of the income reduction for the average grain producer. (4) This support was to follow the producer, *not* the land. (5) A pension system was offered to milk producers. (6) A safety net was provided for farmers who had entered the sector after 1980, to avoid situations of large debts as a direct result of the U-turn of farm policy.

In June 1990, these proposals were adopted by the Swedish Parliament, with certain modifications (the transition period was prolonged to five years, a program of subsidies for new farmers was introduced, export subsidies for beef were granted through fiscal 1992–93, etc.), which were not too damaging for reform (except perhaps the fact that income support should follow the land, not the producer). Even watered down, the Swedish reform shows striking differences with the 1992 CAP Reform (and the 1999 Berlin Council; see below). It imposes large decreases of guaranteed prices (40 percent for grain in four years, 50 percent for ovine meat in 2 years, etc.) in a few years; it covers all the major products (it includes milk); and it relies on transitory income support, with the strongest possible de-coupling between farming activity and income and wealth stability.

The Swedish farm reform did not last long. In late 1990, Sweden announced its intention to join the EC; in spring 1993, the Swedish Parliament decided to reintroduce export subsidies to begin complying with the *acquis communautaire*. In 1995, the EC CAP was fully introduced in Sweden without any transitional period. The results of such a short-lived reform are, of course, limited (see the New Zealand case for full results). However, the reform (the elimination of export subsidies during a few years probably being the single most important measure) reached a few results: (1) The elimination of milk quotas (implemented since 1989) brought no market disturbances. (2) In meat, the adjustment was faster than expected. (3) The number of farms has decreased in accordance with the historical trend (3 percent). (4) Investment and pesticide use have significantly decreased. (5) Consumer prices for food products have risen more slowly. In sum, consumers and environment have begun to get the expected benefits, without serious adjustment costs for farmers.

Box 4.5   The modest decisions of the 1999 Berlin Council

The Berlin Council aimed to prolong the 1992 Reform for 2000–08 by introducing additional cuts in intervention prices, additional (factor-based) compensatory subsidies for cereals and beef, and by introducing the first measures for dairy products (but not before 2005 for this last group of products). One should note that, whereas prices and values before 2000 (reported in table 4.3) are observed in current prices, expected prices and values after 2000 are "constant," because they are expressed in 2000 terms. Table 4.3 describes the major measures, which require three additional remarks. First, concerning sectoral subsidies, the risk of overcompensation is reduced. Additional EC compensatory subsidies (also defined on a ton, head, or hectare basis) compensate only partly (from 50 percent in cereals up to 80 percent in milk) for the revenues that could be lost if market and intervention prices follow the same course (an important condition not fulfilled during the 1990s).

Second, the CAP budget has been stabilized in absolute monetary amounts. This stabilization, which was presented by the Council communiqué as the greatest achievement of the Berlin Council, deserves two caveats. First it rather means, in fact, an average *increase* of roughly 2 percent in the subsidy rate per farmer, because the number of European farmers declines at an average rate of 2 percent per year (an evolution that will continue during the coming decade because almost 40 percent of EC farm workers are aged 55 or more). The second caveat is that it ignores member-state farm budgets, and their possible drift; in 1999, member-states budgeted €12 billion for farmers (€2.5 billion for France, €2 billion for Germany and Italy, €1.4 billion for Finland, and €1.2 billion for Britain) (WTO, *Trade Policy Review: The European Union*, 2000).

Third, all the regulations implementing the Berlin measures include options for "review," which may signal possible reversibility in member-state commitments. They also specify that exports and imports of farm products require licenses, and they explicitly allow for export subsidies.

In addition to these "sectoral" subsidies allocated to specific farm products, the Berlin Council has adopted a "horizontal regulation," by which member-states (and only they) can "modulate" direct subsidies. These subsidies can be reduced by 20 percent at most, on the basis of size-related criteria, such as labor intensity of farms, farm "wealth," global amount of aid received by farms, or "agri-environmental" objectives. But they are reallocated to "rural development," to which the Berlin Council has given a higher degree of visibility—but without clarifying it. Rural development remains a vague concept, which goes from preretirement schemes to aid to young farmers to animal welfare to reforestation—hence, it can be used to increase farm output and productivity, as well as to lower them.

The Berlin Council has introduced many regulatory simplifications in the CAP. There is now only one type of regulated prices (the intervention price which covers wider ranges of products), certain existing regulations have been simplified (e.g., 1 wine regulation has replaced the 23 existing regulations), and so on.[1] All these simplifications have been adopted to facilitate the EC position during the new WTO negotiations. But such simplifications are counterbalanced by two forces: (1) there are a high number of criteria based on production processes or uses to determine subsidies (farm size, irrigation level, stocking density, cattle extensification, product quality level, environmental conditions, and so on); and (2) to the extent that they are expressed in specific terms (euros per unit) and not in ad valorem terms, compensatory subsidies can be a source of important distortions (as seems to be the case between wheat and coarse grains).

---

[1] This effort of simplification is far from complete: many product-specific measures remain, from minimum prices for potatoes for producing starch, to additional compensatory payments for durum wheat, to different subsidies for various types of animals.

prices lower (OECD 2000c). In this case, the EC might try to alleviate its obligations by granting "generous" food aid or export credits at "preferential" rates of interest—all practices that have been lavishly used in the past for manufacturing goods, and that the history of the OECD Consensus on export credits for industrial goods shows as very difficult to discipline.

This perspective is disappointing, all the more because the Berlin Council was preceded by a debate that was much more lively than usual. The Commission proposals, presented in March 1998 in a document called Agenda 2000, were much more promising than the Berlin decisions. Agenda 2000 included an additional immediate 20 percent cut of the guaranteed price of cereals, a 30 percent price cut for beef over three years, and a 15 percent cut for guaranteed dairy prices over four years—but Agenda 2000 also left untouched two key farm products, sugar and olive oil. Discussions addressed the (formerly taboo) question of whether the Community should reform its farm policy before the coming round or wait for the end, in 2003, of the "peace clause" with the United States.

More important, the whole debate revealed increasingly stronger forces in favor of further reforms for *domestic* reasons—the need to reallocate scarce funds to other purposes than agriculture, the necessity of preparing for the accession of Central European countries (some of them having substantial capacities in agriculture in the long run), and last but not least consumers' interests in getting cheaper products (e.g., see European Commission 1997b). In particular, the debate began to clarify the merits of "renationalizing" EC farm subsidies (cofinancing, in EC parlance) in comparison with "modulating" (reducing) them.

A renationalization raises two major problems. First, it would be consistent with EC state-aid rules (see chapter 5) only if the subsidies would not distort intra-EC trade, or if EC member-states would adopt pure income-support schemes. (Farm policy then would come close to social transfers, for which member-states have exclusive competence; see chapter 5.) None of these conditions has been met—and if the second condition were fulfilled, most pending WTO issues would also be solved. Second and more important, it is unlikely that renationalizing EC farm subsidies would lead to the elimination of the CAP. More likely, Germany would save its budgetary transfers to the rest of the EC but it would continue to support its own farmers, whereas the current beneficiaries of intra-EC farm transfers would compensate for vanishing German funds by increasing their own funds. The final outcome would be "15 CAPs" (except for one or two EC member-states, such as Sweden, willing to reestablish their previously more open farm policy), leading to the collapse of the EC common markets in farm products (already de facto anaesthetized by the current CAP) and to more difficulties in opening EC member-state farm markets. Moreover, because renationalization is mostly driven by budgetary concerns, it raises insurmountable problems for the EC enlargement to major Central European countries, such as

Poland and Romania—which are budgetarily poor, but have potential comparative advantages in agriculture (see chapter 6).

The alternative formula—modulating farm subsidies—should ideally combine a degressivity over time of the global amount of EC *subsidies* and a nationalization of the subsidy-cutting formula. There should be an EC common decision to reduce farm subsidies by a certain percentage over a certain period, but each member-state should be left free to use its preferred formula for reaching the common target. Such freedom is required for a simple political reason. If France prefers a formula based on degressivity by farm size, and Britain an across-the-board formula, it is because France has a much larger proportion of small farmers—who could provide the necessary political support for such an approach—than Britain. The combination of an EC-wide freeze on farm aid (a soft version of modulation) and a national subsidy-cutting formula has been the only really positive outcome of the Berlin Council—although EC member-states are implementing it in homeopathic doses, and in a reversible way (as shown by the fact that Germany has not yet abandoned its idea of renationalizing farm aid and cofinancing, as recently illustrated by the Schröder Document; see chapter 7). This timid move may reflect a shift of certain member-states traditionally favoring farm protection toward structural change, hence ongoing deep changes in the EC economies, as is discussed in the section on ongoing changes in the EC economies, below.

Manufacturing: Old Peaks of Protection, New Instruments

On the topic of manufacturing, the texts released for Seattle by the three European institutions are very close, and deal with three issues. First, the EC is looking for "substantial tariff reductions and the elimination of tariff peaks" by introducing a tariff-band approach (based on three bands of low, medium, and high tariffs) and the determination of tariffs at the 6-digit level of the tariff classification; it also proposes an upfront commitment from all industrial countries to implement, no later than the end of the round, duty-free access for essentially all products from less developed countries. However, the EC's zeal for a tariff elimination is tempered by the fact that such changes could be smaller or slower for "sensitive" products, hence reducing the "value" of EC tariff preferences (in particular, for its GSP and Lomé trading partners; see chapter 6).

Second, the Seattle texts are much more modest on "contingent" protection (antidumping, antisubsidy, and safeguards)—the Commission text being the only one opening clearly the prospect of further negotiations on antidumping, because the EC "will have both offensive and defensive interests," a recognition of the worries raised by the worldwide spread of this instrument of protection during recent years. The three texts express support for the WTO dispute settlement mechanism, although the Parliament text mentions "a controversy between trade interests and nontrade concerns." Last, trade facilitation issues (licensing, customs valuation, etc.) are examined at length in the Commission text, with an effort to take into account the converging interests of developing countries and small firms in industrial countries.

This approach—much more positive than in agriculture—reflects the fact that, in sharp contrast to agriculture, there is no doubt about the EC's ability to fulfill its Uruguay Round commitments on *tariff* cuts in the manufacturing sector. This observation leaves open two questions. To what extent has the EC fulfilled its WTO commitments to eliminate NTBs, in particular those contributing to the substantial pockets of protection still existing in EC manufacturing (textiles and clothing, steel, food products, and cars; see chapters 2 and 3)? And what are the consequences of the EC's addiction to antidumping?

Elimination of NTBs: Still Incomplete

Table 2.1 suggests a noticeable decline of EC NTBs between 1990 and 1999. On 31 December 1999, the EC and member-state VERs on Japanese cars were eliminated—fulfilling the EC commitment under the Uruguay Safeguard Agreement. As a result, the EC NTBs officially remaining in force as of January 2000 were the surveillance measures on steel products from Eastern Europe and Asia, and, of course, the VERs on textiles and clothing (the elimination of quotas after 1995 under the Uruguay Agreement on Textiles and Clothing is largely a window-dressing operation; see appendix A, cases 13 and 14).

There are three reasons to believe that this short list may overstate the decline of the EC NTBs—even those defined as "core-NTBs," that is, quantitative restrictions and price constraints. First, the above list relies on EC notifications to the WTO. However, EC trading partners have mentioned additional EC NTBs in the same context. For instance, in 1995, Japan notified import monitoring or licenses on VCRs, forklift trucks, ball bearings, and cotton fabrics, among others (*WTO Trade Policy Report on Japan*, 1995, 81–82). One could argue that this cross-notification may exaggerate EC trade barriers; if the EC partners were right, they should have submitted such cases to the WTO dispute settlement procedure (they would have won them). However, the EC partners may hesitate to do so because their own firms may prefer to keep such NTBs (to keep rents, or escape higher barriers, e.g., antidumping measures; see below). Hence, the question of the exhaustiveness of the EC list of notifications should, at least, remain open.

Second, it is difficult to monitor all the EC safeguard measures effectively. Between 1997 and 1999, the EC removed six safeguard measures: on coal imported in Germany and Spain (but a few months later, a high antidumping specific duty was imposed on coke imports from China); on potatoes delivered to the Spanish Canary Islands; on Japanese cars imported in the whole EC (see appendix A, case 12); on minimum prices on dried grapes and preserved cherries in the whole of EC (WTO, *Trade Policy Review: The European Union*, 2000). However, the EC has a complex set of "import surveillance" schemes, with substantial "chilling" effects, as best illustrated by footwear (Winters 1993b, 1994; Single Market Review 1997c). Moreover, discrete and opaque safeguard measures can be taken in the context of the many EC preferential agreements (e.g., the Europe Agreements with the Central European countries or the Customs Union Treaty with Turkey; see chapter 6), all the more because these agreements provide a wider definition of what can trigger a safeguard than the Uruguay Safeguard Agreement—opening the door more widely to tailor-made bilateral protection, especially because the EC benefits from a strong negotiating position in a bilateral context.

Third, certain international agreements (which are probably inconsistent with WTO rules, but so far not challenged under the WTO dispute settlement procedure) to which the EC is a signatory can limit competition and be substitutes for NTBs. For instance, this may be the case with the 1994 Memorandum of Understanding on aluminum launching joint world "efforts" to cut aluminum output; or with the OECD agreement on shipbuilding and ship repairing—which imposes "fair" competition in the sector by permitting heavy sanctions against noncomplying shipbuilders and related shipping companies, and which could easily be used in a noncompetitive, protectionist way (see below).

Taking into account noncore NTBs would substantially lengthen the list. Some noncore NTBs are covered by WTO disciplines, such as norms or standards (see below) and subsidies (see chapter 5). Indeed, the late 1990s offered several examples of subsidies being substituted for declining border core NTBs. For instance, the French government announced subsidies for the car sector under a massive layoff scheme aiming to substitute young for old workers (a ban on these subsidies by the EC Commission is likely, although its enforcement will almost certainly take a long time). The British government has granted preference to domestic coal (relative to gas) for producing electricity. And the privatization process in the eastern states of Germany has been a source of important subsidies and other NTBs in many industrial sectors (from oil refineries to high-technology production).

Other NTBs are ambiguously covered by WTO disciplines and commitments. "Preferential" rules of origin (justifiable under GATT Article XXIV) may constitute an important source of such additional tailor-made protection (Krueger 1999; Panagariya 1999a), because they are much more stringent than nonpreferential rules of origin, which generally rely on the "change-of-heading" approach. The EC is the nexus of a complex regime of several initially different sets of preferential rules of origin covering the

European Economic Area; Switzerland; the Central European countries; the Mediterranean countries; the African, Caribbean, and Pacific (ACP) countries; and most of the GSP countries.

The efforts to establish a "pan-European" regime of rules of origin covering all these countries (Driessen and Graafsma 1999) are far from having eliminated all the existing distortions, and they have created new ones, as suggested by the following indicative list. (1) Many of the above EC trading partners are small economies, suggesting that inputs imported from outside countries may often constitute a large part of domestic value added, enabling producers in partner countries with the lowest tariffs on inputs to more easily undercut producers in other partner countries. (2) Excluding certain export sectors (clothing) that are key for EC partners from the scope of pan-European rules is equivalent to increasing protection in these sectors. (3) New provisions (e.g., the "no-drawback" clause) in pan-European rules reinforce the central role of the EC economy, to the detriment of the partner economies. (4) In cases of antidumping, the EC may develop specific rules of origin for certain products (such as photocopiers).[8]

The Irresistible Rise of Antidumping Actions

As of January 2000, there were 10 regulations or decisions establishing the EC's specific trade policy instruments. Five deal with antidumping procedures in goods and maritime transport, two with antisubsidy procedures, one with "trade barriers" (often nicknamed EC Section 301), one with the injurious pricing of ships (partly echoing the OECD Agreement), and one with the common rules on imports (see appendix B).

There are several reasons to focus on antidumping in goods. Few cases have been subject to the other regulations, with the limited exceptions of the antisubsidy instrument and the Trade Barriers Regulation.[9] By contrast, the declining role of the EC NTBs has clearly been accompanied by

---

8. So far, the WTO negotiations on the harmonization of nonpreferential rules of origin have not been very productive: After four years of negotiations, solutions have been found for only one-third of the tariff chapters, with pending severe problems in many sectors with high levels of overall protection, e.g., agribusiness, steel products, textiles and clothing, and electronics (Nell 1999).

9. The application of the EC regulation on ship pricing has been suspended, pending ratification by the United States of the OECD Agreement. In April 2000, the EC signed with South Korea (the world's largest shipmaker) "Agreed Minutes Relating to the World Shipbuilding Market" in order to promote "fair" competition and "to work together to stabilize the market, and thereby help raise the level of ship prices to ones that are commercially sustainable," a statement that could reflect an effort to generate large-scale price collusion, http://europa.eu.int/comm/trade/whats_new/korea.htm, 11 April 2000. However, this agreement may not be enough for the EC, which is threatening to go to a WTO panel on Korean subsidies to the shipbuilding industry, despite the fact that the EC has massively subsidized its own shipbuilding industry.

Table 4.4 The pro-collusion impact of EC antidumping measures, 1980–89

EC market share held by complaining and defending firms (level of concentration)	Breakdown of all cases (in percent of all cases)	Percent of cases with an estimated level of injury[a]			
		Higher than 5 percent		Higher than 10 percent	
		Conservative[b]	Plausible[c]	Conservative[b]	Plausible[c]
Less than 100 percent (all cases)	100.0	55.7	31.1	41.0	16.4
Less than 95 percent	68.9	36.1	21.3	26.2	13.1
Less than 90 percent	55.7	29.5	14.8	19.7	8.2
Less than 85 percent	44.3	19.7	11.5	16.4	4.9

EC = European Community.

a. Measured as revenue losses by domestic firms (percent of total revenue).
b. Estimates based on a conservative set of elasticities.
c. Estimates based on a more plausible set of elasticities.

Source: Messerlin (1996a).

the irresistible rise of EC antidumping actions, which allow for quantity and price measures (under GATT Article VI derogatory provisions) so that they can be used as allegedly "GATT-consistent" substitutes for traditional core NTBs. In 1999, the EC initiated 67 new cases—an absolute record in EC antidumping activity for the past 20 years (see appendix B). Eleven industrial products (out of the 14 goods examined in chapter 3) are protected by antidumping measures in the form of specific tariffs, price, or quantity undertakings; appendix B provides more systematic evidence of the use of antidumping measures to both "consolidate" existing VERs and introduce new VERs.

This observation underlines the strongly anticompetitive and pro-collusion bias of antidumping procedures. In many cases, antidumping measures have not only protected EC firms, but they have also encouraged collusive behavior or abuse of market power between EC *and* foreign firms. Table 4.4 suggests that the risks of collusion following antidumping measures are very high because a vast majority of antidumping cases occur in markets held by a few firms. For instance, complainants and defendants that have a joint market share less than 95 percent of EC consumption represent only 68.9 percent of all the EC antidumping cases investigated between 1980 and 1989; lowering the market share threshold to 85 percent would decrease this number to 44.3 percent of all the cases (Messerlin 1996a).

Table 4.4 presents an even more worrisome picture when the level of injury for EC firms due to alleged foreign dumping is taken into account. For instance, complaining EC firms have lost more than 5 percent of their revenues in about 55.7 percent of all cases examined (probably in not more than 31.1 percent if one adopts a less conservative and more plausible set of elasticities for estimating revenue losses). But if one looks at the cases where

EC complainants and foreign defendants hold less than 85 percent of the EC market, EC firms have lost more than 5 percent of their revenues in only 19.7 percent of the cases in question (and more probably in only 11.5 percent of the cases, under the more plausible set of elasticities). In other words, revenue losses are mostly concentrated in cases where EC complainants and foreign defendants hold more than 85 percent of the EC market—that is, in cases where such limited revenue losses occurring in such concentrated markets may just mirror a healthy shift from large monopolistic rents to a more competitive situation, and where antidumping measures are likely to generate, maintain, or amplify anticompetitive practices.

Technical Regulations: Toward a "New" Protectionism?

The texts released for the Seattle WTO Ministerial by the European institutions deal with several topics related to technical regulations: technical barriers to trade (TBTs) per se, and the much wider set of trade, environment, and health (consumer protection) issues. Their general tone and suggestions are similar: (1) On TBTs, the texts underline the need for regulatory cooperation and for strengthening the promotion of international standards, including enforcement and market surveillance. (2) On trade, environment, and health, the texts make frequent reference to "sustainable development," but without defining it, mention "positive synergies" between trade liberalization and environmental protection, and the desire for greater legal clarity on the relations between WTO rules and Multilateral Environmental Agreements, on the question of processes and production methods (e.g., are eco-labeling schemes WTO-compatible?), and on the definition and scope of the "precautionary principle," particularly in the context of trade and food safety.

Technical regulations (TRs), as noted above, consist of mandatory "norms" and voluntary "standards," which, in the WTO framework, are dealt with by the Agreements on Technical Barriers to Trade and on Sanitary and Phytosanitary (SPS) Measures.[10] TRs are introduced for a wide range of reasons, and they can be applicable to products, producers (licensing requirements), or consumers (bans on certain products). The issues they raise can be split into two main categories: designing TRs and enforcing them. *Designing* TRs involves a wide range of actions; if voluntary standards can rely only on private decisions (although they may sometimes need some form of public support), mandatory norms require public intervention. *Enforcing* TRs include (1) conformity-assessment pro-

---

10. The TBT focuses on the nondiscrimination principles in the TR domain, whereas the SPS Agreement insists on the use of scientific methods and risk assessment in the process of domestic regulation making.

cedures (assessing the product's conformity with the relevant TRs of products or production processes requires testing, certifying, marking, etc.), which occur before goods go on sale, and (2) market surveillance procedures once goods are on sale. Conformity-assessment procedures can be ensured by public agencies or private firms (including the producers or distributors of the good in question), whereas market surveillance is generally done by public authorities (general police or specific agencies).

Because they have grown rapidly and steadily since the 1970s, and because they can raise the costs of nondomestic producers more than domestic firms, TRs have been increasingly perceived as a threat to trade (the costs of TBTs have been estimated to be 2 to 10 percent (with peaks of 30 percent) of firms' production costs [OECD 2000f]). This perception has been particularly strong within the EC about intra-EC trade—making internal EC TR policy the core of the Single Market Program in goods. In fact, the past 40 years of EC integration have witnessed more attention to product standards than to labor standards—an essential point for assessing the EC role in the debate on trade and labor standards in the WTO (see chapter 5).

The dynamics of EC trade policy in TR matters raise three major questions: what has been the external impact (on the level of EC protection on foreign goods) of the EC efforts undertaken to solve internal TR problems (intra-EC elimination of TR-related trade barriers) during recent decades? Is the current EC approach favoring the use of mutual-recognition agreements (MRAs) in the WTO likely to last long? Because food safety concerns play an increasingly critical role in the EC, what could be their future impact on EC policy in the WTO?

From the Old to the New Approach: Such a Success?

Since its origin, the EC has been obsessed with the protectionist risks that TRs could represent for the European Common Market, and the Treaty of Rome contains powerful (both direct and indirect) provisions covering TR matters (see box 4.6). But it has been under the Single Market Program that most efforts have been made. As a result, as of May 2000, roughly one-third of the 1,509 directives constituting the whole EC *acquis communautaire* dealt exclusively with TR issues, whereas a substantial part of the directives on agriculture and environment (representing almost 40 percent of the whole *acquis*) dealt also with TR-related provisions.[11]

---

11. There is an interesting parallel to be made on these issues between the EC Single Market Program and the Swiss 1995 Act on Internal Market (with its safeguard clause of "public health"; Guillod 2000) and the 1994 Canadian Agreement on Internal Trade between Canada and its Provinces (Weiler 2000).

Box 4.6   The *Cassis de Dijon* ruling and EC TR policy

Technical regulation (TR) issues in the EC are ruled by four provisions of the Treaty of Rome: (1) Article 28 (ex 30) prohibits quantitative restrictions on imports between member-states and "all measures having equivalent effect." (2) Article 30 (ex 36) is a safeguard allowing for exceptions to Article 28 (ex 30) when "justified on grounds of public morality, policy or security." (3) Article 94 (ex 100) allows the Council to issue directives on TRs if required by the functioning of the Single Market. (4) Article 95:5 (ex 100a) allows member-states to introduce national norms after the adoption of EC measures, conditional on the existence of "new scientific" evidence and on the Commission's approval (the Commission's disapproval can be challenged in the Court of Justice, and overturned, as in the 1994 case of a German ban on PCPs).

The balance between all these articles depends crucially on the definition of "measures having equivalent effect." In its 1979 *Cassis de Dijon* landmark ruling (and its forerunner, the 1974 *Dassonville* ruling), the Court of Justice stated that Germany could prohibit imports of a French beverage (*Cassis de Dijon*) only if it could invoke "mandatory requirements" such as public health, protection of the environment, and fairness of commercial transactions. In other words, the Court introduced a very wide definition of Article 28 (ex 30), so that member-state TRs can be perceived to be almost systematically equivalent to trade restrictions—and hence legitimizing EC TR policy. Within a year, the Commission provided its own interpretation of this ruling (never contested since then): a product lawfully "produced" or "marketed" in one member-state shall be admitted to other member-states for sale, except in cases of mandatory requirements.

Not only did the *Cassis de Dijon* ruling legitimize the creation of an EC TR policy, but it also changed the EC approach to designing TRs by introducing the concept of "mutual recognition." Before the ruling, the so-called Old Approach prevailed: it relied on "harmonization," that is, on substituting newly defined EC TRs for existing member-state TRs—a long and difficult process. Since the *Cassis de Dijon* ruling, a New Approach has been developed, based on two components to be mixed in variable proportions on a case-by-case basis: core common rules are to be harmonized and adopted by all member-states, and the rest of the rules are left to member-state freedom of choice and are subject to mutual recognition by member-states. In fact, the Old Approach is still alive for updating previous Old Approach directives (mostly in the automobile, food, and cosmetics sectors, as is illustrated by the recent updating of the 1973 Chocolate Directive on the relative content of cocoa and other inputs for producing chocolate), whereas the New Approach was preceded by attempts to define limited harmonization (minimal, optional, partial, piecemeal, etc.) or by forerunners (e.g., the 1973 Low Voltage Directive).

The *Cassis de Dijon* ruling has a last feature that is particularly important for EC trade policy. The ruling makes no distinction between goods "produced" and "marketed" in a member-state. This silence has been interpreted as meaning that non-EC goods allowed for sale in a member-state and goods produced in that state should be treated similarly in the rest of the EC, that is, EC mutual recognition is *not* limited to products *made* in the EC. Surprisingly, this silence has never been challenged in the Court of Justice itself (only in member-state courts, e.g., the Baden-Württemberg Oberlandesgericht in 1988, which, so far, have always confirmed the nondiscrimination interpretation).

Until the late 1990s, EC TR policy focused almost entirely on the *design* of TRs, largely neglecting the critical importance of *enforcement* mechanisms. Since the mid-1990s, the preparatory work required for the accession of Central European countries to the EC has revealed the importance of such mechanisms—and the many deficiencies in the exact role and operational conditions of European agencies running conformity assessment procedures (Messerlin 1998c).

Before examining its potential impact on trade, the TR policy deserves a clarification. The New Approach is not the often-celebrated panacea, for three reasons. First, contrary to what is frequently believed, it does not consist only of rapidly negotiated, concise, wide-ranging EC directives. Such directives provide only terms of reference (the "essential requirements," in EC parlance) for the complex task of defining *in detail* the EC core standards. This work is generally done by the European Standardization Bodies (ESBs, such as CENELEC, CEN, or ETSI), which are mandated by the Commission, and often under the close monitoring of dominant EC firms. This process can be a source of misunderstanding and frustration, for instance, because the essential requirements of the directive are too vague (e.g., the Machine Safety and Construction Products directives, for which the Commission was obliged to draft interpretative documents of its own essential requirements). It is also a time-consuming process; in 1998, only 914 (of a total 2,905 mandates granted to the ESBs) were ratified, leaving 1,081 pending approvals and 910 still in preparation. Moreover, these delays tend to be concentrated in new technology sectors and complex products, that is, precisely in activities where *not* delivering TRs in time is particularly costly. Meanwhile, national conformity marks, which tend to fragment EC markets, are burgeoning (European Commission 1999c), as is best illustrated by the fact that, between 1995 and 1999, the EC itself notified 167 TRs to the WTO, whereas the EC member-states notified 977 TRs on their own.

Second, the directives have to be "transposed" (that is, incorporated in EC parlance) into member-state laws—another time-consuming process and source of misinterpretations. The many shortcomings in the adequate application of the mutual-recognition principle by EC member-states often make it still necessary to include mutual-recognition clauses in national legislation, as emphasized by the 1998 *Foie Gras* ruling of the Court.

Third, there are infringements on transposed directives. There were 228 cases during the period 1996–98, often on products well known for their high level of protection (food, spirits and beer, cars, etc.). Only 105 of these cases were resolved through procedures lasting on average 15 months (European Commission 1999f).

There are no strong indications that all these difficulties would vanish in the near future—despite relatively stringent obligations about information and notification imposed on EC member-states by Directive 98/34. In 1998–99, EC member-states with a high rate of creating national technical regulations (Austria, Germany, and the Netherlands) showed little sign of decreasing activity, whereas two other member-states (Belgium and Denmark) were increasingly active (European Commission 2000a). At this stage, it may be useful to mention that lack of progress in the TR domain may be a key source of the little progress observed in the Single Market for goods (see the controversy between economists, as is illustrated by the discussion of Allen, Gasiorek, and Smith 1998).

Why so many difficulties? The success of a New Approach directive depends on its balance between harmonization and mutual recognition, that is, between ex ante trust and ex post regulatory costs (designing and enforcing common TRs) (Messerlin 1998b). Harmonization reflects the absence of ex ante trust between trading partners, and imposes ex post regulatory costs; mutual recognition reflects the existence of ex ante trust, and imposes no ex post regulatory costs, in addition to those already existing. The *Cassis de Dijon* ruling can be interpreted as a "mandatory" increase of the level of trust between member-states—ideally aiming to establish situations as close as possible to "unconditional" mutual recognition (meaning the complete absence of the harmonization component). In reality, the New Approach directives have been (and still are) based on mutual recognition that is conditional on a harmonization component large enough to impose substantial ex post regulatory costs.

This analysis suggests that the New Approach directives may represent an unstable equilibrium. Member-states may be tempted to go to more harmonization as soon as new problems emerge, or alternatively they may be attracted by unconditional recognition with countries that they really trust and that may happen to be non-EC member-states. This can have important consequences for EC trade and trade policy. In the first instance, the New Approach would be creeping toward the Old Approach, with key consequences for extra-EC trade (see below). In the second case, it might distort extra- and intra-EC trade in a very subtle way.[12]

Internal TR Policy and Its Impact on Protection

Any EC TR Directive could have two effects on EC trade. First, it can be a source of trade diversion, to the extent that it is a successful instrument of *intra-EC* trade liberalization. In this respect, the definition of "measures having equivalent effect" is key. Many rulings of the Court have provided (and still do) such a wide definition that they have not only led to the prohibition of clearly protectionist-minded TRs (the obligation to produce certificates, to make a declaration of origin, etc.), but they have also allowed the banning of measures (such as private selling arrangements) having no protectionist intent (but limiting complainants' commercial freedom, even without involving products from other member-states).

The 1993 *Keck and Mithouard* ruling of the Court limited some of these excesses (Eeckhout 2000). Other counterreactions to the wide definition of "measures having equivalent effect" have emerged. In particular, the wider the definition of such measures is, the higher the demand for Arti-

---

12. Complications may be numerous because, if an EC member-state does not trust another member-state, it may not trust trading partners in their totality (e.g., it may trust certain US states and not others).

cle 30 (ex 36) and for Article 95:5 (ex 100a) by member-states can be, that is, the stronger member-state efforts to trigger the "precautionary principle" can be (see below). Despite these rebalancing forces, the EC case law may have amplified trade diversion related to intra-EC liberalization.

Second, any EC TR directive can reduce *extra-EC* trade to the extent that, in addition to some respectable economic purposes, it includes protectionist elements that create additional extra-EC trade barriers. In this respect, the Old Approach directives are likely to be more harmful than the New Approach directives. For a variety of reasons—ranging from minimizing adjustment costs in the largest (dominant) EC industry to sheer power struggles between member-state industries—New Approach directives tend to reflect the TRs existing in the dominant member-state industry of the product in question (and to be conceptually similar to "endogenous" tariffs in the context of a customs union; Olarreaga and Soloaga 1998). In sum, the risks of protectionist impact of EC TR policy in a given sector may be bigger in the case of a successful Old Approach. What follows provides some evidence on these hypotheses.

Table 4.5 (the two first columns) provides crude estimates of the sectoral value added covered by efforts of harmonization (the Old Approach) or by reliance on mutual recognition (the New Approach).[13] A large proportion of EC value added in manufacturing has been covered by the EC TR policy: 33 percent by the Old Approach and 42 percent by the New Approach directives, with each approach dominating different sectors. The third column provides an "index of failure" of EC efforts to eliminate TR-related trade barriers within the EC, as perceived by the EC business community.[14] As suggested by the above remarks on the complexity of the Old and New Approaches, EC TR policy leaves an impression of rather mixed results, with an average failure index (value-added-weighted) of roughly 1.7, that is, between index 1 (meaning measures implemented,

---

13. For simplicity, table 4.5 aggregates under "harmonization" all the sectors under the Old Approach (roughly 29 percent of EC value added) and a mix of harmonization and mutual recognition (4 percent). It aggregates under "mutual recognition" all the sectors under the New Approach (roughly 18 percent) and a mix of mutual-recognition procedures (Single Market Review 1998, vol. 1, appendix E). All these data are available only in the EC NACE classification, which matches poorly the ISIC classification—hence the absence of some ISIC sectors and the necessity to merge them in one last sector. The high level of aggregation and the poor correspondence between the various classifications used makes it impossible to look at the correlation between intra-industry trade and effective TR liberalization (Baldwin 2000) and at the possibility of TRs accompanied by higher import values (Neven and Röller 2000).

14. This failure index is based on extensive interviews with the staffs of EC firms (Single Market Review 1998). It ranges from 0 (no significant TR issue, so no solution needed) to 5 (serious TR-related problems exist, with no solution adopted). However, indices 4 and 5 have been observed in very rare instances, meaning that de facto the range of the failure index is between 0 and 3. This absence of indices 4 and 5 may reflect an underestimating bias of the interviews to the extent that it does not fit well the EC business surveys, which repeatedly rank high TRs among the most important intra-EC trade barriers.

Table 4.5 EC technical regulation directives and EC imports, by sector, 1995

ISIC classification	Manufacturing sector	Coverage of EC technical regulations[a]			Index of "failure"[b]	Rate of global protection (percent)	EC import structure, by ISIC sector						
		Harmonization	Mutual recognition	Total			Intra-EC imports	World	Extra-EC imports from				
									United States	Japan	CECs	Emerging[c]	ACPs
200	Mining	96		96	1.2	3.4	0.4	2.4	2.5	0.0	1.8	0.6	5.1
311–312	Agribusiness	100		100	2.0	30.4	5.8	3.8	2.1	0.1	6.6	3.5	8.4
313	Beverages and sugar	63	37	100	2.0	22.5	3.2	1.1	0.9	0.1	0.6	0.6	9.5
321	Textiles		59	59	0.9	23.1	3.6	4.2	1.2	0.9	10.3	8.2	3.9
322	Clothing		77	77	1.5	31.4	2.3	5.6	0.6	0.2	16.6	10.2	1.9
323	Leather goods			0		4.7	0.4	1.0	0.2	0.0	0.9	1.0	1.4
331	Wood and wood products		100	100	1.3	4.8	1.9	2.2	1.4	0.0	6.9	3.8	4.7
341	Paper and paper products	63		63	1.4	7.8	4.7	2.5	3.7	0.5	1.8	0.8	0.0
351–352	Chemicals	22	76	98	2.6	7.9	14.7	9.2	14.1	9.1	6.7	3.4	3.0
353	Petroleum refineries	100		100	1.0	4.3	1.5	1.6	0.7	0.0	2.5	0.2	0.3
354	Petroleum and coal products		100	100	2.9	9.0	0.8	8.5	0.0	0.1	0.6	0.0	34.8
355	Rubber and rubber products	54		54	2.4	7.8	3.7	2.1	2.3	2.7	2.4	3.3	0.1
361	Pottery, china, etc.		79	79	1.6	8.4	0.3	0.6	0.3	0.0	0.8	0.0	4.2
369	Nonmetallic products	11	55	66	2.0	4.8	1.9	1.0	0.7	0.9	3.8	0.7	0.0
371	Iron and steel		24	24	2.8	15.8	6.9	7.1	3.7	0.8	9.9	0.6	7.7
381	Metal products		43	43	0.8	6.5	3.1	2.2	1.7	1.3	5.2	2.9	0.1
382	Machinery		93	93	1.9	4.5	14.0	16.5	29.0	32.4	5.8	23.5	0.6
383	Electrical and electronic goods	18	82	100	1.8	8.0	10.0	13.5	18.2	25.5	8.1	25.1	0.5
384	Transport equipment	74	19	93	1.0	9.2	15.6	8.3	11.4	22.4	6.8	4.8	5.7
	Other manufacturing goods		62	62	2.1	5.9	5.3	6.7	5.5	3.1	2.0	6.7	8.0

(table continues next page)

109

Table 4.5   EC technical regulation directives and EC imports, by sector, 1995 (continued)

Sectors	Coverage of EC technical regulations[a]			Index of "failure"[b]	Rate of global protection (percent)	EC import structure, by ISIC sector						
	Harmon-ization	Mutual recog-nition	Total			Intra-EC imports	Extra-EC imports from					
							World	United States	Japan	CECs	Emerg-ing[c]	ACPs
All sectors[d]	33	42	75	1.7	9.5	100.0	100.0	100.0	100.0	100.0	100.0	100.0
TR-covered sectors with:												
An index of failure > 1.5			47	2.1	12.5	57.3	63.6	68.6	69.0	48.6	68.8	68.4
An index of failure > 2.0			28	2.3	15.5	32.3	30.0	22.8	13.2	21.7	13.9	62.5
Harmonization > 50 percent value-added	29			1.5	13.1	26.2	17.2	17.7	18.5	18.7	10.5	23.8
Harmonization > 50 percent value-added and failure index > 1.5	11			2.1	22.8	9.8	5.6	3.9	1.6	8.2	5.7	14.4
MRA > 50 percent value-added		33		1.9	8.2	43.5	56.0	59.1	61.1	47.3	66.1	54.9
MRA > 50 percent value-added and failure index > 1.5		28		2.0	7.8	39.5	51.4	57.1	60.6	34.4	57.4	47.8

ACPs = African, Caribbean, and Pacific countries.
CECs = Central European countries.
EC = European Community.
ISIC = International Standard Industrial Classification.
MRA = mutual recognition agreement
TRs = technical regulations

a. In percentage value-added.
b. For definition, see text.
c. Emerging-market economies; for definition, see text.
d. Value-added weighted averages for index of failure and rate of global protection; sum for the other columns.

Sources: Single Market Review (1997, appendix E); table 2.1; WTO, Trade Policy Review: The European Community, 1997, 139; Messerlin (1998).

but with some barriers remaining) and index 2 (meaning measures adopted, but with implementation or transitional problems still to be overcome). More important, the index of perceived failure is almost similar for the sectors of the New (1.8) and Old (1.6) Approaches—a perception that may announce the existence of permanent pressures within the EC for shifting from mutual recognition to harmonization.

Table 4.5 provides three interesting results. First, sectors with an index of failure higher than 2 (that is, with substantial or severe remaining problems of TR implementation or conception) represent a substantial amount of EC production and trade: 28 percent of value added, 32 percent of intra-EC trade, and 30 percent of EC imports from the world. In these sectors, trade diversion caused by the *EC* TR policy per se is likely to be small—but serious TR-related obstacles remain, *both* between EC member-states and between EC and non-EC countries. Intra-EC examples with ramifications at the world level have recently illustrated this first result. Finland (a producer of cadmium-free phosphate) asserts that cadmium in phosphate is damaging to health—opposing Italy and Spain, which import cheaper phosphates with a high cadmium content from Morocco. Canada is a large exporter of asbestos to the EC, whereas Greece, Portugal, and Spain are large producers, and the rest of the EC is raising questions about the effects of asbestos on human health. Other examples limited to the EC include PCPs (see box 4.6), phtalates, nisin (see below), and so on. In sum, after 30 years of intense efforts, member-states have kept a substantial number of national TRs—giving a strong signal of limited expectations about stricter international norms at the world level.

Second, sectors dominated by the harmonization approach (those with more than 50 percent of their value added under this approach) represent 29 percent of EC value added, 26 percent of intra-EC trade, but 17 percent of EC imports from the rest of world—and only 11 percent of EC imports from the emerging-market economies (Hong Kong, South Korea, Indonesia, Malaysia, Singapore, Taiwan, and Thailand). This difference in coverage is consistent with the potential protectionist impact of the EC harmonization of TRs. However, this impact may be magnified by (or partly due to) the relatively high rate of overall protection (13.1 percent) of these sectors. Sectors with the highest failure indices (higher than 1.5) show even stronger restrictions on trade flows, with a clear discriminatory impact on EC imports from the United States and Japan. This result may mirror strong member-state TRs (this factor itself could explain the failure of the EC policy) or the higher rate of overall protection in these sectors.

Third, sectors dominated by the mutual-recognition approach (those with more than 50 percent of their value added under the New Approach) represent a slightly higher proportion of EC value added than those under harmonization. More important, the antitrade bias observed for the Old Approach is not observed in their case. However, table 4.5 suggests another interesting result (although based on such small changes that extreme caution is required): Although sectors with failure indices higher than 1.5 have a lower rate of overall protection, their trade declines roughly in the same proportion for intra-EC and extra-EC trade, *but* more than proportionally for the Central European countries, the emerging-market economies, and the ACP states—all three evolutions possibly mirroring the discriminatory impact of TRs on exporters from countries in transition or developing economies.[15]

MRAs and EC Trade Policy

During the past decade, the EC has advocated the use of MRAs in many regional or bilateral forums: (1) with Central European countries until 1996 (since 1996, the EC has obliged the CECs to adopt the EC TR directives as an integral part of the *acquis communautaire*); (2) with the United States and Canada in the Transatlantic Business Dialogue (see chapter 6); and (3) with the Asian countries that are familiar with TR issues within the Asia Pacific Economic Cooperation (APEC) framework (e.g., see US National Center for APEC 1999). As a result, the MRAs between the EC and major industrial countries (Australia, Canada, Japan, New Zealand, Switzerland, Israel, and the United States) cover a wide range of 20 sectors (from medical devices to pressure vessels, electrical equipment, and lawnmowers), and the Commission has the mandate to negotiate MRAs with a few more economies (Hong Kong, South Korea, and Singapore) (WTO, *Trade Policy Review: The European Community*, 1997, 139).

The MRAs signed between the EC and its non-CEC partners deal only with *conformity-assessment* procedures. They allow foreign manufacturers to have their exports to the EC tested and assessed for *EC* TRs by recognized agencies (bodies in EC parlance) in their *own* country, and vice versa, for EC exporters (e.g., Article 4 of the 1997 US-EC MRA specifies that the MRA shall not be construed to entail mutual acceptance of standards or technical regulations).

The compatibility of these bilateral MRAs with the WTO regime is an open question. On the one hand, Article 2.7 of the TBT Agreement gives the opportunity to WTO members to conclude such regional MRAs. On the other hand, questions could be raised about the consistency of the existing regional MRAs with GATT Article I on the most-favored-nation principle—stating that any advantage granted to one trading partner must be granted to all other WTO members automatically and unconditionally. In fact, the MRAs signed by the EC do not fulfill the two condi-

---

15. Brenton, Sheehy, and Vancauteren (2000) confirm the differing impact of the EC TR policy on the various CECs. They show that the CECs that are most advanced in their negotiations of accession are those particularly concerned by TRs; e.g., the estimated comparative advantages of the Czech Republic and Poland are concentrated in sectors subject to the New Approach.

tions that would be consistent with GATT Article I: they are not applied in an origin-neutral manner, and they do not allow WTO members other than the signatories to join unconditionally (once the essential requirements accepted by the initial signatories have been fulfilled by the candidates).

Will EC support for the MRA approach in the WTO context continue to be as strong in the next decade as it was in the recent past? The question is not superfluous: *both* the Commission and Council texts released for the Seattle WTO Ministerial do not use even once the terms "mutual recognition" or "mutual-recognition agreement." The answer depends largely on two factors, intertwined to a large extent: the difficulties of implementing MRAs, and the problems raised by the accession of Central European countries.

Despite their limited objective of cost savings in conformity-assessment procedures, the MRAs signed by the EC with non-EC countries can be difficult to implement, as is best illustrated by the EC-US MRA on "veterinary equivalency" on red meat, dairy, fish, hides and skins. In the mid-1990s, following the adoption of food safety directives, the EC aimed to harmonize its import rules (still then under member-state competence) *but* without giving up the principle of "regional protection"—according to which, if an EC "region" (i.e., a member-state) is concerned by a disease, *only* exports originating from this region should be subject to the suitable food safety procedures by EC trading partners (hence, the rest of the EC member-states could continue to freely export their products).

Meanwhile, the United States wanted to refer to its own food safety *testing* rules for meat products (rather than to the EC rules), in accordance with the "equivalence principle" stated by Article 4 of the WTO SPS Agreement (the United States has quite different sanitary tests than the EC, but it is convinced that they achieve the same level of protection as the EC tests). Negotiations were completed in 1997, but the MRA was signed only in July 1999, after the addition of detailed technical provisions—with the EC raising doubts about the quality of US tests on chicken, and the United States about the EC's ability to control E. coli and salmonella. In late 2000, the very slow enforcement of the MRA was a renewed source of United States-EC disputes (see the last section below).

Concerning TR issues related to Central European countries, there are widespread fears in the EC that these countries will not be able to implement properly the existing EC TR regime that they must adopt in its entirety before joining the EC (the asymmetries that TRs can generate between the EC and the CECs are examined in chapter 6). But in the late 1990s, Commission investigations led to an even more surprising—and worrisome—result: conformity-assessment agencies in the *current* 15 EC member-states are working under very different standards of confidentiality, ethical constraints, quality, and so on.

Because conformity-assessment procedures can be handled by a wide range of means—from trust in private behavior (manufacturers have a strong interest in taking care of their reputation because it is an essential part of their capital) to reliance on ad hoc public agencies, there is a wide range of solutions to such problems. At one extreme, one could tighten the grip of EC and member-state authorities by imposing more harmonization on conformity-assessment procedures. At the other end of the spectrum, one could favor the emergence of a healthy competition regime between existing (and possibly new) conformity-assessment agencies. For instance, a conformity-assessment agency located in one member-state could decide to provide the "best" services (for testing, certifying, and marking, or for any subset of these activities) for a limited range of goods (those for which it believes it has the best expertise, i.e., "comparative advantages"). If the conformity-assessment agency in question has correctly evaluated its abilities, it should be able to attract manufacturers from the whole EC (not only those of its member-state of origin, as today) *and* even from outside the EC.[16]

As of today, there are conflicting signals on the choices made by the EC authorities (EC member-states and Commission) between these two alternatives. The benefits of competing conformity-assessment agencies are recognized, but there are also strong requests for more harmonization. The choice between these two options will be important for the future EC trade policy. Choosing more harmonization would have a negative impact in terms of implicit protection of EC products (see above). It would also make it more difficult for EC agencies to provide technical aid in these matters, and more generally in trade facilitation—that is, to fulfill an important task underlined in the Seattle texts.

Impacts of Food Safety Concerns on the Dynamics of EC Trade Policy

Issues related to food safety (or consumer health) are crucial for the EC MRA approach and for the level of EC protection. In Europe, they tend to be more important than issues related to the environment, in contrast to the US situation. In the past few years, food safety concerns have been used as a justification for import bans *within* the EC. In particular, the use of the "precautionary principle," which has attracted a lot of attention both in the WTO and in the intra-EC context, has reached a peak with the "mad cow" disease and the complete disruption of *intra-EC* beef trade (see box 4.7).[17] This principle has two major features. It requires action if

---

16. En passant, this alternative is much more consistent (in sharp contrast with the increasing grip option) with the popular view in the EC, according to which the New Approach and MRAs are a way to promote competition between EC regulators (and their capacity to deliver optimal rules).

17. The TEC mentions the precautionary principle only for environmental matters. According to the February 2000 Commission Communication devoted to this topic, measures based

Box 4.7   Mad cow disease and the Common Agricultural Policy

Mad cow disease (bovine spongiform encephalopathy, or BSE) was first identified in Britain in November 1986. It was identified in Ireland in 1989, in Portugal in 1990, in France in 1991, and since then, progressively, in the rest of the EC member-states (as shown below, time lags may have been due, at least partly, to inappropriate detection methods in Continental Europe). Ten years later, in March 1996, the British health minister evoked the possibility of a relationship between mad cow disease and a new variant of an already existing human illness, the Creutzfeldt-Jakob disease, creating the first severe mad cow crisis (as of April 2001, this possible relation had not yet been totally confirmed). In 2000, several cases of mad cow disease detected in France at the last minute or even too late (after the slaughterhouse) have triggered the second (even more severe) mad cow crisis in Continental Europe.

The major causes of BSE—animal proteins or certain pesticides (the first explanation being by far the most widely accepted)—awaken strong echoes in the CAP. Animal proteins have been developed in Europe as a substitute for soybeans and protein seeds made very expensive by the CAP. In order to decrease the production cost of animal proteins, EC firms have reduced the pressure and heat of the production process, a key factor in the emergence of BSE.

An examination of the sanitary measures adopted by the EC Continental member-states (European Commission 1998b; INRA 2000) shows that mad cow disease has been mostly used as a protectionist device against British beef. Available sanitary measures are of four types: prohibiting both (1) animal proteins and (2) BSE-sensitive beef parts (brains, eyes, tonsils, spinal cords, and offal) for bovine consumption, and banning both (3) beef and (4) BSE-sensitive beef parts for human consumption.

For each of these four types of sanitary measures, the scenario during the past decade has been very similar. Britain takes a sanitary measure roughly two years before Continental EC member-states; meanwhile, these latter countries rapidly ban the British imports. For instance, Britain banned animal proteins for bovine consumption in 1988; France did it in 1990, but only partially (hence paving the way for many errors and fraud in France during the 1990s) and after having banned imports of British proteins in 1989 (although the production techniques for these proteins are largely similar on the Continent). Time lags can be much longer. For instance, Britain banned almost all BSE-sensitive beef parts for human consumption in 1994, whereas in France such a decision required a series of measures from 1996 to 2000. As of today, Britain has taken a key measure that no other EC member-state has adopted: the elimination of almost one-third (4 million head) of its bovine cattle in order to eliminate vintage-related risks.

Lags in domestic safety measures have often been justified by the large difference in the number of declared BSE cases: 175,000 in Britain between 1987 and mid-2000; 499, 452, and 151 in Ireland, Portugal, and France, respectively; a handful of cases in the rest of Europe. However, there are increasingly serious doubts about the quality of detection procedures in Continental Europe, for a variety of reasons (veterinary services depending on the Agriculture Ministry, as in France; mere carelessness; etc.). First estimates of underreporting amount to 4,700 to 9,000 cows in France (Donnelly 2000).

The key point is that the most drastic trade measure taken by the EC Continental member-states has been largely inappropriate—but highly profitable from a political point of view. The trade ban on British "muscle-based" beef (i.e., the meat exclusively consisting of muscles) could not have a serious impact on health safety because

(box continues next page)

Box 4.7 *(continued)*

BSE risks are much lower in muscle-based meat than in the previously specified beef parts. The only impact of this ban has been the elimination of British competition from Continental depressed beef markets. In fact, by eliminating much better-monitored British beef from Continental markets, trade bans have increased health risks for Continental European consumers, whereas trade bans on British BSE-sensitive beef parts have been inefficient in protecting Continental European consumers from the risks of *domestic* products containing BSE-sensitive beef parts.

The strong resistance of Continental European farmers to the systematic and complete elimination of herds including one sick animal, to the systematic detection of the disease, and to stringent and clear safety measures for BSE-sensitive beef parts and on their uses, leaves one question: what will be the reaction of European consumers when they realize how much their health has been endangered by *domestic* farm lobbies using foreign products as a scapegoat for *domestically* produced *malbouffe* (bad food)? The strong reaction of French consumers to the 2000 beef crisis, and the failed attempt by French wine grape growers to use the precautionary principle to eliminate competing EC wines, may be the first signs of a serious erosion of trust between European consumers and farmers. If confirmed and stable, this trend might lead to dramatic changes in the EC approach to farm liberalization.

there is a risk, as long as there is no scientific *certainty* that the risk will *not* exist in the *long* run. And it is very rarely assessed in a context that economists would qualify as "general equilibrium" (in other words, not acting generates other risks): for instance, risks raised by genetically modified corn seed are generally assessed in the context of the corn sector *alone*— leaving aside possible positive effects of the new seed on deforestation (a more productive or resistant corn seed could allow less deforestation while yielding the same crop).

The fact that the precautionary principle has huge popular appeal makes it very attractive to both politicians and vested interests. It offers politicians opportunities to take ostentatious actions (in particular, in trade matters) apparently in the general interest, while it offers to vested interests the possibility of capturing politicians and public opinion under the cover of scientific evidence.

---

on the precautionary principle should be, inter alia, proportional to the chosen level of protection, nondiscriminatory, consistent with similar measures, based on the examination of the potential benefits and costs, subject to review, and capable of assigning responsibility for producing the scientific evidence. However, the Commission has difficulties in clearly defining certain terms (what exactly does "a proportionality test based on the chosen level of protection, and not on the potential risk" mean?; how can "similar" measures be defined?) and in assessing the operational content of others (what does a cost-benefit analysis mean in situations where, by definition, the probabilities of the risks are unknown?).

In the EC, the beef hormone case illustrates this conjunction of interests. In 1989, after eight years of intra-EC conflicts, about-faces, and delays, the EC started to prohibit the use of six hormones for cattle-growth-promoting purposes, and consequently to ban imports of beef bred with such hormones. The ban led to bilateral discussions between the EC and the major beef-exporting partners, then to a GATT dispute case, and finally to a WTO dispute settlement case lodged by Australia, Canada, New Zealand, and the United States. In early 1998, the WTO panel ruled that the EC ban violated the EC's WTO obligations. In February, the Appellate Body upheld this conclusion, on the basis that the EC ban was not based on a sufficiently specific risk assessment to show the existence of residues constituting a risk to consumers. In March, the EC announced its desire to carry out a complementary risk assessment. Fifteen months later, at the end of the period usually allowed for implementing WTO rulings, the EC had not complied with the WTO ruling and was still trying to get scientific support, without much success. In June 1999, Canada and the United States asked for WTO authorization to implement retaliatory tariffs on imports from the EC. In July 1999, the WTO authorized Canada and the United States to impose retaliatory tariffs on imports from the EC of US$116.8 million and C$11.3 million per year.

It has always been clear that the EC prohibition of beef hormones has little to do with food safety. Alleged relations to stilbene-related problems having occurred in the 1980s are remote, and very few experts, including those in Europe, believe that there are serious cancer risks for human health related to beef hormones (indeed, one of the two experts appointed by the EC for the WTO panel concluded that there was no danger). As a matter of fact, the EC authorizes three hormones in beef breeding for therapeutic use. Moreover, there are constant rumors reporting permanent, significant illegal use of beef hormones in the EC—such illegal use being a much more serious source of health concern for humans, because it is probably accompanied by the nonobservance of the correct procedures for using the hormones.

Clearly, the main reason for the 1989 ban was the EC's shrinking beef markets. (The EC consumption of beef meat has declined at an annual rate of 1.3 percent since the early 1980s.) Because hormones allow substantial increases in beef production, they could only create massive stocks in an EC unable to reform the CAP. The real role of the EC ban on beef hormones can thus be seen as equivalent to the mandatory set-aside in cereals: it restricts EC farm production by limiting inputs. The major difference is that it also eliminates foreign competition.

In addition to its general appeal for politicians—and vested interests—in the world, the precautionary principle has an especially strong appeal for European politicians. It is the least costly, most powerful open-ended escape clause to the wide definition of "measures having equivalent effects" of Article 28 (ex 30) of the TEC. In the 1981 *Eyssen* case, the Court of Justice de facto gave such a key role to the precautionary principle by not imposing on EC member-states (invoking the safeguard clause of Article 30 [ex 36]) strong requirements concerning the conclusive proofs to be shown about a possibly harmful product.[18] As a result, the precautionary principle has become the closest available instrument to a safeguard provision in *intra-EC* trade.

The unquestionable political appeal of the precautionary principle raises a key question: could such a principle become an important source of protectionist measures in the long run, or is it self-destructive if used from this perspective?

Any protectionist use of the precautionary principle will be subjected to two counterforces, as illustrated by box 4.7 on the intra-EC mad cow disease. First, the disease could spread in any countries implementing the import ban, turning the heat of the precautionary principle against domestic producers. Second, it may not take long for consumers to realize the profound inconsistency between banning imports of goods that could represent an unknown risk in the future, and not banning imports of products that represent a certain and immediate risk, such as tobacco (reported to kill 60,000 people annually in France), canned or prepared food products (subject to listeria or salmonella), or simply cars.

Such counterforces should make *nonmyopic* governments and vested interests (i.e., those that have some sense of their long-term interests) careful to contain the protectionist use of the precautionary principle in order to avoid devastating boomerang effects. However, the nonmyopic condition is not necessarily met by politicians in democratic regimes, who are subjected to repeated and close elections and hence are biased toward short-term actions and may be insensitive to long-term consequences. Its strength thus depends, to a large extent—quite unreassuringly—on the vested interests that may be more concerned about the long-term impact of their actions. (During the 1990s, the relatively cautious handling of the mad cow issue by the French Chambres d'Agriculture may illustrate such a long-term awareness.)

That being said, the precautionary principle raises a crucial question for the EC, as well as all WTO members—and hence for the WTO itself: is the

---

18. The *Eyssen* case deals with the Dutch government's ban on the use of a preservative (nisin) in processed cheese (sold in the home market). The ban was criticized by cheese producers from other member-states as an unfair trade barrier, because Dutch companies could use nisin for cheese to export (some member-states [France and Britain] permit unlimited use of nisin). However, the Court held that the ban was justified because the acceptable daily intake had not been established, because such an intake depended on the entire dietary habits of an individual, and because such habits varied from one member-state to another (Oliver 1996, 208).

key role given to "scientific evidence" robust enough to solve food safety problems? The answer may well be no.[19]

The notion of scientific evidence on which EC rules (e.g., Article 95:5 [ex 100a]) and WTO rules (e.g., Article SPS 5) are based better fits slow-moving 18th-century science than fast-moving, quite unpredictable 21st-century science. Strong technical progress puts a lot of pressure on the trade regime. On the one hand, it increases the number of trade conflicts because it boosts competition by generating new products or production processes that circumvent existing trade barriers. On the other hand, it makes solutions to these conflicts less easy to reach because strong technical progress is engineered by systematic "scientific doubt" and permanent challenges to established scientific evidence much more than by consensus about a fine line between "excessive" and "reasonable" precautions which is implicitly behind the notion of scientific evidence.

As a result, rapid technical progress makes scientific evidence unlikely to constitute a robust enough basis for facing food safety issues, and the precautionary principle is likely to be hijacked by vested interests—inducing politicians using the absence of unanimity among scientists as a license to take "easy" actions (i.e., to restrict imports and do little about domestic production, as is best shown by the mad cow case). In such a context, it is not astonishing that scientific evidence has become an increasing source of conflict, among scientists and between scientists and politicians.

A good example of conflict among scientists is the statement in 1999 of the French Food Safety Agency (Agence française de sécurité sanitaire des aliments, or AFSSA), according to which British beef still represented a specific risk, a concern that the EC Scientific Steering Committee (SSC) "unanimously does not share" (SSC press release, 29 October 1999). Conflicts between scientists and politicians have also followed the continuous reluctance of Continental member-state governments to take adequate domestic measures, raising increasing doubts about the committee's role. For instance, in June 2000, the French government refused to impose a ban on offal used to make large sausages (andouillettes, cervelas, etc.), despite strong requests from AFSSA. The same inertia can be observed in Germany (despite a high consumption of sausages and patés) or in Spain (despite the fact that, at the time, Portuguese cattle were already considered largely contaminated).

Genetically modified organisms (GMOs) constitute another contentious topic (in particular, between the EC and United States) that illustrates the

---

19. The reasons given for justifying this negative answer are valid even when scientific committees are independent from political masters. This basic condition is not always met in many EC member-states (as is best illustrated by the radioactive "Chernobyl Cloud," which, according to the French scientific committee of that time, was respectfully bypassing France while covering all the rest of Western Europe). Such a heritage makes the issues even more difficult—and labeling an even more appealing solution.

above points (Perdikis 2000; WTO, *Trade Policy Review: The European Union,* 2000). GMOs are a compendium of all the possible problems. They have the same undesirable impact as beef hormones in an unreformed CAP (they increase substantially productivity and output) and they have similarities with the mad cow case (their risks are complex to assess; Kerr 1999). In addition, they raise their own specific sources of conflict. First, there is little doubt that they will involve increasingly large markets (in particular, among developing countries) in which EC and US GMO producers will probably be major competitors. In this context, banning EC markets to US firms on precautionary grounds (making these markets a potential sanctuary for EC firms) could only be a measure aiming to help lagging EC firms to catch up, whereas being the first to move could be seen as giving an advantage to US firms.

Second, GMOs can substantially modify the vertical relationships between farmers and GMO producers. By selling sterile seeds, GMO producers could force farmers to buy these seeds every year, and then use their resulting market power to the point of vertically quasi-integrating farmers (but in this context, not selling sterile seeds could be an attractive policy for competitors in order to get more clients). Third, the international legal background available for dealing with the GMO issues is very messy. In particular, the Preamble of the Montréal Biosafety Protocol signed in 2000 allows socio-economic factors to be considered in the approval process for imports, although these factors have nothing to do with environmental or health issues, and are clearly at odds with trade issues (Phillips and Kerr 2000). Fourth, as was already stated, the precautionary principle puts the GMO issue in a very narrow perspective: it tends to hide the fact that banning GMOs may magnify other environmental issues (such as deforestation in developing countries, which would need more land to feed their population without GMOs than with productivity-enhancing GMOs).

In the context of rapid technical progress, the best approach, therefore, seems to rely on *individually* assessed risks, on the basis of the best available scientific *information* provided by public *and* private sources. This implies that a country-based approach to food safety issues is likely to be nonoptimal. There is nothing such as an "average French" or "average British" consumer. There are simply more or less risk-averse and risk-loving consumers in France and Britain, who should decide for themselves between alternative products with different risk intensities.[20] Public authorities have the responsibility to inform consumers about the existing scientific evidence (with all the honest doubts and opposed views) available in the importing *and* exporting countries. But individual consumers should keep the final choice.

---

20. All other things being constant, consumers with a stable risk aversion over time would smoke less when they are 20 years old (because of the compounding risk over the years) than when they are 70 years old (at this age, tobacco-related health risks become limited relative to other health risks).

Such an approach makes *labeling* a pivotal instrument, as indeed it is in the case of tobacco, and its risks of cancer. The EC could offer an interesting international field of experimentation to see how to reduce or eliminate the protectionist potential of labeling. This potential can be substantial: for instance, it has been estimated that the logo mentioning the French origin of beef has allowed French farmers to increase their sale prices by 4 to 8 percent (Chambres d'Agriculture 2000). But such a protectionist potential would be much reduced if the label (1) is voluntary, (2) relies on product-based criteria, not on the mere indication of the origin country, (3) does not impose a "yes-no" situation (e.g., the lower the segregation threshold between GMO and non-GMO crops, the higher the costs of GMO crops), and (4) is subject to cross-monitoring of adopted TRs between trading partners (e.g., would British experts be allowed to monitor German mad cow detection programs, and vice versa?).

These basic conditions suggest that the labeling rules for beef that were implemented starting in September 2000 in the EC have a protectionist potential. They are compulsory; the cross-monitoring will be limited to rare EC missions; and much more important, the information they convey will be concentrated on the country of origin at the various production stages (a particularly worrisome feature because the EC is constantly asking for rules of origin in MRAs. The country of origin is an irrelevant issue for TRs; either the product meets the TRs, or it does not, independently from its geographical origin of production. All these observations are valid for assessing the current debate on the "traceability" system to be introduced for genetically modified food commodities and related products—an ongoing debate within the EC (in relation to the enforcement of Directive 90/220) and within the WTO forum (in relation to the Codex Alimentarius).

The protectionist potential of labeling often makes non-EC firms reluctant to recognize the value of this instrument. Such firms should not forget two aspects. First, voluntary labeling could also be a powerful instrument of market access. For instance, a label underlining that beef has been raised on Argentinian or Uruguayan vast lands can constitute a key marketing advantage over EC beef intensively raised in stables. Second, EC and non-EC food producers alike have to cope with the fact that consumers in rich countries are implicity making food increasingly close to pharmaceuticals; this consumer behavior forces food firms to adopt marketing strategies increasingly similar to those used routinely by drug producers.

Ongoing Deep Changes in the EC Economies?

The EC indirectly affects world trade by changing the ways in which its member-states interact and respond to shocks in the world economy. In this context, three questions deserve attention. Were the farm and manufacturing sectors of member-states diversely affected by the changes in the common EC trade policy on agriculture and industry made during the 1990s? If yes, what could be the consequences of this evolution on intra-EC coalitions and on EC trade policy during the coming WTO negotiations? And what changes may have been revealed by the EC's approach to the Seattle WTO Ministerial?

EC Member-states: Changing of the Guard in Agriculture?

Despite the modest outcome of the 1999 Berlin Council, are EC member-state positions on farm trade policy evolving? This possibility is suggested by the timid choice of the Berlin Council in favor of direct subsidy "modulation." In particular, has the ongoing trade liberalization of EC agriculture—though minimal as it is—had a significantly different impact on member-states—possibly inducing states to change sides and create new coalitions on farm issues?

In the early 1990s, despite differences in the support granted to various farm products, the overall high level of protection implied a relatively similar level of aggregate support for the farm sector in all member-states, independent of the production mix. Despite all its limitations, the Uruguay Agriculture Agreement has modified this situation; it has tended to lower protection on grains more than on animals—and hence to have a differential impact on member-states with varying mixes of animal and vegetable production.

Table 4.6 attempts to capture this differential impact, although, in what follows, one should keep in mind that CSEs reflect world price changes as well as EC policy changes. For 11 key products in 1990 (wheat, corn, rice, sugar, oilseeds, milk, beef, pork, sheep, eggs, and poultry), the CSE-based tariffs estimated for the whole EC have been weighted by the corresponding output in each member-state. For all but the Mediterranean member-states, these 11 products represent more than 50 percent of total farm output. The resulting production-weighted average CSE-based tariffs by member-state have been calculated for the pre-Uruguay Round agreement period (1990–92) and for the post-agreement period (1996–99).

The table suggests a lesson that sheds some light on the Uruguay Round negotiations per se and is useful for understanding possible member-state approaches in the coming WTO negotiations on agriculture. (Because their specific farm products are not covered, the Mediterranean member-states—Greece, Italy, Portugal, and Spain—are left aside in the following discussion.[21]) The average decrease of the EC-wide CSE-based tariff hides

---

21. The case of the Mediterranean EC member-states (dominated by cotton, fruit and vegetables, olive oil, tobacco, and wine) is difficult to assess. On the one hand, because theirs were not among the major products covered by the CAP during the Uruguay Round negotiations, they tend to be relatively open to progressive liberalization (a point illustrated by table 4.6; Sarris 1992), with certain observers expecting a small impact of the Uruguay

Table 4.6   The differentiated impact of EC trade policy on EC member-states: Agriculture

	CSE-based tariffs[a] (EC-12 = index 100)		Farm output coverage[b]	EC average farm budget (EAGGF, 1995–97)		
	1990–92	1996–99		Euros per job[c]	Percent of value added	Percent of farm income
Belgium	94.3	95.2	67.3	12,273	36.9	81.8
Britain	104.7	100.2	77.3	6,759	20.1	41.6
Denmark	86.5	80.2	82.5	11,673	23.2	85.2
France	102.6	98.3	66.4	8,390	26.1	48.1
Germany	101.2	110.0	75.4	4,848	17.8	49.4
Greece	107.9	96.2	37.9	3,492	46.6	34.2
Ireland	127.9	135.2	90.8	12,552	85.1	113.7
Italy	97.6	91.6	41.6	3,174	30.4	45.5
Netherlands	98.0	111.1	56.0	7,168	9.6	46.6
Portugal	96.1	83.0	51.9	1,319	22.8	41.8
Spain	88.8	76.7	48.2	4,175	33.2	33.6
EC-12	100.0	100.0	62.2	5,139	31.3	47.7
Austria		104.3	72.7	2,692	34.4	42.9
Finland		130.1	74.1	2,730	35.9	34.0
Sweden		115.9	79.5	3,878	34.3	21.3
EC-15		100.0	62.2	4,971	31.1	47.4

CSE = consumer subsidy equivalent.
EAGGF = European Agricultural Guidance and Guarantee Fund.
EC = European Community.

a. At constant 1990 and 1995 (respectively) production pattern.
b. See text.
c. Per person employed in farming.

Sources: European Commission, *Report on Agriculture,* various years, and various documents; *European Economy* (1994); OECD, *Monitoring Agricultural Policies,* various years; OECD (1995); Eurostat.

very different changes among individual member-states. After the Uruguay Round, two member-states increased (Germany and Ireland) and one maintained (Britain) their protection relative to the EC average. Even more interesting, two member-states changed sides: France shifted from more-than-average to less-than-average protection, whereas the Netherlands shifted from less-than-average to more-than-average protection (similar computations based on PSEs by member-states confirm the observations based on the CSEs, with minor nuances). The CSE-based results may explain (assuming perfect information) why, in the traditionally mercantilist multilateral negotiations, France was the most vocal opponent of the Blair House agreement in the EC: it was giving the most important trade concessions (because of its farm production structure).

These results offer an interesting—and to a large extent unexpected—picture of intra-EC forces for the coming round. The EC emerges as composed of a stable set of more-than-averagely protected countries (Germany, Ireland, and Britain), a stable set of less-than-averagely protected countries (Belgium and Denmark), and two countries possibly changing sides (the Netherlands becoming more, and France less, protected than the EC average), again leaving aside the Mediterranean member-states.[22]

The results also confirm the pivotal position of France, and the fact that it could shift toward freer trade positions at any time—as soon as its substantial comparative advantages in agriculture finally become the driving force of its farm trade strategy, and as less weak French governments take the side of French farm export interests (Messerlin 1996b).[23] Increasingly, numerous groups of French farmers are realizing that their comparative advantages have been (and still are) constrained (rather than developed)

Round agreement on Mediterranean products (Tracy 1997). On the other hand, it should be underlined that the EC has overshot its export subsidy commitments for olive oil (OECD 2000d), that CAP subsidies for olive oil almost doubled between 1995 and 1998, becoming almost equivalent to those for dairy products (€2.2 vs. €2.6 billion), and that safeguards have been introduced on imported fruit and vegetables. These changes were mirrored by the fact that, during the Berlin Council, Spain was one of the most inflexible member-states.

22. This paragraph and the following two are limited to the 12 EC member-states at the time of the Uruguay Round. The three member-states that joined the EC in 1995 have a very different background in farm policy. Austria and Finland were at least as protectionist as the EC-12, whereas in sharp contrast, in 1989, Sweden launched a major reform of its farm policy (see box 4.4). It is interesting to note that under the qualified majority rule, Germany (with 10 votes) needs only 16 more votes to create a minority-blocking situation in the EC 15.

23. During the past 40 years, the German position (freer trade in manufacturing and protection in agriculture) has reflected economic logic bound by political constraints. The French acceptance of the same stance defies economic and political logic: why has France accepted freer trade in manufacturing, where its comparative advantages were few, and why has it refused freer trade in agriculture, where its initial comparative advantages were many? Such a miscalculation may reflect more a profound ignorance of the way markets function than the strength of farm lobbies (for an in-depth analysis of French farmers' voting, see Adams 1999). It may also reflect an incredibly weak government.

by the CAP, and that—far from being eliminated from the world markets by freer trade—they could improve their market penetration in non-EC (and EC) markets under a more liberal world trade regime.

Of course, trade policy strategies are not determined by existing relative protection alone. Whether a member-state is more (or less) protected than the EC average does not mean that it will necessarily advocate for protectionist (or freer trade) policy at the EC level. Nevertheless, the presumption that a less-than-averagely protected member-state will be inclined to adopt a more open policy cannot be rejected—particularly if it fits the country's comparative advantages, and a general perception of the major forces present, as are briefly described in the introductions to appendix A, cases 15 to 18.

To take into account the fact that member-states will not define their farm strategy in the coming WTO negotiations on the exclusive (or even maybe dominant) basis of changes in the relative level of protection, table 4.7 presents four other indicators that could play a decisive role in designing the future farm strategy of individual member-states. These indicators are based on the following working hypotheses: a member-state will be more inclined to liberalize further if it has (1) a small share of employment in agriculture, (2) a large share of large farms, (3) a large average farm size, and if it is (4) a net provider of European farm funds.[24] To summarize the information by ranking for each criterion every member-state with respect to the EC average (a plus if the state performs better than the EC average, a minus if the contrary): two member-states (Denmark and France) perform best; they are followed by Britain and Germany, and then by the rest of the member-states.

Growing Differences in Manufacturing?

As in agriculture, the EC common structure of tariffs, NTBs, and antidumping measures for manufactured goods has a differentiated impact on member-state economies that rely on varying mixes of industries. Can this differentiated impact generate new coalitions among member-states in favor of further liberalization?

---

24. Table 4.7 provides "total economic transfers" (capturing all CAP-generated transfers, from price supports through milk quotas to financial rebates granted to certain member-states, e.g., Britain) and the corresponding "rates of return" (pure budgetary transfers) for 1997 (Alix 1998). Discrepancies between total economic transfers and rates of return depend, in particular, on the member-state's involvement in intra-EC trade (which is channeling transfers), on the types of subsidies implemented (price supports favor exporters; direct aid favors producers, independent of their export performance), etc. Simulations based on Agenda 2000 suggest that, relative to the 1997 situation, Spain would be the member-state gaining the most from Agenda 2000, and Britain the member-state losing the most (Alix 1998).

Table 4.7 Select economic aspects underlying political forces in agriculture, by EC member-state

	Farm labor[a] (percent of total labor force)			Farm size structure (farms with > 50ha)			Average land per farm (hectares per farm)			Total economic transfers, 1997		Rate of return, 1997 (millions of euros)
	1979	1990	1998	1979	1987	1997	1979	1987	1997	Millions of euros	Percent of farm output	
Belgium	3.0	2.7	2.2	3.8	5.8	10.0	11.3	14.8	20.6	−285.0	−5.7	−542.5
Britain	2.6	2.2	1.7	31.3	33.3	33.6	63.2	64.4	69.3	344.6	2.1	−258.1
Denmark	8.6	5.5	3.7	9.5	17.2	27.8	22.8	32.2	42.6	810.5	13.4	385.8
France	8.8	5.8	4.4	13.5	18.1	29.7	23.3	28.6	41.7	2,093.9	5.1	1,727.4
Germany	6.0	3.3	2.8	3.7	6.1	14.2	14.3	16.8	32.1	−5,692.9	−19.7	−5,118.9
Greece	30.3	21.6	17.7	n.a.	0.5	0.4	n.a.	4.0	4.3	1,786.6	24.0	1,861.6
Ireland	19.2	13.8	10.9*	7.4	9.0	14.1	23.7	22.7	29.4	1,609.3	41.6	1,448.6
Italy	14.2	8.5	6.4	1.7	1.9	1.8	6.2	5.6	6.4	−1,207.0	−3.9	85.9
Netherlands	4.6	4.5	3.5	2.8	4.4	7.1	13.1	15.3	18.6	−457.3	−3.3	−655.6
Portugal	26.6	17.5	13.7	n.a.	1.9	2.3	n.a.	5.2	9.2	−76.7	−2.0	101.0
Spain	18.8	10.7	7.9	n.a.	6.0	8.2	n.a.	13.8	21.2	1,554.1	6.6	1,585.4
EC-12	8.1	6.2		6.8	6.8		15.3	13.3				
Austria			6.5			4.1			16.3	−76.3	−2.5	−213.7
Finland			7.1			8.8			23.7	−68.5	−3.5	−34.5
Sweden			3.1			21.3			34.7	−334.8	−11.4	−315.0
EC-15			4.7*			8.6			18.4			

EC = European Community.
ha = hectare
n.a. = available

a. Figures followed by * refer to the previous year (latest available).

Sources: European Commission, *Report on Agriculture*, various years; *European Economy* (1994, 90); OECD, *Monitoring Agricultural Policies*, various years; Alix (1998).

Table 4.8 provides evidence about the magnitude of this differential impact by weighting the EC sectoral tariffs and rates of overall protection by value added or by employment for each member-state (using the 1990 [for 1990] and 1995 [for 1999] data on value added and employment patterns from OECD 1997a). It gives three results similar to those found for agriculture. (1) The gap between the most and least protected member-states is again substantial, with the highest average tariff for a state being 1.5 to 1.9 times higher than the lowest average tariff for a state. (2) This gap increases noticeably (to roughly 1.7 to 2) when NTBs and antidumping measures are taken into account. (3) The gap noticeably widened between 1990 and 1997.

These observations again suggest a useful taxonomy of less-than-averagely protected member-states versus more-than-averagely protected ones. In 1990, the first set of member-states included France, Germany, and Britain (this club would have also included Finland and Sweden, meaning that these two new member-states were "reprotected" when they joined the EC). All the other countries could be seen as relatively protected.

That the less-than-averagely protected member-states include France seems at odds with that country's strongly protectionist vocal stance during most of the early 1990s. In fact, France is the member-state closest to the EC average, particularly for labor-weighted indices of overall protection. This "central" position fits well both France's role as a deal-striker within the EC, and France's final rally to the Uruguay Round outcome, despite its inability to get substantial additional concessions from its non-EC trading partners.

Between 1990 and 1999, there were significant changes between the two sets of member-states. In 1999, the less-than-averagely protected member-states included Denmark, Finland, and Sweden—but the French position had deteriorated (it remained relatively open in value added, but not labor). Two more-than-averagely protected member-states (Italy and Spain) moved closer to the EC average. These changes fit well with recent internal EC debates (e.g., antidumping measures on cotton bleach proposed by the Commission and strongly supported by France have been rejected by the Council; see appendix A, cases 13 and 14). They suggest that France may have lost its central position, after the reinforcement of the "pro-freer trade" group of member-states by the three last accessions (in particular, Sweden), and after the softening of the more-than-averagely protected group.

Concluding Remarks

Current EC trade policy and its corresponding domestic policies will not be able to fully cope with the challenges raised by a new round of negoti-

Table 4.8 The differentiated impact of EC trade policy for manufacturing on member-states (percent)

	1990				1999			
	MFN tariffs		Overall protection		MFN tariffs		Overall protection	
Country	Labor weighted	Value-added weighted	Labor weighted	Value-added weighted	Labor weighted	Value-added weighted	Labor weighted	Value-added weighted
Austria	7.6	9.5	11.7	12.7	5.5	6.8	8.0	8.6
Belgium	8.2	8.3	13.1	12.9	6.4	6.9	9.8	9.5
Denmark	8.0	8.3	11.9	12.4	5.3	6.3	7.2	8.2
Finland	7.5	7.6	11.1	10.5	5.1	4.8	7.0	6.4
France	7.6	7.8	11.8	11.2	5.9	6.0	8.9	8.2
Germany	7.2	8.3	10.6	11.2	5.1	5.9	7.6	7.9
Greece	10.8	10.6	17.8	16.7	8.7	9.3	13.4	12.8
Italy	8.1	8.0	12.7	12.2	5.9	6.0	9.8	9.2
Netherlands	8.2	9.6	12.1	12.5	6.4	7.1	8.9	8.9
Portugal	9.0	10.7	15.8	17.2	7.1	8.7	12.5	13.0
Spain	8.3	8.8	13.2	13.1	6.6	7.7	10.1	10.2
Sweden	6.8	7.1	9.6	9.7	4.8	4.9	6.6	6.6
Britain	7.5	8.0	11.3	11.4	5.5	7.3	8.3	9.7
EC12–EC15	7.7	8.2	11.8	11.7	7.0	6.3	8.8	8.6

MFN = most favored nation

Note: Manufacturing includes the agri-food industry (International Standard Industrial Classifications 311 to 314).

Sources: Table 2.1; OECD (1997a).

ations without a marked change of course. Ideally, the EC should react in four domains, which are presented in order of decreasing importance in what follows.

Reforming the CAP: A Two-Track Approach

The EC should undertake the long-overdue *real* reform of the CAP. During the 1960s, EC agriculture was relatively homogeneous (based on small farms), so that one CAP may have made sense—if one leaves aside the questions of the number and type of instruments used, and of the magnitude with which they were used. Today, this homogeneity no longer exists, as is shown by the increasing strains between large and small farmers, even in member-states with a strong tradition of a unique, corporatist, farm trade union. As a result, the EC farm sector requires *two* CAPs: a CAP for large farms, based on the assumption that such farms are capable of adjusting to increasing world competition with much smaller subsidies *and* far fewer constraints (such as set-asides); and another CAP for small farms, which would evolve at a slower pace toward pure income support compatible with an increasingly market-based environment. Of course, such a two-track CAP reform with a strong focus on a liberalization based on large farms in the years to come is not a perfect substitute for a complete reform of the CAP: if it lasts too long, it could generate perverse effects, to the extent that running a large or a small farm will become an endogenous decision of farmers.

But for the coming decade, a reformed "CAP for large farms" would provide enough pragmatic solutions to most of the farm conflicts between the EC and the rest of the world, and would also be the necessary ingredient for the EC's enlargement to Central European countries. It would cover roughly 70 percent of EC farm output, and tackle all the major distortions that the EC generates in world farm trade. It would also allow a better appraisal of the EC's comparative advantages in farm products under market conditions—and thus would reveal how wrong is the wide perception among European politicians that EC agriculture has no comparative advantages and can survive only under a world order based on quotas, closed markets, and compensatory subsidies.

Such a perception of almost no European comparative advantages in agriculture (carefully supported by vested interests) does not fit existing facts. For instance, EC exports of relatively unsubsidized, cost-conscious, differentiated products, such as high-quality wine or cheese, compare favorably with EC exports of highly subsidized farm products. This negative perception among decision makers has been challenged by experts such as Tangermann (1999), who argue that, in the negotiations of the coming round, the EC should advocate for a zero-to-zero approach or for a wider trade-off between increasing market access for certain dairy products (of primary export interest for EC producers) and increasing market access for certain cereals (attractive for the Cairns Group and US farmers).

It is interesting that this two-track CAP reform was timidly initiated by the Berlin Council—with several member-states (including key countries such as France and Britain) "modulating" direct subsidies. But as stated above, this effort remains homeopathic (it involves 1 to 2 percent of CAP aid) and ambiguous (modulated aid is reallocated to rural development, a notion unclear enough to constitute a potential back door to the protectionist status quo). Going further thus requires the full recognition and implementation of a principle of "modulation" based on two elements: an EC common decision to *reduce* farm subsidies by a certain percentage according to an agreed time table, and individual member-states' decisions to use their *own*, politically acceptable, subsidy-cutting *formula* to reach this common target. For instance, the formula could be based on degressivity by farm size in member-states with a mix of large and small farms (France) or on an across-the-board approach for member-states with a more homogeneous farm population (Britain).

A More Competition-Oriented TR Policy

The second topic on which the EC should improve its trade policy concerns *technical regulations*. The EC TR policy is not the often-celebrated success. When applied to intra-EC issues, the mutual-recognition approach is still conditional on too many essential requirements (in other words, it is still too close to harmonization), and competition between conformity-assessment bodies is still too limited. Mutual recognition agreements between the EC and other WTO members have shown severe limits: although they do not deal with substance (EC and partners' TRs are untouched) but only with equivalence of conformity-assessment procedures, they are the source of innumerable difficulties and delays.

This situation is best illustrated by the EC-United States MRA on a wide range of products: for pharmaceuticals (the US Food and Drug Administration is assessing certification equivalence, EC member-state by member-state, and is expected to grant equivalence for Britain and perhaps other member-states by December 2001, which is the supposed date of *complete* entry in force of the MRA); for electrical safety (the EC is insisting that both parties should designate the conformity bodies in each country, whereas the US Occupational Safety and Health Administration (OSHA) says that it has agreed only to allow European laboratories to apply to OSHA for approval to certify products for the US market); etc. The EC has thus both domestic and international incentives to resist the temptation to look for more harmonization, and to expand a more flexible (that is, a more market-oriented and firm-based) approach, which would be based more on trust and reputation, that is, on an increasingly unconditional version of the mutual-recognition principle.

Progress in TR issues is particularly important in agriculture. In Europe, environmentalists should logically be natural allies of a serious CAP reform effort because CAP-driven intensive agriculture has generated (and still does) ecological disasters—for instance, sharp declines in water quality caused by excessive amounts of nitrates in Western France require huge public investment paid for by taxpayers, who have paid (and still do) large subsidies to those farmers who caused the deterioration in water quality. Improving EC TR policy will also be crucial for trade and food safety issues—in particular, for an economically sound approach to labeling. In this respect, the intra-EC mad cow case will be a crucial test for both internal EC TR policy and EC trade policy in the WTO.

If EC member-states fail to put in place a mutually acceptable, workable labeling regime, the EC will be induced, sooner or later, to make food safety a powerful trade barrier not only within intra-EC trade (as shown in the mad cow case, which reveals the CAP as a key source of troubles, and hence as the ultimate destroyer of EC common beef markets; see box 4.7), but also against EC imports from the rest of the world. By contrast, if EC member-states succeed in creating an honest labeling and monitoring regime (including a cross-monitoring system whereby, e.g., British veterinarians can check French cattle, and vice versa), European consumers will develop trust in the authorities that seem more trustworthy, and labeling will lose its potential as a protectionist instrument.

European farm lobbies are well aware of these profound relations between TRs and the CAP. They have noticed the increasing public perception of farmers as polluters, particularly in the rural areas directly exposed to environmental deterioration. This awareness explains why, when defending multifunctionality, EC farm lobbies have shifted away from environment-based arguments and toward food safety considerations, flaunting themselves as protectors of domestic "good" food only to get troubles, as shown in the mad cow case.

Market Access in Manufacturing

EC trade policy should improve its *manufacturing* component in two important ways (leaving aside the question of "preferences" for developing countries, to be examined in chapter 6). The EC attitude toward antidumping reform should shift from loose neutrality to active leadership—if the EC does not want to be seen as hypocritical by suggesting negotiations on antidumping after initiating more antidumping cases in 1999 than in any year since it began to implement such procedures (see appendix B).

Moreover, the EC should launch an initiative for early implementation of the Uruguay Round commitments on textiles and clothing—all the more because the EC industry is repeating that it has made all the adjustment efforts required by the EC commitments under the Uruguay Round agreement, so it is now competitive by world standards. Such early implementation is most likely to be a case of time-asymmetric liberalization in a multilateral context (see chapter 6 for illustrations in a bilateral context), to the extent that, at the end of the coming round, the EC will almost certainly get reciprocal concessions from developing countries in the form of decreased tariffs, and better antidumping disciplines, in this sector and in other sectors.

Free Movement of Goods: A Basic Enforcement Problem

The EC must solve an increasingly worrisome problem: effective respect for the free movement of goods *within* the EC. This problem does not refer to the cases where intra-EC trade is interrupted by inopportune decisions from public authorities (e.g., spare parts for motor vehicles seized between Spain and Italy by French customs). The existing EC legal regime can cope with this first type of problem, although too slowly (the infringement procedure should be made more rapid).

Much more worrisome, however, is the increasing basic law enforcement problem in Europe. A growing number of powerful vested interests (farmers and truck drivers being the best known) have used brute force (blockage of roads and railways, destruction of transported products or trucks, etc.) to extract a systematic exemption from obeying the law, without any noticeable intervention by the police of the member-states involved. In this respect, the EC needs a provision (and the determination to enforce it) much closer to the US Commerce Clause than the existing texts, which consist of a mere Council resolution coupled with a Commission regulation adopted in 1998. Of course, any progress in this domestic domain would also constitute an essential improvement in foreign access to EC markets.

5

Emerging EC Commercial Policy

EC commercial policy is still in its infancy, as it is for most WTO members, but it has already had to cope with topics that, for better or worse, attracted a lot of attention at the Seattle WTO Ministerial: services, trade and labor, trade and competition, public procurement, trade-related intellectual property rights (TRIPS), and investment. This policy is not yet driven by EC Uruguay Round liberalization commitments simply because, so far, as for all WTO members, these are limited, and in some cases even nonexistent. The 1995 Uruguay commitments in services and the 1997 agreements on basic telecommunications (hereafter telecoms) and financial services are mostly standstill commitments. WTO commitments on public procurement consist of general principles to be followed in bidding procedures, and of a list of agencies and bodies that must abide by these principles. And WTO negotiations on international investment, trade-related competition, and labor issues may never be launched. The only topic of commercial policy with EC commitments is TRIPS, but it is included in a much wider, older framework of international treaties.

In the absence of WTO commitments, emerging EC commercial policy is largely shaped by another force: the Single Market Program (SMP). As mentioned in chapter 4, the SMP was launched by a group—the European Round Table of Industrialists—that did not want the scope of reforms to be undertaken by the EC to be limited to manufacturing. The ERT 1985 Plan included opening to intra-EC competition key nonmanufacturing activities, such as telecoms, transportation and other essential infrastructure services, and public procurement. The SMP was officially initiated in 1985, a few weeks after the ERT Plan. It has necessitated (and still does) the adoption of a large number of EC regulations and other legislative instruments, particularly in services and public procurement, which have been slowly and painfully (as shown in this chapter) in the process of being implemented since the mid-1990s.

The dynamic interactions between EC commercial policy and the SMP are (and will be) shaped by the balance of power between the Community and its member-states. Whereas trade policy (defined as dealing with goods and related topics in the introduction to part II) is under the Community's exclusive competence, EC commercial policy is often under the *joint* competence of the Community and its member-states—but with marked nuances. At one end of the spectrum, the Community is dominant, with the Commission's exclusive power to impose discipline on member-state subsidies and its leading role in merger and competition policy.

At the other end of the spectrum, the Community relies on a narrow treaty basis for labor issues, where it plays a very limited role as catalyst. Services, TRIPS, and public procurement fall between these two extremes. The Nice TEC version (2001) has tilted the balance somewhat toward exclusive Community competence by expanding the qualified majority rule to a range of service and TRIPS issues—although this change is much more modest than it appears at first glance (see below).

This delicate balance of power between the Community and its member-states on commercial policy is in permanent flux under the pressure of two additional, unrelated (indeed often opposed) forces. First, the Community relies on the legal basis established by the Court of Justice in the late 1970s and early 1980s—the 1979 *Cassis de Dijon* ruling and a few other key procompetitive rulings for the various topics covered by commercial policy (in particular the 1982 *British Telecom* ruling regarding access to networks in services). This reliance on a legal corpus, not just on negotiations between member-states, is (and will be for the foreseeable future) a major difference between the SMP and WTO perspectives.[1]

During the first 40 years of the Community, the Court mostly dealt with trade in goods, and its rulings gave clear priority to the elimination of intra-EC obstacles—magnifying trade diversion costs, in particular, when such "obstacles" were in fact sound economic practices. However, since the early 1990s, the Court has recognized the intrinsic difficulties of dealing with trade in services and regulatory matters, and the deep differences among member-states on many key issues such as the role of "service of general interest," tolerance of monopolies, etc. As a result, the Court has left member-states more freedom in these domains (indeed, meanwhile, the Court has evolved in the same direction in the domain of goods, as is best illustrated by its 1993 *Keck and Mithouard* ruling; see chapter 4). The resulting, more balanced approach by the Court culminated in

---

1. Indeed, there is a striking parallel between the EC Court of Justice and the US Supreme Court on most of the aspects examined in this chapter; for details, see Goodman and Frost (2000).

its 1994 ruling on joint competence of the Community and its member-states for most commercial policy matters the scope of which has been formally reduced by the Nice TEC version.

The second force that has shaped the balance of power between the Community and its member-states (and still does) is European politicians' perspectives. Until the late 1980s, member-states were jealous of their trade policy prerogatives (the communitarization of trade policy has not been an early, rapid, or easy process, as seen in the previous chapters), and most European politicians resisted devolving more power to Brussels. By contrast, since the early 1990s, European politicians have looked much more favorably on harmonization. They refer less and less to the concept of "subsidiarity" (actions should be taken at the lowest efficient layer of decision), much celebrated in the late 1980s and early 1990s, but mentioned only once in the Nice TEC version. And they dismiss the fact that regulatory competition between member-states can be an essential source of cost-efficiency and benefits to the EC (for a thorough analysis of the good economic reasons for diversity across countries in domestic policies dealing with the topics covered by commercial policy, and an explanation of why harmonization is not necessarily a welfare-enhancing proposition, see Bhagwati and Hudec 1996).

However, this politicians' call for harmonization is ambiguous, as is best illustrated by the fate of services and TRIPS in the Nice TEC version. The shift, under this Treaty, of a large group of services from unanimity to qualified majority rule does not represent a dramatic change, for either legal or political reasons. Legally, following the "parallelism" approach (in EC parlance), the unanimity rule in services will continue to prevail for all provisions of international agreements (e.g., on taxation or on social issues) that require unanimity in the adoption of intra-EC decisions. Politically, the history of EC trade policy has amply shown that consensus is still often the de facto rule in the many cases where member-states "trade" their signatures on agreements under the majority rule for their signatures on agreements under the unanimity rule. The range of services left under the unanimity rule (audiovisuals, education, and health and social services; to which one should add transport, which remains governed by specific Treaty provisions) is important and large enough to leave many decisions de facto under the unanimity rule.

What then does the proharmonization shift among European politicians mean? It seems much more a mirroring of the fear of regulatory competition (within the EC, and between the EC and the rest of the world) than a desire to really "harmonize". In fact, harmonization is a very convenient argument for European politicians, for three reasons. First, it allows them to put the blame for the necessary regulatory reforms on "Brussels," in sharp contrast to regulatory competition, which would require hard decisions from member-states. Second, it offers to every member-state the opportunity to include national provisions in European regulations, and hence to possibly "grandfather" domestic regulatory key features, as is best illustrated by the notion of "service of general interest" in services (see below). Third, after the introduction of the euro, harmonization appears as a "must" to many European politicians, who tend to believe that a single currency should bring the same price for the same product all over Europe. Hence they are keen to ensure what they call "fair" competition in Europe—inhibiting, by the same token, the procompetitive effects of the euro, by far its possibly most positive feature.

All these aspects are consistent with the "statist" reaction underlined in chapter 1, and they are illustrated again and again by the typical history of SMP directives in services: The Commission tables a relatively procompetitive draft, which is then copiously peppered with harmonization provisions, which are traded between member-states and powerful incumbent vested interests, and which increasingly limit the scope for regulatory competition, to the satisfaction of the remaining "dirigist" clusters of the Commission.

With these driving forces in mind, it is interesting to look at box 5.1 and table 5.1, which aim to capture the implicit preferences of the three key EC institutions (the Council, the Commission, and the Parliament) on the six topics of commercial policy by examining the texts released by these institutions for the Seattle WTO Ministerial.

Box 5.1 suggests organizing the chapter in six sections. The first section deals with services, an important issue for the three institutions and the most important potential source of gains from liberalization. The second section deals with trade and labor, a dominant topic in the three agendas, despite its negative impact in the WTO forum. The third section looks at competition policy, which is important for the three institutions, despite the limited benefits to be expected from internationalization. The fourth section examines public procurement, a domain surprisingly secondary for the three institutions, despite its often-celebrated large benefits from liberalization (a contradiction that will receive some explanation below). The fifth section looks briefly at TRIPS and investment issues, which are both more marginal, but for different reasons. The concluding section summarizes a few proposals that the EC should ideally table in the coming round of negotiations.

The chapter leads to two general conclusions that shed some light on EC commercial policy in the WTO context. First, EC commercial policy has been deeply permeated by services (the only topic certain to be covered by the coming negotiations under the Uruguay Built-in Agenda) with the SMP core focus on regulatory *convergence* (harmonization), to the detriment of regulatory *competition* (liberalization). If unchanged, this feature will make the EC a difficult partner in the coming WTO negotiations. But it will also make multilateral liberalization of services an attractive opportunity for the EC, because it will boost the incomplete, and still partly reversible, *intra-EC* liberalization—a situation not without similarities to the

EC Common Market in manufactured goods, which has greatly benefited
from subsequent GATT rounds (see chapter 1).

Second, by contrast, the EC has unfortunately not drawn from its *own*
internal liberalization the most interesting lessons for the future WTO
round. For instance, it did not underline the benefits of focusing de facto
on two "modes of delivery" of services (cross-border and establishment),
as the EC has progressively learned to do—instead of invoking systematically four modes, as the WTO still does. Nor did the EC make clear the
profound reasons that have induced EC member-states (and still do) not
to link trade and labor issues *within* the EC. And the EC did not emphasize the fact that priority should be given to *national* competition law *and*
its firm enforcement. The EC also did not insist on the fact that its approach to state aid is much better than GATT provisions on countervailing actions. Last, the EC did not recognize the fact that gains from liberalization in public procurement rely more on swift, effective dispute

Table 5.1 EC preparatory texts for the 1999 WTO Seattle Ministerial: Commercial policy topics

Topic and ranking criteria	Commission		Council		Parliament	
	Share (percent)	Rank	Share (percent)	Rank	Share (percent)	Rank
Topic importance by source[a]:						
Text length devoted to the topic						
Trade and labor	13.4	1	15.8	1	10.0	4
Services	5.8	9	7.1	6	15.9	1
Investment	10.1	3	5.3	7	4.9	10
TRIPS	3.6	11	5.2	8	9.4	5
Public procurement	2.9	13	4.7	10	1.7	13
Competition	6.7	8	4.6	11	5.4	9
Reminder:						
Trade policy topics[b]	44.7	—	45.1	—	45.6	—
Trade and development[c]	12.7	2	12.1	3	7.1	7
"Tone" by topic[d]:						
Term frequencies	Services	Public procurement	Competition policy	Trade and labor	TRIPS	Investment rules
Proliberalization terms	43.8	25.0	9.1	33.3	0.0	7.7
Neutral terms	37.5	37.5	36.4	33.3	0.0	23.1
Reluctant terms	18.8	37.5	54.5	33.3	100.0	69.2
Number of observations	16	8	11	3	1	13

TRIPS = Agreement on Trade-Related Aspects of Intellectual Property Rights.
WTO = World Trade Organization.

a. Decreasing order in the Council text.
b. For details, see table 4.1.
c. For details, see chapter 6.
d. Proliberalization terms = competition, liberalization, market access, mutual recognition and open (market). Neutral terms = barriers, disciplines, nondiscrimination, subsidy, transparency. Reluctant terms = harmonization, progressivity, reciprocity, regulation, safeguard.

Source: See text of the chapter.

settlement procedures at the disposal of the bidding firms feeling unfairly treated than on transparency per se.

The EC experience suggests a last general lesson. Because liberalization of commercial policy tends to be done through regulatory reforms, the design of appropriate reform measures should not exclusively rely on political trade-offs heavily loaded by vested interests (as it did too often in the past in the EC)—but it should make increasing use of a cost-benefit approach based on economic analyses.

The EC SMP in Services: In Need of a WTO Boost

In the mid-1980s, the Common Market was limited to the manufacturing sector, amounting only to a fourth or a third of member-state GDP. Most market-based services, representing half to two-thirds of member-state GDP, were left untouched by intra-EC liberalization. To a large extent, this situation reflected the complex provisions of the Treaty of Rome about services, which can be presented in four basic components.

First, the Treaty of Rome relies on the four modes of delivery on which the WTO legal framework is also based. Article 49 (ex 59), which opens the Treaty chapter on services, and Article 39 (ex 48) on labor movement deal with the freedom to provide services in a way that covers both cross-border trade (mode 1 in GATS parlance) and movements of service providers (mode 4). Echoing mode 2 (movements of consumers of services), several articles in the Treaty principle section (for instance, on citizenship) ban restrictions on the free movement of persons. Article 43 (ex 52) bans restrictions on the right of establishment (mode 3 of GATS).

Second, a key issue is whether all these provisions are *directly* applicable (they can be enforced by national courts without specific Community actions) or not (i.e., they require directives to be adopted by the Council of Ministers and translated into member-state laws, i.e., a long process). The international impact of applicability may be considerable. For instance, the second paragraph of Article 49 (ex 59), which is not directly applicable (contrary to the first paragraph), may allow the possibility of discriminatory treatment against non-EC service providers established within the Community—opening the door to an EC reciprocity-based approach to liberalization of services, and to international conflicts.

Article 39 (ex 48) on labor movement is directly applicable, as firmly clarified by the *Bosman* ruling of the Court of Justice, as is Article 43 (ex 52) on the right of establishment. Similarly, the Court of Justice has repeatedly stated, since its 1974 *van Binsbergen* ruling, that the first paragraph of Article 49 (ex 59), on the principle of nondiscrimination between EC service providers on a nationality or residence basis, is also directly applicable. In an approach echoing the legal structure for goods (see chapter

4), the 1991 *Stichting Collectieve Antennevoorziening Gouda* ruling of the Court of Justice made clear that the freedom to provide services under Article 49 (ex 59) can be limited by member-state laws *only* to guarantee the achievement of an "essential public interest," and *without* going beyond what is necessary to achieve that objective.

By contrast, the other Treaty provisions on services are not directly applicable. These provisions require that directives be developed and enforced, and that has been the raison d'être of the SMP. Of course, there are "in-between" cases where the applicability issue becomes very complex. For instance, Article 43 (ex 52) on the right of establishment, although directly applicable in principle, requires de facto specific directives in the case of professional services (under Article 47 [ex 57]) to solve the problem of equivalence of diplomas, an absolute prerequisite for opening the markets for these services in an effective way.

Third, two other clauses of the Treaty chapter on services deserve attention because they have deeply shaped SMP coverage. The first clause, in Article 52 (ex 63), reads: "priority [for liberalization] shall as a general rule be given to those services which directly affect production costs or the liberalization of which helps to promote trade in goods." It reveals the resilience of the negative perception of the economic role of services in Europe. The distinction between infrastructure and "other" services is biased against a uniform (across-the-board) liberalization of services; it increases the level of effective protection which can be granted to goods. (Liberalizing infrastructure services reduces the costs of producing goods, and hence increases the value added of the domestic production of goods, relative to the value added in foreign production, all other things being constant.) In other words, liberalizing infrastructure services favors trade in goods (if the costs of moving goods decline relative to costs of moving information about goods), or international direct investment in goods (if these relative costs increase).

The second clause of the Treaty on services to be examined more closely is in Article 53 (ex 64): "Member-states declare their readiness to undertake the liberalization of services beyond the extent required by the directives issued pursuant to Article 52:1 (ex 63:1), *if* their general economic situation and the situation of the economic sector concerned so permit." (Author's emphasis) It is thus a safeguard provision for the "other" services, which could be of the utmost importance in the coming WTO negotiations: It can be used by an EC member-state as a legal basis for resisting EC *and* WTO liberalization.

Fourth, in addition to its chapter on services in general, the Treaty of Rome has specific provisions on transport.[2] However, Articles 70 (ex 74) to

---

2. Article 51 (ex 61) specifically mentions liberalization in banking and insurance services, but only to stress that it should be "effected in step" with the liberalization of movement of capital (see the section below on investment).

80 (ex 84) cover only "land carriers" (roads and inland waterways). Paradoxically, they have been a source of more uncertainty than clarity because they balance liberalization with other objectives (a common transport policy and a regional policy) that have de facto excluded land transport from the general right of establishment under Article 43 (ex 52), and from competition rules, by permitting the long survival of a complex web of price controls, quota licenses, public monopolies, state aid, and so on. The only unambiguously proliberalization provision of these articles is the nondiscrimination principle for EC land carriers under Article 75 (ex 79), but its implementation was left to decisions to be made later, with almost no progress (even in terms of regulatory framework) until the late 1980s.

This brief survey deserves two final remarks. National administrations tend not to be subject to many of the above disciplines, in the name of public order. Moreover, in the late 1980s, many service providers in the EC were public monopolies (or firms to which member-states grant special or exclusive rights) subject to specific Treaty provisions about competition (see below, and the following section on state-owned enterprises).

Only in 1985 did the EC decide to embark on a major effort to introduce the regulatory reforms of services possible under the Treaty of Rome. Following Article 52 (ex 63), it did so only for a limited number of service sectors—those perceived, at that time, as constituting the "infrastructure" of the EC economy: financial services, telecoms, transport (land, air, and sea), and audiovisuals, this last service illustrating the political flexibility of the infrastructure notion. The late 1990s witnessed painful, and not always successful, efforts to extend the list to electronic commerce, electricity and natural gas, railways, and postal services, whereas the early 2000s are expected to focus on additional liberalization in financial services. As a result, the services currently covered by the SMP amount to roughly one fourth of the EC's GDP.

The SMP in Services: Regulatory Convergence versus Regulatory Competition

The directives adopted under the SMP in services and its successive extensions during the 1990s share a key feature: they focused too much on regulatory convergence, to the detriment of regulatory competition. This is primarily because the principle of mutual recognition de facto was eroded, or even ignored, in the long negotiations between the member-states necessary to draft the compromises embodied in the directive texts—ultimately to the detriment of intra-EC competition in services.

The SMP was not initiated by the member-states or by the Commission but by two landmark rulings of the Court of Justice: the 1979 *Cassis de Dijon* ruling (and its forerunner, the 1974 *Dassonville* ruling), with its key corollary of "mutual recognition" (see chapter 4); and the 1982 *British Telecom* ruling. These were the first of a series of cases confirming the application of competition rules to the service sectors, which in the early 1980s were still largely dominated by public firms or monopolies in the EC that limited access to their networks.

As underlined in chapter 4, the *Cassis de Dijon* ruling raises the crucial issue of the optimal dose of harmonization and mutual recognition. The ruling could have been interpreted as stating the principle of unconditional (or, at least, maximal) mutual recognition in services, and hence of regulatory competition: member-states would have unconditionally accepted cross-border trade in services between them; and they would have unconditionally allowed the establishment of service providers located in other member-states, their operations being regulated by *home* (country-of-origin) disciplines and authorities. Such a fully "home-based" regime would have strongly induced the authorities of each member-state to ensure that their domestic service providers would enjoy competitive advantages by designing and adopting efficient laws and regulations.

The outcome of such a competitive process among member-states could be regulatory convergence or differentiation (depending on the type of services traded, service providers, and consumers, and on the legal capabilities and strategic views on competition of each member-state).[3] Unconditional mutual recognition is not an unrealistic option, as is illustrated by the 1988 draft of the Investment Services Directive on cross-border provision of investment services. The part of this draft directive that deals with stock exchanges combines an EC-wide authorization procedure for market access for investment firms based on mutual recognition with liberalized access to membership in stock exchanges for all EC firms—regardless of their home member-states and without imposing harmonized trading rules, specific market structures for stock exchanges, or transparency requirements (Steil 1996).

But the *final* texts of the directives are almost entirely the outcome of a pure negotiating process between member-states—without the guidance of cost-benefit analyses of the various options for relative doses of harmonization and mutual recognition. This negotiating process leads to a much less liberal approach: mutual recognition then becomes conditional on the adoption of a substantial core of essential requirements, to be embodied in common EC regulations negotiated by member-states.

In other words, the negotiating process has made the SMP a joint exercise about regulatory convergence more than about market access per se.

---

3. Fears that competing regulations would generate the risks of a "race to the bottom" are frequent, even among associations of consumers (despite the fact that they are the ultimate beneficiaries of more competitive regimes). These fears ignore that member-states are anxious about their "reputation," which induces them to design competitive regulations not detrimental to "quality," all the more because the more countries are integrated, the more powerful reputation effects can be. As for technical regulations (see chapter 4) on trade and labor (see below), strong reputation effects are the best guarantee against a race to the bottom, particularly in democratic, relatively "information-intensive" European societies.

For instance, in the example of the Investment Services Directive, half the member-states, led by France and Italy, have spent four years of negotiations "harmonizing" market structures of EC stock exchanges by loading the final text with the concept of "regulated markets." This concept essentially sought to restrict cross-border liberalization in stock exchanges, in an effort to contain the success of the London Stock Exchange Automated Quotation International (which did not fulfill the definition of a "regulated" market) which was launched by the 1986 "Big Bang" unilateral British regulatory reforms, and threatened the other EC financial markets in the late 1980s (Steil 1996, 1998).

In the line of the *Stichting Collectieve Antennevoorziening Gouda* ruling, the 1995 *Alpine Investment* ruling of the Court of Justice aimed to limit such a drift toward harmonization by stating (1) that the freedom to provide services under Article 49 (ex 59) precludes the application of any national legislation that has the effect of making the provision of services between member-states more difficult than the provision of services purely within one member-state; and (2) that the public interest that member-states could invoke to escape Article 49 (ex 59) must be "essential" (such as the need to protect the reputation of the whole domestic financial sector). The general conclusion of the *Gouda* ruling that "it must not be possible to obtain the same result by less restrictive rules" is the best definition of the optimal dose of harmonization and mutual recognition—but, clearly, member-state negotiators of the SMP in services have often ignored this Court criterion.

Regulatory convergence has an important corollary. By nature, it focuses on trade-offs between regulatory provisions *within* each service sector—a tendency facilitated by the majority voting procedure used for adopting the SMP. It has thus shaped the SMP on a sectoral basis, with little attention devoted to cross-sectoral trade-offs between the services involved. (By contrast, unconditional mutual recognition and liberalization would have tended to focus on trade-offs between concessions given in the various service sectors subject to negotiations.) That regulatory convergence and sectoral approach reinforce each other is an important point for understanding the EC approach in the coming WTO negotiations.

The motive behind the choice of regulatory convergence has been essentially political. Each member-state could then hope to insert parts of its own regulations into the common EC regulations in order to bend the latter as much as possible in its favor. This perspective has made the SMP more palatable to the majority of member-states, which in the late 1980s and early 1990s were still very reluctant to adopt market-oriented regulatory reform of services.[4]

---

4. Even Britain, the member-state most keen to liberalize, has been less adventurous about competition than about privatization, with its duopoly-based, "heavy-handed" approach to regulatory reform of services, in combination with large powers (including detailed price fixing) devolved to regulatory agencies (Vickers and Yarrow 1988; Stelzer 1991).

This political incentive was amplified by an economic consideration. In the late 1980s, many SMP services in member-states were characterized by large overcapacities in basic services after decades of public overinvestment in a context of controlled prices, massive subsidies, and public monopolies. For instance, in the early 2000s, the electricity sector has an estimated average overcapacity of 20 percent in almost all the EC countries (up to 30 percent in France); retail banking is still provided through vastly oversized networks of agencies; and the telecom networks of railways or public electricity monopolies are hugely oversized (in the mid-1990s, SNCF, the French railways company, was reportedly using only 10 percent of its own telecom network capacity). In such a context, many EC decision makers feared that liberalization could lead to a fast, rough shift from monopoly to competition: oversized electricity producers could almost instantly compete fiercely; railway or electricity monopolies could rapidly become major competitors of telecom monopolies; and so on.[5]

The short-term political benefits derived from regulatory convergence have generated long-term economic costs. First, regulatory competition has been limited to regulations *not* included in the common core, which, almost by nature, were of marginal importance. Second, and much more important, the EC common regulations have been loaded with notions (monetary policy, service of general interest, universal service), instruments (safeguards and other escape clauses), or procedures (progressive liberalization) that have allowed (and still do) strong, determined vested interests to limit or contain for years the *real* magnitude of liberalization.

In such an arcane and contradictory legal framework, SMP proliberalization provisions (such as the directives' repeated condition that prices should reflect costs) are often not powerful enough to allow the elimination of the antiliberalization provisions in a costless, swift, and secure process. Lawsuits become necessary, and because they could easily last a decade (especially if they require rulings from the Court of Justice), they induce complainants and defendants to settle their disputes at lower costs, that is, to negotiate collusive actions.

Examples of the negative impact of regulatory convergence on competition and liberalization abound. For instance, in telecoms, the "universal service" clause has been used as a severe barrier against entrants; requirements to be classified as an operator have often been (and still are) very costly; and the crucial "last-mile" liberalization (the unbundling of the local loop) will not be implemented before 2001 in several member-states, assuming no legal hurdles (see appendix A, case 22). In accounting,

5. In fact, competition would have required time. More electricity exports require more high-tension lines, telecom activities by railway companies require more expertise from telecom operators, etc. It is interesting to note that Britain has been one of the EC member-states least exposed to overcapacity. This factor has been a push for regulatory reform, but also the source of a costly focus on equipment, as is best illustrated by the telecom case (appendix A, case 22).

the Fourth and Seventh Company Law Directive provisions on harmonized requirements have been recognized by Commission officials themselves as having negative consequences for the comparability of accounts that they were supposed to enhance (Trachtman 1997). In audiovisuals, the Television Without Frontiers Directive has opened the door to subsidies that have *restricted* intra-EC trade in movies (see appendix A, case 20). In electricity, so many options for liberalization have been left to member-state discretionary decisions that they have ended up by favoring strong anticompetitive strategic behavior by large incumbent operators, such as Electricité de France.

The negative impact of regulatory convergence on competition can take time to emerge, as in the stock exchange case. During the 1990s, the above-mentioned "regulated market" provision of the investment service directives did not severely curb competition between EC exchanges, although they have generally refrained from directly competing with each other's products. In fact, major Continental exchanges reacted to the threat from the London Exchange by improving their efficiency through reliance on the huge liberalizing power of progress in information technology and its impact on new financial techniques—best illustrated by the envisaged London-Frankfurt merger, for which its leadership in trading and settlement technologies (the Xetra system) has given Frankfurt some leverage over the much more mature London Exchange. But technical progress may soon turn anticompetitive, with new techniques and concentration among EC stock exchanges generating serious risks to trigger the protectionist capacities of the regulated market clause (ESFRC 2000).

The SMP focus on regulatory convergence has had a last important consequence. It has required a long period—more than 15 years—to adopt the SMP initial regulations and to *begin* to implement them. First, it took eight years (1985–93) for the Commission and the Council to elaborate on and negotiate the 54 directives that constitute the *initial* SMP legal framework in services.[6] Second, "transposing" all these directives into member-state laws is also a long process, with a sizable proportion of directives not properly implemented. From 1997 to 1999, there were roughly 200 "reasoned opinions" (mirroring potential conflicts between the Commission and member-states) on the way directives were transposed in member-state laws and regulations, and the number of annual cases referred to the Court increased from 52 to 74 (European Commission 2000a).

As a result of these complications, in May 2000, almost one-fourth of the directives that should have been transposed by 1996 and 1997 had not yet been transposed; this proportion jumps to two-thirds for the directives that were to be transposed by 1998. Delays are concentrated in certain sec-

---

6. From 1993 to 1997, 36 additional directives for services were adopted. Energy is often associated with services; eight energy directives were adopted between 1985 and 1993, and seven more from 1993 to 1997.

tors: 4 directives out of 18 in telecoms and 32 directives out of 69 in transport were not yet transposed in all member-states. Delays are also concentrated in certain member-states: 17 telecom and transport directives were not yet transposed by Luxembourg and Portugal, 13 by Ireland, and 10 by France.

In sum, it is essential to avoid the confusion often made between the year of *adoption* of a directive and the year of its correct *implementation* in the whole Community. For instance, the last measures opening intra-member-state flights to EC carriers included in the 1992 Third Directive were implemented only in April 1997, 10 years after the adoption of the First Directive on air transport. The First Directive liberalizing basic telecommunications was adopted in 1988, but the first serious steps to open member-state markets occurred only in January 1998 (January 2000 for some states). The 1993 Council Regulation on "road cabotage" began to enter into force only in July 1998; until then, road carriers operated under a quota system.

The EC in Seattle: Regulatory Convergence and Sectoral Approach

The Seattle texts of the European institutions devote surprisingly little space to services; the topic ranks only fourth in commercial policy issues for the Commission and second for the Council (see table 5.1). The Parliament Resolution seems to reserve better treatment for this domain, but half of its section on services consists of statements limiting the scope of liberalization—from the need for subsidies for minority languages and cultures, to the introduction of notions such as "universal coverage" (universal service), to the complete exclusion of certain services (health, education, and culture) from WTO negotiations.

The EC's initial position in the coming round, as sketched in the Seattle Commission text, has been largely permeated by the SMP focus on regulatory convergence and its sectoral approach—despite the clearly manifested preference of the European business community for procompetitive regulations and a horizontal approach (European Services Forum 1999; Cooke 1999). The Seattle Commission text devotes more space to the need for regulatory disciplines than to the market-opening objective. It insists on the "development of a . . . domestic regulatory commitment justified on the basis of specific public policy objectives," and it aims at further market opening "coupled, where necessary, with regulatory disciplines"—two strong statements not really counterbalanced by a quick reference to the development of more procompetitive regulations "where appropriate."

Moreover, the Commission makes a minimal reference to the horizontal (that is, nonsectoral) approach, which is largely counterbalanced by the emphasis on the need to take into account the "sensitivities" of specific sectors, and by the explicit reference to the "infrastructure" dimension of services for developing countries. Since Seattle, most public statements by the Commission have confirmed this insistence on regulatory convergence as a prerequisite for market access with one recent exception (see the conclusion of this chapter).[7]

If maintained, the EC approach based on regulatory convergence may be a source of conflict between certain key WTO trade partners (which are unprepared to compromise their own legal framework, but willing to accept regulatory competition) and EC member-states (which are accustomed to constrain their sovereign rights through regulatory convergence, particularly if it helps to slow down liberalization and to get a politically acceptable pace of adjustment).

It is important to note that the EC sectoral focus opposes two layers of EC joint competence—and hence will also be a source of *intra-EC* conflicts: the layer of the SMP-covered services, where the Community has some preeminence; and the layer of the services left outside the SMP, where member-states have preeminence and could use Article 53 (ex 64) as a safeguard clause (see above), particularly if they feel that the Commission or some member-states are using WTO negotiations to press for *intra-EC* liberalization. Coalition and coordination problems will not be minor for the EC, because the second layer of services consists of large, essential sectors (business services, construction, hospital services, retail and wholesale trade, tourism, etc.)—some of which have already attracted a lot of attention in the WTO forum, and which are politically very sensitive (some others have been explicitly excluded by the Nice Treaty from the majority rule).

Electronic commerce (hereafter e-commerce) offers a quintessential illustration of all the past, present, and future difficulties. This sector was not included in the initial list of SMP activities; in the Europe of the late 1980s and early 1990s, computers were yet too few and telecom prices too high to allow the Community to perceive the potential importance of this new technology. (At this time, the French Minitel experience had already reached its limits because of its hardware rigidity, its software deficiency, and its distorted price structure.) The Commission started to draft the e-commerce directive only in mid-1997. It tabled its final draft in late 1998, after many difficulties in making the new directive "consistent" with all the related "information society" directives on conditional access, distance selling, distance marketing of financial services, data protection, database transparency, etc.—revealing the complexity of injecting a new sector into the already tight web of SMP regulations inherited from 12 years of regulatory convergence.

---

7. See http://europa.eu.int/comm/trade/2000_round/seaserv.htm, April 2000, with the following excerpt: "Looking at individual sectors, the need for regulatory disciplines to underpin market access and national treatment appears increasingly important, and also includes the question of pro-competitive principles."

The draft directive was adopted by the Council in February 2000 and by the Parliament in May 2000. It is thus *expected* to become member-state law by the end of 2002—with the usual caveat about the long delays for transposing directives into member-state laws, a caveat amplified by the fact that by May 2000, none of the above directives closely related to e-commerce had been adopted by *all* the member-states, although most of them had been adopted at the Community level between 1995 and 1998.

Meanwhile, e-commerce has been emerging as a fascinating example of endless intra-EC and extra-EC barriers. For instance, German laws on promotional selling (Zugabeverordnung and Rabattgesetz, adopted in the 1930s, which prohibit—in conjunction with a main product to be sold—offering an additional product, because it would be an "unfair" gift) have been invoked to ban an unconditional guarantee for return of products sold through the Internet on the grounds that such a guarantee is a gift.[8] Another German law, which requires auctioneers to obtain a permit for each auction and to make a public exhibition of goods on the block, has been invoked in order to stop auctions on Internet sites.

In several member-states, publishers can dictate prices to bookshops on the ground and to domestic online ones, because of either a minimum retail price law, as in France, or a private sectoral agreement, as in Germany. These rules have a strong anticompetitive impact. They have forced domestic online bookshops to have several addresses in the EC (the same book in German can be 40 percent cheaper at the British address than at the German address of the same online bookshop). They also have induced Austrian online booksellers to supply discounted books in Germany (and similarly for Belgian booksellers in France). Reactions by vested interests have been swift: threats of retaliation by German publishers forcing Austrian online booksellers to come back to German prices (and triggering investigations by the EC competition authorities on private obstacles to intra-EC trade), and political pressure to impose minimum retail price laws in Austria and Belgium.

Despite this host of internal problems, the EC has not hesitated to push for regulatory convergence in e-commerce in international forums, and its call for new "competitive" rules for Internet service providers has made many corporate leaders in OECD countries nervous.[9] The currently most worrisome aspect of emerging EC policy on e-commerce is the classifica-

8. In July 1999, the Commission decided to refer Germany to the Court of Justice about this legislation, on the basis that it violates Article 49 (ex 59), and in April 2000, the company involved (Lands' End, a United States-based mail-order retailer) also lodged a complaint.

9. The Internet tends to challenge the creative capacities of regulators. It is often said to require new regulations in terms of taxation, tariffs, intellectual property rights, etc. (although, as recently suggested by the French Conseil d'Etat, such new regulations are not needed). Having Internet-specific regulations will run the risk of being self-destructive from a legal perspective. What may be needed are simply appropriate mechanisms to enforce the existing regulations affecting e-commerce transactions.

tion of transactions. Are movies (or music, software, stock exchange services, legal advice, etc.) that are sold through e-commerce goods or services? In a recent note,[10] the Commission has suggested rules that, if adopted by the WTO, would freeze protection at its highest current level, as is best illustrated by the movie case. The first option for buying a movie online is to order a cassette on the Internet and to get it physically delivered. According to the Commission, this option is to be decomposed into four different components: a good (the cassette), an Internet access service (the Internet gate), a telecom service (the telecom firm), and a distribution service (the online seller). The purchase of a movie cassette through e-commerce should thus comply with the combined commitments of the importing country on trade in cassettes (tariff), on the Internet, on telecoms, and on distribution services—hence, it will be limited by the *most* restrictive of all these commitments.

The second option for buying a movie considered by the Commission is the delivery of the movie in electronic form by downloading the film electronically under a pay-per-view regime. According to the Commission, the rules to be applied in this case should be those related to the content itself (in this example, the EC commitments in audiovisual services), not those related to the means of transmission (telecoms) nor to the good (the movie cassette). Clearly, such a rule would freeze at its highest current level the protection of the many services to be delivered through the Internet.[11] In other words, the current EC proposal wipes out the intrinsic e-commerce capacity to reduce the existing level of protection by its *mere* use (without the need for new negotiations).

By contrast (and contrary to its usual approach, which is to consider the SMP as a model for the WTO), the EC has not suggested importing into the WTO a very desirable feature of the SMP—namely, its ability to progressively focus on two modes of supply, cross-border and establishment. For instance, in the e-commerce case, it will be very difficult to allocate many transactions between cross-border trade and consumption abroad so that merging these two modes would constitute substantial progress for WTO negotiations in services (there would be no need for distinct, possibly inconsistent, commitments) and for a straight enforcement of market-access commitments.

To summarize, the Seattle Commission text suggests that the SMP may have already put serious constraints on the EC's approach in future WTO

---

10. See http://europa.eu.int/comm/trade/services/ecommerce/ecom2.htm, March 1999.

11. The Commission text raises two problems of logic. Why are imported recorded cassettes not subject today to service commitments? How would the electronic equivalent of buying a cassette (i.e., downloading the movie for a full purchase, instead of a pay-per-view) be treated? The logic of the Commission text (no difference because of different supports) suggests that the two purchases should be treated equivalently, i.e., they should be subject to the same tariff.

negotiations on services. One could argue that the 1997 WTO agreements on financial services and telecoms (for the success of which the EC has been instrumental) contradicts this conclusion. However, such a comparison is not so relevant, because these two agreements consist mostly of standstill provisions. In fact, there could be a much better argument for supporting the possibility of a positive EC role in the WTO negotiations in services: it is that the SMP has delivered an incomplete, reversible intra-EC liberalization, and that completing the SMP could be best achieved by WTO liberalization.

Intra-EC Liberalization in Services: Incomplete and Reversible

Its focus on regulatory convergence has made the SMP so far unable to deliver a full and irreversible *internal* liberalization in services. In this respect, the SMP differs considerably from the Common Market in industrial goods, which has delivered much faster a much more complete, irreversible internal liberalization: *complete* because most intra-EC border barriers have been removed (see chapter 2); irreversible because member-states could not easily substitute new barriers for old ones (the intra-EC safeguard clause, Article 134 (ex 115), was tightly enforced by the Commission, which also monitored, though less strictly, technical barriers to trade—see chapter 4—and, even less strictly, subsidies, as shown below). What follows presents the main reasons for such an assessment, which is confirmed by the systematic empirical research summarized in box 5.2 and table 5.2.

In fact, the SMP in services has witnessed an irreversible liberalization only when technical progress has been a powerful procompetitive force—with, indeed, technical progress having been sometimes accelerated by the hopeless slowness of regulatory reforms in substitutable services, as best illustrated by mobile telephony, which has been all the more attractive because hopes of fast EC regulatory reforms in wired telephony have faded—and these procompetitive forces have had important spillovers on closely related services, from capital markets to distribution services.

Technical progress, however, is far from having always been a procompetitive force. For instance, the same huge progress in information technology has allowed airlines to improve their ability to design discriminatory prices in their protected markets more rapidly than it has allowed travelers to improve their ability to shop for cheaper prices—eroding severely the procompetitive potential of the "three packages" SMP in this sector (see appendix A, case 21).

Leaving aside the liberalization impact of technical progress, the SMP has had three basic kinds of very mixed results. First, the SMP has remained *incomplete*. Table 5.3 shows how many highly restrictive measures of protection have survived in every service covered by the SMP. Fiscal

Box 5.2 The Single Market in services: Still to come

Recent research from the OECD Secretariat (Nicoletti 2000) allows a more quantitative assessment of how deeply the Single Market Program (SMP) has really bitten so far. On the basis of an international database on the regulations enforced in OECD countries (Nicoletti, Scarpetta, and Boylaud 2000), it provides indicators—from least (0) to most (6) restrictive—of the regulatory and market environment in 1998. Of course, such an exercise faces limits. Incomplete and imperfect information is a pervasive problem, and assessing the effect of regulations on the degree of competition is a matter of delicate judgment. However, statistical techniques (factor and cluster analyses) allow interesting comparisons between countries from this (admittedly imperfect) large set of information.

As shown in table 5.2, the seven services examined by the OECD research make it possible to account for the complexity of the SMP process: Two services (air passenger and road freight) were included early in the SMP (late 1980s); two others (mobile and fixed telephony) were incorporated late in the SMP (early 1990s); two others (electricity and railways) were covered by SMP extensions (mid- to late 1990s). Retail distribution is not part of the SMP.

Table 5.2 provides three major lessons. First, the EC does not appear, on average, more open than the rest of the OECD countries (defined as the OECD countries not pertaining and not candidate to the EC) in all these sectors. Second, the indicators for the various EC member-states do not show the similarity that would reveal a strong impact of the SMP; certain member-states are still among the most open markets in the OECD region, whereas others are still among the most closed ones. Third, these results are observed whether examined services have been subjected to the SMP or not, for a long time or not.

Table 5.2 shows that the countries that are candidates for accession to the EC will have to make huge efforts toward regulatory reforms of services. All these observations confirm the view presented in the main text, according to which the impact of the SMP is so far very limited—hence the large potential benefits that the EC could get from a WTO liberalization of services. Indeed, the fact that EC member-states exhibit an average (of the seven sectors) indicator more restrictive than the indicator of the rest of the OECD countries (last column on the right) suggests that the EC may gain more from a new round than most of its OECD partners.

The OECD studies provide additional results in three services for which it has been possible to generate an external liberalization element. In air and road transport, barriers to entry have been split into a component of public intervention in domestic markets and an element of discrimination against foreign providers. The EC exhibits a smaller indicator for foreign discrimination than the rest of the OECD countries only in air transport. However, this result (which mirrors SMP-related legal aspects, e.g., the definition of what an EC carrier is; see appendix A, case 21) is more than compensated for by a higher indicator for domestic entry barriers.

In telecoms, estimated price deviations from the OECD average have been decomposed for each country into several components, including a foreign discrimination element. This exercise presents the EC member-states as on average more homogeneous than suggested by table 5.2, and as less expensive than the rest of the OECD countries. However, this result is not related to the liberalization component but to an element (the country economic structure) that captures, among other factors, the impact of technology—echoing what is said in the main text on the role of technical progress in the SMP's apparent successes.

Table 5.2 Regulatory and market environment in 1998 (the scale of indicators is 0–6, from least to most restrictive)

	Air passenger transport			Road freight			Mobile telephony		
	Overall indicator for the sector	Market structure indicator	Barriers to entry indicator	Overall indicator for the sector	Market structure indicator	Barriers to entry indicator	Overall indicator for the sector	Market structure indicator	Barriers to entry indicator
European Community									
Austria	3.2	3.4	3.1	2.8	2.7	2.8	3.5	4.0	3.0
Belgium	4.4	5.5	3.3	3.2	3.0	3.3	3.8	4.5	3.0
Britain	2.2	1.1	3.3	1.3	2.4	0.6	0.0	0.0	0.0
Denmark	4.7	5.8	3.6	n.a.	n.a.	n.a.	3.4	3.9	3.0
Finland	3.6	3.4	3.8	1.7	3.6	0.6	2.3	4.6	0.0
France	3.2	2.3	4.1	2.5	2.2	2.6	0.8	1.7	0.0
Germany	3.0	2.6	3.4	3.0	2.7	3.2	3.2	3.5	3.0
Greece	5.5	5.8	5.1	3.6	4.0	3.4	2.4	1.7	3.0
Ireland	4.4	5.6	3.1	n.a.	n.a.	n.a.	3.7	4.4	3.0
Italy	3.3	2.8	3.8	4.6	4.1	4.9	2.2	4.5	0.0
Netherlands	2.7	2.8	2.6	2.4	n.a.	n.a.	2.2	4.4	0.0
Portugal	5.1	5.1	5.1	2.3	2.1	2.4	3.4	3.7	3.0
Spain	2.9	1.9	3.9	3.0	2.3	3.4	4.6	4.6	4.5
Sweden	3.3	3.2	3.4	2.2	2.6	2.0	1.8	3.7	0.0
Candidate countries									
Czech Republic	5.8	6.0	5.5	3.0	3.0	3.1	4.6	4.7	4.5
Hungary	n.a.	n.a.	n.a.	3.4	3.5	3.3	4.3	4.0	4.5
Poland	6.0	6.0	6.0	2.7	2.0	3.1	n.a.	n.a.	n.a.
Turkey	6.0	5.9	6.0	2.7	n.a.	n.a.	3.9	4.9	3.0
Rest of the OECD									
Australia	3.3	3.1	3.5	0.8	n.a.	n.a.	0.9	1.8	0.0
Canada	3.6	3.1	4.1	2.0	2.6	1.6	n.a.	n.a.	n.a.
Japan	3.1	1.5	4.7	2.1	n.a.	n.a.	0.4	0.8	0.0
Korea	3.8	3.2	4.4	1.1	0.5	1.4	1.6	3.1	0.0
Mexico	3.5	2.3	4.7	2.2	1.6	2.6	2.5	2.0	3.0
New Zealand	3.7	5.2	2.2	1.3	2.4	0.6	2.6	5.2	0.0
Norway	2.9	2.6	3.1	2.2	2.9	1.8	3.9	4.9	3.0
Switzerland	4.6	4.1	5.1	3.8	n.a.	n.a.	4.5	6.0	3.0
United States	1.2	0.4	2.0	1.5	1.5	1.5	n.a.	n.a.	n.a.
Averages									
European Community	3.7	3.6	3.7	2.7	2.9	2.7	2.7	3.5	1.8
Rest of the OECD	3.3	2.8	3.8	1.9	1.9	1.6	2.3	3.4	1.3
Candidates	5.9	6.0	5.8	2.9	2.8	3.2	4.3	4.5	4.0
Minima									
European Community	2.2	1.1	2.6	1.3	2.1	0.6	0.0	0.0	0.0
Rest of the OECD	1.2	0.4	2.0	0.8	0.5	0.6	0.4	0.8	0.0
Maxima									
European Community	5.5	5.8	5.1	4.6	4.1	4.9	4.6	4.6	4.5
Rest of the OECD	4.6	5.2	5.1	3.8	2.9	2.6	4.5	6.0	3.0

n.a. = not available

OECD = Organization for Economic Cooperation and Development.

Note: Figures in italics are simple averages of minimum and maximum indicators.

Sources: Boylaud (2000), Boylaud and Nicoletti (2000), Gonenc and Nicoletti (2000), Gonenc, Maher, and Nicoletti (2000), Steiner (2000).

barriers in financial services, slot allocations in air transport, unconditional access to networks in telecoms, and quotas and licensing rules in audiovisuals, untouched in 1997, were still there in mid-2000, almost unchanged—although they may have taken different technical forms, such

Fixed telephony			Electricity			Railways			Retail distribution			Average by country
Overall indicator for the sector	Market structure indicator	Barriers to entry indicator	Overall indicator for the sector	Market structure indicator	Barriers to entry indicator	Overall indicator for the sector	Market structure indicator	Barriers to entry indicator	Overall indicator for the sector	Market structure indicator	Barriers to entry indicator	Simple averages of sectoral overall indicators by country
3.0	6.0	0.0	n.a.	n.a.	n.a.	n.a.	n.a.	n.a.	4.1	3.0	5.5	3.3
3.0	6.0	0.0	5.5	6.0	5.0	6.0	6.0	6.0	3.1	3.6	2.3	4.1
1.0	2.0	0.0	0.0	0.0	0.0	3.0	3.0	3.0	2.5	2.8	2.1	1.4
2.2	4.4	0.0	5.0	6.0	4.0	n.a.	n.a.	n.a.	2.9	n.a.	n.a.	3.6
0.4	0.9	0.0	0.0	0.0	0.0	6.0	6.0	6.0	3.0	2.9	3.0	2.4
3.0	6.0	0.0	6.0	6.0	6.0	6.0	6.0	6.0	4.7	4.5	5.0	3.7
3.0	6.0	0.0	2.1	1.5	2.7	3.0	6.0	0.0	1.2	1.3	1.2	2.6
6.0	6.0	6.0	6.0	6.0	6.0	n.a.	n.a.	n.a.	3.8	n.a.	n.a.	4.5
2.8	5.5	0.0	4.5	3.0	6.0	6.0	6.0	6.0	1.4	1.6	1.0	3.8
3.0	6.0	0.0	6.0	6.0	6.0	6.0	6.0	6.0	3.1	3.3	2.8	4.0
2.9	5.7	0.0	5.3	4.5	6.0	n.a.	n.a.	n.a.	1.4	1.8	0.8	2.8
6.0	6.0	6.0	4.2	3.0	5.3	n.a.	n.a.	n.a.	2.6	2.5	2.8	3.9
3.0	6.0	0.0	3.8	3.0	4.7	4.5	3.0	6.0	2.5	2.8	2.0	3.5
1.7	3.4	0.0	0.8	1.5	0.0	3.0	3.0	3.0	1.7	1.7	1.6	2.1
6.0	6.0	6.0	n.a.	n.a.	n.a.	1.5	3.0	0.0	0.8	0.6	1.1	3.6
6.0	6.0	6.0	n.a.	n.a.	n.a.	3.0	6.0	0.0	1.9	1.5	2.4	3.7
6.0	6.0	6.0	n.a.	n.a.	n.a.	1.5	3.0	0.0	3.6	2.3	5.3	3.9
6.0	6.0	6.0	n.a.	n.a.	n.a.	6.0	6.0	6.0	3.0	n.a.	n.a.	4.6
1.3	2.6	0.0	0.9	1.5	0.3	n.a.	n.a.	n.a.	1.1	1.4	0.7	1.4
0.8	1.6	0.0	6.0	6.0	6.0	3.0	3.0	3.0	1.3	1.7	0.6	2.8
1.1	2.2	0.0	5.0	6.0	4.0	3.0	3.0	3.0	4.1	n.a.	n.a.	2.7
1.9	3.8	0.0	n.a.	n.a.	n.a.	6.0	6.0	6.0	1.3	0.9	1.9	2.6
1.7	3.3	0.0	n.a.	n.a.	n.a.	4.5	3.0	6.0	1.9	2.0	1.7	2.7
1.4	2.8	0.0	0.0	0.0	0.0	n.a.	n.a.	n.a.	n.a.	n.a.	n.a.	1.8
3.0	6.0	0.0	0.0	0.0	0.0	4.5	3.0	6.0	2.2	3.0	1.1	2.7
3.0	6.0	0.0	n.a.	n.a.	n.a.	6.0	6.0	6.0	1.1	1.2	1.0	3.8
0.3	0.5	0.0	4.3	4.5	4.0	1.5	3.0	0.0	n.a.	n.a.	n.a.	1.7
2.9	5.0	0.9	3.8	3.6	4.0	4.8	5.0	4.7	2.7	2.7	2.5	3.3
1.6	3.2	0.0	2.7	3.0	2.4	4.1	3.9	4.3	1.9	1.7	1.2	2.5
6.0	6.0	6.0	n.a.	n.a.	n.a.	3.0	4.5	1.5	2.3	1.5	3.0	4.1
0.4	0.9	0.0	0.0	0.0	0.0	3.0	3.0	0.0	1.2	1.3	0.8	1.2
0.3	0.5	0.0	0.0	0.0	0.0	1.5	3.0	0.0	1.1	0.9	0.6	0.7
6.0	6.0	6.0	6.0	6.0	6.0	6.0	6.0	6.0	4.7	4.5	5.5	5.3
3.0	6.0	0.0	6.0	6.0	6.0	6.0	6.0	6.0	4.1	3.0	1.9	4.6

as the bundling of access in telecoms with specific conditions on mobile or Internet services.

The costs of the EC nonuniform approach to service liberalization have begun to emerge. The many severe entry barriers in sectors not covered by the SMP have reduced the scope and benefits to be expected from liberalization in the sectors that are covered by the SMP. For instance,

Table 5.3 Removing barriers in the Single Market: The situation in 1997

Service	Cross-border service restrictions	Restrictions on establishment	Restrictions on factor flows	Regulatory and technical barriers	Fiscal barriers	Other barriers
Banking	✓✓Discriminatory conditions for cross-border sale of services ✓Restrictions on market-ing and service content	✓✓Discriminatory conditions for licenses	✓✓Capital controls	✓Prudential requirements ✓Consumer protection	✗Tax on savings ✗Investment income tax ✗Death duties	
Insurance	✓✓Discriminatory conditions for cross-border sale of services ✓Restrictions on market-ing and service content ✗Single license for brokers	✓✓Discriminatory conditions for licenses	✓✓Capital controls	✓Consumer protection conditions for sales	✗Taxation of reserves ✗Taxation of premiums	
Road freight transport	✓✓Bilateral quota restric-tions on access to other EC markets ✓✓Price restrictions	✓✓Discriminatory licensing conditions	✓Cabotage restrictions ✓✓Recognition of diplomas	✓✓Weights and dimensions ✓Road safety rules ✓Speed limiters ✓Resting hours	✓✓Excise duties	✓✓Border formalities for goods
Air transport	✓✓Bilateral restrictions on free access to other EC markets ✓✓Price restrictions ✗Slots allocation	✓✓Exclusive rights for licensing of air carriers ✗Ownership rules in third-country bilateral agreements	✓Cabotage restrictions ✓✓Designation and capacity restrictions	✓✓Conditions for sales ✓Security and safety rules ✗Airport charges	✓Value-added tax	✓Border formalities for passengers ✓✓Access to computer reservation systems ✓State aid, unfair practices

Telecom liberalized services	✓Discriminatory conditions for access to network	✓✓Exclusive rights on mobile, data, and satellite services	✓✓Exclusive rights to sell equipment	✓Technical conditions for use of networks	✗Fair access to networks
Television broadcasting services	✓✓Restrictions on cross-frontier broadcasting; ✓Rental and lending rights; ✓Term of copyright protection; ✓Copyright applicable to satellite and cable	✗National licensing rules for broadcasters; ✗Media ownership restrictions; ✗National quotas on programs		✓Technical conditions for use of networks	✓✓Border formalities for goods; ✓Technical barriers on products
Distribution (fast-moving consumer goods)	No restrictions	No restrictions	✓✓Restrictions on free movement of goods	✓Value-added tax	✓✓Border formalities for goods
Advertising	✗Types of products and media; ✗Comparative advertising	No restrictions	✓Restrictions on media	✓Misleading advertising; ✗Content restrictions	

✓✓ Barriers effectively removed.
✓ Barriers partially removed.
✗ Remaining barriers.

Source: European Commission (1996).

restricted entry in retail permits member-state markets of goods to be more segmented than they would be with more competition among retailers, and it has a similar, probably stronger, impact in services, such as banking or transport services; the absence of competition between travel agencies from different member-states contributes to market segmentation and limited competition in air transport; a similar observation can be made about hospital service providers and pharmaceutical markets.

Second, the SMP's implementation has witnessed a *partial reversal* of the liberalization process because of three major forces not observed (at least, to such an extent) in the case of the Common Market in manufactured goods. The first force is that subsidies have been and still are substantial in services (see table 5.4, despite the fact that they are probably recorded with less accuracy), and more frequently granted to public monopolies or firms with "special" rights, as is best illustrated by the €3.3 billion subsidy to Air France (see appendix A, case 21), the €3 billion subsidy to Westdeutsche LandesBank (WestLB)—and, last but not least, the (at least) €20 billion state aid to Crédit Lyonnais, the largest subsidy ever granted to one firm in the EC (alone, it is equivalent to two-thirds of all the state aid granted to the entire EC steel industry during the peak crisis years 1980–85).[12] Moreover, the devolution of the antisubsidy policy in service sectors to the Directorates General in charge of the services involved (in sharp contrast with the antisubsidy policy for goods, which is handled only by the Directorate for Competition) has severely amplified the problems of subsidy monitoring (see the section below on competition policy).

The second force leading to reversals of liberalization is that member-states have been quick to adopt new protectionist measures, often relying on the ambiguities entrenched in the EC directives by the process of regulatory convergence. For instance, joint pressures by governments and competitors have curbed entrant efforts to offer new services (current accounts bearing interest in France, units of closed-end investment funds in Germany) or they have denied access to essential facilities during strategic periods (slots in airports, access to networks, etc.).

The use, or threat of use, of taxes has been another way to deter entrance. Tax equivalents on new entrants have been imposed through extensive interpretations of the "universal service" notion in telecoms (in France, imposing a tax of roughly €665 million in 1998, €435 million

---

12. Assessing the effective impact of these subsidies is difficult because service sectors are also riddled with taxes of all kinds (e.g., certain European airlines might have been indirectly taxed through the obligation to buy Airbus aircraft at prices that reportedly have been higher than prices paid by non-EC airlines). Unfortunately, there is no study giving a sense of the corresponding effective rates of protection.

Table 5.4 Annual average national and EC subsidies, 1990–98

	1990–92	1992–94	1993–95	1995–98
National state aid				
(in millions of euros)[a]				
Agriculture	n.a.	n.a.	10,772	13,339
Fisheries	320	356	333	260
Coal mining	14,773	13,792	11,487	7,227
Manufacturing	39,784	41,439	42,882	32,639
Transport	n.a.	32,375	34,843	32,193
Financial services	n.a.	n.a.	1,147	3,283
Total[b]	n.a.	97,962	10,1464	93,127
EC subsidies				
(in millions of euros)[a]				
Agriculture	32,362	36,212	37,382	43,631
Fisheries	320	417	442	486
Social fund	4,728	6,009	5,151	7,846
Regional fund[c]	1,101	2,743	3,631	5,168
Research and development	1,853	2,168	2,366	3,379
Steel grants	459	465	398	179
Total	40,823	48,014	49,369	60,688
National and EC subsidies				
(in millions of euros)				
Total	n.a.	145,976	150,833	153,815
State aid to manufacturing sector				
(in percent of value-added)				
Austria	—	—	—	1.4
Belgium	7.9	4.8	2.5	1.9
Britain	1.4	0.8	0.8	0.7
Denmark	1.9	2.8	2.7	2.9
Finland	—	—	—	1.6
France	2.7	3.3	2.1	2.0
Germany	3.5	4.8	4.4	2.6
Greece	12.5	10.5	5.2	4.9
Ireland	2.7	3.5	2.4	1.9
Italy	8.9	8.4	6.1	4.4
Luxembourg	3.5	2.9	2.2	2.3
Netherlands	2.5	2.1	1.1	1.1
Portugal	4.6	4.4	2.7	1.0
Spain	2.1	1.7	2.1	2.1
Sweden	—	—	—	0.8
EC[b]	3.8	4.0	3.5	2.3

n.a. = not available
EC = European Community.

a. For EC-12 for the period 1990–95, EC-15 for 1995–98.
b. The total includes a series of small subsidies not reported.
c. Includes the Cohesion Fund after 1993.

Sources: European Commission, Surveys on State Aids, various issues.

in 1999, and €427 million in 2000),[13] or of the "general interest" notion in certain financial services (European Commission 1999f). Income tax advantages granted to certain insurance contracts in 1998 (France) or available to issuers whose securities are quoted for the first time on regulated markets (Italy) favored domestic stock markets over competitors. And Belgian local taxes imposed on satellite dishes on alleged aesthetic grounds (mostly in the Wallonia region) have severely limited entry of audiovisual service providers willing to compete with incumbent TV networks.

Last but not least, the third force leading to reversals of liberalization is that private barriers have also been rapidly erected by incumbents immersed in the collusive mentality prevailing in Europe (Amatori 1999). For instance, European banks have been found to charge fees of on average 17 percent on small-value cross-border transfers in euros (domestic transfers are charged an average 1 percent fee)—inhibiting the deepening of the euro market.[14] There is little doubt that route sharing in air transport allows further restriction of arbitrage between markets and amplifies price discrimination, to the detriment of travelers.

The impact of all these public and private barriers has been amplified by the SMP focus on "commercial presence"—and its correlative neglect of "cross-border" trade. The so-called EC passport (the possibility for a firm to operate in other EC countries from its home member-state) has been shown to not be enough to get rid of markets still segmented by border barriers. Indeed, direct investment has been seen by many incumbents as having the capacity to raise rivals' costs more (or more easily) than cross-border trade. This implicit anticompetitive feature of commercial presence may explain the strong support that it has received from European incumbent service providers (often among the largest firms in the early 1990s) during the drafting of the SMP directives in services.[15]

---

13. See Autorité de Régulation des Télécommunications, http://www.art-telecom.fr

14. See http://europa.eu.int/comm/internal_market/en/finances/payment/2k-505.htm. Such fees also violate the ban on double charging imposed by the Cross-frontier Transfer Directive.

15. The crucial balance between commercial presence and cross-border trade is best illustrated by the retail industry. In the 1970s and early 1980s, most EC member-states adopted regulations limiting the creation of large stores and the legal range of shop opening hours. These regulations had nothing to do with international competition (then almost nonexistent). They intended to face a purely domestic issue: to protect small domestic "mom-and-pop" shops against large domestic firms, with no discriminatory intent against foreign firms. Twenty years later, these regulations have deeply distorted the prices of commercial land, as much as the Common Agricultural Policy has distorted the prices of farmland. Eliminating such regulations will not eliminate land price distortions in one magical stroke, nor the existing geographical misallocation of large stores (with overcapacities in some regions, cities, or even urban districts), which has been one of the many perverse consequences of protecting small shops. Under such conditions, competing through commercial presence requires large investments and a long-term strategy. For example, the largest US retailer, Wal-Mart, had to pay €10 billion to buy the British supermarket chain Asda in early 1999

The third and final mixed result of the SMP is that Community initiatives for harmonization, such as new EC-wide taxes, have also contributed to the reversal of the liberalization process by reducing or eliminating its expected benefits. For instance, environmental and other taxes have been part of the harmonization package in road transport. The swift imposition of these taxes during the SMP liberalization process in road transport has transformed the estimated 4 percent cost decrease due to liberalization measures into an estimated 4 percent cost increase—generating wide differences between EC member-states, because costs have been estimated to increase by more than 7 percent in Spain, but by less than 3 percent in Denmark and Germany (*Single Market Review* 1997b).

It is sometimes argued that dealing with such barriers could be done through competition cases, but this is a slow and uncertain process, particularly if it requires going to the Court of Justice. Moreover, lawsuits can also be launched by incumbents in their own member-state, in order to slow down the liberalization process—a tactic particularly successful when the breakup of the former monopoly was not guaranteed by clear enough rules, when the new regulators were insufficiently separated from incumbents, or when old laws imposed insurmountable constraints on new technologies (see the e-commerce discussion above).

The SMP in Services Needs WTO Liberalization

As is well known, country schedules of General Agreement on Trade in Services (GATS) commitments do not provide good information on external barriers in services. For instance, the EC GATS schedule does not mention large-store or opening-hours regulations as barriers to retail trade. Ironically, the dispute settlement case on bananas was lost by the EC partly because there was no EC reservation on wholesale trade that could have been used as a legal basis for the banana distribution quotas. However, one can reasonably assume that these barriers are still high, as is suggested by the crude sectoral estimates provided in chapter 2, and indirectly confirmed by the studies summarized in box 5.2.

---

and become a sizable player in Britain able to launch a significant price war. By contrast, despite its €1.7 billion purchase of a large German retail firm (Wertkauf), Wal-Mart is not expected to become a sizable player in the German retail industry for a decade (Deutsche Morgan Grenfell 1998), all the more because another large European retailer (Metro) reacted immediately to Wal-Mart's entry by purchasing another large German retailer, leaving Wal-Mart with very few additional possible purchases. It is interesting to note that, in September 2000, the German Federal Cartel Office accused Wal-Mart of inciting a price war in which it (and two German supermarket chains) had illegally sold products at below their wholesale costs. Following this relatively unusual accusation of "unfair" tactics, the Cartel Office ordered the three retailers to raise their prices on a series of products such as milk, flour, butter, rice, and cooking oil ("Germany Tells Wal-Mart to Raise the Price of Food," *International Herald Tribune*, 9 September 2000, 11).

This conclusion strongly suggests that the SMP would greatly benefit from WTO negotiations in services. In fact, this has already been modestly the case; the 1997 WTO Telecom Agreement has helped the EC to eliminate or reduce transitory periods that the least-developed EC member-states were able to extract during the negotiations on the intra-EC SMP in basic telephony.

Despite the large benefits that the SMP could get from the new WTO round, the EC could be reluctant to enter into rapid negotiations because it would be under the pressure of the following argument: during the past decade, EC firms in services have appeared increasingly small in comparison with their foreign (particularly US) competitors. The diminishing relative size of EC firms would make them less and less able to benefit from scale or scope economies, to innovate at the level required by competition, or to spread risks over a large enough portfolio of activities. As a result, EC vested interests may argue for a need for "consolidation" at the European level *before* opening EC markets to foreign competition. Before the Tokyo Round, this argument was made, with some success, for the manufacturing sector (Servan-Schreiber 1967), and it could be reused—despite the fact that the experience of the Common Market in goods suggests that intra-EC mergers and acquisitions (M&As) are not the necessary intermediate step before worldwide M&As—rather, it suggests that EC firms following a well-conceived worldwide strategy become, *on the top of it*, large EC firms.

The strength of this argument will depend on the evolution of the M&As involving European firms during the coming decade. Many EC service providers were small in the 1980s because they were often operating in segmented member-state markets. Firms based in large EC economies, however, could still be relatively large, particularly if they were monopolies or duopolies. But from the mid-1980s to the late 1990s things dramatically changed in many service sectors. US M&As have generally covered the entire US market. By contrast, European M&As have been largely limited to *intra-member-state* operations; more than 70 percent of the M&As between 1990 and 1995 were still intra-member-state operations (roughly the same level as during the period 1986–90), whereas *intra-EC* M&As increased only from 16 to 19 percent (Buigues and Sapir 1999).[16]

It may be argued that this evolution is not surprising because during this time, the SMP was only in its drafting period. Moreover, intra-EC M&As in SMP sectors have been almost openly discouraged by member-states (e.g., the first merger between a French bank and an EC bank was announced in April 2000, and it involved Crédit Commercial de France, which is only the seventh largest French bank) when they have not been inhibited systematically by tax regimes (as is best illustrated by the Ger-

---

16. It is interesting to note that member-state-based M&As tend to increase the risks and costs of asymmetrical shocks under monetary union for these implicit "national" champions.

man 50 percent tax on capital gains, which makes it very expensive for German banks or insurance companies to streamline their portfolios). Governmental disincentives, combined with the collusive mentality still largely prevailing in the Europe of the 1990s and weak anticartel enforcement in Europe (see below), have led EC firms from different member-states to form "alliances" aimed at consolidating national market shares. But such alliances have rapidly shown their limits, particularly their intrinsic instability (as is best illustrated by the many failed attempts to build such alliances in the audiovisual sector; see appendix A, case 22).

However, in 1999, with the first signs in 1997–98, things may have begun to change. The value of European M&As in 1999 was estimated to be $1,500 billion (three times the 1997 value); large deals (of more than $10 billion) represented roughly $700 billion (seven times the 1997 amount), and there were 393 hostile bids (compared with 7 in 1997) (JP Morgan, as reported in *The Economist*, 29 April 2000, Survey, 10). However, the list of motives behind these deals ranks technical progress first (most of these deals were done in sectors under strong technological pressures, as in telecoms) ranks the emergence of the euro (more precisely, its microeconomic impact at the level of competitive pressures in EC markets) second, ranks the privatization process third, and ranks the SMP process *fourth* and last.

Before being qualified as landmark progress, the 1997–99 evolution in European M&As raises four questions. First, will it continue, or will member-states renew their efforts to tilt it toward "national" champions? Second, will firms continue to use M&As more as a consolidation process in their domestic markets than as an instrument for access to new markets? Third, will European M&As be less successful than US M&As because they must face an environment more hostile to changes in labor and capital markets (as is illustrated by the painful reengineering of Hoechst)? And fourth, what will the impact of M&As be on competition in the still very segmented EC markets?

This fourth question is essential. Many of the recent large M&As have been among utilities (often closely tied to member-state governments), public monopolies, public firms to be privatized, or freshly privatized public monopolies, as is best illustrated by deals such as those between VEBA-VIAG and Tractebel-Suez-Lyonnaise des Eaux, EDF and EnBW-Hidroelectrica del Cantabrio, and Deutsche Post and Lufthansa. In other words, current European M&As are much more about market consolidation than about competition in European markets, more so because some of the biggest service firms in member-states have become so powerful at home that they have little choice but to look abroad. Taking into account the history of the EC service sectors, this situation may be inescapable in the medium term, but it sheds some doubts on the expected success rate for these M&As: it could be lower than the corresponding rate (50 percent) in a fully fledged single market, like the United States. And this concentration movement clearly imposes renewed efforts to boost the procompetitive impact of the SMP. This context should make WTO negotiations on service liberalization all the more attractive to the EC.

Trade and Labor Issues

The Commission devotes more space in its Seattle Communication to the topic of trade and labor than to any other issue, as does the Council—but paradoxically not the Parliament, which devotes more space to services, with a marked antiliberalization tone. However, all these long texts on trade and labor leave the general impression that the EC is unwilling to move very far on this touchy topic—echoing the EC's "follower" behavior on this issue at the very end of the Uruguay Round negotiations, when even the most vocal member-states (Belgium, France, and Germany) were ultimately unprepared to go beyond rhetoric.

The Commission text begins by taking note of the EC's failed attempt to create a working group on these matters during the 1996 Singapore WTO Ministerial. It praises the International Labor Organization (ILO) for the work it has done since then (in particular, the adoption of the Declaration on Fundamental Principles and Rights at Work in June 1998), and it recognizes that the ILO is the "body best placed to make real progress in this area"—and that trade and labor issues could easily be used for protectionist purposes. The Commission states that "there is no realistic prospect of consensus for the establishment of a working group within the WTO." Rather, it develops a strategy to be pursued "in parallel" with the new round, which would essentially consist of enhancing cooperation between the WTO and ILO (starting with a WTO-ILO high-level meeting on trade, globalization, and labor issues), and of granting extra benefits (under the Generalized System of Preferences schemes) to developing countries meeting core ILO conventions on labor. The Council text goes even further: it stresses the EC's "firm opposition to any sanctions-based approaches," a clear allusion to the stance of US President Clinton's administration toward the Seattle Ministerial.

The EC's position is not accidental, for three intertwined reasons. First, the Treaty of Rome contains no provision connecting trade and labor issues *within* the Single Market, an approach carefully followed since then as is last illustrated by the new version of Article 137 (ex 118) included in the Nice TEC version, which "excludes any harmonization of the laws and regulations of the member-states" on social matters and which reaffirms the "right of Member-states to define the fundamental principles of their social security systems." Second, in contrast with the WTO texts, the Treaty of Rome recognizes the fundamental right of free movement of labor—a right aiming to interconnect labor markets directly. Third, the

Treaty's approach has been (although to a limited extent) extended to countries closely linked to the EC through international treaties (e.g., Turkey, with the EC-Turkey Agreement, as discussed by the Court of Justice in the 1987 *Demirel* and 1989 *Sevince* cases). For these reasons, it will probably last during the coming round.

EC's Long History of Disconnecting Trade and Labor Issues

Until the late 1980s—hence, during the first 30 years of the Community—raising trade and labor issues within the EC was a nonstarter. Intra-EC trade liberalization was seen as perfectly compatible with nonharmonized member-state labor and social regimes—in sharp contrast with the strong demand for EC harmonization of technical regulations in *product* markets (see chapter 4).

This situation was the consequence of the hot, lengthy debates during the negotiations for the Treaty of Rome. Between 1950 and 1956, Belgium and France opposed Germany on all the issues raised today about trade and labor, from working conditions to wage and social transfer matters. They insisted on the harmonization of labor conditions, wages, and social transfers as a prerequisite for a customs union, whereas Germany argued that such a total or partial harmonization on labor issues would be a recipe for failure, and thus should not be incorporated into the Treaty (Milward 1992; Bean et al. 1998). Fortunately, German views prevailed—ironically, they were based on the "social market economy" notion, which was used by the EC Parliament text released for Seattle to link trade and core labor standards.

As a result, the Treaty of Rome makes no reference whatsoever to *direct* links between trade and labor issues; by insisting on the close *cooperation* between member-states in labor matters, this makes the Treaty impermeable to the notion of using trade sanctions to impose labor standards. The Treaty Preamble and Article 2 make clear that the Community's goal is to raise the standard of living—intra-EC trade and the free movement of labor being two mechanisms to reach this objective. This approach left the initial version of the Treaty with a narrow legal basis on labor issues. The six initial articles (ex 117 to ex 122) on "social provisions" stated objectives that few governments could envisage refusing to sign: improving working conditions, equal pay for men and women, paid holiday regimes, and so on. Some of these objectives were included to grandfather the *principles* of such rights that preexisted in certain member-states. (For instance, the principle of equal pay for equal work was included in the French Constitution before the signing of the Treaty of Rome.) The Commission's efforts to introduce pieces of European social policy during the 1970s on this narrow Treaty basis were insignificant or failed.

In the mid-1980s, things *seemed* to change dramatically. In December 1989, a Charter on the Fundamental Social Rights for Workers (the so-called Social Charter) was tabled by the Commission, and adopted by all EC member-states except Britain. In 1992, it was annexed as Protocol No. 14 on Social Policy to the Maastricht TEC version (Britain was opposed to its introduction into the Treaty itself). In 1997, it was fully incorporated into the Amsterdam TEC version.[17] Meanwhile, the Commission tabled initiatives (the so-called Social Action Programs) in 1989, 1992, and 1995 on a wide range of topics—from uncontroversial training programs to controversial harmonization of national schemes to inform and consult workers. These Action Programs led to the adoption of 52 directives (as of January 1998), under the majority rule (hence applicable to Britain, although not necessarily voted by this member-state), and presented as the embryo of EC social policy.

However, the real impact of these apparently impressive changes is very limited, for four reasons. First, the Social Charter was a mere declaratory statement. Its introduction into the Amsterdam TEC version did not produce very much. It reaffirmed goals that had been present since 1958, such as health and safety in the workplace, plus a couple of general principles on gender equality and paid holidays. And it restated that the Community shall "support and complement" the social activities of member-states, and that unanimity remains the voting rule for the key aspects of social policy, such as social security and protection of workers. As already mentioned, the Nice TEC version of Article 137 (ex 118) reaffirms EC member-state sovereignty in social security matters, with a quite cryptic addition on the "modernization of social protection systems".

Second, the adopted EC directives are less stringent than existing national laws—a feature reflecting the unchanged Treaty obligation that EC rules should state only *minimum* requirements, if any (Article 137 [ex 118]). For instance, the 1993 directive imposed a maximum work week of 48 hours at a time when the effective average work week in member-states varied from 38 to less than 44 hours. As a result, EC "social" directives have almost no impact on actual practices in member-states. This negligible impact is mirrored by the modest funds allocated to the European Social and Cohesion Funds (see table 5.4): 11 percent of EC state aid, or less than 0.1

---

17. The Charter of Fundamental Rights adopted by the Intergovernmental Conference of Nice (2000) has little to do with labor issues. It is a declaratory statement about "people's rights" in general that is not included in the TEC. Its only provision interesting from a trade and labor perspective is Article 32, which prohibits child labor and protects young people at work. However, the ban on child labor is defined in loose terms, e.g., on the basis of the minimum school-leaving age ("the minimum age of admission to employment may not be lower than the minimum school-leaving age"); this condition is easy to circumvent, and may even be counterproductive (it could induce countries to set a low age for leaving school).

percent of the EC GDP (compared to the GDP share of social protection expenditure in member-states, which ranges from 15 to 35 percent).

Third, the controversial initiatives included in the Social Action Programs have not been adopted, or they have been curbed by subsequent or even concomitant measures adopted by member-states or by the Community itself. For instance, the attempt to harmonize schemes to inform and consult workers was abandoned in 1998, and the use of Article 141 (ex 119) for "retroactive" claims on equal pay (made possible by the 1990 *Barber* ruling of the EC Court of Justice) was severely limited by Protocol No. 2 of the Maastricht TEC version (the very same version that included the "Social Charter" as Protocol 14).

Fourth, adopted "social" directives are raising persistent or recurrent difficulties of transposition in most member-states—from Britain to France. In mid-2000, one-fourth of the social directives (12 out of 49) were still not transposed in all member-states, Spain being the only state having transposed all of them. Social directives account for only 4 percent of the total number of directives constituting the *acquis communautaire*, but they represent 5 percent of directives under consultation for member-state infringement, and 18 percent of directives for which the Court of Justice imposed fines for infringement between 1997 and 2000.[18]

In sum, social policy and transfers are always and in all cases a matter for member-states—an EC tradition to which Germany referred to justify its option of "renationalizing" direct aid to agriculture at the 1999 Berlin Council. Moreover, for five other reasons, the EC is unprepared and unwilling to go very far on trade and labor issues in the WTO forum.

First, the EC's evolution since 1958 has given a lot of ammunition to those who believe that increased trade and integration are powerful instruments for "catching up" (the argument behind the German position during the negotiations for the Treaty of Rome). Labor costs, which were lower in Germany than in France in the early 1950s, during the Treaty negotiations, have been higher since the late 1960s. Contrary to a frequent perception, since its origin the EC has included large "poor" regions (those with an income lower than 75 percent of the EC average); already in 1958, poor regions represented 11 to 15 percent of the EC's population,

---

18. Source: http://europa.eu.int/comm/secretariat_general/sgb/infringements/index_en.htm, dated 1 April 2000. The global figure of 18 percent could be split between 12 percent on access to public employment against Greece and Luxembourg, and 6 percent on night work of women against France. Of course, night work of women did exist in France before the EC directive in question (6 night workers out of 10 in the French health sector are women). But it was introduced through a long series of "exceptions" to the 1892 general ban—another illustration of the tortuous ways often used in Continental Europe for circumventing apparently generous labor laws (see below).

compared to 19 percent in the late 1980s. And the EC has shown its capacity to integrate these poor regions without interfering with trade.[19]

Second, the debate on trade and labor issues reemerged in the EC in the late 1980s, a few years after the 1986 accessions of Portugal and Spain and concomitantly with the Uruguay Round final negotiations. As a result, debates in Europe on social dumping (i.e., plants displaced from EC higher-wage member-states to lower-wage locations) have made little difference, if any, between "low-wage" member-states and "low-wage" non-EC countries. In these conditions, linking trade and labor issues in the WTO forum has an immediate boomerang effect on *intra-EC* relations: It is difficult to argue simultaneously that competition with workers in low-wage non-EC countries is unfair, and that competition with low-wage member-states is fair, all the more because the most frequently targeted low-wage non-EC countries (South Korea, Taiwan, etc.) have higher wages than some low-wage member-states. The boomerang effect is certain because some member-states have the world's most expensive labor forces. After all, viewed from (Western) Germany, France is a low-wage, low-labor-standards country.

Third, the fact that the protectionist dynamics of the trade and labor issues in the WTO forum can very easily engulf intra-EC trade will be magnified by the prospect of the accession of low-wage Central European countries. Indeed, the usual argument that closer integration between a richer and a poorer country may increase inequality in the richer country (by adversely affecting the incomes of its poorer citizens in relative, or even possibly absolute, terms) seems weaker in the case of Central Europe, for several reasons. Most Central European economies are very small relative to the EC economy (meaning that their impact on the huge EC economy will be minute), those likely to be the first to join the EC are growing rapidly, and the accession process for all the CECs will be spread over a long period (probably two decades). As one can easily expect, the CECs themselves are strongly opposed to any direct link between trade and labor issues in the WTO context *before* their accession to the EC—as is illustrated by the CEC opposition led by Hungary to the US and EC proposals on trade and labor issues during the preparatory meetings for the Seattle WTO Ministerial.

Fourth, there is an increasing recognition in European public opinion that Continental Europe is not the realm of "equality" it claims to be. A half-century of welfare state in Continental Europe has left so many visi-

---

19. In 1986, the GDPs per capita of Ireland, Portugal, and Spain were 64 percent, 29 percent, and 52 percent, respectively, of the average income per capita of the four largest member-states (Britain, France, Germany, and Italy). In 1999, they were 107 percent, 50 percent, and 67 percent, respectively. However, it remains to allocate these successes among three possible causes—domestic policies, EC influences, and worldwide influences. For a more detailed analysis at the regional level, see Neven and Gouyette (1995).

ble inequalities (in wages, unemployment, occupation, gender, etc.) that there is a relatively large consensus for not seeing trade as the appropriate instrument for action. In fact, low-wage member-states are not the least regulated in labor matters; the OECD index of stringency of employment protection laws is higher in Italy (142) and Portugal (125) than in Germany (120), and in Spain (112) than in France (95) or Denmark (32) (OECD 1994).

For all these reasons, the 1990s slowly made member-states *and* the Commission, initially prone to adopt European social regulations in order to expand its powers, more aware of the costs of these regulations for the workers themselves. The regulations, which were originally meant to protect the poor, consist of provisions that ultimately boost the income of *insiders* (those already employed). The wide acknowledgment of the limits of the welfare state has been reinforced by the fact that during the past decade, EC Continental member-states have developed tortuous ways to make their national labor markets more flexible—with workers realizing progressively how opaque and unfair to entrants or to reentrants into the labor market this flexibility has been (Cohen, Lefranc, and Saint-Paul 1997).

The fifth and last reason for the EC's inability to go very far with trade and labor issues in the WTO forum is the EC environment itself. For instance, a firm may decide to close its plant in a low-wage member-state, and to keep its plant in a high-wage state because redundancy costs are higher in the latter—illustrating the case where the rigid social policy of the high-wage state works as a beggar-my-neighbor policy. Comparing member-states and non-EC countries is also instructive. For instance, if the inequality gap is 60 percent higher in the United States than in France when measured in terms of current wages (i.e., wages earned by employed workers), it dramatically drops to 15 percent when current wages are adjusted (as they should be) for the likelihood of a worker being unemployed *and* the length of unemployment over the working life (Cohen et al. 1997). Of course, such evidence does not stop politicians in an individual member-state, as is illustrated by the recent mandatory reduction in the number of working hours per week in France. But it is difficult for such politicians to make their views prevail simultaneously in such a diverse group as the EC member-states, all the more because they implement different labor and social policies that rely on different instruments, and combine them differently.[20]

---

20. This point is crucial, because labor relations are a political topic by essence. For instance, one could easily argue that a minimum-wage regime prevails all over Continental Europe. But the fact that it is an essential instrument of public relations for the French government and an essential aspect of power devolution in Germany makes almost impossible a communitarization of this measure.

The Single Market: Free Movement of Labor

The Treaty of Rome considers barriers to factor (labor and capital) movements as "trade" barriers. In this context, Article 39 (ex 48) of the Treaty establishes the "freedom of movement of workers" as one of the four pillars of the Single Market (one of the four "freedoms," in EC parlance)—an approach in complete opposition to the WTO framework. This Treaty provision had little impact until the 1995 *Bosman* ruling of the Court of Justice, and its long case law, which gave a precise definition of the direct applicability of Article 39 (ex 48) and a wide definition of the freedom of movement of workers. Moreover, Article 39 (ex 48) triggered several competitive forces, which in the long run will counterbalance the negative effects of EC social policy on labor markets.

The first competitive force flows from the above-mentioned large set of EC directives (63, as of January 1998) aiming to improve *skilled* labor mobility between member-states in accordance with Article 39 (ex 48). The directives are based on mutual recognition of member-state diplomas, conditional on the harmonization of the minimum knowledge judged necessary to provide certain services. By reducing barriers on skilled labor flows, these directives change the available supply of skilled labor in each member-state market—hence, the real impact of EC labor market regulations. The acceptance of diploma is significant in certain professions (e.g., doctors, nurses, veterinarians, teachers, and architects), and in member-states that are ready to import foreign skilled workers (e.g., Belgium, Germany, and Britain) or to export domestic skilled workers (e.g., Netherlands, Sweden, and Britain) (European Commission 1999f).[21]

It should be underlined that this first competitive force is antagonistic to the logic of the Social Plans and their related regulations, which require that workers employed in another member-state should receive *host* (*not* home) country terms and conditions of work—hence slowing down forces in favor of labor mobility. The limits imposed on "competition" between member-state social policies by the host country principle flow from the implicit assumption frequent in the EC that the home country principle would induce member-states to follow a "race to the bottom" policy reducing the social benefits of their workers. It is beyond the scope of this book to fully examine such an argument. But in these respects, the EC experience echoes the major lessons provided by the recent theoretical and

---

21. It is hard to get detailed evidence on these skilled labor flows. E.g., the late 1990s witnessed an outflow of skilled young French people, who found jobs much more easily in Britain or the United States than in France (*International Herald Tribune*, 10 March 1998). On the basis of an official report (Sénat 2000), one can estimate that between 1995 and 1998, 300,000 skilled French people (most of them young) have left France for the OECD countries (mostly Britain and the United States)—that is, more than one-tenth of the annual number of registered French students and roughly one-half the number of university diplomas granted in one year.

empirical literature: the many caveats to the superficially compelling arguments in favor of a race to the bottom in social matters (Bean et al. 1998; Andersen, Haldrup, and Sorensen 2000; Brown 2000); and the lack of correlation between the absence of *core* labor norms and trade performance (meaning that countries without core norms do not fare better than countries with such norms) although the same cannot be said in the case of *non-core* labor norms (OECD 2000a).

The second competitive force flows from the right of establishment that allows firms to be established in one EC member-state and operate in another one. Article 43 (ex 52) of the Treaty of Rome explicitly prohibits "restrictions on the freedom of establishment of nationals of a Member state into the territory of another Member-state," and Articles 44 (ex 54) to 48 (ex 58) specify the ways to implement this key prohibition. These provisions could have a huge impact if they are massively used by self-employed, often relatively unskilled people, such as bakers, haircutters, and shopkeepers (i.e., managers of and workers in very small firms, which so far have not been directly involved in EC internal liberalization). Self-employed people can locate the headquarters of their own firms in the EC member-state offering the best public services (health, police, pension, etc.) at the lowest prices (business taxes, social security contributions, etc.) and yet continue to work in their member-state of origin. For instance, a French haircutter could register his or her firm in Britain (where he/she pays business taxes) and work in France (where he or she pays income tax) without regulatory barriers.

Such cases have already raised public attention (*International Herald Tribune*, "Finding the System Too Taxing, French Flee", 16 April 1998, 1). It is difficult to forecast the future magnitude of this phenomenon. If large, it will change dramatically the balance between trade, capital mobility, and labor mobility in the EC. A large portion of relatively unskilled labor will become de facto as mobile as skilled labor and capital—reducing substantially the scope of the argument (Rodrik 1997) about potential pressures exerted by trade on social cohesion. Of course, the member-states with the lowest ratios of social benefits to social costs are doing their best to limit this outflow of firms and revenues by curbing competition among member-states through fiscal harmonization.

Competition Policy: Market Power and Subsidies

Since the mid-1990s, the Commission has been the strongest advocate of introducing competition policy in the WTO—making no secret that it considers its own competition policy a model for the world trade system. The Seattle Commission text illustrates this stance by ranking competition issues as the third topic in commercial policy matters and devoting more space to them than to services. It describes a wide program: (1) "core" principles and "common" rules on the scope of competition law and on its procedures; (2) "common approaches" on anticompetitive practices with a significant impact on international trade and investment (e.g., hard-core cartels, vertical restrictions, international mergers); (3) international cooperation on notification, consultation, and surveillance; and (4) the use of the dispute settlement system to "ensure that domestic competition law and enforcement structures are in accordance with the provisions agreed multilaterally."

The Parliament and even more the Council have shown less enthusiasm in their texts. This reserve mirrors underlying power struggles within the EC. Member-states are still attached to their own domestic competition policies as recently illustrated by the so-called Schröder Document (see chapter 7). They may feel that the long list released by the Commission for Seattle is a way to use the coming round to expand the Commission's powers in these matters, in particular on issues much debated within the Community (e.g., export cartels or vertical restraints).

EC competition policy has a feature that is essential in the context of WTO negotiations on competition, if there will be such negotiations. The relevant Treaty of Rome articles do not prohibit practices incompatible with competition, only those incompatible with the "common market" (a feature echoed in the Seattle Commission text by the expression "in accordance with the provisions agreed multilaterally") and affecting intra-EC trade. Distortions and restrictions on competition in the EC may thus be permitted, if they fit the common market objective, whereas economically sound practices may be prohibited to the extent that they are perceived as obstacles to intra-EC trade, as has been the case for private selling arrangements (see chapter 4).

The common market objective refers to the other goals mentioned in the Preamble and in Articles 2 and 3 of the Treaty of Rome (see chapter 1): support of small firms, promotion of research and development (R&D), "fair" competition, competitiveness, social and territorial cohesion, subsidiarity, and democracy. Some of these goals have been perceived as important enough to be explicitly restated in the Treaty articles on market power, state-owned enterprises, and state aid (Articles 81:3 [ex 85:3], 86:2 [ex 90:2], and 87:2 [ex 92:1], respectively), when these articles list the exemptions to be taken into account. Other goals have accumulated over time, such as the encouragement of innovation or the promotion of the competitiveness of European firms.

The multiple-goal feature of EC competition policy helps to explain two frequent reactions to EC proposals on these matters in the WTO forum. On the one hand, WTO members with a competition policy that focuses more strictly on competition issues (e.g., the United States) fear that the EC approach will end up loosening the enforcement of their own competition laws. On the other hand, forces hostile to the introduction of a competition law (including among the 52 countries that have adopted such a law in the past decade) are looking at the introduction of the EC approach in the WTO framework as a possible way to dilute the infant enforcement of their own competition law.

It is important to note that the Seattle Commission text does not deal with all the topics that the Treaty of Rome includes under competition policy. It focuses on one of the two "branches" of EC competition policy, that is, market power issues (cartels, vertical and horizontal restrictions, and international mergers). It scatters under various headings the other topics covered by the provisions of the Treaty of Rome on competition policy (state-owned enterprises, antidumping, regulatory reform, and subsidies), an approach that leads to a superficial treatment of these essential issues. In particular, the Commission text leaves almost completely aside subsidy issues ("state aid," in EC parlance), despite the fact that WTO members would benefit from substituting the EC antisubsidy approach for the GATT countervailing notion.[22]

Competition Policy as Seen by EC Commercial Policy

The Seattle Commission text limits the scope of competition policy in the WTO to three major topics: cartels, vertical and horizontal restrictions, and international mergers.

Hard-Core and Export Cartels

The EC and member-state approaches to hard-core domestic (i.e., intra-member-state or intra-EC) cartels are relatively similar. They condemn them, although there are still some key differences in the immunity policy (about denouncing cartel-like practices) and in the available range of sanctions (particularly the existence, or lack, of criminal sanctions against individuals) and in the intensity of enforcement among member-states and the Community (OECD 2000b). These crucial differences may explain why, paradoxically at first glance, the level of cooperation between the EC and the US competition authorities has been minimal in this crucial anti-cartel activity (Waller 2000).

The European position on *extra-EC* export cartels is a much more open question.[23] In accordance with Article 29 (ex 34) of the TEC, the EC Court of Justice bans discriminatory *intra-EC* export restrictions, but it allows

---

22. The EC itself will benefit from such a substitution, because it is using the GATT countervailing approach for *extra-EC* imports with a worrisome drift (see appendix B).

23. The same can be said for export-subsidy policy, which remains within the competence of the member-states and under the discipline of the OECD Agreement on Export Credits. For the latest available year (1995), the export assistance share in total assistance to industry varies from 0 percent (Spain) to 4 percent (Belgium, Britain) to 13 percent (France) to 20 percent (Germany) to 55 percent (Finland) (OECD 1998d).

schemes restricting exports as long as they make no distinction between products to be sold on domestic markets and those to be sold on export markets (the 1979 *Groenveld* ruling). On the one hand, the Commission argues that it has jurisdiction over such export cartels, and it is favorable to a ban. However, the requirements it imposes for the material evidence required to convict firms are so strict that they explain the lack of deterrent effect of this ban. Moreover, the Commission tends to examine the extent to which export cartels hurt other EC firms (e.g., the implementation of the UN Conference on Trade and Development [UNCTAD] Liner Code on maritime routes between French and African harbors that excluded Danish shipping lines), an approach that can lead to tacit acceptance of cartels. Finally, it ignores the impact of antidumping measures on the formation of such cartels (see appendix B).

On the other hand, member-states consider this issue under their own competence—at least for their own national export cartels that have no effect on EC markets (if that is possible). Their views on export cartels vary from prohibition to tacit acceptance—depending on the relative magnitude of the rents that the domestic cartel extracts from domestic consumers and those that it can extract from foreign consumers. This complicated situation leaves doubts about the EC's capacity to have a common position on this topic in the WTO forum.

Horizontal and Vertical Restraints

Article 81 (ex 85) of the Treaty of Rome deals with "concerted practices" and Article 82 (ex 86) with "abuse" of dominant position. In the case of *horizontal* restraints (agreements between producers of substitutable goods and services) other than cartels, EC competition policy—with its multiple goals defined by the Treaty of Rome—has generated a high degree of discretion and subjectivity in implementation. These complexities in turn have created time inconsistencies in EC competition policy, and wide differences of views and actions between EC and member-state competition authorities—even about essential points, such as the definition of what constitutes a restriction of competition, or the interpretation of the "technical or economic progress" that certain restrictive practices could bring (Neven, Papandropoulos, and Seabright 1998).

Differences of views and actions in the EC about *vertical* restraints (agreements between producers of complementary goods and services) are even wider, because the Treaty of Rome does not distinguish between vertical and horizontal restraints (it was written at a time when vertical relations were seen as dangerous for competition as horizontal agreements).

As a result, the Commission has been forced to use a series of convoluted "exemptions" under Article 81:3 (ex 85:3) so as to have a more friendly approach to vertical restraints than to horizontal restraints. "Block" exemptions (for exclusive distribution, purchasing, patent licensing, franchising, R&D cooperation, technology transfer, car distribution, and certain types of agreements in the insurance sector) and "individual" exemptions for other vertical restraints (subject to the fulfillment of specific conditions by the firms involved) have allowed the Commission to take into account the positive aspects of vertical relations.[24] Some exemptions cover key practices in large sectors (distribution of beer, cosmetics, and petrol, liner conferences in shipping, joint capacity planning in air transport, etc.), whereas other exemptions have allowed clear restrictions on *intra-EC* competition, as is best illustrated by the car distribution agreement (see appendix A, case 12)—a paradox only if one forgets the basic Treaty logic, according to which competition policy is an instrument of economic integration, as underlined above.

International Mergers

In the domain of international mergers, the Seattle Commission text evokes the need for "common approaches," and the possibility of incorporating "negative or positive comity" procedures into the WTO framework, in order to solve the informational problems faced by national competition authorities undertaking investigations (but excluding the possibility of binding obligations to investigate on behalf of another country).[25]

The most often mentioned issue in this domain is the extraterritoriality dimension of many merger decisions made by competition authorities—a dimension increasingly unavoidable in a globalizing economy because competition authorities are concerned with consumers' welfare, *not* with the location of producers. On this point, the EC position shows an increasingly extraterritorial reach. Until the late 1980s, the EC was reluctant to assert extraterritorial jurisdiction, but in 1988, the Court of Justice moved toward some extraterritorial reach with the *Wood Pulp* case. However, this ruling focused on the behavior of *all* firms (domestic and foreign) in *European* markets—hence, on enforcing competition disciplines in the domestic market in a nondiscriminatory way, an approach perfectly compatible with GATT Article III on national treatment.

By contrast, in 1997, the Commission approach to extraterritoriality with the *Boeing-McDonnell* case was very debatable. The Commission dealt with

---

24. The provisions for block exemptions for exclusive distribution, purchasing, and franchising have been clearer since June 2000: Vertical agreements between firms whose combined market share is less than 30 percent are immune to Article 81:1 (ex 85:1), unless these arrangements contain blacklisted restrictions. By contrast, the block exemption on car distribution will be under increased pressure until 2002 to be abolished or reformed.

25. These two procedures have been defined in the 1991 and 1998 United States-EC Agreement regarding the application of competition laws. Under the negative comity clause, each signatory takes into account the other's interests when enforcing its own competition law. Under the positive comity provision, the United States and the EC can request the other jurisdiction to enforce its laws with respect to competitive conduct within its borders that is harming the other jurisdiction (Janow 2000). For a detailed assessment of the comity approach, see Griffin (1994) and Evenett, Lehmann, and Steil (2000).

the possible and *indirect* (hard to document in a robust way) effects of a merger between two US firms (Boeing and McDonnell-Douglas) on an EC producer (Airbus) by dictating conditions for the behavior between the *foreign* seller (Boeing-McDonnell) and *foreign* buyers (US airlines) in a *foreign* (US) aircraft market. Such an approach could clearly open a Pandora's box of conflicts about the strategic use of competition policy in the world trade regime—all the more because Airbus has benefited from massive subsidies, and will benefit from additional state aid.

The last essential point is that in implementing Merger Regulation 4064/89 (the EC core legal text in these matters), the EC Commission has increasingly developed an ex ante approach. The extent to which a merger is authorized or not, and the precise conditions for its authorization (in terms of disinvestment) are based on the knowledge, *before* the merger, of the market situation and of its evolution. This approach raises a major issue. It assumes a level of information on the markets and on their ex post developments that is likely to exceed by far the effective level of information available to the Commission, and to the firms involved.

Such an ex ante approach may lead to inappropriate decisions that "overprotect" firms from competition—particularly in a world economy full of unexpected events. The EC Commission and most member-states have followed this approach because, compared to the US Justice Department, they have had few possibilities of acting at a later stage—for instance, by giving criminal immunity to the first cartel member that would reveal the anticompetitive consequences of a merger (e.g., the existence of a postmerger cartel).

Cost-Benefit Analysis of a Two-Layer System

The Commission's advocacy for WTO competition rules modeled on the EC approach relies on the perceived success of the two-layer system of Community and member-state competition laws. It is thus useful to sketch three aspects of the relative benefits and costs of such a system in relation to a "decentralized" regime (i.e., national competition laws with no a priori common disciplines).

First, because competition policy relies more and more on a case-by-case ("rule-of-reason") basis, similarity of rules does not imply similarity of rulings, contrary to the basic assumption underlying the Commission text for Seattle. "Decentralized" competition authorities enforcing the same disciplines could arrive at different outcomes, either because they weight the same ingredients differently or (assuming they use similar weights) because the producers directly involved, the other producers, and consumers are not equally spread among the jurisdictions, a condition almost certain to be met (Neven and Röller 2000; Cadot, Grether, and de Melo 2000). As a result, even assuming a possible world competition authority (leaving aside the touchy question of the fate of the US Supreme

Court and EC Court of Justice in such a context), *common rules* at the WTO level are not a sure recipe for *similar rulings* by WTO members, even for similar cases, hence for fewer international conflicts.

Second, it is often argued that most member-states would not have developed their own competition policy without the Treaty of Rome's seminal Articles 81 (ex 85) and 82 (ex 86). Formally speaking, this is not correct. France, Germany, and Britain have had a competition law since the 1950s and Spain since 1963—leaving Italy (1990) as the only exception among the large EC member-states since the value of a competition law for smaller EC member-states is debatable. Of course, one can argue that until the late 1960s, competition policy in EC member-states was often an exercise in futility (except perhaps in Germany), but this comment could well be applied to EC competition policy itself.

Since the 1980s, the adoption and enforcement of fully fledged competition policies by EC member-states have been related to an increasingly better understanding of the role of markets. The eight member-states (Denmark, Finland, France, Germany, Luxembourg, Netherlands, Sweden, and Britain) with long-standing competition laws revised them between 1986 and 1998, and the other member-states adopted domestic competition laws during the same period. But the convergence of all these laws toward more similar rules (particularly in Germany and Britain) may be seen as the result of emerging better *general* standards—which influence EC competition policy itself, as in the case of vertical restraints—more than the desire to align with EC standards, although the will to reduce potential conflicts with EC competition enforcement is not absent.

The third aspect of these relative benefits and costs is that casting competition rules in an ironclad treaty can be costly. This is illustrated by the integration constraint imposed on competition policy, and by the complicated "exemption" regime imposed by the Treaty's deficient treatment of vertical restraints.

The conclusion to be drawn from the EC experience is that the focus of WTO discussions for the foreseeable future should not be the adoption of WTO competition disciplines, but rather the adoption of a competition law by *each* WTO member of significant economic size. This adoption would best be done in combination with a "soft" convergence, based on "comities" available to WTO members that take seriously their *own* competition rules—to avoid as much as much as possible the strategic use of competition policies in the international trade context.

Other Aspects of Competition Policy: Left Outside Commercial Policy?

The EC rules on competition in the Treaty of Rome include three other topics: public undertakings, antidumping, and regulatory reform. None of these issues is included in the section of the Seattle Commission text devoted to competition, but all are dealt with under other headings in a short and imperfect way—quite ironically since competition law would certainly put such topics high on the reform agenda.

State-Owned Enterprises

The Commission text evokes the issue of state-owned enterprises only in the section devoted to agriculture. Not only does the communication not make a parallel between the many EC intervention agencies that run the Common Agricultural Policy and state-trading enterprises (see chapter 4), but it also remains silent on the many EC state-owned firms still operating in services, from telecoms to banks to airlines.[26]

This silence reflects the ambiguities of GATS Articles VIII (monopolies and exclusive service suppliers) and IX (business practices), which themselves mirror the rather complex treatment of state-owned firms in the Treaty of Rome, articulated in three Articles of the TEC. First, Article 295 (ex 222) affirms the Treaty neutrality with respect to property ownership. Second, Article 31 (ex 37) specifies that no discrimination regarding the conditions under which goods are procured and marketed shall exist in case of state monopolies of "commercial character," and Article 86:1 (ex 90:1) reinforces this principle by stating that public firms, or firms to which member-states grant special or exclusive rights, *shall* observe Treaty competition rules.

Third, however, Article 86:2 (ex 90:2) exempts state-owned firms from this obligation to follow normal competition disciplines when "entrusted with the operation of services of general interest or having the character of a revenue-producing monopoly." Far from simplifying matters, the "statist" reaction in the EC during the 1990s (see chapter 1) generated a new provision (Article 16 [ex 7d] of the Amsterdam TEC version): "Without prejudice to Articles 73 (ex 77), 86 (ex 90), and 87 (ex 92), and given the place occupied by services of general economic interest in the shared values of the Union as well as their role in promoting social and territorial cohesion, the Community and the Member-states . . . shall take care that such services operate on the basis of principles and conditions which enable them to fulfill their missions."

In practice, the effective dose of competition imposed on EC state-owned firms has varied substantially over time. Starting with the 1982 *British Telecom* ruling (see above), the Court of Justice's market-oriented doctrine of the 1980s reached its peak with the 1990 *Höfner* ruling, in which the Court declared that member-states violate Article 86:1 (ex 90:1) if public firms enjoying special or exclusive rights cannot *avoid* abusive behavior when exercising these rights. But one year later, in the 1991 *Corbeau* case, the Court adopted criteria defining "services of general eco-

---

26. There are four state-trading enterprises in the EC: Electricité de France, Gaz de France, Entreprise Minière et Chimique, and the Italian import monopoly for tobacco (WTO, *Trade Policy Review: The European Community*, 2000).

nomic interest" that severely slowed down the pace at which markets where state-owned firms are operating could be opened to competition (Mavroidis and Messerlin 1998).[27]

Antidumping

The Seattle Commission text does not go much further than expressing the EC's willingness to discuss GATT antidumping procedures, in the very short section on "trade defence instruments" (see chapter 4). It does not mention that antidumping is one of the elements to be examined by the WTO Working Group on Trade and Competition, and it does not evoke the anticompetitive impact of many antidumping measures (see appendix B)—in sharp contrast with the Parliament text, which interestingly mentions that "an effective competition policy by the WTO contracting parties could, in the longer term, reduce recourse to the trade protection measures which are still needed as part of an antidumping policy."

During the past two decades, the Court of Justice, the various member-state competition authorities (from Bundeskartelamt to Conseil de la Concurrence), and the Directorate General for Competition of the Commission have been unable, and often unwilling, to address the antidumping issue, as is best illustrated by the following two cases. First, in the 1992 *Extramet* case, the Court of Justice annulled a first antidumping duty for having failed to take into account the anticompetitive practices of the complaining firm. But within a few months, the Commission reopened a new antidumping procedure—imposing minimum prices equivalent to duties more than three times higher than the first measures—that is, sending a clear message of "retaliation" to defending firms daring to have recourse to competition authorities in antidumping cases.

Second, the 1996 *Saint-Gobain-Wäcker* case dealt with a merger between two EC firms that were ready to renounce forever their rights to lodge antidumping actions in exchange for the right to merge their silicon carbide activities. In other words, these firms offered to renounce the use of antidumping (and hence to accept a much freer trade regime for this product, which has been subjected to repeated EC antidumping measures for years) as the ex ante "remedy" to the possible dominant position that their merger would give them in the relevant EC market. The proposal was rejected by the Commission, on the debatable ground that it would be impossible to enforce such an agreement—another illustration of the balance between ex ante and ex post instruments (see the discussion of mergers above).

These two cases reveal the *systemic* danger of introducing competition policy into a WTO framework that allows for antidumping regulations.

---

27. Moreover, in services, EC and member-state competition authorities have often been unable to efficiently rein in the predatory behavior that former public monopolies tend to follow in markets newly opened to competition, because the slow motion inherent in the investigation of competition cases is an implicit cost for entrants (e.g., see appendix A, case 22).

As shown in appendix B, very few antidumping cases deal with predatory pricing (less than 3 percent) or strategic pricing—suggesting that competition policy and dumping practices (as perceived in trade policy) have little in common. By contrast, many antidumping measures have been shown to generate conditions favorable to procartel practices—suggesting that competition enforcement should ideally look at antidumping *policy* (Messerlin 1990). The fact that the two policies have different purposes and constituencies (and very different financial outcomes for domestic complainants) creates a serious risk of subordinating competition policy to trade considerations—rather than the desirable converse. Indeed, the evolution of the Treaty of Rome offers the best illustration of how serious this risk is. The Treaty's initial Article ex 91, which subordinated intra-EC dumping issues to competition enforcement, disappeared in the Amsterdam TEC version—a clear, and worrisome, sign of which policy (competition or antidumping) is the more powerful.

Regulatory Reforms

The Seattle Commission text does not deal with the relations between regulatory reforms and competition policy in the competition section, but rather in the service section (see above) with a minimal reference to *procompetitive* disciplines. Service liberalization has often been perceived as requiring specific, transitory provisions that favor the emergence of new competitors *and* protect them from the most powerful incumbents for a given period. Such "asymmetric" regulations often require very intrusive rules—from imposing mandatory cost-based pricing on the incumbent during the transition period to banning competition from incumbents. These intrusive rules can be discriminatory, even firm-specific, and they can be enforced by ad hoc regulatory agencies. As a result, these rules represent a danger in the long run both for competition disciplines, which are horizontal by nature, and for the WTO principle of nondiscrimination between countries, and a fortiori between firms.

State Aid

The almost complete silence on state aid of the texts released for Seattle by the three European institutions is all the more striking because subsidies are still reported (in the 1999 business survey on obstacles to intra-EC trade) as the third or second most important obstacle to the Single Market by 28 percent of the small and medium-sized enterprises, and by 36 percent of the large firms. (What follows offers an explanation of why state aid seems more important for large than for small and medium-sized enterprises.)[28]

---

28. See http://europa.eu.int/comm/internal_market/en/update/score/score5.htm, dated 2 December 1999.

EC rules on state aid are relatively close to GATT rules on subsidies except that they are also enforceable in services, whereas GATS Article XV on subsidies in services is still largely an empty shell. Article 87:1 (ex 92:1) of the Treaty of Rome states the general principle that "any aid granted by a Member-State or through state resources, in any form whatsoever which distorts or threatens competition by favoring certain undertakings or the production of certain goods, shall, in so far as it affects trade between Member-states, be incompatible with the common market." The rest of Article 87 (ex 92) lists exemptions to this general principle that are close to those included in the Uruguay Subsidy Agreement: (1) sectoral state aid for "structural adjustment" essentially applied to the EC car, coal, shipbuilding, steel, and synthetic fiber sectors; (2) horizontal subsidy schemes for regions, urban districts, environmental, or R&D activities (with certain schemes of utmost importance for the EC enlargement, hence for EC commercial policy; e.g., 46 percent of EC population in 1997 was located in regions eligible for regional aid; see chapter 6); and (3) the systematic possibility of "compensating" all the EC firms for costs related to "services of general economic interest."

Beyond these similarities, there are two essential differences between EC and GATT rules in these matters. The first concerns the *type* of antisubsidy policy to be pursued. In this respect, the traditional GATT approach is notoriously inadequate, because it is not based on the right motive to curb subsidies. It does not perceive a subsidy as a transfer from domestic taxpayers to foreign consumers, but as a support to domestic producers that would be "unfair" to foreign producers. As a result, the Uruguay Subsidy Agreement imposes the wrong instrument to fight trade-related subsidies, namely, "countervailing" duties that the importing country could impose on subsidized imports, that is, on its *own* consumers—instead of leaving them to enjoy available foreign subsidies.

Two recent WTO panels (on Australian leather and Brazilian aircraft) have tried to limit this traditional GATT flaw by suggesting that countervailing duties should be limited to the level of injury suffered, not up to the level of subsidization. This solution is similar to what already exists in antidumping enforcement, and it is likely to drift in a similar way. Investigations will come up with more inflated levels of injury than in the past.

By contrast, EC antisubsidy policy relies on the right instrument: the ban on (or at least alteration of) state aid by the Commission. The experience accumulated during the past 20 years of increasingly tight Commission enforcement provides three major lessons for the WTO. First, the bulk of the visible state aid granted by member-states to the manufacturing sector between 1984 and 1992 remained concentrated in six industries: textiles, clothing, synthetic fibers, glass, steel, and cars. (Anecdotal evidence does not suggest large changes in this sectoral distribution during the 1990s.) The fact that all these sectors are characterized by a higher level of overall protection than the whole EC manufacturing sector (see table 2.1) reinforces the impression conveyed by chapters 2 and 3 of protection peaks in these sectors.

Second, table 5.4 shows the relative stability of the *overall* nominal amount of subsidies in the EC economies between 1990 and 1997, with a significant substitution of EC subsidies for member-state aid. However, contrary to what happened with the communitarization process in trade barriers (see chapter 2), this substitution was accompanied by noticeable changes in the sectoral distribution of subsidies—away from certain industries, and toward agriculture and certain services.

Third, substitutability between the endless forms of subsidies generates an enforcement problem for the EC antisubsidy policy in the long run. Available evidence suggests that the EC's stricter state aid control after 1987 generated a wider range of types and sources of subsidies, which were more difficult to monitor (Messerlin 1999). Examples of endless creativity with subsidies abound—from subsidies for labor costs apparently granted to all labor-intensive activities, but de facto limited to some sectors (textiles, apparel, footwear) to aid for new purposes (increasingly generous preretirement schemes, aid for foreign investment in joint ventures with Central European firms) to subsidies granted by increasingly low levels of subnational entities to subsidized inputs (land, electricity, movie studios) often produced by public enterprises, and to implicit subsidies generated by state guarantees, as is best illustrated by the banking, electricity, and railway sectors.[29]

This evolution suggests the need to interpret with caution the level and decline of EC subsidy rates between 1990 and 1997 that are reported in table 5.4. In fact, the level of subsidization may be significantly higher, as is suggested by a study (Hallaert 2000), according to which, in the mid-1990s, French total subsidies in manufacturing *and* services would still represent 5.8 percent of French GDP (indeed, a result more in tune with the above-quoted business survey than the official figure of 2.1 percent shown in table 5.4).

---

29. E.g., Germany grants state guarantees (*Anstaltslast* and *Gewährträgerhaftung*) to certain banks (*Landesbanken* and *Sparkassen*), that are equivalent to subsidies on the cost of refinancing or to subsidies to capital (Austria has similar regulations) (Koenig 2000; Schneider 2000; Winckler 2000). In the case of WestLB, it has been shown that this indirect aid allowed WestLB to cross-subsidize its activities in the London competitive markets with its protected activities in Germany. The German government tried to grandfather these guarantees by a protocol to the Maastricht TEC version but failed to do so. In July 1999, the Commission ordered WestLB to repay € 0.8 billion in illegal subsidies. However in November 2000, German regional politicians were still struggling with the various alternative plans to reform the *Landesbanken*. The treatment of investments in railway tracks or other large infrastructure of state-owned firms is not without similarities to this guarantee issue.

The subsidy resilience in the EC raises an interesting question for those manufacturing sectors that are considered liberalized but that continue to receive substantial state aid. As stressed by Snape (1987), subsidies become rapidly very costly when trade barriers are eliminated. The observed resilience may thus reflect either lobbies powerful enough to be able to impose the use of a visibly costly instrument, or more likely the fact that certain extra-EC and intra-EC barriers (e.g., antidumping measures and/or technical regulations) have survived past liberalization efforts and reduce the costs of subsidization.

The second essential difference between the EC and WTO subsidy regimes is that in the EC, state aid control is a Commission "monopoly": Article 88 (ex 93) grants to the Commission *alone* the power to ban or modify subsidies found incompatible with the common market, and the Commission "shall keep under constant review all systems of aid existing" in member-states.

This dramatic power devolution is often mentioned as a key advantage of the EC regime—in comparison with the US regime, for instance, where the Supreme Court is the only institution able to restore some control over local subsidies. However, this argument deserves a caveat for the following three reasons. First, if such power devolution undoubtedly allows simpler, stricter monitoring of small-state aid, it rapidly faces its limits when large subsidies are granted to large or to state-owned firms. In these cases, the Commission does not have the necessary political muscle to confront member-states—distorting its monitoring ability. As a result, and paradoxically, the Commission's antisubsidy policy may be the source of more distortions than no antisubsidy policy, to the extent that it increases the subsidy rate of large and massively subsidized firms *relative* to the rate for the other firms, which are subjected to stricter disciplines—this may explain the noticeable difference (in the above-quoted business survey) between the perception of state aid by small and large firms.

Second, such power devolution does not exempt the Commission from balancing distortions on competition generated by subsidies with the pursuit of other economic and social aims, in accordance with the Treaty provisions. Such balancing requires a *political* consensus in the EC, that is, involves *in fine* member-states. As noted by Besley and Seabright (2000, 13) when criticizing the Commission's policy, "The Commission presumes that state aid distorts competition, yet it approves 98 percent of applications, often for social or distributional reasons."

Third, the power devolution has induced the Commission to pay much more attention to the interests of the competitors of aid beneficiaries (Ehlermann 1995)—balancing its acceptance of state aid by imposing restrictions on the strategies of the subsidized firms for accommodating competitors, again opening the door to the strategic use of competition policy, as is best illustrated by the airline and banking industries. In the airline cases, subsidized firms have been prohibited from acquiring other airlines, expanding aircraft fleets, increasing the number of flights or seats on specific routes, and pricing aggressively on specific routes. In banking, operational constraints on subsidized banks have included quantitative limits on growth rates, a mandatory distribution of revenues between shareholders and other possible beneficiaries (both conditions to be met for a few years), and a mandatory stability of the bank solvency ratio (a condition to be fulfilled for many years).[30]

The problem is not so much that all these restrictions make the restructuring of the subsidized firms more difficult—giving them good excuses to ask for new subsidies, and making it more difficult for the Commission to enforce its "one time, last time" principle. It is that such restrictions impose severe limits on the competitive nature of the markets in which subsidized firms and their competitors are operating (and in related markets)—that the restrictions limit the liberalization process. For instance, limiting airline seat capacities ultimately facilitates collusion between subsidized and nonsubsidized airlines; because the constraints imposed on the subsidized firms are public, the nonsubsidized firms can align their own prices or quantities strategically (including with a collusive purpose) with those permitted for subsidized airlines on constrained routes, and they can use the rents resulting from such restricted competition to cross-subsidize their price strategies for other routes.[31]

Because the nonsubsidized firms can be EC or non-EC companies, the EC's failure to address properly the state aid issue becomes a problem of interest for all WTO members. To conclude this discussion of the EC experience of power devolution in state aid matters, it appears that the Commission has been really successful only when it has been able to convince a wide audience that subsidies are not the appropriate instrument— because they do not really address economic and social problems, and can be easily captured by vested interests. This remark echoes the conclusion for competition policy. The economically sound answer to competition issues (all those briefly surveyed in this section) relies much more on *domestic* enforcement than on multilateral initiatives.

---

30. These illustrations refer to the *Air France* and *Crédit Lyonnais* cases, the latter case raising the issues of both state aid rules and regulatory (prudential) supervision (the extent to which the *Crédit Lyonnais* difficulties have been generated or amplified by the failure of the French supervisory authorities, Trésor and Banque de France, is still under investigation).

31. Limiting the collusive impact of antisubsidy policies is as hard as limiting the collusive impact of subsidies. For example, competitors of a subsidized bank are indirectly subsidized if the state aid granted allows keeping the prices of competitors' assets stable, as well as those of the subsidized bank.

Public Procurement: Such a Big Deal?

The Seattle texts released by the European institutions on the topic of public procurement are among the shortest. They are limited to a call for consolidation of the Uruguay Round results. This brevity, which contrasts with the importance of this issue in the Single Market context and for certain EC trading partners during the Uruguay Round, reflects the intrinsic difficulties of liberalizing in this domain, including within the EC, and the almost simultaneity of slow intra- and extra-EC liberalization.

The Treaty of Rome implicitly covers public procurement. Articles 28 (ex 30) on free movement of goods, 43 (ex 52) on freedom of establishment, and 49 (ex 59) on freedom to provide services govern all contracts (however small) awarded by European public bodies. However, the first directives adopted in the late 1970s to implement these general principles were ineffective—hence the need to include public procurement in the SMP. Seven basic SMP directives on public procurement thus were adopted between 1988 and 1993—almost simultaneously with the Uruguay Government Procurement Agreement (GPA), which became part of the EC legal regime in 1996.[32]

The implementation of these Directives has been slow and is still conflictual. Not only have all the directives not been adopted by all member-states, but the adoption process in member-state laws has also witnessed the introduction of inconsistent provisions in more than one-third of the cases—forcing the Commission to launch almost 40 infringement procedures against member-states in the late 1990s. Difficulties are particularly severe with the two directives on utilities, which cover roughly a fourth of EC public procurement markets (see table 5.5).

Detailed evidence about the impact of the EC measures covers the very first years (1987–94) of their implementation. But the available evidence for a more recent year shows very modest changes: in 1998, the value of published tenders represented 2 percent of EC GDP, less than one-seventh of the EC total public procurement market (WTO, *Trade Policy Review: The European Union*, 2000). The overall import penetration rate in procurement markets (the ratio of public-sector purchases of foreign origin to total public-sector purchases) increased from 6 percent in 1987 to 10 percent in

---

32. As of 1999, three directives had dealt with liberalization in "public sectors" on works contracts with Directive 93/37, on supply contracts with Directive 93/36, and on services contracts with Directive 92/50. Directives 90/531 and 93/38 were devoted to procurement procedures of entities operating in the water, energy, transport, and telecom sectors (the so-called utilities or excluded sectors). Two directives dealt with remedies (89/665 for public sectors and 92/13 for utilities). Directive 90/531 is the only one to have reciprocity conditions (based on local content of inputs included in the foreign bids). In 1993, it triggered a dispute with the United States, leading to limited "sanctions" from both sides (exclusion of US and EC firms from public procurement in certain utilities-based markets) that were still in place in 1997 (WTO, *Trade Policy Review: The European Community*, 1995, 69; 1997, 62).

Table 5.5 EC public procurement markets and operators

| Country | Estimated size of the procurement markets | | | Entities covered and capable of letting above-threshold contracts, 1995[a] (number of units) | | | |
| | Government | | Utilities | | | | |
	Total, 1994 (billions of euros)	Above threshold, 1992 (percent)	1994 (billions of euros)	Central	Subcentral	Utilities	Total
Austria	17.6	n.a.	5.6	200	1,000	100	1,300
Belgium-Luxembourg	8.8	58.9	4.6	220	1,926	72	2,218
Britain	97.3	61.2	27.0	841	7,884	351	9,076
Denmark	9.8	16.3	3.8	177	6,480	2,999	9,656
Finland	8.8	n.a.	2.2	150	524	550	1,224
France	85.9	92.6	31.4	1,625	14,854	138	16,617
Germany	179.8	68.0	48.3	733	18,580	10,850	30,163
Greece	4.9	39.8	2.2	660	2,549	241	3,450
Ireland	3.0	21.0	1.2	129	227	173	529
Italy	56.4	63.9	21.7	n.a.	n.a.	n.a.	23,512
Netherlands	16.6	51.9	7.8	n.a.	n.a.	n.a.	472
Portugal	6.3	39.9	2.4	433	1,349	112	1,894
Spain	29.5	44.0	9.8	1,010	5,097	289	6,396
Sweden	22.7	n.a.	5.9	900	3,075	54	4,029
EC-15	547.4	60.5	173.5	7,078	63,545	15,929	110,536

n.a. = not available
EC = European Community.

a. Luxembourg excluded.

Source: Single Market Review (1998, vol. 2, 115–23).

1994 (Gordon, River, and Arrowsmith 1998). But this overall rate adds up direct purchases (made by public bodies) and indirect purchases (made by firms working for public contracts). Indeed, the ratio for *direct* imports alone only increased from 1.4 percent in 1987 to 3 percent in 1994.

Because these two last figures add up intra-EC *and* extra-EC purchases, they suggest a very low percentage for *extra*-EC sourcing. In addition, table 5.6 shows wide variations *among* sectors. In particular, the 22 most heavily protected sectors (see chapter 3) exhibit the lowest rates of direct import penetration in procurement markets, another indication of their higher than average protection (notably, paper suppliers operating in one EC member-state have had no success in winning business in other EC member-states; see appendix A, case 6).

Such large differences between direct and indirect purchases suggest that public procurement relies largely on domestically located suppliers, with foreign companies eager to bid in procurement contracts in a member-state establishing a subsidiary in the member-state in question. As a matter of fact, a study shows that, although 99 percent of the successful bidders in four "sensitive" British sectors (textiles, paper, medical products, shipbuilding) were located in Britain, only 64 percent of these bidders were British-owned companies (Hartley and Uttley 1994). Such a heavy reliance on establishment makes sense. There are good economic motives for a government or a public body to rely on domestic suppliers (transaction costs are smaller when dealing with local firms than with firms located outside the country, so preferences in procurement can be welfare-improving; Mattoo 1996; Evenett and Hoekman 1999).

The fact that establishment is costly suggests that small contracts are unlikely to be the target of foreign competition. Table 5.5 gives a crude estimate of this portion of public works, which could be de facto left untouched by liberalization. "Small" contracts represent 40 percent of EC public procurement concerns, with wide differences among EC member-states, leaving only 60 percent of the EC procurement markets as effective potential candidates for extra-EC, and perhaps intra-EC, liberalization. In sum, gains from opening public procurement (hence, forces in favor of liberalization) may be smaller than generally expected—a conclusion that may contribute to explaining the very low ranking of this topic in the text of the three European institutions.

The SMP experience in public procurement suggests a last essential lesson for the coming WTO negotiations. Transparency is of little help if not associated with swift procedures for dispute settlement in cases of allegedly unfair treatment. As is underlined by Gordon, River, and Arrowsmith (1998), the current situation is far from satisfactory in certain EC member-states (Germany, Portugal, Spain, and Britain)—suggesting similar difficulties for implementing the Uruguay GPA in these member-states. Unfortunately, the Seattle Commission text did not include this key conclusion as a lesson that the WTO could draw from the EC experience.

Table 5.6 Liberalization in select public procurement markets, 1994

ISIC code	Sector or product	Public procurement purchases		Winning new business in:		Public-sector import penetration rate (percent)	
		Percent of total procurement	Percent of sector output	Domestic markets	Other EC markets	Direct	Indirect
321-2	Textiles, clothing, footwear Uniforms	1	2			3	13
341-2	Paper and printing	4	9	12	4	<1	17–19
381	Metal products	3	6	6	0		
	Office furniture			9	2	5	8
	Boilers			12	4	4	9–10
	Power generation			10	4	6–7	11–14
382x	Office machinery	2	13	17	3	4	22–29
383	Electrical goods	4	11				
	Medical equipment			10	2	5–6	19–21
	Telecom equipment			13	7	6–8	18–22
3843	Motor vehicles	2	4	12	3	3–4	16–19
384x	Other transport equipment	2	9				
	Railway rolling stock			12	10	10–11	19–21
—	Civil engineering	34	31	11	4	3	4–7
—	Business services	15	7				
	Consulting engineering			22	4	1	5–6
—	Other goods and services	44					
—	All goods and services	100	11	9–13	3–4	2–4	5–9

ISIC = International Standard Industrial Classification.

Source: Gordon, River, and Arrowsmith (1998, tables 1 and 2).

Rather, it focused almost exclusively on the transparency issue and on regulatory convergence—insisting on the need for a "substantive" multilateral framework of rules, and mentioning only in passing that "effective rules to ensure enforcement will also be vital."

TRIPS and Investment Issues

This section presents only a brief survey of the issues of TRIPS and investment, for two reasons. First, in contrast to public procurement and competition (which also received limited support in the three Seattle texts reviewed in table 5.1), harmonization of TRIPS and investment has already occurred in other international forums, with a long tradition of plurilateral treaties on TRIPS (dating back, in particular, to the 1883 Paris Convention for the protection of industrial property) and on investment (with the International Monetary Fund [IMF] statutes and OECD codes of liberalization on capital movements, investment, and multinational enterprises). Such international harmonization has gone *beyond* what has been achieved within the EC in a substantial number of instances.

Second, there has been a significant international consensus on de facto liberalization in these domains that does not appear to be under serious threat in the near future. The odd accumulation of roughly 1,500 bilateral treaties on investment has worked reasonably well (at least for large firms), especially because it has been boosted by the progressive elimination of exchange controls and the liberalization of capital markets, amplified by technical progress. Intellectual property rights are becoming more widely acknowledged, despite legitimate concerns about their potential anticompetitive impact if they are unchecked.

All these reasons together suggest that the EC has limited incentives to negotiate on these topics in the coming round. This may explain the existence of noticeable divergence among the three European institutions: TRIPS ranks high on the Parliament list, and investment does the same on the Commission agenda, whereas both issues rank low on the other agendas (see table 5.1).

Intellectual Property Rights

The Seattle texts released by the European institutions send a clear message of strong opposition to renegotiating the Uruguay TRIPS Agreement, as suggested by some developing countries. Rather, they focus on better implementation of the existing agreements (including by mobilizing more international aid for better enforcement by developing countries) and on better integration of new agreements (such as the 1996 World Intellectual Property Organization treaties on copyrights and on performances and phonograms) into the WTO framework. The only new topics of negotiations envisaged deal with (1) extension of the existing TRIPS protection (in particular eliminating exceptions to indications of geographical origin, a major issue for certain EC farm sectors, such as wines or spirits, and currently an important provider of dispute settlement cases involving the EC) and (2) the touchy, including within the EC, issues of biological diversity (Commission text) and patents on living organisms (Parliament text).

Article 295 (ex 222) clearly keeps TRIPS under member-state competence: "This Treaty shall in no way prejudice the rules in Member-states governing the system of property ownership." As a result, international harmonization of TRIPS often goes beyond what has been achieved within the EC, at levels of both designing and enforcing disciplines (Drexl 2000; Ritter, Braun, and Rawlinson 2000).[33] For key types of TRIPS (patent, copyright), the coexistence of EC and US legal regimes seems an example of successful regulatory competition. Moreover, the WTO dispute settlement has shown its muscle in cases where the EC was a plaintiff (alcoholic beverages against Japan and South Korea, music rights in the United States). For these reasons, one may wonder whether current efforts to create additional European law in these matters make economic sense—except for eliminating constraints imposed by previous EC directives, such as the mandatory translation of EC-wide patents into *all* EC official languages. The fact that additional harmonization at the EC level may be more costly than beneficial is well illustrated by the 1993 Duration Directive, which extended copyright protection from 50 years (the duration imposed by the multilateral Berne Convention and initially enforced by most EC countries) to 70 years (the initial duration in Germany, and the longest duration in the EC until the directive's adoption).[34]

The major issue raised by TRIPS is less a matter of negotiating additional rights and obligations than of getting the right balance between the *multilateral* regime of transitory monopoly rights generated by TRIPS and the *national* competition laws. This delicate balance raises the issue of "international exhaustion," that is, the geographic limits (e.g., through territorial restrictions specified in a license agreement) to be imposed, or not,

---

33. TRIPS offer rare cases of EC infringement procedures launched against member-states because they have failed to adhere to international conventions (Ireland and Portugal, in the case of copyright and related rights), a situation underlining the importance of international law in the intra-EC context.

34. It is doubtful that such an extension could have any positive impact on creativity. Before the Duration Directive, a German work was protected for 70 years in Germany, whereas an EC work was protected for 50 years in Germany (if the home country of the EC work enforced the Berne duration). The 1992 *Phil Collins* ruling of the Court of Justice stated that a work should be protected for the same duration in a given member-state whatever the duration in the home country might be. This shift from home to host rule means the sacrifice of mutual recognition for harmonization, allegedly in the name of nondiscrimination but more surely for the benefit of vested interests.

on the use (exhaustion) of a given type of TRIPS. In its 1971 *Deutsche Grammophon* ruling, the EC Court of Justice stated that it was against the Treaty provisions (Articles 28 [ex 30] and 30 [ex 36]) for a manufacturer to exercise its copyright conferred upon it by the legislation of a member-state "in such a way to prohibit the sale in that Member-state of products placed on the market by him or with his consent in another Member-state solely because such distribution did not occur within the territory of the first Member-state."

In other words, the Court imposed the exhaustion principle *between* EC member-states; a few years later, this principle was extended to patents and trademarks. In its 1998 *Silhouette* ruling in a trademark case, the Court of Justice made clear that there is no such exhaustion principle with respect to imports from a non-EC country (in other words, an EC right-holder can restrict extra-EC trade by opposing parallel imports) unless there is an international agreement between the EC and the third country. Such a dual approach (exhaustion between member-states, but not between the EC and third countries) increases the capacity of EC right-holders to segment EC and world markets—hence increasing the overall protection granted to EC markets, and harming competition in the EC markets in the absence of effective competition policies (Maskus 1997). These complicated trade-offs between TRIPS and competition enforcement will involve EC and non-EC countries, and their case-by-case examination may end up in the WTO dispute settlement system, keeping a close link between intra- and extra-EC liberalization in TRIPS matters.

Investment

Unlike the Council and Parliament Seattle texts, the Commission text has a long section on investment, but it does not go much further on substance than the two other texts. It consists of a mere catalogue of good intentions. It reaffirms the EC conviction that the WTO is the appropriate forum for negotiation, that the WTO principles of nondiscrimination and transparency are sufficient for dealing with all the issues at stake, and that the WTO bottom-up approach to commitments (already used in services) would be the correct procedure for further liberalization. But the Commission text does little to clarify and reconcile the conflicting goals listed: protection of investment versus the right to regulate, growth objectives versus sustainable development (the latter being implicitly used as a global escape clause with respect to economic reasoning), long-term investment versus short-term capital movements, and so on.

This fluffy approach may reflect the ghost of the failed OECD negotiations on the Multilateral Agreement on Investment. More deeply, it mirrors the fact that intra-EC and extra-EC liberalization of capital flows have been achieved *simultaneously*, because they have been driven by forces or institutions *wider* than the EC. The initial Articles ex 67 to ex 73 of the Treaty of Rome did not include strong commitments on capital liberalization—to the point that in its 1981 *Casati* case, the Court of Justice found no legal basis for imposing unconditional free movement of capital. Moreover, until the 1980s, barriers imposed by member-states on extra- *and* intra-EC investment flows were mostly indirect (they consisted of exchange controls, payment restrictions, discriminatory regulations on interest and stock exchange transactions, and so on).

These barriers have been eliminated either through *unilateral* initiatives (e.g., the 1979 British elimination of exchange controls, or the 1986 "Big Bang" initiative for the London Stock Exchange, both imitated by other EC member-states during the 1980s and 1990s), or by *multilateral* or *plurilateral* actions under IMF, Bank for International Settlements, or OECD auspices (Henderson 1997). Because the EC as such is not a member of the IMF or OECD, member-states *only* have been in the driver's seat in both cases. The EC as such was not in charge, as is best illustrated by the fact that the last two OECD countries to eliminate exchange controls in 1994 were Greece and Iceland—an EC and an EEA member-state. The most recent illustration of the marginal role of the EC texts and institutions in investment matters was given by the Nice TEC version. Investment is not subjected to the majority rule by the new Article 133 (ex 113) (except for services, but this is because the GATS includes establishment as one of the four modes of delivery).

This evolution—largely led by extra-EC forces and institutions—has had two different effects on EC capital markets. On the one hand, it has led to much sharper provisions on capital in the Maastricht and Amsterdam TEC versions. Article 56 (ex 73b) prohibits all restrictions on the movement of capital and on payments, not only between member-states, but also "between Member-states and third countries."[35] In fact, notifications to the OECD of the remaining barriers show that 11 EC member-states have the same reservations for *both* EC and non-EC countries, leaving only four member-states with more reservations for non-EC than for EC countries (in order of decreasing importance, Belgium, Italy, France, and Portugal) (*Single Market Review* 1997b). More important, worldwide liberalization has generated enough competition in EC financial markets to counterbalance protectionist provisions in the Investment Services Directive or in the other investment-related directives.

On the other hand, the marginal role of the EC as such in investment matters has generated difficulties, and hot disputes with trading partners

---

35. Treaty articles on capital and payments have been renumbered twice. The initial Articles ex 67 to ex 73 were redrafted as Articles 73b to 73g in the Maastricht TEC version, which in turn became Articles 56 to 60 in the Amsterdam TEC version. For an excellent treatment of the links between freedom of capital movements and macroeconomic policies, see Pelkmans (1997).

about the scope of the reciprocity concept included in Article 49 (ex 59) in the case of financial services. Under the Second Banking Directive, which is part of the SMP, non-EC banks can enjoy the benefits of the Single Market under the same conditions as EC banks—except if it can be established that reciprocity is not guaranteed by the trading partner (EC banks do not receive national treatment in partner financial markets). This type of reciprocity is permitted by the OECD Code of Liberalization of Capital Movements, but only a few member-states have notified related measures. As a result, the EC-wide reciprocity provision under the Second Banking Directive opens the possibility of introducing *new* reciprocity requirements in the other member-states (something not completely legally impossible in the code context, but certainly fundamentally opposed to its goal of liberalizing capital flows). In other words, it opens the possibility of a decision by an institution, the EC, that is not a member of the OECD, to be implemented by member-states that are OECD members.

As a result, most of the remaining limits on capital in the EC flow either from discretionary (often opaque) decisions from EC member-states (see the discussion above on restrictions in services), or from specific EC directives not directly related to investment issues, such as the definition of what constitutes an EC firm, for instance an EC air-carrier (sectoral regulations), the Works Directive (public procurement), the Merger Control Directive (competition), or the Work-Time Directive (labor issues). These limits reflect either concerns unrelated to capital flows (with no effort to generate consistency between the various provisions) or certain difficulties of the EC to adopt a clear policy of market opening, probably because most of the EC economies are *both* large exporters and importers of capital, an ambivalence existing for other OECD countries (Graham and Krugman 1989).

Concluding Remarks

In Seattle, EC commercial policy included a vast set of topics for negotiation and it adopted very specific ways to address certain issues, particularly in services. The wide range of topics tabled was counterproductive. Because it was in contrast with the EC's reluctant, even hostile, approach to past rounds, such an encompassing approach generated the suspicion among certain trading partners that the EC wanted to bury the coming WTO round under a gigantic Tower of Babel. This suspicion was followed by interrogations when glimpses of the EC's *detailed* proposals often suggested a narrow scope for certain aspects of the negotiations (e.g., a very narrow definition of energy services). Finally, the EC's tendency to "export" the SMP as a model for the WTO—in particular its approach in services, which is heavily loaded with regulatory convergence and sectoral perspective—generated fears among many EC trading partners. As a result, the EC should ideally modify its Seattle stance on commercial policy in two ways.

First, the EC should abandon any effort to include three topics in the coming round: trade and labor issues, competition policy in its market power component, and trade and investment. Such changes should *not* be justified by considerations related to WTO tactics or politics. Rather, they should be seen as deeply consistent both with the philosophy, history, economics, and politics of the Treaty of Rome, and with a sound general economic approach, as shown by Maskus (2000). For instance, it is far more important for the EC to remember the sound economic and political reasons for which it has rejected (and still does, as most recently illustrated by the Nice TEC version) any direct link between trade and labor issues within the Single Market than to recognize that the "pro-labor" provision of the EC Generalized System of Preferences (see chapter 6) has failed (as the Seattle Commission text resentfully did when stating that such a clause "depends on the willingness of developing countries to apply for the incentives offered").

In these three domains, the EC should trust its *own* history, which shows (in a perfect match with economic analysis) that direct, *not* trade-related, instruments and policies are the best ways to reach the goals targeted. If really convinced by the merits of competition policy, the EC should induce every WTO member (including itself) to adopt and enforce such a policy, independent of trade-related considerations—hence protecting it against potential abuse as a strategic instrument in an international environment.[36] The EC should also commit itself to sign a framework agreement on cooperation (based on negative and positive comities) between competition authorities on a *nondiscriminatory* basis—that is, with any WTO member as soon as it fulfills the basic conditions of the agreement. If it is interested in improved labor standards in developing countries, the EC should remember its own history of de-coupling trade and labor issues and of implementing direct aid when necessary, such as intra-EC regional subsidies. In particular, it should focus on aid to education in developing countries (particularly for working children)—a key determinant of labor relations in the long run. Such an action does not require large funds, all the more because there is no reason to grant such aid unconditionally to all developing countries.

The EC should not be afraid of insisting on conditionality in these matters. There is no reason for the EC to give such aid to education in advanced developing countries (such as Brazil) that have reached a level of per capita income comparable to the European level of the early 1900s but

---

36. Quarrels over a possible capture of competition policy by trade interests have already emerged, as illustrated by the debate between US Congress members and EC Competition Commissioner Mario Monti ("Monti rebuffs US attack on merger policy," *Financial Times*, 19 October 2000, 10).

that do not provide the education services (mandatory school) already available in Europe—that is, these countries do not show their will to make their *own* society more equal. Last but not least, the issue of the efficiency of aid is so pressing that the EC should not hesitate to become sympathetic to private initiatives by EC firms or private institutions that could target well-defined social goals (firms may have incentives to fund schools for children working in their plants or living nearby) in an efficient manner.[37]

The second set of ideal modifications to the current EC commercial policy concerns the issues worth being kept on the WTO agenda. They raise two different types of difficulties.

First, there are "constitutional" issues—aiming to improve the WTO's basic legal framework. In particular, four issues could benefit from the EC experience—although, paradoxically and sadly, they are absent from the current EC proposals: (1) facilitating a progressive focus on only two "modes of delivery" of services (cross-border and establishment) in future schedules of commitments, and shifting away from regulatory convergence and a sectoral perspective toward an approach based on as unconditional mutual recognition as possible and on a horizontal (cross-sectoral) approach; (2) making the WTO agreement on antisubsidy measures closer to the EC approach on state aid, that is, banning or curbing aid granted by the subsidizing countries (instead of countervailing them by duties imposed by the importing countries allowed by the WTO), or alternatively, introducing the possibility of compensating for the impact of subsidies by improved market access to other industries in the subsidizing countries; (3) taking into account the fact that gains from liberalization in public procurement rely more on a swift and effective dispute settlement mechanism, at the disposal of the bidding firms feeling unfairly treated, than on general rules on transparency per se; and (4) ensuring that the TRIPS agreement will receive the appropriate counterbalance from competition policy enforcement by WTO members.

All these issues are particularly difficult because they require new interpretations of existing WTO texts—the most arduous thing to get in such a consensus-based institution—and because they make sense only if one adheres to a competition-oriented approach—not really the most popular view in the WTO forum. But precisely because of these difficulties, such issues require the patient, long-lasting support of major WTO

---

37. This "private" option raises the many and complex issues of "labeling" social aid—which are conceptually similar to those evoked in chapter 4 about technical regulations, but much more delicate to address because of their emotional content. The Parliament resolution released for Seattle suggests a code of conduct for EC multinationals operating in developing countries; this is unlikely to be a good tool, because it can be much too easily captured by vested interests (in developing and industrial countries) that have little to do with the social goals targeted.

members, such as the EC, to achieve some noticeable results in the long run—starting with the coming round.

Second, there is the central issue of market access in services—with the perspective of huge gains for the EC, because the EC SMP in services needs a serious external boost to overcome all its limits and become more complete and less reversible. This topic raises a fundamental problem of governance: getting all the expected gains from liberalization requires sound domestic regulatory reforms. In the EC Single Market Program, which is dominated by regulatory convergence, such reforms so far have largely been the outcome of a purely political process. Member-states have been "trading" regulations that could favor or protect their domestic firms—often at the cost of slowing down the whole process of increased competition, and making liberalization much less profitable than initially expected. Most EC member-states still fail to recognize that such a purely political process cannot ensure the best possible regulatory reform, particularly the best possible balance between the elements to be harmonized and those to be subject to mutual recognition.

A ray of hope could come from the new strategy in services launched by the Commission in March 2001 (European Commission 2000b). This strategy relies on the basic fact that services are much more tradable than is generally believed (Messerlin 1993) and it consists of three key components: (1) a horizontal approach, to be supplemented with the sectoral approach; (2) an effort to facilitate cross-border trade in services and to eliminate the unnecessary legal requirements of establishment imposed by member-states; and (3) a review of the existing directives in services (like those in technical regulations) in order to increase the role of mutual recognition by introducing nonlegislative solutions (such as codes of conduct, leaving harmonization at a strictly necessary minimum). If properly enforced (a first indication of that will be how the analyses to be carried over in 2001 will be done), this new strategy would have a dramatic impact on the EC service policy in the WTO. It would make the EC much more in tune with its major trading partners. For instance, the EC would be much more at ease in adopting the new tools of negotiations currently envisaged in the WTO forum, such as "clusters" of services (mixes of sectoral *and* horizontal interrelated services), in addition to the traditional sectoral discussions.

Because it is largely political, the existing SMP process has been and still is almost certain to deliver excessive harmonization. The US experience suggests that "the greatest threat to consumers' welfare is not states and their competition but a uniform national regimen that stifles the power to exit—that is, a monopoly of making" (Easterbrook 1983, 15). The results of the negotiations in the past on core harmonization in services (as in technical regulations) between EC member-states should be analyzed by economically sound cost-benefit analyses. Within the Community, such a task could be initiated by the Commission, but the experience of the *Single Market Review* (38 studies commissioned by the Commission, mostly done by major international consulting firms) has been highly disappointing in terms of quality and independence of mind. Member-states could also contribute to such analyses, but the past has not witnessed a strong interest from them in doing so—although recent initiatives, such as the auditing of the French Cour des Comptes by its Dutch counterpart, may offer interesting perspectives. Last but not least, as indeed is the case in the United States, most of this task should probably be done by independent "think tanks." The problem is that the EC is a place hostile to such institutions, with its combined heritage of inflated member-state bureaucracies of deteriorating quality and a Europe-wide political correctness prone to assume that any criticism of European integration implies hostility to European integration.

Of course, this fundamental problem of governance does not stop at the EC level. It also exists at the WTO level, where the risk of abandoning service liberalization to a pure negotiating process may be even greater than in the EC. Because its own liberalization of services has made the EC more aware of the need for sound cost-benefit investigations and economic analysis, the EC should not be afraid to be a staunch advocate of similar analyses at the world level—preparing WTO negotiations on market access, and assessing their results and implementation in an uncomplacent way.

The EC Addiction to Discrimination: Toward a Slow Ebb?

In 1999, the European Community had contractual and reciprocal bilateral agreements with 22 countries and contractual and nonreciprocal bilateral agreements with 77 countries (WTO, *Trade Policy Review: The European Union*, 2000). The EC is the direct source of 40 percent of all the preferential trade agreements (PTAs, which can be customs unions or free trade areas) notified to the WTO, and because the EFTA and Central European countries have duplicated the EC's approach, the EC was (and still is) the direct or indirect source of two-thirds of the PTAs in the world.[1]

Future EC policy in these matters—and the positive or negative impact of these PTAs on the EC's willingness to reduce trade barriers at the multilateral level—are thus essential for the WTO. It is all the more the case because the EC is the only PTA (along with the EFTA) for which there is convincing evidence of trade diversion on both the import and export sides, with the EC propensities to import *and* export significantly lower in 1995–96 than in 1980–82 (Soloaga and Winters 1999a, 1999b). These results suggest that the EC may have imposed a welfare cost on the rest of the world.

---

1. In this chapter, the "Central European countries" are the 10 countries that signed a "Europe Agreement": Bulgaria, the Czech Republic, Estonia, Hungary, Latvia, Lithuania, Poland, Romania, Slovakia, and Slovenia. The "Balkan countries" are Albania, Bosnia-Herzegovina, Croatia, Macedonia, and the Federal Republic of Yugoslavia. The "Eastern European countries" are all the successor states of the former USSR (except the three Baltic states) located on the European continent.

In April 1997, the Community put on hold all the existing projects of new discriminatory agreements (because PTAs are discriminatory by definition, PTAs and discriminatory agreements are treated as synonymous in this chapter), revealing a growing political fatigue with respect to such an approach. The pause ended with the signing of the framework agreement with Mexico in December 1997. Since then, negotiations with South Africa and Mexico have been concluded in March 1999 and January 2000, respectively, but no major project with the United States, Mercosur, or Asian countries has gone very far (though none has been officially abandoned). The renewal of the Convention with the African, Caribbean, and Pacific countries (ACP) seems more a painful but inescapable burden imposed on the EC by the past than a free choice.

It is interesting that the texts released by the three European institutions for the Seattle WTO Ministerial are very shy on regionalism. The Council text does not refer to regional or preferential agreements—it does not even once use the term "preferences." The Parliament text mentions the term only once, in the context of the trade and labor issue (see chapter 5). The Commission text uses the term "regional" (rather than "preferential" or "preference") in four contexts: investment, trade facilitation, trade and labor issues, and the erosion of the preference margins granted by the EC to developing countries because of the WTO global liberalization process.

In this context, a few dominant themes emerge: (1) continuing EC support for certain of its traditional trade relations, in particular the agreement with the ACP states and the Generalized System of Preferences; (2) several references to "special and differential treatment" of developing countries; (3) attention to the least developed countries (LDCs), in particular by proposing a joint commitment from all industrial countries and the most advanced developing countries (e.g., South Korea or Singapore) to grant tariff-free treatment by 2003 to "essentially" all products exported by LDCs; and (4) EC commitment to support institutional capacity-building in developing countries (both on domestic topics such as competition policy and on international issues such as trade facilitation, implementation of certain Uruguay Round commitments, future trade negotiations, etc.).

Is this short and relative pause a first sign that the EC "addiction to discrimination" (Wolf 1994) will decline over the next decade (while changing its forms, as underlined by Brenton 2000)? Sustained EC activity on discriminatory agreements during the coming decade will depend on two sources, which will be examined in more detail in this chapter, with the help of the framework described in box 6.1. From the demand side (hence focusing on the cost-benefit analysis of EC-related PTAs for EC *partners*), to what extent have the existing agreements been beneficial to current EC partners—a factor determining the attractiveness of PTAs with the EC for countries having not yet negotiated such agreements? From the supply side (hence focusing on the cost-benefit analysis of PTAs for the *EC itself*), do new agreements exist that the EC would prefer to WTO deals because

Box 6.1 A brief overview of the literature on preferential trade agreements

This chapter often refers to the doubts raised in the economic literature about the wisdom of preferential trade agreements (PTAs; e.g., see de Melo and Panagariya 1993, Baldwin 1994, Winters 1996, Bhagwati and Panagariya 1996, and World Bank 2000). This box briefly describes the main headings used in the chapter to present the pros and cons of preferential trade agreements.[1]

First, economic analysis reveals the "static" costs and benefits of PTAs. Costs from trade diversion (producers from PTA partners are substituted for more efficient producers located in the rest of the world, because of the discriminatory reduction of trade barriers) can offset (and more) gains from trade creation (producers from PTA partners are substituted for relatively inefficient domestic producers). This analysis has three useful corollaries for the chapter: (1) PTAs may get voted in precisely when trade diversion is the dominant force (trade diversion makes PTAs more palatable to domestic uncompetitive industries than multilateral free trade). (2) When a PTA is between a high-tariff and a low-tariff country, losses from the PTA to the former can be large, a situation that may be worsened if the low-tariff country is the dominant economy, as is often the case for PTAs with the EC. (3) A PTA member that depends on tariffs for revenue may increase its tariffs on imports from non-PTA countries to compensate for its PTA-caused tariff revenue losses—hence exacerbating the risks of trade diversion.

Second, PTAs could provide three major types of "political" costs and benefits: security (each PTA partner becomes a member of a larger economic area), credibility (each PTA member locks its own trade policy into an international treaty), and insurance (each PTA member locks in the PTA partner trade policy). Many observers of PTAs are satisfied with the possible existence of these benefits. They implicitly consider that, if PTAs exist despite likely net static costs, it should be because of political benefits. This approach is not acceptable; political benefits must be empirically assessed, and compared with the alternative political benefits to be drawn from the WTO system.

Third, PTAs could bring "dynamic" costs and benefits related to changes in production location and investment patterns, either by decreasing trade-related transaction costs (e.g., through the mutual recognition of product standards or service regulations) or by generating foreign direct investment and associated technology spillovers. However, such positive effects can be counterbalanced by new costs. For instance, because they are discriminatory, PTAs require rules of origin that undoubtedly make customs procedures more complex and costly. Foreign direct investment may increase only to avoid external trade barriers (tariff jumping) raised by PTAs.

PTAs are often based on a "hub and spokes" system (e.g., with the EC as the large, dominant economy—the hub—and the EC partners as the spokes), which may make it more expensive to locate investments in the spoke countries than in the hub country. In other words, such a system favors the EC as the investment location to the detriment of its partners. Similarly, mutual-recognition agreements in hub and spokes PTAs may improve market access for the hub more than for the spokes.

---

[1] This brief survey cannot do justice to theoretical counterarguments, such as welfare-enhancing trade diversion or nondiscriminatory spillover effects of reduced frictional costs. However, these aspects do not change the main thrust of the survey: economists' reluctance to support discriminatory trade agreements.

(box continues next page)

they would provide a cost-benefit balance better than, or at least comparable to, the balance that WTO deals could offer?

The chapter argues that, during the coming decade, the EC may slowly shift away from the discriminatory approach. The first section below (on ACP and GSP countries) and the second section (on Central European, Mediterranean, and Balkan countries) suggest that existing PTAs have been disappointing for most EC partners—inducing these countries to look either for EC membership or, if they cannot, for WTO-friendly alternatives. The third section looks at potential PTAs that the EC could envisage with the United States, and with Latin American, Asian, or Eastern European countries; it suggests that most of these agreements would require structural adjustments from the EC comparable to adjustments for WTO rounds, without offering to the EC the same trade-offs in market access and economic benefits. This is because all the possible PTAs of some scale for the EC will, almost inevitably, include large and serious competitors of EC producers in agriculture, industry, or services that have been left outside by the current web of EC discriminatory agreements.

The fourth section of the chapter examines an often neglected dimension of the "regionalism versus multilateralism" debate, namely, the use of the dispute settlement mechanisms offered by these two alternatives. It focuses on the EC's use of the WTO mechanism, for which there is much more information. The fifth section concludes by suggesting a few ideal ways in which EC trade policy should evolve.

It would be surprising for the EC to completely and rapidly abandon a bilateral approach that it has cherished so much and for so long. PTAs have been seen by the Commission as a proxy for a foreign policy that has been (and still is) out of its reach, *and* by EC member-states as a way to maintain or reinforce their own political influence on certain non-EC countries—almost leading each member-state to get "its" own EC PTAs by trading them for comparable requests from other member-states. Rather, for the foreseeable future, the EC may simply try to "rationalize" its web of existing agreements, at a pace largely determined, as in the past, by political considerations. One should not forget that the Conventions with the African, Caribbean, and Pacific countries were a reaction to the independence of these countries: the EC Generalized System of Preferences was a response to the movement among developing countries of the 1960s; the agreements with the Central European countries came in the aftermath of the fall of the Berlin Wall; and the agreements with the Mediterranean and Balkan countries countered the fear of conflicts close to European borders.

EC Nonreciprocal Discrimination: ACP Conventions and the GSP Scheme

The EC's addiction to discrimination was born with the Treaty of Rome. In 1957, three EC member-states were colonial powers on the verge of granting independence to their remaining colonies. To face this change, the Treaty of Rome offered to these colonies, once independent, the possibility of being "associated" with the Community. The treaty draft contained a framework—a *single* free trade agreement between the Community on the one hand and, on the other hand, a unique free trade area for all future associated countries—that was likely to minimize distortions and costs from such an association (Grilli 1993).

This initial framework was never implemented. It limited too much both the inward-looking development policies fashionable among newly independent countries and the vested interests of former colonial powers. As a result, the First Yaoundé Convention—signed in 1963 between the EC and the 18 newly independent countries—inaugurated the quite different system of hub and spokes. The EC became the hub of 18 de facto *bilateral, nonreciprocal* free trade agreements, one with each associated ACP country. Almost concomitantly, in 1965, developing countries were able to impose the adoption of GATT Section IV, allowing a "special and differentiated treatment" of these countries with a nonreciprocal "generalized system of preferences." The EC GSP became the source of a second set of spokes around the EC hub. Box 6.2 briefly presents these two agreements; the rest of this section examines the benefits for EC partners and the resulting problems to be solved during the coming decade.

What Net Gains for ACP and GSP Beneficiaries?

At first glance, the ACP Conventions look favorable for EC trading partners, and they may have been so until the 1990s. However, EC preferences to ACP states are evaporating (European Commission 1999a) for three reasons. First, preferential margins for EC tariffs imposed on ACP exports and non-ACP exports are decreasing because EC *MFN* tariffs are decreasing. In 1996, the average preferential margin granted to the ACP states

Box 6.2 The ACP and GSP agreements

The trade regime of the African, Caribbean, and Pacific (ACP) Conventions (Yaoundé I and II, followed by Lomé I to IV and, since June 2000, by Cotonou) provides for free access (no duty, quantitative restriction, or measure having equivalent effect) to EC markets for all industrial products originating from the ACP states (77 ACP states have signed the Cotonou Convention). Preferential access to EC markets was granted for four farm products (sugar, bananas, beef, and rum). For a few other farm products, preferential reductions were granted on border charges imposed by the EC Common Agricultural Policy. Rules of origin (possible cumulation, value-added threshold, tolerance about nonoriginating materials) are more favorable for the ACP countries than for the signatories to any other EC discriminatory trade agreement. The safeguard clause is also more limited than in other EC regional agreements (to the point that, in practice, it might be difficult to enforce).

This trade component of the ACP Conventions was easily accepted, all the more because it was not seen as the most valuable part of the Conventions. The ACP countries valued much more the aid regime based on partnership between donors and recipients (hence, without much conditionality) and the commodity price stabilization scheme (Stabex).

In 1971, the EC introduced its own Generalized System of Preferences (GSP), and renewed it several times. Contrary to its direct predecessor (which made wide use of tariff quotas), the current GSP (1995–2004) grants preferences in the form of tariff reductions, but these preferences are subject to "modulation," "graduation," and "incentives."

Modulation means that tariff reductions vary by product according to the "sensitivity" of the product for EC producers. Reductions are restricted to 15 percent for "very sensitive" products (textiles, clothing, and ferro-alloys); to 30 percent for "sensitive" products (electronics, cars, and chemicals); and to 65 percent for "semi-sensitive" products. As a result, tariff elimination is limited to "nonsensitive" products. In other words, modulation implies that the EC GSP grants limited benefits to exports for which developing and emerging-market countries tend to have comparative advantages.

Graduation means that tariff reductions are a function of economic and trade features of the beneficiaries, giving least developed countries preferences close to those they receive under the ACP Convention. Conversely, since 1998, EC trading partners with a GNP per capita higher than roughly $8,200 in 1995 have not been able to benefit from the EC GSP. This clause has eliminated Hong Kong, South Korea, and Singapore from GSP coverage. Last but not least, foreign exporters having a share larger than 25 percent of EC imports of a product are not eligible for the GSP tariff reduction associated with the product in question.

Incentives mean that GSP benefits can be "upgraded" (tariff reductions can be larger) if the EC partner fulfills certain conditions regarding environment and labor standards (see chapter 5). This EC initiative to link trade and labor issues has been badly received. As of July 1999, only Moldova had requested the benefit of these provisions.

Additional tariff reductions have been granted to certain South and Central American countries with the "Drug GSP" (1990) or "Hurricane GSP" (1999) to reward antidrug policies or to help countries facing natural disasters. These refinements have met strong opposition among EC partners because they discriminate among developing countries, as is best illustrated by Brazil's request for a WTO panel on the Drug GSP.

was 3.6 percent with respect to the MFN tariff, and 2.5 percent with respect to the GSP regime. In 2000, these margins were reduced to 2.9 and 2 percent (with more than 80 percent of EC industrial imports from ACP countries being duty free, on an MFN basis).

These smaller preferential margins are also becoming less uniformly spread over the range of products. In industry, only chemicals, footwear, and textiles (one-fourth of ACP exports) will still bring substantial preferences. In agriculture, half the ACP exports will lose their preferences, particularly coffee and cocoa (the latter having, in addition, to face increased competition from vegetable fats following the new EC directive on chocolate, see chapter 4), whereas the other half will keep a preferential margin of 10 percent.

A second, more important, source of preference decrease will flow from the elimination, scheduled for 2005, of the indirect protection granted to relatively inefficient ACP textile producers by EC Multi-Fiber Agreement (MFA) restrictions imposed on more efficient producers from the rest of the world.

A third source of preference decrease is the commodity protocols that have generated noticeable transfers of EC tariff revenues to ACP producers—to the point of artificially inducing certain African countries to invest in banana production, and to try to compete with highly competitive Caribbean producers, despite the long-term negative impact of such crops on African land and water resources. These protocol preferences have generated exports worth roughly €1,600 million: €850 million for sugar, €400 million for bananas exported by 12 beneficiary ACP states, €225 million for ACP rum producers, and the rest for beef. However, in 2000, preferences on rum exports were discontinued, and those on bananas were shifted to a new, indirectly less favorable, legal regime (see below and appendix A, case 19). Those on beef, however, depend on the EC intervention price, which has to be reduced by 20 percent in accordance with the Berlin Summit (see chapter 4), a change that may amplify the steady decline of the quota fill rate (from 80 percent in the late 1980s to 50 percent in the late 1990s).

Last, the EC has granted trade preferences to other countries, in particular Mediterranean states, Mexico, and South Africa. The new trade agreements with these countries offer conditions broadly equivalent to ACP Conventions for market access to the EC for key products (fish, fruit, vegetables, tobacco, textiles, and clothing).

Despite their much easier access to EC markets in the past decades, very few ACP countries have had a good growth and trade record since 1965. The key reason is that ACP countries have been very reluctant to liberalize their *own* economies; periods of liberalization have been rare and short, and they have almost invariably been followed by periods of reprotection (Sorsa 1996, Wang and Winters 1997, and Messerlin and Maur 1999).

At first glance, this conclusion suggests that the ACP Conventions have little to do with ACP bad performance, and it underlines the "unimportance of being preferred" (Davenport 1992; McQueen 1998). Such a view is supported by the fact that the 29 percent of ACP exports that have benefited from substantial preference margins (defined as larger than 3 percent in 1996) increased by only 62 percent in volume during the decade 1988–97, relative to 80 percent for the developing countries benefiting only from the GSP. Only *five* ACP states out of 70 have shown a growth rate higher or equal to the average growth rate of developing countries, and even this success seems very fragile. For three of these five ACP states (Jamaica, Madagascar, and Mauritius), it is based on exports of textiles and clothing; exports from developing-country competitors of these ACP states are subjected to high trade restrictions; and the major exports of the two other ACP states (Kenya and Zimbabwe) consist of flowers and fruit, with all the risks associated with the CAP (for fruit in particular).

One can go further and argue that the nonreciprocity approach of the ACP Conventions has been *instrumental* in the fundamentally flawed design of the trade policies of the ACP states. Because ACP exporters were certain to get free access to EC markets, they did not have to lobby their own governments to open their home economies as a quid pro quo for access to foreign markets. In sum, the ACP Conventions have systematically destroyed the domestic political engine (the export lobbies) behind trade liberalization.

This basic problem has been exacerbated by the fact that, at the dawn of independence, subsidiaries of EC firms constituted the core of the "modern" industrial sector in ACP countries, and became the major beneficiaries of growing ACP protectionism—enjoying considerable monopoly rents when things were still going well, and benefiting from subsidies granted by the ACP host countries (and often financed by EC member-state aid funds) when things turned bad. Last, the wave of nationalizations in many ACP countries has often been more useful for the remaining subsidiaries of EC firms than harmful to them. Nationalizations provided the political justification for high trade barriers and high domestic prices, playing the role of "rent-umbrellas," as is best illustrated by the diverging fate of the EC and ACP shipping companies under the cartels organized by the UNCTAD Conference Liner Code.

Turning to the GSP, its potential preferences have been more limited than those under the ACP Conventions. Modulation allows for keeping still-high GSP tariffs on very sensitive or sensitive products because the MFN tariffs on these goods (e.g., textiles and clothing) are generally very high. Graduation introduces a discriminatory treatment between GSP beneficiaries; it excludes the most developed and the largest exporters among the potential beneficiaries (e.g., it has excluded roughly 80 percent of South Korea's or Singapore's industrial exports and still excludes 55 percent of Chinese industrial exports from EC GSP coverage), de facto limiting the GSP to small developing economies. Last, the complicated structure of the

GSP makes its implementation costly, in particular because of complex rules of origin—hence precisely hurting these small ACP partners.

As a result, the GSP preferences have been very small in recent years (Hallaert 2000). For instance, if one excludes temporarily the impact of the graduation mechanism, the average GSP tariff on industrial goods in 1997 was 2.7 percent—half the 5.1 percent average EC MFN tariff and a differential small enough to be easily annihilated by the costs (estimated to be 3 percent of prices; OECD 1998c) of complying with rules of origin. Taking into account graduation (which forces us to look at specific countries) worsens the picture: in 1997, the average GSP tariff on EC industrial imports from China was 3.6 percent, almost three-quarters of the EC MFN tariff, ironically it was 3.2 percent on industrial imports from Singapore.

1970s and 1980s: The EC "Pyramid of Preferences"

This brief survey suggests that the ACP and GSP schemes have not provided large benefits (if any) for EC partners because they reinforced the choice of a protectionist policy (in the ACP case) or offered in fact very limited "preferences" to these countries (in the GSP case). Nevertheless, despite their limitations, these two schemes were used during the 1970s and 1980s as benchmarks by the EC when granting preferences to other countries—leading to an elaborate "pyramid of preferences" (Mishalani et al. 1981) consisting of six main layers.

At the bottom of the pyramid, the first layer consisted of centrally planned economies, generally not GATT members, which faced "conventional" or bilaterally negotiated EC tariffs (often much higher than EC MFN tariffs), as well as many quantitative restrictions, generally defined at the member-state level—and hence subject to intra-EC trade restrictions under Article 134 (ex 115). The second layer consisted of EC partners under MFN status—essentially the non-EC OECD countries. Imports from these countries were subject to EC MFN tariffs, and to relatively few nontariff barriers, except imports from Japan, which were often subject to voluntary export restraints (introduced during the process of the Japanese accession to GATT).

The third through sixth layers consisted of countries benefiting from EC "preferences." The third layer included the developing countries under the EC GSP. The fourth layer consisted of Mediterranean countries that could not have been included in the ACP scheme because they were already independent when the EC was founded, and that had not been left at the GSP layer because of their deep political ties with certain EC member-states. Exports from these countries enjoyed roughly GSP tariff reductions, but they were subject to fewer EC quantitative restrictions than those imposed on GSP partners (e.g., clothing quotas were imposed on Mediterranean exports, but only by one or two EC member-states, and for

Table 6.1   The remnants of the EC "pyramid of preferences," 1999

			Simple average tariff rates (percent)				
Product	MFN bound	MFN applied	GSP + MFN	FTA + MFN	LDCs + MFN	Lomé + GSP + MFN	Lomé + LDCs + MFN
All products	7.0	6.9	4.9	3.5	1.9	1.9	1.8
Agricultural products[a]	17.4	17.3	15.7	16.7	10.3	10.3	9.5
Nonagricultural goods[b]	4.6	4.5	2.3	0.5	0.0	0.0	0.0

FTA = free trade area
GSP = Generalized System of Preferences.
LDC = least developed countries
MFN = most favored nation

a. As defined in annex I of the WTO Agreement on Agriculture.
b. The rest of the products.

Sources: WTO, Trade Policy Review: The European Union, 2000.

less than a handful of clothing categories). The fifth layer consisted of the ACP countries. Last, at the top of the pyramid were the EFTA countries—the only group of countries under *reciprocal* preferences with the EC, with a free trade area for industrial goods (although subject to antidumping and antisubsidy measures), but also with severe limits on farm trade and almost no provision for services.

In 1989, this pyramid collapsed because the bilateral trade agreements between the EC and the Central European countries catapulted those countries from the lowest layer of the pyramid to almost the highest. (The reshuffling of the upper layer between EFTA, EEA, and new members has not affected the pyramid per se, but has underlined its volatility.) Because any "preference" granted to a trading partner is, by definition, a discrimination *against* another trading partner, the upgrading move of the CECs in the pyramid deteriorated the *relative* situation of all the other EC trading partners—generating bitter requests from ACP, GSP, and Mediterranean countries to "upgrade" their status.

However, there are remnants of this past pyramid of preferences. As shown by table 6.1, tariffs decline according to trade status with the EC—from MFN to the GSP, to the various free trade agreements with the EC, to least developed country status, to Lomé-ACP status. This conclusion deserves three remarks (in addition to the fact that table 6.1 relies on 16 million tariff records—a good indicator of the complexity of the EC pyramid of preferences). First, a country can often choose the lowest rate for each product from the various preferential tariffs for which it is eligible—meaning that there are substantial redundancies among all the various EC schemes for trade preferences. Second, tariff preferences are small in agriculture and preferential tariffs are relatively high. Third, the GSP is not the best status for developing countries, a point crucial for the reform of the ACP Conventions.

What Future for ACP and GSP Schemes?

In February 2000, the Lomé IV Convention expired and the EC and the 78 ACP states concluded negotiations on the Cotonou Partnership Agreement (PA) covering five aspects: political issues (peace-building, human rights, democracy, rule of law, and immigration), institutional reforms and involvement of the "civil" society, development strategies (with a focus on poverty reduction, cultural development, and gender equality), trade policy and trade-related issues (competition policy, standardization, trade and environment, labor standards, health safety), and financial aid.

The Cotonou PA trade component has four major features. (1) It will last only eight years compared to 20 years for the nontrade aspects of the PA. (2) During this eight-year period, the EC will basically continue to apply the nonreciprocal Lomé IV Convention, except for the Lomé banana protocol (to be replaced by new provisions in the context of the new EC banana trade regime, see appendix A, case 19). (3) During the same period, the EC will negotiate new trade agreements with 77 ACP states. (4) The PA trade component does not apply to the largest African economy, South Africa, which signed a special trade agreement with the EC in October 1999, raising risks of eroding the PA benefits for the other ACP states, in particular Botswana, Lesotho, Namibia, and Swaziland (Akinkugbe 2000).

If the EC agreement with South Africa has a time frame that is relatively similar to the PA trade component (a transitional period of 10 years for the EC and 12 years for South Africa), its structure is shaped by GSP status. Tariffs will be removed according to product categories defined by sensitivity, as in the GSP. On the whole, EC tariffs are expected to be removed from almost all South African industrial exports but from only 61 percent of South African agricultural exports (a source of severe friction during the negotiations), whereas South African tariffs are expected to be eliminated or reduced on 80 to 85 percent of farm and industrial imports from the EC.

The new PA trade regime with ACP States will have to be compatible with WTO rules. The Lomé Convention infringed on GATT Article I on nondiscrimination because it covered only *certain* developing countries whereas GATT Section IV allows discrimination only in favor of *all* developing countries; and it could not be considered an exception under GATT Article XXIV because it was *non*-reciprocal, contrary to a customs union or a free trade area.

Moreover, if the Lomé sugar protocol got a waiver at the end of the Uruguay Round (although it could still possibly be contested by certain producers, e.g., Brazil), this was not the case for the beef protocol (because traditional ACP exporters are not "substantial suppliers"), and above all, for the banana protocol. The three GATT and WTO dispute cases on bananas have revealed how much the whole Lomé Convention has progressively become the hostage of EC banana trade policy—with the hostility against Lomé increasing among non-ACP developing countries producing bananas (the motives behind the EC banana policy have little to do with the ACP Conventions; see appendix A, case 19).[2] The legal risks generated by the EC's inability to overhaul its banana policy obliged the EC to request a last waiver for the PA for the transitory period 2000–08 from its WTO partners (see appendix A, case 19).

As a result, the new ACP trade regime will be based on *reciprocity*, which conforms to GATT Article XXIV. Starting in 2008 and for a transitional period of at least 12 years (2008–20), ACP states will liberalize their *own* trade regimes with respect to EC exports, with strong possibilities of "backloading" this liberalization. If ACP states do not want to do so, they will benefit from the new SGP regime that the EC will announce in 2004; however, least developed countries (LDCs) can continue, if they wish, to benefit from the nonreciprocal access to EC markets under the "Everything but Arms" initiative (see the concluding section of this chapter). The 2000–08 preparatory period will thus prepare the ACP states for this crucial move to reciprocity. This shift (with a hotly disputed clause about the readmission by the ACP countries of their illegal emigrants to the EC) is the major reason for the huge financial package to be disbursed during the preparatory period: €13.4 billion in newly committed funds, plus €9.9 billion in resources not disbursed during Lomé IV and €1.7 billion from the European Investment Bank; that is, a total of almost €25 billion (in comparison, the GDP of all the ACP countries was estimated to be €200–250 billion in the late 1990s).

What will be the detailed structure and content of the new trade regime to be negotiated before 2008? Currently, the most fashionable proposal in Brussels is to create "regional economic partnership agreements" (REPAs) consisting of free trade agreements between the EC and ACP countries. The envisaged REPAs would be based on the free trade areas already existing between ACP countries: Caribbean Community (CARICOM), East African Cooperation (EAC), Southern African Development Community (SADC), Union douanière et économique de l'Afrique centrale (UDEAC), and Union économique et monétaire ouest-africaine (UEMOA).

A proposed alternative to REPAs could have been to apply the GSP status to ACP states, but this seems to have been abandoned—largely because it would have been costly for the 37 ACP "*non*-least developed countries" (non-LDCs), which represent three-quarters of ACP exports to

---

2. The only exception to these legal uncertainties consists of the sugar tariff quotas, which have been included in the current access quotas under the Uruguay Agreement on Agriculture.

the EC; a margin of tariff preference of roughly 1.9 percent would have been lost, and losses related to the remaining product protocols would have been substantial for 22 non-LDCs (European Commission 1999b).[3]

The REPA-based proposal suggests two remarks. First, the shift of EC policy to reciprocity has been largely triggered by considerations external to the ACP states. As explained above, the EC has been unable (still is, despite the appearances) to change its banana trade policy quickly enough—fueling the hostility against the ACP Conventions among non-ACP developing countries. Moreover, the EC has found it increasingly difficult to grant nonreciprocal preferences to ACP states, whereas Australia, Canada, the United States, and the APEC countries were receiving some privileged access to certain ACP states through initiatives such as the Free Trade Area of the Americas (Caribbean ACP states) or the US African Growth and Opportunity Act (Sub-Saharan ACP states).

Second, an examination of the three possible sources of costs and benefits from discriminatory trade agreements (see box 6.1) suggests that the envisaged REPAs are likely to generate net costs for the ACP states, for three reasons.[4] REPAs are likely to generate large static costs, because they are unlikely to spur noticeable trade creation, but are likely to generate substantial trade diversion. By reducing their tariffs on EC goods, ACP states will transfer part of their corresponding tariff revenues to inefficient EC-based firms—because of the ACP states' high MFN tariffs imposed on imports from the rest of the world (a sad situation, more so because the previous ACP Conventions transferred protectionist rents to inefficient subsidiaries of EC firms located in ACP countries).

Two additional forces may reinforce these static costs: (1) A PTA between two small countries (such as the ACP states) that also trade with a third large country (such as the EC) may harm the small net importing country whenever imports from the large country are subject to tariff and are necessary to clear the market of the small importing country—a typical situation for the LDC ACP states that will use the possible option to reject the reciprocity condition (remaining de facto under a trade regime close to the Lomé Convention) and will also pertain to PTAs between ACP states. (2) A PTA between two low-income countries tends to lead to income divergence and to put at risk the lowest-income country—a possibly frequent situation because REPAs include countries with noticeably different income levels (Venables 1999). Moreover, the REPA approach

---

3. ACP least developed countries could have been shifted to the GSP regime without too many problems, because the GSP and the Lomé regimes are close for this group of countries (see box 6.2).

4. What follows ignores the huge political difficulties of the REPA approach, namely, the fact that 25 ACP countries are not members of any PTA, and that the existing PTAs among ACP states are far from robust.

will be very costly for all the ACP budgets (tariff revenues represent 30 percent of a typical ACP public budget, with peaks up to 50 percent for Sub-Saharan countries), with additional distortions likely to favor "large" ACP countries (e.g., Ivory Coast or Kenya) relative to "small" ACP states pertaining to the same REPA—with the almost certain risk of generating political tensions.

Moreover, REPAs are unlikely to increase substantially the political benefits from discriminatory trade agreements (security and conflict management, credibility, and insurance), relative to those provided by past ACP Conventions. Finally, dynamic benefits from lower transaction costs due to regional agreements are at best dubious if one takes into account ACP administrative capabilities to manage complex rules of origin; and chances of getting rapidly dynamic benefits from increased foreign investment are slim in countries notorious for their sudden and frequent policy reversals.

In terms of pure reciprocity and discriminatory trade agreements, the EC initiative toward REPAs has major flaws. However, it may not be such a bad idea if recast using a conditionality-based approach, as will be suggested in the concluding section of this chapter.

EC Reciprocal Discrimination: Central European, Mediterranean, and Balkan "Spaghetti Bowls"

In the early 1990s, EC discrimination shifted from a nonreciprocity to a reciprocity approach. Paradoxically, this shift was a reaction to the *nonreciprocal* and *nondiscriminatory* sweeping trade liberalizations undertaken by Czechoslovakia, Hungary, and Poland immediately after the fall of the Berlin Wall. These liberalizations brought rapid economic benefits to the three CECs; within a couple of years, their trade patterns changed dramatically, reflecting a return to trade flows based on comparative advantage (Kaminski, Wang, and Winters 1996; Hoekman and Djankov 1997a). They also brought a large—unanticipated then, still unrecognized today—*political* benefit to the three CECs. In particular, they forced an initially reluctant EC to abandon its old formula of "cooperation and trade" agreements with centrally planned economies and to dismantle its barriers on imports from CECs—in other words, they *forced* the EC to knock down its cherished pyramid of preferences.

The EC shift to reciprocal discrimination has been the source of roughly a hundred *bilateral* agreements in Europe *alone*, and this figure is rapidly increasing, with new agreements in the Balkans, and the replication of EC agreements by Turkey under the Customs Union Treaty with the EC (see table 6.2). All these agreements have the same general structure, but they differ in many details: product coverage, time frame, liberalization pace,

Table 6.2 The "spaghetti bowls" of European discriminatory trade bilateralism, 2000

Column groups: EFTA countries = 1–4; CEFTA countries = 5–11; BFTA countries = 12–14; Other WTO members = 15–21; WTO nonmembers = 22–28.

Group or country	EC 15	1	2	3	4	5	6	7	8	9	10	11	12	13	14	15	16	17	18	19	20	21	22	23	24	25	26	27	28
EC-15		EEA	EEA	EEA	F	EA	EA	EA	EA	EA	EA	EA	F	F	F	CU	CU	CU*	CU	CU	ATP	ATP	F*	ATP					
EFTA countries																													
1 Iceland	EEA		F	F	F	F	F	F	F	F	F	F	F	F	F	F							F						
2 Liechtenstein	EEA	F		F	CU	F	F	F	F	F	F	F	F	F	F	F													
3 Norway	EEA	F	F		F	F	F	F	F	F	F	F	F	F	F	F													
4 Switzerland	F	F	CU	F		F	F	F	F	F	F	F	F	F	F	F							F						
CEFTA countries																													
5 Bulgaria	EA	F	F	F	F		F	F	F	F	F	Fs	F	F	F	F													
6 Czech Republic	EA	F	F	F	F	F		F	F	F	CU	F	F	F	F	F							F						
7 Hungary	EA	F	F	F	F	F	F		F	F	F	F	F	F	F	F													
8 Poland	EA	F	F	F	F	F	F	F		F	F	F	F	F	F	F													
9 Romania	EA	F	F	F	F	F	F	F	F		F	Fs	F	F	F	F													
10 Slovakia	EA	F	F	F	F	F	CU	F	F	F		F	F	F	F	F													
11 Slovenia	EA	F	F	F	F	Fs	F	F	F	Fs	F		F	F	F	F*					F		F						
BFTA countries																													
12 Estonia	F	F	F	F										F*	F*	F													
13 Latvia	F	F	F	F									F*		F*	F													
14 Lithuania	F	F	F	F									F*	F*		F													
Other WTO members																													
15 Turkey	CU	F	F	F	F	F	F	F	F	F	F	F*	F	F	F								F						
16 Andorra	CU																												
17 San Marino	CU*																												
18 Cyprus	CU																												
19 Malta	CU																												
20 Croatia	ATP											F												F					
21 Albania	ATP																												
WTO nonmembers																													
22 Macedonia	F*	F			F		F					F				F					F				F				
23 Bosnia-Herzegovina	ATP																												
24 Yugoslavia																							F						
25 Moldova																													
26 Ukraine																													
27 Belarus																													
28 Russia																													

EEA = European Economic Area.
EA = Europe Agreement.
F = free trade agreement
Fs = free trade agreement with substantial exceptions (agriculture)
Note: Boxes illustrate the membership of EFTA, CEFTA, and BFTA, respectively, with the general status in the diagonal cells.

ATP = autonomous trade preferences
CU = customs union
TEC = Treaty establishing European Community.
* signals a notification in process.

BFTA = Baltic Free Trade Area.
CEFTA = Central European Free Trade Area.
EFTA = European Free Trade Area.
WTO = World Trade Organization.

Sources: Notifications to the WTO; EC, Official Journal.

Box 6.3   The spaghetti bowls of European bilateralism: Part I

The EC reacted very cautiously to the Central European sweeping trade liberalizations that followed the fall of the Berlin Wall (Messerlin 1992). In early 1990, it simply shifted Hungary and Poland from MFN to GSP treatment for five years. Later that year, it eliminated all its quantitative restrictions on Hungarian and Polish exports, but only for one year, and not for a substantial list of "sensitive" products. In 1991, the same benefits were granted to Czechoslovakia. They were progressively extended to the other CECs, when they shifted to a market economy.

It is only in 1992 that the EC began to embody these changes in a series of reciprocal, bilateral Europe Agreements (EAs) with the 10 CECs (for more details, see Winters 1992, Rollo 1992, and Sapir 1995), the major provisions of which can be divided into the following sections:

Free movement of goods: A free trade area is established between the EC and each CEC. Tariffs, quantitative restrictions, and measures having an equivalent effect (including state monopolies, to a certain extent) must be eliminated over a maximum five-year transition period for the EC and a 10-year transition period for the CECs. But antidumping procedures are maintained, six different safeguard provisions are included, and complex rules of origin are established. Special protocols deal with "sensitive" products (e.g., textiles and clothing, coal and steel, cars, processed agricultural goods, and fisheries). Concessions in agriculture are particularly limited, the CECs simply getting privileged access to EC tariff-quotas granted under the EC Uruguay Round commitments. Almost all these provisions (except those in agriculture linked to the Uruguay Round) were quickly implemented (after signing, not ratification) by bilateral "Interim Agreements" (the EA portion devoted to free movement of goods).

The *three other freedoms* associated with the Single Market: movement of workers, movement of capital, and right of establishment in services. But the EAs refer to these fundamental principles of the Treaty of Rome in a rather restrictive way. Restrictions on labor flows are maintained (including on skilled labor and recognition of diplomas), and provisions on services are limited to increased "cooperation" between the EC and each CEC for certain infrastructure services (banking, telecoms, transport).

The *legal framework* (one-third of all EA provisions) covers essentially current payments, competition law and state aid, intellectual property rights, public procurement, and "approximation" of laws (i.e., the CECs' regulatory alignment with EC directives on a large range of issues, from customs procedures to technical regulations, banking law, and transport regulations).

All the EAs are bilateral and differ in many details—never insignificantly. Because of their own trade agreements with the EC, EFTA countries have adopted the same approach that the EC has with the CECs.

and so on. The resulting "spaghetti bowls" (Bhagwati 1995) illustrate the emergence of a European "bilateralism" centered on the EC.

This section focuses on the EC's relations with Central Europe, with three questions related to the Europe Agreements (EAs, described in box 6.3). Are there reasons to believe that EAs are costly for the CECs? If yes, what could the CECs do to reduce these costs? Could the CECs substantially influence EC multilateral trade policy *before* becoming full members of the Community? After having examined these points, the section concludes with a brief description of the discriminatory EC agreements with the Mediterranean and Balkan countries.

Are EAs Costly for the CECs?

From the CEC perspective, the balance of the *static* costs and benefits to be drawn from EAs is likely to be disappointing, for two reasons. (For a slightly more optimistic conclusion, see the analysis of the Poland-EC EA [World Bank 2000, 66–67]).[5] First, the value of *additional* preferences granted by EAs to the CECs (the difference between the EC MFN rate and the EC zero rate granted to the CECs) has been limited because the CECs were *already* enjoying substantial access to EC markets for all nonsensitive products *before* the signature of EAs (under the GSP and the 1990–91 measures; see box 6.3). The only noticeable source of additional preferences attached to EAs has been the elimination or suspension of tariffs in 1997, and quantitative restrictions in 1998 on exports of textiles and clothing from the six original CECs.[6]

The often-mentioned other source of additional preferences—the progressive introduction of a pan-European system of cumulation of rules of origin—is less clear. The pan-European system still has limits (described in chapter 4) that make it costly to manage, and that make it more difficult to assess the net impact of preferential rules of origin on trade creation and diversion. This net effect depends on several factors, e.g., the relative importance of traded intermediate versus final goods, the origin or use of these intermediate goods, etc., that play in opposite directions (Panagariya 1999b).

The second reason for likely static costs attached to EAs is the MFN trade policy of the CECs themselves. During the EA negotiations, all the CECs except Estonia *increased* their protection with respect to non-EC countries, sometimes very substantially (e.g., the Polish average industrial tariff increased roughly from 6 percent in 1991 to 18 percent in 1993). This protectionist drift was possible because all the CECs were not GATT or WTO members subject to the discipline of "bound" tariffs at the time of signing their Interim Agreement with the EC—the only exception being Czechoslovakia, which indeed has not increased its GATT-bound tariffs because it was the only Central European fully fledged GATT member be-

---

5. For the EC, the economic benefits and costs of EAs per se are small, for several reasons: The CECs are small markets for the huge EC economy; the value of the additional preferences granted by the EC to the CECs with EAs has been very limited and declining (EC MFN tariffs have declined with the Uruguay Round, the 1996 First Information Technology Agreement, the Customs Union with Turkey, the agreements with Mexico and South Africa, etc.).

6. From 1992 to 1998, EAs granted increasing "outward processing traffic" (OPT) quotas to CEC exports of textiles and clothing, which prepared for the 1997–98 liberalization. OPT quotas also have been beneficial to EC firms because their use was conditional on imports of raw materials or intermediate goods from the EC. In other words, OPT quotas have given EC firms powerful leverage to vertically integrate Central European producers for six years, and to reap the associated rents. The six initial CECs are Bulgaria, the Czech Republic, Hungary, Poland, Romania, and Slovakia.

fore signing the EA. If it reflected domestic pressures in each CEC, this protectionist drift was also fueled, in numerous instances, by pressures coming from EC member-states, the Commission, and firms (as is best illustrated by the car case; see appendix A, case 12).

By increasing their protection on imports from non-EC countries before or during the EA negotiations (and by continuing to do so since then, when possible, e.g., in agriculture, through discriminatory surcharges and other instruments), the CECs have substantially increased the value of the preferences that they grant to EC producers—and with it, the risk of trade diversion and the possibility of welfare costs. The still relatively high level of EC overall protection shown in table 2.1 suggests that a wide range of EC producers could be relatively inefficient by world standards—in other words, that trade diversion is not rare, all the more because CEC imports from the EC are large, often representing 40 to 60 percent of total CEC imports.

Static costs can be compensated for by political and dynamic benefits. However, the *political* benefits of EAs seem dubious. First, it is hard to see how EAs could have enhanced CEC *security* vis-à-vis the rest of the world, in particular the Soviet Union or Russia. The fact that the EC did not show any willingness to compromise on sensitive sectors, despite minute economic effects on the EC huge economy, was not precisely a signal of West European readiness to fight for the CECs, if necessary.

Second, the *credibility* of CEC economic reforms could have been enhanced by EAs, *only* if EAs were not accompanied by a reversal of the CECs' initially open trade policy (see above) and *only* if CECs' commitments would have been more credible when taken vis-à-vis the EC alone than when taken vis-à-vis a group of trading partners, including the EC. Such a condition—that "fewer cops are better than more cops"—would be convincing only if the EC had a better monitoring and retaliating system than its trading partners—a doubtful condition, if one takes into account the post-Uruguay Round tough dispute settlement regime. (The argument that dispute settlement schemes of PTAs are better than the WTO regime because they may give better access to private parties is highly debatable; such a possibility is not available in most PTAs, and the WTO dispute settlement regime is not totally impermeable to private parties.) Last, the EA component of *insurance* against EC trade practices was not very convincing either, after the EC antidumping regime was upheld and introduced several safeguard provisions were introduced in the EAs. Indeed, from 1990 to 1999, the CECs were accused by the EC of alleged dumping in 42 cases, compared to 106 cases during the 1980s (see appendix B).

Dynamic benefits from EAs are more difficult to assess. The available evidence suggests that the CECs that are most advanced in their accession negotiations are those with the largest exposure of their exports to EC technical regulations policy, and in particular to the New Approach (Brenton, Sheehy, and Vancauteren 2000). However, the discussion of the EC system of technical regulations (see chapter 4) does not suggest that the EAs can be powerful enough to eliminate TR-related costs (those costs have been very imperfectly reduced within the existing Community).

The same observation can be made for liberalization in services. If increasing foreign investment in the CECs could provide large benefits (Baldwin, François, and Portes 1997), investment flows to the CECs have so far remained limited, except for Hungary since the mid-1990s and perhaps the Czech Republic since 1999. In 1997, the inward stock of foreign direct investment (FDI) amounted to, respectively, 35 and 23 percent of GDP in Hungary and the Czech Republic but 10 percent or less in the other CECs (preliminary estimates on FDI flows for 1998 do not dramatically change the picture) (UNCTAD 1999). Moreover, some large FDI inflows may have reflected costly investment diversion occurring behind high trade barriers (e.g., in the Polish car industry; see appendix A, case 12).

EAs and CEC Accession to the EC

In the volatile political environment of Central Europe in the early 1990s, Central European politicians focused on the immediate political benefits of trade agreements (e.g., the apparent legitimacy attached to signing EAs) while ignoring their delayed costs, to the extent that they were aware of such costs. When they began to realize EA deficiencies (with the probably excessive trade reallocation and the limit of EC political support), they started to negotiate discriminatory trade agreements between themselves in order to counterbalance EAs (see box 6.4).

But the *bilateral* feature of many of these intra-CEC agreements imposed (and still does) a strong limit on their capacity to reduce the costs of the hub and spokes regime generated by the EAs. This weakness of the intra-CEC approach can be explained by several factors. Certain factors are political and quite specific to the European situation, such as the CEC belief in a rapid accession of their countries to the EC. Other reasons are economic and quite generic to trade agreements between spokes; contrary to multilateral free trade, gains from discriminatory trade agreements flow from increased shares obtained in export markets, whereas costs are imposed by rents abandoned to inefficient producers located in partner countries. As a result, export lobbies in a spoke country focus on the large markets of the hub country, and concentrate their efforts on the risks of domestic protectionist measures in these markets. By contrast, they neglect spoke markets, and possible domestic protectionist reactions from the spoke countries.

Now that the EAs have been implemented and will last for a long time, how can the CECs reduce their costs? Of course, a first possibility is to accelerate the CEC accession process to the EC. Membership is likely to reduce static costs because it will reduce CEC *MFN* tariffs, and it could be

Box 6.4 The spaghetti bowls of European bilateralism: Part II

Almost simultaneously with the EAs, the Central European countries (CECs) have created their own sets of trade agreements: the Central European Free Trade Area (CEFTA) between Czechoslovakia, Hungary, and Poland in 1992, and the Baltic Free Trade Area (BFTA) between Estonia, Latvia, and Lithuania in 1994.

If the BFTA covers both industrial and farm goods, the CEFTA covers industrial goods (excluding foodstuff) and a limited set of farm and food products (but Bulgaria, Romania, and Slovenia, which acceded to the CEFTA later, have been able to benefit from large exceptions in agriculture). Provisions on technical regulations and service liberalization are very limited. This partial coverage reflects two key features of the intra-CEC agreements. They are conceived as complementary to the EAs and accession to the EC, and they have a strong bilateral touch. This touch flows from the CECs' aversion to supranational institutions, generated by a deep-seated hostility to the trade regime that existed under Soviet hegemony, and by a fear that such institutions could endanger their accession to the EC.

The CEFTA and BFTA could have led to a CEFTA-BFTA-EC free trade area, but they failed to do so. Intra-CEFTA tariff reductions were rapidly followed by protectionist counterreactions for a wide range of products (alcoholic beverages, tobacco products, fuels, cars etc.) in the form of import surcharges, technical regulations, and the absence of cumulation of rules of origin within the CEFTA or BFTA (Enders and Wonnacott 1996). Safeguard measures have been implemented more often and strictly on imports from CEC partners than on imports of similar products from the EC.

More recently, several CEC governments have been more vocal about the loss of their fiscal revenues—resulting from intra-CEC trade liberalization—than about the similar (and much larger) consequences of the EAs. This "deflection" of EC-CEC conflicts to intra-CEFTA or intra-BFTA disputes reflects the strength of the political forces backing market opening with the hub, and the weakness of the political forces supporting market opening with the other spoke countries.

In many respects, these difficulties reveal the weakness of the justification for PTAs on the basis of "proximity" and "natural partners." After all, Estonia is as distant from Bulgaria as from France, and the historical links between Poland and France may be closer than those between Poland and Hungary.

expected to increase dynamic benefits related to smaller transaction costs and larger foreign investment flows. However, this option does not depend on the CECs alone; it requires EC acquiescence at the very time the CECs threaten two powerful EC interest groups: farmers and poor EC regions.

It is thus not so surprising that the accession process has been very slow, as described in more detail in box 6.5 and table 6.3. As of April 2001, no negotiations on the difficult topics had taken place, although the process with the Czech Republic, Estonia, Hungary, Poland, and Slovenia (the so-called first wave, or "Luxembourg Group", which also includes Cyprus) had been launched in December 1997 by the Luxembourg European Council (for details, see Mayhew 2000a). During the past two years, the CECs have completed their negotiating position papers on all the chapters for negotiation, and the Commission has begun to draft the EC common positions.

Box 6.5　The enlargement process: Missing a historic opportunity?

Each EA preamble specifies that the "objective of the [name of the CEC in question] is to become a member-state of the EC." The CECs were unhappy with this formulation: they wanted a sentence presenting the accession as the common objective of the CEC in question *and* of the EC.

The EC insisted on keeping such a unilateral formulation because it wanted to make clear its refusal to negotiate any component of the *acquis communautaire* and to use the enlargement process as an opportunity for reforming the EC's badly designed policies. As a result, the existing and future member-states are locked in the existing intra-EC deals (as was first illustrated by the nonnegotiability of CAP when Britain joined the EC), leaving the WTO as the only external source of reforms.

Viewed from the CECs' perspective, it is crucial to realize how much of a moving target the EC is for a candidate country. The Single Market, which was supposed to be firmly established by 1993 (most EAs were already signed by then), has since been relying on more directives every year. The legal framework required by the European Monetary Union (EMU), the Common Foreign and Security Policy (CFSP), and the Justice and Home Affairs (JHA) is continuously expanding. The Copenhagen Council (1993) imposed a few, but politically sensitive for certain CECs, additional requirements such as the protection of minorities. The Madrid Council (1995) added the "adjustment of administrative structures," a condition that few current EC member-states would fulfill. The Berlin Council (1999) made clear that the existing Common Agricultural Policy will not be expanded to the CECs (see main text). Also, the new Accession Partnerships between the EC and CECs have linked the granting of EC preaccession funds to hard conditionalities on CECs. For instance, Poland was asked to restructure its steel industry (a reasonable goal per se but the Partnership Agreement is silent on the key issue of the interactions between EC and Polish steel restructuring, see appendix A, case 11) and to free short-term capital movements (a debatable goal in the short and medium run).

The EC's day-to-day approach to enlargement is compounding all these difficulties. It consists of a bureaucratic and persnickety process: it is aimed at monitoring CECs' fulfillment of the *entire* EC *acquis communautaire before* entering the EC and it tries to minimize the number and the time span of exceptions as much as possible.

Such an insistence on a strict preaccession conformity approach contrasts strikingly with EC's own history when member-states adopted slowly the EC regulations that were difficult for them to introduce, as best revealed by the many infringements on the translation of EC directives into national laws (see chapters 4 and 5) and by "opting-out" options (including under the disguised form of slow privatization). The EC insistence will have long-term costs: it forces CECs to hastily pass hundreds of laws to comply with EC requirements, and hence it risks creating "virtual" legal frameworks (i.e., texts not, or loosely, enforced) in Central Europe, all the more because implementing certain aspects of the *acquis*, such as environment directives (see main text), imposes huge costs on CEC economies.

The enlargement process follows a strict procedure. First, the Commission "screens" the situation of each CEC to identify the difficult issues likely to arise in the negotiations. Then, *bilateral* discussions involving EC member-states, the Commission, and each CEC are "opened" to discussion on a chapter-by-chapter basis (the whole *acquis communautaire* has been split into 30 "chapters," see rows in table 6.3) by the successive EC Presidencies. This was done first for the Luxembourg Group

(box continues next page)

Box 6.5   *(continued)*

of CECs, and then for the Helsinki Group (for a more detailed presentation, see Mayhew 2000a).

On each opened chapter, candidate countries first present their "position" (requests for arrangements). The Commission then presents its own assessment of the situation. Finally EC member-states present their "common position." Once all the contentious points in a chapter to be kept on the table of negotiations are determined, the chapter is "closed." As of April 2001, only about half the chapters have been closed, with the Helsinki Group increasingly catching up with the Luxembourg Group. Once all chapters are closed, real negotiations will begin. As a result, the real negotiation stage has not yet been reached by any CEC—in fact, the common position of the EC member-states is still far from being known for most of the chapters.

Table 6.3 presents two possible definitions of the *acquis communautaire*: the Treaty provisions that are the core of the *acquis* and are undoubtedly nonnegotiable (they make up the EC Constitution), and the "secondary legislation" consisting of roughly 1,500 directives (a nonnegligible number of which could have been subject to review and reform if the EC had been ready to use the enlargement process as an opportunity to improve its own policies).

The breakdown between closed and still open chapters reveals a striking asymmetry: conflicts of interest are concentrated in chapters with a high dose of secondary legislation, whereas the constitutional Treaty provisions do not raise major problems (except the visa issue in Justice and Home Affairs, which is particularly sensitive because, ultimately, it will define "new" borders, cutting traditional links in Central Europe, for instance between Poland, Belarus, and Ukraine, or Hungary and Romania).

This asymmetry of problems suggests that the enlargement process is more about narrow economic interests than about long-term perspectives. This impression is magnified by the EC's unilateral decisions to grant to itself long transitional exceptions from certain *core Treaty provisions*, as best illustrated by the freedom of movement of workers. Under German and Austrian pressures, the Commission has proposed a five-year transition period (with a possible extension for a further two years) during which the current EC member-states will be able to keep their restrictions on workers from CECs (exceptions on such crucial Treaty provisions and for such long transition periods are unlikely to be granted to CECs). Moreover, it remains to be seen if this contrast between EC's lax position on its own obligations and its strict position on CEC obligations will not be amplified when member-states (finally) come to the forefront of the negotiations (as of April 2001, this was not yet the case).

Such an enlargement process reveals a lack of vision on the part of the EC—and maybe also the fact that the EC may feel overwhelmed by an enlargement involving 170 million people (if one includes Turkey) with wide differences of income per capita and culture.

It also shows that the EC has not learnt an essential lesson from its *own* experience: the EC does not trust markets to discipline CEC behavior despite the fact that during the last 40 years, they have disciplined France, Germany, Italy, and a few other member-states reluctant to open goods or services to competition. As a result, the EC is unable to adopt a strategic approach of enlargement—that is, to focus on the few core components of the *acquis communautaire* to be included in the preaccession exercise (for instance, a robust banking sector), leaving the other aspects to market forces and to postaccession compliance by the CECs.

This lack of vision and focus could add huge political costs to the economic opportunity costs of an enlargement process expressly not used as an opportunity to deliver domestic reforms. The EC may then have lost a historic opportunity.

These negotiations have been made more complicated, and probably slower, by the December 1999 Helsinki European Council decision to extend them to the remaining CECs (the so-called second wave, or "Helsinki Group", which consists of the rest of the CECs and Malta), partly as a recognition of their support during the Kosovo war. Last, if the 2000 Nice Inter-Governmental Conference (IGC) between the 15 EC member-states has dealt with institutional issues, such as voting weights and the Commission size in the EC with 25 member-states (all matters for which the Nice Treaty is not really necessary and which could be handled with the Accession Treaties), it has not dealt with the substantive economic problems of accession.

The accession negotiations are likely to be most difficult on three topics, all key in the context of trade and commercial policies: agriculture, regional subsidies, and technical regulations. In addition, they are expected to also be difficult on foreign policy and Russia, two noneconomic issues with clear echoes in trade policy, and on justice and home affairs (which are also related to trade policy, to the extent that they touch CEC capacities for legal enforcement and upholding the rule of law).[7]

Of course, agriculture is the most difficult chapter of negotiations. It is still a large sector (in value added and employment) in CEC economies, including the CECs that have no substantial comparative advantages in this sector (only Bulgaria, Poland, and Romania are considered potentially large producers of farm products in the future). During the 1990s, political pressures on CEC governments increased, with substantial declines in farm production in most CECs (8 percent in cereals, 28 percent in milk), and with the emergence of trade deficits accompanied by increasing market shares for farm imports from Argentina, Australia, and Brazil.

In this difficult context, the 1999 EC Berlin Council made two inconsistent decisions. When dealing with EC farmers, it chose to reject the option of renationalizing farm aid on the (right) basis that the CAP is *not* a social policy (see chapter 4). But this approach would have logically required scheduling a progressive extension of the whole CAP, including farm income support, to the CECs. Far from going in this direction, the Berlin Council included a financial agreement that made it clear that EC direct income subsidies would *not* be extended to CEC farmers by earmarking a maximum amount of €3.4 billion in 2006 for CEC accessions, whereas available estimates of the budgetary costs of extending the *pre*-Berlin CAP to the CECs fall within the range of €5–15 billion for the Czech Republic, Hungary, Poland, and Slovakia, and within the range of €9–23 billion for all the CECs.

The Commission tried to rescue the Berlin Council decisions, but it made things worse. It justified the Council's position with the fact that EC farm-

---

7. For this second wave, very sensitive political issues, such as the status of minorities, democratic institutions, etc., are a precondition for substantive discussions on accession. The EC has announced that it will not set target dates for accession before having a full assessment of each candidate's situation, i.e., before 2002.

Table 6.3 The EC enlargement to Central Europe, April 2001

	The acquis communautaire	
The "chapters"	Major Treaty provisions (new numbering)	Secondary legislation[a]
1 Free movement of goods	TEC 23–31, 94–97	503
2 Free movement of persons	TEC 39–42, 61–69	5
3 Free movement to provide services	TEC 39,43–48,49–55, 94–97	131
4 Free movement of capital	TEC 56–60[b]	48
5 Company law and TRIPS	TEC 133, 295[c]	12
6 Competition policy	TEC 81–89	19
7 Agriculture	TEC 32–38	383
8 Fisheries	TEC 32	4
9 Transport policy	TEC 70–80	49
10 Taxation	TEC 90–93	46
11 European Monetary Union	TEU, TEC 98–124	
12 Statistics	TEC 117	
13 Social policy	TEC 42, 87, 125–130, 136–148	52
14 Energy	TEC 154[d]	21
15 Industrial policy	TEC 157	
16 Small- and medium-sized enterprises	TEC 137, 157, 163	
17 Science and research	TEC 35, 157, 163–173	6
18 Education	TEC 149–150	63
19 Telecom and information technology	TEC 154–156	12
20 Audiovisual and culture	TEC 87, 151	1
21 Regional and structural policy	TEC 76, 101–104, 154, 158–162	
22 Environment	TEC 157, 161, 174–176	144
23 Consumers and health	TEC 33, 34, 81, 82, 87, 95, 152–153	12
24 Justice and Home Affairs	TEU, TEC 61–69	
25 Customs union	TEC 131–135	4
26 External relations	TEU	
27 Foreign and security policy	TEU	
28 Financial control		
29 Financial and budgetary provisions		
30 Institutions	TEU, TEC 189–312	
Provisionally closed chapters		
Opened chapters		1,509
Memorandum items:	Current European Community	
Date of signature of association	—	
Population (million)	377.6	
GDP (euro) per capita (at PPP)	21,200	

* Negotiations for accession of Turkey have not started yet.
TEC = Treaty establishing the European Community.
TEU = Treaty on European Union.
TRIPS = Agreement on Trade-Related Aspects of Intellectual Property Rights.

a. Number of directives in the *acquis communautaire* (in 1997).
b. OECD Codes (see chapter 5).
c. Multilateral ad hoc Treaties for TRIPS (see chapter 5).

ers will suffer income losses due to scheduled price decreases, whereas CEC farmers will not. This justification has two flaws. It ignores the fact that "intervention" prices of agricultural products in certain CECs (Poland and Slovenia) are becoming as high as EC prices, and sometimes even higher; and it would logically require that any "new" EC farmer (being the heir of a retiring EC farmer or an entrant into farming activities) would not be eligible for aid—and that unfortunately is not the case (see chapter 4).

In 2000, the EC tried to improve the situation by offering to the CECs a trade agreement eliminating export refunds and import tariffs on EC-CEC trade in farm goods (pork, poultry, cheese, fruit, and vegetables) that are not heavily dependent on the CAP in place. This marginal liberalization

Table 6.3 *(continued)*

	The Luxembourg Group						The Helsinki Group						Turkey*
Cyprus	Czech Republic	Estonia	Hungary	Poland	Slovenia	Bulgaria	Latvia	Lithuania	Malta	Romania	Slovakia	
XX	X	XX	XX	XX	XX		XX	XX	XX		XX	
O	O	O	O	O	O							
XX	XX	XX	XX	XX	XX	O	O	O	XX		XX	
XX	XX	X	O	O	XX	O	XX	XX	O		O	
X	XX	X	XX	O	X	O	XX	XX	XX	O	XX	
O	O	O	O	O	O	O	O	O	O	O	O	
O	O	O	O	O	O							
X	X	X	X	O	X	XX	O	O	O	O	XX	
XX	O	O	O	O	O		O	O	O		O	
O	O	O	O	O	O		O	O				
X	X	X	X	X	X		XX	XX	XX		XX	
X	X	X	X	X	X	XX	X	X	XX	O	X	
X	XX	XX	XX	XX	XX		O	XX	O		XX	
XX	O	O	XX	O	XX		O	XX			O	
X	X	X	X	X	X		XX	XX	X		XX	
X	X	X	X	X	X	X	X	X	X	X	X	
X	X	X	X	X	X	X	X	X	X	X	X	
X	X	X	X	X	X	X	X	X	X	X	X	
X	O	XX	O	XX	XX	O	O	XX	X	O	XX	
O	O	O	O	O	O		O	O	O		O	
O	XX	XX	XX	O	XX		O	O	O		O	
X	X	X	X	X	X	XX	XX	XX	XX		XX	
O	O	O	O	O	O							
X	X	O	XX	XX	O		O	O	O	O	O	
X	X	XX	XX	X	XX	XX	XX	XX	X	X	X	
X	X	X	X	X	X	X	X	X	X	X	X	
X	O	X	X	X	X		O	O	XX			
O	O	O	O	O	O		O	O	O		O	
21	18	19	19	16	20	9	13	15	16	6	16	
29	29	29	29	29	29	14	26	25	25	12	24	
1972	1993	1995	1991	1991	1996	1993	1995	1995	1970	1993	1993	1973[e]
0.7	10.3	1.4	10.1	38.7	2.0	8.3	3.7	2.4	0.4	22.5	5.4	64.3
17,100	12,500	7,800	10,700	7,800	15,000	4,700	6,200	5,800	n.a.	5,700	10,300	5,900

d. Plus the Treaty on the European Atomic Energy Community.
e. Plus the Customs Union Treaty (1996).

has generated a lot of bitterness among the CECs, for two reasons.[8] First, CEC tariff-free farm products will be subject to internal control for compliance with EC technical regulations in the country of origin; the extent to which such controls will be a substitute for EC border protection remains to be seen in the near future.

Second, this "freer" trade comes at the cost of constraints on production; production quotas will be imposed on CEC farm products included in these trade agreements, raising the question of the level at which these quotas will be fixed. CECs have requested quotas based on their produc-

---

8. Again, the fact that tariff-free farm exports from the CECs to the EC would increase from 37 to 77 percent as a consequence of this agreement is less a measure of the scope of liberalization than of the severe restrictiveness of the CAP for the rest of CEC exports.

tion during the late 1980s, but the EC has argued that such levels of production reflect the distortions of nonmarket economies, and hence are not acceptable. This is not a minor issue: for instance, CEC pork production declined by 24 percent during the 1990s. The bitterness is particularly high in Poland, which is the major CEC producer of most of the products involved (e.g., it produces 40 to 50 percent of CEC pork output). In this context, the Polish WTO strategy during the Uruguay Round (adopting a high level of protection to minimize compensation when joining the EC) is becoming a trap; it has made its farm sector barely competitive, by EC standards, for the products covered by the agreement (e.g., the production price of pork is 5 percent higher in Poland than in France).

The second major issue raised by CEC accessions consists of the considerable increase in the population living in EC regions that could be qualified as "poor," and hence eligible for regional aid. This problem is exacerbated by the fact that part of the farm problem could be handled through this approach. Direct income support to small farmers could be provided under this heading (assuming that the de-coupling principle will be fully respected and tightly monitored to avoid the past and current mistakes of the CAP—a big "if" in the EC context). Traditionally, the regional issue is dealt with by the so-called Structural and Cohesion Fund transfers. However, the Berlin Council decision to cap EC transfers from these funds at 4 percent of the recipient country GDP has had two effects. It reduces, probably severely, the CEC expectations in this domain. And it implies that a large portion (80 percent) of the structural aid currently given to EC regions should be reallocated to CEC regions.

Such a drastic shift is hardly compatible with the view prevailing among current EC member-states, according to which structural aid is an "acquired right." Ireland successfully defended its rights at the Berlin Council, despite the fact that its per capita GDP was 107 percent of the EC average in 1999, and is expected to be 117 percent in 2001. At the Nice Intergovernmental Conference (2000), Spain kept its right to veto decisions on regional aid until 2013 at least. Last, the Financial Framework of the Berlin Council clearly suggests that the EC expects new member-states to pay their full contribution to the budget—raising the question of the balance, during the first years of accession, between full contribution and still incomplete transfers (Mayhew 2000b).

Last but not least, the CEC accessions raise acute problems in the increasingly important domain of technical regulations and work safety regulations (see chapters 4 and 5, respectively). The estimated costs for the CECs to comply with the EC *acquis communautaire* in these matters are huge. For Poland, they have been estimated at 3 percent of current GDP for the directives on standards and safety rules in transport; 4.5 percent for the directives on the environment; and 0.5 percent for the directives on work safety in general, that is, a total of 8 percent, excluding the costs of aligning the other directives related to the Single Market Program (Mayhew and Orlowski 1998). A World Bank study has also estimated that introducing the 320 EC environment directives alone would annually cost Poland $6–$13 billion (4 to 8 percent of its current GDP) for the next 20 years, and roughly half these GDP percentages for the Czech Republic (Mayhew 2000b). If correct, at least part of these sums (the part reflecting "excessive" environmental protection) is likely to represent a huge amount of forgone consumption in the cost-benefit analysis of EAs.

Assuming no sudden, deep changes in the EC approach, this brief survey suggests that the Berlin Council has tilted the rules in favor of the EC's most powerful vested interests (farmers, poor regions) and against the candidate CECs—and that these changes reduce the benefits of full accession expected by the CECs. Moreover, by imposing costly investments to meet EC technical and environmental regulations, the alignment to the EC *acquis communautaire* will impose forgone consumption on the CECs, another source of reduced benefits for the CECs from accession—and hence of increased acrimony in the CECs.

CECs' Influence on EC Multilateral Commercial Policy during the Coming WTO Round

Because the accession process will be based on a gradual approach (as it was for Greece, Portugal, and Spain, which benefited from transitional periods), the coming WTO round likely will see all the CECs outside the EC—with some of them bitter vis-à-vis the EC. This situation raises the following question. What can the CECs' influence be on EC multilateral trade and commercial policy during the coming round? (The question of what the CECs can do to accelerate their accession to the EC is left for the concluding section of the chapter).

If few (if any) CECs will become EC members during the negotiations of the coming WTO round (assuming that these negotiations will be concluded by 2005–09), and most of them will become full EC member-states after 2010, what then could CEC influence be on EC *multilateral* trade policy during the coming WTO round? This question deserves particular attention when the preaccession CECs' level of protection is *lower* than the EC level (when higher, the CECs will be better off to adopt existing EC protection). Such a situation is not rare because, if the CECs have an economy-wide *average* tariff close to the EC average, they have *individual* (by product) tariffs often different from EC ones. The answer differs significantly for industrial products, farm goods, and services.

In manufacturing, the CECs can adopt two attitudes. They may be "neutral" if they do not feel concerned (for instance, if there are no CEC consumers) and hence leave the EC to grant "compensations" (in accordance with GATT rules) to its trading partners for getting the right to align acceding CEC tariffs to EC tariffs (i.e., the right to impose the *acquis communautaire* on the CECs). Alternatively, the CECs may exert pressure on the EC to align its higher MFN tariffs to the corresponding lower preaccession CEC MFN tariffs. The choice between these two attitudes will depend on the intra-CEC balance of interests between producers and consumers for every product. CEC consumers will always be interested in lower postaccession EC tariffs, whereas CEC producers will not necessarily oppose EC tariff decreases to the extent that they are accustomed to lower protection at home, so that they can expect to increase their share of the EC market. The risk that CECs may have a negative influence on EC trade policy is higher for products under nontariff barriers (in particular CEC producers may oppose EC tariff reductions following the elimination of MFA quantitative restrictions on textiles and clothing) and for products for which coalitions of protectionist lobbies can mobilize several CECs (this situation may happen in one-fifth of the CEC industrial sectors; UN-ECE 1996).

In agriculture, the CECs grant a smaller overall support to agriculture than the EC. In 1998, the estimated CSE-based tariffs (based on the old method; see chapter 2) range from 10 percent (Hungary) to 28 percent (Poland), relative to 49 percent for the EC. (Based on PSEs, the gap is even larger, with the EC support being three times higher than Poland's and nine times higher than Hungary's.) This broad view suggests that the CEC accessions will raise the critical issue of the ability of the enlarged EC to meet its WTO commitments, defined as the sum of the EC-15 and CEC commitments. The levels of difficulties ahead differ according to the type of trade barrier—as outlined in the following four points.

First, in terms of tariff commitments, most CEC accessions will be likely to require compensation because CEC tariffs (except for those of Poland and Romania) are lower than EC tariffs: by 20 percent for Hungary, by 50 percent for the Czech Republic and Slovakia, by almost 100 percent for Estonia.

Second, concerning import quotas, adding EC and CEC commitments would increase EC quotas by 15 percent for milk, by 50 percent for cereals and beef, and by 150 percent for chicken. However, EC vested farm interests hope to use the "netting out" technique, which consists of adding the EC and CEC quotas and subtracting the bilateral portion of these quotas (this technique tends to reduce the quota increases following accession; it has been used for the last EC enlargement, although it is still pending approval in the WTO).

Third, in terms of export subsidies, the situation will be very difficult for the enlarged EC. Almost all the CECs have scheduled low levels of export subsidies, and export capacities estimated for 2006 could amount to twice these levels (of course, aligning CEC internal prices to EC prices would worsen the situation by increasing the CECs' need for export subsidies). Moreover, the EC-15 has no room to maneuver because it is already at the limit of its own export subsidy commitments (see chapter 4).[9]

Fourth, concerning domestic support, the EC-15 has enough reserves in unused support under the *current* definition of the AMS to be able to fulfill the commitments of the enlarged EC. But the final situation will depend on how successful the EC will be in keeping unchanged the existing definition of domestic support; see chapter 4).

Solving export subsidy problems and minimizing tariff compensation would require that the EC substantially reduce its protection on farm products (as was noted above for manufacturing). Further reforms of the Common Agricultural Policy during the coming decade should make lower EC prices more consistent with CEC commitments. The Berlin Summit has left very limited scope for decisive moves in this direction (see chapter 4).

Meanwhile, the competitive pressure from CEC farmers on EC farmers may be reduced for two reasons. Barriers on trade of key farm products between the CECs and the EC are still high, and CEC farmers are often inefficient, making them unable to exert the competitive pressure that wide-ranging regional agreements could potentially provide (Josling 1998). They need massive restructuring, but they fear that they will not have the time to do it, both because EC subsidized farm exports will quickly compete with their own products in the open CEC markets and because CECs' cheap land may be quickly bought by rich EC farmers and resold at high prices later, after the CAP introduction in the CECs. Meanwhile, their hope for massive direct financial transfers from Western to Central Europe is fading, all the more because many CEC farms are small, hence unlikely to get much from the existing CAP biased in favor of large farms (see chapter 4). As a result, farmers in certain CECs (Poland) are both increasingly fiercely opposed to enlargement and trying to slow down any further reform of the CAP—amplifying the protectionist drift in CEC farm policies, which can be already observed (Hartell and Swinnen 1998).

In services, the situation is quite different, largely because that joint competence of the Community and member-states in commercial policy (see chapter 5) opens a Pandora's box of potential coalitions—and hence of strategies from vested interests. For those services for which certain member-states have a strong protectionist stance, the CECs may align their position to the *least* open EC member-states so as to eliminate all risk of future claims for compensation. But in turn, that will make more difficult the emergence of a compromise about an EC "common position" among the *current* EC member-states—the protectionist member-states claiming to have external "supporters" of their policy.

---

9. In 1997, Hungary was granted a waiver from its export subsidy commitments on the basis of miscalculations owing to trade conducted in nonconvertible currencies, and set revised commitments (subject to specific annual reports).

In such cases, the WTO compensation mechanism has the perverse impact of inducing the CECs to "maximize" their *current* level of protection, and hence to reinforce the most protectionist interests in the EC in order to minimize compensation in the *future*. This scenario has been illustrated by Croatia, Estonia, and Latvia, which ultimately adopted the most protectionist version of the EC Television Without Borders Directive, at the cost of delayed accession to the WTO (the United States insisted that these CECs adopt the open-minded version of the directive) and of reinforced protectionism in certain EC member states.

Such a negative scenario could be amplified by the fact that foreign direct investment in CEC services has meant the almost complete elimination of CEC firms in many services (including those where CEC firms initially may have had some advantages, such as retail trade) and the dominance of EC firms possibly eager to expand to the CECs the protection they enjoy in the EC. The counterbalance flows from the fact that large EC service firms tend to have a worldwide perspective—that is, they may be ready to exchange protection in small CEC markets for better access in large markets elsewhere.

The Mediterranean and Balkan Countries

Many EC discriminatory trade agreements have been generated by traditional political alliances between *particular* EC member-states and non-EC countries, and the agreements with the Mediterranean and Balkan countries do share this feature (see box 6.6). However, the key motive behind EC trade policy in these two regions is the fear that "doing nothing" for and with these countries could be a source of pan-European troubles or even regional wars, as mentioned during the launch of the Euro-Mediterranean Partnership by the Barcelona Summit (1995). This motive explains the often limited content of these trade agreements. The EC has used them more as a way to guarantee a status quo and traditional trade flows (hence it tends to conceive them as *minimal* variants of EAs) than as the key component of a strategy to open the partners' economies. It also explains the EC's deep and long-lasting hesitations on the Turkish accession case. Of course, such an approach has generated some disillusionment among all these EC partners.

All these agreements are prone to generate static costs, which can be amplified by a temporary increase in the EC partner's effective rates of protection, as is shown in the case of Tunisia (Hoekman and Djankov 1997b).[10] Political benefits to be expected from trade agreements with the

---

10. Indeed, it might be the case that certain measures to be implemented by Turkey (restraints on textiles and clothing) will protect the EC more than the Turkish market (Hartler and Laird 1999).

Box 6.6 The spaghetti bowls of European bilateralism: Part III

The EC agreements with Mediterranean and Balkan countries constituted a "bazaar" of all conceivable trade agreements with different economic concepts and legal structures (customs union, free trade agreement, etc.), different sectoral coverage (agriculture, manufacturing, services, etc.), different GATT-WTO status, and so on (Pelkmans and Brenton 1997).

The EC-Turkey Customs Union goes further than a typical EA in some respects. It requires Turkey to adopt the EC Common Tariff (including EC tariff preferences to third countries, i.e., Turkey must echo the EC discriminatory regime), and to approximate EC customs regulations (rules for imports, administering quotas, antidumping, and other trade remedies, including on textiles and clothing), and the EC policy of technical regulations. But it is a more limited agreement than an EA for the *three freedoms* and the *legal framework*, except for the approximation of competition laws and TRIPS. It does not cover the farm sector (the principle of free movement of farm products is stated, but without a deadline), despite its enormous importance for the Turkish economy (Hartler and Laird 1999). The EC has similar customs union agreements with Andorra and San Marino (two ministate enclaves in the EC territory), Cyprus, and Malta.

The EC agreements with Mediterranean countries (enforced with Tunisia, 1998; Morocco and Israel, 2000; signed with Jordan and the Palestinian Authority, 1997, and with Egypt, 2001; and in negotiations with Lebanon, Algeria, and Syria) replicate the EAs, but in a "limited" form. The *free movement of goods* does not include faster elimination of EC textile quotas; the period of transition for the EC partners is longer (12 years, generally); concessions on agriculture are marginal; and provisions on the right of establishment in services and on competition policy (including state aid) have no specific language and no time frame.

Since mid-2000, the EC trade policy with the Balkan countries has undergone rapid and important changes. Until 2000, it was based on the 1980 Trade and Cooperation Agreement (TCA) with the former Yugoslavia, although the TCA has not been renewed for the Federal Republic of Yugoslavia between 1998 and 2000. TCA provisions have been prolonged by the "Autonomous Preferential Trade" (APT) agreements with Bosnia-Herzegovina and Croatia, extended to Albania in 1992, and expanded by a more generous agreement with Macedonia. All these agreements consisted of EC nonreciprocal tariff reductions on imports from the Balkan partner, with a complicated, extensive system of annual tariff quotas and import surveillance (Messerlin and Maur 1999). In 1999, the EC shifted to Stabilization and Association Agreements, more generous but of reciprocal nature, starting with Macedonia.

In 2000, the EC unilaterally dismantled all its barriers on imports from the successor states of Yugoslavia (except for Slovenia, already under an EA), including those from Serbia and Montenegro after the free elections in these countries. The only exceptions to this unilateral liberalization are fish, baby beef, wine, and certain textile and clothing products (plus aluminum in the case of the Federal Republic of Yugoslavia), for which there are tariff quotas. The EC put one condition to its unilateral move, namely that the beneficiaries shall be "ready to engage [..] in regional cooperation [..], in particular though the establishment of free trade areas [..]" (Council Regulation (EC) No. 2007/2000, Article 2, *Official Journal* L240, 1–9, 23 September 2000).

EC are few, if any: the military security component in the region is out of the reach of the EC and of its member-states, as is illustrated by the Gulf and Yugoslav wars; and the credibility and insurance components are even weaker than for EAs. Dynamic benefits seem limited by the reputation of these countries for red tape creativity and their small capacity for foreign direct investment (Brown, Deardorff, and Stern 1997; Page and Underwood 1997), despite the existence of capital-abundant countries in the Arabian Peninsula as a possible source of FDI flows in the case of the Mediterranean countries (Council on Foreign Relations 2001).

The EC PTAs with the Balkan countries have one interesting feature. The EC's unilateral liberalization of September 2000 has been conditional on the fact that all these successor states of the former Yugoslavia shall be ready to sign PTAs between themselves. However, it remains to be seen whether the countries involved will grasp this condition for liberalizing their trade between themselves *and* vis-à-vis the rest of the world (as they should; see the concluding section).

EC Discriminatory Trade Policy in the 2000s: The End of the Road?

In the mid-1990s, the EC faced a situation that very few observers would have predicted six years earlier. The disastrous 1990 GATT Ministerial in Brussels, which should have closed the Uruguay Round, witnessed a Community hopelessly riveted to its Common Agricultural Policy. By contrast, the 1994 WTO Ministerial in Marrakesh showed the EC among the strong WTO supporters—an impression reinforced by the EC's role during the negotiations on the 1997 financial services protocol. In the late 1980s, EC member-states were bickering over the need for regulatory reform of services. By contrast, the core legal framework of the Single Market Program was delivered almost on time in 1993, fueling the impression of an almost finalized Single Market in goods and services, soon to be completed by a unique currency. Also in the late 1980s, the EC was cosily adapted to a permanently divided Europe. And again in sharp contrast, the EC's web of discriminatory trade agreements in place in 1995 was seen as a sign of its continental hegemony.

In this rather euphoric context of the mid-1990s, the EC took a series of trade initiatives with the United States, Mexico, Mercosur, certain Asian countries, and Russia—that is, far outside the traditional scope of its discriminatory trade policy. As of mid-2001, these initiatives have led to limited results, raising the following question: can such initiatives really fly, or are they doomed to be window-dressing operations, and even to fail, announcing the ebb of EC discriminatory policy?

Transatlantic Partnership with the United States

The EC's efforts to develop a transatlantic partnership have relied on a wide range of political motives, emerging every time when circumstances were favorable. First, the EC feared that the United States could be irreversibly less supportive of the WTO system, increasingly attracted by regional trade initiatives with Asian or Latin American dragons, and irreparably tired of the EC's negative-minded, slow-growing, rent-riddled behavior in trade matters. The EC also feared that considerations attached to US military hegemony would spill over into domains, such as trade, that it felt were more subject to de facto EC-US "condominium"—through US unilateral trade or economic measures, such as the Helms-Burton or Iran-Libya sanctions acts, among many other unilateral sanctions (Bayard and Elliott 1994). Last, the EC hoped that, after 50 years of having been a follower in trade matters, it could again be a world leader—challenging US supremacy in the WTO and becoming "more" equal to the United States in these limited economic matters.

As the incumbent hegemon—but also because of a portfolio of trade and investment flows well balanced among the major world economic regions—the United States has responded to these EC initiatives with a wide range of nuances of coolness, from skepticism to cautious approval (Barfield 1998). The corresponding US-EC discussions have produced many texts: the Transatlantic Declaration (1990), the New Transatlantic Agenda (1995), the Transatlantic Partnership for Political Cooperation (1998), and the Transatlantic Economic Partnership Statement and Action Plan (1998). And they have created many forums: the Transtlantic Business (TABD), Legislator (TLD), Consumer (TACD), Environment (TAED), and Labor (TALD) dialogues. The question is: what have been the substantive results of all these efforts?

The New Transatlantic Agenda package launched in 1995 led to four results in 1998: (1) a mutual-recognition agreement (with a similar MRA signed with Canada) dealing exclusively with conformity assessment procedures on a relatively wide range of industrial products (telecom equipment, electronic and pharmaceutical products, medical devices, recreational marine craft, etc.), but difficult and slow to be implemented (see chapters 4 and 5); (2) a veterinary agreement on a wide range of meat and fish products, even more difficult and slow to be implemented (see chapter 4); (3) a customs cooperation and mutual-assistance agreement; and (4) the agreement on the "positive comity" approach in competition law enforcement (each country could request from the other to take into account its interests when exercising its competence on competition matters; see chapter 5).

These results are not minor, but they can hardly be qualified as outstanding. The most important achievement is the MRA on industrial products, estimated to allow cost savings of roughly €1 billion a year from the nonduplication of conformity assessment (the so-called rule "approved once, accepted everywhere") on €50 billion annual bilateral imports. This result is largely due to the TABD (which is not a negotiating forum, but a source of recommendations from the chief executives of large US and EC firms presented to US and EC administrations). Moreover, the

TABD is intervening heavily every time the MRA implementation faces difficulties, as in late 2000.

These limited results, and the EC's new confidence following the 1997 WTO agreements on financial services and telecoms, led the Commission to table, in March 1998, a New Transatlantic Marketplace Agreement (NTMA) with four key proposals: (1) elimination of all tariffs on an MFN-basis by 2010, conditional on a "critical mass" of other countries doing the same; (2) removal of technical barriers; (3) creation of a free trade area in certain services (financial services, maritime transport, legal and medical services, satellite-based telecoms, and energy services have been mentioned by the European side), which would be based on the "negative list" method of negotiation, on the liberalization of cross-border trade on a host country basis, on the right of establishment without exceptions and restrictions, on the liberalization of market access through provision of national treatment, and on the elimination of regulatory obstacles on the basis of mutual recognition; and (4) liberalization beyond existing WTO commitments in public procurement, investment, and TRIPS.

From an economic perspective, the NTMA project avoided the most blatant risks of static costs associated with discriminatory trade agreements in goods. Provision (1) represented a de facto "normalization" of the EC position; the EC'was catching up with respect to a similar commitment made in 1996 by Japan and the United States within the APEC forum. It was equivalent to a unilateral liberalization of all the countries considered as pertaining to the "critical mass" (a concept close to the "principal-supplier" approach in WTO negotiations). By contrast, the assessment of the economic effects of provisions (2) to (4) is less clear. In particular, it is unclear whether the US-EC MRA agreements would have been automatically and unconditionally open to third parties, that is, would obey the fundamental WTO nondiscrimination principle (for a general discussion of the issues raised by the MRA approach, see chapter 4).

The NTMA project did not live two months. It met fierce opposition from the French government (scared that agriculture and audiovisuals, excluded from the NTMA, could be brought back at a later stage), heavy reluctance from half the other EC member-states (often because of concerns about the NTMA's consistency with the WTO framework) and much skepticism from the United States and the rest of the EC member-states. The major divergence between the US and EC sides was the balance in the proposed NTMA between liberalization (market access) and "regulatory convergence" in services. The United States found too little of the first ingredient (not only because of the exclusion of agriculture and audiovisuals), and too much of the second, with "regulatory convergence" evoking too much the ideas of reregulation and harmonization, possibly coupled with common judicial review. In any case, the NTMA was thought to require the European Council's unanimous approval—and it did not get it.

The London US-EC Summit of May 1998 tried to rescue the NTMA content by launching the Transatlantic Economic Partnership (TEP), and a joint action plan was adopted in November 1998. However, the TEP is much vaguer than the NTMA. Its multilateral component evokes strengthened US-EC cooperation for the preparation of the Seattle WTO Ministerial, whereas its bilateral component focuses on five domains (technical barriers, certain services, government procurement, TRIPS, and food safety and biotechnology). As of April 2001, there has been no concrete result from the TEP.

The 1999 US-EC Bonn Summit was mostly the mere occasion to examine issues of common relevance for the United States and the EC: cooperation on Balkan and Russian crises, exchange of views on telecoms or e-commerce, and so on. In fact, the summit focused more on political matters than on trade-related issues. Meanwhile, the TABD began to face difficulties. On the one hand, it produced new recommendations on technical regulations (e.g., on third-generation wireless standards and on health issues, such as AIDS, tuberculosis, or malaria); it has been increasingly active in emerging US-EC disputes (e.g., on the EC TRs reducing the noise of landing "hush kits" for aircraft, the EC's "metric only" labeling directive, or the use of the precautionary principle in the case of GMOs) by creating an early warning system; and it has taken initiatives in certain domains (biotechnology products, personnel mobility, corruption, international accounting standards, and specific e-commerce issues, e.g., protection of personal data, electronic authentification). On the other hand, a substantial number of TABD requests or proposals have been rejected by the administrations, leaving many pending problems in highly regulated industries, such as chemicals—e.g., the registration of a new crop protection active ingredient requires 2 tons of paperwork, with different sets of registration forms in every EC member-state (Engel 2000).

The TEP's limited results can be explained by the generally unfavorable circumstances that followed the withdrawal of the NTMA project. In December 1998, the OECD-based negotiations on the Multilateral Agreement on Investment collapsed. The US and EC business communities, increasingly frustrated by the legal complexities and turf wars generated by the negotiations, withdrew their support from the project, leaving the OECD Secretariat to fight alone a hopeless media battle with a few nongovernmental organizations determined to kill the initiative (Henderson 1999). More important, perhaps, the TEP initiative was so close to the coming WTO round that the TEP lost most of its raison d'être.

Beyond all these circumstances, there may be more profound reasons for the very limited results of all the transatlantic initiatives. The first flows from the magnitude of the economic gains expected from such initiatives, which are negligible if the initiative is limited to the elimination of tariffs on industrial goods, and which remain modest (real income increases by 0.3 percent in the United States and by 0.8 percent in the EC) if the liberalization includes agriculture, elimination of antidumping remedies, a broadened public procurement agreement, and a reduction in trading costs related to technical regulations (Baldwin, François, and Portes 1997).[11]

Political reasons also play an important role. From the US side, the support for transatlantic initiatives has been at most moderate, because convinced American supporters of such initiatives were divided in two groups so different that they could hardly constitute a broad and effective coalition (Frost 1997). On the one hand are the "Atlanticists," who tend to believe in gains from multilateral free trade and hence are unmoved by the potential economic gains to be expected from preferential agreements but are moved by political considerations, in particular, the fear of increasing political distrust between the United States and the EC. On the other hand are a protectionist-minded but heterogeneous set of "Japan-bashers," trade unionists, and environmental nongovernmental organizations, all interested in creating a big transatlantic trade bloc against new competitors from Asia and elsewhere.

From the EC side, the NTMA and TEP failures have revealed a more realistic portrait of the EC than the euphoric self-portrait of the mid-1990s (see the beginning of this section). The EC has not been able to deliver these initiatives, because its ability to meet all its Uruguay Round commitments in farm trade after 2000 looked increasingly debatable (chapter 4); because the EC solution to the problems raised by technical regulations is less successful than generally stated (chapter 4); because service liberalization in the Single Market emerged as a much more difficult and long-term undertaking than initially thought, with a crucial debate about more regulation or more liberalization (chapter 5); and because EC support for the WTO is blurred by almost a hundred bilateral discriminatory agreements in Europe (see above). Some of these issues were excluded from the negotiations with the United States (e.g., agriculture), but they have nevertheless been used as excuses by reluctant EC member-states.

All these remaining EC (and US) unsettled problems raise the same key issue. Most of the transatlantic liberalization would require almost the same adjustment efforts from the EC as a WTO deal (because in many instances US firms are among the most efficient world producers), although the United States could not offer to the EC the same concessions as those available in such a WTO deal (because US markets are smaller than world markets). In other words, it may be more profitable for the EC to negotiate a WTO agreement than the corresponding transatlantic agreement.

---

11. As a matter of comparison, expanding the widest liberalization scenario to all the OECD countries would result in an estimated 2.4 percent increase in the US GDP and a 3.3 percent increase in the EC GDP.

Spillovers in Eastern Europe, Latin America, and Asia Pacific

Like the United States, the EC is bound to be a "diminishing giant." Its weight in world trade and output is doomed to decline, if and when developing economies grow. From an economic standpoint, this inescapable fate should not generate fears; welfare is far from depending on size (Wolf 1994). And from a political perspective, relatively small countries have proved to be enormously influential—from the Dutch Republic of the 17th century to the role of Australia or Sweden in the GATT or WTO forums (Hellstrom 1999).

Eastern Europe

During the first half of the 1990s, in contrast with the United States, western Europeans were untouched by the diminishing giant syndrome because of the eastward expansion of the EC. But the EC's web of Central European agreements reached its maximum size in the mid-1990s. The EC concluded Partnership and Cooperation Agreements (PCAs) with Russia in 1994 (entered into force in 1997), Azerbaijan, Kazakhstan, Kyrgyzstan, Moldova, and Ukraine. Because most of these EC partners are not WTO members, these PCAs aim essentially to introduce WTO key disciplines into bilateral trade (MFN and national treatment, no quantitative restriction) and include agreements on textiles and clothing, and iron and steel.

Since 1997, the EC has toyed with the idea of a free trade agreement with Russia, and more recently, with the idea of a "wider vision" including Russia, Ukraine, and of the Caucasus countries (Emerson and Gros 1999). But the political realities of the region have frozen all these efforts, probably for a long period, and 1999 witnessed increased protection on both sides, particularly in steel, a product of primary interest for Russia. As a result, the EC seems to have reached its extreme borders at a time when the United States is looking to expand its new discriminatory agreements in the Americas and in Asia, as is best illustrated with the Free Trade Area of the Americas (FTAA) and the US-Singapore Free Trade Agreement. The US moves, combined with the absence of clear perspectives in Russia, have induced the EC to try to be more involved in Latin America and Asia.

Latin America

The EC's most visible efforts concern Latin America. They have been facilitated by the desire of Mexico and Mercosur members to balance their regional (NAFTA, Mercosur, and the future FTAA) and extra-regional interests.

In January 2000, the Commission approved the results of the negotiations on an Economic Partnership, Political Coordination, and Cooperation Agreement with Mexico. The trade component of the agreement aims to eliminate tariffs for most goods by 2003, but farm products sensitive for EC farmers are excluded (only 62 percent of the current bilateral farm trade will be covered by the agreement, which denies Mexican access to EC markets for all the key products under the EC Common Agricultural Policy, from cereals to sugar, with a review scheduled for 2003), and there are complex provisions for certain sectors (cars and car parts, garments) that required long negotiations about the exact regime of preferential rules of origin to be enforced.[12]

In services and public procurement, EC firms will benefit, according to the Commission, from the same treatment as US and Canadian firms, with the exception of audiovisuals, maritime cabotage, and air transport. The agreement also covers TRIPS, set at the "highest international standards," according to the Commission, cooperation in competition law enforcement, an effective dispute settlement mechanism (without prejudice to the parties' WTO rights), and a foreseen start (in 2003) of liberalization in investment (in recent years, the EC has been comparatively more important as a source of investment in Mexico than as a trading partner, a situation probably related to the impact of NAFTA).

As a result of this agreement, Mexico will be, with Israel and Jordan, one of the few countries to have free trade agreements with the United States and the EC—opening the possibility that the new discriminatory agreement between Mexico and the EC will erode some of the distortions generated in the Mexican economy by the previous one. It is unlikely that Mexico could become a full "hub" with respect to the United States and the EC (many biases in favor of the hub being eroded by the size of the two spokes). But such a set of Mexico-centered PTAs should induce Mexico to "multilateralize" its concessions to its three most important trading partners (Canada, the United States, and the EC)—a process that should naturally lead to WTO-based negotiations.

Prospects for an EC-Mercosur (and Chile) agreement are difficult to assess. Negotiations were formally launched in June 1999, but substantive talks on tariff issues (more topics should be covered) will not begin before July 2001. Moreover, the negotiating mandate specifies that negotiations are not expected to be concluded until after the end of the next WTO round. The nature of the agreement is still vague (it may not be a fully fledged free trade area). No outcome is expected before 2005, and no substantial trade liberalization before 2010–15 (IRELA 1999).

---

12. The EC estimates that the agreement is WTO-consistent because, by January 2003, it will cover almost 100 percent of the existing bilateral trade in industrial and fish products, and 62 percent of the existing bilateral farm trade, hence more than the threshold of 90 percent of total bilateral trade considered by the Commission as the threshold for WTO-consistency. However, *current* trade flows reflect *existing* barriers—implying that the 90 percent threshold is unlikely to be reached under *fully* liberalized trade.

Asia Pacific

The EC asked for membership in APEC, then for observer status, but the two requests have been turned down. Finally, the EC established an institutional dialog with the Asian side of APEC through the Asia-Europe Summit Meetings (ASEM). However, the three meetings held in Bangkok (1996), London (1998), and Seoul (2000) have not led to any substantial result in trade and economic relations—the Seoul Summit even witnessing embarrassing official divergences between the EC member-states on whether, how, or when the North Korean regime should be recognized.

EC policy toward China's accession to the WTO has been largely a free-rider on US policy. In the late 1990s, the EC left the United States to play the difficult role of reminding the Chinese authorities that the WTO is essentially about rules (meanwhile, China was benefiting from its EC GSP status, although it was often subject to the modulation and graduation components of this status; see above). In 1999–2000, when Chinese concessions began to be solidified in written bilateral agreements, the EC tried to expand the concessions obtained by the United States to additional goods and services of interest to it.

The resulting key points of the EC-China pre-accession bilateral agreement are: (1) Chinese tariffs will be reduced from 25 to 65 percent to 5 to 10 percent for 150 products (from spirits through cosmetics, leather, footwear, and textiles to machinery, appliances, and building materials); (2) tariff quotas on several farm products (rape oil, pasta, butter, wheat gluten, wine, and fruit) will be increased; (3) Chinese import monopolies on oil and (NPK) fertilizers and its export monopoly on silk will be eliminated; (4) Chinese opening in services will be improved, in particular in telecoms, insurance (with seven licenses guaranteed to EC firms), and distribution; and (5) investment (joint venture) operations will be eased in motor vehicles. Of course, most of the concessions granted in bilateral agreements (with the United States or the EC) will be extended to all WTO members under the GATT most-favored-nation principle.

The coming years will be critical for understanding the exact nature and content of the Chinese accession. In particular, it will be essential to see how often the status of a "nonmarket economy" (NME) in antidumping procedures will be applied against Chinese firms accused of dumping, and how often the "transitional product-specific safeguard" (TPS) provision included in the United States-China bilateral agreement will be invoked (these provisions will last 12–15 years). In both cases, the already relatively important size of many Chinese exporters implies that a frequent use of these instruments may have important direct effects (on the country implementing the measures) and indirect effects (on the other trading partners of China).

As is shown in appendix B, NME status leaves no chance for allegedly dumping firms to defend themselves, and it allows imposition of antidumping measures twice as large as usual ones. Moreover, the TPS allows China to impose countermeasures on imports from a country having imposed safeguard measures on Chinese imports under certain conditions, and as a result, contributes to turning the WTO regime from an instrument for opening markets into an engine generating a sequence of safeguards restricting trade (the United States or the EC imposes a TPS measure, then China imposes countermeasures, to which the United States, the EC, or any other country may react). Because of these two provisions, one can legitimately fear that the Chinese accession could replicate Japanese accession to the GATT: when Japan acceded to the GATT, existing GATT members imposed on Japan many "gray measures" and voluntary export restraints, which have lasted almost 30 years and endangered the whole GATT system.

A last interesting question to raise is the EC's reaction to the emergence of regional trade agreements in Asia Pacific (starting with the expected negotiations for such an agreement between Japan and South Korea). As of mid-2001, it is too early to see whether these Asian PTAs could launch a new wave of regionalism (Bergsten 2000), or whether things will not change much.

So far, only PTAs involving small and relatively open Asian countries have been signed (e.g., Singapore-United States or Korea-Chile). The economic impact of such PTAs is probably minute. Of course, PTAs involving Japan will change the scale of the effects, but the Japan-Korea PTA has not yet officially reached the negotiation stage (as of early 2001). Moreover, estimates suggest that PTAs involving Japan and Korea will be a source of gains only if China is included (Scollay and Gilbert 2001). In other words, economic gains would require political boldness in Asia. In such a fluid environment, it is hard to forecast EC reactions to Asian PTAs, all the more because estimates of the impact of Asian PTAs on the EC (and the US) economy are small.

A Final Remark

In sum, so far, all the EC trade initiatives toward Eastern European, Latin American, and Asia-Pacific countries (except one, with Mexico) have not led to substantial outcomes. This result could be explained by specific circumstances (the Asian or Brazilian crisis, the Russian transition process), by differences in trade doctrine (APEC vs. EC approaches to economic and political integration), or by opposition on key topics (e.g., trade and labor issues).

But there may be a more profound—permanent—reason for the failure of all these initiatives. All the conceivable PTAs of some substantial economic magnitude include EC partners that are and will increasingly be among the world's strongest competitors of EC producers. As a result, opening the EC markets to these exporters has the same economic consequences for EC producers as opening them to all WTO members (assuming that these PTAs will not be mere window dressing). For instance, a substantial free trade agreement with Mercosur will be almost as demanding in competitive pressures and adjustments for the EC farm sector (cereals, meat, sugar) and certain industrial sectors (from food industries to leather products, cars, or even aircraft) as a WTO agreement with the same product coverage.

The same will be true for PTAs with large Asian economies and the EC manufacturing sector, and for a PTA with the US and the EC manufacturing and service sectors. Conversely, all these PTAs have the disadvantage of offering (much) more limited trade-offs than a WTO deal of the same magnitude. The Mercosur economies, for example, cannot provide the same markets for EC exports as a world including the United States and Asia Pacific, and vice versa for the other possible PTAs. Of course, the balance of gains and costs of all these new discriminatory agreements does not have the same magnitude for all the EC because of the magnitude of the EC partners. For instance, a PTA with Russia would be closer to the Europe Agreements examined above than a PTA with APEC or Japan.[13] It remains that the cost-benefit balance of new discriminatory agreements is likely to be less favorable than the balance offered by the corresponding WTO agreements.

Political benefits from all these initiatives are also hard to see for the EC (they constituted the main gain for the EC of the discriminatory agreements examined in the first and second sections above). Asian and Latin American countries have made clear that a trade agreement with the EC should not be perceived by the EC as an act of defiance against the United States—and even less as an act of allegiance to the EC. Political gains to be expected are thus small for the EC, all the more because they can be counterweighted by political frictions with the United States (which would not exist in the context of WTO negotiations).

In fact, one may argue that all these PTAs require the existence of an EC foreign policy. Because it is impossible to negotiate PTAs simultaneously with Eastern European, Latin American, and Asian countries, there is a need to make priorities, that is, to develop a fully fledged foreign policy. In the absence of such a policy, PTAs will be merely "time-buying" devices, and hence a source of large frustrations, as is best illustrated by the EC policy with respect to Turkey. As of mid-2001, the EC does not seem to

---

13. Indeed, Russia is likely to lose from such an agreement, for reasons similar to those suggested for the CECs (Brenton, Tourdyeva, and Whalley 1997; Enders and Wonnacott 1996). An economically sound agreement between the EC and Russia should also include most of the Soviet Union successor states (except for the Baltics, which are already linked to the EC). But such an agreement may be more difficult to sign because a wide definition of Eastern Europe makes the existence of strong competitors of EC firms more likely.

be ready for such a task, so that even from a political perspective, the WTO appears as the most efficient option for the EC.

Regionalism versus Multilateralism: The Dispute Settlement Dimension

The debate about regionalism versus multilateralism is often limited to considerations about trade agreements per se. It ignores the key role of the "remedies," that is, the institutional guarantees that an agreement will be observed. (This point has been indirectly touched upon above, with the "insurance" motive for discriminatory trade agreements.) PTAs signed by the EC are loaded with a tight net of safeguard clauses of many types, certain of them with debatable GATT consistency, and all the disputes occurring within these PTAs are dealt with by bilateral "joint committees."

The key alternative to bilateral remedies is the WTO-based Dispute Settlement Understanding (DSU), with its panels and appellate procedures considerably reinforced since the Uruguay Agreement. During the GATT period, the widespread skepticism about the operational inability of the settlement procedure to deliver enforceable panel recommendations has been shown unjustified to a substantial extent, except when the EC and the US have been involved (Hudec 1993). Even in this case, there have been successes. For instance, the two successive GATT panels (1989, 1991) on the EC oilseed regime led to substantial changes of EC policy in this sector.

However, if the new procedural rules under the Uruguay Round DSU ensure well-functioning settlement procedures, they have brought to the forefront concerns about the *nature* of the remedies, in particular the ultimate option of retaliatory countermeasures—the negotiating value of such measures (for small countries, relative to large partners) and the economic benefits for the domestic economy (of both small and large parties to the cases) being highly questionable (Mavroidis 2000).

The existence of *alternative* (bilateral vs. multilateral) dispute settlement tracks raises several questions about the possible strategic use of these alternative instruments by the EC. In particular, has the EC actively used the WTO dispute settlement procedure? Has it used it in a substitutive or complementary way to bilateral procedures incorporated in EC PTAs? Has this use been targeted at certain trading partners (and, vice versa, has the EC been targeted by certain of its trading partners)? A final set of questions is to examine whether, and how, the WTO dispute settlement mechanism contributes to shaping the dynamics of EC commercial policy.

The EC is an important user of the dispute settlement procedures. Table 6.4 shows that, of the 194 cases initiated between January 1995 and May 2000, the EC was involved in 92 (as a complainant or defendant, leaving aside 28 cases where the EC was a "third party.") Interpreting these ab-

Table 6.4 WTO dispute settlement cases, January 1995–May 2000

	Number of cases involving European Community			Number of cases involving United States		
	Cases facing:				Cases facing:	
Status	All cases	United States	Preferential partners	All cases	EC	Preferential partners
Complainant	51 (39)	16 (10)	0 (17)	54 (33)	33 (11)	5 (18)
Defendant	41 (36)	22 (9)	0 (12)	42 (41)	24 (8)	4 (12)
Subtotal	92 (75)	41 (19)	0 (29)	96 (76)	57 (19)	9 (30)

EC = European Community.
WTO = World Trade Organization.
Note: Figures in parentheses correspond to the number of cases, if they had mirrored trade flows. For the lists of "preferential" partners, see text.
Source: Dirk de Bievre (2000), Database on WTO DS cases, Florence: European University Institute; author's computations.

solute numbers in a meaningful way requires a comparison with trade flows to get a better sense of a possible overrepresentation of the EC.[14]

If perceived as reflecting the fact that the EC is one of the largest markets in the world (Hoekman and Mavroidis 2000), such an overrepresentation seems best measured by the number of cases in which the EC is a *defendant*, namely 41 cases, whereas the trade-based reference figure would suggest only 36 cases. These five "extra cases" may thus be seen as mirroring the healthy role of the WTO. It is the forum in which small trading countries can best defend their interests against large partners (table 6.4 shows one extra case for the United States).

However, the EC's overrepresentation is much higher when it is a *complainant*, namely 51 cases instead of the trade-based reference number of 39. The relatively excessive overrepresentation in cases where the EC is a complainant with respect to cases where it is a defendant may be a measure of a quite different phenomenon: an intrinsic EC "hyperactivity" in the dispute settlement procedures mirroring the EC's dominance of the WTO forum (such hyperactivity can be also observed for the United States). This conclusion fits the fact that several dispute settlement cases lodged by the EC have resulted from the EC Trade Barriers Regulation, by which the EC defends what it considers its rights (see appendix B).

A good understanding of EC hyperactivity would require a comparison with EC use of the bilateral dispute settlement procedures. Unfortunately, there is no information available on such use—this lack of information being certainly a bad practice, and possibly a bad omen. However, table

---

14. What follows relies on the assumption that the structure of merchandise trade flows reflects the structure of merchandise, services, and intellectual property rights. This assumption may underestimate the weight of industrial countries, which may trade more services and property rights than developing countries. Complaining cases are compared with export flows, and defending cases with import flows.

6.4 shows that there is *no* WTO dispute settlement case lodged by the EC against its PTA partners (EEA countries, Switzerland, Norway, ACP countries, CECs, and Balkan and Mediterranean countries), whereas the trade-based reference number of dispute settlement cases for all these countries would have been a dozen. In other words, the EC seems to use the regional and multilateral tracks in a strictly complementary way.

This conclusion is supported by two additional observations. First, *none* of the almost hundred countries that have bilateral trade agreements with the EC has used the WTO dispute settlement procedures against the EC, whereas they have used these procedures against each other, as is illustrated by the cases opposing the Czech Republic, Hungary, and Slovakia. Second, this last feature is not observed for the United States, which has several cases with its two NAFTA partners, although the trade-based reference number of cases with Canada and Mexico is much larger than the observed number. The strict complementary use of bilateral and WTO dispute settlement procedures by the EC reveals the long-lasting repercussions of the EC's discriminatory trade *agreements* through their *remedies*.

The impression of a strategic use of the WTO dispute settlement procedures by the EC and the United States is reinforced when one examines United States-EC relations. As is shown by table 6.4, the EC has complained against the United States 1.6 times more often that what trade flows would have suggested, relative to 1.3 times when all the EC trading partners are included. The United States shows an even more intense targeting of the EC). One could argue that these figures reflect nothing new, but rather the existing stock of long-lasting, recurrent disputes between the EC and the United States on bananas, beef hormone, the Foreign Sales Corporations regime, countervailing duties in the steel industry, and so on (Miller and Wasserman 1992).

Because panel recommendations under the Uruguay Round DSU are much more binding than the mere "moral" victory associated with GATT panels, this targeted use of dispute settlement procedures by the EC (and the United States) may reflect two incentives at work: an effort to get support from independent panels on (often) old-time trade quarrels; and a tactic to balance "lost" cases by "won" cases for public relations purposes. If the first incentive is acceptable, the second is the source of a worrisome drift for the whole WTO system, and another sign of the "privatization" of EC trade policy (i.e., its capture by private interests, an observation that can be extended to the United States).

Table 6.4 focuses on countries—a preliminary approach that makes sense to the extent that it insists on the decision of a government to lodge a case and on the public relations aspects. But as always in international trade, disputes between countries mirror conflicts within industries. Table 6.5, which is based on the industries and topics involved in dispute settlement procedures, confirms, to a large extent, the main observations presented in chapters 2 and 3. First, part A of table 6.5 reveals a concen-

Table 6.5 EC-related dispute settlement cases, by topic and sector

Topic or Sector	Cases with EC as complainant		Cases with EC as defendant		All cases
	United States as defendant	Others as defendants	United States as complainant	Others as complainant	
Cases ranked by topic, as percent of total					
Import measures	25.0	42.9	27.3	73.7	42.4
Contingent protection	18.8	14.3		10.5	10.9
TRIPS	6.3	5.7	36.4	5.3	13.0
Export measures		8.6	4.5		4.3
Domestic taxes	12.5	11.4			6.5
Subsidies			22.7		5.4
Government procurement	6.3	8.6			4.3
Other topics	31.3	8.6	9.1	10.5	13.0
Cases ranked by sector, as percent of total					
Farm products	18.8	11.4	18.2	57.9	23.9
Textiles, clothing, footwear	12.5	14.3		10.5	9.8
Food products		8.6	4.5	10.5	6.5
Chemicals	6.3	8.6	9.1	5.3	7.6
Steel	12.5	5.7			4.3
Electronics	6.3	5.7	13.6		6.5
Cars		11.4			4.3
Beverages		11.4			4.3
Cement				5.3	1.1
Other products	37.5	17.1	31.8	5.3	21.7
Services	6.3	5.7	22.7	5.3	9.8
Total number of cases	16	35	22	19	92

EC = European Community.
TRIPS = Agreement on Trade-Related Aspects of Intellectual Property Rights.

Source: See table 6.4.

tration of the cases in the usual suspects in EC highly protected sectors (farm and food products, textiles and clothing, cement, etc.). In other words, it confirms the capture of the EC trade policy by these well-known vested interests. Second, part B of table 6.5 confirms that if import measures (from tariffs to tariff quotas to import regulations) still constitute the bulk of barriers, new key issues, such as TRIPS, subsidies, and contingent protection, are important sources of worries for the EC trading partners. As one would expect, the range of instruments and sectors involved is much wider when the EC is a complainant; this largely mirrors the fact that EC complaints involve a wide set of countries, and hence a large set of different trade policies.

The above analysis is limited to the initiation of cases. Ideally, it would be important to look at the pattern of *outcomes* of cases. Unfortunately, there is not enough information on this aspect; if a minority of cases do lead to WTO panel decisions, most are terminated by bilateral consultations, on which there is little or no available information (for some detailed analysis of two key dispute settlement cases in which the EC has been involved, see the beef hormone cases in chapter 4 and the banana cases in appendix A, case 19).

A last, key question is: What is the impact of WTO DSU cases on the dynamics of EC trade policy? Looking at the EC implementation of WTO panel rulings leads to a disturbing observation: the EC has been the first WTO member—and so far, the only one—to refuse to comply with WTO panel rulings and to prefer to face countermeasures by complainants—a reaction accompanied by loud criticism in Europe against the Appellate Body rulings, which has fueled suspicions against the WTO (for a balanced analysis of these rulings, see Vermulst, Mavroidis, and Waer 1999).

From a purely legal viewpoint, the EC attitude is consistent with a strict interpretation of WTO reciprocity. But from a WTO systemic perspective, the fact that one of the two largest trading partners prefers to face countermeasures weakens the whole trade regime. Such countermeasures are paid in the form of additional tariffs, or other trade-restrictive measures, imposed by the complaining parties on their EC imports. In other words, not only are existing EC barriers left intact but new barriers are raised in the rest of the world—hardly a benefit for consumers in the EC or in the complaining countries.

One could argue that the EC choice of facing countermeasures simply mirrors the rigidity of EC decisional procedures in trade policy, which were underlined in chapter 1. In other words, the dispute settlement mechanism would be too fast for the current capacity of the EC decision-making process to deliver a decision changing one aspect of its trade policy, despite the fact that, on average, almost three years separate the initiation of a dispute settlement case from the final outcome. This argument is hardly acceptable for the EC's trading partners (especially if they judge the EC reactions against the celerity that the EC requires for US compliance with the Foreign Sales Corporations panel). Why should the rest of the world pay for the incapacity of the EC to make rapid decisions? (The banana and hormone cases in which the EC has accepted to face countermeasures, have lasted for a decade.)

Concluding Remarks

The main conclusion of the chapter is that the EC's addiction to discrimination may be on a slow ebb for two reasons: (1) The EC has realized that many of the PTAs that it has signed in the *past* have been a costly bargain for its partners and an exercise in futility for its own economic interests—hence, a political burden in the long run that more than compensates for the immediate political gains. (2) The EC may realize that all the discriminatory agreements of some size that it could conceivably sign in the *future* offer a cost-benefit balance less positive than the one available in future WTO rounds, simply because they impose on EC firms the same competition pressures and adjustment efforts as equivalent WTO liberalizations (most of these new PTAs would include efficient world producers) without increasing foreign market access for EC products and services to the same extent as WTO deals. Moreover, the coming two decades are likely to witness the disappearance of many (one hundred!) existing EC discriminatory agreements through the enlargement process, improving the functioning of the WTO system, if (a big "if") the EC-25 are as pro-free trade as the current EC-15. All these evolutions are consistent with (1) the discretion with which the EC texts released for Seattle have mentioned the regional approach (the texts are de facto limited to a defense of the existing discriminatory agreements with developing countries, in particular the ACP states), and (2) the interest shown by these texts in the unilateral elimination of all tariffs imposed by the industrial and emerging-market economies on imports from the least developed countries.[15]

What concrete initiatives could the EC undertake to accelerate this desirable evolution? What follows suggests a few ideal actions aimed at amplifying the expected shift of the EC away from its old addiction to discrimination.

ACP States and Developing Countries

The scheduled renunciation of the old-fashioned ACP Conventions is a step in the right direction—above all for the ACP states. But the currently fashionable proposal of REPAs is not the best alternative, because it imposes geographical limits on ACP liberalization and deprives the ACP states of tariff revenues, which constitute their main source of public revenues. Of course, the EC could easily compensate for such losses by adequate transfers. But this is not a good solution; it weakens the ACP states even more by depriving them of the sovereign right to collect taxes, and it assumes that EC taxpayers will accept paying more in order to aid developing countries (an unwarranted assumption in the long run, with the risk of reducing EC public and private efforts in favor of additional development programs, e.g., education; see chapter 5). Moreover, the experience of the past 40 years about the use of EC aid in ACP states is so disastrous that it is hard to imagine that things could be improved on such a basis.

In an apparently paradoxical way, the EC could substantially improve the ACPs' situation by adding a dose of "limited reciprocity" (instead of

---

15. In December 2000, the EC watered down its initial proposal for its own unilateral liberalization with respect to the least developed countries by introducing a tariff-quota regime (imports from least developed countries would be tariff-free only up to a certain amount) on the major LDC exports (sugar, rice, and rum) until 2006–08.

strict reciprocity as it plans to do) to its new agreements with them. More precisely, the EC should make its new trade agreements with the ACP countries conditional upon a commitment by these countries to decrease and bind their *MFN* tariffs on a *nondiscriminatory* and as *uniform* as possible basis (in other words, the EC would request reciprocity from the ACP states limited to a moderate and uniform ACP tariff, instead of a 0 percent tariff, as in the current REPA project).

Such an initiative would greatly benefit the ACP states. They could keep their tariff revenues—it has been estimated for several sub-Saharan countries that substituting a uniform tariff of roughly 15 to 18 percent for the current system of tariff peaks and exemptions would provide the same revenues (Messerlin and Maur 1999). Such an initiative would eliminate the distortions generated in the ACP economies by the existing complicated tariff schedules, which range from 0 to 50 percent or more. Last but not least, it would reduce a major source of state-related corruption in the ACP economies (ACP customs will not be under constant pressure to change import classifications to give exemptions or lower tariff rates, etc.) and a source of tax evasion (being uniform, and levied on the widest possible basis, the uniform tariff can be moderate, hence reducing incentives for smuggling). The gains for the EC will be slightly better market access, a much reduced need for granting the direct aid that is so difficult to manage wisely, no need to push for regional trade agreements between the ACP states, and, above all, ACP partners much better equipped to undergo faster growth.

Indeed, the EC could strengthen its WTO role, and get political benefits, by launching a joint initiative from all the industrial and dynamic economies to provide the ACP states (or the least developed countries) with a worldwide regime based on the notion of "limited reciprocity."

In March 2001, the EC launched the "Everything but arms" initiative, which comprises EC unilateral *suspension* of tariffs on all imports from 48 least developed countries (LDCs). Three products (sugar, rice, and bananas) have a special time frame: tariffs (estimated at 83, 100, and 160 percent, respectively, by the Commission [2000c]) will be completely suspended only in 2006 (bananas) and 2009 (sugar and rice). During the transition period, a tariff quota at zero duty on these goods will be opened by the EC and increased by 15 percent on an annual basis. There are mechanisms allowing suspension of preferences, especially in cases of serious disturbance to the Community markets and their regulatory mechanisms. Such an initiative is estimated to increase LDC exports to the EC by 37 percent ($185 million)—assuming that market access will not be restricted by more cumbersome rules of origin, antidumping, or safeguard measures (Hoekman, Ng, and Olarreaga 2001). Most of the expected export gains are concentrated in sugar, and to a lesser extent in rice and cereals, meaning that LDCs will get the full benefits of the initiative only at the end of the long transition period.

The above suggestion of an EC leadership for a global initiative of developed countries would have several advantages for the LDCs compared to the "Everything but arms" initiative, which has the merit of existing. In particular, it would offer wider market access to LDC exports because it would include almost all the OECD countries, and maybe a few more. This is important because the LDCs do not have the same intensity of business relationships and good reputation in the various OECD markets, and hence do not have the same ability to grasp the opportunity of freer market access. Moreover, the proposal of "limited reciprocity" has the merit to introduce the kind of liberalization in the LDCs that is necessary for improving both the efficiency of their economies and the quality of their governance, and that enables the LDCs to grasp the opportunity of freer market access. One could argue that the difficulties with which the Commission has obtained the mandate "Everything but arms" despite the fact that it was limited to LDCs (which are tiny trading partners of the EC) suggest that a more ambitious proposal would not have survived the powerful EC protectionist interests in sugar, rice, and bananas. However, by initiating liberalization in the LDCs, the proposal based on "limited reciprocity" would have generated a wider coalition of export interests in Europe, hence a stronger counterweight to the narrow coalition of the EC protectionist farm interests.

Central Europe

The major initiatives that the EC could undertake in favor of Central European countries would consist of purely EC *domestic* actions (described in chapters 4 and 5): a profound reform of the CAP, an increasingly strict cap on antidumping and safeguard measures (e.g., by banning such measures for goods subjected to a tariff smaller than a jointly agreed threshold), and a substantial change in the EC approach to technical regulations and services (based on more conditional mutual recognition and on a stronger, market-driven orientation).

All these measures are necessary to accelerate the CECs' accession to the EC. As already mentioned, they would also need to be complemented by a profound change in the EC approach to the enlargement process: focusing on the preaccession adoption by the CECs of only a few core directives of the *acquis communautaire*, ensuring their effective implementation in the CECs, while leaving the rest of the *acquis* for post accession adoption, trusting market forces and the integration dynamics to discipline CECs' behavior, as they have disciplined the behavior of current EC member-states in the past and continue to do so.

CEC accessions will automatically provide a substantial cure for EC discrimination because they will eliminate the hundred agreements currently in force between the EC, CECs, and EFTA countries. But they raise a key question: to what extent will the new EC member-states shift the currently relatively free-trade-oriented EC-15 to a more protectionist stance? The question is not superfluous: many CECs have revealed inward-looking attitudes during the last decade. It has often been claimed (Lawrence 1997; Sapir 1992; Cadot, de Melo, and Olarreaga 1999) that so far, the EC has induced its most protectionist members to open their borders more than they would have probably done without the EC. Whether this remark will have any chance to remain true when the EC has 25 member-states is an open question. Under present conditions, joining the EC will imply for most CECs an increase in their farm protection and a decrease in their protection of manufacturing and services (for estimates, see François and Rombout 2001). This new structure of protection could induce the CECs to increase their farm production and decrease their industrial and service productions, all evolutions that the CECs may want to resist by using EC instruments of protection (e.g., antidumping in goods and regulations in services) in order to rebalance EC protection in their "favor".[16]

Actually, it is more important in the shorter run to underline that the CECs have *alternatives* to EC actions at their disposal for accelerating their accession to the EC and decreasing the current costs of EAs. The CECs could align their MFN tariffs *higher* than the corresponding EC MFN tariffs to the level of these EC MFN tariffs without waiting for the end of the accession negotiations (Messerlin 1996c).[17] By granting tariff concessions that are probably considered almost worthless by their WTO partners (because the CECs will decrease these tariffs to the EC level anyway as a result of their accession to the EC), the CECs will decrease static and transaction costs associated with EAs and improve their own environment for investors. The CECs may also get political gains from their initiative to the extent that it will generate pressure on the EC to shorten the transition period under the accession protocols (because their initiative will make the CECs instantly ready to enforce the EC Common Tariff).

The CECs could magnify the benefits of such an initiative by making this initiative a *joint* decision to be implemented in a common time framework. Given the CEC hostility to common institutions, it is important to note that such an initiative does not carry any institutional requirement. Only a joint declaration is needed, with each CEC specifying its own time frame to reach the common goal within the time frame decided in com-

---

16. Possible CEC abuse of EC protection raises the question of the robustness of the existing EC decision-making process in trade matters. In particular, how would the complex 133 Committee (see box 1.2) work with more than 20 member-states having very different objectives in trade matters?

17. As a result, rules of origin for all the goods with the same tariff in the EC and CECs could be eliminated. Of course, those CEC MFN tariffs that are *lower* than EC MFN tariffs should not be increased—for WTO legal reasons, but more profoundly, for economic reasons (trying to lower the EC tariffs).

mon. The additional gains it would bring would be a reduction of the static costs generated in the CEFTA-EFTA context, and possibly increased joint bargaining power vis-à-vis the EC.

Mediterranean and Balkan States

The existing trade agreements may be limited in economic terms, but they portray the EC as a continental hegemon—a dangerous illusion to the extent that the EC does not have military power, as has been illustrated in Kuwait, Bosnia-Herzegovina, and Kosovo.

A minimal goal for the EC would be to "rationalize" its nexus of agreements in the region. The Helsinki Council (1999) made one step in this direction with the quite unexpected acceptance of Turkey as a candidate country. But this step was largely an inescapable consequence of a long overdue EC promise in 1964, and it should not be overrated. There is still no date for opening negotiations with Turkey, and there is apparently no definitive EC consensus on its accession, as is shown by the fact that the Nice TEC version has not given Turkey seats in the European Parliament and weighting votes in the EC Council. If this uncertainty will last too long, the EC will be wise to give back to Turkey some degree of freedom, for instance by allowing the current customs union to become a free trade area (hence allowing Turkey to take trade initiatives).

In many respects, Mediterranean countries raise the same problems as the ACP states, although in a less dramatic way. The multiplication of Euro-Med agreements has led to massive preference margins granted by each Mediterranean country to the EC, whereas trade barriers between the Mediterranean countries, and between them and the rest of the world, have remained high, except to a large extent for Israel and Jordan because they have a PTA with *both* the United States and the EC. The ideal EC policy with respect to these countries could be similar to the policy sketched above for the ACP states; in particular, it could again be driven by the "limited reciprocity" approach.

Trade policy in the Balkans raises specific issues. Trade between the Balkan countries may still rely on ethnic relations (between Croatia and the Croat-Muslim Entity of Bosnia-Herzegovina, between the Federal Republic of Yugoslavia and the Serb entity of Bosnia-Herzegovina, between Albania and Kosovo) to such an extent that it is hard to know which borders (inter-state or inter-ethnic zone) really count. In such a politically volatile context, nondiscrimination has particularly strong merits. The EC initiative to open its markets to Balkan countries, conditional on the creation of PTAs between these countries, could be an interesting application of the above-mentioned policy of limited reciprocity—if the EC-sponsored regional PTAs strongly induce the Balkan countries to lower their MFN tariffs. Balkan countries not yet members of the WTO could *bind* their tariffs at the level of EC MFN tariffs, but they should *apply* even lower tariffs as often as possible. This policy makes sense both because the accession of the Balkan countries to the EC is far away (not liberalizing as much as possible for such a long period of transition will be very costly for the Balkan countries) and because it eliminates potential problems with the EC (related to the compensation to be paid by the EC when the Balkan countries become EC member-states).

The EC: Ultimately Born to Support the WTO?

Outside Europe, all the PTAs of sizable economic magnitude that the EC could envisage signing include efficient trading partners: Japan, the United States, or groups of Asian or Latin American countries. Hence, they are likely to impose the same adjustment costs on the EC as WTO deals without granting the same benefits as such deals in market access. PTAs of smaller size, such as the Mexico-EC Treaty, may reduce some distortions generated by preexisting agreements (NAFTA, in the Mexican case). But the conflicting provisions and obligations between these PTAs where the hub is a small economy (Mexico) and where the spokes are large economies (the United States and the EC) may induce their signatories to look for a WTO deal to substitute for these PTAs, that is, for a "multilateralization" process of these agreements. In sum, in all these configurations, the EC ends up with robust (because based on its own interests) reasons for becoming a robust WTO supporter.

Being a strong WTO supporter cannot be limited to shifting negotiations from a bilateral context to the multilateral WTO forum. It also requires becoming a careful supporter of the WTO dispute settlement mechanism. The EC has expressed difficulty in using the WTO panel rulings as a support for eliminating domestic protectionist measures favoring blatantly narrow vested interests capable of getting support from foreign vested interests (as is best illustrated by the banana case; see appendix A, case 19).

This weak capacity to keep under control its own vested interests should induce the EC to promote the following key improvement of the WTO dispute settlement procedure, in order to benefit from stronger support from the WTO. Today, a WTO member faces countermeasures if it decides not to follow panel recommendations. This option transforms the WTO from a liberalizing force into an engine of protection because the defendant's protectionist measures condemned by the WTO panels are followed by the complainant's protectionist countermeasures authorized by the WTO. Instead of such countermeasures, WTO members should get additional concessions from the WTO partners refusing to enforce panel rulings, under the renegotiation provisions of GATT Article XXVIII and GATS Article XXI; this option would keep the proliberalization momentum of the WTO texts.

7

European Political Union and EC Commercial Policy

The conclusions of chapters 4, 5, and 6 suggest a very broad agenda for the coming WTO negotiations, covering almost the whole world GDP (agriculture, manufacturing, and market services) and including the most urgent horizontal themes—reforms of contingent protection (antidumping, antisubsidy, and safeguards) and of the WTO dispute settlement mechanism. To save the "broad" qualification for the EC agenda tabled at Seattle because it also includes trade-related investment, labor, and competition issues makes little sense—all the more because insisting on these three topics is, for the EC, inconsistent with its *own* internal approach. The Treaties establishing the EC (from Rome to Nice) have carefully avoided imposing links between *intra-EC* trade, on the one hand, and investment, labor, and competition issues *within* the EC, on the other.[1]

If confirmed in the next WTO ministerial (to be held in Doha, Qatar, in November 2001), EC insistence on these three issues (that neither the United States nor the developing countries are willing to include in the negotiations) will increasingly raise doubts about EC's real objective for the next WTO round. It could suggest that the EC may simply want to buy time in order to start serious talks in late 2002 at the earliest (after the 2001–02 British, French, and German elections in the hope of a more ro-

---

1. The recent German proposals on the EC political constitution (the "Schröder Document", see below) mention explicitly, once again, the key role of EC member-states in competition and social policy matters.

bust common position among EC member-states), or perhaps even later (after the first wave of accessions of Central European countries to the EC expected in 2004 at the earliest).

Of course, this timing question is also related to the well-known difficulties of further reform of the EC Common Agricultural Policy before 2003 (see chapter 4). And it is also influenced by the persistent uncertainty over the elimination of the quantitative restrictions imposed by the EC under the Multi-Fiber Agreement (MFA): it is now certain that the key EC MFA restrictions will be eliminated only in 2005, and that, until then, the EC will try to get additional concessions from developing countries during the implementation process (such as those from Sri Lanka; see appendix A, case 13–14).

Such an EC tactic of delay may indeed please those developing countries that are reluctant to start a new round of WTO negotiations before the full implementation of the Uruguay Round commitments (i.e., 2005). It is often argued that if industrial countries will not fulfill their Uruguay Round obligations to dismantle MFA quantitative restrictions, developing countries will have the option of retaliating by not implementing their TRIPS obligations due in 2005. However, one may wonder whether the *value* of this retaliation is not rapidly declining. In particular, major pharmaceutical firms are increasingly ready to reduce prices of their products in developing countries, decreasing by the same token the value for those firms of the access to developing-country markets granted by the TRIPS Uruguay Agreement, and consequently the retaliatory leverage of the developing countries in case of ultimately incomplete elimination of the MFA restrictions by developed countries.

This chapter aims to go behind such immediate problems and look at a much broader issue, namely the relationship between EC commercial policy and the concrete solutions for an "ever closer" European political union. This question echoes chapter 1, which underlines the high political content of EC trade policy because the EC is an entity in formation, and so has no other way to express its political views than through its commercial policy.

In 2004, a new EC Intergovernmental Conference (IGC) will be convened, which will focus on EC's "political constitution". In late April 2001, the German Chancellor Gerhard Schröder had already launched this debate on constitutional reforms for Europe, by tabling a keynote paper entitled "Responsibility for Europe" for the National Conference of the German Social Democratic Party to be held in November 2001 (*Der Spiegel*, no. 18, 30 April 2001, 17). The so-called "Schröder Document" has been presented as "internal" to Germany to avoid any hard feelings among other EC member-states. But it has, despite its profound ambiguities (see below), already triggered a debate over the whole of EC, with the Dutch supporting German proposals in early May 2001, and the British and French criticizing them, sometimes quite undiplomatically.

This initiative raises a key question: will the EC attitude in the WTO be very different if it aims to become a "federal" entity rather than a more original type of entity—called the "Community" in what follows? This chapter argues that EC's attitude is indeed likely to differ and that Europe will be much more at ease in the world scene if it chooses the "Community" option.

Europa in the Kingdom of Lilliput

Most European politicians continue to treat Europa as Lilliputians treated Gulliver: they believe that multiplying tiny economic chains that tie European economies together will promote the political union, *even* if these chains are costly. This approach of an intensive and mechanical use of Jean Monnet's bold initiative raises two questions: (1) Has the use of economic integration as a political instrument not reached the point of negative productivity and become a recipe for political stalemate *and* economic costs? (2) Is it not the right time to leave European economic integration to follow its *own* path and rationale and to address Europe's political future with political instruments (as suggested by the economic analysis of the adequacy between goals and instruments)?

The impression of rapidly declining productivity of Monnet's approach should not come as a surprise after 40 years of intensive use. Such an "activism" driven by the existing statist bias in European integration (described in chapter 1) has led to an increasing feeling of "virtuality" in Europe. (To be fair, this virtuality started with Article 205 (ex 148) of the Treaty of Rome stating that the *simple* majority is the *rule*, "*except*" as otherwise provided by the Treaties.) An increasing number of texts have been passed by the EC and its member-states, with too little attention paid to their *effective* implementation, and to a careful assessment of their positive and negative consequences.[2]

Moreover, an increasing number of initiatives have objectives that they are unlikely to deliver. The Common Agricultural Policy is severely hurting small farmers, the environment, and health safety, but lavishly subsidizes large farmers. Too heavy a regulatory convergence in services is inhibiting the emergence of an effective Single Market, but tends to favor dominant incumbents and to introduce a harmonization perceived as

---

2. This remark can be extended to political texts, such as the Charter of Fundamental Rights, which was drafted by ad hoc committees that did not enjoy the level of legitimacy needed to oversee such work. The Charter was promptly adopted by the 2000 Nice IGC without being seriously scrutinized by the EC Parliaments, or exposed to public opinion. As a result, and not surprisingly, it contains many poorly drafted provisions, and has the low status of a nonbinding "declatory statement" because it was not acceptable to all member-states.

valueless or even costly.[3] The Social Charter is unlikely to cure unemployment, but it exacerbates tortuous and hidden ways for making more flexible labor markets. The euro is unlikely to be a robust step toward a political union, but a "strong" euro can rapidly generate political strains within the euro zone—to the point that it could put at risk the Single Market itself by opening the possibility of transforming a euro failure into an economic disaster, if a member-state leaving the euro zone were to raise barriers on intra-EC flows of goods and services. Last but not least, the constraints imposed on the candidate Central European countries during the accession process are obliging them to adopt hundreds of laws in haste, a serious source of additional virtuality and future problems in the EC.

This impression of a profound erosion of Monnet's approach and of an increasingly "virtual" Europe is echoed by the annual Eurobarometer polls, which, despite all the usual intrinsic flaws of polls, provide one clear message: the rise until the mid-1990s, and since then the fall, of a positive image of Europe among the European people.[4] The negative outcomes of referenda on European issues in certain EC member-states, such as Denmark on the Maastricht TEC version and Ireland on the Nice TEC version, confirm these polls. Meanwhile, business leaders who played a leading role in the late 1980s (see chapters 4 and 5) in promoting the Single Market have turned their energy to more global, often worldwide, markets, increasingly leaving the European integration process to the member-states, and to the inward-oriented firms and vested interests.

During this long process of erosion of Monnet's approach, EC member-states have been increasingly at odds with what has been their key contribution to European integration. (To be fair, half a century of peace and

---

3. For instance, it is hard to understand the rationale of the European directive on chocolate, when labeling would seem quite an appropriate measure. It is also hard to see the political legitimacy of the European Court of Justice's ruling assessing Sweden's ban of antialcoholic advertising as a barrier to the free movement of (advertising) services within the EC, and the consistency of this ruling with previous Court's rulings limiting competition in insurance matters when consumers are individuals, on the ground that individuals do not have enough information.

4. To the question "Do you think that your country's membership of the EC is a good thing?", 61 percent of responses were positive for the periods 1985–90 and 1991–94, but only 51 percent for the period 1995–99. To the question "Would you say that your country has on balance benefited or not from being a member of the EC?", 52 and 50 percent of responses respectively were positive for the first two periods, but only 44 percent for the last period. To the question "If you were told tomorrow that the EC has been scrapped, would you be very sorry about it, indifferent, or very relieved?", 43 and 45 percent of the respondents respectively said during the first two periods that they would be very sorry, but only 37 percent said so during the last period (however there were only two observations for this period). For all three questions, results are also better for the period 1980–84 (but there is missing information for a substantial number of years of this period) than for the period 1995–99.

prosperity has contributed to these drifts toward complacency and inward-looking policies.)

France's major contribution has been the bold political leap of faith of Jean Monnet and Robert Schuman, leading a country profoundly hurt physically and morally by the Second World War to offer, only six years after the end of this war, a totally new future to its archrival. Since then, French influence has too often shrunk to a fight for the survival of the Common Agricultural Policy and of a few public monopolies (such as electricity or railways), at the cost of French comparative advantages in agriculture and at the detriment of its other interests in manufacturing and services.

Germany's key contribution has been the economic leap of faith of Ludwig Erhard in the role of markets and competition, leading a country emerging from 25 years of economic chaos and managed economy to champion market rules on the European manufacturing sector, *when* the rest of Western Europe was fascinated by central planning and industrial policy. Since then, German influence has often been a rear-guard fight for slowing down competition in agriculture, services, and factor markets—as is best illustrated by the Schröder Document, which pledges for restrictions on free movement of labor from Central Europe, for an operative European police force for reasons largely related to illegal immigration, and, even more worrisomely, for restrictions on free movement of services during the transition phase of the accession of the Central European countries.

Britain's major contribution has relied on Margaret Thatcher's conviction that huge sources of efficiency and growth were remaining untapped in services, leading a country suffering from decades of economic decay to promote bold regulatory reforms in services. Since then, and despite the fact that the EC Single Market in services is mostly a British achievement, British influence has been severely curbed by Britain's long-standing underconfidence in its role in Europe (and long-lasting overconfidence in its role in transatlantic relations).

Until recently, Italy and Spain had limited their roles to the mere defense of their immediate interests (except Italy in the 1950s), whereas "small" member-states have suffocated under the Franco-German duo, which has quickly turned into a cartel.

The excessive use of Monnet's approach during the last 20 years has had, and still does, a perverse effect in the long run. It has profoundly weakened, and still does, EC member-states in the following sense: opening markets to foreign competition and undertaking regulatory reforms are now rarely presented in a member-state as healthy initiatives taken for the sake of the *country's* welfare. Rather, such actions are presented as imposed by "Brussels"—the "faceless, soulless Eurocracy in Brussels, at best boring, at worst dangerous" to quote M. Joshka Fischer, Minister of Foreign Affairs in Germany, often described as a federalist-minded politician—despite the fact that all these actions have been at least discussed, generally negotiated, and often expressly agreed, by member-state governments. Similarly, bad policies are happily implemented by member-states, hiding and protecting their domestic vested interests supporting these bad policies behind convenient EC excuses, as best illustrated by the capture of loudly pro-free trade member-states by the Common Agricultural Policy.

This evolution will be amplified by the EC enlargement to Central Europe. Many Central Europeans want to join the EC because they find their own governments weak and are looking for a "strong" European government. This dangerous motive is amplified by the fact that the current accession process tends to weaken the Central European states, with the EC showing very limited trust in these states—and no trust in market forces to discipline the candidate countries and to induce them to take the necessary reforms (see chapter 6).

Weakened member-states, increasingly perceived by many European people as empty shells at best and as monuments of duplicity at worst, raise a major problem: they cannot be a healthy basis for a robust European political union. This situation is a key factor to take into account when examining the two options available to the EC: a "federation" or a "Community".

Toward a "Federal" European Union?

The European political union can first be conceived in terms derived from the 19th-century federations. Building such a federation would require three basic ingredients. First, it generally needs common historical references, as with Germany and Italy during the 19th century. But, the EC has been so successful that this will not be the case after its forthcoming enlargements. The EC-6 could refer to the Europe of the early Middle Ages; EC-10 and EC-12 to the Western European core of the 17th–19th centuries. But the emerging EC-26 (from Gibraltar to the Baltics, Poland, Slovakia, Romania, and Turkey) never existed.

Second, a federation often requires "federating" events, such as independence wars (from the Boston Tea Party to Prussia's wars against Austria-Hungary and France). So far, the EC has been lucky to be built in a peaceful context and, fortunately, it seems that it will continue—despite the repeated attempts to use anti-Americanism as a federating event. The price to be paid for such a happy situation is that the European political union will require time to mature. Meanwhile, Europe will be unable to gain the institutional clarity associated with nation-states or clear-cut federations.

Third, a 19th century-type federation often requires a "dominant" member-state but none exists in the EC. In what follows, dominance is defined as the *impression* of leadership, and may thus be different from effective influence. (For instance, one could not argue that Britain was dominant in the EC of the 1980s and 1990s although it shaped the whole EC approach in liberalizing services, which accounts for 70 percent of EC value-added.) The French dominance of the 1960s is over. Britain's difficulties in closing the imperial chapter of its history have limited, and still do, its leadership in Europe.

Today, it is fashionable to evoke German dominance by *invoking* the attraction of the German economy for the Central European economies, and the size of the German economy. But, if Central European countries are currently buying many German services, in the future, they will be likely to find those services cheaper elsewhere, or even to produce them themselves—an evolution revealed by the fears of the Schröder Document about competitive pressures on German firms from Central European service providers. Concerning the current size of the German economy, it reflects German population more than German GDP per capita, and should be put in perspective. Germany (as well as any other EC member-state) will face a crucial dilemma during the next 50 years: either it will not accept immigrants (and could shrink to 60 million people by 2050, losing the basis of its current apparent dominance) or it will accept the necessary number of immigrants (roughly 350,000 people per year), in which case how German will such a Germany be? Last but not least, recent German initiatives on European issues, such as the Schröder Document, reflect the concerns of the German Länder and communal governments, which see their autonomy threatened by the EC (particularly in services, with EC irruption in sensitive areas such as subsidies to *Landesbanken* (see chapter 5) or audiovisual regulations) more than a dominant behavior of the German federal government.[5]

In the future, the dominance of one large EC country will be even more problematic, with Italy and Spain recently expressing strong interest in playing a much more active role in EC affairs, and with the future accession of three large Central European countries (Poland, Romania, and Turkey). The convergence of EC incomes, and the fact that there will be five to eight EC member-states with large populations, will make the intra-EC balance increasingly similar to the old European "balance of powers" of the 17th to 19th centuries: fluid coalitions will be the rule, as

---

5. The concerns of the German Länder may be appealing to Central European candidates, which are also small economies and states. This may contribute to the existing impression of German dominance, whereas it merely reflects common concerns.

illustrated by the Schröder Document prompting a Franco-British-Spanish coalition against it.[6]

In sum, none of the above ingredients necessary for a federal Europe exists in the EC now. In fact, the Schröder Document, generally qualified as "federalist" by the press, devotes only three lines in a 550-line text (in its French translation) to European constitutional problems. Moreover, these three lines are profoundly ambiguous. The future Commission is said to become "a strong executive instance" (one among others?), the Parliament is said to get "full budgetary authority" (on which budget exactly?), and the Council is said to become a "Chamber of European Nations" (with what competences?). By contrast, the Schröder paper insists, in repeated instances, on increased power devolution to member-states and subnational entities on Single Market matters (particularly, services), on the need to take precautions against a "creeping" transfer of competencies to the European level, and on ensuring that member-states "retain the flexibility and structural competence to provide for public and social security"—all suggestions mirroring the often forgotten fact that German public opinion is more *reluctant* about a "federal" Europe than public opinion in many member-states.

Or Toward a Fully Fledged—Political and Economic—European Community?

Indeed, is there a need for a 19th-century type of federal state in 21st-century Europe? This is a legitimate question, when centralized states (from Belgium to Spain, and even to Britain and France) or federal states (the United States) are decentralizing their domestic governance. The enlarged EC will reach 500 million inhabitants. There is no example in human history of a classic federal government running such a huge entity in a democratic and wealthy context. If a soft federalism seems unfeasible and inappropriate for Europe, what then could the alternative be?

The essential role of a European political power should be to energize the EC member-states rather than to "unify" them, and to make them *more accountable*. It should be a "provider of political services . . . whose competence, efficiency, and in-built limitations are the best guarantees of

---

6. In fact, this opposition may be triggered by other aspects than the political proposals because the Schröder Document deals with many other issues. For instance, the Document argues for the renationalization of the CAP and regional funds—a solution that would solve German budgetary problems to the detriment of French (CAP) and Spanish (regional funds) budgets. Chapter 4 argues that a renationalization of the CAP is likely to make the EC even less open in agriculture, by creating "15 CAPs" (only one or two member-states, such as Sweden, may be willing to come back to a more open farm trade policy that they have experienced in the past).

legitimacy" [Andréani 1999, 17]. Such an approach seems a much better answer to the multifaceted, multicultural Europe of the 21st century than the soft 19th-century type federalism. It suggests reusing the term "Community", too hastily abandoned for the dull word "Union", and rediscovering the warm feeling it conveys, and its subtle way of revealing that, though Europe does not have a common memory, it is a "community" of memories.

It is beyond the scope of this book to describe the contours of such a European Political Community. Two brief remarks are sufficient for our limited purpose.

First, when one talks about the European political union, one too often forgets, or dismisses, the fact that the EC already has an elaborate Constitution, namely the Treaties, which often goes very far in the federal direction. For instance, the EC rules on budgetary deficit are stricter than those available to the German federal government with respect to the Länder; the Commission's competence in terms of state aid is equivalent to the competence of central authorities in a centralized state; and so on. As a result, in "normal" times, one should simply aim at a smooth evolution of the European institutions at the pace desired by the European people. Ideally, such an evolution should deliver more effective (less virtual) outcomes, under increasingly simpler and clearer structures and procedures, at *constant* competences. For instance, one should devolve the two functions—legislative and executive—of the current Council of Ministers to two different institutions; limit majority votes to two types only (simple and population-weighted); give to the European Parliament certain rights of legislative initiation currently held by the Commission, in order to put an end to the Commission's monopoly; make the European Central Bank accountable to the Parliament; and so on. *Expanding* competences may only be envisaged with a pragmatic and progressive expansion of the European "secretariats" for the Common Foreign and Security Policy and for Justice and Home Affairs.

Second, increasing the Community's competences is a real issue only in cases of international political "crises". In such cases, a fully fledged political European Community would need a procedure by which EC member-states would agree to devolve their sovereign powers to a "federal" structure for a *limited* period—the idea being that times of crises are those allowing the emergence of a European public opinion and that limited duration ensures a more robust level of political legitimacy. Such an approach would not be brand new in European integration: it expands to political issues the constitutional framework already present in the Treaty of Paris (see appendix A, case 11) with the "state of manifest crisis".[7] In

---

7. Such a provision has respectable ancestors, such as ancient Rome when the powers exerted by the two consuls in "normal" times could be devolved to a dictator in case of crises for a limited (six months) period. The various existing proposals on European political

this perspective, the key aspects to be examined by the 2004 IGC would then be threefold: (1) the design of the European federal structure operating in times of crises, (2) the procedure of power devolution (how to declare a "state of crisis"), and (3) the necessary arrangements to be implemented during the "normal" times for giving to the federal structure the effective means it would need in times of crises (for instance, the progressive building of integrated military equipment and forces).

The key advantage of such a more complete *political* European Community is to free *economic* integration of Europe from the obsession of *political* union, hence to develop the *economic* European Community on *economic* grounds. For instance, such a fully fledged Community would be more inclined to devote to strategic international issues the full attention they deserve. A key consequence of this evolution would be a shift of the focus of the EC-US dialogue away from narrow trade issues toward more global problems, such as security issues in the Asia Pacific or the European technological gap in military equipment.[8] As a result, EC-US trade conflicts will be put into perspective and will take more easily the limited importance they have.

On domestic matters, a fully fledged Community would then be in a position to serenely *reexamine* the huge *acquis communautaire* inherited by its too activist approach of economic integration in the past. Forty years of intensive use of the Monnet method has made the EC overregulated. The time has come to eliminate the costs associated with excessive or inappropriate EC *and* member-state regulations, and to consider power devolution from the EC to the member-states, and from the EC and member-states to appropriate subentities (Länder, regions, and so on).

Accountability and *trust-based mutual recognition* are the engines that should define such a power devolution. The Community should thus aim (1) to satisfy the crucial need for increased accountability in modern economies and (2) to review the balance between harmonization and mutual recognition. Chapters 4 and 5 have shown how much the past 20

---

union provide different trade-offs between the scope of the "common" issues to be federalized and the intensity of federalism. At one end of the spectrum, the Schröder Document minimizes the scope of common issues, and goes "far" on the level of federalism (although the exact content of the term "far" is highly debatable, as mentioned above). At the other end of the spectrum, the French counter-proposal enlarges the scope of common issues, and minimizes the federal approach to the point of losing any credibility. So far, no proposal seems to add a third dimension (such as time limit or geographical limits) to the existing two-dimensional trade-offs.

8. For instance, the handling of the problems raised by North Korea has been a permanent embarrassment for the Community, from the public disagreements between EC member-states at the eve of the ASEM meeting in Seoul in late 2000 to the rush of EC officials to Pyongyang in early 2001 (endangering the emerging EC-US understanding on the EC's rapid reaction force).

years have ignored accountability and been biased toward excessive harmonization, both in goods (technical norms) and services (regulatory convergence).

Increased accountability and mutual recognition will constitute the major differences between a fully fledged European Community and a European integration process, which would remain based on the concept of "nation-states". A Europe based on nation-states will have inherent difficulties in including these two key features, simply because European nation-states inherit a deep-rooted tradition of nonaccountability, and because they tend to be suspicious of each other. Such a lack of increased accountability and mutual recognition is particularly clear in the French counterproposal to the Schröder Document (but it may also be present in the Schröder Declaration to some extent, behind the smokescreen of power devolution).

Impact of the Type of Political Union on EC Commercial Policy

The choice between a more federal Union and a fully fledged Community is important for the future development of the EC commercial policy.

Under the federal option, Europe will be more inclined to economic harmonization, internally, and hence externally—an evolution that would thus be a potential source of severe (intra- and extra-EC) trade conflicts. It would be less inclined to pay attention to the right balance between sovereignty and integration in the international trade regime, hence to allow for different (i.e., adapted to each country) complementary policies accompanying the opening of domestic markets to foreign competition (such complementary policies are a key aspect in service liberalization). Last but not least, a federal Europe would be more tempted to believe that the weakening of the United States is good for Europe, precisely at the time when the crucial challenges emerging in the WTO (such as the beneficial membership of China and of a few other large countries) are so huge that they require *joint* EC and US efforts in the decades to come.

By contrast, a fully fledged European Community will be an easier party for its WTO partners. It will be more inclined to recognize that its fantastic success flows from extremely favorable initial conditions. In the mid-1950s, all the EC member-states exported more than 25 percent of their total exports to the rest of the Community, *and* they represented more than 18 percent of intra-EC trade (except Italy with only 11 percent). In other words, all EC member-states have had both high stakes and high power in the EC creation process. That is not denying the EC success, but it is an essential signal for the rest of the world that the EC experience will be hard to transplant elsewhere.

A fully fledged Community will be an easier WTO partner in liberalizing services because it will be more inclined to accept the principle of competition in regulations, and the use of different complementary policies. It will pay more attention to the intrinsic limits of the WTO constitutional regime. For instance, it will be more inclined to impose sensible limits on the dispute settlement system, in order not to substitute the powers of arbitrators for those of negotiators in matters that have not been discussed and negotiated before. It will also be more open to the implementation problems in the WTO. For instance, it will be more sympathetic to give credit to new WTO members, from China to Vanuatu, for the liberalization that they will achieve, by freeing them more rapidly than scheduled from the constraints imposed by the special instruments of contingent protection included in their accession protocols. Lastly, a European Community will be more inclined to treat with care the fragile sovereignty of many developing countries, in particular by requesting limited reciprocity from its least developed trading partners coupled with the implementation of a uniform tariff by them, instead of requesting full reciprocity, which eliminates tariff revenues—that is, an essential share of developing country public budgets and a core component of their emerging national governance that they have to learn to master.

APPENDICES

Appendix A
Case Studies

Case 1: Cement

At first glance, cement does not seem a highly tradable product, because of its low value added and high transport costs. However, international trade in cement can be very profitable: a few concentrated European producers have segmented markets, by appropriately locating their plants, and generated high profits, which have been increased by the large cycles in the building industry.

In fact, during the 1990s, trade in cement was riddled with intra-EC and extra-EC barriers. A first group of barriers consists of technical regulations harming intra- *and* extra-EC trade. The harmonization or mutual recognition of these regulations has proved to be very difficult, at the level of both design and implementation (*Single Market Review* 1998, vol. 1, 135–53), and the failure index of this operation of harmonization/recognition (see chapter 4) is 4 (6 being the maximum index) (Single Market Review 1998, vol. 1, 299).

Trade barriers against exports from non-EC countries have essentially consisted of antidumping actions, particularly against Central European and Mediterranean countries with large production and export capacities. There were 11 cases between 1985 and 1994 against EC neighboring producers (Czechoslovakia, Poland, Romania, Slovenia, Tunisia, Turkey, and Yugoslavia). As underlined by Dumez and Jeunemaître (2000, 157): "Only the antidumping device seems able to put a halt to the [globalization] process, and bring a return to previous local market equilibriums, where imports are under the control of the local producers." This remark about the US market is applicable to the EC market.

Finally, technical regulations and antidumping measures have allowed frequent anticompetitive practices. In 1994, the Commission imposed fines totaling €248 million on 33 producers found to have participated in secret arrangements (*"Cembureau"*) to rig markets since 1983—including by pressuring importers to align with local producers (these practices are consistent with the lodging of antidumping cases followed by withdrawal from the complaining firms) (European Commission 1994). There have been many similar cases at the national and local levels (Dumez and Jeunemaître 2000). Recently, EC cement firms began to buy CEC cement producers, opening the possibility of consolidating anticompetitive practices in the whole of Europe.

Notes

The level of protection taken into account in estimating the costs of protection is the sum of the GATT-bound tariff (3.2 percent) and the antidumping measures estimated at 19 percent, i.e., half the average antidumping margin mentioned by the investigations. There is relatively scarce information on antidumping measures: 7 out of the 11 antidumping cases have been terminated by a "no injury" conclusion, 3 by the "withdrawal" of the complainants from the complaint, and 1 by the Spanish accession to the EC— all outcomes consistent with the use of antidumping as a collusive device.

To our knowledge, there is no estimate of the total-price demand elasticity and of the supply price elasticity for cement. Estimates of the elasticity of substitution between domestic and foreign products range from 2.1 (ISIC 361) to 1.1 (cement hydraulic) (Shiells et al. 1986; Reinert and Roland-Holst 1992). As a result, elasticities of 1, 1 (both set arbitrarily), and 1.5—for demand, supply, and substitution, respectively—have been used to estimate the costs of protection.

Case 2: Fertilizers

During the late 1980s, EC imports of most types of fertilizers (UAN, NPK, urea, potassium chloride, ammonium nitrate, etc.) coming from a wide range of countries (the United States, Central European countries, the Soviet Union, and Mediterranean or Middle Eastern oil producers) were subjected to antidumping investigations. These inquiries led to some of the highest antidumping margins found during this period (up to 150 percent). Most of these cases were terminated by price undertakings, and a few others by the highest antidumping duties imposed during this period (up to 40 percent). Moreover, some EC member-states imposed their own nontariff barriers: global quotas in Greece, nonautomatic licensing in Spain, automatic licensing in the Benelux countries (GATT, *Trade Policy Review: The European Community*, 1991, 209). During the 1990s, new antidumping cases on similar products were lodged more or less every year until 1995, and 1999 witnessed a reactivation of the antidumping cycle with a huge urea case (see appendix B).

Price collusion schemes in certain fertilizers are well-known practices. They have been reported by EC member-state competition authorities since the early 1960s (CTE 1964). Since the early 1970s, there have been reports of anticompetitive practices by fertilizer producers at the world level (UNCTAD 1971). During the 1990s, following a severe downturn in the early 1990s, EC industry witnessed a series of mergers, leading to a handful of major firms. Of course, this activity is a major beneficiary of the subsidies granted to EC farmers by the Common Agricultural Policy (see chapter 4).

Notes

The rate of overall protection in 1990 is the compounded sum of the average GATT-bound tariff (5.2 percent) and of the average antidumping measure taken in the 1986–87 urea cases (26.1 percent), which is likely to be an underestimate.

The literature suggests a total-price demand elasticity ranging from 0.3 to 3.8 (Stern et al. 1976) and an elasticity of substitution between domestic and foreign products ranging from 9.9 (ISIC 351) to 0.4 (agricultural chemicals) (Shiells et al. 1986; Reinert and Roland-Holst 1992). To our knowledge, there is no available estimate of the supply price elasticity. As a result, elasticities of 1, 2, and 1.5 (for demand, supply, and substitution, respectively) have been used to estimate the costs of protection.

Cases 3 and 4: Polyethylene and Polyvinyl Chloride

These two basic chemical products offer one of the best illustrations of the close relations between trade and competition policies (Messerlin 1990). In November 1981, an antidumping action was initiated against polyvinyl chloride (PVC) exports from four Central European countries, representing 44 percent of EC imports from non-EC countries. In September 1982, another antidumping action was initiated against low-density polyethylene (LdPE) exports from three Central European countries and from the Soviet Union, amounting to 33 percent of EC imports from non-EC countries. In both cases, the bulk of the remaining imports was coming from EFTA subsidiaries of firms that also operated in the EC. By early and mid-1983, the two cases were terminated by "undertakings," the nature and the magnitude of which were not specified in the EC antidumping proceedings.

In late 1983, investigations of collusion and market sharing in the LdPE market were launched under Article 85 of the Treaty of Rome. An official proceeding was opened in March 1988. In December 1988, both EC and non-EC firms were heavily fined for involvement in an LdPE cartel. A similar procedure was followed for the PVC market, with the same outcome in December 1988. The EC anticartel proceedings strongly suggest the role of the antidumping actions (if only in terms of timing) as a key device for sustaining anticompetitive practices in EC markets. Individual cases were taken on appeal to the Court of Justice. In the PVC case, the Commission's decision and hence the fines were annulled on a procedural ground (the authentification procedure defining the language in which decisions are binding was not complete). Meanwhile, from early 1983 to 1987–88, antidumping measures remained in force. The 1990s witnessed a long list of cases (19) on products derived from polyethylene and polypropylene, such as binders, twine, sacks, bags, and terephtalates. Greenaway et al. (1995) have shown that there are strong similarities between these cases and the polypropylene cases.

Notes

The estimated rate of overall protection for 1990 is the GATT-bound tariff (12.5 percent), which was the only official trade barrier existing in 1990. It has been assumed that the undertakings imposed by the antidumping actions have been effectively eliminated, as officially stated (in September 1987 for PVC, in March 1988 for LdPE). However, the "chilling" effect of the cases was clear enough to maintain some kind of cooperative behavior between firms—hence the treatment of this case under the imperfect-competition model.

The literature suggests a supply price elasticity of 2 (Hufbauer and Elliott 1994) and an elasticity of substitution between domestic and foreign products ranging from 8.6 (ISIC 351) to 1.7 (plastics) (Shiells et al. 1986; Reinert and Roland-Holst 1992). To our knowledge, there is no estimate of the total-price demand elasticity. As a result, elasticities of 1, 2, and 4 (for demand, supply, and substitution, respectively) have been used to estimate the costs of protection.

Case 5: Hardboard

In the early 1990s, the wood industry was protected by a wide range of measures restricting *both* intra- and extra-EC trade. In particular, hardboard was subjected to technical regulations (different standards and major differences in conformity assessment procedures) that constituted severe barriers. The index of failure of harmonization and mutual recognition of technical regulations for semifinished wood products and carpentry components (see chapter 4) is 4 (6 being the highest index of failure) (Single Market Review 1998, vol. 1, 304). Moreover, hardboard activity benefited from large production subsidies in certain member-states (such as France) during the 1980s and early 1990s.

On the extra-EC side, antidumping cases recur: 1981 (2 cases), 1982 (1), 1985 (4), and 1997 (6) for hardboard; to which one should add 7 cases on standard particle board (in 1984) and one case on flat pallets (1995). These cases have two characteristics: They generate many more antidumping reviews than in any other industry; and they are terminated by particularly opaque decisions (no official measure, despite the existence of dumping).

Notes

The estimated rate of overall protection in 1990 is the sum of the average GATT-bound tariff (10 percent) and the antidumping measures taken under the 1985 case (13.6 percent). Because antidumping measures consist of undertakings, they are treated as a source of rents, not of tariff revenues. There is no available estimate of the amount of subsidies granted by certain member-states, and thus of their ad valorem tariff equivalents.

The literature suggests a total-price demand elasticity ranging from 0.3 to 1 (Stern et al. 1976), a supply price elasticity ranging from 0.4 to 0.7 (Stern et al. 1976), and an elasticity of substitution between domestic and foreign products ranging from 0.3 (ISIC 331) to 1.73 (hardwood) (Shiells et al. 1986; Reinert and Roland-Holst 1992). As a result, elasticities of 1, 0.5, and 1.7 (for demand, supply, and substitution, respectively) have been used to estimate the costs of protection.

Case 6: Newsprint

In the early 1990s, newsprint production was protected by often opaque EC member-state measures. First, the paper industry was plagued with technical regulations (it is an environmentally sensitive industry), which may have had a substantial protectionist impact, as illustrated by Baldwin (2000).[1] Indeed, technical regulations have been (and still are) a major source of conflict between the EC and certain Central European countries (e.g., Poland) for the adoption of the *acquis communautaire* in technical regulations.

---

1. In the early 1990s, the EC attempted to impose the inclusion of a certain fraction of recycled paper in new paper, a proposal without advantages from the environmental perspective, but which could reduce severely the resource-based comparative advantages of Finnish and Swedish producers relative to French and German producers (the latter produce paper on the basis of recycled paper, whereas the former produce paper on the basis of new trees). The proposal has not been adopted.

Second, the sector has benefited from massive production subsidies in certain member-states, as is best illustrated by France, which put €0.5 billion between 1984 and 1987 into one producer (La Chapelle-Darblay, leading to a national record in subsidy per head for its 1,000 workers) (*Financial Times*, 30 March 1990). These subsidies have taken very opaque forms. For instance, Electricité de France has agreed to charge preferential prices for electricity to five paper producers. These preferential prices have been equal to or lower than those charged the largest electricity users, though for quantities one thousand times smaller, with electricity representing 20 to 30 percent of the total costs of producing paper (Rouam 1998, 14).

Third, an examination of the EC public procurement function has shown that paper suppliers operating in one EC member-state have had very little (in fact, no) success at all in getting business in other member-states (see table 5.6).

There have been persistent reports of anticompetitive practices in this sector. In particular, the Commission has monitored closely the ways Finnish and Swedish newsprint producers operate. In 1998, while recognizing the strongly oligopolistic nature of this market (there are six firms in the EEA) the Commission approved important mergers. One merger was between Repola and Kymmene (both from Finland). The other, more important, merger was between Enso (from Finland) and Stora (from Sweden), which together represent 75 percent of the European production capacity for newsprint; this merger was accepted on the grounds that purchasers of newsprint, such as press groups, have enough purchasing power (European Commission 1999d, 59). These two firms also produce cardboard, and Stora has been deeply involved in an important competition case concerning the European cardboard cartel, which was terminated in 1994 by the imposition of €132 million in fines (European Commission 1994, 405).

Notes

The estimated rate of overall of protection in 1990 has been assumed to be the average GATT-bound tariff, that is, 7 percent, because there is no known estimate of ad valorem tariff equivalents of technical barriers to trade, or of the associated possible quantitative restrictions and cooperative behavior. It is thus likely to be a substantial underestimate.

The literature suggests a total-price demand elasticity ranging from 0.7 to 0.8 (Coursey and Taylor 1982) and an elasticity of substitution between domestic and foreign products ranging from 1.8 (ISIC 341) to 1 (paper mills) (Shiells et al. 1986; Reinert and Roland-Holst 1992). To our knowledge, there is no estimate of the supply price elasticity. As a result, elasticities of 0.8, 1, and 1.5 (for demand, supply, and substitution, respectively) have been used to estimate the costs of protection.

Case 7: Artificial and Synthetic Fibers

Trade barriers on imports of artificial and synthetic fibers (ASF) have consisted of many instruments. In addition to MFN duties, 49 antidumping cases were initiated between 1980 and 1999, covering all the major ASF types—with antidumping duties doubling in the early 1990s, and then tripling the level of protection granted by MFN duties. Moreover, ASF are indirectly influenced by the Multi-Fiber Agreement (see cases 13 and 14 below).

However, the two most interesting aspects of ASF protection are its "crisis cartel" status and the massive member-state subsidies that have to a considerable extent shaped the EC ASF industry (for details, see de Ghellinck and Huveneers 1995).

The ASF industry tried to benefit from the EC "crisis cartel" status between 1972 and 1986. The legal basis for this status is Article 81:3 (ex 85:3) of the Treaty of Rome, which states that agreements between firms can be acceptable if they "contribute to improving the production or distribution of goods or to promoting technical and economic progress, while allowing consumers a fair share of the resulting benefit." However, the ASF firms withdrew their notification in 1972 because the Competition Directorate was opposed to such an agreement, and because they had received enough support from their respective member-states.

A second attempt to introduce a crisis cartel agreement was made in 1978 for a five-year period. Again, the tabled agreement was challenged by the Competition Directorate, because the cartel scheme included production and delivery quotas. But the agreement was not formally rejected: it has been implemented, with several amendments, and has led to a 20 percent cut from the 1977-level production capacities. However, it has virtually frozen the market shares of all the firms involved, with few eliminations of inefficient plants.

In 1982, a third crisis cartel agreement was tabled by the industry, and accepted in 1994 by the Competition Directorate. The *XIIth Report on Competition Policy* (European Commission 1982) laid down the requirements for the constitution of a crisis cartel: structural overcapacity for a prolonged period, output decline, substantial operating losses, and the absence of an expectation of lasting improvement in the medium run. Moreover, the crisis cartel should provide a permanent and irreversible reduction in overcapacity, in combination with moves to specialization by individual firms, timing capacity reduction so as to minimize social dislocation. In 1985, the EC ASF producers benefiting from a crisis cartel represented 85 percent of the installed EC production capacity and had market shares ranging from 55 to 78 percent for the various products involved.

Excess capacity has been largely due to massive subsidies, particularly in Italy. A first EC subsidy "code" aimed at making member-state and Community subsidies conditional on capacity reductions was implemented in 1977. Since then, it has been followed by a series of other codes, the last one having been enforced in 1996 for a period of initially three years, extended to five years, with the possibility of being extended under regional aid schemes. All these codes have been increasingly detailed by product and production process, hence de facto almost by firm or plant. For instance, the 1996 code tightens the notification procedure for aid (for fibers based on polyester, acrylic, or polypropylene) and modifies the rules for authorization of investment aid—making them dependent not only on significant capacity reductions (as usually), but also on product innovation and on the size of enterprises (for small enterprises, aid will be authorized at a higher percentage of the authorized ceilings) (Rouam 1998, 100).

This increasingly detailed approach has required ever closer contacts between the industry and the Commission, a situation that has generated confusion and a strong feeling of subjectivity in the code implementation by the Commission—all the more because there have been no ex post controls of announced capacity reductions, and no tight recovery procedures for illegal aid. There is little doubt that the codes have favored subsidized multiproduct and multiplant incumbents over more efficient entrants with a narrower range of activities.

Notes

The estimated rate of overall protection for 1990 is the sum of the average GATT-bound tariff (8.9 percent) and of the average ad valorem antidumping duty taken under the 1985, 1986, and 1987 cases (12.9 percent). Since then, the industry has been increasingly protected: the average antidumping duty in cases in the 1990s is roughly 15 percent. There has been no attempt to estimate the ad valorem equivalents of the subsidies and crisis cartel status.

To our knowledge, there are no available estimates of the total-price demand and supply price elasticities. Estimates of the elasticity of substitution between domestic and foreign products range from 9.8 (ISIC 351) to 0.7 (Shiells et al. 1986; Reinert and Roland-Holst 1992). As a result, elasticities of 1, 1, and 2 (for demand, supply, and substitution, respectively) have been used to estimate the costs of protection.

Case 8: Videocassette Recorders

Videocassette recorders are one of the best illustrations of the difficult communitarization of trade policy. In autumn 1982, the French government "unilaterally" imposed a luxury tax on all videocassette recorders (VCRs), to be collected in Poitiers (a small customs office in the middle of France) or in the French VCR factories. This move hurt almost everybody in Europe. First, it was counterproductive for the French "national champion" (Thomson) producing VCRs, the alleged originator of the measure. Because Japanese VCRs got unexpected publicity from this measure (French VCR sales started slowly) French consumers rushed to buy Japanese VCRs—hence giving no time to Thomson to react.

Second, major member-states (Britain, Germany, the Netherlands) made clear their opposition to any action against Japanese VCRs at several Council of Ministers meetings in early 1982. They were even more opposed because the French luxury tax was imposed on their *own* production (Thorn-EMI, Telefunken, Philips), whether located in the EC or in France.

Third, the Commission analyzed the procedure for implementing the French luxury tax as an intra-EC trade barrier, favoring Thomson over EC competitors. The jurisprudence, based on Article 28 (ex 30) of the Treaty of Rome, considers a mandatory point of entry as having the equivalent effect to a quantitative restriction (indeed, it would have been difficult to find an entry point more costly for German or British producers than Poitiers). The Commission had two other reasons not to be amused. It had just passed Regulation 288/82 (see chapter 2) aimed at limiting member-state actions setting up new trade barriers (in this context, the VCR case appeared a bad omen for the survival of the regulation); and the Commission had to defend the French action at the GATT dispute settlement panel that Japan requested.

Internal Market Commissioner Etienne Davignon tried to escape all these difficulties by convincing the Association of Firms with a Common Interest in the Video 2000 System to lodge an antidumping complaint. That was done within a few days (van Marion 1993). The notice of initiation of the case was published in December 1982. In February 1983, the Commission came to a VER with the Japanese Ministry of International Trade and Industry (MITI). In March 1983, the association "withdrew" its complaint "following the implementation of the unilateral decision taken by the Japanese authorities to moderate in 1983 and 1984 the exports of VCRs from Japan and to set up an export floor-price system" (EC, *Official Journal*, 1983, L86/23).

In fact, the 1983 VER contained quantity and price elements (Hindley 1985, 1986; van Marion 1993). Quantitative targets were based on sales forecast in the EC for 1983 and 1984. European producers (including EC production located in Austria) got a stable share of 21 percent of the sales and Japanese producers the rest (split into two subsets: one for direct imports from Japan, and one for Japanese plants in the EC, in the proportion of 69 to 10 percent for 1983, and 62 to 17 percent for 1984). Moreover, minima prices for three categories of Japanese VCRs (low, medium, and high-end) were imposed. These were reduced a year later—leaving quantitative targets as the key instrument. This evolution is likely to have accelerated the rise of the VHS standard (JVC-Matsushita) and the fall of the V2000 (Philips) and Betamax (Sony) standards.

In 1987, a new antidumping case was initiated against Japanese and South Korean exports, followed in 1989 by an anticircumvention case against Japanese plants located in the EC, and in 1995 by an antidumping case against VCRs and parts from Korea and Singapore. All these cases were accompanied by a host of antidumping cases on related products: videocassettes from Hong Kong and Korea (1987) and from China (1990); audiocassette tapes from Japan, Korea, and China (1989); and compact-disk players, first from Japan and Korea (1987 and 1991), then from Malaysia, Singapore, and Taiwan. In almost all these cases, Philips was the key complainant, often accompanied by two or three small EC producers—sometimes its own subsidiaries.

Notes

The estimated rate of overall protection is the compounded sum of the GATT-bound tariff (12.5 percent) and of the average antidumping duty taken under the 1987 and 1989 cases, that is, 15.7 percent. This figure is likely to be conservative; Hindley (1985) has estimated that under the VER, prices could have gone up to 24 percent.

The literature suggests a total-price demand elasticity ranging from 1.1 to 1.8 for household appliances (Coursey and Taylor 1982), and an elasticity of substitution between domestic and foreign products ranging from 7.5 to 1.4 (Shiells et al. 1986; Reinert and Roland-Holst 1992). As a result, elasticities of 1.2, 1, and 3 (for demand, supply, and substitution, respectively) have been used to estimate the costs of protection.

Case 9: Integrated Circuits

This case focuses on two major types of integrated circuits of the late 1980s and early 1990s: DRAMs and EPROMs, two key inputs in computers and electronic products. The antidumping complaint against Japanese exporters of DRAMs was lodged in February 1987 by Siemens from Germany, Thomson from France, SGSM from Italy, and Motorola (the EC subsidiary of the US firm) from Britain. As underlined by Greenaway et al. (1995), it was extended to non-Japanese (South Korean) producers of DRAMs (in 1990, with smaller antidumping duties than the estimated measures taken against the Japanese producers) and to Japanese producers of complementary goods, in particular EPROMs (in 1987).

The presence of Motorola is interesting for several reasons. Motorola was considered an EC firm in the EC antidumping case (see the opposite fate of Canon in case 10 below on photocopiers). In the United States, however, it was among the US producers considering, but ultimately *not* lodging, an antidumping complaint and a 301 petition (the antidumping complaints were lodged by a small firm, Micron, for the 64K DRAMs in 1985, and initiated by an unprecedented de officio action of the US Department of Commerce for the 256K DRAMs in 1986). These two US cases were lodged against the same exporters targeted by the EC case—illustrating the "echoing" among antidumping cases (several cases are launched in several countries against the same exporters by the same importers; see appendix B). These transatlantic antidumping echoes have been followed by the US antidumping EPROM case lodged in 1985 and the US anti-dumping case against South Korean producers of DRAMs (1992).

Notes

The estimated rate of overall protection for 1990 is the compounded sum of the GATT-bound tariff (13.5 percent) and of the ad valorem tariff equivalent of the antidumping measures taken under the 1987 DRAM case (estimated at 30 percent). This figure of 30 percent appears quite con-servative for the following reasons: In the DRAM case, the average mar-gin of dumping amounted to almost 89 percent, and the provisional and final ad valorem antidumping duties to 60 percent (possibly "watered" duties); moreover, the ad valorem antidumping duty in the 1987 EPROM case amounted to 94 percent.

The literature suggests a total-price demand elasticity from 1.5 (Flamm 1996; Baldwin 1990) and a supply price elasticity range of 2 (Hufbauer and Elliott 1994). To our knowledge, there is no available estimate of the elasticity of substitution between domestic and foreign products. As a re-sult, elasticities of 1.5, 2, and 2 (for demand, supply, and substitution, re-spectively) have been used to estimate the costs of protection.

Case 10: Photocopiers

In August 1985, an antidumping photocopier case was initiated by four firms: Xerox from the Netherlands and Britain, Océ from the Netherlands, Olivetti from Italy, and Tetras from France. (A fifth firm, Develop from Germany, joined the complaint initially, but when it was bought by Mi-nolta in 1986, it was eliminated by the Commission from the right to com-plain.) In August 1986, provisional antidumping duties ranging from 7.2 to 15.8 percent were imposed. In February 1987, definitive antidumping duties were on average 3 points higher than provisional duties, despite the fact that the final margins of dumping were on average 2 points lower than the provisional margins. No undertaking (i.e., a commitment by an exporting firm to charge export-minimum prices or to export maximum quantities) was accepted (with one minor exception), a relatively unusual decision at this time.

On 17 November 1988, an anticircumvention investigation pursuant to Article 13(10)(c) of the EC Regulation was initiated against Canon, Konica, Matsushita, Minolta, Ricoh, Sharp, and Toshiba. The complaint was lodged by the same EC firms that had alleged that "the value of the parts used [by the Japanese firms] for the assembly operations and originating in Japan exceeds the value of all the other parts used by more than 50 percent" (EC, *Official Journal*, 1988, C 44/3). In December 1988 and May 1989, similar cases were initiated against the EC plants of Sharp (Britain) and Ricoh (France) (the plant built in December 1989 by Sharp in France has not been subject to such a procedure). Estimating the ad valorem rates of protection equivalent to the anticircumvention measures taken is made difficult by the fact that all the cases have been terminated by undertakings or by specific duties followed by undertakings.[2] When computed on the basis of the method described by Vermulst and Waer (1990), ad valorem equivalent duties in the anticircumvention case range from 7 to 20 percent, with an unweighted average of 15 percent.[3] These ad valorem rates of protection should be interpreted with care because no firm has paid such duties (by design, anticircumvention measures are cost-raising instruments, because they are local-content requirements imposed on Japanese Euro-plants).

Notes

The estimated rate of overall protection in 1990 is the sum of the average GATT-bound tariff (7.2 percent) and of the antidumping measures taken (in February 1987) under the 1985 case (24.7 percent).

To our knowledge, there is no estimate of the total-price demand elasticity and the supply price elasticity for photocopiers. Estimates of the elasticity of substitution between domestic and foreign products range from 2 (photographic goods) to 1.4 (communication equipment) (Shiells

---

2. According to the computations of the EC antidumping office, the average proportion of parts of Japanese origin in the Japanese European plants is 66.4 percent—a figure very close to the 60 percent threshold imposed by EC regulations. That is a weighted average, the weights being the relative capacities of production of the Japanese European plants. It should be noticed that EC practices in determining the origin of parts were considerably changed during the photocopier cases by the antidumping office, as is shown in detail by Vermulst and Waer (1990). Moreover, the models of copiers inherited from Develop and Olivetti by Minolta and Canon (respectively) and still produced and sold by the two Japanese companies have been excluded from the scope of the investigation.

3. In application of Article 13(10)(c) of the Regulations, the anticircumvention duty is the product of the antidumping duty times the proportion of parts of origin from the exporting country. In the case of the three specific duties imposed, dividing the specific duty by the average unit value of the import (a proxy for the average price) gives the following ad valorem equivalent duties (depending on the bases used): from 16.7 to 21.1 percent for Konica, from 14.3 to 18.0 percent for Matsushita, and from 2.1 to 2.6 percent for Toshiba.

et al. 1986; Reinert and Roland-Holst 1992). As a result, elasticities of 1, 1, and 2 (for demand, supply, and substitution, respectively) have been used to estimate the costs of protection.

Case 11: Steel

Under the Treaty of Paris, which covers most but not all of the EC steel products,[4] EC member-states have been de jure in charge of trade policy, except in two situations: (1) The Commission is in charge of antidumping and antisubsidy procedures against foreign dumping and subsidies; (2) in case of "manifest crisis" as defined by Article 58 of the treaty, the Commission can impose minimum prices or mandatory production quotas on each EC steel firm, and it can impose fines on violators. These two situations combining trade and domestic measures emerged when the world and EC steel markets collapsed in the late 1970s. This collapse occurred in three successive steps.

From 1974 to 1977, the Commission analyzed the steel crisis as a cyclical fluctuation. Its intervention was limited to encouraging "cooperative" behavior among large European steel firms that were relying on oxygen-furnace technology (following the experience of the "rationalizing groups" in the German steel industry of the late 1960s; Stegemann 1977)—to the detriment of the emerging and more efficient "mini mills," such as the Bresciani for long steel products (particularly rebars).

In 1977, the continuous fall of steel demand in the OECD zone and the relatively higher prices in Europe (partly caused by the "cooperative" behavior among EC steelmakers generated by the Commission) created a situation perceived by many observers as requiring the Commission's intervention under the "manifest crisis" provisions. EC capacity utilization in crude steel production declined from 87 percent in 1974 to 65 percent in the late 1970s, and the share of extra-EC imports in European Coal and Steel Community (ECSC) steel production increased from 2.7 percent in 1974 to 6.7 percent in 1979, with a peak of 7.9 percent in 1977.

In May 1977, the Commission refused to invoke Article 58. Rather, it introduced the first Davignon Plan (after Etienne Davignon, then the commissioner for industrial policy), consisting of *voluntary* minimum prices ("guidance" prices) on most steel products covered by the Treaty of Paris. However, the Commission imposed *mandatory* minimum prices on rebars, a key product for the Bresciani, confirming its bias in favor of large steelmakers and against small steel producers.

Third, in 1980, EC prices collapsed after the closure of the US market (new US antidumping complaints were lodged during the second half of

---

4. Steel products covered by the Treaty of Paris are often called European Coal and Steel Community steel products.

1979) and an additional decline of demand. As a result, the first Davignon Plan fell apart. In October 1980, the Commission adopted a "second" Davignon Plan based on Article 58, imposing *mandatory* production quotas (based on the site-level monthly production performance between July 1977 and June 1980) and minima prices for most of the ECSC steel products. In addition to these major domestic measures, this second Davignon Plan included export and import measures.

EC *export measures* flowed from VERs imposed by the United States, and scheduled to be enforced until March 1992. Although allowing the transferability of export licenses between EC steel producers and merchants, these export quotas favored collusive behavior between EC steel firms in their main export market (the United States)—hence, they reinforced the incentives to collude in the EC steel markets themselves. In fact, the Commission was much in favor of a worldwide cartel. In 1977, it requested the creation of a Steel Committee at the OECD, hoping to generate "cooperative" behavior at the world level, comparable to that being generated in the EC.

On the *import side*, the Davignon Plan had two components, depending on whether the foreign country was a small or a major steel exporter to the EC. Small exporters were subject to "basic" (minimum) import prices, roughly similar to the US "trigger" price mechanism. Major exporters were subject to "autolimitation agreements" (VERs), which contained detailed provisions on export quantities and prices to be renewed every year.

These quantity provisions allowed for the maintenance of "traditional patterns of trade" under the so-called "triple clause", i.e., imposition of a spreading of foreign deliveries over the year, throughout the whole EC, and across the product range. Price provisions banned the possibility of undercutting EC prices by more than 6 percent (4 percent for specialty steels). In cases of conflicts between foreign exporters and the EC, consultations were to be held. In case of price infringements, the EC could impose sanctions, in addition to antidumping actions. From 1979 to 1984 (the crisis climax), autolimitation agreements covered a dozen countries—and roughly 70 percent of extra-EC steel imports.

From 1985 to 1988, the world and EC steel markets began to recover slowly, and the Commission progressively relaxed barriers on EC imports. In particular, the autolimitation agreements evolved in three directions: (1) EFTA candidates to EC accession were increasingly treated according to the provisions of the Treaty of Paris and the EC steel policy, and they begun to behave accordingly. (2) Central European countries became increasingly subject to autonomous quotas imposed by certain member-states (Belgium, Germany, Italy, Luxembourg, the Netherlands). (3) The other major steel exporters were progressively put under the exclusive threat of antidumping measures. As a result, the autolimitation agreements covered less than 15 percent of extra-EC steel imports in 1989.

This slow "re-liberalization" came close to an end in 1992–93, when the world and EC steel markets were again depressed. The VERs on EC exports to the United States, which were scheduled to expire in March 1992, were quickly followed (in June 1992) by a new salvo of US antidumping actions against EC and Asian exporters. In mid-1992, four EC member-states (Belgium, France, Germany, and Italy) had imposed bilateral quotas on Central European exports, despite the recently signed Europe Agreements. In November 1992, the Commission announced the possibility of a $1.1 billion package in "restructuring subsidies," conditional on planned cuts by the industry.[5] Finally, the Multilateral Steel Agreement—which could have been part of the Uruguay Round and which aimed to eliminate domestic subsidies and trade barriers erected in the 1970s—was definitively abandoned in 1994.

However, the 1992–93 crisis did not resuscitate the EC policy based on a manifest crisis under Article 58. The EC imposed new trade barriers (see below), but not as many as in the late 1970s and early 1980s, and the coverage of the EC autolimitation agreements continued to be reduced. In 1996, it represented less than 10 percent of extra-EC steel imports, mostly steel exports from Russia and a couple of other countries of the former Soviet Union.

This apparent liberalization of the early 1990s raises a question, because it left EC imports from the United States and Japan marginal (almost 6 percent of total ECSC imports in 1996) and even smaller than in 1979, whereas it did not boost EC imports from Central European countries, which showed strong ups and downs. The contradiction between an apparently more open regime and small changes in trade flows (in 1996, steel imports still represented less than 9 percent of ECSC production, a very similar ratio to that of the late 1970s for a similar tonnage of ECSC production) can be explained by four mutually reinforcing elements.

First, EC antidumping actions against steel imports have played an increasingly key role since 1976. During the late 1970s, they were used to gain compliance with the autolimitation system from the major foreign exporters—hence the salvo of 77 EC antidumping cases against large as well as small exporters from 1976 to 1980. Since the early 1980s, antidumping measures have been used as the ultimate threat and barrier against foreign exporters. Between 1980 and 1999, there were 111 antidumping cases lodged in steel, that is, almost 15 percent of all the EC antidumping cases, for an industry that represents 4 percent of EC manufacturing production or employment.

Antidumping measures have been taken in 88 percent of all these cases (relative to 71 percent for all manufacturing), and their ad valorem tariff equivalent is roughly 29 percent (relative to the 5 percent average tariff on

---

5. The Braun Report (after Fernand Braun, a well-known EC steel industrialist) detailed capacity cuts totaling 19 to 26 million metric tons of hot-rolled products (15 to 20 percent of 1992 EC crude steel production), 50,000 job losses (14 percent of total employees), and a total cost of $7.1 billion over three years.

steel products). In 1998 (the Asian crisis), 15 cases out of 24, and in 1999, 10 cases out of 67 were initiated in the steel sector. Because antidumping measures in steel are routinely undertakings (minima prices and VERs), they have strongly contributed to limiting competition and reinforcing price collusion in EC steel and world markets.

Second, the Europe Agreements entailed the immediate elimination of EC tariffs on steel exports from Central European countries. However, as soon as the agreements began to be implemented, steel imports from the Czech Republic and Slovakia were put under unilateral quotas by France, Germany, and Italy, from March to December 1992. Then, from 1992 to 1995, these imports were under tariff quotas for the whole EC. Since 1996, these tariff quotas have been eliminated and replaced by a surveillance system of *ex ante* "double checking," allowing a tight monitoring of trade flows enforced on all steel imports from Bulgaria, the Czech Republic, Poland, Romania, and Slovakia.

Concerning Eastern Europe, with huge production capacities, but often outdated products, the quotas imposed in 1995 on steel exports from Kazakhstan, Russia, and Ukraine (based on preexisting EC autonomous quotas) were increased in volume between 1995 and 1999 in the context of Partnership and Cooperation Agreements. The EC has declared its readiness to fully open its market to the three countries by 2001, but conditional on the emergence of "normal competitive conditions," particularly regarding competition policy, subsidies, and environmental protection—all conditions too stringent to make the EC pledge for openness credible. For all these countries, antidumping measures remain a severe and permanent threat.

Third, the past policies of the United States, EC, and other large steel producers may have generated strong incentives to collude at the *world* level. Alan Wolff (1995) provides information supporting the existence of a cartel (the "East of Burma" cartel), which would severely limit trade flows between Europe and Asia—and hence complement US and EC antidumping measures. Within the EC, strong forces toward collusion have been revealed by the relatively large number of competition investigations terminated by large fines, as was recently illustrated by the price-fixing arrangement of December 1993 for flat stainless steel products involving six large steelmakers (the case investigation, terminated in February 1998, imposed €27 million in fines).

The fourth and last aspect to be taken into account when assessing the level of competition and openness of EC steel markets is the role and magnitude of subsidies. If the provisions of the Treaty of Paris tend to inhibit *price* competition, they also tend to exacerbate competition through *investment*. The mid-1960s witnessed all the EC major steelmakers building new plants with large public subsidies from their member-states (except Germany). In the mid-1970s, when the steel market began to plunge, EC steelmakers requested and got even more subsidies to solve their "excessive capacity" problems (capacity was excessive mostly because of the excessive—subsidized—investments granted in the past and the sticky prices imposed by the Davignon Plan).

Of course, the by far major effect of all these additional subsidies has been to exacerbate the adjustment problems they were supposed to solve. Steelmakers have used these subsidies to compensate for their losses without adjusting their capacities, making their competitors' adjustment even more difficult. In 1980, a first Code on State Aid, making new subsidies conditional on plant closures, was adopted. This code, in its successive versions, has had limited effects because delays, exceptions, and infringements have been massive and recurrent. The 1993 "restructuring" plan was never implemented because the reduction commitments effectively offered by EC steel firms amounted to only 11 million tons, far from the minimum of 19 million tons suggested by the Braun Report. As a result, in October 1994, the Commission decided to cancel all aid to the steel industry, except that for social purposes. In 1996, the Sixth Code (to be valid until 2002, after which the subsidy rules of the Treaty of Rome are expected to be applied) gives the Commission the power to request suspension of the disbursement of any financial support *before* its approval.

In sum, the EC steel industry may be one of the best illustrations of the magnified costs of trade barriers in a noncompetitive environment. As stressed by Winters (1995), the key question is to get the most accurate description of the EC steel sector. Is it an oligopoly coordinated by member-states and the Commission, in drastic need of rationalization and elimination of large excess capacities? Or is it a noncooperative oligopoly, but in a position to get rents because of the limited number of existing firms? The importance of the question is underlined by the recent and huge consolidations in the EC and Japanese markets: the concentration among Usinor, Arbed, and Aceralia (leading to the world's largest steelmaker, with 40 percent of the EC steel market) coupled with the agreement between Usinor and Nippon Steel;[6] the merger in Japan between NKK and Kawasaki (leading to the world's second largest steelmaker); and the talks between NKK and ThyssenKrupp. Whether the EC steel sector is a quasi-cooperative oligopoly coordinated by the member-states and the Commission or a noncooperative oligopoly is an important question because the costs of opening trade for the EC are much smaller in the former situation than in the latter (which attributes shocks to changes in trade policy rather than to rationalization). And it underlines the fact that a pan-European steel rationalization would be beneficial only if—a big if—it is not "managed" by

---

6. The Usinor-Nippon Steel agreement includes exclusivity provisions in terms of investment: Usinor will not invest in Southeast Asia without discussing such operations with Nippon Steel, and Nippon Steel will do the same in Central and Eastern Europe. Moreover, Usinor and Nippon Steel will act jointly in China and Russia. The Usinor-centered "consolidation" and the Usinor-Nippon Steel agreement will be key tests for EC competition authorities.

the Commission, the EC member-states, or Western European steelmakers, probably to the detriment of the Central European steel industries. For instance, this "nonmanaged" condition is crucial for getting an economically sound implementation of the condition for steel restructuring imposed by the Accession Partnership on Poland (see box 6.5).

As underlined by Moore (1998), the major problem of the EC steel industry has been the reciprocal reinforcement of restrictive external *and* domestic measures (in contrast with the US focus on trade measures)—a theme underlined in chapters 2 and 3. The Treaty of Rome is certainly better equipped for promoting competition (hence making unsustainable the cooperative equilibrium in the steel industry) than the Treaty of Paris. This observation underlines the importance of the *effective* shift of the steel industry to the TEC by 2002. In this context, one may wonder (taking into account the importance of available information in collusive games) exactly what is the meaning of the provision included in the Nice TEC version, according to which the existing statistical framework for the steel industry should be maintained until December 2002 (pending proposals by the Commission).

Notes

In 1990, the bulk of EC protection in steel was provided by VERs, subsidies, and antidumping measures. There is little information on the ad valorem equivalents of the VERs, and even their exact scope and magnitude is not well known. Table A.1 provides the available information on the subsidies granted between 1980 and 1985 (the crisis peak). It suggests an average subsidy of $26–$30 per net ton, if one relates the subsidies to the steel tonnage produced in the EC during the *whole* of the 1980s (a conservative assumption, if only because more subsidies were granted after 1985, in particular in France, Germany, Italy, and Spain). Crandall (1994) estimated the average difference between the EC and Japanese export prices (the latter being the best proxy for the world price) as $60 per net ton in the 1980s. Adding the $30 average subsidy per net ton to Crandall's estimate leads to a price differential of $90 with the Japanese export price, or 30 percent.

If one assumes that Japanese steelmakers were not subsidized in the 1980s and early 1990s, a substantial portion of this differential percentage represents the rate of protection of the EC steel industry, excluding antidumping measures. Considering that half of the differential (15 percent) can be attributed to protection granted through VERs and subsidies seems a conservative guess, which is used in table 2.1 to fill the NTB column. Concerning antidumping measures that have been substituted for NTBs, they are known only for a small amount of cases, for which the average antidumping duty is 16.3 percent. The fact that this figure is close to

Table A.1 Case 11: Total subsidies to the steel sector approved by the European Commission, 1980–85

Country	Subsidies for closures		Subsidies for continuing operations		Aid to investment and research and development		Total
	Millions of US dollars	Percent	Millions of US dollars	Percent	Millions of US dollars	Percent	Millions of US dollars
Belgium	117	2.8	3,381	80.3	711	16.9	4,209
Britain	1,024	18.4	2,735	49.1	1,815	32.6	5,574
Denmark			67	83.8	13	16.3	80
Germany	612	16.1	1,920	50.5	1,268	33.4	3,800
France	299	3.3	5,733	63.4	3,004	33.2	9,036
Ireland			261	100.0			261
Italy	1,041	8.7	9,066	76.0	1,823	15.3	11,930
Luxembourg	15	2.4	174	27.9	435	69.7	624
Netherlands			219	48.7	231	51.3	450
EC-10	3,108	8.6	23,556	65.5	9,300	25.9	35,964

EC = European Community.

Source: Howeel (1988), 64.

the estimated protection granted through NTBs fits well the likely possibility that antidumping cases are a substitute for NTBs, and hence provide roughly the same level of protection.

In sum, combining the GATT-bound tariff (4.8 percent) and the 16.3 percent of antidumping protection leads to an overall rate of protection of 21.9 percent. The literature suggests a total-price demand elasticity ranging from 0.5 to 2.0, depending on the steel products considered (Crandall 1981), a supply price elasticity ranging from 1.4 to 3.5 (Crandall 1981, 132), and an elasticity of substitution between domestic and foreign steel of about 3 (Shiells et al. 1986; Reinert and Roland-Holst 1992). As a result (and taking into account the fact that EC protection focuses on cold-rolled steel and long products), elasticities of 1.4, 2, and 3 (for demand, supply, and substitution, respectively) have been used to estimate the costs of protection.

Case 12: Passenger Cars

Until 1991, quantitative restrictions on imports of Japanese passenger cars were imposed by several EC member-states on a national basis (for a detailed legal history until the mid-1990s, see Eeckhout 1994).[7] In 1952, Italy and Japan signed a bilateral agreement limiting direct imports from both sides to 2,200 cars per year, reportedly at the request of the Japanese industry, which was afraid of competition from the Italian car industry. In 1977, the Japanese car producer association signed an agreement with the British carmakers' association limiting Japanese exports to Britain to 11 percent of British annual car sales.

Also in 1977, the French president declared that Japanese carmakers would not be allowed to have a share of the French market larger than 3 percent of French sales, a restriction that became binding only in 1980–82, when Japanese car sales reached the 3 percent threshold. Last, Spain limited its direct imports of Japanese passenger cars to 1,000 units, and Portugal imposed a ceiling of 20,000 units on imports of non-EC cars. As a result of all these restrictions, the only large EC market that remained apparently unrestricted in the late 1980s was the German market, although a tacit agreement might also have limited Japanese market share there (*Handelsblatt*, 5 May 1986, 3; *Financial Times*, 9 October 1986, 16; Deutsch 1999).

All these bilateral agreements implied that there was not a single European car market, and that severe intra-EC nontariff barriers were in place (Buigues, Ilzkovitz, and Lebrun 1990). The segmentation of EC car markets was made possible by a combination of several instruments. Article 115 could be used, except by France and Britain, because these two member-

---

7. There also have been quantitative restrictions on certain other types of vehicles (in particular, light commercial and 4-wheel drive vehicles), which are ignored in this case.

states imposed their own restrictions on an "informal" (nongovernmental) basis. Technical standards (notably in Britain) and national certification procedures (notably in France) have made almost impossible any trade between EC member-states without a domestic producers' agreement. Last but not least, legal limits on competition between car distributors based on EC Regulation 123/85 granted a "block exemption" from EC competition law, on the basis of alleged benefits for the consumers in car maintenance and the availability of spare parts.

All these intra-EC barriers have been very effective: All the efforts to generate "parallel" imports of Japanese cars have failed, and indirect imports of Japanese cars have been kept to very small numbers.[8] Discriminatory pricing has been maximized, as best illustrated by the January 1998 Commission decision to impose a fine of € 102 million on Volkswagen for instructing its Italian dealers not to supply "foreign" (i.e., EC non-Italian) customers.

The last source of distortions in EC car markets has been the large subsidies granted by member-state governments and subnational entities to national firms, in particular to those that are state-owned or that invest in greenfield plants in areas benefiting from EC structural funds (Single Market Review 1997d, 104; European Commission 1998c, 16, and 1999g, 14). It is estimated that, between 1977 and 1987, EC carmakers received total aid of more than € 25 billion (Rouam 1998), that is, 12 percent of the 1990 turnover of the industry. In 1989, the Commission tried to rein in this state aid, but it did not go very far. National and European subsidies remained acceptable for (1) offsetting the "cost disadvantages" of producing in certain regions (e.g., the Fiat and Opel-Volkswagen plants in the Mezzogiorno and in Eastern Germany), (2) introducing innovative products or processes (the *Valeo* case), or (3) addressing the "danger of reemergence of overcapacity" (the *Rover* case).

All these conditions have led to the same arcane debates as in the synthetic fiber or steel industries (see cases 7 and 11 above), with the same impression of arbitrariness (e.g., the ban on state aid to Daewoo, and the authorization of state aid to Mercedes, both in Spain). Moreover, during the mid-1990s, the French, Italian, and Spanish governments further circumvented the limited EC disciplines on subsidies to carmakers by granting state aid to car *buyers* (in these two member-states, national carmakers still had a dominant market share). These subsidies were large—roughly € 1.4 billion in the French case. Ironically, consumers used them mostly to buy *non*-national cars (from other member-states or non-EC countries).

---

8. "Parallel" importers of Japanese cars have sued the Commission before the European Court of Justice on the basis of Article 30 (prohibition of quantitative restrictions) and Article 85 of the Treaty of Rome (prohibition of collusion), but they have been unable to get the Court's support. The estimated 100,000 car dealers in the EC sell, on average, 266 new cars per year and per dealer outlet, compared with 674 in the United States (WTO, *Trade Policy Review: The European Community*, 1997, 103).

For instance, it is reported that the biggest beneficiaries of the French subsidies were Fiat and Volkswagen.

To cope with this high and discriminatory level of protection, Japanese carmakers developed two strategies during the 1980s and 1990s. First, they competed with EC firms in *non*-EC markets, to contain EC firms as much as possible in EC markets. Until the mid-1990s, the proportion of EC sales to total sales of the EC carmakers increased for almost all of them, despite its already high level (in 1990, it ranged from 92 percent for Fiat to 53 percent, the lowest, for Volkswagen).[9] EC carmakers could hardly react because of their less efficient plants. In 1989, 36.2 person-hours were required to assemble a vehicle in Europe, against 16.8 in Japan and 21.2 in the United States (Womack, Jones, and Roos 1990, 92).

Second, Japanese carmakers built plants in the EC, with European subsidies in certain cases, whereas no EC firm (except Mercedes and Volkswagen) was able to develop and keep large plants outside Europe during the 1990s. Japanese plants have been located in Britain (Nissan, Honda, Isuzu, and Toyota), in Spain (Nissan), in Germany (Toyota with Volkswagen, Mazda with Ford), and most recently in France (Toyota).

As a result, the late 1980s witnessed one major goal for the EC policy: to communitarize member-state quotas on Japanese cars.[10] This goal was achieved in July 1991, with the signing of an agreement between the EC Commission and the Japanese MITI—the Car Consensus (hereafter, the Consensus).[11] According to the Consensus, six export "levels" were set for 1999, as shown in table A.2: an export level for the whole EC, and five export levels for the five more "restricted" markets (France, Italy, Portugal, Spain, and Britain). These export levels were based on market forecasts of domestic demand; consequently, they have been subject to changes in order to cope with changes in market forecasts, particularly during the severe downturn of EC car markets between 1992 and 1998.[12]

---

9. Large EC carmakers were very dependent on their member-state market; this share amounts to 45 percent, on average, the highest (in 1990) being Fiat (62 percent) and the lowest, Volkswagen (26 percent).

10. Limiting the future output of the Japanese-owned EC plants has never been a widely accepted goal in the EC. Britain has always been strongly opposed to it, often supported by other member-states interested in getting Japanese plants, and many Commission officials have felt such a goal to be a breach of the Common Market.

11. The Commission appears to have negotiated directly with the industry, and sometimes presented the Council with a fait accompli (Holmes and Smith 1995, 132). The Consensus covers passenger cars, off-road vehicles, light commercial vehicles, light trucks (up to five tons), and the same vehicles in wholly knocked down form (CKD sets).

12. In fact, exact Japanese shipments to the EC are determined by bilateral consultations on market trends and annual "supply forecasts" for the EC as a whole and for the five restrictive member-states. The Consensus also contains asymmetric obligations in case of upward or downward market trends: EC carmakers are granted one-third of any EC market increase, whereas Japanese carmakers have to absorb two-thirds of any EC market downfall.

Table A.2 Case 12: The 1991 Car Consensus between the European Community and Japan

Group or country	Situation in 1999, as anticipated in 1991				Effective situation in 1999			
		Japanese cars				Japanese cars		
	Forecasted total car demand	Imports from Japan	Japanese cars from EC plants[a]	Total	Total car registrations	Imports from Japan	Japanese cars from EC plants[b]	Total
In thousands								
European Community	15,100	1,223	1,193	2,416	14,633	1,035	612	1,640
"Restricted" markets								
Britain	2,700	190	456	646	2,198	158	175	333
France	2,850	150	105	255	2,148	76	36	112
Italy	2,600	138	96	234	2,326	109	71	180
Portugal	275	23	29	52	275	32	1	33
Spain	1,475	79	130	209	1,404	61	24	85
The German case	—	—	—	—	3,804	264	146	410
In market shares (percent)								
European Community	100.0	8.1	7.9	16.0	100.0	7.1	4.9	11.2
"Restricted" markets								
Britain	100.0	7.0	16.9	23.9	100.0	7.2	8.0	15.1
France	100.0	5.3	3.7	9.0	100.0	3.5	1.7	5.2
Italy	100.0	5.3	3.7	9.0	100.0	4.7	3.1	7.7
Portugal	100.0	8.4	10.6	19.0	100.0	11.5	0.5	12.0
Spain	100.0	5.4	8.8	14.2	100.0	4.3	1.7	6.0
The German case	—	—	—	—	100.0	6.9	3.9	10.8

a. As the Japanese side has not released figures about transplant market shares, these figures are based on internal Commission documents quoted by Mason (1994).

b. Differences between EC registrations of Japanese cars and car exports from Japan.

Sources: Mason (1994); WTO, *Trade Policy Review: The European Community*, 1997, 1030; *Ward Automotive Journal* (2001); author's computations.

In addition to these restrictions on direct imports of Japanese cars, the Consensus contained forecasts of intra-EC trade flows from Japanese transplants, the exact status of which has been the subject of hot debate. Initially, the Commission pledged to impose no restrictions on Japanese investments in the EC and no controls on the free circulation of Japanese cars produced in the EC, while the Japanese government (MITI) agreed to convey to Japanese carmakers the message that the sales of Japanese cars made in the EC should not be "concentrated" in national (member-state) markets in order to avoid "serious disruption." However, in the oral declaration presenting the Consensus to the international press, the Commission mentioned a "working assumption" of transplant production of roughly 1.2 million cars, suggesting by the same token possible restrictions on Japanese output *in* the EC. The Japanese did not challenge this figure, although they felt that the Commission did not act fairly and was using this working assumption as a last-minute twist on the Japanese delegation.

The Car Consensus has been the only agreement notified by the Community under the Uruguay Round Safeguard Agreement.[13] It was scheduled to be eliminated on 31 December 1999—and indeed, it was. Table A.2 presents the 1999 situation, first as forecasted in the 1991 Consensus, and then as actually prevailing in 1999. It shows that, in 1999, the Japanese carmakers did not reach the maximum forecasted import shares (and they were even further away in terms of transplant shares) in the three restrictive markets (France, Italy, and Spain) with "genuine" domestic production (Rover was largely associated with Honda, then with BMW).[14] The reasons for this situation are numerous (structural and macroeconomic difficulties in Japan, a depressed EC market during most of the 1990s, etc.), and their examination goes beyond this case.

Since the elimination of the Consensus on 1 January 2000, protection of the EC car industry has relied mostly on tariffs, technical norms, and the large entry costs due to the distribution regime. The EC tariff on passenger cars is still high (10 percent)—higher than in Japan, South Korea, or the United States—tariffs are even higher for buses (16 percent) and trucks (22 percent). The tariff on cars was not reduced during the Uruguay Round. Conversely, the few efforts by the EC industry to lodge antidumping complaints against imports of Japanese and Korean passenger cars have all failed so far (somewhat surprisingly, considering the many biases in antidumping procedures).

---

13. Strangely enough, the Consensus has been notified to GATT, although it does not legally exist because it has never been formally endorsed by the Council.

14. For information, the "monitoring" level of demand of Japanese cars forecasted for September 1999 was 1,245 thousand units for total EC demand, 190 thousand units in Britain, 114.7 thousand units in France, 129.5 thousand units in Italy, 92.7 thousand units in Spain, and 50 thousand units in Portugal.

Can the elimination of the Consensus be considered as the end of EC protection against Japanese carmakers? (This case does not deal with possible protection against Korean carmakers.) The answer depends on four key parameters. First, what will be the impact of the most recent Japanese transplants (e.g., the French Toyota plant, starting in 2001 with a full capacity of 200,000 cars per year) on European markets? These markets were under structural overcapacity during most of the 1990s, and may soon go back to such a situation if EC growth again becomes sluggish.

Second, what will be the ultimate fate of the recent subsidy packages promised to the car sector? For instance, in January 1999, the French government promised to Peugeot and Renault a €400 million package to finance the early retirement of 43,000 workers (one-fourth of the labor force in the French car industry) and the hiring of 12,000 younger workers. Such a subsidy scheme is unlikely to ultimately pass Community rules on state aid (as shown by a previous scheme launched unsuccessfully in the French textile industry). But because it can begin to be implemented before being condemned, it can distort competition.

Third, to what extent will the protectionist elements of the technical regulations and certification procedures be effectively removed?[15] In 1997, the EC acceded to an additional number of 78 technical regulations of the UN Economic Commission for Europe (UN-ECE); in 1998, an EC-wide type of approval was introduced; and in 1999, the EC adopted the "parallel agreement" under the UN-ECE setting global technical regulations for cars and parts. However, it remains to be seen whether these improvements will be implemented uniformly and nondiscriminatorily by the EC member-states.

Fourth, to what extent will the block exemption of car distribution from EC competition law (to be reviewed in 2002) stay unchanged or be removed—thus introducing more competition at this level, with the emergence of strong multibrand retailers, as in the United States?

All these questions are raised in a dramatically new environment dominated by new intercontinental alliances between carmakers, such as DaimlerChrysler and Renault-Nissan. Of course, these alliances may favor the further dismantlement of the trade barriers protecting the EC industry. They may turn the EC industry toward market access to third countries, as illustrated by the progressive opening of the Mexican market until 2007 under the PTA (see chapter 6) or by the fact that the EC has been a complainant in three WTO dispute settlement cases (on Canadian local-content rules, the Indonesian "national car" program, and the South Korean certi-

---

15. Harmonization of norms and standards in the car industry represents 201 directives (out of a total of 503 directives in January 1998 on technical barriers to trade; see chapter 4) and it has required (and still does) huge efforts: e.g., the directive on brakes for motor vehicles and trailers has been revised seven times in less than 20 years, and its latest version is 150 pages long.

fication system). But these huge alliances may also generate substitutes for trade barriers, under the form of tacit market sharing and collusion—all the more because they are fragile (one of these alliances is led by a car-maker, Renault, with a long history of subsidies and state support). And if they collapse, they may trigger strong negative reactions in Europe—if only because they have been, so far, very costly for the EC firms involved.

EC trade policy on cars deserves a last comment. The fragmentation of the EC car market of the early 1990s has been mirrored in several Central European countries, following the Europe Agreements (see chapter 6). In 1992, Poland raised its tariff on car imports from 15 to 35 percent and adopted an investment policy mostly favoring Fiat, to the detriment of the other EC carmakers, by introducing a tariff quota for EC cars. The Czech Republic and Hungary followed the same policy less visibly with Volkswagen (Skoda, Audi), curbing Japanese and South Korean carmakers.

Notes

Initially (in the late 1970s and early 1980s), restrictions against Japanese exports might have introduced a high level of discriminatory protection. However, because the car industry is a highly differentiated industry, and because a portion of the EC car industry remained relatively exposed to competition (possibly in Germany, more surely in all the small EC markets and in the rest of the world), intra-EC competition has permitted the substitution of competitive European cars for Japanese cars (Messerlin and Bécuwe 1987). As a result, in the late 1980s and early 1990s, the level of EC protection was more limited and less discriminatory than it had been initially.

To take into account this aspect, and to be as conservative as possible in our results, calculated costs of protection are based on the lowest available estimate (6.3 percent) for the ad valorem tariff equivalent of the existing VERs (Digby, Smith, and Venables 1988).[16] As a result, the 1990 MFN average tariff being 10.2 percent, the estimated rate of overall protection is 17.1 percent. Such a low estimate tends to erode the complications caused by the fact that in 1990, the EC major markets were still not subject to the same level of protection—hence implying that the shift from national quotas to an EC-wide quota should reduce prices in initially relatively protected regional markets, and increase prices in initially relatively nonprotected regional markets (Winters 1989).

The literature suggests a total-price demand elasticity ranging from 0.8 to 3 (with most of the studies using an elasticity of 1.6 following Hess

---

16. For comparison's sake, Smith and Venables (1991) show that in 1988, the "tariff equivalent" to the VER for the French market (defined as the one that keeps the production level of French producers constant) would be 34.9 percent, instead of the existing 1988 tariff of 10.3 percent.

1977), a unitary supply price elasticity, and an elasticity of substitution between domestic and foreign cars ranging from 1.2 to 2 (Shiells et al. 1986; Reinert and Roland-Holst 1992). As a result, elasticities of 1.4, 1, and 1.6 (for demand, supply, and substitution, respectively) have been used to estimate the costs of protection.

Cases 13 and 14: Textiles and Clothing

The EC textile and clothing industries have enjoyed high protection from imports until nowadays (for a detailed legal history until the mid-1990s, see Eeckhout 1994). Since 1974, the Multi-Fiber Agreement—a framework agreement negotiated in GATT, completed by specific bilateral agreements, and renewed every four to five years—has been the backbone of this protection. The third MFA, enforced between 1981 and 1986, was the peak of EC protection in these sectors. EC trade policy under MFA IV was more ambiguous. On the one hand, the EC reduced from 23 to 19 the number of exporting countries under MFA bilateral agreements, it eliminated some products from MFA coverage, it agreed on higher growth rates of imports and less severe flexibility conditions for developing countries that were small or new suppliers, and it renounced combining the use of the MFA and the general GATT safeguard clauses. On the other hand, "price clauses" (minimum prices) were imposed on imports from Central European countries; during the MFA implementation period, the EC extended MFA coverage to new textile products (linen and silk) on the basis of the "basket exit mechanism;"[17] and last but not least, EC antidumping and antisubsidy procedures to be used increasingly on MFA products, despite the fact that they were already under quantitative restraints.

Table A.3 describes the EC textile and clothing regime in December 2000, which is based on three different types of trade agreements on textiles and clothing. The first group consists of the 14 countries remaining subject to the MFA successor, the Uruguay Agreement on Textiles and Clothing (ATC). As shown by table A.3, the EC imposes restrictions on a total of 52 product "categories" (which are standardized aggregates of tariff lines in textiles and clothing).[18] The number of product categories covered by EC restrictions ranges from a handful for some countries (four for Argentina) to a large number for others (44 for South Korea).

---

17. Under this mechanism, imports can be subject to new quantitative restrictions when they reach predetermined thresholds (which vary according to the type of product in question and the trading partner).

18. There is a total of 145 categories under the ATC. The 52 product categories subjected to EC restrictions are aggregated into four groups according to the degree of "sensitivity" of the EC industry to foreign competition.

Table A.3 Cases 13 and 14: EC trade barriers in textiles and clothing, 1990–2000

Group or economy	Share of EC imports 1990 (percent) (1)	Number of ATC product categories concerned			Imports to be liberalized^d (5)	Share of EC imports to be liberalized in 2002 and 2005 (percent)			
		1990^a (2)	1995^b (3)	1998^c (4)		Yarns (6)	Fabrics (7)	Made-up textiles (8)	Clothing (9)
World									
Not subject to limits		93	9	11					
Subject to limits		52	0	12					
Total		145	9	23					
Countries under the ATC (52 product categories are subject to EC limits)									
India	3.1	19			71	22	35	17	26
Pakistan	2.7	14			89	15	47	16	21
Hong Kong	1.9	30		3	91	1	15	1	83
Indonesia	1.5	14			90	14	49	2	36
South Korea	1.4	44		7	59	17	29	3	50
Brazil	1.3	11		1	86	70	20	4	7
Thailand	1.3	19			59	24	28	10	39
Malaysia	0.5	10			92	7	29	1	63
Macau	0.3	20		1	93	0	10	0	90
Argentina	<0.3	4		1					
Peru	<0.3	2							
Philippines	<0.3	12							
Singapore	<0.3	8							
Sri Lanka	<0.3	4							
Total	15.0	211	0	13					

Economies subject to other ATC-like agreements						
China[e]	3.3	55	5	21	19	56
Taiwan[e]	1.3	48	20	49	5	26
Belarus, Uzbekistan, Vietnam[e]						
Memorandum items:						
Turkey[f]	3.6	76	32	16	8	44
Central Europe[g]						
Morocco[h]	0.8	85	7	5	3	84
Tunisia[h]	0.5	81	1	13	2	84

— = Import share smaller than 0.3 percent.
ATC = Agreement on Textiles and Clothing.
QRs = qualitative restrictions

a. Base year.
b. Phase I.
c. Phase II.
d. In percent of total imports in volume terms, based on 1990 amounts.
e. QRs under bilateral agreements.
f. All QRs eliminated in 1996, with Turkey introducing measures parallel to the European Community.
g. All QRs eliminated in 1998 (for the list of countries, see text).
h. Surveillance eliminated in 1998 (as for Malta).

Sources: Galloway (1994); Baughman et al. (1997); WTO, *Trade Policy Review: The European Union*, 2000.

The second group includes eight countries subject to bilateral agreements similar to the ATC regime: Belarus, China, North Korea, Taiwan, Ukraine, Uzbekistan, Federal Republic of Yugoslavia, and Vietnam. These countries cannot be subjected to the ATC because they are not WTO members.

The third group (not shown in table A.3) consists of countries subject to "surveillance" or other types of "administrative cooperation" (e.g., a "double custom checking" at the export and import points): Albania, Bangladesh, Cambodia, China, Egypt, Estonia, Kazakhstan, Kyrgyzstan, Laos, Latvia, Lithuania, Moldova, Mongolia, Nepal, Russia, Tajikistan, Turkmenistan, Ukraine, United Arab Emirates, Uzbekistan, Vietnam, and the successor states of Yugoslavia. In early 2001, certain barriers had been relaxed on imports from Sri Lanka, Ukraine, the Baltic states, and the successor states of Yugoslavia.

Lastly, table A.3 (part D) shows that the EC has liberalized imports of textiles and clothing within the framework of the Europe Agreements (in 1998), the Customs Union with Turkey (in 1996), and the Euro-Med agreements. However, at least Turkey has been obliged to adopt certain quantitative measures mirroring those maintained by the EC.

The Uruguay ATC provides for the progressive elimination of all the quantitative restrictions on textiles and clothing by 2005, in four successive phases freeing 16, 17, 18, and 49 percent of total imports (expressed in volumes based on 1990 amounts) in 1995, 1998, 2002, and 2005, respectively. As is well known, the ATC liberalization raises a key issue. It is initialized on the basis of *all* textile and clothing products, including those that were *already* free of nontariff restrictions at the time of its signing (1994). As shown in table A.3, in 1995 (phase 1), the EC only "liberalized" product categories (9 in total) that were *not* subjected to EC restrictions before 1994. In 1998 (phase 2), again 11 categories not subjected to restrictions before 1994 were "liberalized." Only 12 categories subjected to EC restrictions were liberalized; almost all of them involved only one EC trading partner, and they dealt with product categories considered as nonsensitive by the EC.

As a result, almost all the *effective* liberalization remains to be done—in 2002 or 2005. Column 5 of table A.3 presents the shares of EC imports that remain to be liberalized; columns 6 to 9 present the product category structure of the EC imports to be liberalized. The high import shares that can be observed for clothing (the subsector where the EC is most unlikely to have comparative advantage) are in all cases higher than their share in total imports before liberalization began. Even more important, Baughman et al. (1997) show the wide discrepancy between the situations of the member-states during phases 3 and 4. The remaining product categories to be liberalized cover only 39 percent of German production, whereas they cover 53, 77, and 88 percent, respectively, of Italian, Portuguese, and Greek production—meaning that the industries of these EC member-states will really be subject to foreign competition only in 2005. This situation suggests a serious potential source of difficulty for the EC in fulfilling its commitments in textiles and clothing.

EC trade policy for textiles and clothing deserves three last remarks. First, until 1994 all restrictions on imports of textiles and clothing were specified on a member-state basis (although after 1987 there was a limited scheme of quota transfers between member-states), and this required heavy use of Article 115. The Single Market Program and the Uruguay Round ATC have generated strong forces to communitarize the EC quantitative restrictions. The new licensing system based on EC-wide quantitative restrictions entered into force in 1995. However, communitarizing an import quota regime raises three difficult issues: (1) the choice between eliminating or communitarizing "regional" quantitative restrictions (in this context, "regional" refers to member-states); (2) the possible introduction of an "anticoncentration" clause authorizing a member-state in which all EC imports concentrate to take measures; and (3) the possible introduction of a "regional" (by member-state) safeguard clause for EC-wide quantitative restrictions.

In the EC textiles and clothing case, more than 80 out of the 110 "regional" quantitative restrictions existing in 1994 have been eliminated, and the rest have been consolidated into 12 EC-wide quantitative restrictions. The liberalization element was necessary to make acceptable to EC trading partners the introduction of an anticoncentration clause and of a regional safeguard provision. But this liberalization component seems to have been somewhat eroded by the complexity of the EC import regime, which, despite a high level of communitarization, leaves nevertheless a nonnegligible degree of freedom to member-states (Galloway 1994).

Second, an important aspect of the EC protection of textiles and clothing with respect to the Central European countries—and of the 1998 liberalization—has been the so-called outward processing traffic (OPT) quotas (Corado 1995). OPT quotas allow imports under preferential conditions (larger quantities, with tariffs imposed only on the value added), if these imports are made of inputs coming from the EC (mostly from EC producers, to the detriment of EC retailers). As a result, they have offered a negotiating leverage to EC textile firms with respect to foreign clothing firms operating under OPT provisions (EC firms have been able to establish quasi-vertical integration links with CEC firms)—a potentially negative side of the 1998 liberalization.

Third and last, but not least, an increasing number of antidumping actions were lodged in textiles and clothing starting in 1993–94, during the last months of the Uruguay Round negotiations. There were 15 antidumping cases between 1980 and 1989, 12 between 1990 and 1993, and 39 between 1993 and 1999 (not counting artificial and synthetic fibers). Resulting antidumping measures have been high—on average 23 percent. EC antidumping actions in textiles and clothing show some particularly worrisome specific features: no sufficient effort by the Commission to ensure that the companies involved actually exist; and little, if any, consideration of the logical possibility of dumping and injury when minima prices and maxima quantities are already determined by MFA agreements. These features may explain the relatively low level of success of antidumping cases in textiles and clothing relative to other sectors. Only half of the cases are terminated by official measures (though it is always possible that the absence of official measures hides secret price or quantity undertakings.) They may also explain the quite remarkable and persistent reluctance of some member-states to agree on antidumping measures proposed by the Commission in the bleached cotton case (Hindley 1997).

Notes

These cases cover a very large number of products (roughly 1,000 tariff lines for textiles and 220 lines for clothing) aggregated in two broad sectors (textiles and clothing). For each aggregated sector, the tariff is the unweighted average of all the tariff lines involved in the sector; and the ad valorem equivalent of nontariff barriers is the unweighted average of the estimated ad valorem tariff equivalents of the VERs, which can be found in the existing literature, despite the fact that these VERs vary by source of imports, by type of quota ("regular" vs. OPT) and by product. Concerning clothing (by far the most protected sector), Spinanger (1994) has estimated quota prices charged by Hong Kong exporters for five major categories during the period 1987–90. His estimates vary from 8.2 percent of unit values (exports to Germany) to 14.1 percent (exports to Britain), that is, for two of the most open EC member-states. Harrison et al. (1996) provide even bigger estimates: on average, 13.4 percent for textiles and 23.6 percent for clothing (for 1992). To be conservative, the ad valorem tariff equivalents of VERs adopted are 11 percent (textiles, to which one should add 0.4 percent for antidumping measures) and 19 percent (clothing) for 1990 (and, respectively, 9 and 19 percent for 1995, as is illustrated in table 2.1). A recent study contains information roughly confirming the cost estimates (François, Glismann, and Spinanger 2000).

For textiles, the literature suggests a total-price demand elasticity ranging from 0.3 to 0.5 (Tarr and Morkre 1984; Stern et al. 1976), a unitary supply price elasticity (Cline 1987; Trela and Whalley 1990), and an elasticity of substitution between domestic and foreign products ranging from 0.7 to 2.58 (Shiells et al. 1986; Reinert and Roland-Holst 1992). As a result, elasticities of 0.5, 1, and 2 (for demand, supply, and substitution, respectively) have been used to estimate the costs of protection.

For clothing, the literature suggests a total-price demand elasticity ranging from 0.3 to 0.9 (Coursey and Taylor 1982; Cline 1987), a unitary supply price elasticity (Cline 1987; Trela and Whalley 1990), and an elasticity of substitution between domestic and foreign products ranging from 0.5 to 2.5 (Shiells et al. 1986; Reinert and Roland-Holst 1992). As a result, elasticities of 0.8, 1, and 1.5 (for demand, supply, and substitution, respectively) have been used to estimate the costs of protection.

Estimated costs of protection deserve a last comment specific to the textiles and clothing cases. There has been discriminatory liberalization in favor of Central European countries and Turkey, which raises the following question: Do the results obtained overestimate the costs of protection in the EC existing in the late 1990s?

The real impact of this partial liberalization depends mostly on three factors: the importance of trade between the EC and "liberalized" (CECs and Turkey) trading partners, the concentration of this trade in the most protected textile and clothing categories, and the pricing behavior of the "liberalized" exporters. In 1990–93 (the last year for which all these countries were still constrained), exports from these countries respectively represented 12 and 11 percent of the total textile and clothing imports of four key EC member-states (Germany, Italy, Sweden, and Britain). The respective figures were 14.2 and 15.4 percent for 1994–96, and Spinanger (1998) underlined the clear increase in market shares in these 12 countries after 1993 (once OPT quotas had been increased).

However, the extent to which these trade shifts lead to welfare gains depends on the cost structure and pricing behavior of firms located in these "liberalized" countries. Locating textile and clothing production closer to the EC (in the CECs and Euro-Mediterranean countries) may provide efficiency gains in a fashion industry obsessed by quick fashion response, rapid reordering, and so forth. However, even in this case, "liberalized" exporters may reduce their prices only by the smallest amount, allowing them to undercut imports from constrained MFA exporters—an evolution consistent with shifts in the EC trade pattern in the late 1990s away from MFA-constrained Asian countries and in favor of the "liberalized" countries. Such an evolution raises doubts about a substantial decline in the costs of protection in EC textiles and clothing, all the more because MFA agreements may have reduced the efficiency of foreign exporters. In sum, full liberalization may be necessary for full competition, as is suggested in chapter 3.

Cases 15–18: Introduction to Farm Product Cases

This brief introduction aims at shedding some light on key forces in EC agriculture. Table A.4 uses a broad political perspective, which helps in understanding the relative situations in EC member-states, and thus completes the more economic information on the EC farm sector, based on labor, farm size, and financial transfers between EC member-states, which is provided in table 4.7 (see chapter 4).

Table A.4 Cases 15–18: An overview of the EC agricultural sector, by major product, 1998

Commodity	Share (percent) in total EC farm			Output concentration in the EC		Key products for EC member-state[d]	EC share (percent) in world trade		EC export share in EC output
	Output	Budget	Ratio[a]	Concentration index[b]	Shares (percent) of major member-states[c]		Imports	Exports	
Milk	18.0	6.7	0.37	0.1286	Germany 22.0	Luxembourg 45.4	3.0	28.0[e]	n.a.
					France 19.8	Finland 38.1	12.4	21.9[f]	9.0
					Italy 10.9	Sweden 34.9			
					Britain 10.6	Ireland 34.7	10.7	37.8[g]	6.6
					Netherlands 9.4	Germany 26.3	3.1	31.9[h]	36.5
					Spain 5.4	Denmark 24.2			
						Britain 22.8			
						Netherlands 22.3			
						Austria 22.0			
Beef	10.0	13.3	1.33	0.1437	France 26.7	Ireland 33.4	4.6	13.4	6.8
					Germany 15.9	Luxembourg 24.5			
					Italy 15.0	Austria 15.3			
					Spain 8.6	Belgium 13.6			
					Britain 6.9	France 12.4			
					Ireland 6.9	Germany 10.6			
					Netherlands 6.8	Sweden 10.0			
						Finland 10.0			
Pork	10.0	0.6	0.06	0.1167	Germany 20.0	Denmark 31.6	2.4	41.1	3.6
					Spain 15.2	Belgium 21.1			
					France 13.4	Austria 17.3			
					Italy 10.2	Portugal 16.2			
					Denmark 9.2	Germany 13.2			
					Netherlands 8.2	Sweden 12.5			
					Belgium 6.2	Spain 12.1			
					Britain 6.0	Finland 11.0			
						Netherlands 10.7			

Product									
Fresh vegetables	9.4	2.2[i]	<0.24	0.1563	Italy 26.7 Spain 19.2 France 15.2 Netherlands 9.5 Britain 8.0 Germany 6.6 Greece 5.6	Italy 15.1 Spain 14.5 Greece 12.8 Belgium 12.5 Netherlands 11.8 Portugal 10.2	n.a.	n.a.	n.a.
Wine	6.6	1.8	0.27	0.3353	France 49.8 Italy 26.3 Spain 9.3 Germany 9.2	France 15.1 Italy 10.3 Luxembourg 10.3 Portugal 8.3 Austria 7.5	20.9	45.4	9.1
Fresh fruits	6.4	2.2[i]	<0.34	0.1920	Italy 29.2 Spain 25.7 Germany 13.3 France 11.8 Greece 7.6	Spain 13.3 Greece 11.8 Italy 11.2 Portugal 9.7 Austria 6.3	n.a.	n.a.	n.a.
Poultry	5.4	0.2	0.04	0.1754	France 31.5 Britain 17.0 Italy 16.2 Spain 10.1 Germany 7.6 Netherlands 5.7	Britain 11.1 France 7.9 Belgium 5.4	3.5	19.0	11.5

(Table continues next page)

Table A.4 Cases 15–18: An overview of the EC agricultural sector, by major product, 1998 (continued)

Commodity	Share (percent) in total EC farm			Output concentration in the EC		Key products for EC member-state[d]	EC share (percent) in world trade		EC export share in EC output
	Output	Budget	Ratio[a]	Concentration index[b]	Shares (percent) of major member-states[c]		Imports	Exports	
Cerealsʲ	9.0	46.3	5.14	0.1896	France 34.2 Germany 15.4 Italy 13.1 Spain 12.3 Britain 11.7	France 14.4 Britain 12.5 Denmark 11.5 Sweden 10.0 Germany 9.5 Spain 9.0	3.2	10.3	9.2
Sugar	2.5	4.6	1.84	0.1479	Germany 24.2 France 22.9 Italy 12.3 Spain 8.2 Britain 7.6 Netherlands 6.0 Belgium 5.2	Belgium 4.4 Sweden 4.1 Germany 4.0 Austria 3.8 France 2.6	5.1	17.7	36.2

n.a. = available
EC = European Community.

a. Budget/output ratio.
b. Herfindahl-Hirschmann index (see text).
c. EC member-states producing more than 5 percent of total EC farm output.
d. Product shares (in EC member-state total farm output) larger than the product share in EC output.
e. All milk products.
f. Butter.
g. Cheese.
h. Milk powder.
i. Fresh fruits and vegetables.
j. Except rice.

Source: European Commission, The Agricultural Situation in the European Union (2000).

Columns 1–3 compare the shares of major farm products in EC production and their budgets; they show agricultural products that have captured the EC's attention (those with a budget/production ratio higher than 1) and those that have not. Columns 4–6 examine the concentration of EC output by member-states in major farm products: they give a sense of whether product deals may involve few or many member-states (a low concentration index suggests that many member-states may want to be part of the deals on the farm product in question and a high index reveals the dominance of a few member-states). Columns 7 and 8 show the domestic share of an agricultural product in the total farm output of a member-state when this share is larger than the overall EC share given in column 1, whether the member-state is a large EC producer or not. This reflects the potential weight of vested interests in a product in a member-state, hence the incentive for this member-state to be involved in deals on the product in question. Columns 9–11 show EC import and export shares in world trade flows and the product share of EC exports in EC output in order to capture the sensitivity of world trade to EC trade changes and of EC production to EC trade (exports).

Following are a few specific points on four farm products examined in more detail in cases 15–18.

Cereals (case 15). In 1998, EC accounted for 17 percent of the world production of cereals, excluding rice. Other large producers were the United States (12 percent), Australia, and Canada (4 percent each). Cereals are the best example of how a group of products captured the EC CAP with a budget/production ratio larger than 5, despite the fact that cereals are not the largest EC farm product: they represent only 9 percent of total EC output, having declined steadily since the early 1990s (the share of cereals in total EC farm output was 12 percent in 1990). This remarkable capture may be related to the concentration of EC cereal production in five countries, with no EC member-state that does not pertain to the large producer group having a significant cereal sector (i.e., domestic share larger than the overall EC share of 9 percent).

Meat (case 16). Table A.4 includes only beef, pork, and poultry because lamb represents less than 2 percent of total EC farm production.

In 1998, the EC accounted for 14 percent of the world's production of beef. Other large producers were the United States (22 percent), Brazil (11 percent), China (10 percent), and India, Argentina, Russia, and Australia (between 5 percent and 4 percent each). Beef is the second largest product of total EC farm output, with almost all the member-states having a high stake in it: seven EC member-states produce more than 5 percent of EC beef output and in five others beef represents more than 10 percent (overall EC share) of their domestic farm output. In such a favorable configuration of political interests, the budget/production ratio larger than 1 appears a rather "modest" outcome, particularly when compared to the cereal ratio. The EC's influence on world exports is noticeable, as is the impact of EC exports on EC output.

In 1998, the EC was the second largest producer of pork in the world (20 percent), between China (44 percent) and the United States (10 percent). The pork sector is similar to beef but for three important differences: the budget/production ratio is among the lowest (suggesting that the EC's rank in world production tends to reflect mostly market forces, unlike the two previous groups of products), and EC influence on world trade is huge, whereas the impact of world trade on EC production is barely noticeable. The major difference in the budget/production ratio between beef and pork shows that, despite their importance, political forces are insufficient to fully explain the level of capture of the CAP by this group.

Poultry production is relatively concentrated in the EC, with six major producing member-states and a share larger than the overall EC share for Belgium only. The trade aspects are substantial, with a large proportion of EC poultry being exported, thus representing a large share in world exports.

Milk (case 17). Milk products cover a wide range of goods and account for the largest share in EC farm production. They show the same features as beef or pork: a low concentration index based on a large number of large producers and a substantial number of EC member-states where the milk share in domestic output is larger than the overall EC share. It is difficult to compare the budget/production ratio in milk with the corresponding ratios for other farm products because by definition the budget does not include the rents (transfers) associated with the milk production quota system. As liquid milk is not easily stored or traded long distance given existing technologies, case 17 focuses on tradable "manufactured" milk products: cheese (14 percent of EC milk production), concentrated and skimmed milk (8 percent), and butter (4 percent). In 1997, the EC was a major producer of butter, accounting for 28 percent of world production, followed by India (22 percent), the United States (8 percent), Pakistan (6 percent), and New Zealand (5 percent). It is the largest world producer of cheese (44 percent), followed by the United States (24 percent). Similarly, the EC is the largest world producer of milk powder (35 percent), followed by the United States and New Zealand (10 percent each), Australia (6 percent), and Russia (5 percent).

Sugar (case 18). EC accounts for 14 percent of the world production of raw and white sugar, the largest world producer being Brazil (15 percent). Following the EC are India (11 percent), China (7 percent), and the United States (6 percent). Sugar, the smallest of the products examined in table A.4, shows the second highest budget/production ratio. It is also a relatively widely produced farm product: seven member-states are major producers and in two other member-states sugar producers may represent a noticeable political force. The interactions between EC and world exports, and between EC exports and production, are significant.

Three additional products are included in table A.4, though they are not examined in the following cases. Despite their wide-ranging definitions, fresh vegetables and fruit exhibit noticeable concentration indexes and budget/production ratios. By contrast, wine is the most concentrated product, with a relatively low budget/production ratio.

Case 15: Cereals

The Common Market Organization (CMO) for cereals offers a good illustration of the CAP protectionist drift and its strong bias in favor of a few "basic" farm products. It was established in 1965. Until the 1992 CAP Reform, it relied almost exclusively on price supports: six intervention prices (common wheat, durum wheat, rye, barley, maize, and sorghum), three indicative prices (common wheat, durum wheat, and other cereals) and eight threshold prices (the six cereals mentioned, plus flours and semolina).

During its first 20 years of implementation (except in 1973–75), EC threshold prices fluctuated around 150 to 200 percent of the third-country offer prices. In 1973, the EC shifted from a net importer of cereals to a net exporter. In the mid-1980s, increasingly huge supply and stocks forced the Community to take measures to restrain quantities: "co-responsibility" levies, quality constraints, "extensification" aids aiming to reduce productivity, conversion aids aiming to shift production capacities to non-surplus farm goods, and set-aside programs and early retirement schemes aiming to reduce land and labor. All these "soft" measures proved to be insufficient; in the late 1990s, the EC was still a large net cereal exporter (with a "self-sufficiency" ratio of roughly 120 percent), and the cereal CMO absorbed more than 40 percent of the entire EC budget for CMOs—more than four times the cereal share of EC total farm production.

The cereal situation was made more difficult when, during the Kennedy Round, the EC agreed to impose low *bound* tariffs (from 0 to 6 percent) on products such as oilseeds and manioc. These concessions were made to keep the level of protection of EC cereals high. As a result, cheap imports of these products were rapidly substituted for expensive EC cereals to feed livestock (the largest market for cereals). The EC then decided to support the domestic production of these cereal-substitutes. As EC bound tariffs made impossible the creation of CMOs based on price support (similar to the cereal CMO), the EC adopted two CMOs based on production subsidies (a mechanism almost absent from the initial cereal CMO) for rapeseed (in 1983) and soya (in 1985). Any difference between the world price and the Council-fixed indicative price of these products could be compensated for by subsidies to be paid to the manufacturers buying EC oilseeds and transforming them into food for livestock. These two CMOs added to the cereal glut and generated bitter GATT-WTO disputes (see below).

July 1993 witnessed the first noticeable reform of the cereal CMO. Intervention prices were reduced, on average, by 35 percent; and compensatory subsidies for production and set-asides were increased by more than 80 percent and almost 30 percent, respectively (see table 4.3). In the 1999 Berlin Council, an additional 15 percent reduction of the support price of wheat was made—with less generous compensation for both production and set-asides. Market prices decreased slowly; their decline between 1993 and 1998 (25 percent in effective buying-in prices) was almost perfectly matched by the increase in subsidies between 1993 and 1995.

As a result of all these policy changes, subsidies reached new heights and revealed the two major perverse effects of a policy mix based on direct area payments and set-asides: it favors large farmers, to the detriment of small farmers because these instruments are based on land, even if set-asides are limited to large farms; and it favors incumbent (large and small) farmers, to the detriment of new entrants.

Until 1995, the cereal CMO relied on variable levies on imports and on export refunds, with all imports and exports subjected to licenses. Variable levies were defined (on a weekly basis) as the difference between the EC threshold price and a "world" price *calculated* by the Commission on the basis of the price c.i.f. Rotterdam and on the "best" buying opportunities available in the world. By contrast, export refunds were largely arbitrary: the Commission could impose a zero export refund if it considered the export in question inappropriate, and it could impose discriminatory rates of refunds, depending on the country of destination.

In 1994, the *tariffication* exercise required by the Uruguay Agreement on Agriculture involved 106 tariff lines (including rice) in the EC case, and it manifested a protectionist drift.[19] For instance, the specific duty on wheat was estimated to be equivalent to an ad valorem tariff of 155.6, whereas the ad valorem equivalent tariff for the years 1986–88 was estimated to be 103 percent, that is, it was a "dirty" tariffication amounting to more than 52 percent; it implied that in 2000–01, the EC could still be more protected than in 1988, all other things being constant (Ingco 1996). EC commitments on reductions for these inflated initial tariffs were, on average, 37 percent in cereals between 1995 and 2001 (OECD 1997b).

EC *minima market access* commitments in cereals under the Uruguay Round mirrored bilateral agreements, such as the duty-free quota of 300,000 tons of wheat (almost entirely limited to Central European countries) or already existing market access (such as 2, out of 2.5, million tons of maize). Moreover, for the EC as for other WTO members, tariff-rate quotas (TRQs) granting lower tariff rates for small imported quantities provide limited, if any, opportunities for competition for two reasons: in-quota tariffs are still high (45.7 percent for maize); and imported quantities

---

19. In fact, the tariffication exercise has not completely eliminated the variable levy mechanism because of the ambiguous notion of "maximum duty-paid price" (when prices are firm, the duty-paid price has a similar impact on the market to the threshold price).

are so small that there is almost no incentive for foreign exporters to charge low prices. Rather, they are induced to capture the tariff differentials as rents. Evidence gathered by the OECD (2000d) confirms these predictions.

On the *export-subsidy* side, the EC has been committed to reducing subsidized exported quantities for wheat and wheat flour (from 19.1 million tons in 1995 to 13.4 million tons in 2000) and for coarse grains (from 12.2 million tons in 1995 to 10 million tons in 2000). (All figures are for EC-12.) Since the end of the Uruguay Round, high world prices have prevailed, reducing to a considerable extent the need for EC export subsidies—and even requiring the EC to replace export subsidies by export taxes between mid-1995 and mid-1996. In the future, however, fulfilling the commitments on export subsidies is likely to require further substantial reductions in support prices.

Notes

Table A.5 provides the CSEs, the PSEs, and the CSE ad valorem tariff equivalents for wheat for the EC and three other OECD countries. In addition, a composed index for cereals has been computed for the EC based on weights given by the share of three types of cereals in the total EC cereal output. It suggests a CSE-based tariff of 63 percent as the rate of overall protection for 1990 (based on the average for 1988–90, and used in chapter 3). This indicator dramatically declined until 1997, but has increased again since then. The PSE figures show the same evolution—with the striking difference that the protection granted in 1999 to the EC producers is close to the level in the late 1980s and early 1990s. This divergence between the CSE and PSE evolutions since 1996 reflects the change of instruments favored by the Uruguay Round.

According to the literature, the total price demand elasticity ranges from 0.1 to 0.7 (Stern et al. 1976) and the price domestic supply elasticity from 0.2 to 0.4 (Stern et al. 1976; Schmitz 1979); the elasticity of substitution between foreign and domestic cereals would be large (OECD 1990). As a result, elasticities of 0.4, 0.5, and 4 (for demand, supply, and substitution, respectively) have been used to estimate costs of protection.

Case 16: Meat

There are four CMOs covering meat: beef (1968), pork (1975), poultry (1975), and lamb (1980). All of them rely essentially on price supports, but their many differences reflect the strong CAP bias in favor of beef—one of the "basic" farm products. These four CMOs present decreasing levels of protection. (In fact, the poultry CMO can be seen as trying to minimize the

Table A.5 Case 15: Producer and consumer subsidy equivalents in wheat and cereals, 1978–99 (percent)

Commodity and country	1978–86	1986–88	1988–90	1990–92	1993–95	1995–97	1997	1998	1999
Wheat									
Producer subsidy equivalents (PSEs)									
European Community	33	63	49	62	66	53	54	67	70
Japan	96	101	97	97	102	101	99	100	101
United States	28	54	37	46	37	45	56	80	95
Australia	9	11	6	9	7	10	16	11	12
Consumer subsidy equivalents (CSEs)									
European Community	25	53	36	46	27	2	–1	19	21
Japan	38	64	55	53	51	44	48	52	52
United States	1	14	9	19	12	2	1	1	1
Australia	5	4	1	0	0	0	0	0	0
CSE-based ad valorem tariff equivalents[a]									
European Community	39	112	60	87	39	3	–1	24	27
Japan	71	180	122	112	104	81	93	106	108
United States	1	18	10	24	15	0	–1	–1	–1
Australia	6	5	1	0	5	0	0	0	0
All cereals in the EC[b]									
PSEs	34	60	47	61	66	52	52	66	66
CSEs	27	53	37	47	31	7	3	23	19
CSE-based tariffs	44	119	63	90	48	9	3	31	24

a. Consumer nominal assistance coefficients minus 100.
b. PSEs and CSEs for wheat, maize, and other cereals weighted by shares in EC total cereal output.

Sources: OECD, *Agricultural Policies Monitoring and Outlook*, various years; author's computations.

damage done by the high level of protection imposed by the cereal CMO on poultry production.)

The Beef CMO

The initial beef CMO was based on two cornerstone prices—the "guide" and intervention prices, where the guide price is the price considered as desirable for producers under "normal" market conditions. In contrast with the cereal CMO, intervention was not automatic, and it was done not at the intervention-price level but at the level of specific regional "buying-in" prices, a combination of the intervention price, set coefficients, and conversion factors. Moreover, intervention involved only limited quantities (defined ex ante as "normal" intervention purchases). Also in contrast with the cereal CMO, the beef CMO relied since its origin on production subsidies to be granted to suckler cows (as opposed to milk cows) and to bulls. The EC has been a relatively (by world standards) large net beef exporter since the 1980s. In 1996, the beef CMO represented 13 percent of the EC farm budget (3 percentage points more than the share of beef in EC total farm output).

The 1992 CAP Reform entailed a 15 percent reduction in the beef intervention price and a 55 percent reduction (from 750,000 to 350,000 tons) in "normal" intervention purchases, with an increase in the compensatory subsidies by more than 120 percent (see table 4.3). They consist of a complex set of direct headage payments (with unintended effects, because the possibility of claiming a subsidy twice in an animal's life tended to increase the beef supply by increasing the animal's weight at slaughter time) subject to restrictions on stocking density, limits per holding, regional reference herd sizes, and so forth. The 1999 Berlin Council decided on an additional decrease of the intervention price by 20 percent, with additional increases in subsidies (from 38 to 93 percent), including in those from the member-states.

Until 1995, EC protection in the beef sector consisted of tariffs and variable levies. Levies depended on the difference between the world and guide prices (modified by several conversion factors to account for the type of meat) *and* on the difference between the market price observed in the EC and the guide price (as a result, one could get different variable levies for one import price). Variable levies were reduced or even eliminated for exports from countries that had signed a VER with the EC (Argentina, Australia, Canada, Hungary, Poland, United States, Uruguay, Yugoslavia, and a few ACP countries). Special levies could be imposed on foreign beef sold at "abnormally low" prices. Export refunds were similar to those granted in the cereal CMO.

The Uruguay *tariffication* exercise (involving 239 tariff lines) also witnessed a protectionist drift in the beef sector (as it did for cereals; see case

15 above). For instance, the ad valorem tariff equivalent for beef is estimated to be 125.4 percent, showing a "dirty" tariffication of 42 percent (Ingco 1996). Committed tariff reductions of these initial inflated tariffs are 36 percent for all kinds of beef meat for the period 1995–2000.

Minima market access commitments involved 175,000 tons (40 percent of the total imports for the reference years 1986–88). More than 85 percent of these commitments correspond to the pre-1995 VERs. As with cereals, in-quota tariffs (in the TRQs system) are under high tariffs (20 percent), and again, the tariff differentials are likely to be captured as rents by market participants (Tangermann 1998).

On the *export-subsidy* side, EC commitments under the Uruguay Agreement include a reduction of export subsidies for bovine meat from 1,118 thousand tons in 1995 to 817 thousand tons in 2000 (both figures are for EC-12). These commitments include processed meat as well as fresh meat, a flexibility that is likely to favor producers of fresh meat.

The Sheepmeat CMO

The sheepmeat CMO was introduced relatively late (only after the British accession) after long and acrimonious intra-EC discussions (the "lamb war"). It combines a French-inspired price-support regime (relying essentially on the "basic" price) and a British-inspired deficiency-payment regime (based on the difference between the basic price and the observed regional market price, coupled with a slaughter subsidy that is fully enforced only in Britain). This remarkable duality in the CMO design, and the differences in CMO enforcement among member-states, has imposed the upholding of certain restrictions on intra-EC trade flows (most notably, between Britain and the rest of the EC). It also explains the relatively high share of lamb in the EC farm budget (3.3 percent in 1996), along with a greater desire to take into account market forces. The EC lamb subsector has always been a net importer, with an average self-sufficiency ratio of roughly 80 percent in recent years.

Until 1995, EC protection of the sheepmeat sector consisted of a variable levy coupled with VERs with Argentina, Australia, New Zealand, Uruguay, and five Central European countries (Bulgaria, Hungary, Poland, Romania, and the former Yugoslavia). Imports under VERs represented almost 100 percent of all EC lamb imports.

Under the Uruguay Agreement on Agriculture, the EC has *tariffied* its NTBs on top of its 20 percent duty. To our knowledge, no estimate of the ad valorem equivalent of the resulting protection is available). For the period 1995–2000, tariff reductions are committed to be 36 percent. In terms of *minimum market access*, the EC has transformed its country-specific VERs on sheepmeat imports into zero-tariff quotas, again suggesting a likely capture of tariff differentials as rents by market participants. There are no EC commitments about *export subsidies*.

The Pork CMO

Despite widespread pork production in the EC, the intervention measures allowed by the pork CMO (related to the "basic" price) have been rarely used, and the main instrument has been to subsidize private stocks in case of excess supply. The average self-sufficiency ratio is 103 to 106 percent for recent years, and it has been relatively stable since the origin of the Community. Until 1995, protection against pork imports consisted of a variable levy derived from the difference between the basic price and an estimate of production costs in the rest of the world (*"prix d'écluse"*).

Under the Uruguay Round *tariffication*, the estimated ad valorem equivalents of specific tariffs ranged from 47 to 53 percent, with a modest tariff escalation (OECD 1997b). The dirty tariffication problem has remained modest enough (11 percent for a *pre*-Uruguay-based initial tariff of 51 percent) to be eliminated by the committed tariff reductions of 36 percent for all kinds of pork (Ingco 1996). In 2000, *minima market access* commitments involved almost 180,000 tons (relative to 1986–88 total imports of 96,000 tons) under moderate tariffs (13.3 percent) (Tangermann 1998), but the bulk of this tonnage (100,000 tons) corresponds to quotas open to Central European countries. Last, *export subsidy* commitments led to a decline from 490,800 subsidized tons of pork (1995) to 401,800 subsidized tons (2000) (both figures are for EC-12).

The Poultry CMO

The poultry CMO is quite different from the three other CMOs. Its main goal is to eliminate the negative "effective" rate of protection on poultry, that is, the fact that the high level of protection on cereal inputs imposes a tax on EC poultry production. This feature explains the relatively low share of poultry in the EC farm budget (0.4 percent in 1996, i.e., one-tenth of its value share) coupled with the high average rate of EC self-sufficiency, ranging from 105 to 109 percent in recent years.

Variable levies and export refunds compensate for the difference between cereal costs in the EC and in the rest of the world, to induce poultry-producers to buy EC cereals and food. However, "supplementary" variable levies can be imposed, with the aim of protecting the EC poultry sector from foreign competition. Bulgaria, Poland, and Romania have signed price undertakings exempting them from these supplementary variable levies.

Since the Uruguay Round *tariffication*, the average ad valorem equivalent of specific tariffs on poultry is 44.5 percent, with two interesting features: the existence of tariff deescalation (OECD 1997b), and the absence of dirty tariffication (the starting Uruguay Round tariff may have been even lower than the 1986–88 estimate, by a small margin of –6.5 percent) (Ingco 1996). Committed tariff reductions are 36 percent for all kinds of poultry. In 2000, *minima market access* commitments dealt with almost 130,000 tons (relative to 1986–88 total imports of 86,000 tons), but the bulk of this tonnage (93,000 tons) corresponds to quotas open to Central European countries. In-quota tariffs are close to industrial tariffs (8.1 percent) (Tangermann 1998). On the *export-subsidy* side, EC commitments under the Uruguay Agreement included a reduction of export subsidies for poultry from 440.1 thousand tons in 1995 to 290.6 thousand tons in 2000.

Notes

Table A.6 provides the CSEs, the PSEs, and the CSE ad valorem tariff equivalents for beef for the EC and three non-EC OECD countries. In addition, a composed index of the indicators for beef and lamb has been computed for the EC (based on weights given by the relative shares of these two types of meat). It seems reasonable to distinguish between beef and lamb, on the one hand, and pork and poultry, on the other hand, because the PSEs of the first group have been more than three times those of the second group (the CSEs of lamb have substantially declined since 1996). The CSE-based tariff (95 percent in 1990, based on the average for 1988–90) has been used to estimate the rate of overall protection.

According to the literature, the price demand elasticity for the various kinds of meat ranges from 0.4 to 1.2 (Stern et al. 1976; European Commission 1980); the price supply elasticity ranges from 0.3 to 0.8 (Stern et al. 1976; Schmitz 1979); and the substitution elasticity between foreign and domestic meat is estimated at 1.7 (Reinert and Roland-Horst 1992).[20] As a result, elasticities of 0.6, 0.5, and 2 (for demand, supply, and substitution, respectively) have been used to estimate the costs of protection.

Case 17: Manufactured Milk

The CMO for milk was introduced in 1968. It reflects the constraints imposed on the wide variety of milk products. If it relies on one indicative price for liquid milk, three intervention prices are defined for the three main families of manufactured milk products (butter, skimmed milk, and

---

20. Australian Bureau of Agricultural Economics (1985) underlines the many problems between meat and milk on the supply side, which was torn apart by several conflicting CMOs.

Table A.6 Case 16: Producer and consumer subsidy equivalents in beef and sheepmeat, 1978–99 (percent)

Commodity and country	1978–86	1986–88	1988–90	1990–92	1993–95	1995–97	1997	1998	1999
Beef									
Producer subsidy equivalents (PSEs)									
European Community	49	49	46	58	43	50	59	62	62
Japan	38	47	38	33	45	40	38	38	38
United States	7	7	6	6	5	5	7	5	6
Australia	10	10	8	6	7	7	7	5	5
Consumer subsidy equivalents (CSEs)									
European Community	43	48	44	55	33	34	43	47	49
Japan	30	45	38	30	33	32	31	30	29
United States	1	1	0	0	0	0	0	0	0
Australia	0	0	0	0	0	0	0	0	0
CSE-based ad valorem tariff equivalents[a]									
European Community	79	95	79	126	50	52	75	89	95
Japan	45	83	63	44	50	46	44	42	40
United States	1	1	0	0	0	0	0	0	0
Australia	0	0	0	0	0	0	0	0	0
Beef and sheepmeat in the EC[b]									
PSEs	51	53	51	61	46	53	59	62	58
CSEs	44	51	47	55	32	32	38	42	43
CSE-based tariffs	83	110	95	127	49	49	66	79	83

EC = European Community.

a. Consumer nominal assistance coefficients minus 100.
b. PSEs and CSEs of the two kinds of meat weighted by their relative shares.

Sources: OECD, *Agricultural Policies Monitoring and Outlook,* various years; author's computations.

two types of cheese). Its 12 threshold prices are all defined for products derived from liquid milk (lactoserum, lactose, several kinds of skimmed and concentrated milk, and several types of butter). The very high support prices prevailing until the late 1980s generated massive and persistent overproduction (the "butter mountains"), resulting in the EC's shift from net importer to net exporter to an extent unknown for other farm products.

In the early 1980s, the EC share of world exports ranged from 36 percent (casein) to 48 percent (cheese); in the late 1980s, it ranged from 42 percent (skimmed milk) to 80 percent (concentrated milk). Production quotas (introduced in 1984; tightened in 1987 and 1989) and lower support prices (lower by 15 percent in real terms) have reduced these distortions to some extent. The share of EC expenditure on dairy products in the entire EC farm budget has decreased from 40 percent (1985) to 10 percent (late 1990s). But the level of protection remains very high (see below), and it continues to generate artificially high average self-sufficiency ratios: 100 to 105 percent (butter), 105 to 110 percent (cheese), 115 to 120 percent (skimmed milk), 130 to 140 percent (concentrated milk), and more than 200 percent (whole milk powder).

Market imbalances of such a magnitude and for such a long period of time have had severe consequences, and will continue to do so. In the milk case, the most important consequence is that new, more productive techniques of production are more difficult to adopt in the EC than in more market-based economies. For instance, the hormone-based BST technique is reported to increase cow milk production by up to 25 percent; all other things being constant, countries with persistent excess supply (such as those in the EC) are likely to delay the adoption of such a technique, whereas countries with more sound markets are likely to adopt it.

Until 1995, the milk CMO imposed variable levies based on the difference between an average border price calculated by the Commission (twice a month) and the threshold price of the product in question. The *tariffication* exercise under the Uruguay Agreement on Agriculture has dealt with 108 tariff lines in the EC, which has adopted very high specific tariffs. The average ad valorem equivalents for dairy products are estimated at 288.5 percent, revealing a huge "dirty" tariffication of 111.5 percent (the ad valorem rate for 1986–88 was estimated at 177 percent; Ingco 1996). The rates of reduction of these tariffs between 1995 and 2000 are very similar (36 percent) for all milk products, with one of the very few exceptions in the EC schedule of commitments (the tariff on powdered milk is subject to a reduction rate of only 20 percent) (OECD 1997b).

There are *minima market access* commitments for butter (and butter oil), skimmed milk powder, cheese, and other milk products, with high in-quota tariffs ranging from 33.2 to 47.8 percent (Tangermann 1998). All of them tend to essentially benefit Central European countries. The EC has undertaken commitments to reduce *export subsidies* for butter and butter oil (from 447.2 thousand tons in 1995 to 366.1 thousand tons in 2000), skimmed milk powder (from 297.2 thousand tons in 1995 to 243.3 thousand tons in 2000), cheese (from 406.7 thousand tons in 1995 to 305.1 thousand tons in 2000), and "other milk products" (from 1,161.4 thousand tons in 1995 to 938.4 thousand tons in 2000) (all figures are for EC-12).

Notes

Table A.7 provides the CSEs, the PSEs, and the CSE ad valorem tariff equivalents for milk for the EC countries and three non-EC OECD countries. It shows very high, relatively stable protection in all the countries (even Australia exhibits a noticeable rate of protection). The 1990 CSE-based tariff (104 percent, based on the average for 1988–90) has been used to estimate the rate of overall protection.

Because this case deals with manufactured milk products, some precalculations have been necessary to estimate the sector's basic data. Exports and imports are based on data available for three categories of the tariff classification: 0402 (milk powder and similar products), 0405 (butter and similar products), and 0406 (cheese). Production tonnage and employment data are based on the ratio of manufactured milk products (defined by these three groups of products) to total milk output (European Commission 1995, 13–30, table 2). The production value is obtained by multiplying the production volume by the average intra-EC trade unit value (which is very similar for imports and exports).

According to the literature, the price demand elasticity for the various manufactured products, such as butter and cheese, ranges from 0.2 to 0.7 (Stern et al. 1976; Australian Bureau of Agricultural Economics 1985), the price supply elasticity ranges from 0.3 to 1.3 (Australian Bureau of Agricultural Economics 1985); and the substitution elasticity between foreign and domestic manufactured milk products is between 1 and 2, depending on the products considered (Reinert and Roland-Holst 1992). As a result, elasticities of 0.6, 0.5, and 2 (for demand, supply, and substitution, respectively) have been used to estimate the costs of protection.

Case 18: Sugar

The CMO for sugar was adopted in 1967. As with the cereal CMO, it relies on price support. But these prices are not defined on "primary" sugar products (cane or beet), because sugar beet (the main source of sugar in the EC) is not a tradable product. As a result, the sugar CMO relies on price support for "intermediate" sugar products: two intervention prices (on white and raw sugar), one indicative price (for white sugar), and three threshold prices (for raw sugar, white sugar, and molasses).

Table A.7 Case 17: Producer and consumer subsidy equivalents in milk, 1978–99 (percent)

Country	1978–86	1986–88	1988–90	1990–92	1993–95	1995–97	1997	1998	1999
Producer subsidy equivalents (PSEs)									
European Community	52	56	51	57	55	51	50	56	58
Japan	82	89	85	88	87	82	81	84	87
United States	61	65	55	58	48	44	48	64	60
Australia	27	30	26	36	25	21	23	20	17
Consumer subsidy equivalents (CSEs)									
European Community	40	52	47	53	49	45	44	52	54
Japan	62	77	71	74	74	66	63	67	70
United States	51	52	46	51	42	39	42	58	55
Australia	21	30	27	36	25	20	22	19	17
CSE-based ad valorem tariff equivalents[a]									
European Community	87	139	104	132	108	89	84	118	127
Japan	203	373	255	285	289	204	176	210	239
United States	129	146	93	110	79	65	74	140	125
Australia	29	45	38	55	33	25	28	24	20

a. Consumer nominal assistance coefficients minus 100.

Source: OECD, Agricultural Policies Monitoring and Outlook, various years.

The sugar CMO differs from the other CMOs presented in this book in another essential aspect: it imposes production quotas aimed at "self-financing" the CMO. Quotas A (derived from the historical production of the early 1960s in the founding member-states, and adjusted for the successive accessions of the new member-states) benefit from the full intervention price mechanism. Quotas B (originally up to 35 percent of quotas A) are subject to production levies aimed at financing losses for exporting surplus EC production.

Any sugar production above quotas A and B constitutes "quotas C"—a misleading term to the extent that there is no quantitative limit on the production of sugar quotas C. Sugar under quota C is subject to two constraints: it cannot be sold on EC markets except by paying a tax equivalent to the variable levy imposed on foreign sugar, and it has to be exported without any EC support (i.e., at the world price).[21] This complicated quota system was felt necessary because it had been clear from the origin of the CMO that the high support prices granted to inefficient producers (Germany and Italy) would trigger huge excess supply from efficient suppliers (Belgium and France). Initially, the quota system was to be eliminated in 1975.

In 1977, the EC (until then a net importer) became a net exporter, and very high EC prices (two to three times the world prices) boosted the EC as one of the world largest net exporters. In 1987, special levies were introduced, with the aim of reinforcing the self-financing feature. A 2 percent levy on the base price on quota A sugar and a 37.5-percent levy on quota B sugar finance a Sugar Fund mainly used for the disposal of excess production on world markets.

Despite these measures, there has been (and still is) an ongoing debate on whether this self-financing principle has been realized. Between 1990 and mid-1994, there remained an average annual difference of €1 billion between levy revenues and expenditures on export subsidies and intervention. In 1998, sugar support represented 4.6 percent of total EC farm support expenses, almost twice the sugar share of EC farm output. But the CMO self-financing motto and the CMO capacity to generate rents (reinforced by the fact that quotas are not tradable because they are allocated by member-states) seem to shield the CMO from any reform: there was no change in the 1992 CAP Reform or in the 1999 Berlin Council.

Until 1995, EC imports of sugar were subject to variable levies (there was no tariff), and exports were subject to export refunds with certain additional levies on import of "primary" sugar products and on sugar confectioneries (WTO, *Trade Policy Review: The European Community*, 1997, 181). The Accession Treaty of Britain granted preferential conditions of imports to Commonwealth members, which were extended to ACP coun-

---

21. Producing "sugar C" flows largely from the nontransferability of quotas A and B, which are "unevenly" distributed among EC member-states and regions (generating rents and status quo).

tries and EC overseas territories. These preferential imports consist of quotas benefiting from guaranteed prices and exempt from variable levies. Because the EC produces too much sugar, a portion of these preferential imports (or an equivalent quantity of EC sugar) is reexported (but these exports are excluded from the self-financing scheme). The benefits of these preferences for the ACP countries are often questioned; they are likely to be offset, at least partly, by the depressing impact of the CMO on the world sugar price, and by the incentives generated by the CMO to create sugar substitutes (e.g., aspartame, isoglucose).[22] It is notable that the sugar CMO was extended to isoglucose in 1981.

The Uruguay Round *tariffication* exercise has involved 36 tariff lines in the EC, and it has led to cases of "dirty" tariffication. Ingco (1996) has estimated the average ad valorem tariff equivalent on the main sugar products at up to 297 percent—with a dirty tariffication of 63 percent. Between 1995 and 2000, tariffs were to be reduced by 20 percent on raw sugar, an exception to the frequent average 36 percent reduction in EC agricultural farm commitments.

The EC *minimum market access* obligations do not exceed existing bilateral commitments toward the ACP countries and India (again, most of these imports are reexported), with the result that tariff differentials are likely to be captured by market participants.

In terms of *export subsidy* commitments, the EC has agreed to a reduction of its sugar exports (excluding ACP and Indian sugar) from a subsidized volume of 1,560.4 thousand tons to 1,277.4 thousand tons (quota B sugar). (All figures are for EC-12.) Of course, this reduction could be counterbalanced by a rise in EC exports of quota C sugar. Last, it is important to note that the EC has initiated several antidumping actions against sugar substitutes (aspartame from the United States and Japan in 1990).

Notes

Table A.8 provides the CSEs, the PSEs, and the CSE ad valorem tariff equivalents for sugar for the EC member-states and three non-EC OECD countries. It shows very high, stable CSEs and PSEs. The rate of overall protection is estimated on the basis of the CSE-based tariff, that is, 117 percent in 1990 (which in turn is based on the average for 1988–90).

The literature suggests a total price demand elasticity ranging from 0.1 to 0.5 (Gemmill 1976; Tarr and Morkre 1984), a price supply elasticity ranging from 0.3 to 1.1 (Schmitz 1979), and a high substitution elasticity between foreign and domestic sugar (OECD 1990, 93). As a result, elastic-

---

22. Isoglucose is an artificial sugar that was developed—and has been very successful—largely because it allowed large sugar consumers (e.g., the producers of sweet drinks) to buy a much less expensive sugar substitute.

Table A.8　Case 18: Producer and consumer subsidy equivalents in sugar, 1978–99 (percent)

Country	1978–86	1986–88	1988–90	1990–92	1993–95	1995–97	1997	1998	1999
	Producer subsidy equivalents (PSEs)								
European Community	52	64	46	55	45	41	47	49	58
Japan	68	74	67	70	72	70	67	72	75
United States	47	63	48	52	50	46	48	61	73
Australia	10	15	12	11	11	8	5	7	7
	Consumer subsidy equivalents (CSEs)								
European Community	50	69	51	58	49	46	49	53	59
Japan	60	74	62	65	60	57	53	65	67
United States	41	56	39	43	41	38	40	52	66
Australia	3	43	35	31	19	12	0	0	0
	CSE-based ad valorem tariff equivalents[a]								
European Community	132	229	117	148	106	88	101	117	156
Japan	135	196	149	186	153	133	121	185	202
United States	106	131	66	78	72	60	65	106	196
Australia	39	77	55	46	23	15	0	0	0

a. Consumer nominal assistance coefficients minus 100.

Source: OECD, Agricultural Policies Monitoring and Outlook, various years.

315

ities of 0.4, 0.5, and 4 (for demand, supply, and substitution, respectively) have been used to estimate the costs of protection.

Case 19: Bananas

In 1957, the signing of the Treaty of Rome was delayed by several days because France and Germany were unable to agree on a compromise for the trade regime to be applied to bananas. Germany enforced a complete free-trade policy, and as a result imported bananas from Latin American countries, whereas France and Italy followed an almost autarkic policy favoring their domestic producers. At the last minute, German Chancellor Konrad Adenauer obtained for bananas one of only two additional protocols to the treaty, grandfathering the import policy of member-states (the other protocol was for green coffee).

This legal situation lasted unchanged until 1993 (for a detailed legal history until the mid-1990s, see Eeckhout, 1994). During all these years, there were as many import regimes for bananas as member-states. For simplicity's sake, all the trade regimes existing in 1993 can be classified in three main groups. Group I consisted of six member-states that imposed quotas on bananas coming from Latin America—often nicknamed "dollar bananas" because they are mainly processed and distributed by three US firms, Chiquita, Del Monte, and Dole Foods. For four out of the six member-states, these restrictions aimed to protect domestic banana growers on Caribbean islands (France), Crete (Greece), Madeira (Portugal), and the Canary Islands (Spain), whereas the two others (Italy and Britain) maintained quantitative restrictions favoring former colonies (Belize, Jamaica, Suriname, the British Windward Islands, and Somalia) and their own fruit companies (Fyffes and Geest).

Group II, which consisted of five member-states (Belgium, Denmark, Ireland, Luxembourg, and the Netherlands), merely enforced the Community's common external tariff (20 percent in 1993) and imported almost exclusively dollar bananas. Group III consisted only of Germany, which was exempted from the EC tariff under a zero-tariff quota for almost all its consumption (Austria, Finland, and Sweden were in the same situation before their 1995 accession to the Community).

The total incompatibility among all these trade regimes implied a systematic use of Article 115 by Group I member-states. As a result, intra-EC trade in bananas between the three groups of states was very small. Moreover, the price of bananas varied widely among states: In 1991, for instance, the c.i.f. import price in France, Italy, Spain, and Britain was, respectively, 14, 30, 34, and 63 percent higher than in Germany or Group II member-states. These differences mirrored the severity of protection imposed by Group I member-states: "traditional" suppliers from domestic and other preferential sources benefited from quotas equivalent to 100 percent of domestic consumption (Spain), 90 percent (France), 75 percent (Britain), and less than 20 percent (Italy).[23]

The early 1990s saw the implementation of the Single Market, and the banana situation became a complete oddity. In February 1993, the Community reached an agreement on a CMO for bananas (Regulation 404/93), which began to be implemented in July 1993. Table A.9 summarizes the four major features of the CMO.

The first feature is that there are three major quotas: Quota I guarantees a certain tonnage of imports to EC-grown bananas; Quota II does the same thing to "traditional" ACP bananas, and Quota III to dollar bananas and bananas grown in those ACP countries that are not classified as "traditional." Quotas I and II are not constraining, in the sense that they grant to the beneficiaries quantities much above their export capacities: over the past 10 years, EC production has never been larger than 650 thousand tons, and traditional ACP production has reached a peak of 580 thousand tons. All these quotas are split into several subquotas: 4 for Quota I, 12 for Quota II, and 6 for Quota III. As is well known, such a feature tends to reinforce the distortionary impact of trade barriers. The second feature is that imports above these three quotas were subject to a de facto prohibitive duty of almost 100 percent. The third feature is that EC-grown bananas (from overseas territories) are eligible for production subsidies (so-called compensatory aid) ranging from €200 to €300 per ton between 1994 and 1996 (roughly 40 to 60 percent of the import values) and granted to a limited, but large, tonnage of EC bananas. Last but not least, the fourth feature is that there is a licensing scheme (described in detail below) associated with Quota III that magnifies the quota's protectionist impact by transferring market shares from US and Latin American companies to EC or ACP firms.

This incredibly complex CMO represented a shift from completely or largely open markets (Groups II and III, i.e., six to nine member-states) to a single closed market. As a result, it immediately triggered two reactions from the trading partners of the EC.

First, Latin American producers focused on the *border* protection element of the CMO, that is, the discriminatory split in two quotas (II and III) of non-EC bananas that are subject to very different conditions in terms of tariffs and quantities. At the end of the Uruguay Round negotiations, the EC signed the so-called Banana Framework Agreement with four Latin American countries (Colombia, Costa Rica, Nicaragua, and Venezuela), by which the EC granted specific subquotas of Quota III to these countries

---

23. A high, specific consumption tax was imposed on bananas in Italy. Moreover, special agreements have been concluded with certain ACP countries (including in Latin America, e.g., Dominican Republic or Haiti), implying that all these regimes had no common definition of "traditional" suppliers (this term could cover different ACP countries and overseas territories for each Group I member-state).

Table A.9 Case 19: EC banana import and distribution schemes, 1993–2001

				The Common Market Organization (Regulation 404/93) from 1993 to June 2001	
Border restrictions					
Annual quotas		**EC tariff**		**Nonborder restrictions** (licensing scheme and subsidy)	**The EC-US Agreement of April 2001: Phase I[d]** (only changes with respect to Regulation 404/93 are mentioned)
Tons (000)	Origin	(Euro/ton)	percent[a]		
Quota I. Imports of EC bananas: Total amount 854 thousand tons					
369.0	France	0.0	0.0	Quota allocated among 4 member-states of Group I.	Not mentioned
15.0	Greece	0.0	0.0	Quota allocated to EC companies.	
50.0	Portugal	0.0	0.0	Producer price support subsidy ("compensatory aid") of 622.5 euros per ton.	
420.0	Spain	0.0	0.0		
Quota II. Imports of ACP "traditional" bananas: Total amount 857.7 thousand tons					
155.0	Ivory Coast	0.0	0.0	Quota allocated by EC member-state and by preferred exporting (ACP) country.	**TRQ: Same amount as Quota I**
155.0	Cameroon	0.0	0.0	Quota mostly allocated to EC-ACP companies.	For bananas of all origin.
127.0	Sainte-Lucie	0.0	0.0	Various subsidy schemes.	Tariff of 300 euros/ton.
105.0	Jamaica	0.0	0.0		Tariff preference of 300 euros/ton for ACP bananas.
315.7	8 other ACPs[b]	0.0	0.0		Licensing regime still unknown in April 2001.
Quota III. Import of "other" bananas: Total amount 2,553 thousand tons[c]					
90.0	Nontraditional ACPs	0.0	0.0	Quota mostly allocated to EC-ACP companies.	**TRQs: Same amount as Quota III**
597.4	Costa Rica (23.4 percent)	75.0	8.7	The licensing scheme imposes de facto that 30 percent of the quota goes to EC-ACP companies.	For bananas of all origin. Tariff of 75 euros/ton.
536.1	Colombia (21.0 percent)	75.0	8.7		Licenses granted to companies, not to countries.
76.6	Nicaragua (3.0 percent)	75.0	8.7	(Ecuador is among the most efficient producers.)	Licenses based on firms' 1994–96 performances.
51.1	Venezuela (2.0 percent)	75.0	8.7		83 percent of licenses granted to "traditional" operators.
1201.8	Other "dollar bananas"	75.0	8.7		"Nontraditional" operators cannot become "traditional" operators in subsequent years.
Imports above Quota III					
	Nontraditional ACPs	750.0	87.5	Tariffs to be reduced by 20 percent over the period 1995–2000.	Not mentioned
	Other "dollar bananas"	850.0	99.1		

ACP = African, Caribbean, and Pacific countries.
TRQ = Tariff Rate Quota.

a. Estimates based on a price of 857 euros per ton.
b. Belize, Cape Verde, Dominica, Granada, Madagascar, Saint Vincent, Somalia, and Suriname.
c. Initially 2,000 million tons in 1993, increased to 2,100 million in 1994 and 2,200 million in 1995, and to 2,553 million following the 1995 EC enlargement.
d. Phase I begins in July 2001. For Phase II, see text.

Sources: Various EC Regulations; Inside US Trade, 2001.

on the condition that they not lodge a complaint at the WTO against the banana CMO before 2002 (the year for the CMO review).[24]

Second, the United States focused on the *nonborder* protection granted by the licensing scheme under Quota III. This scheme added discrimination in terms of firms ("operators") and activities to the first layer of discrimination based on import origin. Without the licensing scheme, a large portion of the 1,202.8 million tons of dollar bananas subject to non-country-specific Quota III would have normally been handled by the US fruit companies. But the licensing scheme is estimated to have "granted" 30 percent of the corresponding licenses to EC (and ACP) firms that could use them for their own operations or sell them to other firms (including to US firms). In other words, the licensing scheme introduced a pure transfer of the quota rents from US firms to EC firms.[25]

In 1996, the four major Latin American producers left out of the Banana Framework Agreement that were WTO members (Ecuador, Honduras, Guatemala, and Mexico) and the United States requested a dispute settlement panel at the WTO (for a detailed legal analysis of the successive GATT/WTO banana panels, see Komuro 2000).[26] The panel report was issued in May 1997, and it was confirmed by the Appellate Body ruling of September 1997; both decisions stated that many of the provisions of the banana CMO violated EC obligations under GATT Articles I and XIII and under GATS Articles II and XVII, and were inconsistent with the GATT-WTO waiver attached to the Lomé Convention. In particular, the fact that Quotas II and III (and all the corresponding subquotas) bear no resemblance to the import shares that would prevail in the absence of restrictions was condemned.[27]

Following the WTO rulings, the EC Commission presented a new Regulation, which was adopted by the EC Council in June 1998 (Regulation 1637/98) but made little progress on the key points of contention. In November 1998, the United States announced its intention to impose retaliatory measures if no further changes were introduced in the CMO. In April 1999, the WTO Dispute Settlement Body authorized the United States to

24. These four subquotas were regulated by "special export certificates" managed by the exporting country involved and monitored by the EC—constituting a classic example of voluntary export restraints with double checking (see also cases 13 and 14 above on textiles and clothing).

25. There were restrictions on the resale of licenses, but these restrictions were irrelevant for the large EC and ACP firms such as Fyffes or Pomona.

26. Latin American producers had already launched two panels of dispute settlements under GATT rules that both condemned the EC. But under the then weaker GATT disciplines on dispute settlement, it was easy for the Community to ignore these rulings.

27. Quota I per se was not a topic of debate, because it corresponds to a nondiscriminatory (pure) element of protection to the extent that it reserves a market to EC producers. By contrast, the import-licensing scheme—which grants to EC producers certain rights to import dollar bananas—was a subject of conflict.

suspend concessions to the EC equivalent to the level of nullification and impairment—meaning 100 percent customs duties on imports from the EC worth US$191.4 million (except on imports from Denmark and the Netherlands, which have always voted against the 1993 banana regime). In May 2000, Ecuador got a similar authorization by the WTO Dispute Settlement Body for the amount of US$201.6 million.

In December 2000, the EC agriculture ministers approved a new, transitory tariff-quota regime to be implemented from April 2001 to December 2005. The main novelty was the explicit adoption of a tariff-only system to be enforced starting January 2006. However, the new EC regulation left two key variables undefined: the type of licensing regime to be implemented for managing the quotas until 2006 and the level of the tariff to be imposed in 2006.

In April 2001, the EC and the United States quite unexpectedly reached an agreement based on two phases. During Phase I (starting in July 2001), Quota III is divided into two tariff-rate quotas, A and B (replicating the two sources of Quota III—that is, the EC-12 quota and the autonomous quota following the 1995 EC enlargement). Tariff-rate quotas (TRQs) A and B will be subject to the same licensing regime, which will no longer be defined on a country basis (meaning that ACP and Latin American bananas could be sold under these two TRQs) but on an "operator" (company) basis. For 83 percent of TRQs A+B, import licenses will be distributed to each "traditional" banana operator (defined as a company that either grows or buys green bananas to sell them to the first point of sale in Europe) on the basis of its average reference volume during the period 1994–96. The remaining 17 percent of TRQs A+B will be distributed to "nontraditional" operators. The tariff applied to TRQs A+B will not exceed €76/ton (the current tariff).

The new licensing regime for TRQs A+B is accompanied by a major rebalancing of market shares among major companies. In particular, Chiquita is expected to get back some of its past business in Europe—that is, to get licenses for 35–40 million boxes of bananas annually, compared to its current share of 28–31 million boxes and in the pre-1993 period of 50 million boxes (*Inside U.S. Trade*, 2001, Banana Deal Locks Out Competition, vol. 19, no.15, 13 April, 24). Consequently, it raises severe adjustment problems for Ecuador (the largest and one of the most efficient banana producers) because many of its banana companies will not fulfill the conditions to be considered as a "traditional operator" (except Noboa). The same could be observed for exporters from Costa Rica, Colombia, and other signatories of the Banana Framework Agreement.

In addition to TRQs A+B, the EC creates a TRQ C, equivalent in size to the current Quota II (see table A.9) and subject to a tariff of 300 euros/ton. TRQ C is also open to bananas from any origin, but ACP bananas will have a tariff preference of 300 euros/ton within (and outside) TRQ C, making this TRQ the de facto heir of Quota II. At the beginning of Phase II, a quantity of 100,000 tons will be shifted from TRQ C to TRQs A+B. TRQ C will then be reserved exclusively for bananas of ACP origin, benefiting from the (GATT Article XIII) last waiver that the EC is looking for in the context of the Cotonou Convention with the ACP states until 2008 (see chapter 6).

Phase II can begin only when the EC Council and Parliament have adopted the amendments necessary for implementing this agreement, in particular the shift of 100,000 tons between TRQ C and TRQs A+B. Phase II, which will last until December 2005, may also witness changes in computing the historical reference volume in the licensing regime of TRQs A+B, although the proximity of the final shift to a tariff-only import regime (January 1996) makes such changes unlikely.

Two weeks after the EC-US Agreement, the EC reached an agreement with Ecuador on detailed management of the provisions governing the "nontraditional" operators. At the time of this writing, there was no precise information on this management: the official communiqué simply states that "a very significant share of the trade will be reserved for non-traditional operators working within an open and competitive environment, thus facilitating access for small- and medium-sized businesses."

The April 2001 EC-US agreement is a step toward an EC tariff-only regime for bananas. It allows the EC to obtain the elimination of US sanctions, and, even more important, to get US support for the waiver that the EC wants for the transitory phase (2000–08) of the Cotonou Convention. But, serious obstacles remain before a complete settlement of this issue: (1) the EC member-states have to agree on what is so far only a Commission proposal; (2) the EC has to agree with the rest of the Latin American countries to ease their transitory adjustment problems and to get their support for the Cotonou waiver; (3) last but not the least, the EC has to define the tariff rate to be enforced on 1 January 2006.

It is important to note that, from an economic perspective, the April agreements will not significantly reduce the costs of protection for EC consumers. The sizes of the TRQs remain relatively unchanged (under Phase II, Latin American growers will get at the most 190,000 additional tons, that is, almost 8 percent more than in 2000) and the tariff levels are unchanged. As a result, the EC-US agreement will mostly consist of a big shift of rents—away from the beneficiaries of the 1993 regime and back to traditional operators.

In the short run, the EC-US agreement may even increase the costs of EC protection to the extent that it reinforces the anticompetitive nature of EC banana markets, and generates anticompetitive forces in the traditionally open EC markets, such as Germany or Sweden. In particular, it regrettably excludes the possibility for nontraditional operators to become traditional operators, hence prohibiting entry into 83 percent of TRQs A+B and granting this large market share to a few large firms: Chiquita and Dole, Fyffes (Britain-Ireland), Noboa (Ecuador), and possibly Del Monte. Moreover, what is known (at the time of this writing) about the competitive aspect of the EC-Ecuador agreement is not very reassuring: it suggests a government-led market organization. These conclusions reveal how crucial a rapid definition of the level—hopefully low—of the EC tariff will be. In the absence of a quick decision, the persistence of large rents allowed by the EC-US and EC-Ecuador agreements may simply imply that the EC bananarama may be far from over.

Notes

The level of protection for bananas is more delicate to estimate than in the other cases examined in this study because in 1990, protection was member-state based *and* led to large price differences among the various EC markets (the EC banana CMO was created only in 1993). Moreover, protection was (and still is) generated at two different stages: EC production and imports (border protection), and distribution in the EC (nonborder protection through import licensing). The second stage is important because both the wholesale and retail banana trade are costly in Europe relative to the United States. For instance, in 1989–91, retail prices were more than twice those prevailing in the United States (FAO 1997), and Borell (1996) reports that distribution margins in protected European markets were twice those in the United States, and up to 50 percent higher than in the open German market. Such differences in distribution costs may be due to factors unrelated to the EC banana trade regime, such as population density and wholesale or retail general structures. In this case, border protection would be the only aspect to look at in estimating the level of protection. But the differences in distribution costs can also be caused by the limited competition that the various licensing schemes imposed (and still impose), all the more because licenses were granted by member-states—generally in favor of their own fruit companies.

As a result, there are three possible estimates of the level of protection for the portion of EC markets protected in 1990, that is, roughly 60 percent of the total EC market (Germany, and to a lesser extent, the Benelux countries, can be considered open). First, the lowest estimate of the ad valorem tariff equivalent of the EC member-state quotas is based only on border barriers as measured by the import price differential between bananas imported from the EC overseas territories and bananas imported from other sources (ACP countries, as well as Latin American countries). In 1990, this differential was 61.2 percent.[28]

---

28. The difference was only 6.9 percent for the years 1994–96. This decline results from a large decline in import unit values from EC overseas territories and a modest increase in unit values of imports coming from constrained exporting countries. The price decline of EC-grown bananas was accompanied by a huge increase in quantities. These two shifts seem the logical consequence of the large subsidy scheme in the EC 1994 Regulation (see text above). Calculations, including EC state aid, lead to a minimum price differential of 57.5 percent with dollar bananas (the upper estimate of the ad valorem tariff equivalent of the subsidy scheme is 65.6 percent), i.e., they suggest a very stable level of protection of EC bananas.

Second, the medium-range estimate is based on retail price differentials, as defined by the difference between the average retail price (weighted by national market sizes) observed in protected member-states and the unweighted average of the US and German retail prices. Such prices are available, on a monthly basis, for the four largest EC markets (FAO 1997). Using the German-US prices aims to capture the fact that distribution costs could be higher in the EC than in the United States for reasons exogenous to the banana sector. In 1990, this price differential amounted to almost 82 percent.

Third, the highest estimate is based on the reasonable hypothesis that retail prices include excess costs in distribution caused by anticompetitive practices that existed before 1993, preceding the licensing scheme of the 1993 Regulation, which has de facto reinforced and amplified such practices. Such collusive practices have been observed. For instance, in 1990, the French Council of Competition provided evidence of collusion (organized by the Comité Professionnel Bananier and the Groupement d'Intérêt Economique Bananier) on the French banana market between French firms and imposed substantial fines (Conseil de la Concurrence 1990). For the years 1989–91, this last price differential can be estimated to be 123.2 percent. As a result, the costs of protection estimated in this last approach reflect to some extent imperfect competition (although the Hufbauer-Atje model is not used in this case).[29]

The literature estimates price demand elasticity within the range of 0.5–0.8 (Borell 1994; Laroche-Dupraz 1998), and a 0.7 demand elasticity was used. The EC domestic supply elasticity has been assumed to be relatively low (0.5), but the results are not sensitive to substantial changes in this choice. Substitution elasticity has been assumed to be relatively large (3)—if only to account for the fact that dollar bananas are often considered of better quality than EC bananas.

On the basis of the three price differential estimates and these parameters, the estimated costs to consumers of EC protection for 1990 range from €600 to €825 and to €1,327 million, respectively. Quota rents represent more than half these costs: they range from €338 to €473 and to €743 million.

Has the 1993 banana CMO improved the situation or made it worse? As underlined by Borell (1996), it has caused severe deterioration of the EC-wide situation. Again, there is the problem of measuring price differentials. Only estimates based on mere ad valorem tariff equivalents and

---

29. This imperfect competition aspect is important because many opponents of the liberalization of the EC banana markets argue that there is a strong risk of anticompetitive behavior if US firms are free to operate in the EC market. It should be noted that the world market for bananas shows a global market share of 70 to 75 percent for the 3–6 largest firms, i.e. (as underlined by Borell 1994), a share lower than in many other food or raw material markets (World Bank 1992).

on retail prices as mirroring anticompetitive practices (as described above) have been done for 1995 because the German market reflects less and less efficiency, and because it is protected as much as the other EC markets.

In 1995, the lowest costs of protection amounted to €1.2 billion (twice the corresponding figure for 1990) and the highest estimates amounted to €1.9 billion (almost 50 percent higher than the corresponding figure for 1990). Quota rents also increased to €660 million in the first subcase (almost the equivalent of the lowest *total* costs of protection estimated for 1990), and to €1.2 billion in the second subcase (almost the equivalent of the *highest total* costs of protection estimated for 1990).

Case 20: French Films

This case is limited to the French *film* industry (television productions are excluded from the estimated costs of protection) for two reasons: (1) there are no available consistent data for the whole EC, and (2) France is a good illustration, with a rich dataset, of protection of audiovisuals in the EC (for a detailed legal analysis of the EC situation until the mid-1990s, see Eeckhout 1994).

The extreme French position in the debate on liberalization of audiovisual services and the profusion of instruments of protection observed in France may lead to the belief that the level of French protection is much higher than the level in other large EC member-states. This conclusion is not correct, for two reasons. First, the lush profusion of French instruments of protection is accompanied by a substantial amount of redundancy. As is shown below, the rate of aggregate protection is not the sum of the protection rates of each separate instrument. Indeed, several instruments are imposing constraints on French filmmakers (Cocq 2000)—to the point of improving, in relative terms, the situation of foreign film producers (a kind of "negative" protection).

Second, as is well known, the *effective* level of protection is more difficult to estimate for services than for goods. For instance, the shares of American "fiction works" broadcast in France and in Britain were not so different in the mid-1990s (see table A.10, 4th column). However, one could argue that the corresponding effective level of protection granted was quite different. In Britain, BBC channels broadcast relatively few American movies, while BSkyB broadcasts such films almost exclusively, whereas *every* French TV channel broadcasts at most 40 percent American movies, as described in more detail below. In other words, a British viewer equipped with satellite TV has a less restricted choice at any time of the day than a French viewer: he or she can always see an American movie, although the French viewer can compensate for his or her disadvantage by using a VCR (see below).

Table A.10 Case 20: EC audiovisual markets: Cinema theaters, television channels, videos, 1996–97 and subsidies, 1995

Country	Theaters[a] US films, 1994–97	Theaters[a] EC films, 1997	TV channels[b] US films, 1996	TV channels[b] US fiction works, 1996	Videos VCR penetration rate,[c] 1997	Videos Blank cassettes,[d] 1997	All subsidies (to production and distribution) Total (millions of euros), 1995	All subsidies (to production and distribution) Non production[e] (percent), 1995	Subsidies to production of films and TV works Total (millions of euros), 1995	Subsidies to production of films and TV works Automatic (percent), 1995	Subsidization rates (percent), 1995
Austria	n.a.	0.0	64.6	26.6	75.3	4.7	21.9	n.a.	n.a.	n.a.	n.a.
Belgium	71.9	0.1	34.1	31.1	68.4	4.1	23.8	44.0	13.3	28.4	1,078.3
Britain[f]	80.5	4.8	75.3	19.8	83.0	3.1	31.0	9.3	28.1	0.0	8.8
Denmark	70.2	0.2	65.6	27.4	79.0	5.0	26.1	32.5	17.6	16.6	147.7
Finland	72.7	0.1	67.0	14.8	72.2	4.4	11.5	34.4	7.5	0.0	299.9
France	55.7	10.2	36.2	18.9	77.5	6.3	371.6	49.9	186.3	70.5	47.5
Germany	78.6	3.7	65.2	35.5	77.3	3.4	147.2	50.1	73.5	9.9	42.6
Greece	n.a.	0.0	n.a.	20.2	55.7	1.5	5.2	8.9	4.7	0.0	239.3
Ireland	n.a.	0.0	n.a.	27.1	72.7	2.1	3.8	0.0	3.8	0.0	390.0
Italy	59.9	2.2	61.6	23.6	59.2	2.3	95.5	4.3	91.3	8.0	71.3
Netherlands	86.6	0.2	72.4	22.7	67.3	4.0	34.6	16.3	29.0	0.0	174.6
Portugal	80.8	0.1	n.a.	19.0	52.0	1.3	11.6	50.5	5.7	31.6	695.3
Spain	72.7	1.9	69.0	28.1	72.1	1.9	27.3	21.2	21.5	48.2	42.3
Sweden	67.2	0.4	n.a.	29.7	79.2	4.9	25.7	40.8	15.2	25.0	81.6
EC-15	72.4	1.7	61.1	24.6	73.6	3.5	838.1	37.9	498.6	33.8	52.2
United States	95.4	n.a.	n.a.	n.a.	92.8	n.a.	n.a.	n.a.	n.a.	n.a.	n.a.
Japan	41.3	n.a.	n.a.	n.a.	90.8	n.a.	n.a.	n.a.	n.a.	n.a.	n.a.

n.a. = not available
VCR = videocassette recorder

a. In percent of total seats sold.
b. In percent of hours broadcast (weighted by audience).
c. In percent of households.
d. Expenditures in current euros per person.
e. Percentage of subsidies not directly allocated to production of films or TV works.
f. Share of EC films goes up to 8.7 percent if UK-US films are included.

Sources: European Audiovisual Observatory, *Statistical Yearbook*, 1998 and 1999; Messerlin (2000); Messerlin and Cocq (2001).

But another consideration also should be taken into account in assessing the restrictive effects of these two shares. In each country, the above share of American "fiction works" is roughly half the share of the audience watching American movies in cinemas (80 percent in Britain, and 60 percent in France). This suggests a not too different effective level of protection (in fact, all the indicators for which there are more recent data, e.g., the share of American films in cinema theaters, are rapidly converging in Europe).

As a result, what follows considers the level of protection granted to films in France as not so different from the level of protection in the other large member-states.[30] The situation may be different for small member-states; some of them are relatively open, but others can be even more protectionist than the large member-states, as is best illustrated by Belgium, which imposes strict *internal* barriers protecting Belgian French- and Dutch-speaking movies (without much opening to French or Dutch productions).

Before describing French protection, "cultural" goods and services raise an important preliminary question: how should "national" cultural goods and services be defined (Messerlin 2000)? Quite ironically, in France, a film is considered French once it has been "agreed on" (*agréé*) by the Centre National de la Cinématographie (CNC)—hence, when it has received French subsidies, because most subsidies are automatically attached to the agreement procedure. Of course, this agreement requires certain conditions, in particular French nationality for actors and technicians and the use of the French language for the script and shooting. But a recent official report of the Cour des Comptes has underlined the wide circumvention of these conditions.[31] The crucial point is that the quite bizarre "rule of origin" is discriminatory. The CNC agreement cannot be granted to films made by firms that are "controlled by firms established outside European countries," a provision that specifically excludes firms from the United States and a few other economies (Hong Kong, Japan, South Korea, and Taiwan) with which France has not signed bilateral agreements.

The protection of the so-called "French" film industry relies on three main groups of instruments: indirect taxes, quotas, and subsidies (for details, see Messerlin and Cocq 2001). First, an indirect tax of roughly 11 percent is levied on every seat sold in French cinemas, independent of the nationality of the film presented. The seat tax is thus a nondiscriminatory

---

30. This conclusion is consistent with the similar content and number of pages (seven pages for France and four pages for Britain) devoted by the association of the US major film producers to the description of protectionist measures in these two countries (Motion Picture Association of America 1995).

31. The Cour des Comptes reported a case where a movie was considered French, although it was done in English, as a British coproduction, with seven American and two British actors. The film was *agréé* because it was based on a French novel, used some French elements of scenery, and had one French actress involved (Cour des Comptes, *Report to the President of the Republic*, 1993, 106).

excise tax imposed on both foreign and French films. But the seat tax is also one of the sources of the subsidies granted to the film sector. It finances *two* different subsidies: those granted to French producers for making French movies, and those granted to French cinema owners for improving their theaters—with *American* movies as the main beneficiaries of this second subsidy type, because they constitute the largest share of movies shown.[32] As a result, the impact of the seat tax (in its *use*) is discriminatory, although in a complex way.

The second instrument of protection consists of public subsidies granted to French filmmakers. There are roughly 80 major types of *direct* subsidies available for film production, covering all possible aspects of the business.[33] First, there are subsidies related to production: "*soutien automatique*" (automatic support granted as soon as the film has been agreed on by the CNC), *avances sur recettes* (advances on revenues, which are equivalent to subsidies because they are generally never reimbursed), subsidies for scripts, subsidies for film music, subsidies for coproductions, subsidies for "regional" films, subsidies "expressly granted by the minister for ambitious projects," and so on. Second, there are subsidies attached to film distribution, such as for film development or for making film copies. Last, there is an astounding diversity of subsidies granted to cinemas (many cinemas are run by film producers, such as Gaumont): to new cinemas, to cinemas located in areas with insufficient public transport, to cinemas for films "*d'art et d'essai,*" for better sound equipment, for independent cinemas, for "proximity cinemas," and so on.

In addition to all these direct subsidies, there are *indirect* subsidies: special unemployment benefits for the workers and actors in the "*industrie du spectacle*"; subsidy schemes based on fiscal deductions (SOFECA); subsidies related to the launching of (already outdated when launched!) satellites; and last but not least, EC subsidies (the Media programs). Table A.10 provides a summary of a recent study on subsidies to film *and* TV productions in Europe (European Audiovisual Observatory 1998), and it estimates the subsidization rates (defined as subsidies divided by the turnover of the film *and* TV industries) for EC member-states.[34] As one would expect, subsidies tend to increase for the EC member-states with

---

32. The supporters of the tax believe that it hurts American producers (although, as a tariff in a relatively competitive environment, it does not have this capacity) and that it has a positive impact on the French film industry (although, in fact, it is a tax on successful French movies and a subsidy to unsuccessful French films—hence, a cost for the whole French film industry).

33. The movie industry is the only French industry to have its own book devoted to explaining all the subsidies available.

34. Being based on public accounting, the data on subsidies in table A.10 ignore the implicit subsidies flowing from investment quotas, particularly in the case of Canal Plus (see below, on investment quotas).

small audiences (Belgium being divided in two, the French- and Dutch-speaking regions).

The French subsidy scheme is so complex that it is almost impossible to monitor it; indeed, that was the main conclusion of the report of the Cour des Comptes. It is also crucial to note that subsidies related to "culture" constitute only a *minority* proportion of the whole system—*at most*, one-third during the past 20 years (even less in the most recent years). This point will be essential in the coming debate on the liberalization of audio-visual services in the WTO context (Messerlin 2000).

Quotas are the last instrument of protection. There are three major types of quotas. First, there are quotas based on the country of origin of the films: TV channels have to broadcast at least 40 percent "French" (or rather, more accurately, CNC-agreed-on) films and 20 percent "European" films, leaving a maximum share of 40 percent for movies from the United States and other countries without bilateral agreements. Second, there are quotas that limit the freedom of TV channels to broadcast films: a global ceiling for the year (different for each TV channel), a ban on broadcasting during certain days or hours (Wednesday afternoons, because children are then supposed to go to the cinemas; Saturday afternoons and Sundays until 8 pm; during certain peak hours), and specific quotas on movies older than a year, on recent movies, on the frequency of broadcasting the same movie, and so on. Last but not least, there are quotas on investment: TV broadcasters (in particular, Canal Plus) are required by law to invest a given amount of their annual resources in filmmaking (according to very complex rules)—a source of indirect subsidies roughly as important as public subsidies.

It is important to note that all these quotas have different, and sometimes conflicting, effects. Quotas by origin are pure import quotas. Quotas on time constraints for broadcasting films are protecting cinemas against competition from TV channels; they are nondiscriminatory with respect to American movies, although restricting the global amount of time available for broadcasting films does indirectly favor foreign films. Last, quotas on investment are equivalent to a system of indirect subsidies to French films. But they generate a lot of inefficiency from the subsidizers' point of view (because of the complex rules to follow, which leave very little room for picking up only the best films).[35]

It is useful to end this survey with a glance toward the legal situation at the Community level. Out of the six EC directives dealing with audio-

---

35. These quotas also regulate competition between TV film producers, TV broadcasters, and other domestic film producers. In particular, they have favored strong vertical integration links between all the segments of the audiovisual sector (including the film industry). For instance, in 1995, Canal Plus alone represented 25 percent of the total French investment in film production and had stakes in 72 percent of all the French films produced that year. Such vertical integration creates serious problems of competition—a deadly characteristic from a cultural point of view.

visuals, only the Television Without Frontiers (TWF) Directive has been enforced by all the member-states. It is best known for the provision extending the regime of broadcasting quotas (described above) by origin to all member-states—with the famous caveat of "when available" allowing states to be lax if they wish so.

More important, the TWF has so far missed its core objective: to allow freedom of *cross-border* audiovisual services within the EC.[36] Today "pan-European" TV broadcasters are mostly of non-EC origin; they are still very marginal (12 percent of the total number of channels, less than 2 percent of TV advertising revenues, and only 0.7 percent of total TV revenues). When providing services, a typical European TV broadcaster still establishes subsidiaries in each member-state and slips into the host country rules—instead of beaming programs across European borders. As a result, cross-border programs are very limited, despite significant differences in their prices.

This still strong segmentation of EC markets makes emerging alliances between European TV broadcasters unstable and defensive; they tend to gang together, essentially to consolidate their own position at home. These coalitions minimize competition and in the long run they may generate risks of "excessive" entry.

It would be wrong to provide estimates of costs of protection in audiovisuals without a brief remark on the "culture" aspect. In fact, these estimates do not take into account the *perverse* impact of the many existing protection schemes on French culture in a dynamic setting. By nature, protection induces domestic producers to take the place of foreign producers, and it protects some domestic producers to the detriment of others. Films do not escape these two laws. French filmmakers, protected from American movies, have tried to produce films that are "clones" of American movies—in particular, after the 1989 Plan Lang (named after the then minister of culture, Jack Lang) focusing on films with "large" budgets (large in the French definition meaning budgets roughly equivalent to the average size of the advertising budget *alone* of American movies with "large" budgets). In sum, public incentives "Americanized" new French talents and eroded the "French difference" at a stronger and faster pace.

Notes

The first point is to estimate the ad valorem rate of protection imposed by all the existing restrictions. The seat tax could be seen as equivalent to a tariff only to the extent that it exceeds the level of investment that American moviemakers would have been ready to consider for purely com-

---

36. According to TWF, Article 3, "member-states shall remain free to require television broadcasters under their jurisdiction to lay down more detailed or stricter rules in the areas covered by this Directive."

mercial purposes. For instance, in 1994, American moviemakers paid FFR280 million because of the seat tax, a sum that represented 60 percent of the FFR467 million in subsidies granted to improve French cinemas. However, it is not certain that the American moviemakers would have needed to invest all this money in theaters to attract the same number of viewers (subsidies to French cinemas are likely to inflate investments in theaters). As a result, the seat tax of 11 percent is treated in what follows as a pure tariff on foreign films.

The tariff equivalent of quotas by origin can be estimated by assuming that, in their absence, French viewers would have the same behavior in front of their TV screen as when they go to cinemas. On the basis of this assumption, the degree of bindingness of the quotas by origin was almost nil in 1986 (when they were officially created); at the time, 43 percent of the French going to the cinema watched American films. The year 1990 was the second since then to witness a jump in this proportion, to 55 percent; as a result, the 40 percent broadcast quota was equivalent to a cut of 25 percent (15/55) of the French audience for American films on TV, although this quota-bindingness was partly relaxed by the use of videos, France being among the EC member-states best equipped with VCRs.[37] However, as the costs of protection are estimated for 1990, taking into account this source of protection would have overestimated these costs for the following reason. Successful films tend to be shown on TV screens one or two years after their presentation in cinemas. In other words, the real impact of the surge of interest in American movies among French viewers was translated into the TV market only in 1991 or 1992.

Turning to subsidies, direct public subsidies to the film industry alone (*excluding* TV work) amounted to more than FFR800 million per year in 1989–90 (and to more than FFR1 billion per year after the mid-1990s). The corresponding ad valorem "subsidy rate" (the ratio of the subsidies received by the film industry with respect to the film revenues raised by cinemas) was 65.8 percent for the same three years.[38] The difference with the subsidy rate of 47.5 percent shown in table A.10 is due to the focus on film production alone (TV productions are less subsidized). There has been no attempt to include indirect subsidies in this estimate; a back-of-envelope

---

37. It is interesting to note that American films represent roughly 55 percent of movies made available by private TV channels in Germany and Italy. In the late 1990s, the quota-bindingness increased to roughly 35 percent because American movies had a market share of 60 percent of the films shown in French cinemas.

38. As shown in appendix C, the 65.8 percent subsidy rate corresponds to an ad valorem tariff equivalent of 90.4 percent. Computing the subsidy rate on cinema revenues alone is appropriate because, for the years in question, cinema revenues still represented a major portion of total film revenues. For more recent years, it would be better to estimate the subsidy rate on total revenues, which should increasingly include important TV and video fees (for which there is only crude information).

computation would suggest that taking them into account would multiply the estimated subsidy rate by a factor of 2.

In sum, the rate of overall protection in 1990 is the sum of the tax seat (11 percent) and the tariff equivalent of subsidies (65.8 percent). The price elasticity of demand for motion pictures has been estimated in the United States to be 0.7 for 1950–80 (Coursey and Taylor 1982). The domestic price elasticity of supply has been set at 1, and the substitution elasticity at 5 (to reflect the plausibly high degree of substitution between French and American films). As a result, elasticities of 0.7, 1, and 5 (for demand, supply, and substitution, respectively) have been used to estimate the costs of protection.

Case 21: Passenger Air Transport

This case deals only with passenger air transport.[39] The European air transport market is generally divided into "scheduled" and "charter" (nonscheduled) flights or routes (for a detailed legal analysis of the EC situation until the mid-1990s, see Eeckhout 1994). The division dates back to the 1950s, when a few EC member-states (mostly Austria, Germany, Sweden, and Britain) allowed market forces to play a dominant role on a very limited number of "charter" routes almost exclusively devoted to tourists, such as Mediterranean islands (McGowan and Trengove 1986).[40] By contrast, "scheduled" passenger air transport was completely protected through route duopolies granted to "flag" (national) carriers, which were often publicly owned. Each route monopoly was based on a bilateral agreement sharing the scheduled route between the flag carriers based at the two ends of the route, generally on a 50–50 basis, in accordance with the complex set of rules drawn up by the 1944 Chicago Conference.

In the mid-1980s, the charter market represented 50 percent of the total EC air passenger market (in number of passengers). Despite its size, it exerted almost no competitive pressure on scheduled markets because routes and operating airlines were completely different: prices in EC charter markets were estimated to be close to US prices for similar routes and conditions, whereas prices on EC scheduled routes were estimated to be 45 to 75 percent higher than US prices for similar routes (McGowan and Trengove 1986). These percentages can be interpreted as estimates of the

---

39. EC freight air transport has been liberalized since 1991. Air cargo is liberalized to the extent that there is no direct governmental intervention in pricing and services, but there is no "international" liberalization in the sense that only EC carriers can compete (although foreign carriers operate through EC-controlled associate companies). Of course, a host of indirect barriers can be imposed (through airport availability under rules about noise, timing, etc.).

40. Charter carriers have a lot of flexibility in terms of ownership. Several British charter carriers were owned by foreign capital (Swiss and Canadian).

Table A.11a Case 21: Legal framework of EC liberalization in airlines

Year/reference	Nature	Content
1981		British White Paper on Airline Competition Policy
1984		Britain-Netherlands bilateral agreement
87.3975	MRA/harmonization	First package: Application of competition rules to air transport[a]
87.3976	Liberalization	First package: Application of the treaty to certain categories of agreements and practices[a]
87.601	Liberalization	First package: Directive on air fares
87.602	Liberalization	First package: Capacity sharing and market access[b]
89.2299		Computer reservations systems (CRSs)[c]
90.2342	MRA/harmonization	Second package: Air fares[c]
90.2343	MRA/harmonization	Second package: Market access[c]
90.2344	MRA/harmonization	Second package: Application of the Treaty to certain categories of agreements and practices[a]
91.294	MRA/harmonization	Air cargo (freight and mail) liberalization[c]
92.2407	Liberalization	Third package: Licensing of air carriers[c]
92.2408	MRA/harmonization	Third package: Market access[c]
92.2409	Liberalization	Third package: Air fares and rates[c]
93.95		Slot allocation and airport scheduling arrangements[c]
93.3089		Computer reservation systems (CRSs)[c]

EC = European Community.
MRA = mutual recognition agreement

a. Council recommendation.
b. Council decision.
c. Council regulation.

range of the ad valorem tariff equivalents of the protection granted to EC flag carriers on scheduled routes in the mid-1980s.

Since the mid-1980s, EC passenger air transport has been subject to a lengthy process of liberalization, which table A.11a summarizes. The process started in Britain, marked by the Civil Aviation Authority Review and the White Paper on Airline Competition Policy (1984) and by the privatization of British Airways (1987). In 1984–85, bilateral air services agreements, mostly between Britain and other EC member-states, expanded the liberalization process to a limited number of intra-EC scheduled routes (e.g., London-Dublin or London-Amsterdam). These routes were opened to non-flag carriers (governments agreed to restrain their intervention in terms of "designation," i.e., in terms of designating an airline to operate a route) and fares became less firmly fixed by governments.

The success of these bilateral liberalizations helped to launch the progressive liberalization of the whole Community (plus Iceland, Norway and Switzerland). In what follows, there are three types of markets to consider: extra-EC markets (between an EC member-state and a non-EC country), intra-EC markets (between two member-states), and intra-EC member-state (hereafter, intra-MS) markets (i.e., the domestic market of a member-state). The intra-EC liberalization takes the form of three successive "packages" of measures. But it is only the third package that introduced (1) an effective plurilateral (EC-wide) regime of air transport regulation (instead of a network of bilateral agreements) including intra-MS traffic, and (2) the definition of a "Community air carrier."[41] This progressivity implied that EC flag carriers were diversely affected by the EC packages because of their different initial mix of the three markets; for instance, in the early 1990s, the share of *intra*-MS and intra-EC ranged from 80 percent of airline revenue (for the Scandinavian airline SAS) to less than 30 percent (for the Dutch airline KLM), and the share of the intra-MS market alone ranged from 40 percent of airline revenues (Iberia, the Spanish flag carrier) to zero (KLM).

Table A.11b presents the existing legal situation in more detail. It shows that, for EC carriers, few regulatory constraints remain on intra-EC routes and (only since April 1997, except for member-states having used the freedom to open routes in advance) on intra-MS routes. In both cases, carriers decide the routes to operate on a commercial basis (free entry); their decisions about seat capacity and pricing are free from government intervention (except, in the case of pricing, if "unfair" practices are observed; in such cases, member-states or the Commission can take appropriate action; but so far there have been very few such actions).

Table A.11a shows that new Community rules and EC-based competition cases have faced increasing difficulties in two key markets closely related to passenger air transport. First, travel agents are using computer reservation systems (CRSs) to pick up, book, and sell tickets to travelers (tourists and businesspeople alike). In the 1987 *Ahmed Saeed* case, the Court of Justice found legal the practice of cross-border ticketing (the fact that a travel agent purchases tickets for a specific cross-border route in the cheaper directional market). However, since then, EC air carriers have successfully inhibited wide use of arbitrage in ticketing (generally with member-state support). Second, EC airports constitute particularly severe entry barriers: The few large EC airports are congested, relatively close to each other, and connected to each other in a very inefficient way. For all

---

41. According to OECD (1988), these bilateral liberalizations led to a 3–5 percent increase in passengers, higher regular fares, and much lower charter fares.

Table A.11b Case 21: Overview of "building blocks" of competition in air transport

Building block	EC: International scheduled passenger transport			EC: Intra-EC air transport
	Fare type	Percent of reference fare	Approval conditions	
Fares	Fully flexible	>106	Unless double approval	All fares
	Normal economy	95–105	Automatic	Free pricing, except member-state or Commission's actions against:
	Discount	80–94	Automatic	(1) "excessive basic" fares
	Deep discount	30–79	Automatic	(2) "sustained downward development"
	All others		If double approval	
Designation	Multiple designation allowed by a member-state if 100,000 passengers or 600 round-trip flights			No longer applicable
Capacity	Capacity shares of a member-state of up to 60 percent. Capacity can be increased by 7.5 percent a year			Unrestricted
Route access	3rd/4th freedom between all airports. 5th freedom allowed up to 50 percent of capacity. Public service obligations. Protection for new regional routes. Scope for traffic distribution rules. Restrictions related to congestion and environmental protection. A 3rd/4th freedom can be matched by an airline from the other member-state			Full access to intra-EC routes. Cabotage unrestricted (April 1997). Public service obligations. Protection for new regional routes. Scope for traffic distribution rules. Restrictions related to congestion and environmental protection

Competition rules	Group exemptions regarding: 1. Some capacity coordinations 2. Tariff consultations 3. Slot allocations at airports 4. Common "computer reservation systems" 5. Ground handling of aircraft, freight, and passengers; inflight catering	Group exemptions regarding: 1. Some capacity coordinations 2. Tariff consultations 3. Slot allocations at airports 4. Common "computer reservation systems" 5. Joint operations of new thin routes
Licensing of air carriers	Full freedom to start an airline: uniform conditions across EC Concept of Community ownership and control Specified requirements for financial fitness Small carriers subject to looser regulatory requirements	
Air cargo	Free access (except cabotage) and free pricing	

EC = European Community.

Source: Adapted from *Single Market Review* 1997a, 20.

these reasons, the relatively inert allocation of airport slots tends to perpetuate the situation that existed during the regulatory period.

EC competition policy on air transport deserves a few specific remarks. Sixteen years of legal battles and a ruling of the Court of Justice (in 1974) were necessary to put air transport within the reach of Articles 85 and 86 of the Treaty of Rome. However, this effort has been severely hampered by three factors: (1) "Block exemptions" from competition rules were granted to CRSs, to tariff consultations for the scheduled carriage of passengers and frequent flyer programs, and to slot allocation and airport scheduling. (2) All the mergers in the airline sector so far have been accepted by the Commission (in sharp contrast with audiovisuals; see case 20)—even when the merger in question resulted in high market shares on certain routes or airports. (3) Last but not least, EC competition policy includes disciplines on subsidies (state aid).

This last aspect deserves some comment because the mid-1990s witnessed a surge in state aid (only Lufthansa—to a certain extent—and Luxair did not benefit from state aid). The amount of aid was often huge—on average, 15 percent of operating revenues (the estimate is based on data provided by Single Market Review 1997a, 26–28). When trying to limit this state aid, the Commission imposed many conditions, which turn out to have been quasi-anticompetitive devices. For instance, out of the 16 conditions under which the Commission authorized the €3 billion French aid to Air France (in 1994), several were ultimately blatantly anticompetitive: the prohibition to increase the number of planes above a threshold of 146 units until 1996, the imposition of various sets of quotas on Air France's traffic on European routes (a kind of "[in]voluntary export restraints," including annual growth rates), the prohibition on Air France charging tariffs lower than its competitors' tariffs, and similar provisions for Air Charter (the Air France charter subsidiary). No official detailed information on the monitoring of these drastic conditions is available.

In sum, passenger air transport liberalization in the EC has been a mix of pro- and anticompetitive provisions and measures. It is not astonishing that the result is quite mixed: if in 1997 the routes with more than two carriers represented 10 percent of all the cross-border EC routes, compared to 2 percent in 1992, they have brought an additional decrease of only 5–10 percentage points of the airfares observed for the routes under the traditional duopoly situation (WTO, *Trade Policy Review: The European Union*, 2000, 133–34). This positive outcome may be threatened by the beginning of consolidation through alliances that can already be observed in the EC passenger air transport sector. Meanwhile, technical regulations have been made stricter (e.g., the use of hush kits in old aircrafts), and airports have been shown to develop highly discriminatory pricing policies (equivalent to ad valorem tariffs of 40–50 percent) in favor of the flag carrier.

Notes

In 1990, there was almost no liberalization. As tested by Marin (1994), the first package did not make any noticeable impact during the period 1982–89 (the only source of liberalization being bilateral treaties on some European routes). As a result, it seems reasonable to aggregate both intra-EC and extra-EC markets as "foreign" markets for member-state flag carriers.

Balance of payments data have been used for estimating the size of the "foreign" air market. The European Commission (1995) provides intra-EC and extra-EC exports and imports data for the whole EC (hence, limiting the problem of double counting as much as possible). Of course, such data do not make any distinction between scheduled and charter flights; but the assumption that German air travelers do not use British charters seems an acceptable approximation for the early 1990s (as seen above, in the *Ahmed Saeed* case).

Estimating a "domestic" air market has two aspects. First, there are the flights to and from foreign destinations for travelers of the same nationality as the flag carrier in question. This component can be estimated on the basis that flag carriers tended to have slightly more than 50 percent of the international air flights connected to their countries; what follows assumes that this first component of EC flag carriers represents 1.05 times the size of the intra-EC and extra-EC markets, as defined above. Second, there are the flights corresponding to the *intra-MS* market, *stricto sensu*, which are estimated on the basis of the proportion of revenues accruing to the involved member-state flag carrier; this would amount to 10 percent of all EC flag carrier revenues.

The last step is to provide a reasonable "guesstimate" of the rate of protection. Taking into account the almost endless capacity for price discrimination in the airline business, such a rate could give only an order of magnitude. In what follows, it is defined as the differentials between the intra-MS fully flexible fare on the one hand, and the intra- or extra-EC corresponding fares on the other hand. The absence of a single EC market would require measuring such differentials for each member-state. What follows has used a simpler method consisting of measuring these differentials only for Britain (the least distorted market). This method suggests an estimate of 71 percent, on the basis of data provided by the Single Market Review (1997a, 184–87).

The literature suggests a total-price demand elasticity ranging from 0.2 (for business travelers) to 0.4 (pleasure travelers) (Morrison and Winston 1986). There is no estimate of the supply price elasticity and of the elasticity of substitution between domestic and foreign air carriers. Because business travel is dominant in the EC scheduled market, elasticities of 0.3, 0.5, and 0.4 (for demand, supply, and substitution, respectively) have been used to estimate the costs of protection.

Case 22: Telecommunications

Assessing the costs of protection in EC telecommunications (hereafter, telecoms) is as difficult as in air transport, for three reasons. Telecom regulations have an impact on the level of efficiency of the markets unsurpassed in other service sectors, except perhaps financial services. Telecom services can be subject to almost endless differentiation, if regulations permit. And there is no such a thing as a country that has fully liberalized its telecoms and that consequently could be used as an unequivocal benchmark for assessing the costs of protection in the EC. For instance, as stressed by Crandall (1997), US liberalization, although it started in the 1950s, is far from complete. Competition has developed in the long-distance markets through a combination of rules and a series of accidents, and the 1996 US Telecommunications Act—aiming to create a framework for global competition—has been caught in long legal battles.

As a result, the approach adopted in this case study is modest. It aims to assess the costs of having *delayed* the introduction in the EC of the dose of competition that Finland, Sweden, and Britain have imposed in their telecom sectors.[42] In other words, the costs of protection are estimated on the basis of the wedge between average British-Finnish-Swedish (BFS) *prices* and EC *prices* in telecoms. Such an approach goes far to estimate the costs of protection on the same basis as cases about goods—where benchmarks consist of fully liberalized and efficient foreign industries. As explained below, the British liberalization in telecoms has been subject to a trial-and-error learning process in key aspects—meaning that, by the early 1990s, British prices were still far out of touch with costs, and that cross-subsidies (in particular, transfers from nonlocal calls to local calls) were still large. Finnish and Swedish liberalizations have also been specific enough to leave doubts about their price-cost alignment.

Despite its imperfections, the British liberalization opened the path to EC regulatory reforms in telecoms (for a detailed legal history until the mid-1990s, see Eeckhout 1994). Table A.12a presents the 36 most important EC Directives and legal documents that are the sources of these reforms (out of a total of 117 texts, as of January 1999). One can distinguish three successive steps in EC liberalization. The first step was opening markets for telecom equipment and decoupling the strong links between European Public Telecom Operators (PTOs) and domestic equipment

---

42. Excluding the Finnish and Swedish experiences would have decreased the estimated price wedge by roughly 10 percent. On the one hand, it is correct that these two experiences involve countries that were not member-states in 1990 and, more important, that have very particular geographical size, population concentrations, etc. On the other hand, the current liberalization in the EC shows the key role of Finnish and Swedish firms as entrants promoting competition (e.g., Tele2 has entered the French market on an offer of half the existing price, i.e., a price decline equal to all the price decreases of the previous three to four years).

Table A.12a   Case 22: Legal framework of EC liberalization in telecommunications: Selected directives and documents

Year and reference	Scope (regulation)	Nature	Content
1981			*British Telecommunications Act*
1987			*Commission Green Paper on European Telecommunications services and equipment*
87.372	Services	MRA	Harmonized frequences for global system for mobile communications (GSM)
88.301	Goods	Liberalization	Competition for terminal equipment[a]
90.387	ONP	Liberalization	Harmonized conditions for open access to public telecom networks and services ("Open Network" or "Framework" Directive)
90.388	Services	Liberalization	Competition for telecom value added and data services on wired infrastructures ("Services" Directive)[a]
90.544	Services	MRA	Harmonized frequencies for the European Digital Radio-Messaging System (ERMES)
1990			*Commission Green Paper on Satellite Communications*
1991			*Judgment of the Court of Justice (French Government vs. Commission), 19 March 1991*
91.263	Goods	MRA	Mutual recognition of tests and approvals for terminal equipment (modifies Directive 86.361)
91.287	Services	MRA	Harmonized frequency for Digital European Cordless Telephone (DECT)
1991			*General Guidelines on the application of the treaty's Competition Rules in the Telecommunications Sector*
91.396	Services	MRA	Adoption of a unique European emergency phone number ("112")
92.264	Services	MRA	Adoption of the standard international prefix ("00")
92.044	ONP	Liberalization	Application of open network provision to leased lines
1992			*Judgment of the Court of Justice (Spanish Government and others vs. Commission), 17 November 1992*
1993			*Council resolution to extend competition to all telecommunications services from 1 January 1998*
93.097	Goods	MRA	Mutual recognition for ground station equipment for satellite communications (supplements Directive 91.263)
94.046	Services	Liberalization	Competition for satellite services (modifies Directives 88.301 and 90.388)

(table continues next page)

339

Table A.12a Case 22 *(continued)*

Year and reference	Scope (regulation)	Nature	Content
1994			*Commission Green Paper on Mobile and Personal Communications*
1994–95			*Commission Green Papers on Infrastructure and Cable TV Network Liberalization*
95.046	Services	Protective regulation	Protection of processing personal data and the free movement of such data
95.051	Services	Liberalization	Authorization to use cable TV networks for carrying services liberalized under Directive 90.388 ("Cable" Directive)
95.062	ONP	Liberalization	Application of open network provision to voice telephony
96.002	Services	Liberalization	Competition for personal mobile telephones (modifies Directive 90.388)
96.019	Services	Liberalization	Competition for all telecom services (including voice telephony) and infrastructure ("Full Competition" Directive)[b]
97.013	Services	Liberalization	Harmonized framework for general authorizations and individual licenses in telecom services ("License" Directive)
97.033	ONP	Liberalization	Harmonized framework for interconnection and universal service ("Interconnection" Directive)
97.051	ONP	Liberalization	Competition for leased lines (modifies Directives 90.387 and 92.044)[c]
97.066	Services	Protective regulation	Protection of personal data and privacy in the telecom sector
1997			*Adoption of WTO Agreement on Basic Telecommunications Services[a]*
98.010	Services	Liberalization	Application of open network provision to voice telephony and universal service
98.013	Goods	MRA	Mutual recognition of conformity for terminal equipment and satellites
1998			*Guidelines on Application of Competition Rules to "Access Agreements" in telecommunications sector*
98.061	ONP	Liberalization	Harmonized number portability and carrier preselection (amends Directive 97.033)

MRAs = mutual recognition agreements
ONP = Open Network Provision.

Note: Legal sources other than Council or Commission Directives are in italics.

a. Commission Directive under Article 90.
b. Derogation for 2003 for Greece, Ireland, Luxembourg, Portugal, and Spain.
c. Parts of the Directive can be transposed until October 2000.

Source: European Commission, *Status Report on EU Telecommunications Policy*, 1998

manufacturers: that has required a series of "mutual recognition agreements" (MRAs). The second step of EC liberalization was introducing competition in "new" telecom services rather than in infrastructure. This move also requires MRAs, but in services, such as the adoption of a unique emergency phone number or prefixes to Europeanwide definitions of frequency bands. The last step was opening all markets (including voice telephony) through a series of "open network provision" directives aimed at making transparent and nondiscriminatory the access of entrants (eager to compete for services) to incumbents' telecom structures (the "interconnection" issue, which is still far from being satisfactorily solved, see below).

Table A.12a provides two useful lessons. First, almost a decade separates the EC ONP Framework Directive (1990), the first major EC step toward services liberalization, from the Telecommunications Act (1981) launching the British liberalization. This long delay was imposed by powerful Continental PTOs reluctant to abandon their monopoly position. But it was, to a certain extent, useful because it allowed the EC to benefit from the British efforts. The "duopoly" policy in long-distance services (based on privatized British Telecom, or BT, and private Mercury) followed by Britain between 1983 and 1991 proved to provide a too limited impetus to competitive forces, despite the fact that Mercury was a subsidiary of Cable and Wireless (an heir of the British imperial telecom network, with anchors all around the world).[43] In many respects, these remarks imply that assessing the costs of protection in EC telecoms by using the British-Finnish-Swedish (BFS) benchmark tends to *underestimate* the gains from full liberalization (as shown below).

Second, as underlined by Waverman and Sirel (1997), the initial British focus was on liberalization and competition for telecom *infrastructure* rather than for telecom *services*. This focus was fueled by the dominant perception in Britain of the technical backwardness of the British telecom system in the early 1980s. It has drawn British liberalization somewhat away from what later became the EC focus (which was possible because Continental networks in the early 1990s were better developed than the British network in the early 1980s): providing interconnection at cost and reselling existing capacities. It has also given a special shape to the British telecom sector—in particular, with strong competition between BT and cable TV operators for local calls. In many respects, these remarks imply that assessing the costs of protection in EC telecoms by using the BFS benchmark tends to *underestimate* the gains from full liberalization.

---

43. In 1983, a "price-cap" regime was introduced in order to improve the functioning of the duopoly, but at the cost of increased regulations. Ex ante mandatory decreases of the real prices of telecom services have been imposed and monitored by a powerful regulatory body (OFTEL).

Table A.12b Case 22: A brief survey of the status of competition in EC telecoms, 1997–2001

	Competition with respect to PTOs				Digital mobile telecoms		
	Market shares of new operators[a]						
	Number of PSTNs (2001)	Local (1999)	National (1999)	Inter-national (1999)	Number of licensed operators (2001)	Market share of two largest operators (2000)	Restriction on foreign ownership (2001)
	1	2	3	4	5	6	7
Austria	65	1.8	15.0	n.a.	4	89	no
Belgium	19	0.0	n.a.	n.a.	3	98	no
Britain	487	15.4	n.a.	54.6	5	59	no
Denmark	n.a.	0.4	n.a.	43.7	4	82	no
Finland	126	0.4	62.1	48.5	4	99	no
France	49	0.0	20.0	27.1	3	84	20 percent[d]
Germany	173	1.0	40.0	40.0	4	85	no
Greece[c]	1	0.0	0.0	0.0	3	73	no
Ireland	46	2.4	n.a.	n.a.	3	100	no
Italy	n.a.	0.0	15.0	32.0	n.a.	95	no
Luxembourg	9	0.0	n.a.	n.a.	2	100	no
Netherlands	n.a.	0.1	16.0	15.0	5	85	no
Portugal	19	0.0	0.0	0.0	3	81	no
Spain	75	1.7	14.3	12.9	3	94	10 percent[e]
Sweden	30	1.0	14.0	38.0	4	83	no

n.a. = not available
AIC = average incremental cost
EDC = embedded direct costs
FDC = fully distributed costs
LRAIC = long-run average incremental cost
LRIC = long-run incremental costs
nyop = not yet operational
PSTNs = public switched telephone networks
PTOs = public telecom operators

The second lesson to be drawn from table A.12a is that the EC liberalization process has just started. The bulk of the EC liberalization effort was designed in the mid-1990s, but its implementation by member-states started only in the late 1990s, as is best illustrated by the Full Competition Directive, adopted in 1996 and enforced only since January 1998. If a noticeable portion of EC mobile telephones and data communications was opened by 1995, competition based on leased lines and PTO infrastructure started only in 1998, which happens to be the pivotal year for most of the OECD countries and the EC. The index (100 for 900) of total (fixed plus usage) telephone charges in the OECD countries was still at 94 (individuals) and 91 (business) in 1998 before declining to 83 and 68 respectively in 2000 (OECD 2001, 199). Price decreases show the same acceleration in the EC (European Commission 2000d).

De jure liberalization does not mean *effective* liberalization, as illustrated by table A.12b. Columns 1 to 7 show the main achievements of past liberalization. A large number of licensed telephone networks (PSTNs) are now operating in most of the EC member-states and substantial market shares have been taken by entrants in a handful of EC member-states (Denmark, Finland, Germany, Sweden, and Britain). However, local telephone mar-

Local access: Local loop unbundling		Planned cost method for inter-connection charges	Price for a 10-minute call (in August)					
			Local call		Intra-EC calls		EC to US calls	
Status (September 2000)	Year of full access[b]		Euros (2000)	Change (percent) (2000/1997)	Euros (2000)	Change (percent) (2000/1997)	Euros (2000)	Change (percent) (2000/1997)
8	9	10	11	12	13	14	15	16
yes	1999	FDC	64	31	310	-47	430	-53
no	(2001)	FDC	52	-10	470	-1	630	-21
nyop	(2000)	LRIC/FDC	56	0	400	0	330	0
yes	1998	FDC	33	9	170	-28	380	-30
yes	1996	Company specific	19	5	160	-28	500	-32
no	(2001)	FDC	42	-7	250	-44	250	-63
yes	1998	LRAIC	43	1	250	-50	250	-67
no		FDC	41	96	430	-39	430	-53
no		FDC	55	-13	170	-50	320	-37
nyop	(2000)	FDC	29	7	320	-45	320	-62
no		FDC	39	0	210	-54	210	-72
yes	2000	EDC	32	-13	80	-85	80	-91
no		FDC	33	-13	450	-44	520	-55
no	(2001)	Multistandard	35	42	460	-24	540	-31
no	(2000)	AIC	28	17	100	-51	100	-77

a. Share of switched minutes (percent).
b. Years for scheduled access are in parentheses.
c. Monopoly until 2001.
d. Restrictions on companies outside the European Economic Area for mobile phones.
e. Administrative authorization for acquiring more than 10 percent of Telefonica equity.

Sources: European Commission (2000d); OECD (2001).

kets remain almost completely protected in all the member-states (except Britain, to some extent). Similarly, all the EC member-states have at least three digital mobile phone operators, which have been a powerful source of competition for incumbent PTOs during the last three years. However, most EC mobile markets are still based on duopoly (as shown by the cumulated market share of the two largest mobile operators), except in Britain. Lastly, there is a remarkable absence of restrictions on foreign direct investment, except in France and, to a lesser extent, in Spain.

By contrast, columns 8 to 10 of table A.12b illustrate the pending issues that are crucial for the future success of the Internet in the EC. In early 2001, local access (local loop unbundling) was still not available, de jure or de facto, in most EC member-states, a situation that has induced the Commission to propose replacing 28 existing legal measures with 5 new directives (a new Framework directive and directives on authorization, access and interconnection, universal service, and data protection) coupled with a regulation on the unbundling of the local loop. Even more worrisome is the fact that the most common method for calculating the interconnection charges is FDC (fully distributed costs). The FDC method is often known to lead to prices that are at least 10 percent higher than those based on the more economically sound pricing method of long-run incremental costs (LRIC). This choice may be a substantial source of potential competitive distortions in EC telecom markets in the future.

Lastly, columns 11 to 16 of table A.12b provide information on the average prices for a 10-minute call (local, intra-EC, and EC to the United States) in August 2000 in the EC member-states and on their rate of decline between August 1997 and 2000 (it should be noted that the average EC price of a call from the EC to the United States is still higher than the price of the corresponding call from the United States to EC). These price evolutions reflect the mix of ongoing liberalizations and remaining obstacles. It is interesting to note that the price wedge between the BFS group and the rest of the EC may have slightly declined to 17–35 percent, compared to the wedge of the early and mid-1990s. But that is due to Britain: the price wedge between Finland and Sweden on the one hand and the rest of the EC on the other hand remains within the range of 20 to 135 percent, showing little sign that the rest of the EC is catching up with these two leading member-states.

The last two years show that governments and national regulatory agencies (NRAs) still have a heavy hand in markets. First, governments (not NRAs) are still involved in granting licenses (France and Germany) or in pricing controls (France and Spain). Second, NRAs dominate spectrum allocation and interconnection, as well as pricing controls (and their role will be enhanced by the 5 new directives mentioned above). If free individual negotiations on interconnection agreements are almost the rule, NRAs have considerable freedom to intervene (either directly or through review) in these contracts, which, in accordance to EC directives, should be based on costs plus benchmarks, although so far the EC has said little concrete on benchmarks. In sum, there are still noticeable risks of public intervention, all the more because the privatization process is far from completed in many member-states (Austria, Belgium, Finland, France, Germany, Greece, Luxembourg, the Netherlands, and Sweden) and because in almost all member-states, bodies of appeal are administrative courts that are particularly badly equipped to address the issues raised by the transition to a market-based environment.

The fact that telecoms are regulation-intensive multiplies the sources of potential conflict. For instance, equal access (consumers can select the carrier that will deliver calls to their final destination by dialing the same number of digits irrespective of the carrier's identity) can allow discriminatory treatment (for instance, in favor of network-based operators in Britain). Or there is the problem of being entrenched in legal battles (e.g., in France, the one-digit approach adopted for "national" operators implicitly meant that the authorities did not expect more than seven competitors, strongly underestimating the number of potential competitors). Another important pending issue is the coverage of the universal service concept in the EC. Its definition is potentially wider than in the United States, and member-states have a large degree of freedom for implementing it; for instance, the costs of the universal service fund were nil in Britain but have reached a peak of roughly €665 million in France since 1998.

All these observations lead to two concluding remarks. First, the future evolution of the EC liberalization in telecom services relies on the answer to a basic question: what is the Community's desired trade-off between market integration and intensity of competition? As stressed by Grout (1996), telecom services are the realm of differentiation at a time of huge technological progress; these forces push for price discrimination—therefore they should induce regulators to allow for maximum flexibility, hence for price discrimination between member-states. But to many European people, price discrimination is antagonistic to European integration. This key issue has been already raised in relation to goods within the context of the use of Article 30 and of the communitarization of EC trade policy.

The second remark concerns EC commitments in the WTO Telecommunications Agreement. At first glance, the EC final offer is very liberal: all services are open on a facilities and resale basis, with a few short delays (most of them only until 2000, except for Greece, until 2001).[44] However, table A.12b suggests viewing the liberality of these commitments with some caution. EC member-states still have enough regulatory discretion to restrain competition from non-EC firms. They are unlikely to use this power to block foreign entry completely. But they can use it to negotiate "reciprocal" entries from trading partners, or to force foreign firms to make joint ventures with domestic entrants, instead of entering the member-state market alone.

Notes

The following estimates of the costs of protection in the EC rely on two working hypotheses. First, as mentioned at the beginning of this case, costs of protection are assessed with respect to a "competitive" benchmark "country" (an aggregate of Finland, Sweden, and Britain), despite the fact that trials and errors in regulatory reform in these three countries may have limited the gains to be expected from full liberalization. This implies that the estimated costs of protection are likely to be underestimated—or, alternatively, our approach recognizes the fact that optimal regulations are not provided free of charge, without a costly trial and error process.

The second working hypothesis is that *all* (local, long distance, domestic, and international) telecom services are taken into account. Under pre-

---

44. Except the severe restraints related to broadcasting or the stringent restrictions on foreign-equity limits, with two member-states (France and Portugal) imposing ceilings of 20 and 25 percent, respectively.

vious noncompetitive regimes, local calls (and fixed user charges) were systematically underpriced in relative terms, whereas nonlocal calls were always overpriced. As already mentioned, liberalizing telecom services imposes a rebalancing of prices between the former and latter calls. However, recent developments in telecom technology and competition suggest that even local calls will benefit from regulatory reform (this point was questioned a few years ago). On the basis of these hypotheses, the non-British EC telecom market in 1990 amounted to €62.7 billion. Using the import-export proportion of Eurostat estimates (unfortunately, based on balance of payments), extra-EC (non-British) imports and exports can be estimated at €3.2 billion and €3 billion, leaving an intra-EC (non-British) market of €56.5 billion.

The ad valorem equivalent of the protection granted to EC PTOs is mirrored by the price difference between call prices in member-states sticking to old regulatory regimes and call prices in the more competitively based regulatory framework introduced in Finland, Sweden, and Britain. The OECD regularly publishes access charges and expenses for a representative basket of phone calls. Data for 1990 suggest a price wedge on calls between the "BFS" reference and the other EC member-states of 45.2 percent. This figure has been taken as the ad valorem equivalent of the delayed liberalization of EC telecom.

Demand price elasticities of long-distance services vary from 0.25 to 1.2, depending on the type of services to be provided (Hausman, Tardiff, and Belinfante 1993), with 0.7 as the most frequent estimate (Crandall and Waverman 1996, 162). For nonlocal calls, authors tend to choose price elasticities in the upper range: from 0.49 (suggested as a short-run estimate; Kahai, Kaserman, and Mayo 1996), to 0.4 (national long-distance calls) or 0.6 (international calls) (OFTEL 1995), to near unity (Waverman and Sirel 1998). Domestic supply price elasticity has been estimated only once; the available estimate of 4.48 (Kahai, Kaserman, and Mayo 1996) for fringe suppliers seems reasonable when one considers that a majority of EC member-states enjoy large available infrastructures (if one includes those owned by railways, electricity companies, etc.) and that new entrants' market shares have increased from 0 to 60 percent in certain cases. However, a supply elasticity of 2 has been used, to remain on the safe side. Last, it has seemed reasonable to adopt a substantial elasticity of substitution of 3. As a result, elasticities of 0.8, 2, and 3 (for demand, supply, and substitution, respectively) have been used to estimate the costs of protection.

Appendix B
EC Contingent Protection: Antidumping and Other Trade Instruments

After a brief survey of the EC antidumping cases initiated between 1980 and 1999, the first section of this appendix examines whether EC antidumping cases are dealing with competition issues. It reaches the conclusion that they are not—a conclusion that completes one of the chapter 4 results (antidumping measures are procartel actions). The second section briefly presents the other instruments of contingent protection available to the EC.

Antidumping

As is well known, the EC's most important instrument of contingent protection is the antidumping regulation, which was lately amended several times, in 1995, 1996, and 1998 (for a survey of the post-Uruguay EC regulations from a legal perspective, see Bronckers [1995]). These repeated amendments aim at conforming the EC provisions to the Uruguay Antidumping Agreement, but they also reflect tense negotiations between member-states on EC's internal procedures, such as the voting system for adopting or rejecting antidumping measures. Conflicts between EC member-states, and between member-states and the Commission, have been recurrent. They have even generated proposals by member-states to shift antidumping enforcement out of the Commission to an "independent" (from the Commission, not from the Council) authority, although it is hard to know whether these proposals were genuine, or prompted by pressure for tougher use of antidumping (the French proposal on such an independent authority followed a series of failures to adopt antidumping measures in cotton fabric cases requested by small, but politically powerful, French firms).

From a WTO consistency perspective (a point of some interest, although far from being one of the most essential aspects of the antidumping problem, as underlined in chapter 4), the existing EC antidumping regulations raise two main issues. First, they include two procedures that are not covered by the Uruguay Antidumping Agreement: an 'antiabsorption' procedure (dealing with prices that are not increased by the full amount of the imposed antidumping duties) and an 'anticircumvention' procedure (dealing with assembly operations in the EC or in third countries, or other similar practices, which could allow escaping payment of antidumping duties [Holmes 1995]). Both these procedures have been subject to recent inquiries by WTO members (one may recall that following a complaint by Japan, the initial EC anticircumvention procedure introduced in 1987 to target Japanese 'screwdriver plants' in the electronics sector had been found inconsistent with GATT provisions before the end of the Uruguay Round).

Second, the WTO Antidumping Agreement requires WTO members to make available judicial review mechanisms that enable the "prompt" review of antidumping measures. Such mechanisms are hardly available in the EC: procedures are cumbersome, slow, and hardly available to exporters who did not participate in the antidumping investigation. (The best way to challenge antidumping measures may be to go to national courts.) Moreover, the EC Court of Justice and the national courts have consistently refused to look at the substance of the cases: they have limited their decisions to cases of manifest errors of law by the Commission. The only case (the 1988 calcium metal case) where the Court of Justice looked at substance—by underlining the necessity to take into account the impact of the adopted antidumping measures on the level of competition in the markets involved—has ultimately delivered a very negative signal: a few months after the Court's ruling, the Commission Trade Directorate General reinitiated the case *ex officio*, and the new investigation has led to duties more than three times higher than the initial ones, sending a clear message that antidumping measures dominate competition aspects (all the more because the Court and the Commission Competition Directorate General did not react).

A Census of EC Antidumping Cases, 1980–99

Table B.1 presents the total number of EC antidumping cases by year for the period 1980–99. EC antidumping cases are defined as complaints

Table B.1 Major outcomes of EC antidumping cases, 1980–99

| | All cases | Provisional measures | | | Definitive measures | | | | | | | "Direct impact" ratio[a] |
| | | | | | Ad valorem duties | | | Specific duties | | Undertakings | | |
Year	(total number)	Number of cases	MDG	AvD	Number of cases	MDG	AvD	Number of cases	MDG	Number of cases	MDG	
1980	25	12	14.1	13.2	11	13.4	11.7			1	9.6	48.0
1981	47	10	49.9	23.6	2	21.6	22.0	1	41.8	31	39.5	72.3
1982	55	24	46.6	22.6	6	44.1	19.6	9	49.8	25	45.0	72.7
1983	43	13	33.2	17.0	3	17.7	19.7	3	46.3	21	22.1	62.8
1984	42	11	44.0	19.4	6	33.5	17.3			17	38.0	54.8
1985	35	3	79.6	18.0	3	79.5	17.4			17	57.9	57.1
1986	31	21	64.2	26.0	5	47.6	26.5	3	50.7	13	57.3	67.7
1987	36	25	33.0	19.7	16	20.8	16.2	4	49.3			55.6
1988	43	18	32.7	16.4	9	19.6	17.0	5	32.0	10	33.9	55.8
1989	28	10	49.5	34.2	4	45.1	28.2	1	38.7			17.9
1990	45	28	30.1	18.2	20	22.7	16.3	7	45.6	6	20.1	73.3
1991	24	14	37.5	24.2	10	54.7	37.4	3	49.7	4	30.1	70.8
1992	42	23	29.7	20.9	13	22.2	20.6	8	47.7	2	37.5	54.8
1993	21	19	41.8	41.8	9	38.8	38.7	7	43.6	1	33.3	81.0
1994	44	20	45.7	40.1	11	37.8	35.0	5	52.5	4	54.4	45.5
1995	36	12	40.2	27.9	16	38.1	25.0	3	19.6			52.8
1996	28	20	23.1	22.8	11	37.0	37.3	2	18.2	4	15.2	60.7
1997	50	37	36.3	25.8	24	48.2	28.3	1	31.7	6	13.3	62.0
1998	24	16	50.3	35.3	3	38.0	30.6			11	56.1	58.3
1999	67	41	27.4	21.5	28	28.9	23.0	5	41.2	6	35.7	58.2
	Sum	Sum	Average	Average	Sum	Average	Average	Sum	Average	Sum	Average	
All years	766	377	37.6	24.7	210	33.5	24.2	67	43.7	179	39.5	59.5
1980–84	212	70	38.6	18.4	28	25.3	16.2	13	48.4	95	36.5	64.2
1985–89	173	77	45.4	22.5	37	31.5	19.2	13	42.1	40	51.7	52.0
1990–94	176	104	36.1	29.0	63	32.6	27.0	30	47.3	17	33.3	62.5
1995–99	205	126	33.5	25.5	82	37.8	27.1	11	30.3	27	36.0	58.5

AvD = ad valorem antidumping duties (see text)
MDG = margin of dumping (percent).

a. Number of cases terminated by official measures, as a percentage of all the cases initiated.

Sources: EC Official Journal; author's computations.

lodged by EC producers and initiated by the Commission for a given product and exporting country. There current or expiring cases. However, table B.1 leaves aside the reviews, despite the fact that they can extend two or three times the time length of the measures (in fact, reviews largely annihilate the impact of the five-year "sunset" clause imposed by the Uruguay Antidumping Agreement).[1] Moreover, table B.1 gives a limited view of EC antidumping activity to the extent that there is no information about the cases for which the Commission has received an antidumping complaint, but that it has rejected: these cases are said to represent at least one-third of the officially initiated complaints, and they may have an indirect protectionist (deterrent) impact.

Table B.1 shows two main results. First, there is no correlation between the initiation of cases and the EC business cycle. EC antidumping enforcement became stable after a peak in the early 1980s. This peak could leave the impression of a relationship between increased demand for protection and the more difficult economic conditions of the time; but it is smaller than the previous peak, which occurred in the late 1970s, despite a better economic environment then. The 1999 peak is not related to the EC business cycle: 1999 was the best year for EC growth in a decade or two (this peak in EC antidumping was justified by the Commission because of alleged dumping by Asian firms, after the Asian financial crisis).

Second, table B.1 reveals the frequency, rapidity, and severity of EC antidumping measures. EC cases can be terminated by four different measures: ad valorem duties, specific duties, undertakings (commitments by foreign firms to raise their export prices in the EC market to an agreed level or to restrict their quantities exported to the EC to an agreed level), or no official measure of protection (because of no dumping or no injury, or because the Community is not interested in taking such a measure) and withdrawal of their complaint by the plaintiffs.[2]

Table B.1 allows for three observations. First, the likelihood of measures of protection is high, as shown by the average of 61 percent for the "impact" ratio (the number of cases not terminated by negative outcomes, as

---

1. As a result, it is difficult to give a precise mean duration of the measures enforced since it depends on the definition of what a "case" is (does it include reviews or extensions?). A conservative estimate is six to seven years for the EC cases (compared to four years in Australia and 11 years in the United States) (CBO 1998). However, it is not rare to find in the EC *Official Journal* the official recognition of a much longer duration: for instance, 11 years on ferrosilicium imported from Brazil (EC *Official Journal*, L42, 14 February 1998, 1), 13 years on artificial corundum from China (EC *Official Journal*, L276, 9 October 1997, 9), etc.

2. A case can be terminated by a mix of these five basic outcomes (such mixed outcomes are not shown independently in table B.1). All the estimates presented in this section are unweighted averages of the antidumping duties imposed on specific firms and of the antidumping "residual" duties (i.e., the duties imposed on firms that have not provided information during the investigations or on firms that have not been taken into account for various reasons during the investigations) when these residual duties have been expressly mentioned in the EC *Official Journal*.

a percentage of the total number of cases). This direct impact ratio provides a *minimal* estimate of the impact of EC antidumping activity because it does not take into account the withdrawals of complaints, which can be the result of private agreements between EC plaintiffs and foreign firms, and because it ignores the fact that the termination of the investigation by a "no dumping" or "no injury" conclusion can send a clear message to foreign firms to restrain their competitive pressures in the future.

The second observation is that almost 50 percent of the cases initiated are subject to provisional measures, which are taken rapidly (within a few months) and which already represent high trade barriers (on average, roughly 24 percent).[3] This feature becomes more marked with time.

The third observation is that the average amount of the *definitive* antidumping duties imposed during the entire period is 24 percent—two to three times the EC average *ad valorem* applied GATT tariffs, and may increase further (see table 2.1). This feature also becomes more marked with time: average antidumping duties have increased from 16 percent in the early 1980s to 27 percent in the late 1990s. This result leaves aside the *ad valorem* equivalents of specific duties, undertakings, or mixed measures on which information is scarce. However, available *ad hoc* evidence suggests that all these measures are also very high—the dumping margins on which they are based being generally higher than those leading to *ad valorem* antidumping duties (see table B.1).

Information on the number of tariff lines and average antidumping measures by industry has already been provided in table 2.1 (see chapter 2). It suffices to say here that the mere number of cases (the "unit" of information used in this appendix) does not fully reflect the level of "harassment" accompanying a substantial number of cases. Harassment can flow from recurrent cases: a noticeable number of tariff lines are common to several antidumping cases (and are increasing since the late 1990s, see chapter 2), as best illustrated by the 1994, 1996, and 1997 cotton fabric cases. It can also be observed within a given case: for instance, between April 1998 and May 1999, the 1996 Atlantic salmon case led to no fewer than 10 different decisions on the measures to be imposed, with a strongly protectionist drift from an initial decision imposing a specific duty on "salmon" to a final decision establishing a set of minimum prices on 12 types of salmon products.

Table B.2 provides basic information on the coverage of antidumping cases by trading partner. From an economic perspective, such information is less important than the breakdown of cases by industry. But it sheds

---

3. All the estimates presented in this appendix are unweighted (as they should be) averages of the antidumping duties imposed on specific firms and of the antidumping "residual" duties (i.e., the duties imposed on firms that have not provided information during the investigations or on firms that have not been taken into account for various reasons during the investigations) when these residual duties have been expressly mentioned in the EC *Official Journal*.

Table B.2 EC antidumping cases: Shares in cases by trading partner, 1980–99

Group/country	All cases (total number)	Provisional measures			Definitive measures							"Direct impact" ratio[a]
					Ad valorem duties			Specific duties		Undertakings		
		Number of cases	MDG	AvD	Number of cases	MDG	AvD	Number of cases	MDG	Number of cases	MDG	
1980–89												
OECD countries	146	55	29.7	17.5	34	20.5	15.0	7	41.1	37	38.8	53.4
Portugal, Spain	20	3	19.4	15.0	1	25.6	14.2	2	11.2	6	30.5	45.0
Austria, Finland, Sweden	11	2	31.8	4.9	1	6.1	6.7			6	19.1	63.6
EEA, EFTA members	5									3	26.8	60.0
Turkey	10	4	18.8	13.0	2	13.9	8.8			2	59.8	40.0
Yugoslavia	28	10	42.5	16.1	3	25.7	16.1	3	46.2	9	52.8	53.6
United States	28	15	13.8	13.8	14	13.4	11.8			6	49.6	71.4
Japan	36	17	37.2	25.2	13	28.8	19.9			3	30.8	44.4
Other OECD countries	8	4	42.9	15.0				2	63.3	2	37.1	50.0
Non-OECD countries	239	92	49.7	22.6	31	38.0	20.7	19	46.8	98	41.8	61.9
Central Europe	106	26	59.0	25.7	3	46.0	22.4	4	62.3	67	43.8	69.8
Eastern Europe	20	11	83.6	19.1	4	72.1	22.9	3	89.9	7	59.9	70.0
Euro-Med countries	4	1	5.8	5.8				1	5.8			25.0
Asian Tigers	37	14	25.9	13.8	10	20.5	13.6	2	31.5	3	12.5	40.5
China	26	16	55.9	30.2	7	46.5	28.3	2	56.9	8	37.7	65.4
Other Asian countries	8	4	32.3	19.1	1	6.7	6.7	2	40.8	1	58.0	50.0
Mercosur countries	15	7	24.4	13.2				3	16.6	6	25.3	60.0
Mexico, South Africa	9	5	32.8	20.3	3	26.3	15.9	2	28.4	2	37.7	77.8
Other countries	14	8	48.6	28.6	3	44.8	31.8			4	30.4	50.0
All countries	385	147	42.2	20.7	65	28.9	17.7	26	45.3	135	41.0	58.7

1990–99

OECD countries	61	26	41.8	23.0	20	50.5	33.4	5	60.8	8	29.2	54.1
Portugal, Spain	2	6	14.1	13.1	3	16.1	11.7	1	10.6	1	11.2	100.0
Austria, Finland, Sweden												
EEA, EFTA members	16	3	41.6	29.0	1	56.1	15.4			2	19.4	31.3
Turkey	10	5	52.1	21.2	3	31.3	21.4	2	88.3	5	36.7	60.0
Yugoslavia	8	11	54.3	28.8	12	66.1	45.1	2	58.4			62.5
United States	23	1	19.6	13.6	1	18.0	12.0					60.9
Japan	2											50.0
Other OECD countries												
Non-OECD countries	320	204	33.8	27.5	125	33.1	26.0	36	40.0	36	36.3	61.6
Central Europe	42	29	21.3	19.5	5	27.7	17.6	4	26.1	20	21.1	69.0
Eastern Europe	41	24	49.1	41.1	7	34.1	31.0	16	46.1	6	57.9	70.7
Euro-Med countries	8	5	16.0	16.4	1	12.7	11.7			2	35.6	37.5
Asian Tigers	65	36	21.7	19.0	34	21.3	18.1	11	41.0			52.3
P.R. China	59	39	47.8	39.9	26	56.7	38.9	2	5.8	4	45.1	62.7
Other Asian countries	82	59	29.8	26.6	44	30.3	25.5	2	43.7	1	12.3	61.0
Mercosur countries	10	7	36.1	25.3	5	22.6	19.3	1	46.8	3	90.7	80.0
Mexico, South Africa	9	4	80.1	45.2	2	34.1	37.4					66.7
Other countries	4	1	36.8	3.9	1	40.0	16.8					25.0
All countries	381	230	34.7	26.9	145	35.5	27.0	41	42.5	44	35.0	60.4
1980–99												
All countries	766	377	37.6	24.5	210	33.5	24.7	67	43.7	179	39.5	59.5

AvD = ad valorem antidumping duties (see text)
EEA = European Economic Association.
EFTA = European Free Trade Association.
MDG = margin of dumping (percent).
OECD = Organization for Economic Cooperation and Development.

a. Number of cases terminated by official measures, as a percentage of all the cases initiated.

Sources: EC Official Journal; author's computations.

some light on the relations between the EC and its trading partners: as a result, table B.2 groups these partners by the type of agreements with the EC.[4] It provides five main results. First, there is a shift (in absolute and relative terms) of the main targets of the EC antidumping activity, away from OECD countries to non-OECD countries—in particular, the Asian Tigers, China, and other Asian emerging economies (this geographical shift mirrors a change in the EC industries using antidumping procedures, and, in particular, the emergence of the electronics and textile industries as heavy users). Second, being candidates to the EC or being close to concluding a preferential trade agreement with it does not necessarily grant protection from EC antidumping, as best shown by the Central European and EuroMed countries. Third, the frequency of provisional measures largely differs by country: less than 50 percent for most of the OECD countries, but up to 70 percent for Central Europe, China, EuroMed, Mercosur, and other Asian countries. Fourth, the level of antidumping duties imposed varies hugely—with peaks on imports from Japan, Mexico, South Africa, and the nonmarket economies (former USSR and China). Lastly, the type of antidumping measures differs noticeably, with countries under preferential agreements getting undertakings more easily than the others.

Antidumping and Predation

Is there any evidence that EC antidumping cases have been related to "monopolizing" behavior (predation or strategic dumping) from foreign exporters? Inquiries about antidumping cases as protecting competition from predation are mostly related to the importing market, whereas inquiries about strategic dumping are more related to the exporters' markets. Because this appendix relies on the information provided in the antidumping procedures published by the EC *Official Journal*, it is adequately equipped only to examine predation. What follows thus presents five successive simple tests ("screens") about the following question: is there any evidence showing that antidumping cases are antipredation cases (for details, see Bourgeois and Messerlin 1998)?[5]

---

4. EEA and EFTA members include Iceland, Norway, and Switzerland. The other OECD countries refer to the 1985 definition of the OECD. Central Europe includes the countries under the Europe Agreements (except Slovenia); Eastern Europe refers to the former USSR (except the Baltics); the Asian Tigers include Hong Kong, Korea, Macau, Singapore, and Taiwan; and the other Asian countries cover all the emerging economies (from Indonesia, Malaysia, or Thailand to India or the Philippines).

5. The method used has the advantage of relying exclusively on information published in the official proceedings of EC antidumping cases—hence on sources that are not biased in favor of the conclusion finally reached by the appendix (i.e., there is almost no evidence of antidumping as an antipredation device).

The first screen aims to assess the capacity of the foreign firms involved in antidumping cases to behave as predators. At first glance, it seems reasonable to assume that plausible predatory behavior would require as a precondition a *dominant* position of the foreign firm in the EC market. Under such a hypothesis, a precise set of circumstances for predation must coexist: (1) very important static or dynamic economies of scale for producing the good in question; (2) a large size of the exporter's home market, both in absolute and relative (vis-à-vis the EC markets) terms; (3) closure of the exporter's home market to EC firms (either because EC firms cannot export to the exporter's home market, or because they do not own subsidiaries in the exporter's home market); and (4) significant size of each independent exporter's share of the home market.

Absent this set of circumstances, a foreign firm with a small market share in the EC markets is unlikely to behave as a predator; it could not quickly supply a dominant part of the EC market, and lacking dominance, it would be unable to exercise market power. The concrete criteria used to assess possible dominance are drawn from the history of competition enforcement in the EC, which, in general, suggests a market share of 40 percent as necessary for a dominant position.

However, an approach much more severe than this reasonable hypothesis has been adopted in the appendix to allow for the possibility of rapid entry of foreign firms into EC markets—that is, to allow for very successful predation. Instead of merely screening out all the antidumping cases where a foreign firm would have an observed market share lower than 40 percent of the EC market for the last year examined by the antidumping investigation, the first screen is based on the foreign firm's *forecasted* market share, namely, the foreign market shares that would have existed in the first year *after* the year of the decision to take (or not) antidumping measures. Because of the average duration of antidumping investigations, this approach assumes that when EC petitioners make the decision to launch a complaint, they are looking two years ahead. Moreover, the forecasting method chosen is very conservative, so that it tends to provide high estimates of the computed market shares.[6]

A last problem has to be solved. In many cases, EC antidumping proceedings do not provide market shares by individual foreign firm. They merely provide the aggregate EC market share of all the foreign firms involved in the same case, whether these firms are originating from one or

---

6. The forecasting method chosen rests on the annual compound growth rate computed on the basis of the initial and final market shares given by the official investigations. These calculated growth rates are then used to extrapolate the market shares that the foreign firms would have enjoyed in the EC market for the product examined one year after the end of the investigation and after the imposition of the antidumping measures (should these measures not have been taken). Because this approach ignores the likely correlation between low growth rates and large foreign firms' market shares, it tends to overestimate the likelihood of predation—and all the more when foreign firm market shares start from a very low base.

several exporting countries. For all these cases, the first screen thus tests for forecasted aggregate market share of 40 percent or more held by foreign firms in the EC—making the approach adopted in the appendix even more conservative. In sum, the first screen eliminates only the cases where the foreign firms' market shares—once extrapolated (for the year following the decision about imposing antidumping measures), and aggregated when no data by exporting firm are available—are lower than 40 percent.

This severe first screen can be imposed on only the 461 cases (out of 658 cases initiated between 1980 and 1997) for which information on foreign market shares in the EC markets is available in the official proceedings. Table B.3 presents the breakdown of the 461 cases by industry. The 197 cases left out of this first screen (because of no available information) can be split into three groups. First, there are anticircumvention cases, which are the aftermath of some of the 461 antidumping cases eliminated by the screening procedure at one stage or another. Second, there are cases not terminated by *official* antidumping measures (including the cases terminated by the withdrawal of the complaint by the EC firms); however, one should consider the possibility that these antidumping procedures have been used (at least partly) to monitor or enforce "grey area" barriers. Third, there are a few cases terminated by antidumping measures but for which the official proceedings give no information.

Table B.3 shows that the first test screens out 311 cases of the 461 cases examined. It seems useful to test the robustness of this result—by assuming even longer forward forecasts—with the following question: How often would the market share threshold of 40 percent have been reached during the second year (or the third year, etc.) after the end of the investigation? The answer is: not often. The 40 percent threshold is projected to have been reached in only 55 additional cases during the second year after the investigation (i.e., two to three years after the lodging of the complaints and the initiation of the investigations), in 93 cases (including the previous 55) during the third year, in 132 cases (including the previous 93) during the fourth year, and in 165 (including the previous 132) cases during the fifth year—only half of the 311 cases screened out. As a result, the market share reached at the end of the first year seems a robust basis for the screening exercise.

The second screen examines the 150 cases left by the first screen; it consists of eliminating the cases terminated by a *negative outcome*. There is no reason to consider antidumping cases a response to predatory behavior where the EC investigations have concluded that "no injury" or "no dumping" was present.[7] When the information is based on market share

---

7. A foreign firm can behave as a predator in its home and export market without "dumping." This possibility is not covered by GATT Article VI in a straightforward manner—confirming that antidumping has never been really concerned with predation per se.

Table B.3 Five tests for screening EC antidumping cases, 1980–97

ISIC Code	Industry	Total number of cases	Cases with information		Cases left after screen				
			Number	Percent	No. 1	No. 2	No. 3	No. 4	No. 5
321	Textiles	64	36	56.3	8	8	2	1	
331	Wood products	27	7	25.9					
351	Industrial chemicals	204	164	80.4	53	46	19	16	5
362	Glass products	13	13	100.0	12	12			
369	Other nonmetals	17	12	70.6	1				
371	Iron and steel	86	67	77.9	14	13	4	1	1
372	Nonferrous metals	24	16	66.7	3	2	2	2	2
381	Metal products	24	21	87.5	10	10	4	4	
382	Nonelectrical machines	41	23	56.1	5	5	5	1	
383	Electrical machines	81	49	60.5	17	16	9	4	
	Subtotal	581	408	70.2	123	112	45	29	8
	Other industries	77	53	68.8	27	24	16	15	4
	Total	658	461	70.1	150	136	61	44	12

Sources: EC Official Journal; author's calculations.

for all the exporters involved in the same case, a conservative approach has been taken; only cases terminated by negative outcomes for all the countries involved have been eliminated. On the basis of this conservative assumption, 14 cases can be screened out—leaving 136 cases to be examined more closely in the third screen.

The third screen takes into account the *number of countries* involved in a given case. The two previous screens have been based on the implicit assumption that all the foreign firms are able to collude perfectly for predatory behavior whether or not they are based in different countries. It seems reasonable to relax this hypothesis. If four or more countries are involved in simultaneous antidumping actions on the same product, the possibility of joint predatory behavior seems rather low; collusion between firms coming from so many countries (and particularly from nonmarket economies, as is often the case) would have required a level of coordination and consistency that is implausibly high.[8] Table B.3 shows that 75 cases can be screened out on this basis.

The fourth screen looks at the 61 cases left by the third screen. It aims to take into account another aspect of the costs of colluding: the *number of firms* involved in a given case. If a case involves eight or more different firms, the possibility of predatory behavior seems rather low, because the costs of colluding required by joint predatory behavior among so many firms are likely to be very high, and because the costs of maintaining a "joint monopoly" in such circumstances are likely to be even higher. The figure chosen—of eight firms—happens to be convenient for several reasons: there is no case with six firms; several cases with eight firms involve two different trading partners; and if one excepts four cases with nine firms, all the other cases involve 10 to 19 different firms. This fourth test screens out 17 more cases, leaving 44 cases—already less than 10 percent of the total number of cases under examination in this screening procedure.

The fifth and last test introduces the information available on the *EC firms* involved in the 44 remaining cases, which can be divided into two groups. Group I consists of 16 cases for which the only additional information available on the EC firms is their number. Although this limited information does not allow us to go very far, in two cases, foreign firms held market shares that were very small (4.5 and 6.1 percent) in the final period examined in the official investigations, whereas these firms faced five and nine EC firms, respectively. Both reasons (low foreign market shares and many EC competitors) do not suggest the existence of noncompetitive markets favorable to predatory behavior. It thus seems reasonable to screen out these two cases and to leave the remaining 14 cases of Group I without a definitive conclusion because of the lack of information.

---

8. The criteria used for the last two screens are usually those most commonly found in the economic literature (see, e.g., Scherer 1980, 56–57).

For the 28 cases of Group II, information is available on the number of EC firms and on their aggregate market shares (for both the initial and final periods considered in the investigations) of EC consumption. Hence, it is possible to compute two Herfindahl-Hirshmann indices (HHIs) for each of the two periods.[9] Minimum HHIs are based on the assumption that the aggregate market share for the foreign firms is split equally among them and that the aggregate market share for the EC firms is split equally among them. Maximum HHIs are based on the assumption that all foreign firms except one have market shares close to zero and all EC firms except one have market shares close to zero.[10]

These indices allow the division of the 28 cases into three subsets. First, four cases have both minimum and maximum indices in the final period lower than the threshold of 0.18; thus they can be safely screened out. Second, 12 cases exhibit minimum HHIs lower than 0.18 (for both the initial and final periods) and maximum indices higher than 0.18 (also for both the initial and final periods): despite such a high stability of the pairs of indices, a definitive conclusion is not possible without information on individual market shares by firm. Third, 12 cases exhibit both minimum and maximum HHIs higher than 0.18 in the final period.

To conclude, the final test of the 44 antidumping cases having passed the four previous screens suggests keeping these last 12 cases—that is, only 2 percent of the 461 cases screened—as *mere* possible candidates for a closer examination of possible predatory behavior. This conclusion is very conservative for three reasons: seven of these 12 cases exhibit declining or stable minimum and maximum HHIs between the initial and final periods; four other cases involve China (for which our HHI estimates always assume the existence of one producer and exporter, and hence systematically underestimate the level of competition and overestimate the HHIs); and none of these 12 cases involves sophisticated products for which entry barriers could be high.

Four Final Comments

In sum, the past 20 years of EC antidumping enforcement have clearly not addressed predation issues. This result—which is similar to what has been found for US antidumping cases (Shin 1997)—deserves four important final remarks.

---

9. The Herfindahl-Hirshmann index (HHI) is defined as the sum of the squares of the market shares held by all the firms operating in the market examined. An index close to zero means that the market is not concentrated (there are many firms with similar weights), whereas an index close to one means that the market is close to monopoly (there is one firm with a very large market share).

10. Maximum HHIs have been computed by assuming that all foreign firms but one have zero market shares and that all EC firms but one have zero market shares.

First, these five tests have examined only the mere possibility of the existence of the *first* stage of predatory pricing: the acquisition of a large market share. But they have not looked at the *second* (and necessary) stage of a predatory pricing analysis: the capacity to exercise and keep market power once a large market share is obtained—a stage that the theoretical and empirical studies of industrial organization suggest as very difficult.[11]

Second, antidumping actions are industrial disputes more than international conflicts. There are many cases where EC complaining firms are owners of the respondents or of the firms used for determining the dumping margins, where foreign respondents supply EC complaining firms, where foreign firms export from several countries to the EC, where foreign firms produce in the Community, and so on. All these links make assessing the existence of predation more complex. In particular, the screening tests have ignored an alternative hypothesis for the emergence of dominant positions by foreign exporters: the fall of highly dominant positions held by EC firms.[12]

Third, there have been endless suggestions for "improving" (making less protectionist) the EC antidumping regime. One of the most interesting set of suggestions comes from the Kommerskollegium (1999) in Sweden, because it reflects the views of the "free trade" group of EC member-states. After noting the risk of even more protectionist use of the antidumping instrument by the EC, once Central European countries accede to the EC, the Kommerskollegium suggests 10 recommendations: (1) dumping should be the *principal* cause of material injury; (2) "*double*" protection (antidumping measures on top of quantitative restrictions) should not be allowed; (3) measures should last 5 years *at most*; (4) the Commission should produce short *disclosure* documents; (5) *cumulation* should be restricted (and banned under WTO rules)[13]; (6) "*zeroing*" (only export transactions that have been found dumped are used to calculate dumping margins) should be abandoned (all export transactions should be used); (7) *repeated* initiations in a short period of time should not be allowed; (8)

---

11. The EC and US competition laws are very different with respect to predation. The US law requires the recoup step (*Brooke Group* case, 1992), whereas the EC law requires showing the existence of pricing below marginal cost (*Tetrapak* case), making predation similar to price discrimination.

12. This is a hypothesis well documented in 1 of the 12 cases left by the five tests: In the glycine case against Japan (1984), the EC antidumping proceedings discuss the point that EC antidumping measures might protect the sole EC competitor more than they protect competition.

13. Tharakhan et al (1998) have shown the huge impact of cumulation on the type and level of antidumping measures taken: cumulation increases the probability of taking an antidumping measure by nearly 42 percent, and the capacity to find injury by about two in cases terminated by undertakings. It should be noted that the European Commission, unlike the US antidumping authorities, is not obliged to follow that practice.

aggregating products under the *"one single product"* procedure should be restricted; (9) the EC member-states should get *more* time before meetings in the WTO antidumping committees (currently they get only half an hour in the morning on the day of the meeting); and (10) the *"de minimis"* rule should be expanded (and EC practices conformed totally with WTO requirements). In this context, it is interesting to note that the recent (2001) WTO dispute settlement requested by India against an EC case (bed linen) has led to an Appellate Body ruling stating that "zeroing" (suggestion f) is inconsistent with the Uruguay Antidumping Agreement.

Lastly, in recent years, certain EC exports have been subject to an increasing number of antidumping measures taken by EC trading partners—roughly 50 cases per year since 1997. One may argue that this situation may induce the EC to be less active in implementing its own antidumping regulations. This argument is not very convincing for two reasons. First, the markets closed to EC products by foreign antidumping measures are generally much smaller than the EC markets closed to foreign products—a situation unlikely to be perceived by the Commission or the EC member-states as a reason to constrain the use of antidumping by EC firms (and the persistence of EC antidumping cases against US imports confirms the weakness of the argument). Second, many foreign antidumping cases echo EC antidumping cases: they deal with the same or very similar goods (canned fruit, paperboard, LdPE and PVC-based products, steel goods, ball bearings, etc.). In other words, they may contribute to the same goal as the corresponding EC cases—segmenting the world markets—and, to that extent, they may well be seen as a "positive" development by EC plaintiffs.

Other EC Trade Instruments

There are four major trade instruments in the EC legal apparatus. First, there are two EC antisubsidy regulations (one for iron and steel products subject to the Treaty of Paris, the other for all other products) with their latest versions reflecting the WTO Agreement on Subsidies and Countervailing Measures. Until 1996, these regulations were barely used: ten cases were initiated between 1977 and 1983, and only two between 1984 and 1996. These antisubsidy cases duplicated antidumping cases, and antisubsidy measures were not enforced (only antidumping measures were). Since 1996, one witnesses an increasing use of this instrument by the EC—mostly against India, South Korea, and Saudi Arabia on steel and chemicals (polypropylene, polyethylene).

These few recent cases, which often echo antidumping cases, deserve two remarks. One, antisubsidy investigations have allowed the EC to indirectly take into account some new arguments in favor of protection, such as the trade and labor issue; for instance, the investigation in the salmon case against Norway has examined whether differentiated social security schemes constitute countervailable subsidies. Two, the antisubsidy procedures have been subject to biases leading to protectionist measures (in particular, a very limited scope for deductions) as shown in detail by Waer and Vermulst (1999).

Second, the Trade Barriers Regulation (TBR, nicknamed EC Section 301) came into force in January 1995. If trading activities in third countries are being affected by obstacles imposed by a foreign country, or if there is a threat of future damage, an individual firm, group of firms, or EC member-state can submit a formal complaint to the Commission for investigation. Trade barriers include tariffs and nontariff barriers to trade in goods and services, and the protection of TRIPS and they include practices forbidden by the WTO rules as well as those not forbidden but considered as having adverse trade effects on EC firms (it must be shown that EC company exports or imports are being prevented, impeded, or diverted). About 15 cases have been submitted to the TBR procedure, covering a wide range of countries, products, services, and intellectual property rights: leather (Argentina and Japan), cognac, sorbitol, and regional aircraft (Brazil), pharmaceuticals (Korea), musical works (Thailand and the United States), geographical indication (Canada), and the US Antidumping Act of 1916. The TBR has been related to the "market access database" initiative, which allows the Commission to collect the information provided by EC firms on trade barriers in third countries (echoing similar initiatives in the United States and Japan). A key goal of the TBR is to prepare the initiation of WTO dispute settlement cases by the EC: indeed, many of the above cases have led to EC complaints in the WTO dispute settlement system.

Third, there is an antidumping regulation in the shipping services industry, the first-ever antidumping procedure in services. It has been used only once (against the Hyundai Shipping Company operating between Europe and the Pacific Islands), clearly to protect the existing market-sharing of the route between EC shipping companies. There is also an instrument concerning the sale of newly built ships, the so-called Injurious Pricing Regulation. Application of this regulation has been suspended pending the ratification by the United States of the OECD agreement on shipbuilding and ship repairing, but the EC threatens to initiate a WTO dispute settlement case against Korean subsidies.

Fourth, the EC (following a request by a member-state) can impose safeguard measures in accordance with GATT Article XIX. (These measures can be Community-wide or regional, that is, for specific member-states.) There is no specific EC regulation for such cases. As noted in chapter 4, the EC has recently (between 1997 and 1999) removed six measures: on coal in Germany and Spain (but a few months later, a high antidumping specific duty was imposed on coke imports from China), on potatoes in the Canary Islands (Spain), on Japanese cars (the whole of EC), and on minimum prices for dried grapes and for preserved cherries (the whole of EC) (WTO, *Trade Policy Review: The European Union*, 2000). Moreover, the EC considers two types of measures as safeguards: quotas on imports of footwear, porcelain, and ceramic tableware from China similar to safeguards (ironically they are incorporated into EC Regulation 519/94 establishing free importation (meaning "no quantitative measures", in EC parlance) as the general rule of the EC Common Import Regime); and the "surveillance" regime based on a system of automatic import licensing.

Appendix C
Models

The Computable Partial Equilibrium Model

To facilitate international comparison, the same computable partial equilibrium model that was used to compute the costs of protection in the United States, Japan, South Korea, and China is used in this book.[1] Compared with the computable general equilibrium approach, this partial equilibrium model is simple and easy to use. However, the methodology has several limitations (see chapter 2). The four key assumptions of the computable partial equilibrium model are:

- Domestic and imported goods are not perfect substitutes.
- The supply schedule for imported goods is flat (perfectly elastic).
- The supply schedule for domestic goods slopes upward (less than perfectly elastic).
- All markets are perfectly competitive.

The static effects of removing a trade barrier (either a tariff or a quota) are illustrated in figures C.1 and C.2. In figure C.1, the supply curve for imports (Sm) is flat, corresponding to a "small country" with an open economy. According to a fundamental assumption of this model, a small country is a "taker" of world market prices and does not influence them

---

1. The computable partial equilibrium model was devised by Peter Uimonen (see Hufbauer and Elliot 1994).

Figure C.1 Effects in the import market of removing a trade barrier

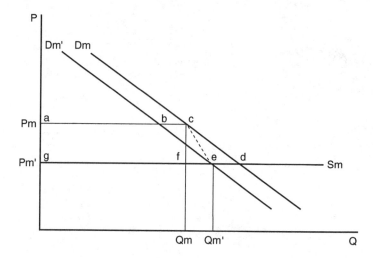

With the trade barrier in place, the price of the import in the protected market is *Pm,* and the quantity imported is *Qm.* Following liberalization, the price falls to *Pm',* the world price. Then, responding to a lower price in the domestic market (see figure C.2), the demand schedule for the import shifts from *Dm* to *Dm',* and the quantity imported settles at *Qm'.*

Figure C.2 Effects in the domestic market of removing a trade barrier

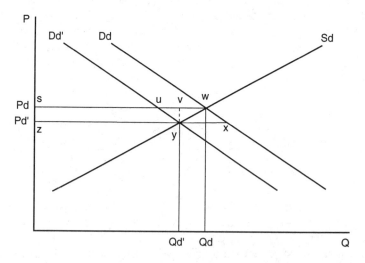

With the trade barrier in place, the price of the import-competing domestic product is *Pd,* and the quantity demanded is *Qd.* Following liberalization and the decline in the import price (see figure C.1), demand for the domestic substitute falls, shifting the demand curve from *Dd* to *Dd',* the quantity consumed falls to *Qd',* and the price drops to *Pd'.*

(see the last section of chapter 3, which examines the case of the EC as a "large" country). Pm' is the world market c.i.f. price (expressed in euros); with the trade barrier in place, the landed price of imported goods in the protected home market is Pm (expressed in euros):

$$Pm = Pm' (1 + t + n),\qquad(1)$$

where t is the tariff rate (percent ad valorem) and n is the tariff equivalent of nontariff barriers (percent ad valorem).

After liberalization (assuming the removal of all trade barriers), the landed price falls to Pm'. Then, responding to the lower price in the domestic market (see figure C.2), the demand curve for imports shifts from Dm to Dm', and the quantity imported settles at Qm', which is higher than the initial quantity imported, Qm. Trade liberalization will have a series of welfare effects. The consumer surplus gain from liberalization in the import market is approximated by the area $aceg$ (figure C.1). Area $acfg$ represents transfers to consumers from the government in the form of lost tariff revenues and transfers to consumers from those who controlled quotas in the form of lost quota rent. The import market will also experience an efficiency gain because resources will be better utilized.

Before liberalization, the wedge between the landed price of imports and the world market price lured resources toward the production of import substitutes and away from other sectors that could have made more efficient use of those resources. After liberalization, the process is reversed. The efficiency gain following liberalization is represented by the area cef. Areas $acfg$ plus cef add up to area $aceg$, the total gains realized by consumers.

In figure C.2, the supply curve for the import-competing domestic product (Sd) slopes upward. With the trade barrier in place, the price of the domestic product is Pd (expressed in euros), and the quantity demanded is Qd. Following liberalization and the decline in the import price (figure C.1), the demand curve for the domestic substitute shifts from Dd to Dd', the quantity consumed falls to Qd', and the price drops to Pd'. The consumer surplus gain from lower domestic prices may be approximated by the area $swyz$, which is just offset by the producer surplus loss.

To summarize the welfare effects on the two markets following liberalization, the efficiency gain is the area cef, and the total consumer surplus gain is the area $aceg + swyz$. Of this total, area $acfg$ is the transfer to consumers from the government and quota rent collectors, and area $swyz$ is the transfer to consumers from domestic producers.[2] Because the model

---

2. The tariff revenue plus quota rent (area $acfg$) may be estimated as $Qm(Pm - Pm')$. The efficiency loss due to protection (area cef) may be estimated as $(1/2)[(Pm - Pm')(Qm' - Qm)]$. The consumer surplus loss in the domestic market due to protection (area $swyz$) may be estimated as $Qd'(Pd - Pd') + (1/2)[(Pd - Pd')(Qd - Qd')]$.

only calculates static welfare, it might substantially underestimate the contribution that trade expansion makes to economic growth.

To derive solutions for individual industries, a computable partial equilibrium model corresponding to figures C.1 and C.2 was devised. The model assumes that supply and demand relationships are not linear in their absolute terms, but rather that they are linear in their logarithmic terms. This assumption enables the parameters associated with the price terms to be interpreted as elasticities.

The underlying domestic supply and demand functions are specified according to the following equations:

$$Qd = aPd^{Edd}Pm^{Edm} \tag{2}$$

and

$$Qs = bPd^{Es}. \tag{3}$$

In equation 2, Edd is the own-price elasticity of demand for the domestic good, while Edm is the cross-price elasticity of demand for the domestic good with respect to the price of the imported good. In equation 3, Es is the own-price elasticity of supply of the domestic good. Because the domestic good and the imported good are imperfect substitutes in this model, equilibrium in the domestic market requires that domestic demand equal domestic supply (i.e., $Qd = Qs$).

Assuming that the supply of the import is perfectly elastic, the demand and supply equations in the import market are:

$$Qm = cPd^{Emd}Pm^{Emm} \tag{4}$$

and

$$Pm = Pm'(1 + t + n)(1 + Rv)/(1 - Rc) \tag{5}$$

In equation 4, Emd is the cross-price elasticity of demand for the imported commodity with respect to the price of the domestic commodity, while Emm is the own-price elasticity of demand for the imported commodity. Equation 5 represents the assumption that the supply of the imported commodity is perfectly elastic, and that the world market c.i.f. price, Pm', is therefore the same regardless of import quantity. In equation 5, Rv represents the value-added tax rate for imports, and Rc represents the consumer tax rate.

This system of supply and demand functions may be converted into a system of linear relationships by taking the logarithms to the base e (shown by ln) of equations 2, 3, 4, and 5:

$$\ln Qd = \ln a + Edd \ln Pd + Edm \ln Pm \qquad (6)$$

$$\ln Qs = \ln b + Es \ln Pd \qquad (7)$$

$$\ln Qm = \ln c + Emd \ln Pd + Emm \ln Pm \qquad (8)$$

$$\ln Pm = \ln[Pm'(1 + t + n)(1 + Rv)/(1 - Rc)] \qquad (9)$$

Equations 6, 7, 8, and 9 are used to calculate the welfare effects of liberalization.

A Generalized Armington Import Model

This note summarizes the nonlinear Armington model developed in Francois and Hall (1997). They define the demand system for product X as a CES, where the elasticity of demand is σ and the CES weights are designated as α. This gives equation (1) as follows.

(1) $\qquad Q = \left[\sum_{i=1..n} \alpha_i X_i^\rho \right]^{1/\rho}$

(2) $\qquad \left[\dfrac{\alpha_j}{P_j} \right]^\sigma P^{\sigma-1} E - k_{si} \left[\dfrac{P_j}{(1+t_j)} \right]^{\varepsilon_{sj}} = 0 \quad j = 2..n$

(3) $\qquad \left[\dfrac{\alpha_i}{P_i} \right]^\sigma P^{\sigma-1} E - k_{si} \left[\dfrac{P_i}{(1+t_i)} \right]^{\varepsilon_{si}} = 0 \quad i = 1$

(4) $\qquad k_A P^{NA+1} - E \qquad\qquad = 0$

(5) $\qquad \left[\sum_{i=1}^{n} \alpha_i^\sigma P_i^{1-\sigma} \right]^{1-1/\rho} - P \qquad = 0$

$n + 2$ equations and unknowns

P, E, P_i

From the first order conditions, they are then able to derive excess demand for a given national variety (indexed by $i=1\ldots n$) as in equation (2) above for the case of imports. Note that they have assumed that import supply is subject to a constant supply elasticity of ε_s. In equation (2), the term t is an import tax. In equation (3), they then have excess demand for the competing domestic variety, where it is also potentially subject to an output/production tax or subsidy at rate t_i. Equation (5) then defines the prices for the CES composite good Q, while equation (4) relates this composite price to demand for the CES composite, subject to composite demand elasticity NA.

Note that equations (2) through (5) define a system of $n+2$ equations, and $n+2$ unknowns. Working with a nonlinear solver (like that provided in Excel) they can use this system to solve explicitly for a calibrated version of the model, and to then apply the numeric model to examine the impact of changes in tariffs on prices, import volumes, and the implied welfare and consumer and producer surplus changes that follow from trade policy changes.

This model can be downloaded from http://www.intereconomics.com/handbook/.

References

Abbott, Philip. 1998. Competition Policy and Agriculture. Paper presented at an OECD workshop on emerging trade issues in agriculture. Paris: OECD. Photocopy (October).

Adams, W. James. 1999. The Political Economy of Agriculture in France's Fifth Republic. *Explorations in Economic History* 36: 1–29.

Akinkugbe, Oluyele. 2000. The European Union and South Africa Free Trade Agreements: An Exploratory Partial Equilibrium Analysis of Potential Effect on ACP-EU Trade Flows. *Journal of World Trade* 34, no. 3: 95–109.

Alix, Kareen. 1998. Les effets redistributifs de la politique agricole commune entre les états-membres. Paris: Ministère de l'Economie, des Finances, et de l'Industrie, Direction de la Prévision. Photocopy (September).

Allen, Chris, Michael Gasiorek, and Alasdair Smith. 1998. The Competition Effects of the Single Market in Europe. *Economic Policy* (October): 441–85.

Amatori, Franco. 1999. European Business: New Strategies, Old Structures. *Foreign Policy* (Summer): 78–89.

Andersen, Torben M., Niels Haldrup, and Jan Rose Sorensen. 2000. Labour Market Implications of EU Product Market Integration. *Economic Policy* (April): 107–33.

Anderson, Kym. 1995. *The Political Economy of Coal Subsidies in Europe*. CEPR Discussion Paper 1089. London: Centre for Economic Policy Research.

Anderson, Kym, Erwidodo, and Merlinda Ingco. 1999. Integrating Agriculture into the WTO: The Next Phase. Paper presented at a WTO-World Bank conference, Washington (20–21 September).

Andreani, Gilles. 1999. *Europe's Uncertain Identity*. London: Centre for European Reform.

Armstrong, Mark, Simon Cowan, and John Vickers. 1994. *Regulatory Reform: Economic Analysis and British Experience*. Cambridge, MA: MIT Press.

Atje, Raymond, and Gary Hufbauer. 1996. The Market Structure Benefits of Trade and Investment Liberalization. Washington: Institute for International Economics. Photocopy.

Australian Bureau of Agricultural Economics. 1985. *Agricultural Policies in the EC*. Policy Monograph 2. Canberra: Australian Government Publishing Services.

Baldwin, Richard. 1990. *The U.S.-Japan Semiconductor Agreement*. CEPR Discussion Paper 387. London: Centre for Economic Policy Research.

Baldwin, Richard. 1994. *Towards an Integrated Europe*. London: Centre for Economic Policy Research.

Baldwin, Richard E. 1995. A Domino Theory of Regionalism. In *Expanding European Regionalism: The EU's New Members*, eds. R. E. Baldwin, P. Haapranta, and J. Kiander. Cambridge: Cambridge University Press.

Baldwin, Richard E. 2000. Regulatory Protectionism, Developing Nations and a Two-Tier World Trade System. Geneva: Graduate Institute of International Studies. Photocopy (March).

Baldwin, Richard E., R. Forslid, and J. Haagland. 1995. Investment Creation and Investment Diversion in Europe. *The World Economy* 19, no. 6: 635–59.

Baldwin, Richard, Joseph François, and Richard Portes. 1997. The Costs and Benefits of Eastern Enlargement: The Impact on the EU and Central Europe. *Economic Policy* (April): 127–76.

Barfield, Claude. 1998. The Deceptive Allure of a Transatlantic Free Trade Agreement: A U.S. Perspective. *Intereconomics* (September/October): 203–11.

Baughman, Laura, Rolf Mirus, Morris Morkre, and Dean Spinanger. 1997. Of Tire Cords, Ties and Tents: Window-Dressing in the ATC? *The World Economy* (July): 407–34.

Bayard, Thomas O., and Kimberly Ann Elliott. 1994. *Reciprocity and Retaliation in U.S. Trade Policy.* Washington: Institute for International Economics.

Bean, Charles, Samuel Bentolila, Giuseppe Bertola, and Juan Dolado. 1998. *Social Europe: One for All?* Monitoring European Integration 8. London: Centre for Economic Policy Research.

Bergman, Lars, Chris Doyle, Jordi Gual, Lars Hultkrantz, Damien Neven, Lars-Hendrik Röller, and Leonard Waverman. 1998. *Europe's Network Industries: Conflicting Priorities in Telecommunications.* Monitoring European Deregulation-MED 1. London: Centre for Economic Policy Research.

Bergsten, C. Fred. 2000. *The New Asian Challenge.* Working Paper Series no. 00-4. Washington: Institute for International Economics.

Besley, Timothy, and Paul Seabright. 2000. The Effects and Policy Implications of State Aids to Industry: An Economic Analysis. *Economic Policy* (April): 15–53.

Bhagwati, Jagdish. 1993. Regionalism and Multilateralism: An Overview. In *New Dimensions in Regional Integration*, eds. J. de Melo and A. Panagariya. Cambridge: Cambridge University Press.

Bhagwati, Jagdish. 1995. U.S. Trade Policy: the Infatuation with Free Trade Areas. In *The Dangerous Drift to Preferential Trade Agreements*, eds. Jagdish Bhagwati and Anne O. Krueger. Washington: American Enterprise Institute.

Bhagwati, Jagdish N., and Robert E. Hudec. 1996. *Fair Trade and Harmonization: Prerequisites for Free Trade?* Cambridge, MA: MIT Press.

Bhagwati, Jagdish, and Arvind Panagariya. 1996. *Preferential Trading Areas and Multilateralism: Strangers, Friends or Foes?* Washington: American Enterprise Institute.

Bomberg, Elizabeth, and John Peterson. 1996. *Decision-Making in the European Union: Reflections on EU Governance.* CEPS Working Document 98. Brussels: Centre for European Policy Studies.

Bonnefous, Edouard. 1952. *L'Europe en face de son destin.* Paris: Presses Universitaires de France.

Borell, Brent. 1994. *EU Bananarama III.* Policy Research Working Paper 1386. Washington: World Bank.

Borell, Brent. 1996. *Beyond EU Bananarama 1993: The Story Gets Worse.* Canberra: Centre for International Economics.

Bourgeois, Jacques, and Patrick A. Messerlin. 1998. *The European Community's Experience.* Brookings Trade Forum. Washington: Brookings Institution.

Boylaud, Olivier. 2000. *Regulatory Reform in Road Freight and Retail Distribution.* OECD Economics Department Working Paper 255. Paris: OECD.

Boylaud, Olivier, and Giuseppe Nicoletti. 2000. *Regulation, Market Structure and Performance in Telecommunications.* OECD Economics Department Working Paper 237 (April). Paris: OECD.

Brenton, Paul. 2000a. The Changing Nature and Determinants of EU Trade Policies. Brussels: Centre for European Policy Studies. Photocopy (June).

Brenton, Paul. 2000b. Antidumping Practices in the EU and Trade Diversion. Brussels: Centre for European Policy Studies. Photocopy (July).

Brenton, Paul, John Sheehy, and Marc Vancauteren. 2000. *Technical Barriers to Trade in the EU: Importance for Accession Countries.* CEPS Working Document 144. Brussels: Centre for European Policy Studies.

Brenton, Paul, Natalia Tourdyeva, and John Whalley. 1997. The Potential Effects of an FTA between the EU and Russia. Brussels: Centre for European Policy Studies. Photocopy.

Bronckers, Marco C. E. J. 1995. WTO Implementation in the European Community: Antidumping Safeguards and Intellectual Property. *Journal of World Trade* 29, no. 5: 73–95.

Brown, Drusilla K. 2000. International Trade and Core Labor Standards: A Survey of the Recent Literature. *OECD Labour Market and Social Policy Occasional Papers*, no. 43. Paris: OECD.

Brown, Drusilla K., Alan V. Deardorff, and Robert M. Stern. 1997. Some Economic Effects of the Free Trade Agreement between Tunisia and the European Union. In *Regional Partners in Global Markets: Limits and Possibilities of the Euro-Med Agreements*, eds. Ahmed Galal and Bernard Hoekman. London: Centre for Economic Policy Research.

Buigues, Pierre, Fabienne Ilzkovitz, and J. F. Lebrun. 1990. The Impact of the Internal Market by Industrial Sector: The Challenge for the Member States. *Brussels: European Economy*, special edition.

Buigues, Pierre, and André Sapir. 1999. L'impact du marché unique sur les grands pays européens. *Revue d'économie politique* 109, no. 2: 177–97.

Bureau, Dominique, and Jean-Christophe Bureau. 1999. Agriculture et negociations commerciales, Conseil d'Analyse Economique. Paris: La Documentation Française.

Cadot, Olivier, Jaime de Melo, and Marcelo Olarreaga. 1999. Regional Integration and Lobbying for Tariffs against Nonmembers. *International Economic Review* 40, no. 3: 635–57.

Cadot, Olivier, Jean-Marie Grether, and Jaime de Melo. 2000. Trade and Competition Policy: Where Do We Stand? *Journal of World Trade* 34, no. 3: 1–20.

CBO. 1998. Antidumping Action in the United States and Around the World: An Analysis of International Data, CBO Paper (June). Washington: Congressional Budget Office.

Centre for Economic Policy Research. 1992. *Is Bigger Better? The Economics of EC Enlargement.* Monitoring European Integration 3. London: Centre for Economic Policy Research.

Chambres d'Agriculture de France. 1993. L'agriculture en Nouvelle-Zélande. Février, supplément au 811. Paris: Assemblée Permanente des Chambres d'Agriculture.

Chambres d'Agriculture de France. 1994a. L'Accord du GATT du 15 Décembre 1993. Février, supplément au 819. Paris: Assemblée Permanente des Chambres d'Agriculture.

Chambres d'Agriculture de France. 1994b. La réforme de la Politique Agricole Commune. Avril, supplément au 821. Paris: Assemblée Permanente des Chambres d'Agriculture.

Chambres d'Agriculture de France. 2000. Traçabilité et Etiquetage: Un Dossier en Perpétuelle Évolution, no. 887 (Avril): 7. Paris: Assemblée Permanente des Chambres d'Agriculture.

Cline, William R. 1987. *The Future of World Trade in Textiles & Apparel.* Washington: Institute for International Economics.

Cocq, Emmanuel. 2000. Analyse économique de la politique française du cinéma. PhD thesis. Paris: Institut d'Etudes Politiques de Paris.

Cohen, Daniel, Augustin Landier, Arnaud Lefranc, and Alexandre Vincent. 1997. Une comparaison des marchés du travail en France et aux Etats-Unis. Paris: CEPREMAP. Photocopy (October).

Cohen, Daniel, Arnaud Lefranc, and Gilles Saint-Paul. 1997. French Unemployment: A Transatlantic Perspective. Economic Policy 25. London: Centre for Economic Policy Research.

Colson, François, and Vincent Chatelier. 1998. Agenda 2000 et modulation des aides directes en agriculture. Paris: Institut National de la Recherche Agronomique. Photocopy (June).

Conseil de la Concurrence. 1990. *Décision relative à des pratiques relevées sur le marché de la banane.* Décision no. 90-D-20. Paris: Conseil de la Concurrence.

Cooke, John. 1999. Trade in Services: Pro-Competitive Regulation. London: Association of British Insurers. Photocopy (September).

Corado, Cristina. 1995. The Textiles and Clothing Trade with Central and Eastern Europe: Impact on Members of the EC. In *European Union Trade with Eastern Europe*, eds. Riccardo Faini and Richard Portes. London: CEPR.

Council for Asia-Europe Cooperation. 1997. *The Rationale and Common Agenda for Asia-Europe Cooperation.* London: International Institute for Strategic Studies.

Council on Foreign Relations. 2001. *Towards a Growth Strategy for the Middle East.* New York: Council on Foreign Relations.

Coursey, Don L., and Lester D. Taylor. 1982. Consumer Demand in the United States: Revisions and Extensions. Burlington, MA: Strategic Information. Photocopy (January).

Cowles, Maria Green. 1995. Setting the Agenda for a New Europe: The ERT and EC 1992. *Journal of Common Market Studies* 33, no. 4: 501–26.

Crandall, Robert W. 1981. *The U.S. Steel Industry in Recurrent Crisis: Policy Options in a Competitive World.* Washington: Brookings Institution.

Crandall, Robert W. 1994. The Economic Effect of Antidumping Policies on International Trade in Steel. Washington: Brookings Institution. Photocopy (September).

Crandall, Robert W. 1997. Telecommunications Liberalization: The U.S. Model. Paper presented at the Tripolar Meeting sponsored by the Brookings Institution, Tokyo (6–7 October).

Crandall, Robert W., and Leonard Waverman. 1996. *Talk Is Cheap: The Promise of Regulatory Reform in North American Telecommunications.* Washington: Brookings Institution.

CTE (Commission Technique des Ententes). 1964. Entente dans l'industrie du superphosphate. Paris: *Journal Officiel*, 7 February.

Daly, Michael, and Hiroaki Kuwahara. 1998. The Impact of the Uruguay Round on Tariff and Non-Tariff Barriers to Trade in the "Quad." *The World Economy* 21, no. 2: 207–34.

Davenport, Michael. 1992. Africa and the Unimportance of Being Preferred. *Journal of Common Market Studies* 30, no. 2: 233–51.

Deutsch, Klaus G. 1999. *The Politics of Freer Trade in Europe: Three-level Games in the Common Commercial Policy of the EU, 1985–97.* New York: St. Martin's Press.

Deutsche Morgan Grenfell. 1998. Wal-Mart and German Hypermarket Retailing. In *Focus on German Hypermarkets.* Paris: Deutsche Morgan Grenfell.

Devedjian, Patrick. 1993. *Le libre-échange: une chance pour la France.* Paris: Assemblée Nationale.

Devuyst, Yonuri. 1992. The EC's Common Commercial Policy and the Treaty on European Union. *World Competition* 2: 67–80.

Digby, Caroline, Alasdair Smith, and Anthony Venables. 1988. Counting the Cost of Voluntary Export Restrictions in the European Car Market. Southhampton, UK: University of Southampton. Photocopy.

Dobson, Wendy, and Pierre Jacquet. 1998. *Financial Services Liberalization in the WTO.* Washington: Institute for International Economics.

Donnelly, C.A. 2000. Likely size of the French BSE epidemic. *Nature* 408 (14 December): 787–88.

Drexl, Joseph. 2000. Existing Legal and Institutional Mechanisms for Cooperation and Coordination: The Case of Intellectual and Industrial Property. In *Transatlantic Regulatory Cooperation: Legal Problems and Political Prospects*, eds. George A. Bermann, Mathias Herdegen, and Peter Lindseth. Oxford: Oxford University Press.

Driessen, Bart, and Folkert Graafsma. 1999. The EC's Wonderland: An Overview of the Pan-European Harmonised Origin Protocols. *Journal of World Trade* 33, no. 4: 19–45.

Dumez, Hervé, and Alain Jeunemaître. 2000. *Understanding and Regulating the Market at a Time of Globalization: The Case of the Cement Industry.* New York: St. Martin's Press.

Easterbrook, Frank H. 1983. Antitrust and the Economics of Federalism. *Journal of Law and Economics* XXVI (April): 23–40.

Eeckhout, Piet. 1994. *The European Internal Market and International Trade: A Legal Analysis.* Oxford: Clarendon Press.

Eeckhout, Piet. 2000. After Keck and Mithouard: Free Movement of Goods in the EC, Market Access, and Non-Discrimination. In *Regulatory Barriers and the Principle of Non-Discrimination in World Trade Law*, eds. Thomas Cottier, Petros Mavroidis, and Patrick Blatter. Ann Arbor, MI: University of Michigan Press.

Ehlermann, Claus-Dieter. 1995. State Aid Control in the European Union: Success or Failure? *Fordham International Law Journal* 18, no. 4: 1212–29.

Emerson, Michael, and Daniel Gros. 1999. *The CEPS Plan for the Balkans.* Brussels: Centre for European Policy Studies.

Emiliou, Nicholas. 1994. Opening Pandora's Box: The Legal Basis of Community Measures before the Court of Justice. *European Law Review* 19: 489–507.

Enders, Alice, and Ronald J. Wonnacott. 1996. The Liberalization of East-West European Trade: Hubs, Spokes and Further Complications. *The World Economy* 19, no. 3(March): 253–72.

Engel, Hans-Ulrich. 2000. The TABD from the European Chemical Industry's Point of View. In *Transatlantic Regulatory Cooperation*, ed. George A. Bermann. New York: European Legal Studies Center, Columbia Law Center.

ESFRC (European Shadow Financial Regulatory Committee). 2000. *Towards a Single Market in European Securities Trading: An Agenda for Reform of the ISD.* London: ESFRC.

European Audiovisual Observatory. 1998. *Comparative Analysis of National Aid Mechanisms* 1. Strasbourg, France: Council of Europe.

European Commission. 1980. *A Systematic Approach to Agricultural Forecasts.* Information on Agriculture 77. Brussels: European Commission.

European Commission. 1982. *XIIth Report on Competition Policy.* Luxembourg: Official Publications of the EC.

European Commission. 1994. *XXIVth Report on Competition Policy.* Luxembourg: Official Publications of the EC.

European Commission. 1995. *Panorama of the EC Industry.* Luxembourg: Eurostat, Official Publications of the EC.

European Commission. 1996. *The Single Market and Tomorrow's Europe.* Brussels: European Commission.

European Commission. 1997a. *The Agricultural Situation in the European Union: 1996 Report.* Luxembourg: Official Publications of the EC.

European Commission. 1997b. *Situation and Outlook: Cereals, Oilseeds, Protein Crops.* Directorate General for Agriculture, Working Document CAP 2000. Brussels: European Commission.

European Commission. 1997c. *Special Sectoral Report No. 1: Public Procurement.* http://europa.eu.int/dg15.

European Commission. 1998a. *Public Procurement in the European Union.* Communication XV-5500-98. Brussels: European Commission.

European Commission. 1998b. *Second Bi-Annual BSE Follow-Up Report* (18 November). Brussels: European Commission.

European Commission. 1998c. *Sixth Survey on State Aid.* Brussels: Commission-DG-IV.

European Commission. 1999a. An Analysis of Trends in the Lomé IV Trade Regime and the Consequences of Retaining It. Report CE/TFN/GCEC3/09-ACP/61/002/99. Brussels: European Commission. Photocopy.

European Commission. 1999b. Consequences for the ACP Countries of Applying the GSP, Joint Analysis by EU and ACP Experts, Group 3. Report CE/TFN/GCEC3/29-ACP/00/177/99. Brussels: European Commission. Photocopy (20 April).

European Commission. 1999c. *Economic Reform: Report on the Functioning of Community Product and Capital Markets.* Report presented by the Commission in response to the conclusions of the Cardiff European Council, (20 January). Brussels: European Commission.

European Commission. 1999d. *The European Competition Policy.* Luxembourg: Official Publications of the EC.

European Commission. 1999e. *The European Union's Commercial Policy for the Automotive Sector.* http://europa.eu.int/comm/dg01/polauto.htm.

European Commission. 1999f. *Mutual Recognition in the Context of the Follow-up to the Action Plan for the Single Market.* Communication from the Commission to the European Parliament and the Council, COM99, 232 final, (11 May). Brussels: European Commission.

European Commission. 1999g. *Seventh Survey on State Aid.* Brussels: Commission-DG-IV.

European Commission. 2000a. *Single Market Scoreboard No. 6.* http://europa.eu.int/comm/internal_market/en/update/score/score6.htm (May).

European Commission. 2000b. An Internal Market Strategy for Services, COM (2000) 888 (December). Brussels: European Commission.

European Commission. 2000c. Everything but Arms Proposal: Possible Impact on the Agricultural Sector (December). Brussels: European Commission.

European Commission. 2000d. Sixth Report on the Implementation of the Telecommunications Regulatory Package (December). Brussels: European Commission.

European Services Forum. 1999. Declaration of the European Services Industries towards the Millennium Round. Brussels: UNICE. Photocopy (25 October).

Evenett, Simon J., and Bernard Hoekman. 1999. Government Procurement of Services: Assessing the Case for Multilateral Disciplines. Washington: World Services Congress. Photocopy.

Evenett, Simon J., Alexander Lehmann, and Benn Steil, eds. 2000. *Antitrust Goes Global: What Future for Transatlantic Cooperation?* Washington: Brookings Institution.

FAO (Food and Agriculture Organization). 1997. *Banana Statistics, April, CCP: BA-97/2.* Intergovernmental Group on Bananas. Rome: Food and Agriculture Organization.

FCO (Foreign & Commonwealth Office) and DTI (Department of Trade and Industry), United Kingdom. 1996. *Free Trade and Foreign Policy: A Global Vision.* London: Foreign and Commonwealth Office.

Federated Farmers of New Zealand. 1999. *Life after Subsidies: The New Zealand Farming Experience,* (November) (revised edition). Wellington: Federated Farmers of New Zealand.

Flamm, Kenneth. 1996. *Mismanaged Trade? Strategic Policy and the Semiconductor Industry.* Washington: Brookings Institution Press.

François, Joseph, Hans-Heinrich Glismann, and Dean Spinanger. 2000. *The Cost of EU Trade Protection in Textiles and Clothing.* Kiel Working Paper no. 997. Kiel, Germany: University of Kiel, Kiel Institute of World Economics.

François, Joseph F., and H. Keith Hall. 1997. Partial Equilibrium Modeling. In *Applied Methods for Trade Policy Analysis: A Handbook,* eds. Joseph F. François and Kenneth A. Reinert. Cambridge: Cambridge University Press.

François, Joseph F., and Kenneth A. Reinert, eds. 1997. *Applied Methods for Trade Policy Analysis: A Handbook.* Cambridge: Cambridge University Press.

François, Joseph F., and Machiel Rombout. 2001. *Trade Effects from the Integration of the Central and East European Countries into the European Union.* Working Paper no. 41. Brighton, UK: Sussex European Institute.

Frost, Ellen L. 1997. *Transatlantic Trade: A Strategic Trade Agenda.* POLICY ANALYSES IN INTERNATIONAL ECONOMICS 48. Washington: Institute for International Economics.

Fundación de Economía Analítica. 1998. State Aid and Convergence in the European Union. Barcelona: IESE. Photocopy (June).

Galloway, David. 1994. L'achèvement du marché intérieur pour le régime à l'importation des produits textiles dans la Communauté. *Revue du Marché Commun et de l'Union européenne,* no. 379 (June): 362–71.

Gemmill, G. 1976. *The World Sugar Economy: An Econometric Analysis of Production and Policies.* Agricultural Economics Report 313. East Lansing, MI: Michigan State University.

de Ghellinck, Elizabeth, and Christian Huveneers. 1995. Chemical Fibres Industry. In *European Policies on Competition, Trade and Industry,* eds., Pierre Buigues, Alexis Jacquemin, and André Sapir. Aldershot, UK: Edward Elgar Publishing.

Gibson, Paul, John Wainio, Daniel Whitley, and Mary Bohman. 2001. *Profiles of Tariffs in Global Agricultural Markets*. Agricultural Economic Report no. 796 (January), Economic Research Service. Washington: US Department of Agriculture.

Gissurarson, Hannes H. 2000. *Overfishing: The Icelandic Solution*. Studies on the Environment 17. London: Institute of Economic Affairs.

Gonenc, Rauf, and Giuseppe Nicoletti. 2000. *Regulation, Market Structure and Performance in Air Passenger Transportation*. OECD Economics Department Working Paper no. 254. Paris: OECD.

Gonenc, Rauf, M. Maher, and Giuseppe Nicoletti. 2000. *The Implementation and the Effects of Regulatory Reform: Past experience and current issues*. OECD Economic Department Working Paper no. 251. Paris: OECD.

Goodman, Richard M., and John M. Frost. 2000. *International Economic Agreements and the Constitution*, WP00-2 Working Paper Series, no. 2000-2 (March). Washington: Institute for International Economics.

Gordon, Harvey, Shane River, and Sue Arrowsmith. 1998. The Economic Impact of the European Union Regime on Public Procurement: Lessons for the WTO. *The World Economy* 21, no. 2 (March): 157–87.

Graham, Edward M., and Paul R. Krugman. 1989. *Foreign Direct Investment in the United States*. Washington: Institute for International Economics.

Grant, Wyn. 1997. *The Common Agricultural Policy*. London: Macmillan.

Greenaway, David, T.A. Lloyd, Chris Milner, W.O. Morrissey, Geoffrey Reed, and Geoffrey Hutton. 1995. The European Union's Antidumping Policy and Non-Tariff Barriers to Trade, A Report to H.M. Treasury and the Department of Trade and Industry. University of Nottingham, UK: CREDIT. Photocopy.

Griffin, Joseph P. 1994. International Antitrust Guidelines Send Mixed Message for Robust Enforcement and Comity. *World Competition* 18, no. 1 (September): 5–31.

Grilli, Enzo R. 1993. *The European Community and the Developing Countries*. Cambridge: Cambridge University Press.

Grout, Paul A. 1996. Promoting the Superhighway: Telecommunications Regulation in Europe. *Economic Policy*, no. 22: 111–54.

Guillod, Olivier. 2000. Market Integration in a Small Federal State (Switzerland): The Role of Public Health. In *Regulatory Barriers and the Principle of Non-Discrimination in World Trade Law*, eds. Thomas Cottier, Petros Mavroidis, and Patrick Blatter. Ann Arbor, MI: University of Michigan Press.

Gulbrandsen, Odd, and Assar Lindbeck. 1973. *The Economics of the Agricultural Sector*. Stockholm: Almquist and Wicksell.

Hagdahl, Thomas. 1996. *The Price of Protection: Customs Duties at the End of the 20th Century*, no. 1. Stockholm: Industriförbundet Handelspolitik.

Hallaert, Jean-Jacques. 2000. Un bilan à mi-parcours du SPG européen. Paris: Groupe d'Economie Mondiale. Photocopy (May).

Hamilton, Carl B. 1986. An assessment of voluntary restraints on Hong Kong's exports to Europe and the USA. *Economica* 53: 339–50 (August).

Hamilton, Carl B. 1990. *Textiles Trade and the Developing Countries*. Washington: World Bank.

Harrison, Glenn, Thomas Rutherford, and David Tarr. 1996. Quantifying the Uruguay Round. In *The Uruguay Round and the Developing Countries*, eds. Will Martin and L. Alan Winters. Washington: World Bank.

Hartell, Jason G., and Johan F.M. Swinnen. 1998. Trends in Agricultural Price and Trade Policy Instruments since 1990 in Central European Countries. *The World Economy* 21, no. 2: 261–79.

Hartler, Christina, and Sam Laird. 1999. The EU Model and Turkey: A Case for Thanksgiving. *Journal of World Trade* 33, no. 3: 147–65.

Hartley, K., and M. Uttley. 1994. The Single European Market and Public Procurement Policy: The Case of the United Kingdom. *Public Procurement Law Review* 3: 114–25.

Hatakeyama, Noboru. 2000. Political Perspective, Public Opinion and Policy Options for the Global Trade Agenda. Paper presented at 5th Evian Group Meeting, sponsored by Japan External Trade Organization, Tokyo. October.

Hathaway, Dale E., and Merlinda D. Ingco. 1995. Agricultural Liberalization and the Uruguay Round. In *The Uruguay Round and the Developing Economies*, ed. L. Alan Winters. Washington: World Bank.

Hausman, Jerry, Timothy Tardiff, and Alexander Belinfante. 1993. The Effects of the Breakup of ATT on Telephone Penetration in the United States. *American Economic Review, Papers and Proceedings* 83, no. 2: 178–84.

Head, Keith, and Thierry Mayer. 1999. Non-Europe: The Magnitude and Causes of Market Fragmentation in the EU. *Weltwirtschaftliches Archiv*, Band 136, no. 2: 284–314.

Hellstrom, Mats. 1999. *A Seamless Globe? A Personal Story of the Uruguay Round in GATT*. Lund, Sweden: Hjalmarson and Hogberg.

Henderson, David. 1997. The Role of the OECD in Liberalising International Trade and Capital Flows. *The World Economy, Global Trade Policy 1996* 11: 28.

Henderson, David. 1999. *L'accord multilatéral sur l'investissement: leçons d'un échec*. Groupe d'Economie Mondiale. Paris: Institut d'Etudes Politiques, and London: Royal Institute of International Affairs.

Herin, Jan. 1986. *Rules of Origin and Differences between Tariff Levels in EFTA and in the EC*. EFTA Occasional Paper 13. Geneva: European Free Trade Area Secretariat.

Hess, A.C. 1977. A Comparison of Automobile Demand Equations. *Econometrica* 45, no. 3: 683–701.

Hindley, Brian. 1985. European Venture: VCRs from Japan. In *What Britain Pays for Voluntary Export Restraints*, eds. David Greenaway and Brian Hindley. London: Trade Policy Research Centre.

Hindley, Brian. 1986. EC Imports of VCRs from Japan, a Costly Precedent. *Journal of World Trade Law* 20, no. 2 (March-April): 168–84.

Hindley, Brian. 1997. EC Antidumping: Has the Problem Gone Away? *Annual Review of Trade Policy 1996–97*. London: Centre for Policy Studies.

Hindley, Brian, and Martin Howe. 1996. *Better Off Out?* Occasional Paper 99. London: Institute of Economic Affairs.

Hoekman, Bernard. 2000. Towards a More Balanced and Comprehensive Service Agreement. In *The WTO After Seattle*, ed. Jeffrey J. Schott. Washington: Institute for International Economics.

Hoekman, Bernard, and Simeon Djankov. 1997a. Determinants of the Export Structure of Countries in Central and Eastern Europe. *World Bank Economic Review* 11: 471–87.

Hoekman, Bernard, and Simeon Djankov. 1997b. Effective Protection and Investment Incentives in Egypt and Jordan during the Transition to Free Trade with Europe. *World Development* 25, no. 2: 281–91.

Hoekman, Bernard, and Petros Mavroidis. 2000. WTO Dispute Settlement, Transparency and Surveillance. *The World Economy* 23, no. 4: 527–42.

Hoekman, Bernard, Francis Ng, and Marcelo Olarreaga. 2001. Tariff Peaks in the Quad and Least Developed Country Exports. Washington: World Bank. Photocopy (February).

Hoeller, Peter, Nathalie Girouard, and Alessandra Colechia. 1998. *The European Union's Trade Policies and Their Economic Effects*. Paris: OECD.

Holmes, Peter, and Alasdair Smith. 1995. Automobile Industry. In *European Policies on Competition, Trade and Industry: Conflict and Complementarities*, eds. P. Buigues, A. Jacquemin, and A. Sapir. Cheltenham, UK: Edward Elgar Publishing.

Holmes, Simon. 1995. Anti-Circumvention under the European Union's New Anti-Dumping Rules. *Journal of World Trade* 29, no. 3 (June): 161–80.

Howeel, Thomas. 1988. *Steel and the State*. Boulder, CO: Westview Press.

Hudec, Robert E. 1993. *Enforcing International Trade Law: The Evolution of the Modern GATT Legal System*. Salem, NH: Butterworth.

Hufbauer, Gary, and Kimberly A. Elliott. 1994. *Measuring the Costs of Protection in the United States*. Washington: Institute for International Economics.

Hulsman, John C. 2001. *The World Turned Rightside Up: A New Trading Agenda for the Age of Globalization*. Occasional Paper 114. London: Institute of Economic Affairs.

IATRC (International Agricultural Trade Research Consortium). 1994. *The Uruguay Round Agreement on Agriculture: An Evaluation*. Commissioned Paper no. 9. Davis, CA: University of California.

Ingco, Merlinda. 1996. Tariffication in the Uruguay Round: How Much Liberalization? *The World Economy* 16, no. 4: 425–46.

INRA (Institut National de la Recherche Agronomique). 2000. http://www.inra.fr/Internet/Produits/dpenv/vfol_e.htm.

IRELA. 1999. *Economic Relations between Mercosur and the EU: Prospects for the Coming Decade*. Madrid: IRELA.

Jacquemin, Alexis, and André Sapir. 1991. Competition and Imports in the European Market. In *European Integration: Trade and Industry*, eds. Alan L. Winters and Anthony Venables. Cambridge: Cambridge University Press.

Janow, Merit E. 2000. Transatlantic Cooperation on Competition Policy. In *Antitrust Goes Global: What Future for Transatlantic Cooperation?* eds. Simon J. Evenett, Alexander Lehmann, and Benn Steil. Washington: Brookings Institution.

Johnson, D. Gale. 1995. *Less Than Meets the Eye: The Modest Impact of CAP Reform*. London: Centre for Policy Studies.

Johnson, R.W.M. 2000. *Reforming EU Farm Policy: Lessons from New Zealand*. Occasional Paper 112. London: Institute of Economic Affairs.

Josling, Timothy. 1998. *Agricultural Trade Policy: Completing the Reform*. Policy Analysis in International Economics 53. Washington: Institute for International Economics.

Kahai, Simran K., David L. Kaserman, and John W. Mayo. 1996. Is the "Dominant Firm" Dominant? An Empirical Analysis of ATT's Market Power. *Journal of Law and Economics* 39, no. 2: 499–517.

Kaminski, Bartlomiej, Zhen Kun Wang, and L. Alan Winters. 1996. Export Performance in Transition Economies. *Economic Policy*, October: 423–42.

Kerr, William A. 1999. International Trade in Transgenic Food Products: A New Focus for Agricultural Trade Disputes. *The World Economy* 22, no. 2: 245–60.

Koedijk, Kees, and Jeroen Kremers. 1996. Market Opening, Regulation and Growth in Europe. *Economic Policy* no. 23: 445–67 (October).

Koenig, Christian. 2000. State Guarantees for the German Landesbanken and the EC State Aid Regime. In *State Aid Control in the European Union: Selected Problems*, eds. Giuliano Amato and Claus-Dieter Ehlermann.

Kommerskollegium. 1999. Further Actions within the EU in the Field of Antidumping. Kommerskollegium [National Board of Trade], Stockholm. Photocopy (17 June).

Komuro, Norio. 2000. The EC Banana Regime and Judicial Control. *Journal of World Trade* 34, no. 5: 1–87.

Krueger, Anne O. 1992. Government, Trade, and Economic Integration. *American Economic Review, Papers and Proceedings* 82, no. 2: 109–14.

Krueger, Anne O. 1999. Rules of Origin as Protectionist. In *Trade, Theory and Econometrics: Essays in honour of John Chipman*, eds. J. Melvin, J. Moore and R. Riezman. New York: Routledge.

Krugman, Paul. 1991. *Geography and Trade*. Leuven, Belgium: Leuven University Press.

Langhammer, Rolf J. 1990. Fuelling a New Engine of Growth or Separating Europe from Non-Europe? *Journal of Common Market Studies* XXIX, no. 2 (December): 133–55.

Laroche-Dupraz, Catherine. 1998. *Politique de restriction des importations et gestion des droits à importer: le cas de la banane dans l'Union Européenne*. Rennes, France: Ecole Nationale Supérieure Agronomique de Rennes.

Lawrence, Robert. 1997. *Regionalism, Multilateralism, and Deeper Integration*. Washington: Brookings Institution Press.

Lequesne, Christian. 1999. Quand l'Union européenne gouverne les poissons: pourquoi une politique commune de la pêche? *Les Etudes du CERI [Centre d'études et de recherches internationales]* 61. Paris: Fondation Nationale des Sciences Politiques.

London Economics. 1994. *The Economic Impact of Television Quotas in the European Union.* Report for Sony Entertainment. London: London Economics.

McGowan, Francis, and Chris Trengove. 1986. *European Aviation: A Common Market?* IFS Report Series 23. London: Institute for Fiscal Studies and Monash University.

McQueen, Matthew. 1998. Lomé versus Free Trade Agreements: The Dilemma Facing the ACP Countries. *The World Economy* 21, no. 4: 421–43.

Mahé, Louis, and François Ortalo-Magné. 2001. *Politique agricole: un modèle européen.* Paris: Presses de la Fondation Nationale des Sciences Politiques.

Mahé, L. P., and T. L. Roe. 1996. The Political Economy of Reforming the 1992 CAP Reform. *American Journal of Agricultural Economics* 78: 1314–23.

Marin, Pedro L. 1994. Competition in European Aviation: Pricing Policy and Market Structure. *Journal of Industrial Economics* 43, no. 2: 141–59.

Marre, Béatrice. 1998. *La Politique Agricole Commune en quête de nouvelles missions.* Délégation pour l'Union européenne, rapport 1247. Paris: Assemblée Nationale.

Maskus, Keith E. 1997. Implications of Regional and Multilateral Agreements for Intellectual Property Rights. *The World Economy* 20, no. 5: 681–94.

Maskus, Keith E. 2000. *Regulatory Standards in the WTO: Comparing Intellectual Property Rights with Competition Policy, Environmental Protection, and Core Labor Standards.* Working Paper Series 00-1. Washington: Institute for International Economics.

Mason, Mark. 1994. Elements of Consensus: Europe's Response to the Japanese Automotive Challenge. *Journal of Common Market Studies* 32, no. 4: 433–53.

Mattoo, Aaditya. 1996. The Government Procurement Agreement: Implications of Economic Theory. *The World Economy* 19, no. 6: 695–720.

Mavroidis, Petros. 2000. Remedies in the WTO Legal System: Between a Rock and a Hard Place. *European Journal of International Law* 11, no. 4: 763–813.

Mavroidis, Petros, and Patrick A. Messerlin. 1998. Has Article 90 ECT Prejudged the Status of Property Ownership? In *State Trading in the Twenty-First Century,* eds. Thomas Cottier and Petros C. Mavroidis. Studies in International Economics, World Trade Forum, vol. 1. Ann Arbor, MI: University of Michigan Press.

Mayhew, Alan. 2000a. *Enlargement of the European Union: An Analysis of the Negotiations with the Central and Eastern European Candidate Countries.* Working Paper 39. Brighton, UK: Sussex European Institute. Photocopy (December).

Mayhew, Alan. 2000b. *Financial and Budgetary Implications of the Accession of Central and East European Countries to the European Union.* Working Paper 33. Brighton, UK: Sussex European Institute. Photocopy (March).

Mayhew, Alan, and W. Orlowski. 1998. The Impact of EU Accession on Enterprise Adaptation and Institutional Development in the EU-Associated Countries in Central and Eastern Europe. London: European Bank for Reconstruction and Development. Photocopy.

de Melo, Jaime, and Arvind Panagariya, eds. 1993. *New Dimensions in Regional Integration.* Cambridge: Cambridge University Press.

Messerlin, Patrick A. 1989. The EC Antidumping Regulations: A First Economic Appraisal, 1980–85. *Weltwirtschaftliches Archiv* 125, no. 3: 563–87.

Messerlin, Patrick A. 1990. Antidumping Regulations or Procartel Law? The EC Chemical Cases. *The World Economy* 13, no. 4: 465–92.

Messerlin, Patrick A. 1992. The Association Agreements between the EC and Central Europe: Trade Liberalization vs. Constitutional Failure? In *Trade, Payments and Adjustment in Central and Eastern Europe,* eds. John Flemming and Jim Rollo. London: Royal Institute of International Affairs.

Messerlin, Patrick A. 1993. Services. The EC as a World Trade Partner. *European Economy,* no. 52: 143–75. Brussels: European Commission.

Messerlin, Patrick A. 1996a. Competition Policy and Antidumping Reform: An Exercise in Transition. In *The World Trading System: Challenges Ahead*, ed. Jeffrey J. Schott. Washington: Institute for International Economics.

Messerlin, Patrick A. 1996b. France and Trade Policy: Is the French Exception "Passée"? *International Affairs* 72: 292–309.

Messerlin, Patrick A. 1996c. Trade Policy in Central European Countries: Key Issues. Paris: Institut d'Etudes Politiques. Photocopy (December).

Messerlin, Patrick A. 1997. *European Film Policy: "La Grande Illusion."* London: Centre for Policy Studies.

Messerlin, Patrick A. 1998a. Central Europe. In *Unilateral Trade Liberalization*, ed. Jagdish Bhagwati. Washington: American Enterprise Institute.

Messerlin, Patrick A. 1998b. Liberalisation in Services Trade and the Strategy of European Multinationals. In *Asia and Europe: Beyond Competing Regionalism*, eds. Kiichiro Fukusaku, Fukunari Kimura, and Shujiro Urata. Brighton, UK: Sussex Academic Press.

Messerlin, Patrick A. 1998c. Technical Public Regulations and Industry Standards: The EC Regime. Washington: World Bank. Photocopy (July).

Messerlin, Patrick A. 1999. External Aspects of State Aid. In *State Aid and the Single Market*, *European Economy*, vol. 3. Brussels: European Commission.

Messerlin, Patrick A. 2000. Regulating Culture: Has It "Gone with the Wind?" In *Achieving Better Regulations of Services*, eds. Australian National University and Australian Productivity Commission. Canberra: Australian Productivity Commission.

Messerlin, Patrick A., and Stéphane Bécuwe. 1987. French Trade and Competition Policy in Cars. In *Costs of Import Restrictions: The Car Industry*, ed. OECD. Paris: OECD.

Messerlin, Patrick A., and Emmanuel Cocq. 2001. Preparing Negotiations in Services: EC Audiovisuals in the Millennium Round. American Enterprise Institute and Groupe d'Economie Mondiale, Washington and Paris. Photocopy (March).

Messerlin, Patrick A., and Jean-Christophe Maur. 1999. Six Sub-Saharan Countries and the WTO: The Situation and the Options. Groupe d'Economie Mondiale, Paris. Photocopy (December).

Messerlin, Patrick A., and Yoshiyuki Noguchi. 1991. The EC Antidumping and Anticircumvention Regulations: The Photocopier Case. Institut d'Etudes Politiques, Paris and Nomura Research Institute, Tokyo. Photocopy (May).

Meunier, Sophie, and Kalypso Nicolaidis. 1999. Who Speaks for Europe? The Delegation of Trade Authority in the EU. *Journal of Common Market Studies* 37, no. 3: 477–501.

Miller, Randy E., and Jessica A. Wasserman. 1992. Trade Relations between the EC and the U.S.: An Overview of Current Issues and Trade Policy Instruments. *Boston College International and Comparative Law Review* 15, no. 2: 393–442.

Milward, Alan S. 1992. *The European Rescue of the Nation-State*. London: Routledge.

Mishalani, Philip, Annette Robert, Christopher Stevens, and Ann Weston. 1981. The Pyramid of Privilege. In *EEC and The Third World: A Survey*, ed. Christopher Stevens. London: Overseas Development Institute.

Molander, Per. 1994. The Swedish Food Policy Reform: Background, Principles, and Problems of Transition. *European Economy* 5: 229–62.

Moore, Michael. 1998. European Steel Policies of the 1980s: Hindering Technological Innovation and Market Structure Change. *Weltwirtschafliches Archiv* 134: 43–68.

Morrison, Steven A., and Clifford Winston. 1986. *The Economic Affects of Airline Deregulation*. Washington: Brookings Institution.

Motion Picture Association of America (MPAA). 1995. *Trade Barriers to U.S. Filmed Entertainment: Report to the United States Trade Representative*. Washington: MPAA.

Nell, Philippe G. 1999. WTO Negotiations on the Harmonization of Rules of Origin: A First Critical Appraisal. *Journal of World Trade* 33, no. 3: 45–71.

Neven, Damien, and Claudine Gouyette. 1995. Regional Convergence in the European Community. *Journal of Common Market Studies* 33, no. 1: 47–65.

Neven, Damien, Pénélope Papandropoulos, and Paul Seabright. 1998. *Trawling for Minnows: European Competition Policy and Agreements between Firms*. London: Centre for Economic Policy Research.

Neven, Damien, and Lars-Hendrik Röller. 2000. The Allocation of Jurisdiction in International Antitrust. *European Economic Review* 44: 845–55.

Nicoletti, Giuseppe. 2000. *Regulation in Services: OECD Patterns and Economic Implications*. OECD Economics Department Working Paper (16 October). Paris: OECD.

Nicoletti, Giuseppe, Stefano Scarpetta, and Olivier Boylaud. 2000. Summary Indicators of Product Market Regulation with an Extension to Employment Protection Legislation. OECD Economics Department Working Paper 226. Paris: OECD (April).

OECD (Organization for Economic Cooperation and Development). 1988. Deregulation and Airline Competition. Paris: OECD.

OECD (Organization for Economic Cooperation and Development). 1990. Modelling the Effects of Agricultural Policies. OECD Economic Studies, Special Issue no. 13 (Winter). Paris: OECD. Photocopy (February).

OECD (Organization for Economic Cooperation and Development). 1994. *Jobs Study (Part II)*. Paris: OECD.

OECD (Organization for Economic Cooperation and Development). 1995. *Adjustment in OECD Agriculture: Issues and Policy Responses*. Paris: OECD.

OECD (Organization for Economic Cooperation and Development). 1997a. *The OECD Stan Database for Industrial Analysis*. Paris: OECD.

OECD (Organization for Economic Cooperation and Development). 1997b. *The Uruguay Round Agreement on Agriculture and Processed Agricultural Products*. Paris: OECD.

OECD (Organization for Economic Cooperation and Development), 1998a. *Agricultural Policies in OECD Countries: Monitoring and Evaluation 1998*. Paris: OECD.

OECD (Organization for Economic Cooperation and Development). 1998b. *National Accounts*. Paris: OECD.

OECD (Organization for Economic Cooperation and Development). 1998c. *Open Markets Matter: The Benefits of Trade and Investment Liberalisation*. Paris: OECD.

OECD (Organization for Economic Cooperation and Development). 1998d. *Spotlight on Public Support to Industry*. Paris: OECD.

OECD (Organization for Economic Cooperation and Development). 1999a. *Agricultural Policies, Markets and Trade in OECD Countries: Monitoring and Evaluation*. Paris: OECD.

OECD (Organization for Economic Cooperation and Development). 1999b. Distributional Effects of Agricultural Support in Selected OECD Countries. Paris: OECD. Photocopy (November).

OECD (Organization for Economic Cooperation and Development). 1999c. Preliminary Report on Market Access Aspects of Uruguay Round Implementation (Report and Annex). Paris: OECD. Photocopy (June).

OECD (Organization for Economic Cooperation and Development). 2000a. *Hard Core Cartels*. Paris: OECD.

OECD (Organization for Economic Cooperation and Development). 2000b. *International Trade and Core Labor Standards*. Paris: OECD.

OECD (Organization for Economic Cooperation and Development). 2000c. *OECD Agricultural Outlook, 2000–2005*. Paris: OECD.

OECD (Organization for Economic Cooperation and Development). 2000d. Preliminary Report on Domestic Support Aspects of the Uruguay Round Implementation. Paris: OECD. Photocopy (February).

OECD (Organization for Economic Cooperation and Development). 2000e. Preliminary Report on Export Subsidy Aspects of the Uruguay Round Implementation. Paris: OECD. Photocopy (February).

OECD (Organization for Economic Cooperation and Development). 2000f. *Transition to Responsible Fisheries: Economic and Policy Implications*. Paris: OECD.

OECD (Organization for Economic Cooperation and Development). 2000g. *An Assessment of the Costs for International Trade in Meeting Regulatory Requirements*. Paris: OECD. Photocopy (February).

OECD (Organization for Economic Cooperation and Development). 2001. *Communications Outlook*. Paris: OECD.

OFTEL (UK Office of Telecommunications). 1995. *Beyond the Telephone, the Television and the PC*. London: OFTEL.

Olarreaga, M., and I. Soloaga. 1998. Endogenous Tariff Formation: The Case of Mercosur. *World Bank Economic Review* 12: 297–320.

Oliver, Peter. 1996. *Free Movement of Goods in the European Community*. London: Sweet and Maxwell.

Olmi, Giancarlo. 1991. *Politique agricole commune*. Commentaire Mégret. Brussels: Institut d'Etudes Européennes, Editions de l'Université Libre de Bruxelles.

Page, John, and John Underwood. 1997. Growth, the Maghreb, and Free Trade with the European Union. In *Regional Partners in Global Markets: Limits and Possibilities of the Euro-Med Agreements*, eds. Ahmed Galal and Bernard Hoekman. London: Centre for Economic Policy Research.

Panagariya, Arvind. 1999a. The Regionalism Debate: An Overview. *The World Economy* 22, no. 4: 477–511.

Panagariya, Arvind. 1999b. *Regionalism in Trade Policy: Essays on Preferential Trading*. Singapore and London: World Scientific.

Pedler, R. H., and M. P. C. M. van Schendelen, eds. 1994. *Lobbying the European Union*. Aldershot, UK: Dartmouth Publishing Company.

Pelkmans, Jacques. 1997. *European Integration: Methods and Economic Analysis*. Open University of the Netherlands. Harlow: Addison Wesley Longman Limited.

Pelkmans, Jacques, and Paul Brenton. 1997. Free Trade with the EU: Driving Forces and the Effect of "Me Too." Centre for European Policy Studies Working Paper 110. Brussels: Centre for European Policy Studies.

Pelkmans, Jacques, and Antonia Giulia Carzaniga. 1996. The Trade Policy Review of the European Union. *The World Economy* (Global Trade Policy 1996): 81–100.

Perdikis, Nicholas. 2000. A Conflict of Legitimate Interests or Pandering to Vested Interests? *Estey Centre Journal of International Law and Trade Policy* 1, no. 1: 51–65.

Phillips, Peter W.B., and William A. Kerr. 2000. Alternative Paradigms: The WTO versus the Biosafety Protocol for Trade in Genetically Modified Organisms. *Journal of World Trade* 34, no. 4: 63–75.

Preda, Daniela. 2001. The Schuman Plan: The First Step to European Unity and the First European Antitrust Law. Genova: Dipartemento di Ricerche Europee, Università degli Studi di Genova. Photocopy (March).

Reinert, Kenneth A., and David W. Roland-Holst. 1992. Disaggregated Armington Elasticities for Mining and Manufactured Sectors. *Journal of Policy Modelling* 14, no. 5: 631–39.

Richardson, Keith. 2000. Big Business and the European Agenda. Working Paper 35, Sussex European Institute, Brighton. Photocopy (September).

Rieben, Henri. 1954. *Des ententes de maîtres de forges au Plan Schuman*. Lausanne: Centre de Recherches Européennes.

Ritter, Lennart, W. David Braun, and Francis Rawlinson. 2000. *European Competition Law: A Practitioner's Guide*. The Hague: Kluwer Law International.

Rodrik, Dani. 1997. *Has Globalization Gone Too Far?* Washington: Institute for International Economics.

Rojko, A., D. Regier, P. O'Brien, P. Coffing, and L. Bailey. 1978. *Alternative Futures for World Food in 1985*. US Department of Agriculture Report 146. Washington: US Government Printing Office.

Rollo, Jim. 1992. The Association Agreements between the EC and the CSFR: Hungary and Poland: A Half-Empty Glass. London: Royal Institute of International Affairs. Photocopy.

Rouam, Claude. 1998. *Le contrôle des aides aux entreprises dans l'Union européenne*. Paris: Economica.

Sapir, André. 1992. Regional Integration in Europe. *Economic Journal* 102: 1491–1506.

Sapir, André. 1995. The Europe Agreements: Implications for Trade Laws and Institutions. In *Foundations of an Open Economy*, ed. L. Alan Winters. London: Centre for Economic Policy Research.

Sapir, André. 1996. The Effects of Europe's Internal Market Program on Production and Trade: A First Assessment. *Weltwirtschaftliches Archiv* 132, no. 3: 457–75.

Sapir, André. 1997. *Domino Effects in West European Trade, 1960–92*. CEPR Discussion Paper 1576. London: Centre for Economic Policy Research.

Sapir, André. 1998. The Political Economy of EC Regulation. *European Economic Review* 42: 717–32.

Sapir, André. 2000. Trade Regionalism in Europe: Towards an Integrated Approach. *Journal of Common Market Studies* 38, no. 1 (March): 151–62.

Sarris, Alexander. 1992. Consequences of the Proposed CAP Reform for the Southern Part of the EC. Athens: University of Athens. Photocopy (January).

Scherer, Frederic M. 1980. *Industrial Market Structure and Economic Performance*, 2d ed. Chicago: Rand-McNally.

Schmitz, P.M. 1979. EC Price Harmonization: A Macroeconomic Approach. *European Review of Agricultural Economics* 6: 165–90.

Schneider, Uwe H. 2000. State Aid and the Banking Sector. In *State Aid Control in the European Union: Selected Problems*, eds. Giuliano Amato and Claus-Dieter Ehlermann.

Scollay, Robert, and John Gilbert. 2001. *New Regional Trading Arrangements in the Asia Pacific*. Washington: Institute for International Economics.

Sénat. 2000. Rapport d'information sur l'expatriation des jeunes Français, Séance du 7 Juin 2000. Paris: Sénat de la République Française.

Servan-Schreiber, Jean-Jacques. 1967. *Le défi américain*. Paris: Denoel.

Shiells, C.R., A. Deardorff, and R. Stern. 1986. Estimates of the elasticities of substitution between imports and home goods for the United States. *Weltwirtschaftliches Archiv*, Band 122, no. 2: 497–519.

Shin, Hyun Ja. 1997. *The U.S. Experience*. Brookings Trade Forum. Washington: Brookings Institution.

Shirotori, Miho. 1997. Fishery Sector: The Post Uruguay Round Trade Environment. Division on International Trade and Commodities. UNCTAD, Geneva. Photocopy (July).

Single Market Review. 1997a. *Air Transport*. Subseries II, vol. 2. Luxembourg: European Commission.

Single Market Review. 1997b. *Capital Market Liberalization*. Subseries III, vol. 5. London: Kogan Page/Earthscan.

Single Market Review. 1997c. *External Access to European Markets*. Subseries IV, vol. 4. Luxembourg: EC Office for Official Publication.

Single Market Review. 1997d. *Motor Vehicles*. Subseries I, vol. 6. London: Kogan Page.

Single Market Review. 1998. *Dismantling of Barriers: Technical Barriers to Trade*. Subseries III, vols. 1 and 2. Luxembourg: EC Office for Official Publications.

Smith, Alasdair, and Anthony Venables. 1991. Counting the Cost of Voluntary Export Restraints in the European Car Market. In *International Trade and Trade Policy*, eds. Elhanan Helpman and Assaf Razin. Cambridge, MA: MIT Press.

Snape, Richard. 1987. The Importance of Frontier Barriers. In *Protection and Competition in International Trade: Essays in Honor of W.M. Corden*, ed. Henryk Kierzkowski. Oxford: Basil Blackwell.

Soloaga, Isidro, and L. Alan Winters. 1999a. *How Has Regionalism in the 1990s Affected Trade?* Policy Research Working Paper 2156. Washington: World Bank.

Soloaga, Isidro, and L. Alan Winters. 1999b. *Regionalism in the Nineties: What Effect on Trade?* Discussion Paper Series 2183. London: Centre for Economic Policy Research.

Sorsa, Piritta. 1996. Sub-Saharan Africa's Own Commitments in the Uruguay Round: Myth or Reality? *The World Economy* 19, no. 3: 287–305.

Spinanger, Dean. 1994. *Profiting from Protection in an Open Economy: Hong Kong's Supply Response to EC's MFA Restrictions.* Kiel Working Paper no. 653, September. Kiel, Germany: University of Kiel, Kiel Institute of World Economics.

Spinanger, Dean. 1998. Textiles beyond the MFA Phase-Out. *The World Economy* 22, no. 4: 455–75.

Stegemann, Klaus. 1977. *Price Competition and Output Adjustment in the European Steel Market.* Kieler Studien 147. Tübingen: J.C.B. Mohr (Paul Siebeck).

Steil, Benn. 1996. *The European Equity Markets.* London: Royal Institute of International Affairs.

Steil, Benn. 1998. *Regional Financial Market Integration: Learning from the European Experience.* London: Royal Institute of International Affairs.

Steiner, Faye. 2000. *Regulation, Industry Structure and Performance in the Electricity Supply Industry.* OECD Economics Department Working Paper 238 (April). Paris: OECD.

Stelzer, Irwin M. 1991. Regulatory Methods: A Case for "Hands Across the Atlantic." In *Regulators and the Market: An Assessment of the Growth of Regulation in the UK,* ed. Cento Veljanovski. London: Institute of Economic Affairs.

Stern, Robert M., Jonathan Francis, and Bruce Schumacher. 1976. *Price Elasticities in International Trade.* Trade Policy Research Centre, London: The MacMillan Press Ltd.

Stetser, Bradley W. 1996. L'économie politique des quotas de diffusion. Institut d'Etudes Politiques de Paris, Paris. Photocopy (September).

Swinbank, Alan. 1997. The New CAP. In *The CAP,* 2d ed., ed. Christopher Ritson and David Harvey. New York: Cab International.

Swinbank, Alan. 1999. EU Agriculture, Agenda 2000 and the WTO Commitments. *The World Economy* 22, no. 1: 41–54.

Tangermann, Stephan. 1994. The European Union and the Uruguay Round. In *The Uruguay Round Agreement on Agriculture: An Evaluation,* ed. International Agricultural Trade Research Consortium. Davis, CA: University of California.

Tangermann, Stephan. 1998. Implementation of the Uruguay Round Agreement on Agriculture by Major Developed Countries. In *Uruguay Round Results and the Emerging Trade Agenda,* eds. Harmon Thomas and John Whalley. Geneva: UNCTAD.

Tangermann, Stephan. 1999. Europe's Agricultural Policies and the Millenium Round. *The World Economy* 22, no. 1: 1155–78.

Tarr, David. 1990. A Modified Cournot Aggregation Condition for Obtaining Estimates of Cross-Elasticities of Demand. *Eastern Economic Journal* 16, no. 1: 257–64.

Tarr, David G., and Morris E. Morkre. 1984. *Aggregate Costs to the United States of Tariffs and Quotas on Imports.* Washington: Bureau of Economics, US Federal Trade Commission.

Tharakhan, P. K. M., G. Greenaway, and J. Tharakhan. 1998. Cumulation and Inquiry Determination of the European Community in Antidumping Cases. *Weltwirtschafliches Archiv* 134, no. 2: 320–39.

Trachtman, Joel P. 1997. Accounting Standards and Trade Disciplines: Irreconcilable Differences. *Journal of World Trade* 31, no. 6: 63–98.

Tracy, Michael. 1997. *CAP Reform: The Southern Products.* Genappe: Agricultural Policy Studies.

Trela, Irene. 1998. Phasing Out MFA Restrictions in the Uruguay Round. In *Uruguay Round Results and the Emerging Trade Agenda,* eds. Harmon Thomas and John Whalley. Geneva: UNCTAD.

Trela, Irene, and John Whalley. 1990. Global Effects of Developed Country Trade Restrictions on Textiles and Apparel. *Economic Journal* 100: 1190–1205.

Tyers, R., and Kym Anderson. 1992. *Disarray in World Food Markets: A Quantitative Assessment.* Cambridge: Cambridge University Press.

UNCTAD (UN Conference on Trade and Development). 1971. *Report on Restrictive Business Practices.* TB/B/C.2/104/Rev. 1. New York: UNCTAD.

UNCTAD (UN Conference on Trade and Development). 1994. *The Outcome of the Uruguay Round: An Initial Assessment.* Geneva: UNCTAD.

UNCTAD (UN Conference on Trade and Development). 1999. *World Investment Report: Foreign Direct Investment and the Challenge of Development.* Geneva: UNCTAD.

UN-ECE (UN Economic Commission for Europe). 1996. The Re-emergence of Trade Among the East European and Baltic Countries: Commercial and Other Policy Issues. *Economic Bulletin for Europe* 48: 75–91.

US National Center for APEC (Asia-Pacific Economic Cooperation). 1999. *The APEC Food System.* Seattle, WA: US National Center for APEC.

van Marion, Marcel F. 1993. *Liberal Trade and Japan.* Heidelberg and New York: Physica-Verlag.

Venables, Anthony J. 1999. *Regional Integration Agreements: A Force for Convergence or Divergence?* Photocopy (June). Washington: World Bank.

Vermulst, Edwin and Paul Waer. 1990. Anti-Diversion Rules in Antidumping Procedures: Interface or Short-Circuit for the Management of Interdependence? *Michigan Journal of International Law* 11, no. 4 (Summer): 1119–94.

Vermulst, Edwin, Petros Mavroidis, and Paul Waer. 1999. The Functioning of the Appellate Body after Four Years—Towards Rule Integrity. *Journal of World Trade* 33, no. 2: 1–50.

Vickers, John, and George Yarrow. 1988. *Privatization: An Economic Analysis.* Cambridge, MA: MIT Press.

Vincent, Daniel. 1998. Le transport: nouveau moteur ou laissé pour compte de la construction européenne. Groupe d'Economie Mondiale, Fondation Nationale des Sciences Politiques, Paris. Photocopy (September).

Waer, Paul, and Edwin Vermulst. 1999. EC Antisubsidy Law and Practice after the Uruguay Round: A Wolf in Sheep's Clothing? *Journal of World Trade* 33, no. 3: 19–43.

Waller, Spencer W. 2000. Anticartel Cooperation. In *Antitrust Goes Global: What Future for Transatlantic Cooperation?* eds., Simon J. Evenett, Alexander Lehmann, and Benn Steil. Washington: Brookings Institution.

Wang, Zhen Kun, and L. Alan Winters. 1997. *Africa's Role in Multilateral Trade Negotiations.* Policy Research Working Paper 1846. Washington: World Bank.

Waverman, Leonard, and Esen Sirel. 1997. European Telecommunications Markets on the Verge of Full Liberalization. *Journal of Economic Perspectives* 11, no. 4: 113–26.

Waverman, Leonard, and Esen Sirel. 1998. A Comparison of Liberalization in the United Kingdom and France. Paper presented at the Tripolar meeting, Tokyo (6–7 October).

Weiler, Todd. 2000. International Regulatory Reform Obligations. *Journal of World Trade* 34, no. 3: 71–94.

Weiss, Frank. 1992. Trade Policies in Germany. In *Handbook of Comparative Economic Policies,* vol. 2, *National Trade Policies,* ed. Dominick Salvatore. New York: Greenwood Press.

Winckler, Antoine. 2000. State Guarantees for Financial Institutions: Of State Aid and Moral Hazard. In *State Aid Control in the European Union: Selected Problems,* eds. Giuliano Amato and Claus-Dieter Ehlermann. Forthcoming.

Winters, Alan. 1989. The Market for Cars in the Enlarged European Community. Center for Economic Policy Research, London. Photocopy (December).

Winters, L. Alan. 1992. The Europe Agreements: A Briefing Note. Centre for Economic Policy Research, London. Photocopy (March).

Winters, L. Alan. 1993a. The European Community: A Case of Successful Integration. In *New Dimensions in Regional Integration,* eds. Jaime de Melo and Arvind Panagaryia. Cambridge: Cambridge University Press.

Winters, L. Alan. 1993b. Import Surveillance as a Strategic Trade Policy. In *Empirical Studies of Strategic Trade Policy,* eds. Paul Krugman and Alasdair Smith. Chicago: University of Chicago Press.

Winters, L. Alan. 1994. VERs and Expectations: Extensions and Evidence. *Economic Journal* 104: 113–23.

Winters, L. Alan. 1995. Liberalization of the European Steel Trade. In *European Union Trade with Eastern Europe: Adjustment and Opportunities,* eds. Riccardo Faini and Richard Portes. London: Center for Economic Policy Research.

Winters, L. Alan. 1996. *Regionalism versus Multilateralism.* Policy Research Working Paper 1687. Washington: World Bank.

Wolff, Alan. 1995. The Problems of Market Access in the Global Economy: Trade and Competition Policy. In *New Dimensions of Market Access in a Globalising World Economy,* ed. OECD. Paris: OECD.

Wolf, Martin. 1994. *The Resistible Appeal of Fortress Europe.* London: Centre for Policy Studies.

Wolf, Martin. 1996. The Dog that Failed to Bark: The Climate for Trade Policy in the European Union. In *The World Trading System: Challenges Ahead,* ed. Jeffrey J. Schott. Washington: Institute for International Economics.

Womack, J.P., D. Jones, and D. Roos. 1990. *The Machine that Changed the World.* London: Maxwell-Macmillan.

World Bank. 1992. *Market Outlook for Major Primary Commodities,* vol. 2. Washington: World Bank.

World Bank. 2000. *Trade Blocs.* New York: Oxford University Press.

Zonnekeyn, Geert A. 2000. The Status of WTO Law in the EC Legal Order: The Final Curtain? *Journal of World Trade* 34, no. 3: 111–25.

Zuleeg, Manfred. 1997. The European Constitution under Constitutional Constraints: The German Scenario. *European Law Review* 22: 19–30.

Index

Air France—*continued*
    competition policy rulings, 173–74, 181
    computer reservation systems, 333
    flag (national) carriers, 331
    liberalization in, 66, 70, 146, 150, 151*b*, 154*t*, 156, 156*n*, 158
    market indicators, 152*t*
    subsidies, 336–37
Albania, 227*b*
Algeria, 227*b*
Alpine Investment ruling (1995), 143
aluminum, 100
AMS. *See* aggregate measures of support (AMS)
Amsterdam Treaty (1997), 5
    antidumping policy, 178
    Article 16 (ex 7d), 176
    Common Agricultural Policy design, 79*n*
    goals of, 11*t*–12*t*, 13
    investment issues, 190, 190*n*
    social policy, 164
Andorra, 227*b*
Anstaltslast, 180*n*
anti-Americanism, as federating event, 254
anticircumvention measures, 274, 274*n*
anticoncentration clause, 293
antidumping, 29, 347–58
    ad valorem tariff equivalent of, 35, 64
    aggregation procedure, 33–34
    cancellation of, 13, 64*n*
    cases
        number of, 64
        outcome of (1980–99), 348–54, 349*t*
        screening tests (1980–97), 356–59, 357*t*
        by trading partner (1980–99), 352*t*–353*t*
    collusion bias of, 102*t*, 102–03
    combining NTBs and tariffs with, 31–34
    community protection via, 30–31
    and competition policy, 177–78
    and domestic price increases, 53
    fisheries, 81*b*
    in goods, 102
    for industrial sectors, 75, 102
    in manufacturing, 98–99
    and market structure, 57–58
    nonmarket economy in, 235–36
    and predation, 354–59, 357*t*
    reform of, 131
    regime improvement, 360–63
    and rents, 52
    rise of, 101–103
    and rules of origin, 101, 326
    sector concentration of, 34–35
    systemic incorporation of, 24
    textiles and clothing, 293–94
    time span of, 33*n*
    unilateral reform of, 360–63
antisubsidy measures, 361–62
    and collusion, 182, 182*n*
    in goods, 101

in manufacturing, 98–99
    types of, 179, 193
APEC. *See* Asia Pacific Economic Cooperation (APEC)
APT. *See* Autonomous Preferential Trade (APT)
Argentina, 219
Armington import model, 369–70
Article 115, 30, 30*n*, 282, 293
artificial and synthetic fibers (ASF), 269–70
Asia-Europe Summit Meetings, 235
Asia Pacific, 235–38. *See also* African, Caribbean, and Pacific countries (ACP) Conventions; *specific country*
Asia Pacific Economic Cooperation (APEC), 112, 230, 235–37
    preferential trade agreements, 209
Association of Firms with a Common Interest in the Video 2000 System, 271
Atlanticists, 232
audiocassette tapes, 272
audiovisual markets, 325, 325*t*, 327–30
Australia, 179, 209, 219
Austria, 69–70, 124*n*
autolimitation agreements. *See* voluntary export restraints (VERs)
Autonomous Preferential Trade (APT), 227*b*
avances sur recettes, 327
Azerbaijan, 233

Baden-Württemberg Oberlandesgericht (1988), 105*b*
balance of powers, 255–56, 258–59
Balkan countries
    definition of, 197*n*
    preferential trade agreements with, 201, 210, 226–28, 227*b*, 247–48
Baltic Free Trade Area (BFTA), 216*b*
Banana Framework Agreement, 317–18, 320
bananas, 5, 159, 202*b*, 203, 207–09, 240, 243*n*, 244
    case studies, 316–24, 318*t*
Bank for International Settlements, 190
banking. *See also* financial services; investment
    liberalization in, 144, 154*t*, 156, 158, 191
    mergers and acquisitions, 160–61
    subsidies, 180*n*, 180–82, 182*n*
Banque de France, 182*n*
Barcelona Summit (1995), 226
barley, 92
BBC, 324
beef
    from ACP countries, 202*b*, 207–08
    case studies, 296*t*, 299–300, 305–06, 309*t*
    hormone case, 117–20, 240
    labeling rules for, 121
    mad cow disease, 114, 115*b*–116*b*, 117–19, 131
    reform of, 85*b*, 95*b*–96*b*, 224
Berlin Council (1999), 79, 94–98, 96*b*
    and CAP reform, 85*b*, 86*t*–87*t*, 88
    and Central European countries, 217*b*, 219–23, 225

Financial Framework, 222
subsidy modulation, 122, 130, 203
Berlin Wall, fall of, 13, 201, 210, 212b
Berne Convention, 188
BFTA. *See* Baltic Free Trade Area (BFTA)
biological diversity, 188
Blair House agreement (1992), 94, 124
block exemptions, 172–173, 173n, 287
blue box subsidies, 78, 93
BMW, 286
Boeing-McDonnell ruling (1997), 173–74
Bonn US-EC Summit (1999), 231
bookshops, online, 148
border effects, intra-EC, 56
border nontariff borders, 24
Bosman ruling (1995), 139, 168
Bosnia-Herzegovina, 227b
Botswana, 207
bovine spongiform encephalopathy (BSE). *See*
mad cow disease
Braun Report, 277n
Brazil, 179, 202b, 207, 219
British Airways, 332
British Telecom (BT), 134, 141, 176, 341
Brittan, Leon, 17
Brussels, role of, 253
Brussels Ministerial (1990), 228
BSE (bovine spongiform encephalopathy). *See*
mad cow disease
BSkyB, 324
business cycle, antidumping cases and, 350
butter, 308, 310–11. *See also* dairy products

cadmium, 111
Cairns Group, 130
Canada. *See also* Quad countries
Agreement on Internal Trade between Canada
and its Provinces (1994), 104n
and beef hormone case, 117
mutual-recognition agreement with, 229
preferential trade agreements, 209
technical regulations policy, 111, 112
Canal Plus, 327n, 328
Canon, 274
capital gains tax, 161
capital liberalization, 189–90
Car Consensus, 284–286, 285t
Caribbean Community (CARICOM), 208. *See also*
African, Caribbean, and Pacific countries
(ACP) Conventions; *specific country*
cars, 35, 58, 173
case studies, 282–89, 285t
Japanese industry, 29, 31, 66, 99–100, 282–88
stability of protection, 64–65
subsidies, 66, 100, 179, 283–84, 287
cartels
crisis, 48
export, 171–72
hard-core, 171–72
Casati ruling (1981), 190

case law. *See* European Court of Justice; *specific
ruling*
case studies, 263–346
air transport, 331–38, 332t, 334t–335t
artificial and synthetic fibers, 269–70
bananas, 316–24, 318t
beef, 296t, 299–300, 305–06, 309t
cars, 282–89, 285t
cement, 263–64
cereals, 298t, 299, 301–03, 304t
dairy products, 296t, 300, 308–12, 312t
farm product cases, 295–300, 296t–298t
fertilizers, 264–65
French films, 324–31, 325t
hardboard, 266–67
integrated circuits, 272–73
meat products, 296t, 299–300, 303–08, 309t
newsprint, 267–68
photocopiers, 273–75
polyethylene, 265–66
polyvinyl chloride, 265–66
steel, 275–82, 281t
sugar, 298t, 300, 311–16, 315t
telecommunications, 338–46, 339t–340t,
342t–343t
textiles and clothing, 289–95, 290t–291t
videocassette recorders, 270–72
Cassis de Dijon ruling, 105b, 107, 134, 141–42
CCP. *See* Common Commercial Policy (CCP)
CEFTA. *See* Central European Free Trade Area
(CEFTA)
Cembureau, 264
cement, 64, 263–64
Central European countries (CECs)
accession of, 5, 69–70, 245–46, 250, 252, 254
process of, 216–19, 217b–218b, 220t–221t
agreements within, 215, 216b
agriculture policy, 78, 89, 97–98, 129, 214, 217b,
219–22, 224–25, 246
car imports, 288
and commercial policy, 223–26
credibility of reforms in, 214
definition of, 69n, 197n
EC initiatives for, 245–47
and Europe Agreements, 213–15, 215–23
exports from, 30–31
Helsinki Group, 219
initial group, 213n
Interim Agreement, 213
labor issues, 166, 218b
Luxembourg Group, 216, 217b–218b
manufacturing, 223–24, 246
political content, 210, 214, 218b, 219n, 246
preferential trade agreements, 197, 201, 206,
210–28, 245–47
services, 225–26, 245–46, 255
steel industry, 276–77, 280
and technical regulations, 105b, 112n, 112–13,
214–15, 222–23, 245
textiles and clothing, 293

European Council, Seattle preparatory texts. *See*
    Seattle Ministerial (February 2001)
European Court of Justice, 6*b*. *See also specific*
    ruling
  air transport rulings, 336
  antidumping rulings, 348
  commercial policy rulings, 134–35, 140–43
  competition policy rulings, 171–77
  intellectual property rights rulings, 188*n*,
    188–89
  investment rulings, 190
  labor rulings, 163, 168
  market-oriented push of, 13, 14*b*, 15*t*–16*t*
  steel trade policy ruling, 30
  technical regulations rulings, 105*b*, 106–08
European Defense Community, collapse of, 2
European Economic Area, 69
European fiscal pact, 169
European Free Trade Area (EFTA), 24, 69, 74*n*,
    197, 206, 212*b*, 247, 276
European institutions (Commission, Council,
    Parliament), Seattle Ministerial preparatory
    texts. *See* Seattle Ministerial (February
    2001)
European Investment Bank, 208
European Monetary Union (EMU), 217*b*
European Parliament
  Seattle preparatory texts (*See* Seattle Ministerial
    (February 2001))
  weighting votes in, 13, 15*t*–16*t*
European Political Community, meaning of, 257
European Roundtable of Industrialists (ERT), 74,
    74*n*, 133
European Standardization Bodies (ESBs), 106
European Union, *versus* European Community, 1*n*
Euroskeptics, 3
euro zone, 252
Everything but Arms initiative, 63*n*, 208, 244–45
exclusive economic zones (EEZs), 80*n*
exemption regime, in competition policy, 172–73,
    173*n*, 287
exhaustion principle, 188–89
export cartels, 171–72
export policies, progressive harmonization of, 7*b*
export subsidies, 24, 63*n*, 64, 89–90, 224–25, 225*n*
  beef, 306
  cereals, 302–03
  milk, 310
  pork, 307
  poultry, 307–08
  sugar, 314
export taxes, 92
Extramet ruling (1992), 177–78
Eyssen case (1981), 118, 118*n*

factor-based subsidies, 85
failure index, 108*n*, 108–11
fair competition, 136
farm(s), size of, 129–30
farm entrepreneurs, 88–89

farmers, 45*n*
  demonstrations by, 84
  and environmental issues, 131
  overcompensation of, 87–88, 92, 96*b*
  subsidy entitlement, 88–89
farm income, 84, 93*n*, 93–94
farm market-support payments, 82
farm policy. *See also* agriculture
  Austria, 124*n*
  case studies, 295–300, 296*t*–298*t*
  Denmark, 125
  Finland, 124*n*
  France, 93, 93*n*, 124–25
  Germany, 124*n*, 124–25
  Ireland, 124
  New Zealand, 94, 95*b*
  protective measures, 29
  reform of, 94, 95*b*
  Spain, 122*n*, 124*n*, 125*n*
  Sweden, 94, 95*b*, 124*n*
  United Kingdom, 7, 88, 124, 125, 125*n*
  United States, 89
farm subsidies, 63–64, 78, 82
  blue box, 93
  Central European countries, 219–22
  compensatory land-based, 85*b*, 87–88, 90–91,
    93–94, 96*b*
  demand, 82
  entitlement to, 88–89
  export, 89–90
  factor-based, 85
  French, 93, 93*n*
  green box, 93
  level of, determination of, 88–89
  modulation of, 98, 122–25, 129–30
  OECD *versus* CAP, 82, 83*t*
  and overcompensation, 87–88, 92, 96*b*
  price-support, 82, 84–85, 94, 95*b*
  renationalization of, 97–98, 219–22
  sectoral, 96*b*
  supply, 82
farm supply control, 82
favored nation (MFN) status, zero tariffs, 28, 244
FDC. *See* fully distributed costs (FDC)
FDI. *See* foreign direct investment (FDI)
federation, 254–56
fertilizers, 264–65
Fiat, 283–84, 288
fibers, artificial and synthetic, 179, 269–70
films, 37, 52, 58, 66, 70, 145, 149, 149*n*, 180
  case studies, 324–31, 325*t*
financial services, 141–45, 150, 158, 230. *See also*
    banking; investment; stock exchanges
Finland
  accession of, 69–70
  farm policy, 124*n*
  manufacturing policy, 127
  paper industry, 268
  technical regulations policy, 111
  telecommunications industry, 338, 338*n*, 341–42

Fischer, M. Joshka, 253
fisheries, 79, 80b–81b, 229
Foie Gras ruling (1998), 106
Food and Drug Administration (U.S.), 130
food products. *See also* agriculture; farm policy
  consumer prices for, 95b, 97
food safety issues, 63, 114–21, 130–31
  and consumer behavior, 120–21
  labeling, 121, 131
  and scientific evidence, 119n, 119–20
  as source of trade barriers, 75, 78, 103–04
  and technical regulations, 113, 114, 117
footwear, 203
Ford, 284
foreign direct investment (FDI), 215, 226, 227–28
foreign policy, trade policy as substitute for, 4,
  200–01, 251, 258
Foreign Sales Corporations regime, 240, 242
Fortress Europe, 24, 35
forward mechanism, 90n
four freedoms, intra-EC, 10, 168, 212b, 227b
France
  banana regime, 316
  car industry, 284, 286–87
  environmental issues, 131
  farm policy, 93, 93n, 124–25
  film industry, 52, 66, 324–31, 325t
  labor issues, 167n, 168n
  mad cow disease, 115b–116b, 118
  major contributions of, 253
  manufacturing policy, 127
  souverainistes, 3
  state aid, 180, 182n
  VCR tax, 270–71
Franco-German Treaty of Commerce, 9
François-Hall model, 49, 54t–55t, 69–70
free movement
  of goods, 212b, 227b
  of labor, 162–63, 168–69, 218b, 253
  of services, 253
Free Trade Area of the Americas (FTAA), 209, 233
French Safety Agency (Agence française de
  sécurité sanitaire des aliments), 119
fruit, 297t
full-compensation principle, 91
fully distributed costs (FDC), 343
Fyffes, 316, 321

GATS. *See* General Agreement on Trade in
  Services (GATS)
Gaz de France, 176n
Geest, 316
General Agreement on Tariffs and Trade (GATT),
  2, 25
  antidumping policy, 177
  Article I, 112, 207, 319
  Article III, 173
  Article VI, 102
  Article XIII, 319, 321
  Article XIX, 362–63

Article XXIV, 100, 207, 208
Article XXVIII, 27, 248
banana import negotiations, 5
beef hormone case, 117, 240
competition policy, 171
fisheries negotiations, 81b
and intra-EC liberalization, 18
Japanese accession to, 205, 236
Leutwiler Group, 74n
and mutual recognition agreements, 112
preferential trade agreements, 207–08
Section IV, 201, 207
settlement procedures, 238
subsidy rules, 179
General Agreement on Trade in Services (GATS),
  159
  Article II, 319
  Article VIII, 176
  Article IX, 176
  Article XV, 179
  Article XVII, 319
  Article XXI, 248
  investment issues, 190
general equilibrium approach, 40, 116
general interest, 158, 179
Generalized System of Preferences (GSP), 50n,
  162, 192, 198, 201–28
  application to ACP countries, 208–09
  drug, 202b
  future for, 207–10
  history of, 202b
  net gains for, 201–05
  pyramid of preferences, 205–07, 206t
genetically modified organisms (GMOs), 116,
  119–20
Geneva, agricultural negotiations, 78
German miracle, 10
Germany
  banana regime, 316
  car industry, 284
  Cartel Office, 159n
  dominance of, 255
  eastern states of, privatization process in,
    100
  farm policy, 124n, 124–25
  intellectual property rights cases, 188n
  labor issues, 167n
  Länder, 255, 255n, 257
  major contributions of, 253
  manufacturing policy, 127
  PCP ban, 105b, 111
  political content, 3
  promotional selling laws, 148, 148n
  retail industry, 159n
  Social Democratic Party, 250
  state aid, 180, 180n
  Gewährträgerhaftung, 180n
  glycine, 360n
  GMOs. *See* genetically modified organisms
    (GMOs)

International Monetary Fund (IMF), 187, 190
International Standard Industrial Classification
   (ISIC) sectors, 22t–23t, 26–27, 108n,
   109t–110t
International Steel Cartel (Entente Internationale
   de l'Acier), 9
Internet services, 147–149, 148n, 153, 343
intervention prices, 78, 85b, 87, 90–91, 94, 96b, 203,
   220
   beef, 305
   cereals, 301–02
   milk, 308
   sugar, 311
   versus world prices, 90–92, 302
intra-EC barriers, elimination of, 10
intra-EC border effects, 56
intra-EC cartels, 171–72
intra-EC liberalization, 18, 136, 147
   caused by technical regulations, 107
   in services, 150–59
intra-EC mergers and acquisitions, 160–62
intra-EC technical regulations policy, 104–11,
   131–32
investment, 6b, 187, 189–91
   foreign direct, 215, 226–28
   international, WTO negotiations on, 133, 137b
   and Latin American agreements, 234
investment services, 142, 145, 158. See also
   financial services
Investment Services Directive, 190
Iran-Libya sanctions act, 229
Ireland, 124, 188n, 222, 252
ISIC sectors. See International Standard Industrial
   Classification (ISIC) sectors
isoglucose, 314, 314n
Israel, 227b, 247
Isuzu, 284
Italy, 127, 176n, 253, 286
ITQs. See individual transferable quotas (ITQs)

Jamaica, 204
Japan. See also Quad countries
   car industry, 29, 31, 66, 99–100, 282–88, 285t
   DRAM industry, 272–73
   GATT accession, 205, 236
   glycine case against, 360n
   intellectual property rights cases, 188
   Ministry of International Trade and Industry
      (MITI), 271, 284, 286
   photocopier industry, 273–74, 274n
   preferential trade agreements, 236–37
   steel industry, 276–77, 279–80
   technical regulations policy, 111
   VCR industry, 271–72
Japan-bashers, 232
jobs. See also labor; workers
   and costs of protection, 41, 53–56, 54t–55t
Jordan, 227b, 247
judicial activism, to reintroduce statism, 10
Justice and Home Affairs (JHA), 5n, 217b, 218b

Kawasaki, 279
Kazakhstan, 233
Keck and Mithouard ruling (1993), 107, 134
Kennedy Round (1962–67), 18, 81
Kenya, 204
KLM, 333
Kommerskollegium (Sweden), 360
Konica, 274, 274n
Korea. See North Korea; South Korea
Kosovo, 219
Kymmene, 268
Kyrgyzstan, 233

labeling, 121, 131
   of social aid, 193n
labor, 162–169, 192. See also jobs; workers
   and competition, 166
   core norms, 169
   free movement of, 162–63, 168–69, 218b, 253
   harmonization in, 163
   political content of, 167, 167n
   treaty basis for, 133–34, 137b, 139–40
labor costs, 165–67
labor flows, 168n, 168–69
labor-intensive industrial sectors, 45–48
labor relations, and aid to developing countries,
   192–93
labor standards, 104
   costs for workers, 167
labor-weighted tariff averages, 27–28, 36
land-based subsidies, compensatory, 85b
Länder (Germany), 255, 255n, 257
Landesbanken, 180n
land prices, 84, 158n
large country, EC as, 66–70, 67t–68t
large-store regulations, 158n–159n, 159
last-mile liberalization, 144
Latin America, 233–34, 236–38. See also African,
   Caribbean, and Pacific countries (ACP)
   Conventions; specific country
   banana regime, 317–18, 321
law enforcement
   competition, 66n, 229, 234
   technical regulations, 103–04, 105b, 132
Law of the Sea, 80n
LdPE. See low-density polyethylene (LdPE)
leadership, 255
Lebanon, 227b
legal basis. See European Court of Justice; specific
   ruling
less developed countries (LDCs), 198, 206, 208, 244
Lesotho, 207
Leutwiler Group, 74n
Liechtenstein, 69n
limited reciprocity, 243–44, 247
Lomé Convention, 202b, 206–09, 319
London Stock Exchange, 145, 190
   Automated Quotation International, 143
London US-EC Summit (1998), 231
long-run incremental costs (LRIC), 344

modeling of, 367–70
modes of, 149
supply control, 82
supply subsidies, 82
Supreme Court (U.S.), 134*n*, 174–75, 181
surveillance regime, 363
sustainable development, 103
Swaziland, 207
Sweden
    accession of, 69–70
    ban on antialcoholic advertising, 252*n*
    farm policy, 94, 95*b*, 124*n*
    manufacturing policy, 127
    paper industry, 268
    telecommunications industry, 338, 338*n*, 341–42
Switzerland, 69*n*, 104*n*
Syria, 227*b*

TABD. *See* Transatlantic Business (TABD) dialog
TACD. *See* Transatlantic Consumer (TACD) dialog
TACs. *See* total allowable catches (TACs)
TAED. *See* Transatlantic Environment (TAED) dialog
Taiwan, 272
TALD. *See* Transatlantic Labor (TALD) dialog
tariff(s)
    1990–2000, 25–28
    combining NTBs and antidumping measures with, 31–34
    costs for levying, 50
    6-digit level classification, 98
    Kennedy Round cuts, 18
    reshuffling, 22*t*–23*t*, 27, 35
    revenues, 46*t*–47*t*, 50, 52–53, 53*n*, 244
tariff averages, 24
    on industrial goods, 205
    labor-weighted, 27, 28, 36
    production-weighted, 122
    value-added-weighted, 27, 28
tariff-band approach, 98
tariff-cap formula, 92
tariff-rate quotas (TRQs), 320–21
taux de retour (rate of return), 88, 125*n*
taxes
    capital gains, 161
    and commercial policy, 156–58
    EC-wide, 159
    environmental, 159
    export, 92
    income, 158
    luxury, 270–71
    seat, 326
transportation, 159
tax revenues, 52
TBR. *See* Trade Barriers Regulation (TBR)
TCA. *See* Trade and Cooperation Agreement (TCA)
technical barriers to trade (TBTs), 103, 103*n*, 112, 230. *See also* technical regulations (TRs)

technical progress
    and competition policy, 172
    and food safety issues, 119–20
    and services, 145, 150, 151*b*, 161
technical regulations (TRs), 29, 29*n*, 73–74, 103–21, 131
    car industry, 283, 287
    and Central European countries, 105*b*, 111, 111*n*, 112–13, 222–23, 245
    costs of, 104
    and country of origin, 121
    cross-monitoring of, 121, 131
    design of, 103, 105*b*
    enforcement of, 103–04, 105*b*, 132
    and Europe Agreements, 214–15
    European Court's treatment of, 13
    hardboard, 266–67
    impact on protection, 104–11, 131
    intra-CEC agreements on, 216*b*
    labor (*See* labor standards)
    paper industry, 267–268
    telecommunications industry, 338, 344–46
    at world level, 111
telecommunications, 133, 144, 144*n*. *See also* telephony
    antidumping measures, 58
    case studies, 338–46, 339*t*–340*t*, 342*t*–343*t*
    commercial policy, 133, 144, 144*n*
    level of protection, 37
    liberalization of, 66, 70, 146, 150, 151*b*, 152*t*–153*t*, 153, 155*t*, 156, 158, 230, 341–42
    mergers and acquisitions, 161
    WTO negotiations on, 18
Telecommunications Act (U.K.; 1991), 341
Telecommunications Act (U.S.; 1996), 338
Telecommunications Agreement (1997), 160, 345
telephony, 150, 151*b*, 152*t*–153*t*, 153, 160
television broadcasting services, 154*t*, 158, 324, 325*t*, 327–28
Television Without Frontiers Directive, 145, 226, 328*n*, 328–29
TEP. *See* Transatlantic Economic Partnership (TEP)
terms of trade losses, 66–60, 67*t*–68*t*
Tetras, 273
textiles, 29, 99, 131, 179, 203, 204, 213, 226*n*, 227*b*
    case studies, 289–95, 290*t*–291*t*
Thatcher, Margaret, 253
theaters, 325*t*, 326, 327
Thomson, 271, 272
threshold prices
    cereals, 301–02
    milk, 310
    sugar, 311
ThyssenKrupp, 279
TLD. *See* Transatlantic Legislator (TLD) dialog
tobacco, 176*n*
Tokyo Round, 160
Toshiba, 274, 274*n*
total allowable catches (TACs), 80*b*–81*b*
total economic transfers, 125*n*

Toyota, 284
TPS. *See* transitional product-specific safeguard
    (TPS)
traceability system, 121
Tractebel-Suez-Lyonnaise des Eaux, 161
Trade and Cooperation Agreement (TCA), with
    former Yugoslavia, 227*b*
trade barriers, removal of
    effects in domestic market, 365–67, 366*f*
    effects in import market, 365–67, 366*f*
Trade Barriers Regulation (TBR), 101, 362
trade creation, and preferential trade agreements,
    199*b*
trade diversion
    caused by technical regulations, 107–11
    and preferential trade agreements, 197, 199*b*
trade dynamics, 73–132
    impact of dispute settlement on, 242
    impact of food safety issues on, 114–21
    and preferential trade agreements, 199*b*,
        214–15, 227–28
    in technical regulations policy, 104
trade flows
    based on comparative advantage, 210
    effect of technical regulations on, 111, 131–32
trade liberalization. *See also specific area of trade*
    climate for, 8
trademarks. *See* intellectual property rights
trade-related intellectual property rights (TRIPS),
    133–35, 176, 187–89, 193, 250
    and Latin American agreements, 234
trade shocks, 73
Transatlantic Business Dialogue (TABD), 112, 229,
    231
Transatlantic Consumer Dialogue (TACD), 229
Transatlantic Declaration (1990), 229
Transatlantic Economic Partnership (TEP), 231–32
Transatlantic Economic Partnership Statement
    and Action Plan (1998), 229
Transatlantic Environment Dialogue (TAED), 229
Transatlantic Labor Dialogue (TALD), 229
Transatlantic Legislator Dialogue (TLD), 229
Transatlantic Partnership for Political
    Cooperation (1998), 229
Trans-European Networks, 10
transfers from protection, beneficiaries of, 52–53
transitional product-specific safeguard (TPS),
    235–36
transparency, 31, 185, 189, 193
transportation, 133, 151*b*, 152*t*, 154*t*, 156. *See also*
    air transport; cars; trucking
    equipment, 13, 35
    taxes, 159
    treaty basis for, 140–41, 146
travel agencies, 156
Treaty-based trade policy, 2, 4–8. *See also specific
    treaty*
Treaty Establishing the European Community
    (TEC), 5, 5*n*
    Article 28 (ex 30), 117

Article 29 (ex 34), 171
Article 31 (ex 37), 176
Article 295 (ex 222), 176, 188
precautionary principle, 114*n*
statist bias in, 8–13
steel industry, 280
Treaty of Paris (1951), 4, 6*b*
    Articles 71–73, 30
    pricing rules, 9
    sector bias, 13
    statism of, 9, 10
    steel trade policy under, 30
Treaty of Rome (1957), 2, 4, 5
    ambiguities of, 10
    Article 2, 163, 170
    Article 3, 170
    Article 28 (ex 30), 105*b*, 118, 183, 189, 271
    Article 30 (ex 36), 105*b*, 107–08, 118, 189, 283*n*
    Article 32, 164*n*
    Article 32 (ex 38) to 38 (ex 46), 79–81
    Article 33 (ex 39), 79–81
    Article 39 (ex 48), 139, 168
    Article 43 (ex 52), 139–41, 169, 183
    Article 44 (ex 54) to 48 (ex 58), 169
    Article 49 (ex 59), 139–40, 143, 148*n*, 183, 191
    Article 51 (ex 61), 140*n*
    Article 52 (ex 63), 140–41
    Article 53 (ex 64), 140, 147
    Article 58, 275–276
    Article 70 (ex 74) to 80 (ex 84), 140–41
    Article 75 (ex 79), 141
    Article 81 (ex 85), 172, 173*n*, 175, 269
    Article 82 (ex 86), 172, 175
    Article 85, 266, 283*n*, 336
    Article 86, 336
    Article 87 (ex 92), 179
    Article ex 91, 178
    Article 94 (ex 100), 105*b*
    Article 95:5 (ex 100a), 105*b*, 108
    Article 134 (ex 115), 150
    Article 137 (ex 118), 162, 164
    Article 141 (ex 119), 165
    Article 205 (ex 148), 251
    banana regime, 316
    Common Agricultural Policy design, 79*n*, 79–81
    Common Commercial Policy, 6*b*
    Common External Tariff, 18
    Common Fisheries Policy, 80*b*–81*b*
    competition policy, 170–71, 175–78, 192
    farm subsidies, 94
    goals of, 11*t*–12*t*
    labor issues, 162–63, 168–69
    market-economy option, 10
    political content, 9–10
    Preamble, 163, 170
    preferential trade agreements, 201, 212*b*
    on public procurement, 183
    renumbering of articles, 6*n*
    revised versions of (*See* Amsterdam Treaty
        (1997); Maastricht Treaty (1992))

scope of, 74
sector bias, 13
services policy, 139–41
social provisions, 163
subsidy rules, 179, 279
technical regulations policy, 104, 105*b*
transport provisions, 140–41
Treaty on the Single European Act (1986), 4
Trésor, 182*n*
triple clause, 276
TRIPS. *See* trade-related intellectual property
    rights (TRIPS)
TRQs. *See* tariff-rate quotas (TRQs)
TRs. *See* technical regulations (TRs)
trucking, 132, 151*b*, 152*t*, 154*t*
Tunisia, 227*b*
Turkey, 163, 226*n*, 247
    Customs Union with, 210, 213*n*, 227*b*

Ukraine, 233
unanimity rule, in services, 6*b*, 135, 164
UNCTAD. *See* United Nations (UN), Conference
    on Trade and Development (UNCTAD)
UN-ECE. *See* United Nations (UN), Economic
    Commission for Europe (ECE)
uniform principles, 6*b*
unilateral actions, 39
Union douanière et économique de l'Afrique
    centrale (UDEAC), 208
Union économique et monétaire ouest-africaine
    (UEMOA), 208
United Kingdom
    air transport industry, 332
    CAP budget waiver, 88
    car industry, 282, 284
    competition policy, 360*n*
    domestic coal preference, 100
    elimination of exchange controls, 190
    Euroskeptic approach, 3
    farm policy, 7, 88, 124–25, 125*n*
    film and television, 324
    mad cow disease, 115*b*–116*b*, 119
    major contributions of, 253
    manufacturing policy, 127
    NAFTA membership, 3
    public procurement issues, 185
    regulatory reform in services, 143, 143*n*, 144*n*
    social policy, 164
    telecommunications industry, 338–41, 339*t*–340*t*
United Nations (UN)
    Conference on the Law of the Sea, 80*n*
    Conference on Trade and Development
        (UNCTAD), 172, 204
    Economic Commission for Europe (ECE), 287
United States. *See also* Quad countries
    banana regime, 5, 316–22
    bilateral agreement with China, 235–36
    Commerce Clause, 132
    competition policy, 173*n*
    costs of protection in, 51, 61

customs cooperation with, 229
dispute settlement cases, 240
farm policy, 89
film and television industry, 324–329, 325*n*,
    327*n*, 329*n*
food safety issues, 116–20
industrial products agreement, 229
intellectual property rights cases, 188
mergers and acquisitions in, 160–62
mutual-recognition agreement with, 130, 229
peace clause, 78, 97
political content, 228–229, 232
preferential trade agreements, 209, 228–32, 247
steel industry, 276–77
subsidy rules, 181
technical regulations policy, 111–13
telecommunications industry, 338
veterinary agreement with, 229
United States-Singapore Free Trade Agreement,
    233
universal coverage, 146
universal service, 144–45, 156
Uruguay Agreement on Safeguards, 31
Uruguay Agriculture Agreement
    ability to fulfill, 79
    Article 20, 75–76
    versus CAP Reform, 78, 84–89
    escape clause, 93
    implementation of, 89–94, 122
    market access issues, 90–91, 208*n*
    reference period for tariffication, 89
    tariffication exercise, 302, 302*n*, 305–07, 310, 314
Uruguay Government Procurement Agreement
    (GPA), 183, 185
Uruguay Round, 6*b*, 21
    Agreement on Textiles and Clothing (ATC), 31,
        99, 131, 292–93
    agricultural commitments, 18, 75
    Built-in Agenda, 78, 136
    developing countries commitment to, 250
    Dispute Settlement Understanding (DSU), 238
    good trade commitments, 74
    level of liberalization achieved by, 17, 17*n*
    overall protection rate after, 34
    Safeguard Agreement, 99–100, 286
    services commitments, 133
    Subsidy Agreement, 179
    tariff commitments, 24, 63
    TRIP Agreement, 187
Usinor, 279, 279*n*
utilities, 161. *See also* infrastructure services;
    specific service
    public procurement directives, 183, 183*n*, 184*t*

Valeo, 283
value-added-weighted tariff averages, 27, 28
van Binsbergen ruling (1974), 139
VEBA-VIAG, 161
vegetables, 297*t*
Venezuela, 317

Other Publications from the Institute for International Economics

* = out of print

POLICY ANALYSES IN INTERNATIONAL ECONOMICS Series

BOOKS

IMF Conditionality*   John Williamson, editor
1983   ISBN 0-88132-006-4
Trade Policy in the 1980s*   William R. Cline, editor
1983   ISBN 0-88132-031-5
Subsidies in International Trade*
Gary Clyde Hufbauer and Joanna Shelton Erb
1984   ISBN 0-88132-004-8
International Debt: Systemic Risk and Policy
Response*   William R. Cline
1984   ISBN 0-88132-015-3
Trade Protection in the United States: 31 Case
Studies*   Gary Clyde Hufbauer, Diane E. Berliner,
and Kimberly Ann Elliott
1986   ISBN 0-88132-040-4
Toward Renewed Economic Growth in Latin
America*   Bela Balassa, Gerardo M. Bueno, Pedro-
Pablo Kuczynski, and Mario Henrique Simonsen
1986   ISBN 0-88132-045-5
Capital Flight and Third World Debt*
Donald R. Lessard and John Williamson, editors
1987   ISBN 0-88132-053-6
The Canada-United States Free Trade Agreement:
The Global Impact*
Jeffrey J. Schott and Murray G. Smith, editors
1988   ISBN 0-88132-073-0
World Agricultural Trade: Building a Consensus*
William M. Miner and Dale E. Hathaway, editors
1988   ISBN 0-88132-071-3
Japan in the World Economy*
Bela Balassa and Marcus Noland
1988   ISBN 0-88132-041-2
America in the World Economy: A Strategy for
the 1990s*   C. Fred Bergsten
1988   ISBN 0-88132-089-7
Managing the Dollar: From the Plaza to the
Louvre*   Yoichi Funabashi
1988, 2d ed. 1989   ISBN 0-88132-097-8
United States External Adjustment and the World
Economy*   William R. Cline
May 1989   ISBN 0-88132-048-X
Free Trade Areas and U.S. Trade Policy*
Jeffrey J. Schott, editor
May 1989   ISBN 0-88132-094-3
Dollar Politics: Exchange Rate Policymaking in
the United States*
I.M. Destler and C. Randall Henning
September 1989   ISBN 0-88132-079-X
Latin American Adjustment: How Much Has
Happened?*   John Williamson, editor
April 1990   ISBN 0-88132-125-7
The Future of World Trade in Textiles and
Apparel*   William R. Cline
1987, 2d ed. June 1990   ISBN 0-88132-110-9

Completing the Uruguay Round: A Results-
Oriented Approach to the GATT Trade
Negotiations*   Jeffrey J. Schott, editor
September 1990   ISBN 0-88132-130-3
Economic Sanctions Reconsidered (2 volumes)
Economic Sanctions Reconsidered: Supplemental
Case Histories
Gary Clyde Hufbauer, Jeffrey J. Schott, and
Kimberly Ann Elliott
1985, 2d ed. Dec. 1990   ISBN cloth 0-88132-115-X
                      ISBN paper 0-88132-105-2
Economic Sanctions Reconsidered: History and
Current Policy
Gary Clyde Hufbauer, Jeffrey J. Schott, and
Kimberly Ann Elliott
December 1990   ISBN cloth 0-88132-140-0
                      ISBN paper 0-88132-136-2
Pacific Basin Developing Countries: Prospects for
the Future*   Marcus Noland
January 1991   ISBN cloth 0-88132-141-9
                      ISBN 0-88132-081-1
Currency Convertibility in Eastern Europe*
John Williamson, editor
October 1991   ISBN 0-88132-128-1
International Adjustment and Financing: The
Lessons of 1985-1991*   C. Fred Bergsten, editor
January 1992   ISBN 0-88132-112-5
North American Free Trade: Issues and
Recommendations*
Gary Clyde Hufbauer and Jeffrey J. Schott
April 1992   ISBN 0-88132-120-6
Narrowing the U.S. Current Account Deficit*
Allen J. Lenz
June 1992   ISBN 0-88132-103-6
The Economics of Global Warming
William R. Cline/*June 1992*   ISBN 0-88132-132-X
U.S. Taxation of International Income: Blueprint
for Reform*   Gary Clyde Hufbauer, assisted by
Joanna M. van Rooij
October 1992   ISBN 0-88132-134-6
Who's Bashing Whom? Trade Conflict in High-
Technology Industries   Laura D'Andrea Tyson
November 1992   ISBN 0-88132-106-0
Korea in the World Economy*   Il SaKong
January 1993   ISBN 0-88132-183-4
Pacific Dynamism and the International Economic
System*
C. Fred Bergsten and Marcus Noland, editors
May 1993   ISBN 0-88132-196-6
Economic Consequences of Soviet Disintegration*
John Williamson, editor
May 1993   ISBN 0-88132-190-7
Reconcilable Differences? United States-Japan
Economic Conflict*
C. Fred Bergsten and Marcus Noland
June 1993   ISBN 0-88132-129-X

Australia, New Zealand, and
Papua New Guinea
D.A. Information Services
648 Whitehorse Road
Mitcham, Victoria 3132, Australia
tel: 61-3-9210-7777
fax: 61-3-9210-7788
e-mail: service@dadirect.com.au
http://www.dadirect.com.au

Canada
Renouf Bookstore
5369 Canotek Road, Unit 1
Ottawa, Ontario K1J 9J3, Canada
tel: 613-745-2665
fax: 613-745-7660
http://www.renoufbooks.com

United Kingdom and Europe
(including Russia and Turkey)
The Eurospan Group
3 Henrietta Street, Covent Garden
London WC2E 8LU England
tel: 44-20-7240-0856
fax: 44-20-7379-0609
http://www.eurospan.co.uk

India, Bangladesh, Nepal, and Sri Lanka
Viva Books Pvt.
Mr. Vinod Vasishtha
4325/3, Ansari Rd.
Daryaganj, New Delhi-110002
India
tel: 91-11-327-9280
fax: 91-11-326-7224
e-mail: vinod.viva@gndel.globalnet.
ems.vsnl.net.in

Japan and the Republic of Korea
United Publishers Services, Ltd.
Kenkyu-Sha Bldg.
9, Kanda Surugadai 2-Chome
Chiyoda-Ku, Tokyo 101
Japan
tel: 81-3-3291-4541
fax: 81-3-3292-8610
e-mail: saito@ups.co.jp
For trade accounts only.
Individuals will find IIE books in
leading Tokyo bookstores.

Southeast Asia (Brunei, Cambodia,
China, Malaysia, Hong Kong, Indonesia,
Laos, Myanmar, the Philippines, Singapore,
Taiwan, and Vietnam)
Hemisphere Publication Services
1 Kallang Pudding Rd. #04-03
Golden Wheel Building
Singapore 349316
tel: 65-741-5166
fax: 65-742-9356

Thailand
Asia Books
5 Sukhumvit Rd. Soi 61
Bangkok 10110 Thailand
tel: 662-714-0740-2 Ext: 221, 222, 223
fax: 662-391-2277
e-mail: purchase@asiabooks.co.th
http://www/asiabooksonline.com

Visit our Web site at:
http://www.iie.com
E-mail orders to:
orders@iie.com